Sibylle Baumbach, Birgit Neumann, Ansgar Nünning (eds.)
with Mirjam Horn and Jutta Weingarten

A History of British Drama

Genres – Developments – Model Interpretations

WVT-HANDBÜCHER ZUM LITERATURWISSENSCHAFTLICHEN STUDIUM

Band 15

Herausgegeben von
Ansgar Nünning und Vera Nünning

Sibylle Baumbach, Birgit Neumann, Ansgar Nünning (eds.)
with Mirjam Horn and Jutta Weingarten

A History of British Drama
Genres – Developments – Model Interpretations

WVT Wissenschaftlicher Verlag Trier

A History of British Drama
Genres – Developments – Model Interpretations /
Ed. by Sibylle Baumbach, Birgit Neumann and Ansgar Nünning
with Mirjam Horn and Jutta Weingarten. -
Trier : WVT Wissenschaftlicher Verlag Trier, 2011
     (WVT-Handbücher zum literaturwissenschaftlichen Studium; Bd. 15)
     ISBN 978-3-86821-333-1

Cover design: Brigitta Disseldorf

© WVT Wissenschaftlicher Verlag Trier, 2011
ISBN 978-3-86821-333-1

No part of this book, covered by the copyright hereon,
may be reproduced or used in any form or by any means
without prior permission of the publisher.

WVT Wissenschaftlicher Verlag Trier
Bergstraße 27, 54295 Trier
Postfach 4005, 54230 Trier
Tel.: (0651) 41503 / 9943344, Fax: 41504
Internet: http://www.wvttrier.de
E-Mail: wvt@wvttrier.de

TABLE OF CONTENTS

1. An Outline of the Features, Objectives, and Premises of *A History of British Drama*   1
   SIBYLLE BAUMBACH, BIRGIT NEUMANN & ANSGAR NÜNNING

2. Early English Drama: Morality Plays and Mystery Cycles   19
   SIBYLLE BAUMBACH

3. Genres and Developments in Elizabethan Drama: Christopher Marlowe's *Doctor Faustus*   31
   ENNO RUGE

4. Shakespeare's Comedies: *A Midsummer Night's Dream* and *Twelfth Night*   47
   INA HABERMANN

5. Shakespeare's History Plays: *Richard III* and *Henry V*   63
   STEPHAN LAQUÉ

6. Shakespeare's Tragedies: *Hamlet*   77
   SIBYLLE BAUMBACH

7. Jacobean City Comedies: Ben Jonson's *The Alchemist* and Thomas Middleton's *A Chaste Maid in Cheapside*   95
   JOACHIM FRENK

8. Restoration Comedies: William Wycherley's *The Country Wife*, Aphra Behn's *The Rover*, and William Congreve's *The Way of the World*   113
   MARION GYMNICH

9. Restoration Tragedy and Heroic Drama: John Dryden's *All for Love, or The World Well Lost*   129
   INGO BERENSMEYER

10. Sentimental Comedy: Richard Steele's *The Conscious Lovers*   143
    VERA NÜNNING & IRINA BAUDER-BEGEROW

11. Domestic Tragedy: George Lillo's *The London Merchant, or The History of George Barnwell*   159
    BIRGIT NEUMANN

12. Eighteenth-Century Comedy of Manners: Richard Brinsley Sheridan's
    The School for Scandal 177
    JÜRGEN KAMM

13. Romantic Verse Drama: Joanna Baillie's *De Monfort* and Percy Shelley's
    The Cenci 193
    UTE BERNS

14. Victorian Melodrama: Thomas Holcroft's *A Tale of Mystery* and
    Douglas William Jerrold's *The Rent Day* 207
    GABRIELE RIPPL

15. Aestheticist Comedy of Manners: Oscar Wilde's
    The Importance of Being Earnest 223
    PETRA DIERKES-THRUN

16. Naturalist Drama – 'Problem Plays' or 'Plays of Ideas'?
    Bernard Shaw's *Mrs Warren's Profession* and John Galsworthy's *Justice* ... 237
    GERHARD STILZ

17. The Emergence of Irish Drama in the Early Twentieth Century:
    John Millington Synge's *The Playboy of the Western World* and
    Sean O'Casey's *The Plough and the Stars* 251
    HEINZ KOSOK

18. Realist Plays by the Angry Young Men and Kitchen-Sink Drama:
    John Osborne's *Look Back in Anger* and Arnold Wesker's
    Chips with Everything 267
    KLAUS PETER MÜLLER

19. The Theatre of the Absurd: Samuel Beckett's *Waiting for Godot* and
    Harold Pinter's *The Homecoming* 285
    ECKART VOIGTS-VIRCHOW

20. Political Drama: Edward Bond's *Saved* and David Edgar's *Maydays* ... 305
    ANETTE PANKRATZ

21. Biography, History, and Memory Plays: Brian Friel's *Making History* and
    Peter Shaffer's *Amadeus* 319
    ANSGAR NÜNNING & SIBYLLE BAUMBACH

22.	Feminist Theatre: Pam Gems' *Queen Christina* and Caryl Churchill's *Top Girls*	337
	BEATE NEUMEIER	
23.	New Forms of (Tragi-)Comedy: Alan Ayckbourn's *Absurd Person Singular* and *Comic Potential*	353
	ALBERT-REINER GLAAP	
24.	Adaptation, Intertextuality, and Metadrama: Tom Stoppard's *Rosencrantz and Guildenstern are Dead*, Peter Nichols' *A Piece of My Mind*, and Michael Frayn's *Look Look*	367
	JANINE HAUTHAL	
25.	Contemporary British Drama: In-Yer-Face or Post-Political Theatre? Sarah Kane's *Blasted* and Mark Ravenhill's *Shopping and Fucking*	381
	ROGER LÜDEKE	
26.	Drama and Postmodernism: Martin Crimp's *Attempts on Her Life* and Patrick Marber's *Closer*	399
	SARAH HEINZ	
27.	The Documentary Turn in Contemporary British Drama and the Return of the Political: David Hare's *Stuff Happens* and Richard Norton-Taylor's *Called to Account*	413
	ANNEKA ESCH-VAN KAN	
28.	Black British Drama: debbie tucker green and Kwame Kwei-Armah	429
	DEIRDRE OSBORNE	

1. An Outline of the Features, Objectives, and Premises of *A History of British Drama*

Sibylle Baumbach, Birgit Neumann & Ansgar Nünning

1. Introducing the Main Features and Objectives of this History of British Drama

Although the answer to the question recently raised by Hans Ulrich Gumbrecht in the title of his essay "Shall We Continue to Write Histories of Literature?" (2008) may indeed be an open and hotly debated one, students and other readers who would like to gain an overview of the main genres, developments, and plays in the history of British dramatic literature will probably be more interested in that history itself than in the debates over the alleged (im-)possibility of the writing of literary histories. And although one of the many insights of the theory of literary history is that "[it] used to be impossible to write; lately it has become much harder," as Lipking (1995: 1) observed, literary historians continue to write histories of literature, more often than not from new theoretical angles like a comparative or transcultural perspective (cf. Lindberg-Wada 2006). They may do so for many reasons, but the fact that not only students have to come to terms with the intricacies of literary history, but that the common reader, too, continues to be interested in the literary works of earlier ages is probably not one of the least important ones.

Nonetheless, one might just as well ask, 'Why *this* history of British drama?' The first duty falling on anyone who wishes to introduce a book entitled *A History of British Drama* is to explain what distinguishes it from the burgeoning collection of similar titles that might be found alongside it on the literary history shelf. Indeed, the present volume might best be introduced precisely by the ways in which it differs from traditional literary histories, which it does in five main respects:

- Firstly, this book is resolutely a history, rather than an attempt to be the (i.e. the definitive) history of British drama. Both the individual contributions and the collection as a whole are presented in full consciousness that they are selective and exemplary. In contrast to those traditional literary histories that aim to create an illusion of comprehensiveness – surely never more than a working fiction –, this volume focuses on some of the key areas, periods, and genres in the history of British drama.
- Secondly, rather than covering up the main choices that the editors have made, this history of British drama already flaunts its focus in the subtitle: It explores the main features and developments of major genres in selected periods. The individual chapters do not (and indeed could not) treat their topics exhaustively. Instead, they engage with and work through the main features of the genres and periods in

question, discussing and analysing problems and issues that each respective contributor finds most important in a given genre or in the selected plays.
- Thirdly, the present volume offers both a theoretically oriented form of literary history and very practical analyses of a wide range of plays. In contrast to those more traditional literary histories that present themselves as comprehensive and neutral surveys of the entire domain, each of the contributors here take as their respective points of departure a theoretical approach or a specific literary-historical problem pertaining to the respective genre, period, and play(s). Thus, in the title of each contribution, it is not only the genre and period treated that is denoted, but also the specific play or plays that is/are the subject of an exemplary analysis in each chapter.
- Fourth, this history aims not only to provide a state-of-the-art contribution to literary histories of British drama and to the selected genres. Above all, it is firmly oriented towards the needs of students seeking topics to work on in their own studies. The student perspective has been kept in mind by the contributors and editors alike at all times to create *A History of British Drama* that provides not only a source of information on its literary historical object, but a broad selection of theoretical and methodological models of how students and researchers might approach and analyze it: the analytical tools, as it were, as well as the materials for the study of British drama.
- Fifth, this history of British drama consists of a diachronically structured series of introductions to the main genres and exemplary analyses and interpretations of plays that serve as paradigm examples for the respective genres. The chapters that follow will thus introduce readers to both the main features of a broad range of dramatic genres and developments in the history of British drama and to an equally broad range of important plays, while also showing how the latter can be interpreted by using the analytical tools, concepts, and methods developed by literary studies in general (for an introduction, cf. Nünning/Nünning 2009) and the theory and analysis of drama in particular (cf. e.g. Pfister 1988; Pickering 1998, 2005; Baumbach/Nünning 2009).

These five distinguishing features already hint at the primary objective of this volume. It aims to give students concise information on key areas of English dramatic literary history and to provide them with the means to carry out their own independent study, analyses of individual plays, and research. As a result of this main goal, the chapters place the key features and developments of a given genre and period at the centre, providing readers with a historically and theoretically informed overview of the most prominent genres and periods in the history of British drama.

This book is primarily directed at all those students who want to gain an overview of the history of British drama and wish to conduct independent research as part of their studies (be it in preparation for a seminar paper or exam, or in developing a Bachelor's or Master's thesis). The volume should also prove helpful to all those who wish to deepen their expertise in British drama and explore new approaches to the major periods and genres. The goals of this book have been crucial in the selection of topics. The order of contributions is based roughly on the diachronic sequence of the major eras of British dramatic history, with the emphasis within the selected periods leading naturally to a focus on the dominant genre or genres of the time.

2. Introducing the Theoretical Premises: On the Problems of Writing Literary Histories

The articles in this volume are based on the premise that literary history, including literary-historical 'objects' such as genres, periods, and contexts, are not given but constructed by the literary historian who uses explicit theories or proceeds from intuitive assumptions. The ways in which we fabricate such constructs as literary and/or cultural histories also depend on the theories, models, and metalanguages we employ. If one accepts the view that "literary-historical 'objects' [...] are constructed, not given or found, then the issue of *how* such objects are constructed [...] becomes crucial" (McHale 1992: 3). Let us therefore briefly turn our attention to some of the main processes and challenges involved in the writing of literary histories. Literary history is inevitably confronted with:

- the problem of delimiting the object of enquiry, i.e. defining key concepts like 'literature,' 'context,' or 'culture,' concepts which are themselves subject to historical change (cf. Grabes 1988; Olsson 2006);
- problems regarding the selection of texts and contexts, and the question of the canon;
- problems involved in analysing and interpreting literary texts and contexts;
- the problem of periodization and establishing 'thresholds of new epochs' (*Epochenschwellen*; cf. the essays in Gumbrecht & Link-Heer 1985; Herzog & Koselleck 1987);
- the problem of selecting a suitable 'mode of emplotment' (sensu Hayden White) by means of which authors and texts can be arranged into narrative sequences;
- the problem of contextualizing works through syntheses and classifications based on concepts like genres, movements, and traditions;
- the problem of contextualizing literary texts diachronically by relating them to various cultural traditions;
- the problem of explanation, i.e. attempting to account for literary change;
- problems inherent in presenting the subject and in finding adequate forms in which to convey sophisticated conceptions of the literature and culture of past ages (cf. Perkins 1992: 53).

Since most of these issues have been discussed in great detail elsewhere, we will merely refer here to the pertinent works of such theorists as David Perkins (1991, 1992) and Robert F. Berkhofer Jr. (1995). The main challenges that have a direct impact on this history of British drama concern the following keywords: selection and canonization; periodization and genre definition (including questions of writing forms and representational techniques).

The problems of selection and canonization are closely linked to the respective underlying concept of literature at the time of literary-historical assessment. As the various definitions of the term 'literature' show, any history of literature is the result of selection processes based on the criteria of what counts as 'literature' (cf. Grabes 1988). Because selection is not possible without evaluation (cf. Plumpe/Conrady 1981: 375), the question of what aesthetic or other criteria are applied in the selection process is always at stake. In traditional literary histories, this issue is often ignored, although what history is told largely depends on highly specific values and standards. The question is not whether or not historians impose such aesthetic values in their selections, but how aware they are of the criteria and standards that they implement in those selections, and how explicitly they explain these.

Processes of selection and evaluation in literary histories ultimately result in the formation of literary canons. Broadly speaking, the term 'canon' refers to a highly selective corpus of (literary) texts, i.e. to a limited number of works which possess a substantial amount of prestige within the larger framework of culture. (Originally, the term designated a corpus of sacred religious texts based on divine revelation.) In its most basic function, the canon turns the overwhelming plenitude of available texts into a manageable history, "i.e. into a corpus of texts that can be surveyed and retained in collective memory" (Grabes 2008: 314). In a more critical sense, one could say that canons serve societies by controlling which literary texts are kept in the collective memory, taken seriously, or valued as 'good' literature.

Because the literary canon is based on evaluation and is thus inextricably linked to the values of certain groups, it is likely to be subject to "a continuing cultural negotiation that is deeply political" (Felperin 1990: xii). Indeed, for a long time in the history of British literature, canons have been shaped by the values of the ruling classes, i.e. of white upper-class men. In the last few decades the awareness of the negative effects of the selectivity of canons and their suppressive power has increased considerably. After all, the literary canon widely determines which texts remain in a society's cultural memory and are taught in schools and universities, which, in turn, influences the view of the present and the future. No wonder that 'the canon' is frequently and fiercely attacked, in particular by those groups that have long been subject to existing power structures and whose works have thus been conspicuously absent or underrepresented in the canon (cf. Neumann 2010: 12). The debates on the literature of minorities, and issues raised by feminist demands for an adequate account of the literary achievements of women, have raised awareness of the problem of every canon and the need for continuous canon revisions.

Rather than proposing a new canon of dramatic literature, this volume aims at presenting the key stages in the development of British drama from the Middle Ages to the 21st century. In each chapter the focus is set on one specific dramatic genre, whose main features are illustrated by selected examples from one or two major plays of the time. Instead of providing a set list of key dramatic works, therefore, the volume presents a literary history based on exemplary analyses that should enable students to develop the analytic tools to identify and analyse generic features independently and to relate them in meaningful ways to their period of production. Furthermore, the problems arising from any attempt to offer clear-cut definitions of literary periods and genres are addressed in the individual chapters. Each chapter reconstructs preceding and following developments and pinpoints significant overlaps of literary genres and periods. By focusing on processes of hybridization, reception, and revival of genres, the chapters illustrate that the history of British drama cannot be understood as a linear development but rather as a discontinuous process of generic modification, innovation, and blending.

Less controversial but no less problematic than the canon debate is the question of how the selected material can be emplotted, structured, and presented. Literary histories, to give just one example, do not have beginnings; rather, literary historians choose specific dates or literary incidents as their starting point. Where we set off to study the development of British drama and where we decide to begin our history is an important decision because it inevitably influences the literary history we tell. In this history of British drama, we have chosen medieval drama as our starting point – and there are indeed good reasons for doing so. The first dramatic texts scholars localized in Britain are liturgical plays of the 10th century (cf. Goodman 1990), followed by manuscripts of late-14th-century mystery cycles and moralities in the mid-15th century. After the decline of performances of Roman plays in Britain following the conversion of the Roman Empire to Christianity, drama seems to have reinvented itself. Based on the changing performance conditions, it established not only a new kind of theatrical space, but also a new time, form, and dramatic structure, which sets it apart from its predecessors. The closing of the Roman theatres – not unlike the closing of the theatres in 1616 – seems to have given rise to a new kind of drama. As there was no longer a designated public 'place of viewing' (*theatron*), plays were performed in churches and monasteries as well as outdoors in streets and market places. Their time of performance was restricted by Christian holidays, and their structure broke with the 'dramatic unities' of time, place, and action observed in ancient drama. What further contributes to the notion of the emergence of English drama during this period are the multiple forms of drama that developed independently from each other. The coexistence of liturgical drama, clerical drama, moralities, Corpus Christi cycles, and secular dramatic entertainment not only counters the belief in an evolutionary history of British drama, but also supports the notion that British drama could have set off right there – with the reinvention of drama after the closing of the Roman theatres.

Yet, even this beginning is somewhat arbitrary. After all, beyond and around what we can readily classify as medieval drama is a long tradition of Roman theatre. The history of theatre in Britain starts as early as the 1st century with the building of Roman theatres, which held performances of plays by the great Roman dramatists, such as the comic playwrights Plautus and Terence, who wrote in the tradition of Greek new comedy. It is likely, therefore, that Roman and Greek theatre (and also theatre architecture) had some impact on the development of British drama: Both are based on cultic rituals, for instance, and scholars have claimed that the large spectacles shown in amphitheatres influenced the productions of medieval cycle plays. It is equally likely that the dramatic tradition never died in Britain, but that it was kept alive by mimes and other performances and that we simply lack the textual evidence to confirm its continuous, even if small, presence. After all, medieval plays were not designed for reading and the manuscripts that have survived are only a fraction of the overall performance tradition. The scarce documentation might also explain the peculiar absence of antitheatrical sentiments following the reinvention of drama in the monastic choirs, which scholars have found puzzling, given the vast criticism against the theatre in the late empire which led to the closure of theatres. Rather than assuming the emergence of medieval drama, therefore, it is important to bear in mind that beginnings in literary history are often doubtful because written records were subject to casual destruction and natural decay, as well as edited or suppressed by various groups in power.

Constructing beginnings is only the beginning of a complicated process of narrative emplotment that underlies any history of literature. Authors of literary histories have to arrange the selected texts in a readable form. Hence, they have to impose order on the selected texts, link them with one another, employ specific narrative patterns to mark distinctions and use tropes to fabricate a meaningful story (cf. Perkins 1992: 19). In order to establish a sense of coherence and structure the vast amount of literature literary histories frequently draw on two basic categories: periods and genres. Genres and periods enable us to break down the multitude of texts into manageable units. The construction of periods, i.e. periodization, is based on the premise that many literary works produced in a specific time have significant features in common. Similarly, genre constructions proceed from the assumption that texts can be classified according to similarities in content, form, and/or function (cf. Fowler 1982).

Of course, in both cases, the act of identifying representative features raises a number of problems because it usually involves reasoning in a hermeneutic circle: We cannot know which texts are to be classified as, for instance, 'sentimental comedy,' unless we already have a concept of comedy and sentimentalism. We must derive these concepts, however, from sentimental comedies (cf. Perkins 1992: 113). Periods and genres are therefore inherently slippery categories, which allow for different understandings and definitions.

That periods and genres are not predetermined 'natural forms' does not, however, diminish their benefits as concepts in literary history. As the following inventory indicates, periods and genres are not only useful for literary history, but indispensable. They fulfil

- explanatory and cognitive functions: With the help of periods and genres, the premises and classification criteria of literary histories can be explicitly stated, and tacitly presupposed assumptions are made overt;

- heuristic functions: With the aid of genre- and period-concepts, research questions and hypotheses can be formulated;
- definitional and descriptive functions: They enable us to distinguish, identify, name, and describe phenomena in the field of literary history;
- ordering functions: They allow us to typologically differentiate phenomena, synchronically and diachronically, to structure the object area and correlate texts in literary history;
- shorthand descriptive functions: The labeling of a literary work as a 'sentimental comedy,' or as an example of the Early Modern or Romantic period already implies a (more or less) differentiated description of the respective set of features, without which thematic and formal features would continually need to be re-named and re-described;
- comparative functions: Period and generic terms are useful as a benchmark for comparative studies (for both intra- and inter-epochal comparisons within a national literature as well as across comparative literatures) and to make the specificities of works and literary movements visible;
- application-oriented, communicative, and didactic functions: These are not only useful functions in terms of interpretation but are also evident in their teaching and communicative roles. Genre and period concepts form the basis for teaching, and learning about, literature in terms of historical relationships (whether in the context of courses or that of independent reading) and for inter-subjectively comprehensible understanding on matters of literary history (not least, of course, in exams).

Because of this range of functions, genre and period have been selected as the structural principles underlying this volume. By discussing issues of selection and periodization, the articles attempt to provide a general sense of how literary histories are created, thus inviting readers to consider the challenges of literary history.

If the practice of literary history does not want to fall behind the findings of contemporary literary theory, it must replace the idea of *the* literary history with that of *a* history among many possible versions. This volume builds on such literary-theoretical awareness in its conception of period and genre, but goes one step (or two) further in deciding not to tell one particular history of British dramatic history and its development with a single theoretical framework, but rather to approach it through many. The concept of a polyphonic and theoretically informed literary history is something Steinwachs has suggested putting into practice – an approach "that, conscious of its methodology, pluralizes literary history" (1985: 320; our transl.).

If we take the insights of the modern theory of history seriously, it seems that a diverse range of theoretical and analytical approaches ideally suits the purpose of providing a multiperspectival literary history of the diachronic and synchronic diversity of British drama. The different genres and periods are too varied to be pressed into a single, particular theoretical scheme, just as the object of study here is too multi-faceted and complex to be adequately covered by one observer alone. It is, indeed, precisely the rich variety of different perspectives brought together here, each emanating from different theoretical standpoints and approaching differently delineated literary issues, problems, and themes that allows this volume to provide so vivid an impression of the great diversity of British drama past and present.

3. Introducing the Concept of Genre and Main Dramatic Genres

Since this volume is organized around the main dramatic genres that have emerged in British drama over the last 500 years, a brief look at both the concept of genres and some of the genres treated in greater detail in the chapters that follow may be helpful. One of the most important, and the most useful, categories in literary history and literary studies at large is the concept of 'genre,' or 'text type,' in the case of non-fictional texts. The term 'genre' is derived from the biological term *genus* and refers to a group of literary works that share significant characteristics in terms of content, form, and/or function. Such 'generic features' or 'generic conventions' not only serve as a classificatory system for literary works, but they are also important signposts for authors and recipients.

Genres are constructs based on socio-cultural, literary, and social consensus (cf. Voßkamp 2000: 256), which manifest themselves in the form of groups of texts. Genres, then, "are pragmatic constructs through and through" (Fohrmann 1988: 282). Although in theory there is a system of distinct genres and types, the different kinds of texts actually form a continuum, with permeable boundaries between the various categories. Moreover, genres are historically conditioned modes of communication and forms of convention and therefore subject to historical change.

This is immediately evident in the development of comedy. The emergence of Restoration comedy, for instance, largely responded to the cultural and political changes that occurred subsequent to the restoration of the British monarchy in 1660. Half a century later, in the 18th century, comedy then frequently took the form of sentimental comedy. This generic development again needs to be seen in the context of larger cultural developments, namely in the increasing emphasis put on sentiment, morality, and benevolence, which were now deemed as central virtues improving the mind of the individual and society in general. Hence, as the present volume shows, literary periods are characterized by the privileging of different literary genres, and these privileged genres are often interrelated with pressing cultural issues of the time. Only a diachronic approach, therefore, allows us to pinpoint genre modifications over time and to identify the prevalence of specific genres in certain periods.

Of course, just as with the assignment of individual texts to literary periods, their assignment to genres is often ambiguous. Contemporary genre theory stresses that genres change over time and that literary works always incorporate features of several different genres. One and the same text can therefore often be assigned to different or various genres. Hence, the object changes according to the parameters upon which the distinction of genres is based. In order to define, typologically account for, and characterize the multitude of genre manifestations, precise categories need to be applied in a reflected way. These categories have to be terminologically clear and rationally defined, and they have to be related to each other in a systematic way.

In most histories of drama in English the organization of the heterogeneous material is based on the basic distinction between comedy and tragedy; frequently, they also devote a chapter or two to other dramatic genres and modes like farce and burlesque. The questions, however, of how these genres are constructed and which features can be deemed typical of them, are often ignored, although what story is told largely depends on these (admittedly slippery) genre constructions.

In the last quarter of the 16th century, English drama diverged into three broad types: comedies, tragedies, and histories. The first major innovations were in comedy, introduced by John Lyly in his pioneering courtly comedies *Campaspe* (1584) and *Endymion* (1591). Whereas previous comedies were traditionally written in verse, Lyly introduced an ornate prose style. Moreover, his placing of verbal play and love between the sexes at the heart of comic writing proved influential for further Elizabethan comedies (cf. Keenan 2008: 82). Following Lyly's plots, Elizabethan comedy was mainly romantic, "joining magic, music, clowning and pastoralism to tales of love and imaginative adventure" (Gossett 2000: 167). Typically, these comedies concentrate on issues of mistaken identity, erotic adventure, and (thwarted) persecution (cf. Carroll 2003: 175). The relation between men and women, negotiations of gender roles and the freedom of women to act and think independently in courtship and marriage therefore move centre stage in many comedies. The plot frequently unfolds during a provisional festive time of release from established cultural restraints (cf. Hiscock 2008: 166). The pursuit of unexpected liberties on the part of the characters opens up a space where conventions of the time can be turned upside down. Social rules are subverted; norms are broken while disguise, misunderstanding, and deception rule.

Like comedy, tragedy is a genre that has its roots in the drama of ancient Greece and Rome, but the first tragedies in English were not written until the Renaissance (cf. Keenan 2008: 89). Broadly speaking, tragedy sketches the fall from fortune of a great man (only very rarely of a woman) as a consequence of pride or mistake in judgement. British tragedy is often said to begin around 1587: In this year, Thomas Kyd's *The Spanish Tragedy* and Christopher Marlowe's *Tamburlaine the Great* appeared; in the early 1590s Marlowe's *The Tragical History of Doctor Faustus* was performed and Shakespeare's *Titus Andronicus* was probably first staged in 1594. These tragedies have in common a larger-than-life hero, a detailed political framework, and an interrogation of pressing cultural issues, such as the limits of patriarchy, the conflict between individual aspiration and established authority, or the state's ability to provide justice (cf. Gossett 2000: 161). In so-called revenge tragedies, a popular subgenre especially during the Elizabethan and Jacobean era, the murder of a sovereign and the naming of an avenger sets off the tragic action, which involves disguise, masking, and intrigues, and culminates in the fulfilment of revenge and the death of the avenger. The most famous revenge tragedies are Kyd's *The Spanish Tragedy* and Shakespeare's *Titus Andronicus* as well as *Hamlet*. Whereas comedy eventually leads its protagonists to happiness and joy, tragedy takes the opposite route: It depicts the progression from good to bad fortune and culminates in destruction, usually in the death of the protagonist.

Next to tragedies and comedies, history plays became particularly fashionable in the 1590s. History plays dramatize the stories of (allegedly) historical characters and events, typically exploring the male-dominated worlds of politics and rule (cf. Keenan 2008: 98). Like their sources, namely the popular historical chronicles produced in increasing numbers at the end of the 16th century, these plays testify to the widespread interest in history and the lessons to be learned from it for the present. Marlowe contributed considerably to the popularizing of the history play, but the playwright who had the largest impact on the popularity of histories was Shakespeare. Exploring the national history, and in particular the English history of the 15th century, history plays served as powerful vehicles for the construction of the emergent national consciousness and for the consolidation of royal power. Most history plays, such as Shakespeare's *Henry VI* and *Richard III*, negotiate the legitimacy of royal rule, political power, and the struggles between conflicting loyalties. Elizabethan history plays are powerful reminders of the complexities of national identity and the ambivalences, indeed problems, of power (cf. Gossett 2000: 165).

These comedies, tragedies, and histories quickly established themselves as an essential part of popular British metropolitan and courtly culture. "The pervasive theatricality of Renaissance culture helps to explain the special currency of the 'life as theatre' metaphor in the period and, perhaps, informed the contemporary fascination with drama" (Keenan 2008: 59). Although many contemporaries condemned plays as morally corrupting, maintaining that they taught spectators to be wicked by presenting them with images of vice and subversion, comedies, tragedies, and histories were culturally extremely significant to the Tudor world. Cultural discourses on rightful authority, on marriage, on class relations, and on the nation were discussed in them (cf. Neumann 2010: 65).

In the further history of British drama, the generic conventions of tragedy, comedy, and history have been continuously modified and handled in very creative and intricate ways. The 17th century saw the rise of satiric or black comedy, such as Ben Jonson's Jacobean city comedy *Volpone* (1606), whose buffoonish tone and sexual innuendo follows the tradition of Greek old comedy, as well as that of the comedy of manners, which, like Roman comedies by Plautus and Terence, feature amorous intrigues, double entendres, and attack the artificial conduct of higher classes. The comedy of manners reached its peak with the Restoration comedies of George Etherege, William Wycherley, and William Congreve.

At the dawn of the 18th century, comedy began to strike a more sincere note: As reaction against the witty Restoration comedies, in sentimental comedy – a reformed version of comedy with a melodramatic ending – it is the communication of values and morals as well as the *pathos,* the excess of emotions that take centre stage. As with other dramatic genres, there is no linear development here, much less a succession of one genre by the other, as the comedy of manners was revived towards the 18th century by Oliver Goldsmith and Richard Brinsley Sheridan.

In contemporary theatre, a more extreme type of comedy, farce or absolute comedy, has gained grounds again. Whereas comedy usually retains some degree of seriousness, almost anything goes in farce to produce laughter: The action presented does not have to be probable, but only possible. In fact, the comic in farce often arises in the gap between the plausible and the implausible, the logical and the illogical. In Michael Frayn's *Noises Off* (1982), or Alan Ayckbourn's *Communicating Doors* (1995), for instance, the focus is set on misunderstandings, confusions, and caricature to expose irrational, vain, and nonsensical behaviour.

It is particularly the blending of different dramatic forms and the concomitant blurring of boundaries and genre distinctions that has become increasingly popular, as indicated by the rise of new, hybrid forms such as tragicomedy, sentimental comedy, and domestic tragedy. As indicated by the term, 'tragicomedy,' for instance, is a blend between tragedy and comedy, embracing elements of both. A potentially tragic plot leads to a happy ending or comic elements are continuously mingled with the serious. While often debased as mongrel in Early Modern times, tragicomedy became *the* dramatic genre in post-World War II British theatre and the theatre of the absurd (see chapter 19). Another hybrid is domestic tragedy (see chapter 11), which embraces a tragic plot but breaks with conventions of (neo-)classical tragedy insofar as its protagonists are neither kings nor heroes but ordinary people from the newly emerging middle classes. These trends of hybridization, which we can only sketch briefly here (for a more detailed overview see Baumbach & Nünning 2009: 23-36), not only point to the development of genres, but also suggest how productive it is to focus on genre writing in the history of British drama.

4. A History of British Theatre:
The Cultural and Social Power of Drama

As indicated by this very brief overview of the main dramatic genres, British drama can hardly be understood without taking into consideration its historical contexts, including its cultural performances and stage history. As plays are often exclusively studied in their written form, it is easy to neglect their performative dimension and performance history. However, the original circumstances of staging and the sociopolitical conditions for which they were written are crucial components of any play and indispensable for their comprehension. As Styan notes,

> [a] play lives in its ability to create something of an electric circuit between the actor and his audience, and this interchange also reflects the relationship of the theatre and society, between the implicit role of the stage and the community that nourishes it. It follows as the night the day that the merits of a play may not be fully understood without a sense of

how it worked, or failed to work, when it was played under the conditions for which it was written. (1996: xiii)

The theatre, the 'seeing place,' not only provides a space for representing the world and its inhabitants, as suggested by the concept of *theatrum mundi*, but drama in general serves as a most effective vehicle for the critical reflection of human conditions, the dissemination of knowledge, and communication of values: Drawing both on visual and verbal communication, its language is immediate (performances or rather theatrical events are happening 'here and now') and easily accessible for the educated and the common man. Furthermore, drama can be performed anywhere at any time: All that is needed for a play to come into being are an actor, an audience, and any space that can be used for performance, be it a marketplace, a street, a wagon, or an actual theatre. The space of performance has a considerable impact on a play's design and the way in which it was perceived. Medieval plays that were staged on pageant wagons and were 'on the move' across the city, or Shakespeare's drama that was written for the Globe Theatre allowed a much more intense interaction between actors and audiences than, for instance, the proscenium or picture frame stage that prevailed in 19th- and 20th-century theatres. Similarly, whether a play is performed in an "empty space" (Brook 1984 [1968]), a bare stage virtually void of decorations and props, like Shakespeare's drama, or embedded in a lavishly decorated setting has an impact on both the language of the play and actor-audience communication.

In addition to aesthetic laws for performance and the complex system of theatrical communication (cf. Baumbach/Nünning 2009: 44-75), a history of drama must take into consideration the sociopolitical contexts which the plays considered originated in. Drama is a highly political and intertextual genre: It not only presents characters who interact with society and struggle with the norms and values of the time, but often alludes to historical figures, events or discourses on gender, ethnicity, identity, and so forth, as well as to previous dramatic and aesthetic traditions. Consequently, the following chapters pay special attention to the conditions of performance as well as to the cultural or political contexts of the plays in question, while providing an outlook on the further development of the respective genre that helps students get to grips with dramatic traditions.

5. The Structure of Individual Chapters: Aims and Objectives

Even though the individual chapters differ as a result of the nature of the respective periods and genres and the theoretical and methodological approaches taken, there is a common ground in the conceptual basis and principal aims of these different journeys through British dramatic history, which may be outlined as follows. Each chapter makes a sustained attempt

- to illustrate the problems of periodization and the criteria used for the delineation of (sub-)genre,

- to highlight the main thematic concerns and formal or representational techniques that are characteristic of each genre and period with examples from selected works. Where detailed interpretations or summaries have been omitted because of shortage of space, bibliographic references point to recommended anthologies of interpretation and other relevant publications.
- In their shared aim to present theoretically informed literary history, the articles gathered here showcase the diverse possibilities for the synchronic and diachronic structuring of British drama. They illustrate the benefits of structured, genre-typological, thematic, formal, and function-historical criteria over a mere chronological arrangement of the texts in attempting to identify and describe the main trends of genres and periods, as well as characteristics of sub-genres and individual works.
- Each chapter includes a bibliographical selection of relevant primary and secondary sources, which provides an overview of the important research literature on the topic and invites further reading.

Just as this volume does not claim to be *the* comprehensive history of British drama, the dramatic genres and plays it covers do not, of course, entirely exhaust the variety of genres and periods in British drama. However, if this volume manages to provide an overview of the major periods and genres of British dramatic history and facilitate independent research, then it will have fulfilled its main purpose. And if the volume were also to encourage readers to dig deeper into the history of British drama – and, more widely, encourage an awareness of the constructedness of any literary history –, it will have fulfilled a no less important aim.

Bibliography

Companions and Introductions to the Theory and Analysis of Theatre and Drama

Allain, Paul & Jen Harvie. 2006. *The Routledge Companion to Theatre and Performance*. London: Routledge.
Aston, Elaine & George Savona. 1991. *Theatre as Sign System: A Semiotics of Text and Performance*. London: Routledge.
Balme, Christopher B. 2008. *The Cambridge Introduction to Theatre Studies*. Cambridge: Cambridge UP.
Baumbach, Sibylle & Ansgar Nünning. 2009. *An Introduction to the Study of Plays and Drama*. Stuttgart: Klett.
Bentley, Eric. 2008. *The Theory of the Modern Stage*. London: Penguin.
Birch, David. 1991. *The Language of Drama*. Houndmills, et al.: Palgrave.
Boulton, Marjorie. 1988 [1960]. *The Anatomy of Drama*. London: Routledge.
Carlson, Marvin. 1989. *Places of Performance: The Semiotics of Theatre Architecture*. Ithaca: Cornell UP.

Elam, Keir. 1980. *The Semiotics of Theatre and Drama*. London/New York: Methuen.
Nünning, Ansgar & Vera Nünning. 2009 [2004]. *An Introduction to the Study of English and American Literature*. Stuttgart: Klett.
Pfister, Manfred. 1988. *Das Drama*. München: Fink.
—. 1993 [1988]. *The Theory and Analysis of Drama*. Cambridge: Cambridge UP.
Pickering, Kenneth. 1998. *How to Study Modern Drama*. London: Macmillan
—. 2005. *Key Concepts in Drama and Performance*. Houndmills, et al.: Palgrave.

On the Writing of Literary History

Assmann, Aleida & Jan Assmann. 1987. "Kanon und Zensur." In: *Kanon und Zensur: Archäologie der literarischen Kommunikation II*. München: Wilhelm Fink.7-27.
Berkhofer, Robert F., Jr. 1995. *Beyond the Great Story: History as Text and Discourse*. Cambridge, MA/London: The Belknap P of Harvard UP.
Felperin, Howard. 1990. *The Uses of the Canon: Elizabethan Literature and Contemporary Theory*. Oxford: Clarendon P.
Grabes, Herbert. 1988. "Selektionsprinzipien und Literaturbegriff in der anglistischen Literaturgeschichtsschreibung." In: *Germanisch-Romanische Monatsschrift* 38: 3-14.
— (ed.). 2001. *Literary History/Cultural History: Forcefields and Tensions*. REAL: Yearbook of Research in English and American Literature 17. Tübingen: Narr.
— (ed.). 2005. *Literature, Literary History, and Cultural Memory*. REAL: Yearbook of Research in English and American Literature 21. Tübingen: Narr.
—. 2008. "Cultural Memory and the Literary Canon." In: Astrid Erll & Ansgar Nünning (eds.). *Cultural Memory Studies: An International and Interdisciplinary Handbook*. Berlin/New York: de Gruyter. 311-19.
Gumbrecht, Hans Ulrich. 2008. "Shall We Continue to Write Histories of Literature?" In: *New Literary History* 39.3: 519-32.
— & Ursula Link-Heer (eds.). 1985. *Epochenschwellen und Epochenstrukturen im Diskurs der Literatur- und Sprachhistorie*. Frankfurt/M.: Suhrkamp.
Herzog, Reinhart & Reinhart Koselleck (eds.). 1987. *Epochenschwelle und Epochenbewußtsein*. München: Fink.
Lindberg-Wada, Gunilla (ed.). 2006. *Studying Transcultural Literary History*. Berlin/New York: de Gruyter.
Lipking, Lawrence. 1995. "A Trout in the Milk." In: Marshall Brown (ed.). *The Uses of Literary History*. Durham/London: Duke UP. 1-12.
McHale, Brian. 1992. *Constructing Postmodernism*. London: Routledge.
Nünning, Ansgar. 1996. "Kanonisierung, Periodisierung und der Konstruktcharakter von Literaturgeschichten: Grundbegriffe und Prämissen theoriegeleiteter Literaturgeschichtsschreibung." In: *Eine andere Geschichte der englischen Literatur: Epochen, Gattungen und Teilgebiete im Überblick*. Trier: WVT. 1-24.

—. 2001. "No Literary or Cultural History without Theory: Ten Teutonic Theses on the Deconstruction and Reconceptualization of two Complex Relationships." In: Grabes 2001. 35-66.
Olsson, Tord. 2006. "Delimiting the Objects of Literary History." In: Lindberg-Wada 2006. 63-65.
Perkins, David (ed.). 1991. *Theoretical Issues in Literary History*. Cambridge, MA: Harvard UP.
—. 1992. *Is Literary History Possible?* Baltimore: Johns Hopkins UP.
Plumpe, Gerhard & Karl Otto Conrady. 1981. "Problem der Literaturgeschichtsschreibung." In: Helmut Brackert & Jörn Stückrath (eds.). *Literaturwissenschaft: Grundkurs 2*. Reinbek bei Hamburg: Rowohlt. 373-92.
Rees, Cees J., van. 1984. "Wie aus einem literarischen Werk ein Meisterwerk wird. Über die dreifache Selektion der Literaturkritik." In: Peter Finke & Siegried J. Schmidt (eds.). *Analytische Literaturwissenschaft*. Braunschweig: Vieweg. 175-202.
Steinwachs, Burkhart. 1985. "Was leisten (literarische) Epochenbegriffe?" In: Gumbrecht & Link-Heer 1985. 312-23.
Styan, J.L. 1996. *The English Stage: A History of Drama and Performance*. Cambridge: Cambridge UP.

Introductions to Genre Theory and to Dramatic Genres

Aebischer, Pascale. 2010. *Jacobean Drama*. Houndmills/New York: Palgrave Macmillan.
Bermel, Albert. 1982. *Farce: From Aristophanes to Woody Allen*. New York: Simon and Schuster.
Bonheim, Helmut. 1990. *Literary Systematics*. Cambridge: D.S. Brewer.
Booth, Michael R. 1965. *English Melodrama*. London: Jenkins.
Chernaik, Warren L. 2007. *The Cambridge Introduction to Shakespeare's History Plays*. Cambridge/New York: Cambridge UP.
Cohen, Ralph. 1986. "History and Genre." In: *New Literary History* 17.2: 203-18.
—. 1988. "Do Postmodern Genres Exist?" In: Perloff 1988a. 11-27.
—. 1991. "Genre Theory, Literary History, and Historical Change." In: Perkins 1991. 85-113.
— (ed.). 2003a. "Introduction." In: *New Literary History* 34.2: v-xv.
— (ed.). 2003b. "Introduction: Notes Toward a Generic Reconstitution of Literary Study." In: *New Literary History* 34.3: v-xvi.
Dimock, Wai Chee. 2006. "Genre as World System." In: *Through Other Continents: American Literature Across Deep Time*. Princeton: Princeton UP. 72-106.
—. 2007. "Introduction: Genres as Fields of Knowledge." In: *Remapping Genre. PMLA* 122.5: 1377-88.
— & Bruce Robbins (eds.). 2007. *Remapping Genre. PMLA* 122.5.

Duarte, João F. (ed.). 1999. *Reconceptions of Genre. EJES* 3.1.
Duff, David (ed.). 2000. *Modern Genre Theory*. Harlow: Longman.
Ellis, Frank H. 1991. *Sentimental Comedy: Theory and Practice*. Cambridge/New York: Cambridge UP.
Esslin, Martin. 1991 [1980]. *The Theatre of the Absurd*. London/New York: Penguin.
Fishelov, David. 1991. "Genre Theory and Family Resemblance Revisited." In: *Poetics* 20: 123-38.
—. 1993. *Metaphors of Genre: The Role of Analogies in Genre Theories*. University Park: The Pennsylvania State UP.
—. 1995. "The Structure of Generic Categories: Some Cognitive Aspects." In: *Journal of Literary Semantics* 24.2: 117-26.
—. 1999. "The Birth of Genre." In: *Reconceptions of Genre. EJES* 3.1: 51-63.
Fohrmann, Jürgen. 1988. "Remarks towards a Theory of Literary Genres." In: *Poetics* 17: 273-85.
Foster, Verna A. 2004. *The Name and Nature of Tragicomedy*. Aldershot: Ashgate.
Fowler, Alastair. 1982. *The Kinds of Literature: An Introduction to the Theory of Genres and Modes*. Oxford: Clarendon P.
—. 1989. "The Future of Genre Theory: Functions and Constructional Types." In: Ralph Cohen (ed.). *The Future of Literary Theory*. New York/London: Routledge. 291-303.
Frow, John. 2006. *Genre*. London: Routledge.
Gymnich, Marion, Birgit Neumann & Ansgar Nünning (eds.). 2007. *Gattungstheorie und Gattungsgeschichte*. Trier: WVT.
Hempfer, Klaus W. 1973. *Gattungstheorie*. München: Fink.
Hornby, Richard. 1986. *Drama, Metadrama, and Perception*. Lewisburg: Brucknell UP, London/Toronto: Associated UP.
Kamm, Jürgen. 1996. *Der Diskurs des heroischen Dramas: Eine Untersuchung zur Ästhetik dialogischer Kommunikation in der englischen Restaurationszeit*. Trier: WVT.
Malkin, Jeanette. 1999. *Memory-Theater and Postmodern Drama*. Ann Arbor: U of Michigan P.
Muir, Kenneth. 1970. *The Comedy of Manners*. London: Hutchinson.
Mukherji, Subha & Raphael Lyne (eds.). 2007. *Early Modern Tragicomedy*. Cambridge: Brewer.
Nelson, T.G.A. 1990. *Comedy: An Introduction to Comedy in Literature, Drama, and Cinema*. Oxford: Oxford UP.
Neumann, Birgit & Ansgar Nünning. 2007. "Probleme, Aufgaben und Perspektiven der Gattungstheorie und Gattungsgeschichte." In: Gymnich, Neumann & Nünning 2007. 1-28.
Paget, Derek. 1990. *True Stories? Documentary Drama on Radio, Screen, and Stage*. Manchester/New York: Manchester UP.
Pankratz, Anette. 1998. *Werterepertoires der englischen Restaurationskomödie*. Essen: Blaue Eule.

Patterson, Michael. 2003. *Strategies of Political Theatre: Post-War Playwrights*. Cambridge: Cambridge UP.
Perloff, Marjorie (ed.). 1988. *Postmodern Genres*. Norman/London: U of Oklahoma P.
Sierz, Aleks. 2001. *In-Yer-Face Theatre: British Drama Today*. London: Faber and Faber.
Voßkamp, Wilhelm. 2000. "Gattungen." In: Helmut Brackert & Jörn Stückrath (eds.). *Literaturwissenschaft: Ein Grundkurs*. Reinbek bei Hamburg: Rowohlt. 253-68.
Wallace, Jennifer. 2007. *The Cambridge Introduction to Tragedy*. Cambridge: Cambridge UP.
Weitz, Eric. 2009. *The Cambridge Introduction to Comedy*. Cambridge: Cambridge UP.

Selected Histories of Theatre & Drama in English

Aston, Elaine & Janelle Reinelt (eds.). 2000. *The Cambridge Companion to Modern British Women Playwrights*. Cambridge: Cambridge UP.
Bain, Carl E. (ed.). 1973. *Drama: Norton Introduction to Literature*. New York, et al: Norton.
Brater, Enoch & Ruby Cohn (eds.). 1990. *Around the Absurd: Essays on Modern and Postmodern Drama*. Ann Arbor: U of Michigan P.
Brook, Peter. 1984 [1968]. *The Empty Space*. New York: Atheneum.
Brown, Laura. 1981. *English Dramatic Form, 1660-1760: An Essay in Generic History*. New Haven/London: Yale UP.
Carlson, Julie Ann. 1994. *In the Theatre of Romanticism: Coleridge, Nationalism, Women*. Cambridge/New York: Cambridge UP.
Carter, Ronald & John McRae. 2001 [1997]. *The Routledge History of Literature in English, Britain and Ireland*. London: Routledge.
Courtney, Richard. 1982. *Outline History of British Drama*. Littlefield: Adams & Company.
Dillon, Janette. 2006. *The Cambridge Introduction to Early English Theatre*. Cambridge: Cambridge UP.
Gibbons, Brian. 1980 [1968]. *Jacobean City Comedy*. London/New York: Methuen.
Goodman, Jennifer R. 1990. *British Drama Before 1660: A Critical History*. Boston: Twayne.
Gossett, Suzanne. 2000. "Dramatic achievements." In: Arthur F. Kinney (ed.). *The Cambridge Companion to English Literature 1500-1600*. Cambridge: Cambridge UP. 153-77.
Grabes, Herbert. 1998. *Das amerikanische Drama des 20. Jahrhunderts*. Stuttgart: Klett.
Hiscock, Andrew. 2008. "The Renaissance, 1485-1660." In: Paul Poplawski (ed.). *English Literature in Context*. Cambridge: Cambridge UP. 110-210.
Holdsworth, Nadine & Mary Luckhurst (eds.). 2008. *A Concise Companion to British and Irish Drama*. Malden, MA: Blackwell.
Keenan, Siobhan. 2008. *Renaissance Literature*. Edinburgh: Edinburgh UP.

Krieger, Gottfried. 1998. *Das englische Drama des 20. Jahrhunderts*. Stuttgart: Klett.
Luckhurst, Mary (ed.). 2006. *A Companion to Modern British and Irish Drama 1880-2005*. Malden, MA: Blackwell.
McMillin, Scott. 1997 [1993]. *Restoration and Eighteenth-Century Comedy*. New York/London: Norton.
Mehl, Dieter (ed.). 1970. *Das englische Drama: Vom Mittelalter bis zur Gegenwart*. 2 vols. Düsseldorf: Bagel.
Müller, Klaus-Peter. 1993. *Englisches Theater der Gegenwart: Geschichte(n) und Strukturen*. Tübingen: Narr.
Neumann, Birgit. 2010. *A Short History of English Literature until 1900: A Survey of Periods, Genres and Major Writers*. Stuttgart: Klett.
Nünning, Ansgar (ed.). 1996. *Eine andere Geschichte der englischen Literatur: Epochen, Gattungen und Teilgebiete im Überblick*. Trier: WVT.
Orr, John. 1991. *Tragicomedy and Contemporary Culture*. Hong Kong: Macmillan Academic and Professional Ltd.
Patterson, Michael. 2003. *Strategies of Political Theatre: British Playwrights in the pre-Thatcher Era*. Cambridge/New York: Cambridge UP.
Reitz, Bernhard & Marc Berninger (eds.). 2002. *British Drama of the 1990s*. Heidelberg: Winter.
Schabert, Ina. 2000 [1972]. *Shakespeare-Handbuch: Die Zeit – Der Mensch – Das Werk – Die Nachwelt*. Stuttgart: Kröner.
Seller, Maxine S. 1983. *Ethnic Theatre in the United States*. Westport: Greenwood P.
Shepherd, Simon & Peter Womack. 1996. *English Drama: A Cultural History*. Oxford: Blackwell.
Tönnies, Merle (ed.). 2010. *Das englische Drama der Gegenwart: Kategorien – Entwicklungen – Modellinterpretationen*. Trier: WVT.
Trussler, Simon. 1994. *The Cambridge Illustrated History of British Theatre*. Cambridge: Cambridge UP.
Wells, Stanley & Lena Cowen Orlin (eds.). 2003. *Shakespeare: An Oxford Guide*. Oxford: Oxford UP.
White, Martin. 1998. *Renaissance Drama in Action: An Introduction to Aspects of Theatre Practice and Performance*. London: Routledge.
Zarrilli, Phillip B., Bruce McConachie & Gary Jay Williams. 2006. *Theatre Histories: An Introduction*. New York, et al.: Routledge.

2. EARLY ENGLISH DRAMA:
MORALITY PLAYS AND MYSTERY CYCLES

SIBYLLE BAUMBACH

1. Early English Drama and Medieval Theatricality

Often underestimated in their significant role in the development of dramatic structures and forms, early English plays tend to be neglected in the study of English drama and at times remain *terra incognita* for many students of English literature, disregarding the fact that one of the most popular plays widely performed on contemporary stages is a medieval one: *Everyman* (cf. McKinnell 2008 [1994]: 316). Despite being a translation of the Dutch drama *Elckerlijc*, this play, which deals with the question of what a man can do to be saved from death, is still ranked amongst the English morality plays and, in its adaptation by the Austrian playwright Hugo von Hofmannsthal, continues to be performed every year across Germany and Austria. The success of *Everyman* (c. 1495) points to a vivid dramatic tradition of early English drama, whose main features and developments this chapter aims to outline.

Even though the roots of the dramatic tradition in England fall into what is known as the later medieval period, it is more accurate to speak of 'early English drama' than 'medieval drama,' as the major dramatic genres which came into being at that time remained popular well into the 16th, and in some cases even the 17th century (cf. Beadle & Fletcher 2008 [1994]). The beginnings of early English drama are no less contested, partly because the term 'play' or its Latin equivalent *ludus* was less clear-cut than it is today, insofar as it could not only refer to a theatrical performance, but was also applied to any kind of game or festivity, thus embracing both dramatic and non-dramatic events. There seems to be consensus, however, that the first dramatic performances in England reach back into the 10th century and were enacted in private liturgical ceremonies or during the Introit ceremony on Easter morning, which marked the opening of the Eucharist celebration in the Roman Catholic Church (cf. Ricks 1987 [1971]: 13). At the Introit, a biblical text describing the encounter of the three Marys with the angel before Christ's empty sepulchre was sung by two or more alternate voices. Not unlike the development of Greek drama, which derived from the separation of one singer from the chorus and their dialogue, the *Quem quaeritis* ('whom do you seek?') dialogue between the angel and the Marys, which is regarded as the first example of 'liturgical drama,' might have paved the way for more elaborate performances to develop.

The precise nature of the relationship between the origins of English drama and liturgical ceremonies, however, remains an area of speculation, just like the question of when exactly these religious *ludi*, which were performed in Latin or French (cf. Goodman 1990: 51) and required an educated audience, moved from the monasteries and churches into an open public space where they could be viewed by a greater laity audience. What scholars widely agree on, however, is that it was the same institution that attempted to suppress drama during the Dark Ages, during which the theatre largely disappeared, that eventually (re-)instituted dramatic performance and put it in its service. While the so-called cycle-plays that marked the beginning of vernacular drama in England received clerical support, the early Church had attacked the practice of acting and theatrical devices such as face-painting as heretical, and did so strongly, referring to Deuteronomy: "The woman shall not wear that which pertaineth unto a man, neither should a man put on a woman's garment: for all that do so are abomination unto the Lord thy God" (Deuteronomy 22.5, qtd. in Styan 1996: 2). Banned by the clerics, drama survived mainly through itinerant players, street mimes, or 'joculators,' and was kept alive by acrobats or wandering minstrels, who travelled from town to town, gathering large audiences, and sung about miracles of the saints, biblical stories, and Christian heroes, thus preparing for the re-invention of drama in the 14th century.

One of the reasons why biblical and moral drama could be staged in Christian England despite the church's condemnation of theatrical practices is that these liturgical plays were not associated with the 'theatre' in our modern understanding, as they were part of Christian festivals and their content was pious, their action symbolic. Thus, they differed significantly from the ancient *theatron*, the place of spectacle, which was connected with obscene, licentious, and impudent pagan practices (cf. Clopper 2001: 2 f.).

Unlike in early modern times, the centre of dramatic activity was not London, but village greens and the country at large. While churches provided the chief theatrical space for the first performances of liturgical drama, a wide variety of outdoor locations and open spaces, including fields, gardens, streets, and market squares, were used as natural 'stages' wherein plays could be performed (cf. Normington 2009). It was especially the transition from liturgical to vernacular drama that led to a changed and more experimental use of theatrical space. To understand the semiotics of the medieval stage, the two concepts of *platea* and *locus*, often referred to as 'place' and 'scaffold,' respectively, which Robert Weimann developed in connection with Shakespeare's theatre (cf. Weimann 2000: 180-208) prove helpful. While the *locus* marks a demarcated space that represents a specific location (i.e. a door or scaffold that stands for a house, heaven or hell, or any other conceptual place), the *platea* is an open space whose boundaries are fluid and which is defined in and through performance. Whereas there can be several symbolically encoded *loci* in a performance, there is only one *platea*.

One of the greatest challenges concerning a study of early English drama lies in the oral tradition of the time. Performances were addressed mainly to an illiterate audience who were accustomed to hearing, not reading a play. The great flexibility of stories that were transmitted orally not only supported the interaction between actors and audience, as performances could be tailored to the spectators' responses, but also encouraged changes in performance, which makes the analysis of medieval drama difficult, as it is based on an essentially unstable and variant texts.

For a deeper understanding of early English drama, therefore, it is vital to take into account the theatrical conditions, musical traditions, and iconography of the time as well as the intense interaction between actors and audiences during the performance. As Meg Twycross reminds us, "there was no such thing as casual theatregoing" (2008 [1994]: 26). Plays were restricted to and regulated by the annual religious and agricultural festivals as well as occasional special celebrations such as weddings and coronations (cf. Ricks 1987 [1971]: 29). The motives for putting on a play depended on both the patron and the place(s) of performance. The medieval mystery cycles, for instance, were not only part of a religious festival, but also a great tourist attraction. Hence, "their players could draw on a charge of heightened religious emotion and civic pride which we can never recreate" (Twycross 2008: 26). As indicated by Twycross, the understanding of early English drama is intertwined with an understanding of its theatricality. Therefore, this chapter will attempt to do both: to provide a brief overview of key plays in the dramatic tradition up to the 16th century as well as offer an insight into early modes of performance.

Since professional drama did not develop until the 16th century (when it developed rapidly), medieval actors were predominantly amateurs, i.e. guildsmen or clergymen drawn from the community or itinerant performers and nomadic players who were not sponsored by the church but staged mummings or masques at festive events. As suggested by the acting conventions of the time, theatre was conceived as artifice, pretence, or a game. Instead of aiming for illusion, metadramatic reference such as the actor's blunt announcement of his role ("I am St George of Merry England, / Bring in the morris-men, bring in our band," *St. George's Play*, Oxfordshire, qtd. in Styan 1996: 6) and repeated addresses to the audience assured that the play was perceived as a play.

The successful representation of religious and legendary figures was based on the audience's familiarity with the iconography of the time. Specific garments, properties, or indicative colour were thus sufficient to identify religious and legendary heroes: keys pointed to St. Peter, a traditional blue gown was commonly worn by the Virgin Mary and Judas Iscariot could be recognized by the red hair (cf. Ricks 1987: 44).

The fact that actors were often taken from the community contributed to the widespread notion that the world is a theatre and "all the men and women merely players" (Shakespeare, *As You Like It* 2.7.139) which dominated medieval thinking and suffused early English drama. This dramatic world view derives from Augustine's (354-430) conception of the world as a theatre where God is the audience, watching mankind acting out its brief existence on earth, a view that – in a secularized form, discarding divinity – would remain prevalent well into the 16th century, as suggested by Shakespeare's Globe and the popular parallel between the theatre and the *theatrum mundi* (see chapters 4-6). Insofar as medieval theatre focussed on the fall from grace to redemption through repentance and atonement to the return to grace, plays combine elements of both tragedy and comedy and can best be described as hybrid, "invariably tragic-comic" (Ricks 1987: 46) drama. Rather than using generic classifications such as 'tragedies,' 'comedies,' and 'histories,' therefore, scholars of early English drama commonly distinguish, according to form and content, between 'miracle cycles' or 'mystery plays,' 'moralities,' 'interludes,' and 'saints plays,' which dealt with the legendary lives of martyrs, apostles, and

Christian saints, such as the late 15th-century *Mary Magdalene* and the *Conversion of St. Paul* (cf. Görlach 1998). The former is a case in point with regard to generic ambiguity: "[T]he play cannot be said to cross generic boundaries because it does not even recognize them. Moral allegory, biblical narrative and hagiographic fantasy all inhabit a single dramatic world" (Shepherd & Womack 1996: 16).

As with other generic distinctions, it is important to bear in mind that there are overlaps between these different kinds of drama and that these terms were not used in the medieval period, but applied in retrospect, and thus remain somewhat unsatisfactory and ambivalent. There remains some doubt, for instance, whether plays that appear as cycle plays or fragments thereof were in fact compiled many years later or performed individually (cf. Dillon 2006: 144). For want of a better terminology, however, these distinctions are still prevalent and used for convenience.

2. Mystery Plays

Cycle, mystery, or miracle plays, referred to as 'popular civic religious drama,' allowed a predominantly illiterate audience to access biblical narratives and religious mysteries. These plays were performed annually to celebrate religious festivities and holy days, such as Corpus Christi Day, even though the anonymous Corpus Christi plays were not exclusively staged on or around the corresponding church festival, despite what the cycle's title might suggest (cf. Dillon 2006: 144 f.). Only few cycles have survived, most notably those of York, Chester, 'Towneley' (or Wakefield), Coventry, and N-Town (possibly from Lincoln). The latter may have toured, as the 'N' may stand for the Latin *nomen* or 'name,' which might have been a placeholder for different cities. These plays present the history of the world and mankind, beginning with the creation of Heaven and Earth and culminating in the Last Judgement.

These plays were staged over the course of one (York) to three days (Chester) and presented either as processional performance (York and Chester) or in a fixed location (N-town). In processional staging, the cycles were divided into individual episodes that were presented on different mobile stages or pageants. The wagons, which were delegated to separate crafts or religious guilds that were responsible for a smooth performance of the production as well as for the props and costumes required for different pageants, were pulled through the streets, stopping at different designated stations along a set route in the city. At each stop, actors would perform 'their' sequence before giving way to the following pageant and moving on to the next station, where they performed the same episode again. With regard to the York plays (c. 1350), for instance, the best documented surviving cycle, which embraces 48 pageants, the audience gathered at around twelve different stations across the city and could see the whole sacred history staged from Creation and the Fall of Lucifer, which was shown on the first pageant, to Judgement Day, in one single day. The pageant carts often had elaborate machinery or scenery and frequently had three different levels to represent Heaven, Earth, and Hell.

Besides the great challenges processional performances posed to actors, there was a further disadvantage: The plays gave an opportunity for collecting money from the crowd to support the church or community; however, as the audience moved around in the open space and could leave before the box went round, this aim was not always met. What was the downside of open air street performances, laid the foundation for the commercial theatre. Dedicated playing spaces were established where people had to pass the box office before being admitted. In 1576 the first public theatre, 'The Theatre,' was founded by James Burbage in Shoreditch. Its location outside the jurisdiction of the city of London made performances independent from the restrictions of the religious calendar and provided a space for new dramatic structures and themes (cf. de Grazia 1997: 13-18).

It would be misleading to assume, however, that the cycle plays were limited to the communication of biblical narratives. While their primary aim was to mediate religious culture, they also provided a ritual space for the community to reflect the social and political concerns of the audience, including conflicting attitudes towards religious differences, conspiracy, rebellion, authority, representations of gender (in depictions of female virtue as in the *Nativity* plays of York, *Mary Play* of N-Town, depiction of female culpability in *Adam and Eve* or *The Fall of Man* [cf. Normington 2004; Coletti 2004]), as well as regional and class conflict (in the Chester *Shepherds' Plays*). For more straightforward lessons in human conduct and virtues, however, there was another, popular kind of drama: the morality play.

3. Morality Plays

The majority of the non-cycle plays make up what is commonly referred to as 'morality plays,' 'morals,' 'moral plays,' or simply 'moralities.' Like the cycle plays, the moralities present a stylized Christian narrative, including the temptation, fall, reversal, and restitution of the main character called Everyman or Mankind, who represents a human being the audience could immediately identify with. They also rely on iconographical conventions, and are deliberately didactic. It would be wrong to conclude that the moralities are an extension of the mystery cycles. Such Darwinian evolutionary hypotheses not only belie the fact that the history of drama is no regular succession, but also disregard that it is the differences between the mystery and morality plays which are striking, not the similarities.

In contrast to the mysteries, morality plays were not connected to any particular holy day, and did not require clericals as actors, but could be performed several times a year by priests or by tradesmen. They were considerably shorter than the cycles, which made them more apt for touring across the country, and highly allegorical. The *dramatis personae* represent personified abstract principles and qualities (such as the three cardinal virtues – Faith, Hope, and Charity – or the seven deadly sins – Sloth, Pride, Covetousness, Anger, Envy, Greed, Lechery); human categories (such as Fellowship) or supernatural beings (God or the Bad Angel). Rather than providing lessons in biblical narratives, morality plays aimed at refining their audience, offering instructions on how to distinguish between virtue and vice, which are both fighting for man's soul: "[I]f the source of the texts of the Cycles was the *lectio*, or readings from the Latin Bible, the source of the texts of the Moralities was the single vernacular item within the liturgy, the sermon" (Ricks 1987: 21 f.).

Of the five medieval English moralities that survived – *The Pride of Life* (c. 1350), *The Castle of Perseverance* (c. 1405-25)*, Wisdom* (c. 1460-65), *Mankind* (c. 1465-70), and *Everyman* (c. 1495) – the earliest play that has survived almost intact is *The Castle of Perseverance* (cf. Bevington 1975: 796-900), which comprises many dramatic features characteristic of the moralities, even though it is unusually long (over 3600 lines) and includes an uncommonly large number of characters (35 speaking parts). The play describes the life of Mankind and the temptations he is faced with from his birth to his death when he is judged before the throne of God.

Mankind, who enters the play as a newborn, naked child, is wavering between the Good and the Bad Angel. In the course of his life, he is tempted by World, Flesh, the Devil, and Covetousness, but saved by Penitence and Confession, and enters the Castle of Perseverance. After the virtues won the battle against the vices that laid siege to the castle, Covetousness lures Mankind out of its walls whereupon his soul Anima is carried to Hell. The four daughters of God – Mercy, Truth, Righteousness, and Peace – appear to plead for their father's mercy, which is granted, and Mankind is admitted to God's scaffold, for one purpose, as the audience is reminded, "To save you fro sinninge" (*The Castle of Perseverance*, line 3646; Bevington 1975: 900).

What is particularly interesting about this play is the graphic plan for its performance, which survived, and which illustrates the symbolic universe erected in this *platea* (see figure 1 and 2; cf. also Belsey 1974).

The Castle of Perseverance was designed for an open-air performance in a round space. Mankind's castle was in the centre, surrounded by a ditch of water, which has been read both as a barrier to demarcate the acting space and as a symbolic frame and allegorical feature for the action (cf. Styan 1996: 44), all the more so as it connects to references within the text, such as Sloth's attempt to dig a channel to let other Deadly Sins enter the siege (cf. King 2008 [1994]: 242). Some scholars suggest that the audience was excluded from the defensive rim around the castle but could move around between the scaffolds. They could thus also physically follow the places of conflict between Mankind and the awesome forces surrounding his castle while being banned from the "personal armament of the protagonist" (ibid.). Others claim that they also filled part of the *platea* and that the "stytelerys" mentioned in the stage plan were ushers who parted the audience when actors needed to move through the crowd (cf. Bevington 1975: 798). Both the scaffolds and the central arena bustled with action. As suggested by the stage directions, special effects and rich costumes were used, too. "And he that shall play Belial look that he have gunpowder burning in pipes in his hands and in his ears and in his arse when he goeth to battle" (cf. stage plan). The four daughters of God are symbolically dressed in white (Mercy), red (Righteousness), green (Truth), and black (Peace) robes.

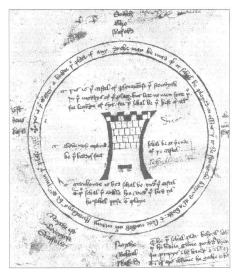

Figure 1: Stage map of *The Castle of Perseverance* as it was appended to the Macro manuscript (Bevington 1975: 796).

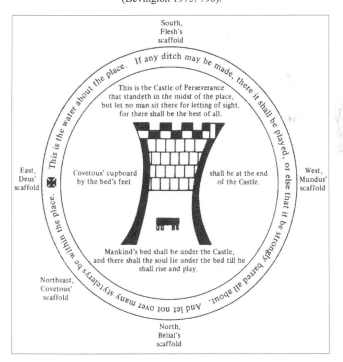

Figure 2: A modernized version of the stage map of *The Castle of Perseverance* (Bevington 1975: 797).

The play is not only highly allegorical, it is "essentially an animated sentence, a play on words, [...] a systematic series of puns" (Shepherd & Womack 1996: 23). Take, for instance, World's greeting of Mankind when the latter, successfully lured by World's obedient servants, Lust-Liking and Folly, dressed in rich clothes arrives at its mansion to enter its service:

> Now, Foly, faire the[e] befall,
> And Luste, blissyd be thou ay!
> Ye han browth Mankinde to min[e] hall
> Sertys, in a nobyl aray. [...]
> Mankinde, I rede that thou reste
> With me, the Werld, as it is beste. (ll. 725-735; Bevington 1975: 819 f.)

Folly and Lust persuade Mankind to serve the world and turn his back on God. What we find enacted here, as in so many other scenes in the play, is a straightforward ethical maxim. "The drama takes the flat proposition, as it were, and projects it into three dimensions, so that its verbs become physical actions, its nouns actors, its adjectives costumes and its prepositions spatial and social relationships" (Shepherd & Womack 1996: 23).

Like other moralities, such as *Mankind*, in which the protagonist is attacked by Nought, New-Guise, and Nowadays, the boasting of World, Flesh, or the Devil, and also like the cycle plays, which often included grim humour, *The Castle* creates comic moments in a tragic context (even though, considering the final revelation of man, these plays could qualify as comedies), which might have inspired the comic moments in Marlowe's *Doctor Faustus* or Shakespeare's Fool in *King Lear* (cf. Styan 1996: 48).

In contrast to the elaborate staging of *The Castle of Perseverance,* the stage requirements of the shorter and more famous *Everyman* are less demanding, even though including multiple levels and locations, making its staging much simpler. The play is based on the Dutch *Elckerlijc*, which attests to the cross-fertilization of early drama, and was the first of its kind to be performed on modern stages (cf. King 2008 [1994]: 251). The action sets in at the end of Everyman's life. Once Death has introduced himself to him, announcing his final journey, Everyman begs Fellowship, Kindred, Riches, Beauty, Strength, and Discretion to accompany him, to no avail. In the end he faces death with only Good Deeds by his side before the Angel leads him to Heaven. Alongside common themes such as the inevitability of death and the Last Judgement, *Everyman,* as is the case with other moralities, reveals the protagonist's whole life in a subtle time scheme which reflects the limited nature of man who is gradually but perpetually abandoned by the "goods of fortune" and the "goods of the soul" (King 2008: 254). Unlike other morality plays, *Everyman* does not revolve around the difficulty of defining evil, but of defining what is good and virtuous. What furthermore distinguishes morality plays from the cycles is their expansion from the ethical into the socio-political realm, which was further developed in shorter plays labelled as the 'interludes' during the Tudor period (1485-1603).

4. Tudor Interludes and the Political Dimension of Early English Drama

'Interlude' became the umbrella term for secular plays that were thought to have been performed in intervals during celebrations. While embracing a wide variety of genres and contents, the most common features of these interludes include "[r]elatively *uncomplicated staging* with few scenic requirements [...], *music, song and dance* [...] [*s*]*ymbolic costumes and properties,* as well as *two-dimensional characterization*" (Styan 1996: 62 f.). Henry Medwall's *Fulgens and Lucrece* (c. 1491-1501), the earliest purely secular English interlude that survived, is a case in point insofar as it compares social values of the Republican Rome with newly emerging ones under the reign of Henry VII, thereby promoting humanist learning. With John Bale and Sir David Lyndsay, drama soon became a vehicle for Reformation polemic.

> The technique was simply to equate the Pope, Cardinals, monks and friars with Lucifer and the Deadly Sins on the one hand, and Henry VIII and the pioneers of the reformed religion with the heavenly virtues on the other and to substitute Commonwealth or Widow England for the Everyman or Mankind figure of the earlier plays. (Ricks 1987: 24)

While pre-Reformation moralities focussed on redemption through man's actions, the abstinence from the seven deadly sins, and the figure of Vice, who embodies diabolic forces, in post-Reformation moralities, the Catholic doctrine was undermined to promote Protestantism: the Vice would be a Catholic and biblical narratives became vehicles to justify sinning.

Similar to *Fulgens and Lucrece*, John Skelton's *Magnyfycence* (c. 1519) theme is neither didactic nor religious, but political. The play, in which Fancy leads Magnificence to destruction, has often been read as an implicit attack against the young Henry VIII and a satire about corruption, vanity, and intrigue at his court. In Nicholas Udall's *Respublica* (1553) not only the state ruler is called to account, but the play also exposes conflicts and abuses within society, "[t]o shewe," as the Prologue announces, "that all Commen weales Ruin *and* decaye / from tyme to tyme hath been, ys, and shalbe alwaie, / whan Insolence, Flaterie, Opression, / and Avarice have the Rewle in theire possession" (lines 18-22). The play shows how Insolence, Flattery, and Oppression, disguised as Authority, Honesty, and Reformation, enter the service of Lady Respublica and flourish, supported by Avarice, masked as Policy, and Flattery in the guise of Honesty (cf. Walker 2008 [1994]: 83 f.). The "cultural work of early drama" (ibid.: 82) did not only include the intervention in social and political debates but also the deployment of "the panoply of emotive and affective devices at its disposal to sway royal or aristocratic audiences towards particular policies and against others" (ibid.: 85).

5. Developments

As suggested by the satirical content and comic banter between characters, such as A and B in *Fulgens and Lucrece*, the predominant dramatic form in the Tudor period was comedy which was gradually freed of any moral underpinning. Inspired by the Roman New Comedy of Plautus and Terence, plays such as Nicholas Udall's *Ralph Roister Doister* (c. 1553), full of comic trickery and treachery, included character types such as the braggart and the *miles gloriosus*. Likewise inspired by classical influence, following a five-act structure, adhering to the Aristotelian unity of time and place, and employing stock characters like the Vice figure (or a comic version of it, which conceived of the vice less as an incarnation of the devil than as a cunning and dramatically useful schemer or gadfly, the precursor of the popular clown figure), *Right Pithy, Pleasant, and Merry Comedy Gammer Gurton's Needle* (c. 1553) is an interlude whose plot revolves around the loss of needle and the caricature of an old mother Gurton. While comedy provided room for satire, tragic drama was more adequate for more complex reflections and criticism of political issues. Like the comedies, they often combined comic and tragic elements, as suggested by the title of Thomas Preston's play, which is announced as *A lamentable tragedy mixed ful of pleasant mirth, conteyning the life of CAMBISES King of PERCIA* (1569). Preston's drama furthermore illustrates the transition from the medieval moralities to the tragic and historical drama of the early modern era insofar as the list of *dramatis personae* includes both allegorical (Diligence, Cruelty) and historical figures (Cambyses).

As suggested by Preston's play, it is especially the morality plays and interludes that had a strong influence on early modern drama. Thus, we find morality characters like the Good and Bad Angel, the Seven Sins, God and the Devil, and, of course, the Vice revived in some of the most popular early modern plays, such as Christopher Marlowe's *Doctor Faustus* (1604) or William Shakespeare's *Richard III* (1592). Due to the Christian ideology they transported, however, plays that dealt with traditional religious subjects were banned from the English stages by an Act of Parliament that was released in 1572 and persisted (more or less successfully; cf. Clopper 2001: 268-94) under the final years of Henry VIII's reign, and the Protestant reigns of Edward VI and Elizabeth I. While most of these biblical plays did not enter the English theatres again until their re-opening in 1660, they remained an important part of cultural and theatrical memory, shaping the drama of Marlowe, Shakespeare, and Jonson. In fact, the knowledge of early English theatre is essential for the understanding of early modern drama, which we might read differently against the background of the medieval heritage. The loud banging on the gate in the porter scene in Shakespeare's *Macbeth* (1606), for instance, might have reminded the audience of the "Harrowing of Hell," an episode of the English Miracle Cycles, in which Christ breaks down the gates of hell and descends into the underworld to free the righteous. This background knowledge would have affected the way the audience saw Macduff, who enters the gate in *Macbeth*. Similar references to the medieval tradition can be found in the Christ-like figure of the silently suffering Lavinia in Shakespeare's *Titus Andronicus* (1592), or in the final scene of *King Lear* (1605), when Lear enters with the dead Cordelia in his arms, evoking the image of the *pietà*. When we read early modern drama, therefore, we should be aware of the dramatic foil established by biblical imagery, stock characters, and the rituals or ceremonial contexts of performance of early English drama, which early modern theatre could either draw on or deviate from, but which, regardless, remained a potent foundation for dramatists to work with and set themselves apart from in the process of creating new dramatic structures and forms.

Bibliography

Primary Sources

Bevington, David (ed.). 1975. *Medieval Drama*. Boston: Houghton Mifflin.
Greg, W. W. (ed.). 1952. *Respublica: An Interlude for Christmas 1553, Attributed to Nicholas Udall*. London: Oxford UP.

Annotated Bibliography

Cox, John D. & David Scott Kastan (eds.). 1997. *A New History of Early English Drama*. New York: Columbia UP.
A highly recommended collection of 25 essays by distinguished scholars in the field, providing excellent insights into the physical and social space of early English drama as well as conditions of performance and publication.
Normington, Katie. 2009. *Medieval English Drama: Performance and Spectatorship*. Cambridge/Malden: Polity P.
A comprehensive study of the contexts and locations of medieval performances.
Woolf, Rosemary. 1973. *The English Mystery Plays*. Berkeley/Los Angeles: U of California P.
A detailed survey of the genre including in-depth analyses of chosen plays.

Further Secondary Literature

Beadle, Richard & Alan J. Fletcher (eds.). 2008 [1994]. *The Cambridge Companion to Medieval English Theatre*. Cambridge: Cambridge UP.
Belsey, Catherine. 1974. "The Stage Plan of *The Castle of Perseverance*." In: *Theatre Notebook* 28.3: 124-32.
Briscoe, Marianne G. & John C. Coldewey (eds.). 1989. *Contexts for Early English Drama*. Bloomington: Indiana UP.
Clopper, Lawrence M. 2001. *Drama, Play, and Game: English Festive Culture in the Medieval and Early Modern Period*. Chicago: U of Chicago P.
Coletti, Theresa. 2004. *Mary Magdalene and the Drama of Saints: Theater, Gender and Religion in Late Medieval England*. Philadelphia: U of Pennsylvania P.

de Grazia, Margreta. 1997. "World Pictures, Modern Periods, and the Early Stage." In: Cox & Kastan 1997. 7-24.
Dillon, Janette. 2006. *The Cambridge Introduction to Early English Theatre*. Cambridge: Cambridge UP.
Görlach, Manfred. 1998. *Studies in Middle English Saints' Legends*. Heidelberg: Winter.
Goodman, Jennifer R. 1990. *British Drama Before 1660: A Critical History*. Boston: Twayne.
Griffin, Benjamin. 2001. *Playing the Past: Approaches to English Historical Drama*. Woodbridge: D. S. Brewer.
Happé, Peter. 1999. *English Drama Before Shakespeare*. London/New York: Longman.
Ingram, William. 1992. *The Business of Playing: The Beginnings of Adult Professional Theater in Elizabethan London*. Ithaca/London: Cornell UP.
Kermode, Lloyd Edward, Jason Scott-Warren & Martine van Elk (eds.). 2004. *Tudor Drama Before Shakespeare, 1485-1590: New Directions for Research, Criticism, and Pedagogy*. Houndmills/Basingstoke: Palgrave.
King, Pamela M. 2008 [1994]. "Morality plays." In: Beadle & Fletcher 2008. 235-62.
McKinnell, John. 2008 [1994]. "Modern Productions of Medieval English Drama." In: Beadle & Fletcher 2008. 287-325.
Meredith, Peter & John Tailby. 1983. *The Staging of Religious Drama in Europe in the Later Middle Ages: Texts and Documents in English Translation*. Kalamazoo, MI: Medieval Institute Publications.
Moseley, C. W .R .D. 2007. *English Renaissance Drama: A Very Brief Introduction to Theatre and Theatres in Shakespeare's Time*. Tirril: Humanities-Ebooks.
Normington, Katie. 2004. *Gender and Medieval Drama*. Cambridge: Brewer.
Ricks, Christopher. 1987 [1971]. *English Drama to 1710*. New York: Peter Bedrick Books.
Shepherd, Simon & Peter Womack. 1996. *English Drama: A Cultural History*. Oxford/Cambridge, MA: Blackwell.
Styan, J. L. 1996. *The English Stage: A History of Drama and Performance*. Cambridge: Cambridge UP.
Twycross, Meg. 2008 [1994]. "The Theatricality of Medieval English Plays." In: Beadle & Fletcher 2008. 26-74.
— & Sarah Carpenter. 2002. *Masks and Masking in Medieval and Early Tudor England*. Aldershot: Ashgate.
Walker, Greg. 2008 [1994]. "The Cultural Work of Early Drama." In: Beadle & Fletcher 2008. 75-98.
Weimann, Robert. 2000. *Author's Pen and Actor's Voice: Playing and Writing in Shakespeare's Theatre*. Cambridge/New York: Cambridge UP.
Wickham, Glynne. 1987. *The Medieval Theatre*. Cambridge: Cambridge UP.
—. 2002. *Early English Stages*. 4 vols. London: Routledge.

3. Genres and Developments in Elizabethan Drama: Christopher Marlowe's *Doctor Faustus*

ENNO RUGE

1. Introduction

Though widely used, labels like Georgian poetry or the Victorian novel are problematic because they suggest that literary works of a certain genre written and/or performed during the reign of a certain king or queen share special characteristics and that these characteristics can be directly related to that monarch's rule. 'Elizabethan drama,' for example, is a label applied to a variety of literary periods none of which coincides precisely with the reign of Queen Elizabeth I (1558-1603). It may refer, for example, to the years covered by Shakespeare's career as a playwright (c. 1590-1616), or to the period beginning with the opening of the first purpose-built open-air theatres in London in the mid-1570s and ending with either the Queen's death in 1603 or the closure of the theatres by the puritans in 1642. This usage, however, tends to obscure the fact that there are earlier theatrical traditions which may also be called Elizabethan and which have their roots in even older popular traditions, for example the saints or miracle plays, the moralities and customary household and community theatre. The importance of these traditions for the drama of the Renaissance has long been recognized.

In fact, 'Elizabethan drama' is often used as a synonym for 'Renaissance' or 'early modern drama.' In that sense it usually denotes a new departure in the history of drama, "the beginning of a theatrical tradition that, while interrupted by the closing of the public theatres in 1642 (and the subsequent destruction in the following years), continued on in the performing of Shakespeare and his contemporaries in the Restoration and beyond, down to the present day" (O'Connell 2010: 60). It has been argued that the plays by Shakespeare and others have been so influential and still speak to us today because they register problems caused by critical processes of modernization, a general loss of certainties in a time of radical religious, social, and political change, problems that, in a way, are still ours. This explains why some of the Elizabethan heroes, notably Shakespeare's Hamlet and Marlowe's Faustus, have become myths of the western world (Pfister 2004: 125).

2. Elizabethan Drama

In his extraordinary poetological essay "The Defence of Poesy" (written c. 1580-1585, published 1595) Sir Philip Sidney complained about plays that be neither right tragedies, nor right comedies, mingling kings and clowns, not because the matter so carrieth it, but thrust in the clown by head and shoulders to play a part in majestical matters with neither decency nor discretion, so as neither the admiration and commiseration, nor the right sportfulness, is by their mongrel tragi-comedy obtained. (Sidney 2002 [1595]: 244)

Modern critics who have found the comic scenes in Christopher Marlowe's *Doctor Faustus* (c. 1589) at odds with the tragedy's general argument of high seriousness (cf. Healy 2006: 174) seem to echo Sidney's critical opinion that a "tragedy should be still [i. e. always] maintained in a well-raised admiration" (ibid.), since comic scenes, "fit to lift up a loud laughter, and nothing else" (ibid.), threaten to displace the tragedy's 'message' and to spoil its desired cathartic effect.

Sidney did not live to see Marlowe's drama; his criticism was directed at plays like Richard Edwards' comedy *Damon and Pythias* (c. 1567) and Thomas Preston's tragedy *Cambyses, King of Persia* (c. 1570) which combined classical subject matter or stories of eminent historical persons with low life scenes involving clowns and ruffians. The fact that Preston's play, which dramatizes the rise and fall of the powerful Persian ruler Cambyses II, is emphatically called "a lamentable tragedy mixed full of pleasant mirth" (Preston 1570: title page) does not only indicate that this kind of 'mongrel tragi-comedy' was in vogue at the time but also suggests that the dramatist did not fear that by "mingling kings and clowns" (Sidney 2002: 244) he would compromise the play's central didactic purpose of presenting the Persian king's "odious death by God's Justice appointed" as a punishment for "his many wicked deeds and tyrannous murders" (Preston 1570: title page). Apparently, Sidney's firmly Aristotelian point of view was out of tune with the theatrical practice of his time.

The list of *dramatis personae* of Preston's tragedy includes allegorical representations of virtues and vices such as "Diligence" and "Crueltie" (ibid.), a fact that clearly shows the play's indebtedness to the morality tradition. In contrast to the mystery or miracle plays, morality plays like *Everyman* (c. 1495) or *Mankind* (c. 1465) did not use stories from the Bible or the lives of the saints, but staged an exemplary externalized battle between personified virtues and vices for the human soul. These plays were designed as popular entertainments and contained comic scenes and characters which were, however, not allowed to detract from the homiletic message: resist temptations, repent, and rely on God's justice and mercy.

For a while after the Reformation, religious drama became the vehicle of protestant anti-catholic propaganda, as in John Bale's *Kyng Johan* (c. 1536), which is often considered the first English history play. Even after the more radical protestants turned against the theatre, transformations of religious drama continued to be performed, for example *A Looking Glass for London and England* (c. 1590), written by Thomas Lodge and Robert Greene, a play which presents the fate of Biblical Nineveh as a warning to the people of Elizabethan London and England; a similar strategy used in countless sermons throughout early modern London. Moreover, as Brian Gibbons (1968) has shown, the morality plays were a major influence on Jacobean city comedies.

Although early-Elizabethan homelitic tragedies were often parodied in later plays for their bombastic style, creaking fourteen-syllable verse, predictable didactic morals and unbelievable psychological characters – as is for example Preston's *Cambyses* by William Shakespeare in *Henry IV* (c. 1597) – playwrights, companies and audiences were well aware of the influence of the tradition on early modern English drama. Even Thomas Norton's and Thomas Sackville's *Gorboduc* (1562), the tragedy singled out for praise by Philip Sidney for its "stately speeches and well sounding phrases" (2002: 243), echoes the moralities. The various political counsellors in the play, which stages the division of King Gorboduc's kingdom and its disastrous consequences, thus anticipating Shakespeare's *King Lear* (1604/05), can be seen as traditional embodiments of good and evil struggling for the human soul. One of the authors, Thomas Sackville, was the initiator of a collection of cautionary tales about the fall of great men, entitled *A Mirror for Magistrates* (1559), which was modelled on medieval *de casibus* tragedies. Accordingly, *Gorboduc* offered an indirect advice to England's monarch, the unmarried Elizabeth I, before whom the tragedy was performed in 1562, warning her against leaving her succession perpetually unsettled.

Sidney exempted *Gorboduc* from his general condemning verdict for its "climbing to the height of Seneca's style" (ibid.); for those educated at the new English humanist schools and universities, Seneca's tragedies, dating from the 1st century AD, were the model of dramatic decorum. As is well known, however, Elizabethan drama did not strictly observe the classical rules for tragedy set up in Aristotle's *Poetics* (c. 335 BC) that informed Seneca's plays. Even *Gorboduc*, the first blank-verse tragedy in English, which adopted the division into five acts from its Latin model, was found "faulty" with regard to the unities of place and time, much to Sidney's disappointment. "For […] the stage should always represent but one place, and the uttermost time presupposed in it should be, both by Aristotle's precept, and by common reason, but one day […]" (ibid.).

Even though later Elizabethan playwrights did not follow Sidney's instructions, they certainly realized and exploited the dramatic potential of Seneca (whose works were now available in translations even to those who had no humanist education), in particular the sensationalist aspects of his revenge-plots. The most important example is Thomas Kyd's *Spanish Tragedy* (first recorded performance 1592, but probably performed earlier), one of the most popular and influential Elizabethan stage-plays. Two Senecan characters, a dead man's ghost, and the personification of Revenge serve as the tragedy's chorus. However, *The Spanish Tragedy* also violated classical decorum by showing shocking horrors on stage that were only related verbally in Seneca, for example the brutal murder of Horatio. Hieronimo, Horatio's father and avenger, is a new kind of tragic protagonist. His insidious revenge plot clearly violates Elizabethan legal and religious norms, but he still retains the audience's sympathy through his soliloquies which show him as a wronged, grieving, shattered outsider struggling for his sanity, who keeps postponing his revenge but is ultimately driven to it. Even though *The Spanish Tragedy* had gone out of fashion at the beginning of the 17th century, it set a pattern for the revenge tragedies that followed, most notably for Shakespeare's *Hamlet* (c. 1600; cf. Watson 1990: 317-34; see chapter 6).

Together with Marlowe's tragedies, *The Spanish Tragedy* marked "the breakthrough to greatness" (Watson 1990: 312) for the Elizabethan tragedy and, arguably, for the Elizabethan drama in general. The rapid development and fruition of the powerful new kind of tragedy was made possible by the evolution of professional playing companies who had established themselves in purpose-built, permanent playhouses in the suburbs of London, exempt from the hostile city's jurisdiction. The most important of these so-called public playhouses were the Theatre, erected in 1576, followed by the Curtain (1577), in Shoreditch, and the Rose (1587), the Swan (1595), the Globe (1599), on Bankside, south of the river Thames (cf. Foakes 1990). These commercial playhouses, targeting large audiences from all classes – some, like the Globe, could take up to 3.000 people –, needed spectacular tragedies like those by Kyd and Marlowe, which were both popular and artistically refined. Nevertheless the status of the theatre was ambivalent. Favoured on the one hand by aristocrats and the court, playwrights and players were, on the other hand, still not regarded as respectable. The fact that many playhouses stood next to brothels and dicing houses did not help either. Even though the theatre had many enemies, the puritans were at the forefront of its detractors. In 1612, the preacher Thomas Sutton deplored that the masses kept flocking to the "wanton theatres" to see "profane & obscœne stageplaies" and called acting a "trade of sinne" (Sutton 1616: 27 f.). To be sure, though, theatre owners, companies, and playwrights exploited the notoriety of the theatrical spectacles.

3. *Doctor Faustus* and the 'Marlowe Effect'

If it is true that the acting companies operating at the great public playhouses of Elizabethan London were constantly on the lookout for sensationalist plays which promised food for thought as well as spectacle and perhaps a bit of scandal into the bargain, *Doctor Faustus*, the tragedy of a great scholar who sells his soul to the devil in his thirst for knowledge and power, must have been just their play. Even more so, because of the growing notoriety of its author, Christopher Marlowe, as a man involved in various illicit activities and engaged in secret government service, who was arrested no fewer than four times, a freethinker, a blasphemer, and even an 'atheist' (cf. Levin 1954; Riggs 2004).

The first recorded performance of *Doctor Faustus* was on 30 September 1594, after Marlowe's violent death at the age of 29, but it had certainly been performed earlier. As most scholars now believe, it was probably written and initially performed in 1588 or 1589 (cf. Bevington & Rasmussen 1993: 1-3, 48 f.), that is after the sensational success of *Tamburlaine the Great* in 1587, a tragedy in two parts, which made Marlowe famous as a playwright but also earned him notoriety. For example, it provoked Marlowe's rival playwright Robert Greene to accuse him "of daring god out of heaven with that Atheist Tamburlan" (qtd. in Cheney 2006: 1). *Doctor Faustus* invited similar reactions. In 1633 the puritan anti-theatrical writer William Prynne reported an incident during a performance of *Doctor Faustus* at the otherwise little known Belsavage theatre (probably in 1588 or 1589),

> the visible apparition of the devil on the stage of the Belsavage playhouse, in Queen Elizabeth's days, to the great amazement of both the actors and the spectators, whiles they were there playing the History of Faustus, the truth of which I have heard from many now alive, who well remember it, there being some distracted with that fearful sight. (qtd. in Bevington & Rasmussen 1993: 2)

The anecdote of the devil himself mingling with the actors on stage, pretending to be devils, is presented by Prynne as 'evidence' that a theatre was indeed "sathans synagogue," as the polemicist Philip Stubbes had called it in 1583, where people went "to worship the deuil" (qtd. in Chambers 1923, IV: 223). The puritans' view that conjuring up the devil on stage could make the powers of darkness actually appear on the scene was certainly extreme, but a tendency towards theatrical extravagance and excess, an unmistakable desire for notoriety, became something like a trademark of Marlovian drama, a phenomenon which Tom Healy calls "the Marlowe effect" (Healy 1994: 2).

Although initially connected with Marlowe's enigmatic personality, the Marlowe effect also seems to have worked independently of the author. After Marlowe's death in 1593 his plays continued to be popular on stage, even though – in the case of *Doctor Faustus* at least – in substantially revised form. Considerable portions of the successful versions acted after Marlowe's death and, it is to be inferred, of the two earliest textual versions that have come down to us, printed in 1604 and 1616 respectively, are certainly not originally by Marlowe. In 1602 Philip Henslowe, the owner of the Rose theatre on Bankside, paid two playwrights, William Birde and Samuel Rowley, four pounds for "ther adicyones in docter fostes" (Foakes 2002: 206), and these revisions were probably not the last and possibly not even the first (Healy 2006: 179).

The daring, impetuous personality of Marlowe's heroes, which, according to those critics who read the plays biographically, correlated with their author's, is a distinguishing feature of Marlovian drama, but it may also be seen as the signature of a dramatic form not fully developed. According to Robert N. Watson (1990: 312), Marlowe's tragedies "have the kind of naïve power that often characterizes artifacts from young cultures discovering their strength". Accordingly, critics of *Doctor Faustus* have pointed out the imbalance of the composition, the lack of dramatic unity and the episodic structure. Indeed the plot seems to have little dramatic suspense. Faustus' initial pact with the devil is followed by a series of practical jokes and conjuring tricks until the magus finally meets his promised end.

Critical discussions tend to privilege the scenes with a tragic dimension that touch upon serious questions of metaphysics, while the scenes of farce are often explained away as the inheritance of the medieval morality tradition. In keeping with this view, critics now prefer the 'darker,' morally more ambiguous and thus more 'modern,' so-called A-text, published in 1604, rather than the 'milder,' more 'conventionally orthodox' B-text, printed in 1616, in which the comic parts are expanded (Healy 2006: 183). Moreover, the underlying assumption for preferring the earlier to the later text is its being closer to Marlowe's 'original.' My brief analysis is based on the A-text which does not mean, however, that I agree with all the arguments in favour of the earlier version; neither is it my intention to completely dispose of the B-text. If the B-text's "additions and variations show a sensitive understanding of the pattern of ideas, images and motifs that inheres in the shorter version" (MacAlindon 1994: xi), in other words, if the A-text is 'complete' as it is, then it is to be preferred; nevertheless the B-text can help us to interpret Marlowe's tragedy (Healy 2006: 184). Unless otherwise indicated, all quotations are from the A-text in David Bevington's and Eric Rasmussen's critical edition (2008), which the editors have plausibly divided into five acts.

4. Morality Play and / or Tragedy

Marlowe's principal source for his tragedy was *The History of the Damnable Life and Deserved Death of Doctor John Faustus*, a translation of the original German "Faustbuch," the *Historia von D. Johann Fausten / dem weitbeschreyten Zauberer und Schwartzkünstler* (1587). The date of the earliest surviving print, 1592, was taken by some editors as proof that Marlowe's tragedy cannot have been written before that date, but it is now generally assumed that the 1592 edition was not the first. Like the German original, the English Faustbook, from which the tragedy takes the central elements of the story, including the comic scenes, is a cautionary tale warning against intellectual pride, exhorting its readers to repent (cf. Wootton 2008). The source's moralizing tone matches that of the morality tradition which Doctor Faustus also makes use of. The apparitions of the good and bad angels struggling for Faustus' soul and the show of the seven deadly sins could be taken directly from a morality play and even the mysterious old man who admonishes Faustus in the final act and Mephistopheles may be seen as traditional embodiments of good and evil. What is more, the prologue and the epilogue framing the dramatic action suggest that in the play Faustus is presented as a moral exemplum. The figure of the Chorus announces that the players "must perform / the form of Faustus' fortunes, good or bad" (Prologue 7 f.). With dramatic economy the chorus sums up in a few lines Faustus' early years, which Marlowe's source narrates in great detail, and his successful studies at the university of Wittenberg (the university of Martin Luther where Shakespeare's Hamlet studies as well) until he is

> graced with doctor's name
> Excelling all whose sweet delight disputes
> In heavenly matters of theology;
> Till, swollen with cunning of self-conceit,
> His waxen wings did mount above his reach,
> And melting heavens conspired his overthrow.
> For, falling to a develish exercise,
> And glutted more with learning's golden gifts,
> He surfeits upon cursèd necromancy;
> Nothing so sweet as magic is to him,
> Which he prefers to his chiefest bliss. (Prologue, 17-27)

The language of the prologue marks Faustus as a sinner form the start. Having "glutted" himself with knowledge (gluttony is the deadly sin of overeating) he moves on to the "develish exercise" of "necromancy," i. e. black magic. His sin is intellectual pride which induces him to pursue things above human reach. For this purpose he is even prepared to abandon his "chiefest bliss," i. e. the hope of salvation. However, like the mythical Icarus, who flew too close to the sun, he foolishly overestimates his power and will be punished accordingly for his transgression by divine powers.

The epilogue, again spoken by the Chorus, concludes the play in much the same tone:

> Cut is the branch that might have grown full straight,
> And burnèd is Apollo's laurel bough
> That sometime grew within this learnèd man.
> Faustus is gone. Regard his hellish fall,
> Whose fiendful fortune may exhort the wise
> Only to wonder at unlawful things,
> Whose deepness doth entice such forward wits
> To practise more than heavenly power permits. (Epilogue, 1-8)

However, the homiletic message of prologue and epilogue is undermined by much of what happens in between. As Tom Healy (1994: 31) points out,

> Marlowe's drama is a sustained assault on preconceptions about a didactic role for literature, imagining it to improve the human condition through representing reductive attitudes about moral improvement. Marlowe's scepticism about this role of writing, and of the values which underlie it, reflects the cultural diversities of sixteenth-century life.

Marlowe, however, does not cite the moralistic pattern simply to dismiss or satirize it. Faustus is a man of exceptional intellectual abilities but he is also an Everyman facing perplexing choices in a radically changing world of conflicting values and ideologies. In *Doctor Faustus* "[t]he schematic battle among allegorical figures is still plainly visible," Robert N. Watson (1990: 334) observes, "but tied into the real temptations of a psychologically plausible human life. The vicious circle of pride and despair becomes less demonology than psychopathology."

The central choice Faustus is facing is that between worldly ambition and Christian humility or *contemptus mundi*. Whereas the Middle Ages had regarded ambition, honour, glory, curiosity, desire, or passion as dangerous desires threatening the divine cosmic and social order, the Renaissance came to see them as positive human driving forces (cf. Pfister 2004: 137). The Elizabethans admired accomplished individuals and their personal achievements and self-fulfillment in this world. It was "a culture enthusiastically engaged in gaining the world (through imperialism, commerce, science and humanistic philosophy)" (Watson 1990: 334). At the same time, however, the protestant reformers, in particular the Calvinists dominant in England, put renewed emphasis on the traditional Christian disregard for the temporal world. Believers were urged to disdain worldly ambition and success, to withstand the temptation of 'glittering trifles' and to aspire to higher things instead, that is to the eternal life of the soul. As the body was considered the temporal dwelling, or even the prison, of the soul, this contempt for the world included a disdain for sensual pleasures. *Doctor Faustus* dramatizes the conflict between these ideals.

In the expository first act, Faustus, having dismissed the academic disciplines he excelled in, philosophy, law, medicine, and theology, as insufficient to satisfy his desire for knowledge, is resolved "to practise magic and concealèd arts" (1.1.104). Significantly, knowledge is only one thing among others which he hopes to gain with the help of black magic, as he says in one of his first soliloquies. The spirits he intends to conjure up are not only to resolve him of "all ambiguities" (1.1.82), read him "strange philosophy / And tell the secrets of all foreign kings" (1.1.88 f.); but perform "what desperate enterprise [he] will". He might want the servile spirits to "fly to India for gold, / Ransack the ocean for orient pearl, / And search all corners of the new-found world / For pleasant fruits and princely delicates" (1.1.83-87). With the acquired wealth he plans to finance an army for which the spirits will invent new terrible weapons, so that he can help the protestant cause to triumph and "reign sole king in all our provinces" (1.1.96). "Magic appeals to Faustus because it allows intellectual activity to control the material world; he is betrayed, as were many Renaissance aspirations, by the impossibility of freeing himself from the material sphere and materialist motives." (Watson 1990: 335) In fact, Faustus is denied the secret knowledge he so craves after he has sold his soul to Mephistopheles in exchange for his services. The devil provides him with all kinds of magic books but leads him by the nose when it comes to serious questions, for example in an astrological debate about the Ptolemaic system (2.3.33-66). When asked "who made the world," Mephistopheles flatly refuses to answer (2.3.66 f.). Some of Faustus' materialistic wishes are granted, but the world he commands with his magic has nothing to do with his earlier grand vision of "a world of profit and delight, / Of power, of honour, of omnipotence" (1.1.55 f.). "In exchange for his forfeited soul, Faustus receives merely some slapstick revenge, a little money, praise from the ignorant, unfulfilling fulfilments of his sexual fantasies, and a horrible spiritual emptiness." (Watson 1990: 335) On stage the clown-scenes which parody Faustus' erroneous pursuit of happiness soon make clear that Faustus has made a rather bad bargain. Robin the clown (i. e. a rustic, coarse buffoon) is so desperate that he is ready to "give his soul to the devil for a shoulder of mutton" (1.4.8). When Faustus' foolish apprentice Wagner, imitating his master, offers to teach Robin the trick of turning himself "to a dog, or a cat, or a mouse, or a rat, or anything," the clown retorts:

> How? A Christian fellow to a dog or a cat, a mouse or a rat? No, no, sir. If you turn me into anything, let it be the likeness of a little, pretty, frisking flea, that I may be here and there and everywhere. O, I'll tickle the pretty wenches' plackets! (1.4.60-64)

Faustus is a grave scholar, a sophisticated man with good manners, but he is also "wanton and lascivious" (2.1.140 f.) and his desires are not so different from Robin's naughty fantasy. In fact, the first and the last thing he asks Mephistopheles to do for him concern the satisfaction of his sexual desire.

5. Faustus as Entertainer

As it turns out, Faustus continues to debase himself. Practically all of the third and fourth act is devoted to cheap tricks which Faustus performs with Mephistopheles' help. In act 3 he visits Rome where he is made invisible by Mephistopheles and upsets the Pope's dinner, terrifying the prelates. In act 4 he establishes a reputation for himself as a magician touring the great European courts. The scene in the Vatican has extra significance for a 16th-century protestant audience who was told incessantly by the religious authorities that the Pope was an embodiment of Antichrist. Not surprisingly, then, the scene has strong anti-catholic overtones. However, Faustus' snatching food from the Pope's plate, boxing him on the ear, and throwing fireworks does not substantially further the protestant cause. In the B-text Faustus and Mephistopheles free the German antipope Bruno from his imprisonment in the Vatican, but even that action can be seen as simply more adolescent tomfoolery. "In the assault on the Pope, the reformation has become vandalism" (Watson 1990: 336). In the scenes in which Faustus astounds the Emperor Charles V by conjuring up the spirit of Alexander the Great (4.1.) and pleases the Duke of Vanholt's pregnant wife with "a dish of ripe grapes" (4.2.10 f.) the magus is reminiscent of those scientists and alchemists who were (like John Dee) summoned to the great European courts to work wonders for financial rewards. In marked contrast to his great vision of omnipotence, Faustus acts like a servant of the powerful, and the social order remains perfectly intact.

As we have seen, the burlesque scenes have an important function as illustrations of Faustus' self-degradation as he wastes his powers (paid for, after all, with his soul) on pranks and cheap showmanship. Nevertheless, critics have often regarded them as insignificant, perhaps even as degrading the tragedy's great metaphysical concerns. They may be significant, however, precisely for what they are. When Faustus' heart sinks after signing the contract, Mephistopheles wants to divert him with a show of dancing devils. Asked what this show means, the devil answers: "Nothing, Faustus, but to delight thy mind withal / And to show thee what magic can perform" (2.1.84 f.). Here the play dramatizes the anti-theatricalists' insinuation that the theatre is "sathans synagogue" (Howard 1994: 22), the devil's trap. According to them, the sole purpose of playing is to distract unstable minds from the right course, not, as the theatre's defenders claimed, to teach moral lessons. This is also demonstrated in the grotesque parade of the Deadly Sins (2.3.106-55) which "are meant to be ridiculous. Relics [...] of medieval outlook they pose no threat as itemized sins. It is his sitting down for the diverting pastime that expresses Faustus's jeopardy." (Stachniewski 1991: 307) When Faustus announces that he has benefited greatly from the performance ("O, this feeds my soul"), he is reprimanded by Lucifer acting as stage-manager: "Tut Faustus, in hell is all manner of delight." (2.3.164 f.) In act 4, where Faustus acts in effect as an illusionist pleasing his audiences with mere representations of the real thing, he shows that he has finally learned his lesson.

Are we to understand, then, that in the Elizabethan theatre all is "manner of delight," too, that Elizabethan drama has no 'meaning'? The farcical scenes in *Doctor*

Faustus may indeed, as the metatheatrical references suggest, provocatively confirm the anti-theatricalists' accusation that diversion is the whole purpose of playing – especially, if we take into account that the 'serious' scenes also provide ample opportunity for theatrical spectacle, fireworks and all. Does it follow that the "play's preoccupation with creating theatre, with organizing performances" should be seen as "its ultimate rationale" (Healy 2006: 189) – in other words that there is no *Tragical History of Doctor Faustus* at all?

It is doubtful, I believe, whether the play's exuberant theatricality "completely displaces any attempt at serious drama" (ibid.: 185). On the contrary, instead of taking off the edge of Faustus' tragic predicament, the frequent self-conscious reminders that the audience is watching a frivolous entertainment add to the play's ambiguity. After all, the playgoers have come to be distracted from serious thoughts, an activity which will, as they are about "to see from Faustus's fate, condemn them" (Stachniewski 1991: 307).

6. A Tragedy of Damnation

If Faustus is betrayed, who, then, is his betrayer? Does he foolishly deceive himself, as the moralistic prologue suggests, is he led astray by Mephistopheles or is it the heavenly powers themselves that conspire his overthrow? Or is he even merely Fortune's fool, like the heroes of the old *de casibus* tragedies, and is all which takes place *necessary*? Does Faustus have a choice, either to resist temptation in the first place or to change his ways when he realizes his mistake, or is his fate sealed from the beginning? The tension between self-determination and heteronomy is characteristic of Elizabethan tragedy. Students of *Macbeth* (1606) are familiar with the difficult question whether Macbeth brings about his own downfall or whether the witches have arranged everything for him. In *Doctor Faustus* the problem is complicated by the Calvinist doctrine of double-predestination, according to which God has decreed before the creation of the world whose soul will be saved and whose will be damned. Although Calvinism was officially endorsed by the Church of England in the late 16th century, the doctrine of double-predestination was far from uncontested (MacAlindon 1994: 110 f.).

When Faustus makes up his mind to turn to black magic he seems to be fully aware of the consequences, but he is nevertheless resolved to go through with it. He brusquely informs Valdes, one of the men who provide him with the necessary books, "as resolute I am in this / As thou to live" (1.1.136 f.). Significantly, he neither hears the good angel's warning nor the bad angel's cheer at this point (cf. 1.1.72-79). The thought that he is risking salvation does not worry him, as he assures Mephistopheles: "There is no chief but only Beelzebub, / To whom Faustus doth dedicate himself, / This word 'damnation' terrifies not him" (1.3.57-59). He mocks the fallen angel's suffering for "being deprivèd of the joys of heaven" and haughtily advises the devil: "Learn thou of Faustus manly fortitude, / And scorn those joys thou never shalt possess" (1.3.85-87). He even denies the existence of hell itself.

> FAUSTUS. Come, I think hell's a fable.
> MEPHISTOPHELES. Ay, think so still, till experience change thy mind.
> FAUSTUS. Why, think'st thou then that Faustus shall be damned?
> MEPHISTOPHELES. Ay, of necessity, for here's the scroll
> Wherin thou hast given thy soul to Lucifer.
> FAUSTUS. Ay, and body too. But what of that?
> Think'st thou that Faustus is so fond
> To imagine that after this life there is any pain?
> Tush, these are trifles and mere old wives' tales.
> MEPHISTOPHELES. But, Faustus, I am an instance to prove the contrary,
> For I am damnéd and am now in hell.
> FAUSTUS. How? Now in hell? Nay, an this be hell, I'll willingly be damned here. What?
> Walking disputing, etc.? (2.1.127-39)

As long as life in hell is like life at a university, it is alright for Faustus. At this point he is still so self-assured that he enjoys playing the sceptic, believing he is the master of his fate.

After Mephistopheles coolly refuses to reveal the secrets of the universe, however, Faustus suddenly realizes that he has been deceived and blames the devil for his plight: "'Tis thou hast damned distressèd Faustus' soul" (2.3.75). At the end of the B-Text a passage is added where Mephistopheles confirms the truth of this accusation (cf. 5.2.91-97), whereas the A-text leaves the matter open. At this crucial moment of crisis, Faustus seriously wonders whether it is not too late for him to repent. The good angel (whom he now can probably hear, cf. 2.1.7) reassures him that it is "[n]ever too late, if Faustus can repent" (2.3.78). The B-text has "if Faustus will repent" instead of "can". For some critics the different auxiliaries, together with other changes, signal "doctrinal differences" between the two texts (Marcus 1996: 47; Hopkins 2008: 31). According to these readings (which, arguably, can be seen as symptoms of what Honigmann [1991:174] calls "the tendency to overexplain" Marlowe's play), the theological position of the A-text is radically Protestant, or rather Calvinist, as Faustus, being damned, is denied free will and the ability to repent, whereas the B-text appears to support the position (variously described as "Lutheran," "latitudinarian Anglican," "Arminian," "Anglo-Catholic," etc.) that "repentance is possible if the person chooses it" (Hopkins 2008: 47), because God never gives up a penitent sinner.

The difference between the two texts is most obvious in the final speech of the mysterious "old man," the last attempt to urge Faustus to repent before he dies. In the A-text the old man severely reprimands Faustus in the style of an Old Testament prophet (or an early modern puritan):

> Ah, Doctor Faustus, that I might prevail
> To guide thy steps unto the way of life,
> By which sweet path thou mayst attain the goal
> That shall conduct thee to celestial rest!
> Break heart, drop blood, and mingle it with tears –
> Tears falling from repentant heaviness
> Of thy most vile and loathsome filthiness,

> The stench whereof corrupts the inward soul
> With such flagitious crimes of heinous sins
> As no commiseration may expel
> But mercy, Faustus, of thy Saviour sweet,
> Whose blood alone must wash away thy guilt. (5.1.35-46)

The B-text reads:

> O gentle Faustus, leave this damnèd art,
> This magic, that will charm thy soul to hell
> And quite bereave thee of salvation!
> Though thou hast now offended like a man,
> Do not persever in it like a devil.
> Yet, yet thou hast an amiable soul,
> If sin by custom grow not into nature.
> Then, Faustus, will repentance come too late;
> Then thou art banished from the sight of heaven.
> No mortal can express the pains of hell.
> It may be this my exhortation
> Seems harsh and all unpleasant. Let it not,
> For, gentle son, I speak not in wrath
> Or envy of thee, but in tender love
> And pity of thy future misery;
> And so have hope that this my kind rebuke,
> Checking thy body, may amend thy soul. (5.1.34-50)

The second speech is obviously "milder and gentler" (Marcus 1996: 48), and, arguably, poetically weaker. In marked contrast to the relentless wording of the A-text, the old man emphasizes that he does not speak "in wrath," but "in tender love". However, both texts want to show the erring Faustus a way to save his soul. The A-text emphasizes the corrupt nature of fallen mankind, only to be overcome by acknowledging Christ's atonement for the sins of mankind (which Faustus has mocked repeatedly, not least by sealing his pact with the devil with Christ's final words "*Consummatum est!*" [2.1.74; cf. also 1.1.39-50]). In comparison the B-text is more optimistic. Here the old man tries to win Faustus over by flattery, claiming that it is not too late for him.

However, the readings which see the two texts as addressing opposing theological positions do not account for the fact that in either case Faustus is eventually denied the ability to repent, despite all the rhetoric of forgiveness. In the end it makes little difference for Faustus whether he is damned because of man's inborn sinful nature or because sin has "by custom" grown "into nature". The punishment of a wrathful god is certain. In either version the good angel and the old man are obviously powerless. Rather, Faustus feels that their exhortations mock his helplessness, which is why he asks Mephistopheles (in both versions) to "torment" the old man (5.1.75). Until the very end he oscillates between hope and despair, even in his grand final soliloquy:

> Now thou hast but one bare hour to live,
> And then thou must be damned perpetually.
> Stand still, you ever-moving spheres of heaven,

> That time may cease and midnight never come!
> Fair nature's eye, rise, rise again, and make
> Perpetual day; or let this hour be but
> A year, a month, a week, a natural day,
> That Faustus may repent and save his soul!
> O lente, lente, currite noctis equi!
> The stars move still; time runs; the clock will strike;
> The devil will come, and Faustus must be damned.
> O, I'll leap up to my God! Who pulls me down? (5.2.58-69)

In his despondency Faustus wishes he had no immortal soul, i.e. he yearns to be out of the Christian belief system, which has become his "psycho-theological prison" (Stachniewski 1991: 331). This is why he would rather live in the pre-Christian world of the ancients, represented here by the philosopher Pythagoras (even though Faustus is mistaken about Pythagoras' doctrine of metempsychosis, which was after all grounded in the immortality of the soul), and mythical Helen of Troy, whose spectre he conjures up to spend his final hours with, compared to whom "all is dross" (5.1.96) and who "sucks forth" his soul (5.1.93).

Depending on the point of view, Faustus' delusion either proves that he is hopelessly lost and that God's punishment is just (a reading the B-text may lend itself to more readily). Alternatively it may be seen as the outcry of a tormented soul against the oppressive constraints of religion, be it traditional or reformed (cf. Dollimore 2004: 114). Admittedly, the view that Faustus is a sceptical rebel against conventions and superstition owes much to modern conceptions of religion, but it seems plausible that Elizabethan audiences would have found his downfall disturbing nonetheless, as it may have teased out "latent fears conditioned by a shared religious nervous system" (Stachniewski 1991: 306). Faustus cannot have been much good as a moral example. Most people in the audience will have found they could never achieve assurance of salvation like the pious, ascetic old man whose 'saving faith' protects him against temptations and enables him to bear tribulations patiently. It is much more likely that they would have compared themselves with the foolish and frail sinner in his anguish, perhaps wondering how to account for their own sins, including idling away their precious time in a playhouse, "only to wonder at unlawful things" (Epilogue, 6).

7. Conclusion

Christopher Marlowe's *Doctor Faustus* may be called a quintessential Elizabethan drama. It stages the contradictions of Elizabethan culture. The (over-)ambitious scholar Faustus is at the nexus of two conflicting ideals characteristic of the age: on the one hand the age admired 'Renaissance man' for testing the limits of human potential; on the other hand it valued moral reform, moderation and Christian humility. *Doctor Faustus* transforms older moralizing types of drama into a morally ambiguous tragedy. Marlowe's Faustus is not merely a moral *exemplum*, but also a tragically erring individual questioning conflicting norms and conventions, who eloquently expresses his ambition, inner conflicts, and growing despair in moving soliloquies, thus enabling the audience to empathize or even identify with him. Like Marlowe's other Elizabethan tragedies, *Doctor Faustus* looks back to older theatrical traditions and at the same time marks a new beginning in the history of European theatre. It paves the way for the great tragedies of William Shakespeare, Thomas Middleton, and John Ford, but also for Jacobean city comedy, notably Ben Jonson's *The Alchemist* (1610). If *The Tragical History of Doctor Faustus* still speaks to us today, it is perhaps because we, having lost confidence in philosophy, science, and religion, like Faustus, at times catch ourselves thinking that in exchange for having absolute power over the material world we would sell our souls.

Bibliography

Primary Sources

Kyd, Thomas. 2009 [c. 1592]. *The Spanish Tragedy*. James R. Mulryne (ed.). London: Methuen.
Marlowe, Christopher. 2008 [1995]. *Doctor Faustus and Other Plays*. David Bevington & Eric Rasmussen (eds.). Oxford World's Classics. Oxford: Oxford UP.
Norton, Thomas & Thomas Sackville. 1970 [1562]. *Gorboduc or Ferrex and Porrex*. Irby B. Cauthen (ed.). London: Arnold.
Preston. Thomas. 1975 [c. 1570]. *Cambyses, King of Persia*. Robert Carl Johnson (ed.). Salzburg: Inst. f. Engl. Sprache u. Literatur.

Annotated Bibliography

Altman, Joel B. 1978. *The Tudor Play of Mind: Rhetorical Inquiry and the Development of Elizabethan Drama*. Berkeley: U of California P.
A seminal study in the field, which examines dramatic structure and its origin in rhetorical theory. According to Altman, Elizabethan drama functions as a medium of intellectual and emotional exploration of received norms, values and ideas.
Bevington, David M. 1962. *From Mankind to Marlowe: Growth of Structure in the Popular Drama of Tudor England*. Cambridge: Harvard UP.
A classic study on Marlowe's use of the morality tradition.
Cheney, Patrick (ed.). 2006. *The Cambridge Companion to Christopher Marlowe*. Cambridge: Cambridge UP.
An excellent collection of essays by leading Marlowe-scholars.
Dollimore, Jonathan. 2004 [1984]. *Radical Tragedy: Religion, Ideology and Power in the Drama of Shakespeare and His Contemporaries*. Hemel Hempstead: Harvester Wheatsheaf.

As the title indicates, this key text of the cultural materialism emphasizes the tragedies' potential for subversion of dominant ideologies. There is an important chapter on Doctor Faustus.

Gurr, Andrew. 2009 [1970]. *The Shakespearean Stage 1574-1642*. Cambridge: Cambridge UP.

Still the best study of Elizabethan and Jacobean theatre history.

Hattaway, Michael (ed.). 2010. *A New Companion to English Renaissance Literature and Culture*. 2 vols. Oxford: Blackwell.

One of the most useful comprehensive handbooks on the period.

Healy, Thomas. 1994. *Christopher Marlowe*. Plymouth: Northcote House.

A brilliant, concise exploration of Marlowe's drama.

Levin, Harry. 1954. *The Overreacher: A Study of Christopher Marlowe*. Cambridge: Harvard UP.

Another seminal study. Levin's image of Marlowe as a political and religious radical was immensely influential. Levin has been criticized, however, for aligning the author's personality (as he understands it) with Faustus' and that of all of Marlowe's other heroes.

MacAlindon, Thomas. 1994. *Doctor Faustus: Divine in Show*. Toronto/New York: Maxwell Macmillan.

A lucid interpretation of Marlowe's tragedy.

Oz, Avraham (ed.). 2004. *Marlowe*. Basingstoke: Palgrave Macmillan.

This very useful collection assembles recent criticism on Marlowe.

Riggs, David. 2004. *The World of Christopher Marlowe*. London: Faber and Faber.

Among the still growing number of Marlowe-biographies one of the more stimulating reads.

Further Secondary Literature

Barber, C. L. 1988. *Creating Elizabethan Tragedy: The Theater of Marlowe and Kyd*. Richard P. Wheeler (ed.). Chicago/London: U of Chicago P.

Chambers, Edmund K. 1923. *The Elizabethan Stage*. 4 Vols. Oxford: Clarendon P.

Cheney, Patrick. 2006. "Introduction: Marlowe in the Twenty-First Century." In: Cheney. 2006. 1-23.

Foakes, R. A. 1990. "Playhouses and Players." In: A. R. Braunmuller & Michael Hattaway (eds.). *The Cambridge Companion to English Renaissance Drama*. Cambridge: Cambridge UP. 1-52.

— (ed.). 2002 [1961]. *Henslowe's Diary*. Cambridge: Cambridge UP.

Gibbons, Brian. 1968. *Jacobean City Comedy: A Study of Satirical Plays by Jonson, Marston and Middleton*. London: Hart-Davies.

Grantley, Darryl & Peter Roberts (eds.). 1996. *Christopher Marlowe and English Renaissance Culture*. Aldershot: Scolar P.

Healy, Thomas. 2006. "Doctor Faustus." In: Cheney 2006. 174-92.

Honigmann, Ernst. 1991. "Ten Problems in Dr Faustus." In: Murray Biggs, et. al. (eds.). *The Arts of Performance in Elizabethan and Early Stuart Drama: Essays for G. K. Hunter*. Edinburgh: Edinburgh UP. 173-91.

Hopkins, Lisa. 2008. *Christopher Marlowe: Renaissance Dramatist*. Edinburgh: Edinburgh UP.

Howard, Jean Elizabeth. 1994. *The Stage and Social Struggle in Early Modern England*. London: Routledge.

Marcus, Leah S. 1996. *Unediting the Renaissance: Shakespeare, Marlowe, Milton*. London: Routledge.

O'Connell, Michael. 2010. "Continuities between 'Medieval' and 'Early Modern Drama.'" In: Michael Hattaway (ed.). *A New Companion to English Renaissance Literature and Culture*. Vol. 2. Oxford: Blackwell. 60-69.

Pfister, Manfred. 2004 [1991]. "Die Frühe Neuzeit: Von Morus bis Milton." In: Hans Ulrich Seeber (ed.). *Englische Literaturgeschichte*. Stuttgart/Weimar: Metzler. 43-148.

Sidney, Philip. 2002 [1595]. "Defense of Poesy." In: Katherine Duncan-Jones (ed.). *Sir Philip Sidney: The Major Works*. Oxford: Oxford UP. 212-50.

Stachniewski, John. 1991. *The Persecutory Imagination: English Puritanism and the Literature of Religious Despair*. Oxford: Clarendon P.

Sutton, Thomas. 1616. *England's first and second summons: Two Sermons Preached at Paul's Crosse*. London: Matthew Law.

Watson, Robert N. 1990. "Tragedy." In: A. R. Braunmuller & Michael Hattaway (eds.). *The Cambridge Companion to English Renaissance Drama*. Cambridge: Cambridge UP. 301-51.

Wootton, David. 2008. "Marlowe's *Doctor Faustus* and the *English Faust Book*." In: Lorna Fitzsimmons & Peter Werres (eds.). *Lives of Faust: The Faust Theme in Literature and Music: A Reader*. New York: de Gruyter. 145-55.

4. SHAKESPEARE'S COMEDIES:
A MIDSUMMER NIGHT'S DREAM AND *TWELFTH NIGHT*

INA HABERMANN

1. Early Modern English Comedy

Early modern English comedy is a mongrel, or, in more academic terms, an extremely hybrid genre. Among the many influences which combine to shape this theatrical phenomenon, I want to point out seven strands which have been interwoven to produce the intricate fabric of Shakespearean comedy. First, playwrights drew on classical models, both on Greek comedy (with its origin in ancient Greek ritual) by such authors as Aristophanes and on the Latin comedy of Plautus and Terence, which was well-known as part of the humanist curriculum at schools and universities. Nicholas Udall's *Ralph Roister Doister* (1552) or the anonymous *Gammer Gurton's Needle* (c. 1553) are early examples of the genre as it developed in England. Roman comedy had a satirical bent and supplied stock figures such as the boastful soldier (*miles gloriosus*), the learned doctor, the shrewish wife, or the witty servant as well as a plot line dramatizing love against the odds, where two young people are forced to defend their love against a hostile society. In Udall's comedy, the eponymous character was modelled after the Plautine *miles gloriosus*, and *Gammer Gurton's Needle* is a satirical take on English village life. Second, in addition to drama, classical poetry and the epic provided a rich source of stories, characters, and images for plays. Here, the work of Homer and Virgil must be mentioned, and above all Ovid, particularly his *Metamorphoses* (c. 8 AD). These often tragic and violent stories of shape-shifting and transformation exerted a strong influence on Renaissance minds, and Shakespeare was greatly indebted to Ovid for plot elements, a lyrical style, esteem for poets and their social significance, and for a philosophical dialectics of continuity and change.

Third, along with the classical heritage, more recent developments in Italian drama were also crucial, both the more sophisticated *commedia erudita* and the *commedia dell'arte*, a form of Italian satirical drama played with masques. A fixed set of characters, like the learned Dottore, the Capitano, descendant of the *miles gloriosus*, the lady with her servant, a young lover, and a number of clever and stupid servants would improvise around set *scenari*, satirizing respectable citizens. Beyond plot and characters, Shakespeare's Italian settings, which include Verona, Padua, Venice, and Messina, testify to this influence. *The Merry Wives of Windsor* (1602) is his only comedy set in England, and although the foreign settings must not be interpreted in an overly realist manner since the plays always respond at one level to events in contemporary London, the spatial displacement does introduce resonances of a pan-European richness and variety. Fourth, related to this, literary prose romances were very popular in the 16th century, for example Robert Greene's *Pandosto* (1588), which inspired Shakespeare's romance *The Winter's Tale* (c. 1610). Novella such as Boccaccio's *The Decameron* (c. 1349-53) were influential sources of stories, as were such Renaissance epics as Ariosto's *Orlando Furioso* (1516-32) and *La Gerusalemme Liberata* (1581) by Torquato Tasso. The intricate plots of the romances and novella may have furthered the marked disregard in English drama for the three classical unities of place, time and action. Fifth, the specifically medieval traditions of the mystery plays and the morality plays must not be forgotten (see chapter 2). In comedy, the 'vice figure' from English moralities supplies dramatic interest and satirical humour. The work of Geoffrey Chaucer, particularly *The Canterbury Tales* (1387), must also be considered an important influence.

Sixth, comedy has roots in English folk ritual such as the mummers' play and the feast of the Ass (cf. Barber 1959; Laroque 1991). This could take the form of a festive celebration of community rites and values, but it could also serve to re-enact social conflict and public communal punishments like stang-riding, ducking, the *charivari* and shrew-taming, which could be a source of robust slapstick humour. Shakespeare's early comedy *The Taming of the Shrew* (c. 1593) must be seen as part of this discourse (cf. Boose 1991). Instances of misrule and topsy-turvy situations would be staged regularly, at such times as Candlemas, Shrove Tuesday, May Day, Whitsuntide, Midsummer Eve, Harvest Home, Halloween, or Twelfth Night with the ultimate purpose of restoring order, the most powerful symbols of this restitution in comedy being marriage and a closing dance. Shakespeare's *Twelfth Night* (1601) with its happy matches emerging from a most unpromising confusion of gender and social status is a case in point. Frequently, the 'green world' of comedy, the classic pastoral setting as depicted in Shakespeare's *As You Like It* (1599), provides a counterpoint to established society and its laws and regulations. Seventh, related to the dramatization of social (dis)order, the inns of court, prestigious London institutions for the training of lawyers, were important centres of drama. Here, drama developed out of moot trials and legal debates, and the lawyers also often relied on classical material or translations from Italian comedy. For example, George Gascoigne's *Supposes* (1566), his influential translation of Ariosto's *I Suppositi* (1509), was staged at Grey's Inn in 1566. As legal problems are explored in these plays by acting them out, it emerges that acting is 'supposing,' presenting a case about people's actions and their social consequences. This approach, which acknowledges the structural analogy between the court and the stage, was prominent in the 16th century as the legal system became more established, and Shakespeare's *The Merchant of Venice* (1596-97) with its climactic trial scene and Portia's impersonation of a lawyer is clearly indebted to this tradition. The sexual slander of women is an interesting legal issue which inspired a number of plays, including Shakespeare's *Much Ado About Nothing* (1598-99), *Othello* (1603-04) and *Cymbeline* (1609-10) (cf. Habermann 2003).

Although Shakespeare was not as well educated as, for example, his colleague Ben Jonson, he drew on a wide range of classical and modern materials. *The Comedy of*

Errors (c. 1594), for instance, merges plot elements from Plautus' *Menaechmi* (200 BC) and *Amphitruo* (c. 190 BC), and a number of sources have been identified for almost all of Shakespeare's plays. His genius does not lie in *creatio ex nihilo*, which in any case would not have been appreciated in the early modern period, but in weaving together traditional elements in such a way that they gain new resonance and depth. Among Shakespeare's English predecessors, John Lyly's courtly drama, staged by boy actors, exerted a particular influence on Shakespeare's comedy. The prominent instances of gender cross-dressing clearly look back to Lyly's *Gallathea* (c. 1588), an elegant and courtly mythological play in which two cross-dressed girls have been misled into falling in love with each other. They are rescued by Venus, who brings about the comic and happy closure, promising to transform one of them into a boy at the church door.

Shakespeare's comedies are often subdivided into early comedy (*The Comedy of Errors* [c. 1594], *The Taming of the Shrew* [c. 1593], *The Two Gentlemen of Verona* [1590-91], *Love's Labour's Lost* [1598]), 'festive' or 'happy' comedy (*Much Ado About Nothing* [1598-99], *As You Like It* [1599], *The Merchant of Venice* [1596-97], *Twelfth Night; or What You Will* [1601]), romantic comedy or romance (*A Midsummer Night's Dream* [1595-96], *Pericles* [1606-08], *Cymbeline* [1609-10], *The Winter's Tale* [c. 1610], *The Tempest* [1610-11]), and 'problem plays' (*Troilus and Cressida* [1601-03], *All's Well That Ends Well* [c. 1604], *Measure for Measure* [1603-04]). While these labels are debated and criticized for several reasons, they must be mentioned since they have been and are still widely applied. The label 'early' could be misunderstood to suggest artistic immaturity, the labels 'festive' or 'happy' disguise the fact that almost all these plays include very dark, tragicomic moments which afford at least a glance into the abyss of tragedy, and the label 'problem,' denoting both peculiar knotty issues treated in the plays and difficulties of classification, appears unduly normative and rigid with regard to genre distinctions imposed on rather than extrapolated from the plays actually in existence. The plays formerly gathered under this label now tend to be read *sui generis*.

Shakespeare's first great phase of comedy writing occurred in the 1590s, simultaneous with the production of most of the history plays, after he had joined the prestigious adult company *Lord Chamberlain's Men* (only rivalled by the *Admiral's Men*) in 1594. He wrote for celebrated actors such as Richard Burbage, who impersonated the great tragic heroes, and the flamboyant comedian Will Kempe. The company performed in public theatres (the Theatre, the Curtain, and the Swan) before the Globe was built in 1599 and from 1608 also in the Blackfriars, a smaller, more upmarket indoor theatre – a development which had a marked impact on Shakespeare's last plays. Kempe as the leading comedian with an imposing stage presence starred as Dogberry in *Much Ado About Nothing* and above all as Falstaff in the two parts of *Henry IV* and *The Merry Wives of Windsor*, and Shakespeare's introduction of 'wise fools' such as Touchstone in *As You Like It* or Feste in *Twelfth Night* is associated with Kempe's departure from the company in 1599 and the arrival of Robert Armin (cf. Wiles 1987), who was also an accomplished musician. This helped Shakespeare to extend the range of his comedies beyond banter and slapstick to psychological and philosophical depth. Without belittling the achievement of the playwright, it must be stressed that theatre was, and remains, a collaborative medium, and Shakespeare used the strengths of the actors available to him. It is assumed, for example, that a particularly gifted boy actor inspired some of Shakespeare's spirited heroines, such as Beatrice in *Much Ado* and Rosalind in *As You Like It*. Around the time of Queen Elizabeth's death in 1603 and James I's accession to the throne, Shakespeare's company, now the *King's Men*, appeared to have gone through a process of 'gentrification,' staging more sophisticated drama for socially more elevated audiences. The tone and atmosphere of Shakespeare's work also became darker during this period, and the focus shifted to tragedy for some years.

There are some motifs and comic devices, such as twinning, confusion of identities, overhearing scenes and cross-dressing, which recur in the comedies, and the plays dramatize love plots, rites of passage, lovers' tribulations and the removal of impediments to a happy union. Humour is both situational, as for example in overhearing scenes, and created through language, for instance when characters try to appear educated through the use of complicated words, entangling themselves in misunderstandings, double-entendres, and unconscious bawdry. Constable Dogberry in *Much Ado* trips constantly on slippery linguistic ground: requiring a record of an examination, he sends for "the learned writer to set down our excommunication" (4.1.55 f.). Shakespeare's preferred mode appears to be gentle irony and parody rather than biting satire, and the multi-perspective quality of his plays ensures that even the characters most ridiculed or permanently cast out of the community receive an opportunity to express their point of view. This is a major reason why his plays lend themselves to perpetually new interpretations, both in criticism and on stage. Never advocating a particular cause, they present gestures of inquiry which invite readers and audiences to reflect on the social interactions they see while amusement and laughter, the 'delight' of classical poetics, provide the emotional context for a lasting and potentially transformative experience. Laughter has both a therapeutic and a social function, and it must be noted that the comic is not restricted to comedy; Shakespeare also inserts comic scenes into his tragedies, for example the "porter scene" in *Macbeth* (2.3.1-38), or some grotesquely comic scenes in *King Lear*, which can be seen as a "study of folly" (Ghose 2008: 187). Neither is comedy entirely a laughing matter.

While there are aspects in the comedies which suggest that Shakespeare assumes and explores an unchanging 'human nature,' it must not be forgotten that he also subscribed to the early modern theory of humours derived from antiquity. According to this theory, character can at least partly be explained by the preponderance of a particular body fluid, or humour. Individuals can be dominated by blood, which makes them sanguine, by phlegm, which makes them phlegmatic, by yellow bile, which makes them choleric, or by black bile, which makes them melancholic. The 'malcontent,' a melancholic figure antagonistic to the generally sanguine humour of comedy, is often the cause of disturbance, for example Don John in *Much Ado About Nothing*, who sexually slanders the young virgin Hero and generally cannot accept a harmonious atmosphere. Characters dominated by a bad humour need no further psychological motivation in early modern drama, and if the malcontent prevails, like Iago in *Othello*, tragedy ensues.

Even though drama was very popular in Shakespeare's time and extremely inclusive in terms of the social status of audiences, this was counteracted by a strong anti-theatrical prejudice (cf. Barish 1981), particularly expressed by Puritans who tended to deplore merriment, play-acting, and all other entertainments potentially conducive to sinful behaviour. Some such killjoys also walk Shakespeare's stage in the shape of malcontents like Malvolio, but in the comedies, they fight a losing battle, since comedy's trajectory is harmonious union, a smiling acceptance of the world's imperfections, transformation, and rejuvenation. Importantly, the charming or enchanting atmosphere is enhanced by frequent songs and music, as acknowledged in the very first line of *Twelfth Night*: "If music be the food of love, play on!"

2. *A Midsummer Night's Dream*

The *Dream* is a romantic comedy, first performed in 1595 or 1596, around the time when Shakespeare was also working on his early tragedy *Romeo and Juliet* (1595-96) and on the sonnets. All these texts share a particularly lyrical language, which leads Tom Stoppard in the film *Shakespeare in Love* (USA/GB 1998, dir. John Madden) – a highly creative and enjoyable instance of the 'biographical fallacy' – to suggest that the author himself must have fallen in love around that time. The *Dream* is set in "Athens," a few days before the wedding of Duke Theseus and Hippolyta, his newly conquered Amazon bride. The main plot focuses on a love tangle between four Athenian lovers, Hermia and Lysander, Helena and Demetrius. Hermia and Lysander escape to the woods to avoid Hermia's father who tries to prevent the match, having promised his daughter to Demetrius. Demetrius follows Hermia, persecuted in turn by the infatuated Helena. The woods are ruled by the Fairy King and Queen, Oberon and Titania, and it so happens that they have quarrelled over an Indian boy whom Titania does not want to give up to her husband. There is a lot of traffic in the nightly woods, which become the setting for various characters' existential crises. If the woods are taken to represent the 'green world,' a place where social strictures are suspended and the common order can be seen from a distance, sweet pastoral quickly gives place to jungle law. With a view to resolving the love tangle, Oberon sends his mischievous servant Puck to treat Demetrius' eyes with a love-charm, but Puck initially confuses the two young gentlemen, so that both end up transferring their love to Helena, until Lysander's charm is finally reversed and two happy couples wake up on the edge of the woods after a night of very strange dreams. Meanwhile, Titania also becomes the victim of a love-charm, which makes her fall in love with Bottom the Weaver, who has been bewitched and is carrying the head of an ass. This is the result of a practical joke Puck played on him while Bottom and a group of fellow artisans were assembled in the woods to rehearse a play for Theseus' wedding. Finally, Titania is freed of the charm and reconciled with Oberon, Bottom regains his former shape, the two pairs of Athenian lovers are allowed to marry and the artisans perform their play on Theseus' and Hippolyta's wedding night. As the newly-weds prepare to retire to bed, the fairies take over again, and Puck takes his leave of the audience, suggesting that, if they did not like what they saw, they should consider it all a dream.

In this comedy, Shakespeare fuses classical mythology with indigenous folklore. The world of Athens, Theseus' world of reason, law, and patriarchal domination is contrasted with an English world of homespun craftsmen, mischievous sprites and sensuously evoked nature. Helen Hackett argues that beyond an intertextual dimension, where Shakespeare draws on such English pastoral writings as Edmund Spenser's *Shepheardes Calender* (1579), he conjures up the memory of an agricultural and rural world within an urban context. While tapping into an "urban vogue for fairy literature" (Hackett 1997: 69), however, he grounds his story in a material and potentially sinister reality. The *Dream* attributes disturbances in the rural rhythms to the discord between the Fairy King and Queen, as expressed in Titania's complaint:

> Therefore the winds, piping to us in vain,
> As in revenge have sucked up from the sea
> Contagious fogs which, falling in the land,
> Hath every pelting river made so proud
> That they have overborne their continents.
> The ox hath therefore stretched his yoke in vain,
> The ploughman lost his sweat, and the green corn
> Hath rotted ere his youth attained a beard.
> The fold stands empty in the drowned field,
> And crows are fatted with the murrain flock.
> The nine men's morris is filled up with mud,
> And the quaint mazes in the wanton green
> For lack of tread are undistinguishable. (2.1.88-100)

The country's loss of fertility is attributed to an evil, mythic agency partly personified in Puck. This "shrewd and knavish sprite" (2.1.33) is identified with the hobgoblin Robin Goodfellow from English folklore who "frights the maidens of the villag'ry" (2.1.35), steals cream from the milk and misleads nightly wanderers. The fairy rulers need to resume marital relations, just as Theseus and Hippolyta and the pairs of Athenian lovers need to celebrate their marriage rites in order to restore the natural cycles of fertility. In line with this, the play is infused with an intensely physical eroticism and a potentially threatening sexuality which glance back to the origin of Greek drama in fertility rites, and it is important not to downplay this element in favour of ethereal fairies in frilly frocks, as has often been done in bourgeois interpretations informed by the more squeamish morals often associated with Victorianism. The dramatization of rites of passage and the struggle between generations are common themes in early modern drama, and the *Dream* shows the initiation of the young lovers into adult life, regulated through the institution of marriage. On their way, they have to overcome paternal resistance and the restrictions of the patriarchal order, and they need to shift their allegiance from juvenile same-sex relationships to a partner of the opposite sex within a heterosexual regime. The Amazon Hippolyta has been conquered by Theseus, Titania has to give up the Indian boy, the son of her votaress, to her husband, and Hermia and Helena replace their maiden love with sexual jealousy. These developments in comedy tend to include a phase of gender struggle and the blurring of gender boundaries, often dramatized through cross-dressing, as in *Two Gentlemen of Verona*, *The Merchant of Venice*, *As You Like It*, *Twelfth Night,* and *Cymbeline*, until the social order can be restored again.

This 'anthropological' aspect, however, is only one dimension of an immensely intricate dramatic structure. Another dimension, often amplified in New Historicist or Cultural Materialist discussions of the play, can be seen in the topical allusions. One strand here is the reference to an actual season of bad weather, bad harvests, economic hardship, and social unrest (cf. Patterson 1989). Another is the allusion both to a possible aristocratic marriage where the play could have been staged as part of the celebrations, and to contemporary panegyrics of the reigning monarch Elizabeth I (cf. Montrose 1996: 159-78, *passim*; Williams 1997). The *Dream* recalls the entertainments organized by noblemen for the Queen in progress through her realm, such as those at Kenilworth in 1575 or at Elvetham in 1591 where Elizabeth would be celebrated as the Queen of springtime, associated with the Fairy Queen surrounded by her ladies/fairies. (Again, a connection can be made to Spenser and his epic *The Faerie Queene* [1590/96].) Oberon's description of Titania's bower evokes the iconography of Elizabeth, inserting a reference to the eglantine, a type of white rose with which the Queen was associated:

> I know a bank where the wild thyme blows,
> Where oxlips and the nodding violet grows,
> Quite overcanopied with luscious woodbine,
> With sweet musk-roses, and with eglantine.
> There sleeps Titania sometime of the night,
> Lulled in these flowers with dances and delight[.] (2.2.249-54)

The trajectory here, as Helen Hackett argues, is not exact allegory but the evocation of "floral motifs which were useful in elaborating a poetic image of feminine power" (1997: 68). This example shows how Shakespeare is both of his age and yet "for all time," as Ben Jonson puts it in his dedicatory poem to the Folio edition of Shakespeare's works (Jonson 1902: 14). While he contributes to the contemporary discourse of panegyric, he employs and transforms it in such a way as to transcend the historical moment of production. Another facet of the cult of Elizabeth, the iconography of the Virgin Queen, in which the queen was associated with the Goddess Diana and the moon, is also prominent in the *Dream*. As Oberon tells Puck:

> That very time I saw, but thou couldst not,
> Flying between the cold moon and the earth

> Cupid, all armed. A certain aim he took
> At a fair vestal thronèd in the west,
> And loosed his love-shaft smartly from his bow
> As it should pierce a hundred thousand hearts.
> But I might see young Cupid's fiery shaft
> Quenched in the chaste beams of the wat'ry moon,
> And the imperial vot'ress passed on,
> In maiden meditation, fancy-free. (2.1.155-64)

Contemporaries would make the connection with Elizabeth's long drawn-out marriage negotiations and her final decision to remain married only to her realm and people while simultaneously enjoying the spectacle and savouring the superb poetry.

The *Dream* forges a link between love and sexuality, conceived as a passion bordering on madness, and the poetic imagination. Responding to the lovers' account of the night's strange happenings, Theseus supplies the voice of reason:

> More strange than true. I never may believe
> These antique fables, nor these fairy toys.
> Lovers and madmen have such seething brains,
> Such shaping fantasies, that apprehend
> More than cool reason ever comprehends.
> The lunatic, the lover, and the poet
> Are of imagination all compact.
> One sees more devils than vast hell can hold:
> That is the madman. The lover, all as frantic,
> Sees Helen's beauty in a brow of Egypt.
> The poet's eye, in a fine frenzy rolling,
> Doth glance from heaven to earth, from earth to heaven,
> And as imagination bodies forth
> The forms of things unknown, the poet's pen
> Turns them to shapes, and gives to airy nothing
> A local habitation and a name. (5.1.2-17)

It is a cunning move on the playwright's part to make Theseus, the Duke of Athens, the most powerful man and principal patriarch, look disingenuous to an audience who has just witnessed the 'truth' of the night's happenings and would be more inclined to follow Hippolyta, who believes that "something of great constancy; / But howsoever, strange and admirable" (5.1.26 f.) has indeed taken place. This is a celebration of the power of the poet, because the "forms of things unknown" which his imagination "bodies forth" are not just idle fantasies, but expressions of a deeper truth about the 'soul of man,' to put it in humanist terms. The early modern period had great respect for and fear of the passions and their disruptive and transformative qualities, and the images Shakespeare found for this continue to have great resonance. It should not come as a surprise that in the 20th century, the *Dream* was read in psychoanalytic terms, as a symbolic expression of unconscious drives. It should be noted, however, that psychoanalytic readings which recast the *Dream* as psychodrama also reduce the element of magic, transfiguration, and wonder about an infinitely complex and interrelated world. An eco-critical reading of the play might in turn amplify this dimension.

In any case, this exchange about the "airy nothing" (5.1.16) takes place at the beginning of act 5, when the conflict of the main plot has already been resolved, and immediately before the mechanicals' performance brings the sub-plot to a conclusion. They stage "*The Most Lamentable Comedy and Most Cruel Death of Pyramus and Thisbe*" (1.2.9-10), which could be taken as an intertextual hint towards, or perhaps even an advertisement for Shakespeare's current tragedy of doomed lovers, *Romeo and Juliet*. Their inept performance, which moves the audience to tears of laughter rather than pity, is punctuated by the condescending commentary of the noble spectators, who fail to acknowledge the importance of the craftsmen's perspective. However, their down-to-earth presence points to the analogy between "marital and artisanal joinery" (Parker 1996: 6) as well as to the skill required to 'weave' words into poetry. As regards early modern stagecraft, the play-within-the-play is a common device which Shakespeare also uses repeatedly, for example in *Hamlet* (1600-01), where the play "The Mousetrap" is designed to prove King Claudius' guilt (see chapter 6). There are various dimensions to this emphasis on theatricality. First of all, the Renaissance conceived of the world as a theatre, as expressed by the melancholy Jaques in *As You Like It*: "All the world's a stage, / And all the men and women merely players. / They have their exits and their entrances, / And one man in his time plays many parts" (2.7.138-41), and in a tragic vein by Macbeth: "Life's but a walking shadow, a poor player / That struts and frets his hour upon the stage, / And then is heard no more" (*Macbeth* [1606], 5.5.23-5). Conversely, the theatre could represent the world, which the Chamberlain's Men emphasized through the choice of name for their new playhouse in 1599: the Globe. Thus, the theatrical exploration of life in the *Dream* gains authority through its connection with a basic conceptual metaphor for existence.

At the same time, Puck's epilogue may also serve as an expression of modesty by the playwright and actors, flattering a high-ranking audience and asking for gracious acceptance, particularly if the comedy was indeed performed at an aristocratic wedding. The performance on stage would then mirror the staging of the play itself in a process of *mise-en-abîme*. Even if no occasional performance is assumed, a kind of mirroring process takes place every time the play is performed, and this element of display throws into relief the delightful, enlightening, and 'transfiguring' quality of theatre. The mechanicals' hilariously inadequate performance suggests to the audience that they are to take drama seriously, but not over-literally. When Starveling the tailor enters with a lantern, informing spectators that "this lantern doth the hornèd moon present" (5.1.235) and Snug the joiner assures the ladies that they need not be afraid of him since he is not really a lion, they show that they do not understand the dialectics of illusion, or immersion, and meta-theatrical awareness in an audience's "willing suspension of disbelief" (Coleridge 1983 [1817]: 6). Yet this is instrumental, as the 'mechanicals' are after all instrumental, in making the 'magic' work and reap the reward, as suggested in Puck's (mischievous?) promise: "Give me your hands, if we be friends, / And Robin shall restore amends." (Epilogue, 16 f.)

3. *Twelfth Night*

The link between early modern drama and saturnalia is particularly strong in the title of this 'festive' comedy, which refers to the Twelfth Night after Christmas, i.e. the feast of the Epiphany on January 6, marking the climax of Christmas celebrations and the time of 'misrule' where traditional hierarchies would be suspended or subverted. A performance in the Middle Temple is recorded for 1602, and the first printed version of the text appears in the *First Folio* (1623). Sources include Barnabe Riche's tale "Apollonius and Silla" in *Riche His Farewell to Military Profession* (1581), which in turn drew on Italian and French sources, but while Shakespeare found a number of plot elements and motifs in his sources, the psychological subtlety and sophistication with which he dramatizes them are entirely his own. *Twelfth Night* is perhaps Shakespeare's most accomplished comedy, and the last of the 'festive' comedies. It is set in "Illyria," where Duke Orsino has for some time wooed the Countess Olivia, whose household includes her drunken kinsman Sir Toby Belch and his hapless companion Sir Andrew Aguecheek, the 'wise fool' Feste, the puritanical steward Malvolio and the clever servant Maria. Olivia is in deep mourning for her brother and unresponsive to Orsino's advances. The play begins, as many comedies do, with the arrival of outsiders in this small community. Shipwrecked on the coast of Illyria, the young Viola enters Orsino's service disguised as the boy Cesario. Having fallen in love with Orsino, it pains her to run constant errands to Olivia, who in turn becomes infatuated with Cesario. Meanwhile, Viola's twin brother Sebastian has also been stranded in Illyria, and after a phase of confusion and mistaken identities recalling the *Comedy of Errors*, Olivia can be paired with Sebastian while Orsino transfers his affections to Viola.

The sub-plot deals with a conspiracy against Malvolio, whom the other members of the household want to punish for his bad faith and snobbishness. He is given to understand that Olivia loves him in secret and that he should strut around in cross-gartered yellow stockings to show his responsiveness. As a consequence, he is incarcerated as a madman and tortured. Significantly, the festive conclusion does not include him, and his promise of revenge as well as Feste's wistful comments on the strange ways of the world serve to a certain extent to subvert the play's closure. Shakespeare increasingly transcends the conventions of genre in favour of a drama designed to equal the complexity of life. As Kiernan Ryan puts it, *Twelfth Night* is "a Janus-faced play which looks back to the farcical and the festive romantic comedies that preceded it, and forward to the darker, disenchanted vision of the problem plays and the romances' miraculous, bittersweet tales of shipwreck, grief and kindred reunited." (Ryan 2009: 235)

Twelfth Night is a play about inversions of hierarchy, about upward mobility and wayward desire in a "land where folly holds sway" (Ghose 2008: 109) and where nobody is wiser than the fool. It is a play about deception and self-deception, the discrepancy between being and seeming, the untrustworthiness of appearances and the unreliability of perception. If both the sanity of the individual and the life of the community are based on an agreement about reality, a consensus of interpretation and a memory of past occurrences, then 'Illyria,' whose very name suggests a fusion of illusion and delirium, is a madhouse. Olivia is driven to distraction by her infatuation with Cesario, Malvolio is tricked into behaving like a madman and then treated like one, and Sebastian comes to distrust his senses because he does not know that everyone, including Olivia, takes him for Cesario.

> This is the air, that is the glorious sun.
> This pearl she gave me, I do feel't and see't,
> And though 'tis wonder that enwraps me thus,
> Yet 'tis not madness. […]
> Yet doth this accident and flood of fortune
> So far exceed all instance, all discourse,
> That I am ready to distrust mine eyes
> And wrangle with my reason that persuades me
> To any other trust but that I am mad,
> Or else the lady's mad. […] There's something in't
> That is deceivable. (4.3.1-4; 11-16; 20-1)

At a point when it begins to undermine a character's sense of self, the confusion of identities becomes decidedly unfunny, and Viola, who has violated gender divisions, begins to see that disguise is a "wickedness" (2.2.25). Yet, the moral injunction against disguise is at odds with the fact that disguise propels the action forward and there would be no drama and no pleasure without it. The comedy is thus in dialogue with the contemporary Puritan anti-theatricalism that became ever more vocal. Malvolio, the malcontent and killjoy, is often seen as a representative of the anti-theatrical stance within the play, but he, too, the most unlikely suspect, as it were, is driven to disguise and madness through his desire for social advancement. He trusts a forged letter which he believes to be addressed to him by Olivia:

> In my stars I am above thee, but be not afraid of greatness. Some are born great, some achieve greatness, and some have greatness thrust upon 'em. Thy fates open their hands, let thy blood and spirit embrace them, and to iniure thyself to what thou art like to be, cast thy humble slough, and appear fresh. (2.5.125-30)

The joke that Maria and her friends play on him decidedly goes too far, and Maria, who has plotted Malvolio's downfall, is rewarded with a marriage to Sir Toby. She, too, is motivated by the desire for upward mobility which appeared to require punishment in the steward.

The lady Olivia is the only character who does not eroticize upward mobility, which 'anomaly' is the starting point for the comedy, since she refuses Duke Orsino's advances. Her 'wayward desire' becomes focussed on Viola, who, disguised as Cesario, exhibits a fascinating androgyny. "'Tis with him in standing water between boy and man" (1.5.141-42), as Malvolio reports to his mistress, and Olivia, bored with Orsino's conventional Petrarchan posturing and his overbearing, patriarchal manner, is attracted by his youthful messenger – as Orsino in fact suspected: "Diana's lip / Is not more smooth and rubious; thy small pipe / Is as the maiden's organ, shrill and sound, / And all is semblative a woman's part. / I know thy constellation is right apt / For this affair." (1.5.30-35) Olivia and 'Cesario' start their conversation with a banter about mistaken identities, which, again, carries resonances of madness. Olivia responds to 'Cesario's' description of what 'he' would do if madly in love, and the hypothetical nature of the account makes attractive what is in fact a disturbing stalking scenario: Installed at Olivia's gate, 'Cesario' would "Write loyal cantons of contemnèd love, / And sing them loud even in the dead of night; / Halloo your name to the reverberate hills, / And make the babbling gossip of the air / Cry out 'Olivia!'" (1.5.239-43) The suggestion of something unattainable intrigues the lady: "You might do much." (1.5.246)

In early modern drama, gender cross-dressing suggests itself as a plot device due to the material conditions of the stage. From having boy actors play women, it appears to be only one step to have these boy-women disguise themselves as boys, putting the theatrical convention under pressure only to have it emerge the more triumphantly. Paradoxically, for example, in *As You Like It*, Rosalind's disguise as a boy who enacts Rosalind in order to educate Orlando in matters of wooing serves to make the character of Rosalind more real. Her 'reality' under the layers of illusion in the play ultimately serves to disguise the reality of the boy actor while the resulting androgyny produces erotic frisson, endorsing the Puritans' suspicion that some sort of illicit sexual activity was going on between the body of the boy and the female attire. By blurring the boundaries between the sexes, cross-dressing in drama explores gender and the nature of sexual desire, which appears often to be enhanced by an oscillation between sameness and difference. In *Twelfth Night*, the closure is conventional: when Sebastian appears beside 'Cesario' for the first time, although "[a]n apple cleft in two is not more twin" (5.1.216), there is no doubt that he is the 'real thing.' He knows how to use his sword to fight Sir Andrew, and he has that which will enable him to consummate his marriage with Olivia: "[N]ature to her bias drew in that" (5.1.253). But who would be so churlish, after having seen this charming comedy, to believe that this was the whole truth? Feste's song at the end offers an aptly inconsequential and wistful conclusion to these revels: "A great while ago the world begun, / With hey, ho, the wind and the rain, / But that's all one, our play is done, / And we'll strive to please you every day." (5.1.392-95)

4. Summary and Consequences

Shakespeare was lucky, since he was writing his plays for the London stages at a time of increasing cultural sophistication, relative peace and prosperity, although the "Golden Age"-rhetoric of the Tudor state and Elizabeth's reign in particular often serves to obscure the considerable internal and external violence and the many hardships of the period. Yet, both civic London and the court were thriving, and the theatre united everyone in a way that no other art form or medium did at the time, much like film until recently and the internet at present. This allowed for a fusion of various classical and indigenous traditions which led to a drama never surpassed in richness and complexity. Shakespeare certainly was in the right place at the right time, but it is doubtful whether this astonishing development would have occurred without him, so we, too, are lucky. While the comedy of his influential precursor John Lyly is an acquired taste today, Shakespeare's work has passed the test of time, albeit partly since he helped set the standards by which dramatic achievement is measured. This is more true today than in the late 17th and 18th centuries when classicist tastes prevailed and some of Shakespeare's 'irregularities' appeared to require an improving hand. Needless to say, there are topical jokes and dialogues, particularly in the comedies, which are no longer funny or even intelligible to modern audiences, but these are offset by characters and dramatic constellations which are as hilarious and touching today as they must have been when the "sweet Swan of Avon" (Jonson 1902: 14) first put them on stage.

The plays of the late Elizabethan and early Jacobean period are so dark at times as to stretch the label 'comedy' to breaking point. For example, the sinister machinations of Angelo in *Measure for Measure*, who imposes a strict moral law which he himself is unable to keep, emerge as the almost inevitable consequence of authoritarian rule. When the 'comedy' ends with a prospect of enforced marriages and 'order' arbitrarily and violently restored, this might well be seen as tragic, if tragedy as a classic genre did not require the actual deaths of the protagonists. Shakespeare's only city comedy is *The Merry Wives of Windsor*, and while the popularity of this satirical genre was at its height during the first half of James' reign, Shakespeare left it to Ben Jonson, Thomas Middleton, Thomas Dekker, and others and wrote his great tragedies and romances. Having said this, it does make sense to read *Measure for Measure* both as a city comedy (set in 'Vienna' rather than London) and a 'disguised ruler play' alongside Middleton's and Jonson's comedies.

The romances are epic in scope, and Shakespeare abandons his earlier lyrical language for a simple and clear style with a sparse use of images. Academics still disagree in how far this ought to be interpreted as a "late style" (cf. McMullan 2007). Shakespeare also tried his hand at the new fashionable tragicomedy in which Francis Beaumont and John Fletcher were at that time excelling, and he collaborated with Fletcher on *All is True* (*Henry VIII*; 1612-13), a history play about King Henry VIII's reign up to the birth of Elizabeth, the *The Two Noble Kinsmen* (1613) and the lost *Cardenio* (1613). This shows that even though he lived an increasingly retired life at Stratford, he was still prepared to try innovative forms and support younger playwrights shortly before he died of a fever in 1616 at the age of 52. City comedy, revenge tragedy, court masques, and (pastoral) tragicomedy were fashionable at the time, audiences tended to demand new plays rather than repertory, and the *King's Men* obliged. During the Civil War and the Commonwealth (1649-1660), the theatres were closed, and after the revival of theatre in the Restoration period, French-style comedy was particularly appreciated at court, Shakespearean comedy only being taken up again significantly in the late 18th century. While the comedies continue to stand in the shadow of the great tragedies considered to be the 'noblest' dramatic achievements, in the 20th century and up to the present day, Shakespeare's 'festive' comedies have remained immensely popular with audiences seeking to be reassured delightfully that "Jack shall have Jill, / Naught shall go ill, / the man shall have his mare again, and all shall be well." (*A Midsummer Night's Dream*, 3.3.45-47)

I wish to thank Gordon McMullan for helpful comments on an earlier version of this chapter.

Bibliography

Primary Sources

Shakespeare, William. 1997. *The Norton Shakespeare*. Stephen Greenblatt, et al. (eds.). New York/London: Norton.

Annotated Bibliography

Barber, Charles Laurence. 1959. *Shakespeare's Festive Comedy: A Study of Dramatic Form and Its Relation to Social Custom*. Princeton: Princeton UP.
A groundbreaking study of Shakespeare's dramatization of folk ritual.

Barish, Jonas. 1981. *The Antitheatrical Prejudice*. Berkeley: U of California P.
This is an in-depth analysis of the Puritan anti-theatrical discourse and still the standard account of the issue.

Boose, Lynda. 1991. "Scolding Brides and Bridling Scolds: Taming the Woman's Unruly Member." In: *Shakespeare Quarterly* 42.2: 179-213.
This seminal essay situates Shakespeare's The Taming of the Shrew *in the historical discourse of shrew-taming, arguing that the play romanticizes contemporary misogyny and violence against women.*

Ellis, David. 2007. *Shakespeare's Practical Jokes: An Introduction to the Comic in His Work*. Lewisburg, PA: Bucknell UP.
Rather than discussing comedy as a genre, this helpful study explores what is actually funny in Shakespeare's work, with a focus on the practical joke.

Ghose, Indira. 2008. *Shakespeare and Laughter: A Cultural History*. Manchester: Manchester UP.
This is an inspiring study of laughter in the early modern period, arguing that an automatic connection between laughter and subversion is problematic and offering incisive readings of various plays including Twelfth Night *and* King Lear.

Hackett, Helen. 1997. *William Shakespeare: A Midsummer Night's Dream. Writers and their Work*. Plymouth: Northcote House.

A very instructive and comprehensive, yet concise introduction to the Dream by a specialist on Elizabeth I and the cult of the Virgin Queen.

Laroque, François. 1991. *Shakespeare's Festive World: Elizabethan Seasonal Entertainment and the Professional Stage*. Cambridge: Cambridge UP.

A comprehensive account of Shakespeare's relation to popular culture and the world of festival and holiday, translated by Janet Todd from the French original published in 1988.

Leggatt, Alexander (ed.). 2002. *The Cambridge Companion to Shakespearean Comedy*. Cambridge: Cambridge UP.

A very helpful introduction organized around themes such as love and courtship, language, sexual disguise, or issues of genre.

McMullan, Gordon. 2007. *Shakespeare and the Idea of Late Writing: Authorship in the Proximity of Death*. Cambridge: Cambridge UP.

This wide-ranging study examines the general idea of 'late style' and its ideological and aesthetic implications, taking Shakespeare as a prominent example.

Montrose, Louis. 1996. *The Purpose of Playing: Shakespeare and the Cultural Politics of the Elizabethan Theatre*. Chicago: U of Chicago P.

This study combines a New Historicist account of the cultural politics of Shakespeare's theatre with an extended reading of the Dream focussed on gender, political power, and theatricality.

Parker, Patricia. 1996. *Shakespeare From the Margins: Language, Culture, Context*. Chicago: U of Chicago P.

This study offers fascinating cultural readings of Shakespeare, including the Dream, through meticulous attention to linguistic resonances and historical semantics.

Patterson, Annabel. 1989. *Shakespeare and the Popular Voice*. Cambridge: Blackwell.

This study analyses Shakespeare's representations of the common people, arguing that Shakespeare develops a social vision through dramatic meditations on the structure of English society.

Ryan, Kiernan. 2009. *Shakespeare's Comedies*. Basingstoke: Palgrave Macmillan.

The most recent study of the comedies by an eminent Shakespeare scholar, providing perceptive close readings of the first ten comedies and arguing for a trajectory of increasing disillusion on Shakespeare's part.

Wiles, David. 1987. *Shakespeare's Clown: Actor and Text in the Elizabethan Playhouse*. Cambridge: Cambridge UP.

This is an important contribution to the history of theatre and the conditions which shaped Shakespeare's theatrical work. Wiles also published a historical study of the Dream in 1993 entitled Shakespeare's Almanac.

Williams, Gary Jay. 1997. *Our Moonlight Revels: A Midsummer Night's Dream in the Theatre*. Iowa City: U of Iowa P.

A comprehensive overview of four hundred years of performance history of the Dream *including a discussion of the 'wedding performance' issue.*

Further Secondary Literature

Coleridge, Samuel Taylor. 1983 [1817]. *Biographia Literaria, or Biographical Sketches of My Literary Life and Opinions*. Vol. II. James Engell & W. Jackson Bate (eds.). Collected Works Vol. 7. London: Routledge.

Gay, Penny. 2008. *The Cambridge Introduction to Shakespeare's Comedies*. Cambridge: Cambridge UP.

Greenblatt, Stephen. 1988. *Shakespearean Negotiations: The Circulation of Social Energy in Renaissance England*. Berkeley: U of California P.

—. 2004. *Will in the World: How Shakespeare Became Shakespeare*. New York/London: Norton.

Habermann, Ina. 2003. *Staging Slander and Gender in Early Modern England*. Aldershot: Ashgate.

Jardine, Lisa. 1983. *Still Harping on Daughters: Women and Drama in the Age of Shakespeare*. Hemel Hempstead: Harvester.

Jonson, Ben. 1902. "To the memory of my beloved, the Author Mr. William Shakespeare: and what he hath left us." *Shakespeares Comedies, Histories, & Tragedies being a reproduction in Facsimile of The First Folio Edition 1623*. Oxford: Clarendon P. 13-14.

Schabert, Ina. 2000. *Shakespeare-Handbuch: Die Zeit – Der Mensch – Das Werk – Die Nachwelt*. Stuttgart: Kröner.

Tredell, Nicholas. 2010. *Shakespeare: A Midsummer Night's Dream. Readers' Guides to Essential Criticism*. Basingstoke: Palgrave Macmillan.

5. SHAKESPEARE'S HISTORY PLAYS: *RICHARD III* AND *HENRY V*

STEPHAN LAQUÉ

1. History Play: The Subtle Novelty of a Genre

At first sight, the term 'history play' may come across as a tautology: since etymologically 'story' is but an aphetic form of 'history,' 'history play' turns out to mean no more than a play about a sequence of events – surely, a minimal definition of all drama. Indeed, a wide array of Shakespeare's plays are described as histories on the covers of their Quarto editions, among them *The Famous History of Troilus and Cresseid*, *The Most Excellent History of the Merchant of Venice*, and the *True Chronicle History of the life and death of King Lear and his three Daughters*. To all intents and purposes, *Troilus and Cressida* (1602) and *The Merchant of Venice* (1596-97) tell stories and *King Lear* (1605-06) even tells a history – if by that word we wish to denote the somewhat narrower concept of factual past events. However, the legacy of two men, John Heminges (1556-1630) and Henry Condell (?-1627), forces us to probe further into the finer implications of the term 'history play.' Heminges and Condell were actors with Shakespeare's company who, in 1623, turned into Shakespeare's first editors with the publication of the First Folio edition of the plays. The title page of that edition refers to its content as *Mr. William Shakespeare's Comedies, Histories, & Tragedies published according to the True Originall Copies*. If the "True Originall Copies" refer to the Quarto editions of the plays, the editors have taken exceptional liberty in their handling of the true and original titles and their attribution of the plays to diverse genres. Their division of Shakespeare's plays into 14 comedies, ten histories, and eleven tragedies further complicates matters by introducing the history play as a new third genre which does not enjoy the same Aristotelian and classical pedigree as comedy and tragedy.

The history play sits somewhat uneasily alongside its two illustrious neighbours. However, the fact that the First Folio places the genre *between* the two established types of play can serve as an indication of its nature. History play is a genre in its own right, but its distinction is situated on a different plane from that of both tragedy and comedy. While these can be characterized in terms of dramatic form, the history play is chiefly defined by its subject matter. When it comes to dramatic form, history plays – and Shakespeare's histories in particular – show close ties to both tragedy and comedy, they liberally link and adapt elements belonging to these genres and they are therefore, indeed, situated between and in contact with both of these genres. As E.M.W. Tillyard has astutely observed in his magisterial study *Shakespeare's History*

Plays of 1944: "Shakespeare's Histories are more like his own Comedies and Tragedies than like others' Histories." (1991: 11)

But considering that Shakespeare's tragedies and his comedies are also mixtures of elements taken from both genres, what is left to define a history play? To put it bluntly: an English history play is a play about English history. More specifically, these plays address the relatively recent history of Shakespeare and his contemporaries, the history stretching from King John's reign (1199-1216) to that of Henry VIII (1509-1547). Even though *King Lear* and *Cymbeline* (1610) are likewise plays about British monarchs, the First Folio pronounces them to be tragedies without them being any more 'tragic' and less 'historical' than, say, *Richard II* (1595), which is classified as a history play. Shakespeare's contribution to the genre is traditionally grouped into two units of four plays each, the so-called tetralogies, with *King John* (1596) as a prologue preceding these eight plays and *Henry VIII* (1613) following them as an epilogue. The two tetralogies deal respectively with the Wars of the Roses (c. 1455-1485) and with the events leading up to that conflict. It is customary to label the two groups of plays with the names of the families whose temporary reign they focus on. The Lancaster tetralogy comprises *Richard II*, the two parts of *Henry IV* (1596-98) and *Henry V* (1598-99); the York tetralogy covers the three parts of *Henry VI* (1591-92) and *Richard III* (1592-93). These tetralogies were composed in reverse order with the York tetralogy – which is sometimes referred to as the 'first tetralogy' – written first even though the part of history it covers in fact followed the events recounted in the Lancaster tetralogy. This ranging of the plays according to the chronology of their content is further evidence of the first editors' eagerness to impose order on Shakespeare's oeuvre. The significance of their decision lies in its prioritizing of historical coherence and teleology over artistic evolution. The sequence of events is held to be more important than the dramatic and artistic merit of the individual texts and their affinity with the established genres, with tragedy or comedy. It is this focus which led to the proclamation of the history play as a distinct third genre of Shakespeare's works – a focus which is, therefore, an important aspect in the definition of the genre. Unlike *King Lear* or *Macbeth* (1606), the plays which Heminges and Condell call Histories describe a coherent trajectory of historical *personae* and events. The plays are a sequence of predominantly *de casibus*-plots which recount the fall of English kings and they are woven into a narrative of national identity by foreshadowing, flashback, quotation, and thematic cross-referencing (cf. Danson 2000; Egan 2007; Maguire 2004).

2. The Myth of the 'Tudor Myth'

The histories catered to the patriotic and nationalist fervour of the 1580s and 1590s, a fervour that reached its peak in the wake of the sinking of the Armada in 1588. Thus, early modern history plays were a distinctly Elizabethan fashion with their popularity dwindling from the accession of James I in 1603. In the order which the First Folio imposed on them, the plays describe a historical trajectory which leads up to reign of the Tudor family. Shakespeare's two tetralogies run from the deposition of Richard II and the usurpation of his crown by Henry Bolingbroke (1399), later king Henry IV, to the brief glory of the reign of Henry V (1413-1422) and on to the troubled kingship of Henry VI (1422-1461 and 1470-1471) to culminate in the brutal and iniquitous reign of Richard III (1483-1485) who is eventually defeated by the Earl of Richmond (1485) who, as Henry VII, becomes the first Tudor monarch (1485-1509). This narrative follows a linearity wherein the usurpation of Bolingbroke is expiated through the horrors of civil war. In the end, order is re-established when in the last scene of *Richard III* the crown is offered to Richmond who brings about a peaceful union of the two houses of York and Lancaster. E.M.W. Tillyard has seen this teleological sequence of events as part of Tudor propaganda, of what he famously calls the 'Tudor Myth' (cf. 1991: 36 ff.). According to Tillyard, Henry VII was, on the one hand, eager to promote a notion of ancestry which would justify his claim to the throne without recourse to his descent from the Lancaster family or his marriage into the York family. On the other hand, as Tillyard believed, the monarch was trying to foster the notion that "the union of the two houses of York and Lancaster through his marriage with the York heiress was the providential and happy ending of an organic piece of history" (1991: 36). When *Shakespeare's History Plays* was published, Tillyard's readers were already familiar with his ideas of organic unity and ordered regularity which he had expounded in his seminal 1943 book *The Elizabethan World Picture*. Like the Elizabethan World Picture, the Tudor Myth is a very neat critical construct – so neat, in fact, that Tillyard appears to have got carried away by its unifying momentum claiming that "the two tetralogies make a single unit" (1991: 153). While this teleological reading of the histories was widely accepted in the years after its publication in 1944, critics in the 1970s came to regard it as misleadingly simplistic. Rifts and fissures were shown to prevail in the plays, contradictions and ambivalences which served to unhinge any narrowly providential interpretation. Indebted to both tragedy and comedy, Shakespeare's histories display entirely un-providential traits such as a tragic sense of arbitrary chance and misguided personality or the comic and subversive forces of irony and ambiguity (cf. Chernaik 2007: 15 ff.; Holderness 2000: 3).

3. Writing History – Handling Sources

In order to defend the priority he was attributing to the Tudor myth in his readings of the histories, Tillyard felt compelled to reduce the complexity of Shakespeare's many and diverse sources. Shakespeare was not alone in his interest in history and he could base his plays on a range of newly available historical writing, the so-called Tudor 'chronicles.' Henry VII commissioned Polydore Vergil, an Italian humanist at the English court, to write a history of Britain which was published in 1534 as *Anglia Historia*. In 1548, Edward Hall was to follow Vergil's model with his *Union of the Two Noble and Illustre Families of York and Lancaster*, a book that in fact adopted and translated sizeable passages from Vergil's *Anglia Historia, 1485-1537*. Focused on the

Wars of the Roses, Hall's book does indicate something like a Tudor Myth, a sense of glorious union under Henry VII after painful conflict, although this union is not consistently seen as providential. Some two decades later, the work of Hall was in turn picked up and modified by Raphael Holinshed who hired a team of chroniclers to produce *The Chronicles of England, Scotlande, and Irelande* in 1577. Holinshed had reserved for himself the privilege of writing the history of England in this volume which saw an important reprint "newlie augmented and continued" in 1587 – over half a decade after Holinshed's death. Though heavily indebted to the work of Hall, *The Chronicles* omit most of the providential rhetoric of the earlier text. Tillyard was impatient with this unruly evidence which might challenge his world picture: "Much of the motivation of Polydore and Hall was borrowed by Holinshed but only parrotwise and with little understanding. [...] He blurs the great Tudor myth" (1991: 57). But as Shakespeare's numerous borrowings from the second edition show, Holinshed's book was in fact the more important source – an important source not only for the histories proper but also for the tragedy *King Lear*. Early modern historiography was an instrument of politics, it was an act of commemoration and it was eminently literary in its free combination of fact, rumour and sometimes fantastical fiction (cf. also Kantorowicz 1957; Burke 1969; Hawley 1992; Hattaway 2002, part 1). But history was also and importantly moral and educational and it is in this field somewhere between the non-dramatic histories by Hall or Holinshed and the histories written for the stage that another central source for Shakespeare's histories is situated. *The Mirror for Magistrates* (1559-87) is a popular accumulation of moralizing tragic tales about historical figures in the tradition of Boccaccio's *De casibus virorum illustrium* (1356-1373). As its title explains, *The Mirror* intends to instruct its readers "by examples passed in this realme" (*A Mirrour for Magistrates* title page 1571, qtd. from *The Mirror for Magistrates* 1960 [1938]), by the same material which gave coherence to Shakespeare's histories. However, as Wolfgang Iser (1988: 59) has noted, neither the providential teleology of the Tudor myth nor the edifying moral instruction of *The Mirror* can offer a conclusive answer to the questions which Shakespeare's plays open up.

Though Shakespeare gave the Tudor history play its by far most prominent voice, he did not invent the genre. However, the earlier histories are so markedly unlike Shakespeare's resourcefulness and dramatic effectivity that they appear to have served him as so many more historical sources rather than as models in the art of composing history plays. Shakespeare gleaned information for his *Henry IV* plays and for *Henry V* from the anonymous play *The Famous History of Henry the Fifth* of 1586, and *The Troublesome Reign of King John* of 1588 may have had some pertinence to Shakespeare's own play on that monarch. The equally anonymous *Woodstock* (c. 1592-95) is an often comical and highly unconventional play on the reign of Richard II which may have influenced the composition of Shakespeare's *Richard II*. *Edward II* (1594) by Christopher Marlowe and the two parts of *Edward IV* (1600) by Thomas Heywood are important history plays that were written at the same time as Shakespeare's contributions to the genre. *Edmund Ironside* (c. 1585-95) and *Edward III* (c. 1595) are history plays of unknown authorship but with a potential collaboration by Shakespeare. In fact, *Edward III* was admitted into the Shakespeare canon by Cambridge University Press who decided to publish a critical edition of the play as part of the New Cambridge Shakespeare series in 1998.

4. *Richard III*: History and Morality Play

Richard III and *Henry V* are the culmination and conclusion of the two respective tetralogies. For this chapter, the sequence of composition takes precedence over the historical order of the plays so as to elucidate the development of the genre. The composition of the two plays lies some seven years apart – at the beginning and the end of the 1590s respectively – and they display notable changes in Shakespeare's handling of the genre. For his *Richard III* Shakespeare is indebted to his usual sources Holinshed and Hall. But through Edward Hall it is above everything else Sir Thomas More's *History of King Richard the Third* (c. 1512-1518) that served as a source for the play. Both Holinshed and Hall relied on More's detailed account of Richard's career up to his coronation with Hall quoting More's account verbatim. Among the work of the other chroniclers, More's treatment of Richard is unusually rich in the complexity of its central character and in the psychological insight of his presentation. One can argue that from this source Shakespeare borrowed not only much of the plotline and dramatic detail for his play, but also the concept and technique of shaping a historical character into a powerfully intriguing theatrical force and into one of the most influential stage villains.

With *Richard III*, the York tetralogy and with it the historical trajectory of the two tetralogies ends in the tyrannous reign of the physically and morally deformed Richard Gloucester. Within the frame of Tillyard's Tudor Myth, the punishment which England has to suffer as penance for the murder of Richard II is completed and concluded in the total corruption of royal power at the court of Richard III. Richard is the first of Shakespeare's great speakers of monologues and displays much of the potential which was going to be fully developed in the late tragedies. *Richard III* begins with a long soliloquy by the protagonist who thus acts as his own prologue – a first indication of the exceptional control which he is going to command throughout the play. Richard everywhere steps beyond the confines which the conventions both of common morality and of dramatic convention would impose on him. Speaking his own prologue shows him in command of language and well aware of the strategic power of texts and their application. Richard begins by extolling the ascendancy to the throne of his family: "Now is the winter of our discontent / Made glorious summer by this son of York" (1.1.1 f.). His first words describe historical change as a blessing for the country, but his speech soon turns towards himself and towards his own private discontent which has not even begun to give way to a glorious summer:

> But I, that am not shap'd for sportive tricks,
> Nor made to court an amorous looking-glass;
> I, that am rudely stamp'd and want love's majesty […]
> Deform'd, unfinish'd, sent before my time
> Into this breathing world scarce half made up. (1.1.14-21)

Richard is physically handicapped and palpably haunted by his deformity which he regards as the cause of his isolation. While in *Henry VI* he had claimed lack of love as the cause of his physical shortcomings, in *Richard III* he asserts that his deformity is the reason why he does not experience love and that this lack is the cause for the villainies we are about to witness: "since I cannot prove a lover / To entertain these fair well-spoken days, / I am determined to prove a villain" (1.1.28-30). From the start, Richard is a consummate manipulator of stories, a writer of his own entry in the book of history. Since he is about to show outrageously depraved actions, he tries to use his deformity as an excuse – an attempt that is unlikely to be any more successful than his earlier bid to blame the lovelessness of his mother's womb. But while Richard's deformity can hardly be regarded as the cause of his evil disposition, it is a highly appropriate outward reflection of his inner corruption, a corruption that is, as it were, inscribed on his body.

We know from his pronouncements in *Henry VI* that Richard's foremost ambition is the crown of England. However, his reason for wanting to become king are stranger than a mere hunger for power. Richard plans the deaths of all that stand between him and the throne with King Edward as the last obstacle: "God take King Edward to his mercy, / And leave the world for me to bustle in" (1.1.151 f.). The first instance of what he means by bustling in the world is a foray into the world of love when he sets out to woo, of all people, Lady Anne, the widow of Edward, Prince of Wales, whom Richard killed at Tewkesbury. Richard at first seems to be fighting an uphill battle when Anne takes the better part of act 1, scene 2 to curse him. Her first words to him set the mood for the execrations that follow: "Avaunt, thou dreadful minister of hell!" (1.2.46) Anne proves to be an eloquent condemner and it is all the more remarkable that Richard emerges victorious from the battle of words which he fights against her. Having won Anne over by the power of what she will later describe as his "honey words" (4.1.79), Richard is himself genuinely surprised by and inordinately pleased with his own success: "And I, no friends to back my suit at all / But the plain devil and dissembling looks – / And yet to win her, all the world to nothing!" (1.2.240-42) In act 1 Richard is thus his own prologue and now also his audience who applauds the marvellous role he himself has performed on stage. He does not require the real support of friends since he can count on "the plain devil," the role model of the Medieval Vice-figure, and on his "dissembling looks," the art of the actor, to have effects in the very real world – the real world which is thus cynically reduced to "nothing." There appears to be precious little strategy behind this playacting. Much in keeping with his credentials as a Vice figure, Richard's motivations are often opaque and there is no telling why he woos Anne. He professes to seek this marital bond for some unspecific "secret close intent, / By marrying her which I must reach unto" (1.2.159 f.). Both his playacting and his intention are strikingly founded in his unparalleled egocentricism. By gaining Anne's favour, he has above everything else gained favour with himself: "Since I am crept in favour with myself, / I will maintain it with some little cost" (1.2.263 f.). The favour he has gained immediately translates into a new role, into a new disguise which he will cultivate, as he explains, by buying clothes that will cover his deformity. He will "study fashions to adorn my body" (1.2.262), he will invest in new surfaces.

Richard Gloucester is a historical figure who, in the play, is trying to hide his nefarious intentions behind clothes, behind layers of deception, and behind his clever rhetoric. History is established and passed on in the theatre and on the page and it is here that Richard succeeds magnificently in the role he centrally intends to play: "I am determined to prove a villain" (1.1.30). In that he is made to "prove a villain," the play suggests that this is more than mere playacting. Richard's being a villain is more substantial than his being a lover or a soldier – not, however, because it faithfully reflects some essence of his character, but because Shakespeare's play commands more historiographical authority than Richard's antics. The play makes sure that all the various roles which Richard puts on dovetail into the role of the Vice figure. Indeed, the play is not content to portray Richard as a villain. He has to be made a monster, he has to be turned into a veritable living devil for posterity. This agenda of the play serves to heighten the effect of Richard's death, or rather: it serves to make plausible the effect which the play will ascribe to it. In order to have the coronation of Henry VII at the end of the play appear as an act of redemption and divine grace, the first Tudor monarch has to replace someone more substantial than any average unjust monarch. Richard has to be a worthwhile foe to bring down, he has to impersonate every evil known to man so that his destruction can not only appease but, indeed, redeem England.

But Richard is not alone in promoting his identity as a villain. While Anne relents after her rambling curses, old Queen Margarete is a curser of Richard who will not be taken in by his cleverness. According to the chronicles, Margarete dies in exile well before the events of *Richard III*. Her presence in the play is therefore unhistorical and is a good example of the liberties which Shakespeare took with his sources – sources, needless to say, which were themselves a far cry from being accurate or objective by today's standards of historiographical precision. At first, the banished queen lurks at the side of the stage and offers asides in which she recounts the injustice she has suffered and begins to curse Richard: "Out, devil!" and "leave this world, / Thou cacodemon" (1.3.118; 1.3.144 f.). However, she is totally indiscriminate in casting her ire and bile on everyone present. Her blind retributive malice raises some doubts as to her moral status and her presence thus temporarily removes Richard, who can outwit the old queen with his nimble rhetoric, from the centre of the audience's censure. But apart from briefly suspending and ultimately reinforcing our judgement of the protagonist, Margarete functions like a tragic chorus. Her curses and warnings serve to structure the plot and they derive their force from the power of history for which the old queen can be taken to stand. In an eerily disconcerting way, however, she not only recounts and assesses the past but appears to be actively making history when the curses which she hurls against Richard and the other nobles come true. Richard here emerges as the manager and executioner of Margarete's imprecations. In act 3, he makes the outrageous claim that Margarete's magic has caused his arm to shrivel up and thereby sets a trap for Hastings. As soon as Hastings appears to be only slightly wary of acknowledging the injustice which Richard claims to have suffered, the king straightaway proclaims him a traitor and sends him to the block. Hastings declares that his death is the result of Margaret's curses: "O Margaret, Margaret, now thy heavy curse / has lighted on poor Hasting's wretched head" (3.5.92 f.). Although her elaborate vitriolic tirades tend to come across as a ludicrous sign of her waning mental health, Margarete's curses are a powerful dramatic example of history and historiography in the making – not, needless to say, by magic, but by the dissemination of texts that can variously be dismissed, questioned, reinterpreted, and manipulated. The power of drama can thus serve to turn curses and other rhetoric into historical fact.

The many curses and the figure of the Vice who is constantly referred to as a devil, place *Richard III* in close relation to the medieval mystery plays. Indeed, Richard explicitly places himself in that tradition by remarking in one of his typical asides that he is "like the formal Vice" (3.1.81). Many features of religious drama are retained in the play: devils gloat and demons seduce unsuspecting victims, sinners are punished and martyrs are cruelly killed, curses are uttered and dramatically (if not miraculously) come true. The death of Clarence whom his brother Richard has killed in the Tower in act 1, scene 4 would appear to add nothing to the play that might merit its length were it not for its strong religious vein which serves to highlight the debt which the play as a whole bears to the tradition of medieval religious drama. Clarence recounts a dream in which Richard pushes him off a ship. At the bottom of the sea Clarence sees treasures of sunken ships and in the face of this powerful symbol of earthly vanity, of riches that come to nothing, he drowns. However, his dream continues beyond death and he exclaims that "then began the tempest to my soul" (1.4.44). He finds himself in hell, in "the kingdom of perpetual night" (1.4.47), where ghosts from his past greet him and confront him with his disloyalty to Henry VI. Like sinners in religious drama, Clarence recognizes his sins but fears that it is too late for penance: "I have done these things / That now give evidence against my soul" (1.4.66 f.). However, the two murderers who eventually kill him are not agents of divine retribution, but the henchmen of Clarence's tyrannical brother. Clarence thus dies a repentant martyr whose cause and honesty even serve to convert one of the murderers who uses a biblical image to express his own repentance: "How fain, like Pilate, would I wash my hands / Of this most grievous murder" (1.4.261 f.). Conventional elements of the moralities are here used as tools for the writing of history (cf. Naumann 1978: 16 f.). The line which is drawn between Richard the Vice on one side and Clarence the martyr along with the other repentant and punished sinners on the other heightens the sense of Richard's devilish nature and helps to cast the history of England in religious terms: a country which will at last be redeemed from the sin that is the deposition and murder of Richard II.

The figure of Richard III incorporates a wide range of the Vice's facets: malicious devil, sarcastic clown, sly schemer, and executor of divine providence. A second salient tradition which informs Richard's character is that of the Machiavellian hero, of a politician who dissembles and murders for his own gain – according to the heavily distorted notion which Shakespeare's time had of the thought of Niccolò Machiavelli (1469-1527). On the night before the battle of Bosworth, Richard's victims appear before him as ghosts. Shaken by the apparition of the ghosts and seemingly on the verge of madness Richard stumbles among his men. But unlike Clarence, he regains his composure to dismiss his dreams: "Conscience is but a word that cowards use, / Devis'd at first to keep the strong in awe" (5.3.310 f.). His stereotypical professions of ruthless violence show Richard as his old villainous self devoid of *anagnorisis* and tragic stature. As the *de casibus* plot draws to its conclusion, the last we see of Richard is an obsessed and in every respect reduced warrior in search of his opponent: "A horse! A horse! My kingdom for a horse!" (5.5.13)

Shakespeare's *Richard III* is an important element in a tradition which casts Richard Gloucester as a murderous tyrant – a perception which is not exactly borne out by historical evidence. The short scene in act 3 where Prince Edward muses on Caesar's supposed claim to having built the Tower of London explains the mechanism behind this construction of history. Edward addresses Richard:

> But say, my lord, it were not register'd,
> Methinks the truth should live from age to age,
> As 'twere retail'd to all posterity,
> Even to the general all-ending day. (3.1.75-78)

Even if Caesar's building of the Tower is not a verifiable fact which has been placed on record, it will still be regarded as a fact by posterity. Rumours, prejudice, and stories are thus turned into accepted fact, into history. The Prince is quite explicit in stating that "the truth should live from age to age": from the tradition of stories being handed down results not opinion or belief, but truth itself. Not contingent upon verifiable record, truth can be constructed by hearsay – it is open to manipulation. While Shakespeare's Richard III is an accomplished fabricator of facts, the play which bears his name is a prime example of this very form of fabrication. Though the image of King Richard III as a devilish, raving villain is not registered, *Richard III* has retailed that image to all posterity. Shakespeare has, indeed, made history.

5. *Henry V*: History and Comedy

Henry V is the last play in the tetralogies to be composed by Shakespeare. It concludes the Lancaster tetralogy and marks a moment of respite in the long penance of England after the deposition of Richard II at the hands of King Henry IV. Rather than as an isolated play, *Henry V* can helpfully be seen as making up a trilogy of plays together with the two parts of *Henry IV*. These plays are united in their focus on one character: Henry V, whose formation is recounted from his youth as Prince Hal in *Henry IV* and as Henry V after he takes the crown at the death of his father. In *Henry IV*, prince Hal is a disappointment and a source of concern for his royal father. He shows no inclination to cultivate the virtues required of a king, but enjoys the privilege of youth to be recklessly immature. His shortcomings are illustrated by his position with regard to two entirely unconnected characters in the play: Sir John Falstaff and Percy Hotspur. While Hal is constantly seen in the company of Falstaff, he is the opponent and, indeed, the opposite to Hotspur. Falstaff is a *miles gloriosus*, a cowardly braggart, a hedonistic philanthropist and a likeable crook. His disorderly world in the taverns of Cheapside jars with the serious world at the court of Henry IV and Prince Hal forms a problematic link between the two spaces. So dismal is the prospect of having this undisciplined Hal as a king that his father even dreams of having Percy Hotspur, who defies his authority, for a son (1 *Henry IV* 1.1.86-89). On his death bed he predicts the ruin of his kingdom: "O, thou wilt be a wilderness again, / Peopled with wolves, thy old inhabitants!" (2 *Henry IV* 4.5.137 f.) Against these bleak anticipations of his father, Hal performs a radical change so that the extreme scepticism towards his ascension works as another historiographical device for the creation of contrast: Just like *Richard III* turns Richard Gloucester into a veritable monster so as to heighten the glory of Henry Tudor who defeats him, so Prince Hal is in *Henry IV* shown to be an irresponsible rogue only to increase the effect of his miraculous transformation into the ideal ruler we are shown in *Henry V*.

The epilogue to *Henry IV* ends with a promise to the audience which the author will partly break: "[O]ur humble author will continue the story, with Sir John [Falstaff] in it, and make you merry with fair Katherine of France" (2 *Henry IV* 5.4.26-29). Katherine of France will figure in *Henry V* and her part will be merry, but Falstaff does not appear at all. His death is noted but this reference only further bears out the radical cut in Henry's life. As his wife Nell and his Eastcheap friends note, Falstaff dies as an effect of Henry's rejection: "The King has killed his heart" (2.1.88). There is an element of unease in this claim, but the dominant impression is not that of an act of disloyalty and irresponsibility on Henry's part, but quite the reverse: a 'killing off' of all that has been irresponsible and disloyal to England in Henry's earlier life. With Falstaff dies the world of jest and bawdy laughter which Henry is leaving behind to engage in more serious matters. However, these serious matters of state – the battle of Agincourt – will also lead to comedy, though to comedy of a different kind: Henry triumphs and he marries Katherine of France thus reconciling England with the defeated French. The note of comedy which *Henry V* sounds is thus both romantic and political.

While Richard Gloucester speaks his own prologue in *Richard III*, *Henry V* starts with a formal Chorus presenting the prologue. Like the chorus in Sophocles' tragedies, the Chorus reports and comments on events. Since it starts off every act of the play, its presence is felt throughout. The Chorus offers a formal grounding of the serious yet entirely successful and decidedly un-tragic action of the play, it imparts to it a frame of tragic solemnity. However, the Chorus is exceptional in its insistent reflexivity, in its constant consideration of the workings and shortcomings of the theatre.

> Can this cockpit hold
> The vasty fields of France? Or may we cram
> Within this wooden O the very casques
> That did afright the air at Agincourt? (Prologue, 11-14)

The present of the theatre cannot live up to the glory of the past it purports to represent. However, the answer which the Chorus gives to the question it poses is still affirmative: All that is required to fit the lofty subject into the frame of a play is the audience's imagination. As the Chorus advises: "Into a thousand parts divide one man / And make imaginary puissance" (Prologue, 24 f.). The theatre cannot offer truthfulness or authenticity, but it stands redeemed as an appropriate medium for historiography since far from an ideal of historical precision, it can convey the glory of the events by means that any historian today would reject: dramatic fabrication, rhetorical strategy and imagination.

Richard III displays a noticeable proximity to the medieval morality plays and their religious background as sinners and martyrs meet their deaths, curses fly and are fulfilled, the devil himself walks the palace. *Henry V* is a markedly more secular play. Actions and events are here directed towards national unity and the glory of England. Henry IV wanted to engage the country in a crusade for the very secular purpose of uniting his subjects and of diverting challenges to his questionable claim to the throne. He advises his son to follow a similar course and Henry V is eager to comply by marching against France. In *Henry V*, the figure of the king is introduced in a dialogue between two bishops who are contemplating ways of protecting the assets of the church by encouraging and sponsoring Henry's martial plans. A painfully pedantic and long-winded exposition of Henry's claim to the French throne by the Archbishop (1.2.33-95) complements this scene. This unravelling of the entire royal lineage is a parody of legitimacy and it shows the disconcerting lengths to which politicians in state and church will go to make history conform. In view of these scenes, audiences cannot help but question Henry's political and moral justification for war. However, though these questions are raised, the play accepts the secular agenda of king and church and does not elaborate on moral implications.

The figure of Henry V completely dominates the play. Approximately one third of the lines are spoken by him. In the last analysis, the play only has one character – King Henry V – and moves upward and ahead towards ultimate triumph in one straight and unwavering movement. It is very hard to construct a captivating play around this two-dimensional constellation and especially around what appears to be a very static and two-dimensional protagonist. His straightness and honesty culminates in his fervent encouragement to his soldiers: "Once more unto the breach" (3.1.36), a rhetoric that is markedly free from duplicity and manipulation. However, this almost boringly flawless character is marred by a number of highly questionable actions that – unlike the death of Falstaff – resist assimilation into the glorification of Henry V. While the Chorus offers a popular and idealized image of Henry, the play shows a tainted ruler who bears the seed of tyranny (cf. Chernaik 2007: 149). Talked into a war on France by the bishops, there is the sneaking suspicion that Henry is a calculating warmonger. His way of waging war is compromised when he tries to threaten the town of Harfleur into surrender: "the fleshed soldier [...] / In liberty of bloody hand shall range / With conscience wide as hell, mowing like grass / Your fresh fair virgins and your flowering infants" (3.3.11-14). This rhetoric which threatens slaughter, rape, and total destruction is strikingly reminiscent of Christopher Marlowe's ruthlessly violent tyrant and titan Tamburlaine the Great when he lays siege to Damascus. There is no telling if, unlike Marlowe's Tamburlaine the Great, Henry V is merely bluffing but during the battle at Agincourt he clearly indicates that his fight is not firmly rooted in moral probity. At one point Henry believes that the French have reinforced their troops and that he is in danger of losing the battle. Immediately, he orders the killing of all prisoners (4.6.36-38) – an order which, as Fluellen straightaway notes (4.7.1-4), is a blatant breach of martial law. The question of responsibility in war is another issue where Henry falls short. On the night before the great battle, he mixes with his soldiers without revealing his identity. Two soldiers proclaim that the fate of the soldiers is in the hands of the king, including the purity of their souls should they be forced to sin out of obedience to the monarch. Henry tries to reason with them, but is eventually reduced to undignified self-pity: "We must bear all. O hard condition, / Twin-born with greatness" (4.1.230 f.). Though Henry bids farewell to his youthful drunken irresponsibility, he is having great trouble assuming a mature and truly royal form of responsibility.

6. Conclusion

Up to *Henry IV*, Shakespeare's histories, including, of course, *Richard III*, were largely designed according to the model of the *de casibus* tragedy. Flawed men of high rank – i.e. weak, contested, or morally corrupt monarchs – experience troubled lives and violent or ignominious deaths. With *Henry IV* this pattern changes. Though a usurper, Henry IV dies a natural death and is in his last moments reassured that the future of the monarchy will be bright, that tragedy will at last give way to comedy. More importantly still, *Henry IV* shows tragedy and comedy side-by-side: the troublesome reign of the monarch on one side and the mirthful humour of Prince Hal and his common companions in Cheapside on the other. In *Henry V*, tragedy and comedy blend in a solemn play which is structured by the Chorus of Greek tragedy. Like a tragedy, the play deals with serious matters of state governed by a far from untainted monarch, but in the mode of comedy, the protagonist is allowed to survive the end of the play where he wins a war, unites two countries and marries a princess. While displaying the tragic potential inherent in the power and politics which govern the history of a nation, *Henry V* thus deflects the tragic potential which the genre is wont to pursue and makes way for a happy ending. History plays can in this way create a rich interplay of tragedy and comedy, an interplay which makes them an important tool for the writing and indeed for the creation of history.

During both the 18th and 19th centuries, plays in the genre tended to make history subservient to spectacle, to a melodramatic and romantic sensationalism which catered to the popular taste of the time mixed with an overt didacticism. In this respect, playwrights like Nicholas Rowe (1673-1718), Edward Bulwer-Lytton (1803-1873), and Alfred Lord Tennyson (1809-1892) differ only in degree (cf. Wikander 1986). With George Bernard Shaw (1856-1950), history began to take centre stage. The emerging modern history play in the 20th century by such authors as T.S. Eliot (1888-1965), Robert Bolt (1924-1995), and Edward Bond (*1934) was marked by daring and inventiveness as well as a renewed respect for its sources. To this day, however, Shakespeare's history plays are the most seminal landmark in the genre. His histories are neither superficial in their concern with the past, nor are they subservient either to historical precision or to Tillyard's Tudor Myth. On the contrary: by defying categorization, by forming a genre which explodes the rules and proprieties of both tragedy and comedy, Shakespeare's history plays point out ways in which the full potential of the theatre can produce a living form of historiography which engages readers and audiences to become themselves historians.

Bibliography

Primary Sources

Shakespeare, William. 1960. *Henry IV, Part 1*. A.R. Humphreys (ed.). London: Routledge (The Arden Shakespeare).
—. 1960. *Henry IV, Part 2*. A.R. Humphreys (ed.). London: Routledge (The Arden Shakespeare).
—. 1981. *Richard III*. Antony Hammond (ed.). London: Methuen (The Arden Shakespeare).
—. 1995. *Henry V*. T.W Craik (ed.). London: Routledge (The Arden Shakespeare).

Annotated Bibliography

Chernaik, Warren. 2007. *Shakespeare's History Plays*. Cambridge: Cambridge UP.
   Offers individual interpretations of the entire canon of Shakespeare's histories along with a lucid introduction to the critical debates surrounding their reception.
Danson, Lawrence. 2000. *Shakespeare's Dramatic Genres*. Oxford: Oxford UP.
   Brief discussions of the history plays with a marked focus on questions of genre and a highly relevant discussion of Early Modern genre-theory.

Egan, Gabriel. 2007. *Shakespeare*. Edinburgh: Edinburgh UP.

Chapter 2 offers a very accessible and concise reading of Richard II *and* Henry V *within the context of the tetralogies.*

Hattaway, Michael (ed.). 2002. *Shakespeare's History Plays*. Cambridge: Cambridge UP.

An anthology of both introductory essays and detailed readings of individual plays including chapters on Shakespeare's historical drama set outside Britain.

Holderness, Graham. 2000. *Shakespeare: The Histories*. Houndmills, et al.: Macmillan.

Interprets the histories within a discourse of historical, cultural, and sexual difference. Informed by modern theory, the readings focus on history as a textual process, as a form of writing.

Iser, Wolfgang. 1988. *Shakespeares Historien: Genesis und Geltung*. Konstanz: Universitätsverlag Konstanz.

Based on a thorough introduction into Elizabethan concepts of history and historiography, Iser demonstrates how Shakespeare's history plays do not mirror history, but change and put in relief the reality they are based upon.

Maguire, Laurie E. 2004. *Studying Shakespeare: A Guide to the Plays*. Oxford: Blackwell.

The chapter on "Political Life" links the histories proper to the Roman plays and to the tragedies in a concise consideration of the Elizabethan interrelation between politics and playacting.

Tillyard, E.M.W. 1972 [1943]. *The Elizabethan World Picture*. London: Penguin.

A canonical, albeit much-reviled, portrait of Elizabethan England as a place of cognitive orderliness.

Further Secondary Literature

Burke, Peter. 1969. *The Renaissance Sense of the Past*. London: Edward Arnold.
Campbell, Lily B. (ed.). 1960 [1938]. *The Mirror for Magistrates*. New York: Barnes & Noble, by Special Arrangement with the Cambridge UP.
Hawley, William. 1992. *Critical Hermeneutics and Shakespeare's History Plays*. New York: Peter Lang.
Kantorowicz, E.H. 1957. *The King's Two Bodies*. Princeton: Princeton UP.
Naumann, Walter. 1978. *Die Dramen Shakespeares*. Darmstadt: WBG.
Tillyard, E.M.W. 1991 [1944]. *Shakespeare's History Plays*. London: Penguin.
Wikander, Matthew H. 1986. *The Play of Truth and State: Historical Drama from Shakespeare to Brecht*. Baltimore/London: The Johns Hopkins UP.

6. Shakespeare's Tragedies: *Hamlet*

Sibylle Baumbach

1. How to Do Things with Tragedy

Take an action that is "whole and complete and of a certain magnitude" (Aristotle 1927 [c. 335 BC]: vi.2), a character "in high station and good fortune" who is "good" (ibid.: xv.2), "consistent" (ibid.: xv.7), and shows some fatal judgment, tragic flaw, or error (*hamartia*); present the plot "in language enriched with all kinds of ornament" (vi.2); work towards a cathartic ending, which both incites and purges "pity [*eleos*] and fear [*phobos*]" (vi.2) in the audience, and what you get is not Shakespearean tragedy. Even though it is tempting to apply Aristotle's definition of tragedy to medieval or early modern drama, it is often forgotten that the elements listed in the *Poetics* are derived from Greek plays of the 5th century. Rather than prescribing a tragic model for future dramatists, Aristotle described the dramatic form and content he experienced in the tragedies by Aeschylus, Sophocles, and Euripides. While we might find some connection between Greek and early modern drama, and critics have applied Aristotelian concepts such as *hamartia* to Shakespeare's plays (as, for instance, Bevington 2002: 62-65), concepts such as 'tragic flaw' and the 'unity of action' ultimately fail to account for the complex psychological disposition of characters and the multiple plots in Shakespeare's drama. It is important, therefore, to bear in mind that tragedy, like any other genre, is essentially in flux as it is shaped and reinvented by authors of different eras and cultures.

Shakespeare's tragedies were experimental (cf. Dillon 2007: 5). Unlike John Lydgate or his contemporaries Ben Jonson, John Webster, and Philip Massinger, whose work interacted with theories of tragedy, Shakespeare was, strictly speaking, no tragedian. Instead of following any specific school of tragedy, his tragedies "evade its most characteristic commitments, fulfill them too literally [or] transform them" (Bayley 1981: 5). To an even greater degree than Thomas Kyd and Christopher Marlowe, who paved the way for Renaissance tragedy by promoting a kind of drama that was more daring than its predecessors (see chapter 3), Shakespeare's work exhibits the generic fluidity that is characteristic particularly of early modern drama. His tragedies share no tragic pattern or form: "There is a greater resemblance among Greek tragedies, those in the classic French or Spanish genre, or in the German Romantic tradition, or among the tragedies of Shakespeare's own contemporaries, than there is between *Macbeth* and *Timon of Athens*, *Troilus and Cressida*, *King Lear* or *Coriolanus*" (Bayley 1981: 5). Consequently, as Kenneth Muir pointed out, "[t]here is no such thing as Shakespearean tragedy; there are only Shakespearean tragedies" (1972: 12).

The increasing hybridization of genres is explicitly referred to in *Hamlet*, Shakespeare's most successful tragedy, and notably so by a comic figure: the meddler Polonius, who, when praising the supreme talents of the newly-arrived actors, ridicules the notion of clear-cut genres, thus hinting at the difficulty of classifying early modern drama:

> The best actors in the world, either for tragedy, comedy, history, pastoral, pastorical-comical, historical-pastoral, tragical-historical, tragical-comical-historical-pastoral, scene individable, or poem unlimited; Seneca cannot be too heavy, nor Plautus too light. (2.2.379-383)

With the 1st-century Roman dramatist Seneca and the Roman playwright Plautus (c. 254-184 BC), Polonius points to two major classical influences of Shakespeare's tragedies and comedies, respectively (see chapter 4). Before having a closer look at the particularities of Shakespeare's tragedies, however, let us briefly turn to the term 'tragedy' and its early modern understanding.

2. Mapping Early Modern Tragedy

The English expression 'tragedy' derives from the Greek *tragōdia*, whose literal meaning, 'goat song,' hearkens back to the origins of theatre and the cult of Dionysus, the god of ecstasy (from Greek *ekstasis* = 'standing-out,' 'displacement'). It was originally applied to narrative poems which describe the downfall of man from happiness and prosperity to utmost misery and suffering, as suggested in the prologue to Geoffrey Chaucer's *The Monk's Tale*, written in the late 14th century:

> Tragedie is to seyn a certeyn storie,
> As olde bookes maken us memorie,
> Of hym that stood in greet prosperitee,
> And is yfallen out of heigh degree
> Into myserie, and endeth wrecchedly. (Chaucer 2008: VII.1973-77)

Later definitions, which follow Latin writers such as Donatus (4th century BC) and Horace (1st century BC), rather than being derived from a direct reading of Aristotle's *Poetics*, explain 'tragedy' as a "mournful play being a lofty kind of poetry, and representing personages of great state and matter of much trouble, a great broil or stir: it beginneth prosperously and endeth unfortunately or sometimes doubtfull, and is contrary to comedy" (John Florio, *Latin Dictionary* [1598], qtd. in Dillon 2007: 10). The first English tragedies that appeared around 1560, Thomas Preston's *A Lamentable Tragedy, Mixed Full of Pleasant Mirth, Containing the Life of Cambyses, King of Persia* (1558-1569) and *Gorboduc* (1562) by Thomas Sackville and Thomas Norton, already indicate the mixed, cross-fertilizing tradition in which Shakespeare wrote. Whereas *Cambyses* as a vernacular drama is indebted to medieval morality plays, mixing as it does allegorical characters (Cruelty, Shame, Diligence) with historical figures (King Cambyses), *Gorboduc* follows the Senecan tradition (see chapter 3) and provides a model for tragedies with exceptionally violent content presented in a highly elevated language, which includes short, memorable moral statements or *sententiae*. The didactic quality of tragedy, which answered to the overriding orthodox concern of theatre critics at the time, is stressed in many definitions of the term, such as Philip Sidney's famous description of "high and excellent Tragedy":

> [...] Tragedy, that openeth the greatest wounds and showeth forth the ulcers, that are covered with tissue; that maketh kings fear to by tyrants, and tyrants manifest their tyrannical humours; that, with stirring the affects of admiration and commiseration, teacheth the uncertainty of this world, and upon how weak foundations gilden roofs are builded. (Sidney 1965 [1595]: 177 f.)

Beside so-called domestic tragedies, which focus on a personal conflict, such as adultery, in the middle-class milieu (e.g. *Arden of Faversham* [1591], *A Yorkshire Tragedy* [1608], and Thomas Heywood's *A Woman Killed With Kindnesse* [1607]), the most popular tragedies in the Elizabethan and Jacobean eras were Senecan-inspired 'revenge tragedies,' including Thomas Kyd's *The Spanish Tragedy* (1592), John Webster's *The White Devil* (1612), and John Middleton's *The Revenger's Tragedy* (1607). As well as focusing on violent, repulsive actions, these tragedies share a common plot: the action starts off with the murder of a benign character, usually a sovereign, who returns from the dead to name his avenger, usually his son; what follows is a plot of disguise and intrigue, often involving madness, before the play culminates in the eruption of violence and the death of both murderer and avenger. Shakespeare's earliest, neo-classical tragedy, *Titus Andronicus* (1592), is greatly indebted to this tradition. The gruesome spectacle of slaughter and mutilation, created by immense physical cruelty in speech and action, is condensed in the very memorable stage direction "*Enter a* MESSENGER *with two heads and a hand*" (*Titus Andronicus*, 3.1.232). The play culminates in a Thyestean feast when Titus serves his adversary Tamora a pie made from the flesh of her two sons before killing her, avenging his own children. The extreme gore has led critics to doubt Shakespeare's authorship and attribute the play to Thomas Kyd instead. What the style and content of *Titus* might indicate, however, is the great development of Shakespeare's art of tragedy from a tribute to the Senecan tradition to more experimental, diverse, and challenging forms of tragic plays.

3. Shakespeare's Tragedies

The classification of Shakespeare's drama into comedies, tragedies, and history plays derives from the First Folio edition, published in 1623 (cf. chapter 5). Whereas the 14 comedies and ten histories listed therein are closely linked by generic features – having either love as a central theme, complicated by social and gender confusions, masking and disguise, and ending in harmony and marriage (comedies), or figures and events of English history presented in chronological order (history plays) – the common ground shared by the twelve plays gathered under the lemma 'tragedies' is much harder to define. Shakespeare's tragedies have often been subdivided into the 'great' or 'mature tragedies,' *Hamlet* (c. 1600-01), *Othello* (c. 1603-04), *King Lear* (1604-05), and *Mac-*

beth (1606), and the 'Roman plays,' *Julius Caesar* (1599), *Antony and Cleopatra* (1606), and *Coriolanus* (1608), which present chronicles of Roman history, based on Plutarch's *Parallel Lives* (c. 100 BC), in tragic form. Deviating from these there are the 'early tragedies,' *Romeo and Juliet* (1595) and *Titus Andronicus* (1592), which break ranks insofar as the former starts off as what could evolve into a comedy, and the latter includes extraordinarily gruesome actions; *Timon of Athens* (1607-08), which is arguably a tragedy but due to its irregular plot structure is sometimes, like *Troilus and Cressida* (1602), grouped with the 'problem plays;' and, finally, *Cymbeline* (1609-10), which has been listed as tragedy in the Folio but has also been identified as 'romance.' This categorization, however, cannot belie the fact that the genres are closely intertwined. As Samuel Johnson wrote in his "Preface to Shakespeare" (1806 [1765]: 143):

> Tragedy was not in those times a poem of more general dignity or elevation than comedy; it required only a calamitous conclusion, with which the common criticism of that age was satisfied, whatever lighter pleasure it afforded in its progress.

The key distinction between comedies and tragedies is their different outcome, the former culminating in marriage ("Jack shall have Jill, / Naught shall go ill," *A Midsummer Night's Dream*, 3.3.45 f.), the latter in the death of the protagonist. Apart from this requirement, the tragic often appears on the verge of comedy, and vice versa. *Romeo and Juliet* could potentially develop into a romantic comedy, involving two lovers who meet under adverse circumstances, a masked ball, as well as stock characters such as the *senex* and older authority figures who oppose the relationship – these are all classic elements of comedy. The play, however, takes a tragic turn when the jester, Mercutio, is killed, and Romeo, avenging his friend, slays Tybalt. While Shakespeare's tragedies frequently include comic elements as thematic variation and comic relief, his comedies show tragic potential: Shylock's demand for Antonio's flesh is almost fulfilled in *The Merchant of Venice*, and the maltreated, gulled Malvolio announces his revenge at the end of *Twelfth Night*.

The distinction between history plays (see chapter 5) and tragedies is even more complicated. The two genres are closely connected, as indicated by the title of *The Tragedy of Richard the Third* (1592-93), which was grouped under history plays in the First Folio. While histories employ a different 'cast,' namely personae from English history, they qualify as tragic plays insofar as they present human suffering due to fatal judgement, the violation of a pre-established order, as well as dramatic heroes who find themselves and the world and time they live in "out of joint" (*Hamlet*, 1.5.189).

What, then, are the main characteristics of Shakespeare's tragedies compared with other forms of tragedy? Tragedy revolves around contradictions, displacements (cf. Hammond 2009), a violation of order, and a fierce conflict between the individual and a greater (natural, political, or moral) order or authority. Tragic conflict can arise from a clash between conflicting embodiments of a universal (ethical) power, which eventually is resolved in a state of sublation or *Aufhebung* (G. W. Hegel), or from the contradiction of Apollonian and Dionysian powers (Friedrich Nietzsche), i.e. of reason and control versus passion and ecstasy. Lily Campbell (1973), for instance, regards Shakespeare's heroes as "slaves of passion" insofar as they are driven to extreme and violent action due to their inability to control their jealousy (Othello), ambition (Macbeth), grief (Hamlet), or wrath (Lear). The tragic scheme in Shakespeare's plays, however, is more complex than this might suggest. While early modern theories of the passions and bodily humours (see chapter 4) inform his construction of *dramatis personae*, Shakespeare's characters are more complex and cannot be subsumed under certain types (with the exception of characters derived from the medieval vice-figure, such as Jago or Richard Gloucester).

What further distinguishes Shakespeare's tragedies from his predecessors' is their lack of consolidation, recuperation, and closure. Just like the comedies, whose 'happy endings' are disputable insofar as marriage proposals remain unanswered (*Measure for Measure*) or are almost crushed by much ado about nothing, his tragedies often end with an unsettling outlook: despite the death of the main character, order is not restored. Instead of an equilibrium of previously conflicting forces, we are left with a potentially corrupt promise of restoration, which is based on a disquieting silence (in *Othello*, the villain Iago refuses to disclose his motives) or entails troubling recurrences of the past (in *Macbeth*, Macduff is hailed as new king three times, echoing the way in which Macbeth was hailed Thane by the three 'weird sisters') (cf. Kastan 2003: 18). Redemption is provided only by the recognition that there is no escape from a corrupted world in which the dialectic of destruction and renewal no longer applies. Rather than providing closure, the tragedies announce new rounds of suffering, as if suggesting that "[t]omorrow, tomorrow, and tomorrow" (*Macbeth*, 5.5.18), as the wheel of fortune keeps turning, will bring similar hardship.

The capriciousness of fortune, however, which is a central theme in medieval *de-casibus*-tragedies, has but little room in Shakespeare's drama. Unlike the 'tragical tales' of Giovanni Boccaccio's *De Casibus Virorum Illustrium* (1355-1374), Chaucer's *Monk's Tale* (14th c.), John Lydgate's *The Fall of Princes* (c. 1430-38), or *The Mirror for Magistrates* (1559), a multi-authored collection in which different speakers recall cautionary stories of (famous) men who have fallen from the heights of happiness to wretchedness, Shakespeare's tragedies provide no overtly moral lessons in humility but combine ideas of fortune, providence, and the inherent paradoxes of life with man's subjection to his socio-political environment and the destructiveness of human actions. King Lear divides his kingdom and abdicates, violating divine law; Macbeth murders the king, destroying natural order; and Romeo is banished because he killed Tybault. Even though the gods are invoked in Shakespeare's tragedies (as, for instance, in *King Lear*), they remain silent. The plurality of competing influences and the great variety of dramatic conflicts and themes explain the continuing fascination with Shakespeare's tragedies: they depict the political, social, and religious upheavals as well as the gender and colonialist discourses of the time, and mark the transition from the pre-modern to a modern world, in which the belief in a cosmic world order (cf. Tillyard 1961) gave way to growing scientific and philosophical scepticism and a new focus on the individual. Even though it is a speculative enterprise to fully reconstruct the historical context, Shakespeare's tragedies cannot be isolated from the environment they were originally written and performed in – they have to be set in a material, socio-political, or historical context to examine their relation or dissidence to dominant ideologies of the time.

Due to its popularity across all social classes, the theatre was not only a place of diversion and entertainment, but also provided an arena for the distribution and circulation of knowledge (cf. Baumbach 2009) and the negotiation of competing world views. It thus both appropriated and transformed the cultural landscape of the time (Greenblatt 1988). While Shakespeare's tragedies deal with the dislocation of man in the world, they – or rather, their performances – themselves were displaced: the Globe was located at the margins of urban society, across the Thames and outside the jurisdictional district of London, offering a heterotopia, a space wherein questions of gender, politics, and ideology could be articulated, hegemonic discourses contested, the shaping powers of social and interpersonal relations discussed, and the crises of personal and public life mediated. While it is debated whether the theatre served to circulate and popularize discourses dominating Elizabethan and Jacobean society, or represented dominating ideologies from a different perspective in a subversive manner, or whether it produced ideologies, creating meanings and values that offered solutions to cultural tensions of the time, it seems probable that it fulfilled all three functions (cf. Drakakis 1992: 25).

Take character, for instance. The greater complexity of Shakespeare's *dramatis personae*, which led the critic Harold Bloom (1999) to the audacious claim that Shakespeare 'invented' the human and shaped the ways in which characters are represented in language, went hand in hand with a new consciousness of the individual fuelled by conduct books and manuals of rhetoric circulating at the time: Baldassare Castiglione's *The Courtier* (1528), which promoted stylized forms of interaction that, disguised by the artful effort or *sprezzatura,* seemed natural; Niccolò Machiavelli's *The Prince* (1532), a handbook for gaining and maintaining power in state politics even through unethical means; and Thomas Wright's *The Passions of the Minde* (1601-04), which emphasized the need for performance and "self-fashioning" (cf. Greenblatt 1980) as part of the construction of identity in every-day life, raised new anxieties about the legibility, malleability, and manipulability of characters. These manuals fuelled an augmentation of self-consciousness and point to the early modern discourse on subjection that perceives man as both the initiator (subject) and the object of (i.e. subjected to) social and cultural practices and powers that shape one's identity and individuality. Self-knowledge became one of the prime objectives of the humanist subject. Like plays by Marlowe and Webster, Shakespeare's tragedies experiment with different philosophical or religious notions and representations of the self and investigate questions of interiority (cf. Maus 1995) and identity by exploring the fatal outcome of self-forgetting (cf. Sullivan 2005), which leads to madness and disorientation. Lear's question "[w]ho is it that can tell me who I am" (*King Lear,* 1.4.195) is symptomatic of the tragic hero. Cases of spiritual or erotic self-forgetting can be found in

Marlowe's Faustus or Shakespeare's Antony, respectively, while Macbeth, for instance, forgets his loyalty to Duncan, which prepares the fatal ending of the play. Hamlet, on the other hand, suffers under the burden of memory and the knowledge of his father's murder that sets off the tragic action of Shakespeare's longest and most popular play.

4. *Hamlet*

Shakespeare's *Hamlet* was written around 1600. The precise date of its composition is uncertain, as the text exists not only in two – as most of Shakespeare's plays – but three textual versions: the First and Second Quartos (1603 and 1604-05) and the First Folio (1623). Editions today are based on *The Tragedie of Hamlet, Prince of Denmarke* from the Folio while including passages from *The Tragicall Historie of Hamlet, Prince of Denmarke* that was printed in the Second, 'good,' Quarto. The First Quarto, also referred to as the 'bad quarto,' is generally dismissed as an abridged version of an earlier revision of the play. As with other plays, Shakespeare recycled and reworked existing narratives while drawing from a variety of texts that circulated in his time: besides Seneca's and Kyd's revenge tragedies, major sources include a lost *Ur-Hamlet*, attributed to Kyd, which was performed around 1589, and Saxo Grammaticus' late 12th-century chronicle *Historiae Danicae*, which includes the Norse legend of Amleth, who feigns madness to prevent getting murdered and to exact revenge on his uncle for killing his father.

The plot of *Hamlet* follows the dramatic pattern of revenge tragedies. The play opens with the appearance of the ghost of the dead king, who discloses to his son Hamlet that he was murdered by Claudius, Hamlet's uncle, who meanwhile was elected king and married the widowed Gertrude. Assigned the role of the avenger, Hamlet decides to "put an antic disposition to" (1.5.173) and feign madness while making plans to "catch the conscience of the King" (2.2.582) and make him confess the crime. Supported by a company of actors, he puts on a play, *The Murder of Gonzago*, which re-enacts the murder and upsets Claudius, who abruptly leaves the performance. Hamlet is summoned to his mother Gertrude for an explanation and accidentally kills the eavesdropping Polonius, confidant of the king and father of his beloved Ophelia, mistaking him for Claudius. The king sends Hamlet to England, intending to have him killed on his way, but Hamlet, seeing his true colours, survives. Prior to his return, the grieving Ophelia goes mad and drowns. Supported by Claudius, her brother Laertes seeks revenge for the deaths of his father and sister and challenges Hamlet to a duel. During the fight, both avengers receive a deadly hit by Laertes' poisoned sword, while Gertrude drinks from the poisoned wine that Claudius intended for Hamlet. Reconciled with the dying Laertes, Hamlet kills the king and, before dying himself, commands his friend Horatio to tell his story.

Hamlet raises a number of issues that are characteristic of Shakespeare's tragedies and reflect important aspects of early modern culture. These include questions of character, early modern notions of 'self,' performance, and (meta-)theatre as well as questions of gender, mourning, and memory. *Hamlet* has been described both as "theatre's greatest meditation on death" (Howard 2007: 10), as a reflection upon the limits of language, which comes down to empty "[w]ords, words, words" (2.2.192), and as a play about authority: the authority of a divinity (based on the question of whether it is nobler to suffer in patience or to revenge injustice); of the sovereign (who turns out to be the criminal); of drama whose purpose is to "hold as 'twere the mirror up to nature" (3.2.20: the performance of *The Murder of Gonzago* reveals the murderer); and the actor whose success is based upon the ability to "[s]uit the action to the word, the word to the action" (3.2.16 f.). First and foremost, it is a play about the function and modes of representation, or *mimesis*. Hamlet's advice to the actors to match words and action has been read as indicating a natural rather than a stylized mode of performance in early modern stage practice. Instead of supporting stage illusion, however, the numerous references to the art of acting on "the empty space" (Brook 1968) of Shakespeare's theatre, which lacked scenery and whose minimal props challenged the imaginary faculties of the audience, creates an anti-illusionistic effect. It is especially in *Hamlet* that representations are exposed as what they are, as nothing but representations.

The great intensity of theatricality, which is characteristic of Shakespeare's plays, comes to the fore in the very first line of the play: "Who's there?" (1.1.1) The demand for identification that is expressed by the king's guard, Barnardo, points to the different theatrical levels this play is working on. Imagine the beginning of *Hamlet* as it was performed in the Globe. Even though the first scene is set in a dark winter night, the Globe was flooded by daylight, offering full views of the stage and the actor's faces. In addition to being a theatrical device to identify the characters for the audience, the opening question can be read as an appeal for the stimulation of the imaginative faculties. The thick, inky darkness that unfolds 'before the mind's eye' prepares the appearance of the Ghost by creating impressions of isolation, anxiety, and insecurity of perception. At the same time, however, the opening heightens the audience's awareness for the presence of actors and the conditions of acting – not only in the Globe, but also in the world of the play, and outside the walls of the theatre, in the *theatrum mundi*. It is here that the different levels of the theatrical world, the world of the play, and the 'theatre of the world' intersect in a shared concern with the same pressing questions of identity and identification. Conduct books and manuals of rhetoric that circulated at the time drew new attention to the performative dimension of the 'self' and raised doubts about the authenticity of actions as they opened up new possibilities for simulation and dissimulation, i.e. for the presentation of qualities that are not present or the disclosure of those that are. This trend of self-fashioning in everyday life invites reference to the theatre that operated with similar techniques to allow actors to take on different roles – techniques that not only shook concepts of the 'self' but also met with severe criticism. Actors became the centre of attention for theatre opponents who regarded the mutability of appearances and the capability of crossing the boundaries between different social ranks and gender as threats to one's identity.

The threat posed by protean selves is explored especially in those of Shakespeare's villains who use their deceptive appearances to achieve their mischievous goals: Iago announces at the outset of *Othello*, "I am not what I am" (1.1.65), and Richard Gloucester prepares the audience for his vicious scheme by momentarily lifting his deceitful mask: "I can smile, and murder whiles I smile" (3 *Henry VI,* 3.2.182). These insecurities of identity are played out in *Hamlet*, in which characters take on different roles to protect themselves or deceive others, language is suffused with theatrical metaphors, and "[t]he play's the thing" (2.2.581).

The linchpin of the 'who is who' is Hamlet himself, who takes on many different parts in the course of the action. He is heir to the throne, son, scholar, soldier, courtier, lover, madman, and avenger without bringing any of these roles to perfection, partly because they have already been fulfilled by other characters: Hamlet's "antic disposition" (1.5.173), which enables the prince to assume the role of madman and fool, engage in witty and sarcastic wordplay, and speak the truth unharmed, is countered by Ophelia's true madness; the soldier and future king – parts that should have been Hamlet's – enter the stage with the Norwegian prince Fortinbras; Polonius is a comic counterpart of a humanist scholar; and the avenger is represented several times – in Hamlet's foil Laertes; in Fortinbras, who seeks revenge for his father's death and the loss of his territory; and in Pyrrhus, whose story is told by the First Player and who also demands justice for his father's death.

The question remains, however, what we are to make of Hamlet, "the most discontinuous of Shakespeare's heroes" (Belsey 1985: 41). William Hazlitt's famous claim that "[i]t is we who are Hamlet" (Hazlitt 2004 [1902]: 9) points to the universality of this particular character that has been described as fragile dreamer, hesitating intellectual, and regretful, irresolute thinker. However, such romanticized readings and the demand for psychological realism proposed by Hazlitt, which reached a peak with the critic A. C. Bradley (1904), belie the fact that dramatic 'characters' are constructions, words on the page, and cannot be treated like 'real' people. Measuring their actions through a psychological lens and imputing our attitudes to them is highly misleading, as suggested by L. C. Knights' (1933) provocative question, "How Many Children Had Lady Macbeth?" – an attack against the excessive focus on character. Harold Bloom warns us against another common misperception: "The largest mistake we can make about the play, *Hamlet*, is to think that it is the tragedy of a man who could not make up his mind, because (presumably) he thinks too much" (Bloom 2004: 7). For Hamlet *does* act: He devises a play he calls "The Mousetrap," enacts the role of the madman, and thwarts Claudius' assassination plot against him. Furthermore, he never accepts the Ghost's demand for revenge, but only promises to remember (cf. Foakes 2002: 85):

Remember thee?
Ay, thou poor ghost, while memory holds a seat
In this distracted globe. Remember thee?
[…] thy commandment all alone shall live
Within the book and volume of my brain. (*Hamlet* 1.5.95-103)

The "distracted globe," which alludes to the human skull, the world, and the Globe theatre – representing the personal and cultural dimensions of memory, respectively – and points to the Copernican de-centring of man and 'his' planet in the universe (cf. McAlindon 1991), is but one example of the complex imagery and the numerous meta-theatrical references in the play. Especially *Hamlet* is "obsessed with doubles of all kinds" (Kermode 2000: 100), particularly hendiadys, literally 'one-through-two,' such as "book and volume." These figures of speech intensify the play's predominant concern with identity, difference, and the undoing of unities. The "commandment" also allows for several readings: Hamlet is caught between two commandments, the demand for worldly revenge and the Christian doctrine, which opposes self-justice, a pressing conflict inherent in revenge tragedies. Together with the appearance of the ghost from a Catholic purgatory, "the undiscovered country" (3.1.81), and Hamlet's maximization of mourning, which Reformists regarded as disproportionate (cf. Rist 2008: 65), it prompts speculations on the role of Christian values and the religious positioning in *Hamlet*. Such speculations, however, are ultimately "doomed to inconclusiveness" (Greenblatt 2001: 239), as Shakespeare's plays try out different positions in the process of theatrical enactment.

As in many of Shakespeare's plays, it is the conditions of playing and the theatrical dimension of social behaviour and interactions that take centre stage in *Hamlet*. At the prince's first appearance on stage, the potential discrepancy between inward and outward is briefly discussed and, on Hamlet's part, denied. When Gertrude bids him to doff his mourning ("Good Hamlet, cast thy nightly colour off," 1.2.68), he refuses:

> HAMLET. [...] it is common.
> QUEEN.   If it be,
> Why seems it so particular with thee?
> HAMLET. Seems, madam? Nay, it is. I know not 'seems'.
> 'Tis not alone my inky cloak, good-mother,
> Nor customary suits of solemn black,
> Nor windy suspiration of forced breath,
> No, nor the fruitful river in the eye,
> Nor the dejected haviour of the visage,
> Together with all forms, moods, shows of grief,
> That can denote me truly. These indeed 'seem',
> For they are actions that a man might play;
> But I have that within which passeth show –
> These but the trappings and the suits of woe. (1.2.74-86)

While claiming that all external appearances might be misleading insofar as speech and bodily expressions are prone to manipulation by skilful rhetoric, Hamlet refutes his 'seeming' by pointing to "that within which passeth show." His mourning clothes are no relics of an empty ritual but offer a truthful, if insufficient, representation of his excessive grief. In keeping with early modern doctrine of the humours, Hamlet's black attire points to his melancholic disposition, indicating a character prone to rapid mood changes and scrupulous thinking interrupted by short periods of intensive activity.

What lies within Hamlet has led to speculation: from a delicate soul of a poet suffering from the pressures of the world around him, to an unresolved Freudian Oedipus complex, and political resistance against a corrupt regime, critics have proposed a wide variety of (anachronistic) readings for Hamlet's 'within.' However, as Francis Barker remarked, "there is, in short, nothing" (Barker 1984: 33): By dissociating himself from "actions that a man might play" and referring to 'that within' which surpasses representation, Hamlet gestures toward a modern concept of subjectivity and interiority while his interior ultimately remains a mystery.

The paradox of Hamlet's refusal to adopt a role that lacks substance is that he is part of the socio-theatrical framework at the Danish court and thus bound to follow modes of self-fashioning and theatrical dramaturgy while relying on external appearances to identify other characters. The "antic disposition" (1.5.173) he puts on to carry out the revenge works only within this histrionic framework; the same applies to the play-within-the-play, which holds a mirror up to the usurper Claudius and re-enacts the murder, the act of pouring poison into the ear of the sleeping king. Before commissioning the players to act *The Murder of Gonzago*, Hamlet witnesses a performance which upsets the distinction between appearance and reality. Delivering a speech by the Queen Hecuba, who watches Pyrrhus butcher her family at the fall of Troy, the First Player seems to fuse with the grieving mother and shed her tears:

> HAMLET. Is it not monstrous that this player here,
> But in a fiction, in a dream of passion,
> Could force his soul so to his whole conceit
> That from her working all his visage wanned,
> Tears in his eyes, distraction in's aspect,
> A broken voice, […] And all for nothing.
> For Hecuba! (2.2.528-535)

The player weeps neither for Hecuba, nor instead of her, but with her. In keeping with rhetoric manuals like Quintilian's *Institutio Orator* (ca. 95 AD) and Cicero's *De Oratore* (55 BC), for instance, which advise speakers to use the expression of passions to move and convince their audience, the actor produces tears to provoke compassion. The perfected performance informs Hamlet's later advice to the actors to observe the rules of *decorum* and to "suit the action to the word, the word to the action" (3.2.16 f.). The powerful effect of the performance serves to prove Claudius' guilt by a gauging of his reactions to the play: "I'll observe his looks" (2.2.573). Probing the revealing and deceiving potential of appearances, Shakespeare's plays and particularly *Hamlet* engage in a critical debate about socio-theatrical self-fashioning (cf. Baumbach 2007) while the powerful effect of the performance counters anti-theatrical sentiments of Puritan critics of the time, who attacked the theatre as being fraudulent and inauthentic.

Dramatic shifts from the exterior to the interior can be experienced especially in Hamlet's soliloquies ("[n]ow I am alone," 2.2.523), which create a sense of inwardness. Of all tragedies, *Hamlet* contains the most soliloquies, eight of which are spoken by the protagonist. These rhetorically refined, emotionally intense and complex speeches, in which characters reveal (moral) conflicts that are confined within their minds (cf. Belsey 1985: 43), often include sudden changes of direction and raise critical questions about the theatrical, religious, and philosophical dimensions of the play. Read as one sequence, the soliloquies contain *Hamlet* in a nutshell insofar as they mark and reflect upon crucial moments in the action. The most celebrated soliloquy, "To be or not to be," reveals the intense moral conflict with which Hamlet grapples:

> To be, or not to be; that is the question:
> Whether 'tis nobler in the mind to suffer
> The slings and arrows of outrageous fortune,
> Or to take arms against a sea of troubles,
> And, by opposing, end them. (3.1.58-62)

What begins as a contemplation of suicide evolves into a strategic reflection upon the effectiveness and (moral) implications of Hamlet's planned performance, his motives, and culminates in the question of what makes man "lose the name of action" (3.1.90): "conscience does make cowards of us all" (3.1.85). What remains is an irresolvable dilemma insofar as both to act while fearing the consequences and not to act to avoid them makes man a coward. The 16th-century essayist Michel de Montaigne suggested that "to philosophize is to learn to die" (1991 [1580]: 89), and Hamlet's meditations on death prepare the audience for his final appearance on stage before "[t]he rest is silence" (5.2.300). Hamlet's sense of annihilation voiced in this soliloquy is also expressed in his attacks on Ophelia and Gertrude, whom he accuses of stepping out of their path of female duty. While he blames his mother for marrying again within two months of the king's death ("frailty, thy name is woman," 1.2.146), he dismisses Ophelia, who, obedient to her father, refuses his attentions and returns his letters (cf. Stewart 2008: 256 f.), sending her to "a nunnery" (3.1.137), which in Elizabethan colloquial expression could refer to either a 'convent' or a 'brothel.' While Ophelia and Gertrude are portrayed as greatly dependent on male guidance, Shakespeare offers strong counter-figures to these female stereotypes in other tragedies, such as the Machiavellian heroines Lady Macbeth, Cleopatra, and even Desdemona, who resist patriarchal control, taking on a leading part in the action. The fragile Ophelia, however, rejected by Hamlet and deprived of her father who died by his hand, goes mad, drowns, and is buried on the day Hamlet returns to the Danish court.

The graveyard scene at the beginning of act 5 is at once one of the most tragic and most comic scenes in Shakespeare's tragedies. The absurd conversation between the two gravediggers, who sing and jest while grave-making, offers a grotesque inversion of Hamlet's musings on the devaluation of language, death, suicide, and the authority of a divine being. Such unexpected comic moments in the tragedies temporarily provide comic relief with a satirical purpose: they expose corruption, hypocrisy, and ridicule key themes of the play. Like the Fool in *King Lear*, who comments on the irrational actions of the king, or the Porter in *Macbeth*, who ponders on hell's gates before Duncan's murder is discovered, the gravediggers trigger laughter as a reaction to absurdity and disorder, which intensifies the tragic events that are to follow. In this case, the comic is coupled with a *memento mori*. *Hamlet* is a tragedy: the gravedigger started his work the day Hamlet was born and the court jester, Yorick, is dead when the play sets in. Nonetheless, the play continues to fall back onto elements of comedy in the banter with Polonius, the appearances of Rosencrantz and Guildenstern, and the return of Yorick – as a skull. His remains are a cue for another meta-theatrical allusion, which goes hand in hand with an attack on excessive face-painting, a popular practice at the time, which the 'virgin queen' Elizabeth I was said to have made extensive use of: "Now get you to my lady's chamber and tell her, let her paint an inch thick" (5.1.178 f.). Sent to get some make-up, the skull becomes a medium for negotiating identity. Complementing Hamlet's "antic disposition," which is doffed in act 5, the proposed cosmetic make-over creates a carnevalesque moment, in which identities are blurred and social ranks playfully turned upside down. After the comic interlude, the action progresses to the tragic ending.

Following the duel between Hamlet and Laertes, the stage is littered with corpses: the duellers, Gertrude, and Claudius all die. The tragic conflict seems resolved as the murder is revenged, but the play settles between order and chaos. "We may feel both relief and regret that we are returning to a world of convenient, superficial half-truths. [...] [W]hen order is restored, it comes at the cost of many qualities we admire: truth, humility and moral rightness" (Marsh 1998: 37). Fortinbras' claiming of the throne ("with sorrow I embrace my fortune," 5.2.332) and Horatio's confidence that "All this can I / Truly deliver" (5.2.328 f.) proclaim a new, yet ambiguous beginning: the sincerity of the successor's "sorrow" is debatable, as is Horatio's capability of offering a truthful account of the events. Instead, we are prepared for the fact that Hamlet's story will continuously be retold, adjusted, and ultimately altered in the course of reception. Rather than providing closure, Shakespeare's tragedies leave us with promises of restoration and order that are potentially corrupt, intrinsically ambiguous, and foul and fair at the same time: "The rest is silence" (5.2.300).

5. Where Do We Go from Here?

The rest is not silence: "*Hamlet* is not a problem to which a final solution exists. It is a work of art about which questions can always be asked. Each generation asks its own questions and finds its own answers, and the final test of the validity of those answers can only be time" (Gardner 1964: 70). A great deal of the ongoing fascination with Shakespeare's tragedies in general and *Hamlet*, in particular lies in their mysteriousness, inconclusiveness, and their heterogeneity. It is this resistance to categorization combined with the powerful language which create an imaginative world that maintains a strong connection to the worlds we live in while resisting full intelligibility ("nothing is / But what is not," *Macbeth* 1.3.140 f.) that makes Shakespeare's plays so compelling, universal, and timeless.

However, the course of his tragedies did not run so smoothly. When the theatres reopened in 1660 after an 18-year closure by the Puritan government, it was not only the theatrical conditions that changed radically with the Restoration proscenium stage, which had elaborate decorations, movable sets, and introduced actresses playing female parts. Under the influence of French theatre and the rise of neo-Aristotelian theories in England, Shakespeare's tragedies were dismissed for not following the rules of art and for lacking *bel esprit*. "In Tragedy he appears quite out of his Element," raged Thomas Rymer, one of his severest critics, "his Brains are turn'd, he raves and rambles, without any coherence" (qtd. in Vickers 1974: 2.58). As a consequence, Shakespeare's tragedies were ruthlessly adapted to meet the requirements of the time. John Dryden presented a revised *Antony and Cleopatra*, entitled *All for Love* (1677), that adhered to the unities of time and action; William Davenant, amongst other 'improvements,' cut the Porter's bawdy lines in his version of *Macbeth* (1674), and Nahum Tate rewrote *King Lear*, turning the tragic ending into a happy reunion, saving Cordelia and Lear from undeserved death. In the early 18th century, Shakespeare's heroines were adjusted to fit the drama of sentiment while, at the same time, first scholarly editions of the plays by Nicholas Rowe (1709) and Alexander Pope (1725) made them accessible to readers and helped establish Shakespeare as national poet. Besides inspiring critical pluralism, the tragedies still hold a firm seat in our 'distracted globe': some of the most memorable phrases, metaphors, and puns that have become a part of our cultural memory derive from them; Shakespeare's characters live on in numerous literary (re-)writings, including Samuel Beckett's *Endgame* (1957), Tom Stoppard's *Rosencrantz and Guildenstern are Dead* (1967), and many more. The tragedies themselves have stood the test of time and continue to fascinate readers, spectators, and critics precisely because they resist full explanation and closure.

Bibliography

Primary Sources

Shakespeare, William. 1997. *The Norton Shakespeare*. Stephen Greenblatt, et al. (eds.). New York/London: Norton & Company.

Annotated Bibliography

Belsey, Catherine. 1985. *The Subject of Tragedy: Identity and Difference in Renaissance Drama*. London/New York: Routledge & Kegan Paul.
  A seminal work focusing on questions of subjectivity, subjection, identity, and gender in early modern tragedy.

Bloom, Harold (ed.). 2004. *Hamlet*. Broomall: Chelsea House Publishers.
  A useful collection of major essays on the character Hamlet (by William Hazlitt, A.C. Bradley, Northrop Frye) and new readings of the 'Melancholy Dane.'

Drakakis, John (ed.). 1992. *Shakespearean Tragedy*. London/New York: Longman.
A profound overview of major criticism in the field.

Dutton, Richard & Jean E. Howard (eds.). 2003. *A Companion to Shakespeare's Works*. Vol. 1: *The Tragedies*. Oxford: Blackwell.
An excellent collection of essays covering diverse aspects of Shakespeare's tragedies; good introductory reading.

Hammond, Paul. 2009. *The Strangeness of Tragedy*. Oxford/New York: Oxford UP.
An excellent study, based on readings of Greek, Senecan, and Shakespearean tragedies (esp. Macbeth, Othello, *and* King Lear*), examining forms of estrangement (of time, space, and language) created by tragic drama.*

Hattaway, Michael. 2010. *A New Companion to English Renaissance Literature and Culture*. 2 vols. Oxford: Blackwell.
A highly recommended companion, which contains over 80 scholarly essays on all major aspects of early modern literature and culture.

Marsh, Nicholas. 1998. *Shakespeare: The Tragedies*. New York: St. Martin's P.
A good introduction to Shakespeare's tragedies, focusing on various aspects, including dramatic openings and endings, tragic heroes, society, humour, and imagery.

Maus, Katharine Eisaman. 1995. *Inwardness and Theater in the English Renaissance*. Chicago: U of Chicago P.
A superb study of inwardness and subjectivity in early modern drama.

Poole, Adrian. 2005. *Tragedy: A Very Short Introduction*. Oxford/New York: Oxford UP.
A very concise and engaging introduction to the concept of tragedy, tragic theories, and the development of the genre.

Smith, Emma. 2004. *Shakespeare's Tragedies*. Malden/Oxford: Blackwell.
A highly recommendable overview of criticism from 1590 until 1900 and a useful guide to some of the major areas in criticism with chapters on genre, characters, language, gender and sexuality, history and politics, texts, and performance.

Further Secondary Literature

Aristotle. 1927 [c. 335 BC]. *Aristotle, The Poetics, 'Longinus', On the Sublime. Demetrius, 'On Style.'* W. Hamilton Fyfe (trans.). London: William Heinemann/New York: G. P. Putnam's Sons.

Barker, Francis. 1984. *The Tremulous Private Body: Essays on Subjection*. London: Methuen.

Baumbach, Sibylle. 2007. *'Let me behold thy face'. Physiognomik und Gesichtslektüren in Shakespeares Tragödien*. Heidelberg: Winter.

—. 2009. "Wissensräume im Theater der Frühen Neuzeit." In: Wolfgang Hallet & Birgit Neumann (eds.). *Raum und Bewegung in der Literatur: Die Literaturwissenschaften und der Spatial Turn*. Bielefeld: transcript. 195-212.
Bayley, John. 1981. *Shakespeare and Tragedy*. London/Boston: Routledge & Kegan Paul.
Bevington, David. 2002. "Tragedy in Shakespeare's Career." In: Claire McEachern (ed.). *The Cambridge Companion to Shakespearean Tragedy*. Cambridge: Cambridge UP. 50-68.
Bloom, Harold. 1999. *Shakespeare: The Invention of the Human*. New York: Riverhead Trade.
Bradley, A. C. 1904. *Shakespearean Tragedy: Lectures on 'Hamlet,' 'Othello,' 'King Lear' and 'Macbeth'*. London: Macmillan & Co.
Brook, Peter. 1968. *The Empty Space*. New York: Atheneum.
Campbell, Lily B. 1973. *Shakespeare's Tragic Heroes: Slaves of Passion*. Gloucester, MA: Peter Smith.
Chaucer, Geoffrey. 2008. *The Riverside Chaucer*. Larry Dean Benson (ed.). Oxford/New York: Oxford UP.
Dillon, Janette. 2007. *The Cambridge Introduction to Shakespeare's Tragedies*. Cambridge/New York: Cambridge UP.
Foakes, R. A. 2002. "Hamlet's Neglect of Revenge." In: Arthur F. Kinney (ed.). *Hamlet: New Critical Essays*. New York/London: Routledge. 85-99.
Gardner, Helen. 1964. "The Historical Approach: *Hamlet*." In: Alfred Harbage (ed.). *Shakespeare: The Tragedies: A Collection of Essays*. Englewood-Cliffs, NJ: Prentice-Hall. 61-70.
Greenblatt, Stephen. 1980. *Renaissance Self-Fashioning: From More to Shakespeare*. Chicago: U Chicago P.
—. 1988. *Shakespearean Negotiations: The Circulation of Social Energy in Renaissance England*. Berkeley/Los Angeles: U of California P.
—. 2001. *Hamlet in Purgatory*. Princeton: Princeton UP.
Hazlitt, Willam. 2004 [1902]. "Hamlet." In: Harold Bloom (ed.). *Hamlet*. Broomall: Chelsea House Publishers. 9-14.
Howard, Tony. 2007. *Women as Hamlet: Performance and Interpretation in Theatre, Film and Fiction*. Cambridge: Cambridge UP.
Johnson, Samuel. 1806. *The Works of Samuel Johnson*. Vol. 2 (12 vols.). London: Hansard.
Kastan, David Scott. 2003. "'A rarity most beloved': Shakespeare and the Idea of Tragedy." In: Richard Dutton & Jean E. Howard (eds.). *A Companion to Shakespeare's Works*. Vol. 1: *The Tragedies*. Oxford: Blackwell. 4-22.
Kermode, Frank. 2000. *Shakespeare's Language*. London: Allen Lane.
Knights, L. C. 1964 [1933]. "How Many Children Had Lady Macbeth? An Essay in the Theory and Practice of Shakespeare Criticism." In: *Explorations – Essays in*

Criticism Mainly on the Literature of the Seventeenth Century. New York: New York UP. 15-54.
McAlindon, Thomas. 1991. *Shakespeare's Tragic Cosmos*. Cambridge: Cambridge UP.
Montaigne, Michel de. 1991 [1580]. *The Complete Essays*. Trans. Michael A. Screech. London: Penguin.
Muir, Kenneth. 1972. *Shakespeare's Tragic Sequence*. London: Hutchinson.
Rist, Thomas. 2008. *Revenge Tragedy and the Drama of Commemoration in Reforming England*. Aldershot: Ashgate.
Sidney, Philip. 1965 [1595]. *An Apology for Poetry*. Geoffrey Shepherd (ed.). London: Thomas Nelson.
—. 1989. *Sir Philip Sidney*. Katherine Duncan-Jones (ed.). Oxford: Oxford UP.
Stewart, Alan. 2008. *Shakespeare's Letters*. Oxford/New York: Oxford UP.
Sullivan, Garret A. 2005. *Memory and Forgetting in English Renaissance Drama: Shakespeare, Marlowe, Webster*. Cambridge: Cambridge UP.
Tillyard, E. M. W. 1961. *The Elizabethan World Picture*. New York: Vintage.
Vickers, Brian. 1974. *Shakespeare: The Critical Heritage*. Vol 2: 1693-1733. London: Routledge.

7. JACOBEAN CITY COMEDIES:
BEN JONSON'S *THE ALCHEMIST* AND
THOMAS MIDDLETON'S *A CHASTE MAID IN CHEAPSIDE*

JOACHIM FRENK

Around the middle of the 16th century, London began to explode. The population rose from about 70,000 in 1550 to about 200,000 in 1600, and by 1650 London had about 400,000 inhabitants (cf. Finlay & Shearer 1986). While it had been the unrivalled centre of England since the Middle Ages, in these 100 years London grew into a recognizably (early) modern metropolis, a gigantic marketplace of goods, ideas, bodies, and all kinds of cultural products, of which the new theatre scene was one (cf. Griffiths & Jenner 2000; Manley 1995; Orlin 2000). London's importance both as a place of capital and as an international hub of trade increased dramatically. Two events may serve to exemplify these changes: from 1566 to 1569, Sir Thomas Gresham, a financial genius, built the Royal Exchange, the first burse and shopping mall in London, and on 31st December 1600, the company of London merchants that was later to become the East India Company received their Royal Charter. The city of London provided the national and international luxury goods consumed by both the city elites and the neighbouring court at Westminster. Since the capital dwarfed any other city in the British Isles, its political and cultural predominance was unquestionable. But the rise of the city came at great human cost, since London was also a killer. Mortality rates both among children and adults were high, and only the constant influx of immigrants kept the city growing (cf. Clark & Ross 2008; Porter 1994; Rappaport 1989).

Many contemporary texts give voice to the overwhelming impression London made; the ever-growing city was a wonder to behold, a cynosure of splendour and conspicuous consumption. At the same time, London seemed a monster, a claustrophobic and congested *über*-city of unknown proportions, burdened with increasingly inadequate medieval administrative structures that struggled to get a grip on the uncontrolled growth of the early modern city. In 1632, one Donald Lupton put both his admiration and his unease into words:

> She is grown so great that I am almost afraid to meddle with her. She's certainly a great world, there are so many little worlds in her. She is the great beehive of Christendom; I am sure of England. She swarms four times in a year, with people of all ages, natures, sexes, callings [...]. She may be said to be always with child, for she grows greater every day than other [...]. She is the countryman's labyrinth; he can find many things in it, but many times loseth himself. (Lupton 1632: B-B2v, qtd. in Stock & Zwierlein 2004: 4 f.)

In keeping with an established convention in the representation of cities, Lupton's rhetoric represents the metropolis as an organic entity, an allegorical female figure. However, that whole London is constantly threatened by processes of fragmentation:

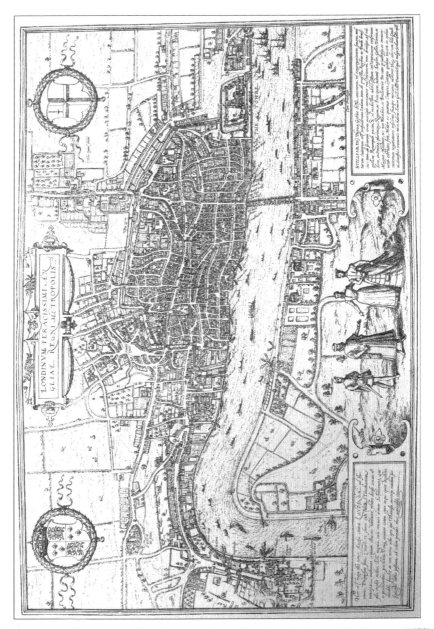

Figure 1: Map of London from Georg Braun and Frans Hogenberg, *Civitates Orbis Terrarum* (1572).

This map of London, which was produced in the 1560s, shows that around the middle of the 16th century the city had already exceeded its walls. Note the connection of the city, the mercantile centre, with Westminster, the political centre on the left margin of the map. This connection would get ever stronger in the following decades.

it is a world consisting of little worlds, a swarming beehive of heterogeneous people. Lupton's imagination seeks to get hold of London through different images; in addition to the beehive, he visualizes a pregnant woman and an unmanageable labyrinth. As an urban phenomenon previously unknown in the British Isles, this new London constantly challenged and inspired the imagination of inhabitants and visitors alike.

1. The City and Comedy

One of the most visibly active centres of the cultural imagination in early modern London was the theatre scene, so it was only logical that London more and more found its way onto the stage. Darryll Grantley has counted the plays with London settings from the mid-16th century onwards:

> After only a sprinkling of surviving early plays locating dramatic narratives there, 8 of 43 Elizabethan comedies are set in London, 10 of 16 histories, and 3 of 18 tragedies. There are also 42 further plays of other genres, 6 of which have some direct London interest. This makes a total of 21 plays with London settings and a 119 set elsewhere. After the Elizabethan period, it is only comedies that are set in London; among Jacobean comedies 40 of 84 are set there, and 44 of 98 Caroline comedies. (Grantley 2008: 7)

It is important to bear in mind that we can only count the plays that are still extant, a minority of the plays written and performed at the time. Yet there is an unmistakable tendency to depict London as a dramatic setting, particularly in the genre of comedy. This tendency is explicable through the changing dramatic genres in the contemporary theatre market. The new theatre scene was not only a market in itself, it was also part of London as an emerging international marketplace, and the theatre, while largely following the logic of this marketplace, also commented upon it. In this way, it thereby contributed to the constructions, deconstructions, and reconstructions of early modern capitalism, London-style (cf. Agnew 1986).

The ways in which London was represented in plays changed considerably from the mid-16th to the early 17th century. The interludes of the mid-16th century were largely written and performed outside London. In these, London figured mostly not as the specific city it was, but as a signifier of the temptations which 'the city' (as an abstract idea) offered to gentle Christian souls. This stage-London, which was heavily influenced by the allegorizing morality plays of the late middle ages, figured as an inherently corrupt and corrupting place in a fallen world, a place of temptation and sin. An Elizabethan play which still clearly shows the influence of the tradition of London as an allegorical place of corruption is Robert Wilson's *The Three Ladies of London* (1584) – the names of the three eponymous ladies are Love, Fame, and Conscience.

The stellar rise of the early modern London population also meant that there were new masses of people craving to be entertained. Permanent theatres in London emerged in the last third of the 16th century, and the plays that were written and performed in these new London theatres entertained new audiences familiar with London's topography. The playwrights quickly realized that the city itself was a topic of interest to these new audiences, and the celebration of London in the spirit of civic pride of the city became a stage convention. William Haughton's comedy *Englishmen for My Money: or A Pleasant Comedy Called, A Woman Will Have Her Will* (c. 1597-98) illustrates the national and civic pride which Londoners came to see on stage. It is set in London, and the main plot shows three English suitors winning the hands of the three daughters of a Portuguese merchant-usurer – against the will of the father and against three foreign suitors. Thomas Dekker's *The Shoemaker's Holiday* (1599), although catering particularly to the tastes of the influential guild of the shoemakers, also celebrates the daily life in and the bourgeois legends of London as illustrated through the madcap shoemaker Simon Eyre's improbable elevation to Lord Mayor. At the festive ending, the king appears and legitimates both the marriage of the romance plot and Simon Eyre's new position as Lord Mayor. The final merry-making takes place in Leadenhall, which is one of many examples of easily recognizable London locales included as settings into the fabric of plays – for diverse reasons, and with diverse functions, as befitted the complexity of the growing city (cf. Dillon 2000; Gibbons 1980; Leggatt 1973).

The spirit of London comedies changed in the Jacobean age. "Jacobean" refers to James I (1566-1625), whose name translated into Latin is Jacobus. In the 1590s, when the Virgin Queen Elizabeth I was visibly aging and it became clear that she would die without an heir, many rightly felt that they were living at the end of an age. In 1603, after the death of the last Tudor monarch, Elizabeth I, the first Stuart king, James VI of Scotland, became her successor as James I of England, Scotland, and Ireland. James' imperial project of a Great Britain, the full political union of England and Scotland, would only be realized in 1707. In terms of personality, James I was radically different from the extroverted Elizabeth I. While she had been an actress in the public eye (in an age which forbade actresses on stage) and had impressively performed the role of the queen for her court and her people, he was a rather withdrawn person who preferred being a privileged onlooker to acting out the spectacle of kingship in public (cf. Hopkins 2009: 103-46). At the same time, James took great pride in his learning, and he was highly interested in intellectual pursuits. He famously commissioned the *King James Bible* (1611), the most important version of the bible in English, and he wrote treatises, for instance on the necessity of witch hunting and on political theory – the latter explicating his view of the divine right of kings. In 1604, after a one-year delay caused by the plague, the new king celebrated his triumphant entry into the city of London. By following the ritual of the new monarch's festive entry into the city, James made sure he had the support of the capital as the economic powerhouse of England.

While there is no particular moment that completely changed the genre of city comedy, Jacobean city comedies on the whole differ from their Elizabethan predecessors in their general representation of London on stage. The progressive change is vividly illustrated in Francis Beaumont's *The Knight of the Burning Pestle* (1607). In quite modern theatrical manner, at the beginning London citizens (who are *dramatis personae*, despite the fact that they sit in the audience) enter the stage, interrupt the

Prologue and thus destroy the stage illusion: A grocer and his wife complain that neither ordinary London citizens nor their tastes matter in the stage business. The grocer has a clear idea what kind of play he wants to see instead of the one that is being announced:

> PROLOGUE. So, grocer, then by your sweet favour, we intend no abuse to the city.
> CITIZEN. No, sir? Yes, sir! If you were not resolved to play the jacks, what need you study for new subjects, purposely to abuse your betters? Why could not you be contented, as well as others, with *The Legend of Whittington*, or *The Life and Death of Sir Thomas Gresham, with the Building of the Royal Exchange*, or *The Story of Queen Elenor, with the Rearing of London Bridge upon Woolsacks*? (Beaumont 2002 [1607]: Prologue, 15-23)

This is clearly a satire of the Elizabethan comedies celebrating London by staging the city's tales about its heroes in the manner of *The Shoemaker's Holiday* or Thomas Heywood's *If You Know Not Me, You Know Nobody, Part 2* (1606) – the latter being one of the few Jacobean examples of this kind of play. By the beginning of James' reign, the commercial London theatres, mostly located in the marginal spaces of the city, had established themselves as an aspect of London's everyday life, often against the resistance of the city-government and religious groups. The satire of *The Knight of the Burning Pestle* targets the conventional way of presenting London on the stage; this unmistakably indicates that new ways of staging London were sought. The two comedies to be discussed both illustrate these new ways of staging London. Further, they demonstrate the wit, the vigour, and the artistic brilliance which Jacobean city comedies achieved in the first quarter of the 17th century, at the very apogee of the genre. Both comedies offer multifaceted stage phantasms of London which were firmly rooted in the city's everyday life, and they throw each other into relief.

2. *The Alchemist*

The Alchemist (1610) was written by Ben Jonson (1572-1637), a Londoner born and bred. While he probably never went to a university, Jonson received a good classical education at Westminster School and remained an avid reader of Greek and Roman literature for the rest of his life. In one of the two poems he contributed to Shakespeare's First Folio in 1623, Jonson famously quipped that his friend had had "small Latine, and lesse Greeke" (Jonson 1623: line 31). Although in the 1590s and in the early 1600s he was repeatedly in peril for criticizing the authorities, including the King himself, Jonson sought the patronage of the nobility and of the city authorities throughout his life. Excepting Christopher Marlowe, who died aged only 29 in 1593, Jonson is the only early modern dramatist whose popularity and influence have approximated that of his friend Shakespeare (cf. Craig 1990; Harp & Stewart 2000; Riggs 1989). However, while the Stratfordian and London immigrant Shakespeare mostly avoided London settings in his plays, Ben Jonson specialized in the depiction and dissection of London life and manners in his comedies: *Every Man in His Humour*

(1598), *Every Man Out Of His Humour* (1599), *Eastward Ho!* (1605; a collaboration with John Marston and George Chapman that briefly landed both Jonson and Chapman in jail) and *Epicoene, or The Silent Woman* (1609) are famous specimen of Jonson's city comedies. But *The Alchemist* and *Volpone, or the Fox* (1605) are regarded as Jonson's most accomplished city comedies. Since the 1590s, Jonson had excelled in the comedy of humours, a subgenre that highlighted and exposed to laughter individual traits of its comic characters. He was also an exceptionally talented poet, and he excelled in masques, lavish, and fantastic court entertainments with allegorically or mythologically inspired plots focusing on elaborate costumes, dancing, and music. For the Jacobean masques, Jonson wrote highly poetical texts while his long-time collaborator Inigo Jones provided the stage designs.

The Alchemist was first performed in 1610, by the King's Men, Shakespeare's company. The comedy announces its London focus even in the Prologue:

> Our scene is London, 'cause we would make known,
> No country's mirth is better than our own,
> No clime breeds better matter, for your whore,
> Bawd, squire, imposter, many persons more,
> Whose manners, now called humours, feed the stage:
> And which have still been subject, for the rage
> Or spleen of comic writers. (Prologue, 5-11)

The play's satiric drift becomes clear right at the outset, with the announcement that it will deal with "whore / Bawd, squire [i.e., a pimp], imposter," i.e., with London's criminal and/or sexually transgressive underbelly, thereby exposing the vices and the human folly woven into the texture of the metropolis.

The play begins with an argument between the two tricksters who are, with their third partner, the prostitute Dol Common, at the centre of the stage action: Subtle, the bogus alchemist of the title, and Face, his business partner, quarrel about their respective claims to the profits they have gained. Face's real name is Jeremy; he is the servant of Lovewit, a gentleman who has flown from his city house because of an outbreak of the plague. Face, a quasi blank, de-individualizing name, is more apt than Jeremy for this shape-shifting character. Face has a face for everybody, but there seems to be no one face behind all his faces – itself a meta-theatrical commentary on acting and actors. Face, Subtle, and Dol use Lovewit's house as their base. Dol has to remind the two querulous men that their common success depends on all three of them working together as a "venture tripartite" (1.1.135). For the time being, Subtle and Face put their differences aside, and their stage-cheating can begin.

The first client is Dapper, a lawyer's clerk whom Subtle, who also claims to be a necromancer, has promised that he will conjure up the Queen of Fairy to help him in his gambling if he subjects himself to certain (ridiculous) rituals. The second client is Drugger, a tobacconist eager to establish a business that will make him rich. The third person seeking the alchemist's help is Sir Epicure Mammon, a nobleman craving to gain possession of the Philosopher's Stone, a much desired and legendary product of alchemy said to secure its owner both immeasurable material riches – it would turn all base metals into gold – and spiritual wealth. The day of the stone's perfection has come, and Sir Epicure is impatient to get it into his greedy hands. Surly, Sir Epicure's friend, voices his contempt of Subtle's and Face's alchemical show. Later, he will disguise himself as a noble Spaniard and seek to expose them. When the Anabaptist Ananias, who is just as greedy as all others, visits Subtle, the alchemist pretends to be annoyed; he sends Ananias away, demanding to speak to his superiors. Moreover, both Subtle and Face covet the hand of Dame Pliant, a rich widow, while fleecing her brother Kastril, a country bumpkin. The ensuing confrontations and complications in this fast comedy keep the audience entertained. In the end, Lovewit returns home, Face / Jeremy is pardoned for making sure that Lovewit can marry Dame Pliant, and Subtle and Dol can only just escape, without any of the riches they hoped to gain. In the words of "The Argument" at the beginning, the animated stage action around the three tricksters goes on "Till it [the Philosopher's Stone], and they, and all in fume are gone." (The Argument, 12)

The Alchemist is quite specific about its setting: Lovewit's house is located in Blackfriars (1.1.17; 4.1.131), a fashionable and heterogeneous area on the south-western margins of the city. Ben Jonson lived there, and so did many Puritans (cf. Dol's acerbic remark on vain Puritans buying feathers in Blackfriars [1.1.128-29]), so the zealot Ananias had real-life counterparts there. London's most important indoor theatre was in Blackfriars; among the plays that premiered there was *The Knight of the Burning Pestle*, and Shakespeare's company, the King's Men, took possession of the Blackfriars in 1608 and played there in the winter months. In spite of the fact that the first documented performance took place in Oxford in September 1610 (the London theatres were closed from July 1610 due to the plague), *The Alchemist* may have been first performed at the Blackfriars in that year's early summer (cf. McEvoy 2008: 96). When a comedy located in Blackfriars was acted in the Blackfriars theatre, the dividing line between the theatrical illusion and the real London outside the theatre was obviously blurred. As the play unfolds, more specific London locations are mentioned (e.g., Lothbury [2.1.33]; Pict-Hatch [2.1.62]; the New Exchange [4.4.47]), but on the whole the exact topography of the city is not at the centre of the play. Jonson's satire rather aims at the greed and the folly of the city as a whole, at the London *Zeitgeist*.

In spite of its title, *The Alchemist* is not, at least not primarily, a satire of alchemy. In the early modern age, the modern science of chemistry had not yet come into existence; alchemy, chemistry's unscientific and 'magical' precursor, was a mixture of mythologically and religiously informed analogical thinking and pre-experimental accumulated knowledge. It was taken at least half-seriously by many; e.g., Queen Elizabeth's influential advisor John Dee (1527-1608; cf. *The Alchemist*, 2.4.20) devoted much of his life to the study of alchemy, and the scholarly inclined James I also showed some interest in it. Subtle and Face are clearly not alchemists; they are fraudsters pretending to know the secrets of alchemy. In addition, however, Jonson quotes extensively from or alludes to important alchemical texts (cf. 2.3, where Subtle and

Face try to impress Surly with arcane alchemical 'knowledge'). The rhetoric of 'real' alchemy is made present on stage. Ultimately, therefore, the play is highly skeptical about alchemy's promises, and Surly's view is also Jonson's: "alchemy is a pretty kind of game, / Somewhat like tricks o' the cards, to cheat a man, / With charming" (2.3.180-82; cf. McEvoy 2008: 97 f.).

In *The Alchemist*, Jonson plays with the idea(s) of alchemy on a number of levels. In addition to its use as a foil for the tricksters' ruses, he uses alchemy as a signifier for what happens in and to early modern London:

> The object of limitless desires, [alchemy] promises infinite wealth and transformative power through operations scarcely less mysterious than the workings of capital, whose fantastic logic had not yet been dulled by familiarity. Alchemy makes a neat metaphor for nascent capitalism. (Haynes 1992: 114)

Moreover, alchemy's promise of turning base metals into gold is elevated to another level in the play, and, arguably, in a way this promise is kept. Reading closely the rhetorical texture of *The Alchemist*, we may claim that in this comedy alchemy serves as an analogue to both language and the theatre. Jonson exposes and satirizes the all-pervasive greed and lust of London, the great marketplace where everything is turned into a desirable commodity. Still, while everybody's voracity is performed on stage, nobody (apart from Lovewit, who is absent while the tricksters and the tricked circle around each other) gets what he or she wants. In the end, the tricksters do not fare one jot better than their victims, even though Jeremy / Face is not punished. Jonson's satire is highly inclusive: no social group is exempt from his exposure of human folly, as the list of those caught in the tricksters' machinations proves: a clerk, a tobacconist, a nobleman, and Puritan (Anabaptist) clerics.

At the same time, at least in some passages, *The Alchemist* celebrates the sheer lust for all worldly matters. The endlessly desiring and tellingly named Sir Epicure Mammon is one of Jonson's most fascinating creatures. As Subtle perceptively comments: "If his dream last, he'll turn the age to gold" (1.4.29). Sir Epicure's extended and magnificently phrased visions of what he will have and do he has the Philosopher's Stone show that language itself can function like alchemy. Language both serves to express a desire for these riches and, in the imagination, it also provides them. Here is one 'Epicurean' passage of many:

> My meat, shall all come in, in Indian shells,
> Dishes of agate, set in gold, and studded,
> With emeralds, sapphires, hyacinths, and rubies.
> The tongues of carps, dormice, and carmels' heels,
> Boiled i' the spirit of Sol, and dissolved pearl,
> (Apicius' diet, 'gainst the epilepsy)
> And I will eat these broths, with spoons of amber,
> Headed with diamant, and carbuncle.
> My footboy shall eat pheasants, calvered salmons,
> Knots, godwits, lampreys: I myself will have
> The beards of barbels, served, instead of salads;

Oiled mushrooms; and the swelling unctuous paps
Of a fat pregnant sow, newly cut off,
Dressed with an exquisite, and poignant sauce;
For which, I'll say unto my cook, there's gold,
Go forth, and be a knight. (2.2.71-87)

A line of lists interrupts the syntax, suggesting an excited breathlessness that revels in the aesthetic effects and the sheer exoticism of the words it invokes ("emeralds, sapphires, hyacinths, and rubies"; "beards of barbels"). Ultimately, Sir Epicure wants to devour the world; his lists are teeming with the luxury goods of London, which are simultaneously conjured up and imaginatively consumed. He is like a child who will accept nothing but the immediate satisfaction of his desires. In act 4, Sir Epicure retreats with Dol (who acts the role of a lord's sister) in order to seduce her, which gives the fraudsters an excuse why he does not get the stone after all – he is not the pure man he has to be in order to deserve it. Sir Epicure's fantasies often violate the borders of good taste and disclose the underlying dark urges, as when he fantasizes about the "newly cut off" teats of the pregnant sow he wants to have. Yet his infinite desire for everything material (and particularly sexual) develops a grasp on audiences when his lines are spoken on stage and when his desiring self is acted out. In a sense, Sir Epicure already possesses the stone he is craving for – his (i.e., Jonson's) rhetorical genius enables him to summon up the riches of the earth from airy nothings. His discourse generates what it pretends to describe; it turns mere words into rhetorical gold. The same may be said about the theatre, which, through Jonson's stage magic, turns the basest matters into artistic – and financial – gold. The last words, spoken by Face, even suggest that the entire play is a kind of trick. The linguistic richness of *The Alchemist*, its superbly balanced structure – Coleridge famously claimed that it has one of the three most perfect plots in literature (cf. 1990: 295) – and its animated stage action both ensure *The Alchemist*'s place in the history of British drama and its lasting popularity on the stage.

3. *A Chaste Maid in Cheapside*

Thomas Middleton (1580-1627) probably wrote *A Chaste Maid in Cheapside* in early 1613; the first print-version appeared in 1630. In his portrayal of London life, Middleton could already draw on a number of plays that had paved the way for his acerbic comedy. The title asks for some explanation 400 years after the play's composition: Cheapside, which derives its name from the Anglo-Saxon "ceap" ("[t]o barter, buy and sell; to trade, deal, bargain"; "cheap, v.," *OED*), had been the chief marketplace of London since the middle ages (cf. Weinreb, et al. 2008: 153 f.). In the early modern age it had emerged as London's most splendid shopping area. Middleton, the son of a bricklayer, was born in one of its side streets. The most impressive part of Cheapside was Goldsmiths Row, which the city chronicler John Stow (1971 [1598; 1603]: vol. 1, 345) in his *Survey of London* described as "the most beautiful frame of fair houses and shops that be within the walls of London, or elsewhere in England". The title of Middleton's play may well have been proverbial in the early 17th century: "A chaste maid in Cheapside? Not likely" (cf. Middleton 2002: 2). Through its seemingly paradoxical linking of chastity and Cheapside, then, to early modern audiences Middleton's comedy indicated in its title what they could expect, the interrelations between sexuality and the marketplace being one of Middleton's favourite topics (cf. also *The Honest Whore*, 1604; this and other plays in Middleton 2007, *passim*). In the highly varying spelling of early modern English, the title also plays on "chaste"/ "chased" – the eponymous chaste maid Moll is chased by two suitors and, later, by her parents. Another early modern connotation: London prostitutes were punished by being 'chased' through the streets behind a cart. Excessive sexual puns, analogies, and *double entendres* pervade the text; Middleton's stage-London is largely driven by lust, carnally and rhetorically.

The stage direction preceding the first scene epitomizes the principal theme of the play: "*Enter* Maudline *and* Moll, *a shop being discovered*". We are in Goldsmiths Row, and we see the wife and the daughter of Master Yellowhammer, a goldsmith, in his shop; women are on the market, in every sense of the phrase. Addressing her daughter Moll, Maudline Yellowhammer, continues the line of sexual innuendo initiated in the title of the play: "Have you played over all your old lessons o' the virginals?" (1.1.1) It was customary for young girls of the Cheapside shopkeepers to learn how to play the virginal, a small keyboard instrument. At the same time, the unmarried Moll is, for all we know, a virgin (which guarantees her value on the marriage market). What follows from here is a racy and unremitting socio-sexual comedy, "a blistering satire whose relentless sexual jests lend a farcical atmosphere; but this can darken to unveil bleak vistas" (Woodbridge 2007: 907). The play is set in the time of Lent, the time of the Christian year between Ash Wednesday and Easter Eve during which Christ's 40 days in the wilderness were to be imitated through fasting and penitence. Clearly, the ascetic, world-renouncing spirit of Lent stands in sharp contrast to the unconstrained worldly desires for sex and riches on stage.

The play very much centres on the tellingly named Sir Walter Whorehound, a knight coming "to the heart of the city of London" (1.1.91 f.) for sex and money. Eager to add the title of a knight to their family, the Yellowhammers seek to marry off their daughter to Sir Walter, who is willing to wed Moll for her dowry. Moll, however, loves the young gallant Touchwood Junior; this plot provides the little romance interest there is in this play. Sir Walter also wants to marry off one of his mistresses, a Welsh prostitute he passes off as his niece, to the Yellowhammers' son Tim, a self-important Cambridge student. Sir Walter (also spelled "Water," a slang term for semen) has a longstanding affair with the wife of Master Allwit, whose name plays on "wittol": "A man who is aware of and complaisant about the infidelity of his wife; a contented cuckold" ("wittol," *OED*). Mistress Allwit's seven children are all Sir Walter's, whose support enables the Allwits to maintain a comfortable lifestyle.

Meanwhile Touchwood Senior, the older brother of Moll's suitor, has to part from his wife because they keep producing too many children; Touchwood Senior is so over-potent that he impregnates every woman he has sex with. It is consistent with the logic of the play, which revels in contrasts and analogies, that Touchwood Senior meets Sir Oliver Kix and his wife, who have been married for seven years but have no child. The Kixes are related to Sir Walter, and if they have a child before Sir Walter produces a legitimate heir, they are entitled to his fortune. The Kixes learn that Touchwood Senior is in possession of "one water" (2.1.288) against infertility. They ask him for help, Touchwood Senior beds Lady Kix, of which Sir Oliver remains ignorant, and begets her with child.

Moll tries to elope with Touchwood Junior, but is caught and imprisoned at home by her parents. On the day before her wedding to Sir Walter, she escapes again, is caught, falls into the Thames and seems to fall fatally ill. Her two suitors fight a duel in which both Touchwood Junior and Sir Walter are wounded. Touchwood Senior reports that his brother has died, which seems to cause Moll's death, and the aggrieved parents agree to a joint burial of the young lovers – for the moment, structurally the play seems to be a tragedy (not unrelated to *Romeo and Juliet*, 1597) while the style and the characters make sure that it cannot.

The Allwits coldly reject Sir Walter, who is injured, penitent of having (allegedly) killed a man, and, due to Lady Kix's pregnancy, ruined. Faced with absolute ruin and death, Sir Walter finally sees the error of his philandering ways: "Gamesters farewell, I have nothing left to play" (5.1.159). At their 'funeral,' the two young lovers rise from their coffins – in a scene reminiscent of conventions from rebirth rituals to the *commedia dell'arte* and to contemporary English plays – and the Yellowhammers now agree to the marriage. Tim Yellowhammer and the Welshwoman have been married earlier, so there are two marriages to celebrate, albeit both marriages have come about through deception. Sir Oliver Kix invites Touchwood Senior and his family to live at his house, unwittingly enabling him to begin a life as a professional adulterer. In keeping with the conventions of comedy, the play ends with Yellowhammer's promise to celebrate the two marriages with a dinner in the hall of the Goldsmiths' Company.

The humour of *A Chaste Maid in Cheapside* covers a wide spectrum, from thigh-slapping sex-jokes and farcical situation comedy to sophisticated structural ironies and topical / topographical allusions. Early modern London springs to life, brimming with unputdownable vitality. Yet the overall image of the city and its citizens is mostly the opposite of celebratory; Middleton's satire is just as deep-cutting and uncompromising as Jonson's. Time and again, we laugh at the play's cynicism only to realize that the matter we are laughing at is at the same time distressing, that the play actually proposes a dark vision of London life and of human existence in general. One case in point is the topic of procreation. Throughout the play, procreation is important on a number of levels: the Kixes' infertility contrasts with Touchwood Senior's super-fertility, and Sir Walter has seven children with Mistress Allwit, but he has so far not produced a legitimate heir. The legitimate offspring of the Yellowhammers, Moll and Tim, both fail to come up to their parents' expectations: Moll refuses to marry the husband her parents have chosen for her, and Tim is married to a penniless prostitute. Tim finally proclaims "I'll love her for her wit, I'll pick out my runts there" (5.4.121 f.); he announces his intention to procreate with his new wife whose "wit" is that of a former prostitute – which calls into question the legitimacy of their potential offspring.

When an unnamed "Wench" presents the super-potent Touchwood with one of his many bastards (2.1.62-105), we witness a meeting of two liars, both of whom could hardly care less about the offspring of their illicit sexual encounter. The Wench first claims that she was a virgin before she met Touchwood only to admit later that this is actually her fifth child (2.1.104 f.), and Touchwood lies to her, gives her what money he has on him and is glad to get rid of her and the baby so easily. Later, the Wench, carrying a basket full of meat, lets herself be caught by 'promoters,' informers who are on the lookout for citizens breaking the fast of Lent. When the greedy promoters let her go for letting them keep the meat basket, they find the Wench's illegitimate child hidden under the meat. The shocking bottom line of this trickster episode is that in London new-born babies equal fresh meat.

Another illustration of the way Middleton's dark humour works on the topic of procreation is the soliloquy of Master Allwit when he hears that Sir Walter has arrived in London to visit his mistress, Allwit's wife. Allwit is delighted of the news:

> The founder's come to town! [...]
> I thank him, h'as maintained my house this ten years,
> And all my family; I am at his table,
> He gets me all my children, and pays the nurse,
> Monthly, or weekly, puts me to nothing,
> Rent, nor church duties, not so much as the scavenger:
> The happiest state that ever man was born to.
> [...]   I am as clear
> From jealousy of a wife as from the charge.
> O two miraculous blessings; 'tis the knight
> Hath took that labour all out of my hands;
> I may sit still and play; he's jealous for me –
> Watches her steps, sets spies – I live at ease;
> He hath both the cost and the torment; when the strings
> Of his heart frets; I feed, laugh, or sing,
> *La dildo, dildo la dildo, la dildo dildo de dildo.* (1.2.12-57)

Convinced that he is the one who most profits from this *ménage a trois*, Allwit rejoices in what is clearly a perversion of married life. He is only a guest in his own house, and there is no love between him and his wife, only a mutual material interest. Allwit loves nobody but himself, not his wife, and certainly not his wife's children that are not his; he treats them without a shred of parental love, as the bastards they are in his eyes (cf. 1.2.115-28). Allwit is a caricature; he brings into focus the loss of accepted norms in a society that threatens to subordinate meaningful human relationships and its family ideal to material greed. Allwit does not realize that he has lost all claims to a position of authority in a household that is no longer his – the play clearly marks how much his wittol existence undermines his masculinity and therefore his role as the head of the (non-existent) family. As a servant tells him when asked to confirm that Allwit is the master of the house: "O you are but our mistress's husband" (1.2.65). At the end of his soliloquy, Allwit sings a song of the dildo; a substitute phallus is all that is left for the vainglorious and symbolically castrated, substitute husband. A servant of the house dryly comments: "Now he's out of work he falls to making dildoes" (1.2.59).

Allwit's bovine self-satisfaction hinges on his effortless material well-being. His is a rhetoric of copiousness, which is typical of the early modern age, in which the idea and the language of modern capitalism began to take shape: "Allwit's speech stands as a dramatic thesaurus of the Renaissance theater's commercial mythology, a mythology centering upon the horn of plenty. He appears to revel in the material accommodation of the wittol relationship" (Bruster 1992: 60). Renouncing accepted norms and responsibilities and focusing exclusively on his material well-being, Allwit "live[s] at ease". When he sees his lifestyle threatened through Sir Walter's intended marriage to Moll, he contacts Yellowhammer and even simulates outrage at Sir Walter's (and his own) lifestyle: "[the whore] whom he has kept this seven years, / Nay, coz, another man's wife, too" (4.1.234 f.). Allwit knows the official moral code, but it does not mean anything to him. But he is able to act as if it did; the official value system serves him as playing material, for acting out what is commonly expected of him.

Allwit's indifference towards the children that are not his is mirrored in the way he watches the pregnant wife that is not his lying in for childbirth:

> When she lies in,
> As now she's even upon the point of grunting,
> A lady lies not in like her; there's her embossings,
> Embroid'rings, spanglings, and I know not what,
> As if she lay with all the gaudy shops
> In Gresham's Burse about her. (1.2.30-35)

The "grunting" woman is physically likened to a beast, while at the same time her material surroundings, provided by Sir Walter, elevate her to the status of a lady. Mistress Allwit, surrounded by precious commodities, is imaginatively located in Gresham's Burse, i.e. the Royal Exchange, London's first shopping mall, where she turns into a commodity herself: Allwit trades her body and her fertility for Sir Walter's money.

The Allwits refuse to support the injured Sir Walter when they learn that he has lost his fortune and is to be accused of manslaughter. In an instant, the two hypocrites establish the façade of average London citizens outraged about Sir Walter's misdemeanour. Allwit acts the head of the household he is not, and Mistress Allwit acts the true and obedient wife she has never been:

> ALLWIT. Cannot our house be private to ourselves,
> But we must have such guests? [...]
> Good he were apprehended ere he go,
> He's killed some honest gentleman. Send for officers!
> [...] I tell you truly
> I thought you had been familiar with my wife once.
> MISTRESS ALLWIT. With me? I'll see him hanged first; I defy him,
> And all such gentlemen in the like extremity. (5.1.146-57)

The threat of public exposure through Sir Walter's downfall brings out the Allwits' fraudster solidarity, not unlike that of Face, Subtle, and Dol in *The Alchemist*. And like the tricksters in *The Alchemist*, the Allwits quickly drop their routine and decamp when their game is up, but in contrast to Jonson's criminal trio they can take their spoils with them. Interested in nothing but material matters, the Allwits change their living arrangements from one moment to the next; as soon as their 'founder' is ruined, they instantly have plans for the future:

> MISTRESS ALLWIT. Let's let out lodgings then,
> And take a house in the Strand.
> ALLWIT.   In troth a match wench:
> We are simply stocked with cloth of tissue cushions,
> To furnish out bay windows: push, what not that's quaint
> And costly, from the top to the bottom. (5.1.169-73)

For the opening of their new business, the Allwits use the household stuff Sir Walter has given to them over the years. The phrasing betrays the kind of lodgings they plan to let out: in early modern London, prostitutes presented themselves in bay windows, and Master Allwit's use of "quaint" – a synonym for "cunt" – spells out that the Allwits will set up a brothel in the fashionable area west of the city wall, in the direction of Westminster, to attract affluent customers. On the whole, the Allwits stick to their trade, only that in the future they will hire out the work Mistress Allwit has so far done herself. At the end, the seven children of Sir Walter and Mistress Allwit are not even mentioned; but they have never been anything but means to an end anyway, objects in the city's circulation of sexual favours and material riches.

Both *The Alchemist* and *A Chaste Maid in Cheapside* cynically criticize the corrosive materialism of London, the city that turns everything and everybody into a commodity. Both use this corruption and turn it into excellent entertainment. This view of London agrees with the stage representations of London in the early and mid-16th century. What distinguishes both comedies from the early interludes is their local specificity, the ways in which they are embedded in the everyday London life of their day, and their refusal to employ didactic sermonizing. What distinguishes them from the self-congratulatory Elizabethan plays of the late 17th century is their all-encompassing satire, their refusal to glorify London, its history and its heroes. In both comedies, the threats and the enemies of London do not come from vaguely conceived foreign countries; rather, the threats are greed and lust, corrupted values and degraded human relationships in the city itself.

The Jacobean age came to an end when King James I died on 27 March 1625. In the Carolean age – King Charles I reigned from 1625 to 1649, when he was beheaded as a traitor by the Parliamentarians – the London theatre scene developed in two directions: first, there were more indoor theatres like the Blackfriars, providing for increasingly exclusive audiences, and second, the cultural scene more and more shifted to the increasingly gentrified area between the city wall and Westminster, where the Allwits intend to move at the end of *A Chaste Maid in Cheapside*. While London continued to be represented and performed on the stages of the capital, often in colourful if sometimes limiting local detail, the verbal fireworks, the brilliant satire, and the all-encompassing social panoramas that made Jacobean city comedy one of the most sparkling genres of early modern British theatre remained largely limited to the first quarter of the 17th century.

Bibliography

Primary Sources

Beaumont, Francis. 2002 [1607]. *The Knight of the Burning Pestle*. Michael Hattaway (ed.). London: A & C Black.
Jonson, Ben. 1623. "To the memory of my beloued, The Avthor Mr. William Shakespeare: And what he hath left us". In: *Mr. William Shakespeares Comedies, Histories, & Tragedies*. London. VI.
—. 1991 [1610]. *The Alchemist*. Elizabeth Cook (ed.). London: A & C Black.
Middleton, Thomas. 2002 [1630]. *A Chaste Maid in Cheapside*. Alan Brissenden (ed.). London: A & C Black.

Annotated Bibliography

Agnew, Jean-Christophe. 1986. *Worlds Apart: The Market and the Theater in Anglo-American Thought, 1500-1750*. Cambridge: Cambridge UP.
   A by now classic study which is also a testimony to the historicizing / contextualizing school of criticism of the 1980s.
Bruster, Douglas. 1992. *Drama and the Market in the Age of Shakespeare*. Cambridge: Cambridge UP.
   Like Agnew's, a key study elucidating the intricate connections between drama and the market. More focused on the time span relevant to this essay.
Clark, John & Cathy Ross. 2008. *London: The Illustrated History*. London: Allen Lane.
   Published by the Museum of London, this is a highly readable and richly illustrated history of the capital.
Gibbons, Brian. 1980. *Jacobean City Comedy*. London: Methuen.
   The founding study of criticism on our topic.
Grantley, Darryll. 2008. *London in Early Modern English Drama: Representing the Built Environment*. Basingstoke: Palgrave Macmillan.
   A readable (hi)story of London on the stage.
Manley, Lawrence. 1995. *Literature and Culture in Early Modern London*. Cambridge: Cambridge UP.
   This study is bursting with meticulously researched detail.

Middleton, Thomas. 2007. *The Collected Works*. Gary Taylor & John Lavagnino (eds.). Oxford: Clarendon P.

The authoritative edition of Middleton's works, meticulously researched and excellently introduced and annotated by a team of scholars. There is also a separate companion to the Collected Works *by the same editors.*

Orlin, Lena Cowen (ed.). 2000. *Material London, ca. 1600*. Philadelphia: U of Pennsylvania P.

Brings the material economies of early modern London life into focus.

Porter, Roy. 1994. *London: A Social History*. London: Hamish Hamilton.

Another good one-volume history of London; an excellent introduction to the topic.

Riggs, David. 1989. *Ben Jonson: A Life*. Cambridge, MA: Harvard UP.

In spite of its occasionally rough-hewn psychoanalytical approach still the definitive biography of Jonson.

Weinreb, Ben, et al. 2008. *The London Encyclopedia*. London: Macmillan.

A treasure-trove of facts on London through the ages.

Further Secondary Literature

Beier, A. L. & Roger Finlay (eds.). 1986. *London 1500-1700: The Making of the Metropolis*. Harlow: Longman.

Coleridge, Samuel Taylor. 1990. *Table Talk: Recorded by Henry Nelson Coleridge* (and John Taylor Coleridge). 2 vols. Carl Woodring (ed.). Princeton, NJ: Princeton UP.

Craig, D.H. (ed.). 1990. *Ben Jonson: The Critical Heritage*. London: Routledge.

Dillon, Janet. 2000. *Theatre, Court and City, 1595-1610: Drama and Social Space in London*. Cambridge: Cambridge UP.

Finlay, Roger & Beatrice Shearer. 1986. "Population Growth and Suburban Expansion." In: Beier & Finlay 1986. 37-59.

Griffiths, Paul & Mark S. R. Jenner (eds.). 2000. *Londinopolis: Essays in the Cultural and Social History of Early Modern London*. Manchester: Manchester UP.

Harp, Richard & Stanley Stewart (eds.). 2000. *The Cambridge Companion to Ben Jonson*. Cambridge: Cambridge UP.

Haynes, Jonathan. 1992. *The Social Relations of Jonson's Theatre*. Cambridge: Cambridge UP.

Hopkins, D. J. 2009. *City/Stage/Globe: Performance and Space in Shakespeare's London*. New York/London: Routledge.

Leggatt, Alexander. 1973. *Citizen Comedy in the Age of Shakespeare*. Toronto: U of Toronto P.

Lupton, Donald. 1632. *London and the Countrey Carbonadoed*. London.

McEvoy, Sean. 2008. *Ben Jonson: Renaissance Dramatist*. Edinburgh: Edinburgh UP.

Rappaport, Steve. 1989. *Worlds within Worlds: Structures of Life in Sixteenth-Century London*. Cambridge: Cambridge UP.
Stock, Angela & Anne-Julia Zwierlein. 2004. "Introduction: 'Our Scene is London …'." In: Dieter Mehl, Angela Stock & Anne-Julia Zwierlein (eds.). *Plotting Early Modern London: New Essays on Jacobean City Comedy*. Aldershot: Ashgate. 1-24.
Stow, John. 1971. *A Survey of London (1603)*. Charles Lethbridge Kingsford (ed.). 2 vols. Oxford: Clarendon P.
Woodbridge, Linda. 2007. "A Chaste Maid in Cheapside." In: *Thomas Middleton: The Collected Works*. Gary Taylor & John Lavagnino (eds.). Oxford: Clarendon P. 907-11.

8. RESTORATION COMEDIES: WILLIAM WYCHERLEY'S *THE COUNTRY WIFE*, APHRA BEHN'S *THE ROVER*, AND WILLIAM CONGREVE'S *THE WAY OF THE WORLD*

MARION GYMNICH

The restoration of the monarchy in 1660, when the Stuart King Charles II returned from exile, had an enormous impact on the situation of the theatre in England. The theatres reopened after having been closed for approximately two decades, due to the English Civil War, which had begun in 1642, and the Puritan Interregnum. During the Restoration, the theatre thrived once again, and a number of significant changes took place, some of which had a lasting influence on the history of the English theatre. Visiting the theatre was a very popular form of entertainment throughout the Restoration period, but, in contrast to the Elizabethan theatre, which appealed to people of all social ranks, the Restoration theatres attracted in particular the higher social classes, partially as a result of comparatively high entrance fees. Moreover, for the first time in English stage history female characters were impersonated by actresses. Several new types of plays emerged during the Restoration period, some of which turned out to be relatively short-lived, however. A particularly successful new type of play was the 'comedy of manners' or 'comedy of wit.'

The term 'comedy of manners' alludes to the fact that comedies from the Restoration period typically display the life style of polite (London) society, featuring predominantly upper-class characters who are aware of current fashions and who seem to spend most of their time paying visits to each other, gossiping, gambling, visiting the theatre, and flirting. As the term 'comedy of wit' suggests, the concept of 'wit' is of crucial importance in Restoration comedies. In the comedies 'wit' first and foremost refers to an individual's capacity of reaching his or her goals by cleverly manipulating others by means of a range of strategies, including the use of rhetorical brilliance and double entendres. Thus, possessing 'wit' implies the ability to see through one's antagonists' motivations, which makes it possible to exploit them for furthering one's own plans (cf. Palmes 1990: 83). Dialogues provide the witty characters with the opportunity of demonstrating their intellectual superiority. Both clever intrigues and rhetorical brilliance, which is presumably most obvious in the so-called 'wit duels' involving two (more or less) equally witty characters (often of opposite sex), are thus indicative of wit. Wit duels constitute one of the recurring courting rituals in Restoration comedies and are simultaneously one of the techniques used to create comic effects.

Restoration comedies tend to feature a contemporary setting. One of the rare exceptions is Aphra Behn's *The Rover* (1677), which is set during the Puritan Interregnum and focuses on the adventures of a group of Royalist Cavaliers in exile. Being set in Naples, *The Rover* is also an exception in terms of its spatial setting, since the overwhelming majority of Restoration comedies are set in London. They often even refer explicitly to specific fashionable meeting places in the city, such as the theatre and the chocolate house (cf. for instance the first scene of Congreve's *The Way of the World* [1700], which is set in a chocolate house). When Restoration comedies present scenes that are set in the English countryside these mainly serve to highlight the contrast between the fashionable lifestyle characteristic of London and the backwardness and naivety of the characters residing in the countryside. In fact, even if there are no scenes that are actually set in the countryside, Restoration comedies regularly feature at least one or two characters from the countryside visiting London who serve as a target of laughter. Thus, Restoration comedies time and again project a contrast between the city, which is celebrated as the epitome of a refined, modern lifestyle, on the one hand, and the countryside, which is depicted as the abode of simple-minded and/or highly conservative characters, on the other hand. Whenever a character from the countryside is introduced in a comedy of manners, the contemporary audience knew exactly what to expect: while the male characters from the countryside are often downright foolish, the younger female characters from the countryside may be inexperienced, but they typically want to escape from the restrictions imposed on them by life in the countryside as soon as they lay eyes on the attractions that London has to offer.

A further characteristic of the Restoration comedy of manners is its tendency to present both male and female characters who display obviously promiscuous behaviour. Flirting, sex, and adultery are among the most important topics of the Restoration comedy, and typically neither male nor female characters who commit adultery show any scruples. Restoration comedies in fact seem to suggest that adultery constitutes an integral part of the modern lifestyle characteristic of city life. The predominant concept of love that comedies of manner project in their love and courtship plots thus is hardly a very romantic, let alone platonic one. Sexual satisfaction is a vital goal for many of the characters (of both sexes), and the comedies are full of sexual innuendoes and of what has been referred to as "racy language" (Bevis 1988: 73). As a result, Restoration comedies have frequently been criticized for propagating immoral behaviour. Both contemporary critics and later literary criticism repeatedly condemned the comedy of manners because of its endorsement of undisguised promiscuity. Contemporary criticism of the promiscuity displayed in the Restoration comedy, which "reached a first peak in Jeremy Collier's *Short View of the Immorality, and Profaneness of the Restoration Stage* (1698)" (Bevis 1988: 98), is one of the factors that contributed to the emergence of a new type of comedy at the beginning of the 18th century, the 'sentimental comedy,' which adopted a radically different approach to the depiction of love and propagated moral values – even at the expense of producing comic effects (see chapter 10).

Restoration comedies tend to present a set of stock characters, who can often be identified already on the basis of their telling names and whose predictable patterns of behaviour are vital for achieving comic effects. One of these stock characters is the 'rake,' a dashing and extremely witty young womanizer who is only interested in his own pleasure; although his actions are certainly not guided by moral principles, he is typically 'rewarded' at the end of the play by achieving his goals. The rake's disillusioned and cynical notion of human nature shows the impact of the philosophies of Hobbes and Machiavelli (cf. Schabert 1997: 253). More often than not, the protagonist of a comedy of manners is a rake. Many of the comic effects created in Restoration comedies are based on the rake's wit, i.e. on scenes in which he displays his intellectual superiority to most other characters, who are time and again fooled and exposed to ridicule by him. The audience is thus clearly invited to 'laugh with' the rake. Another stock character of the comedy of manners, the 'fop,' is ridiculously vain; moreover, he is in love with everything French (in particular French fashion, the French language, etc.). He is typically one of the targets of the rake's satirical comments, and the audience is invited to 'laugh at' him. Telling names such as 'Sir Fopling Flutter' (in George Etherege's *The Man of Mode*, 1676) and 'Lord Foppington' (in John Vanbrugh's *The Relapse*, 1696) are associated with this particular stock character. Similar to the fop, the 'witwoud,' a third type of stock character, tries to fulfil the norms of polite society, but invariably fails to do so. The witwoud is convinced of his own rhetorical brilliance and his equality with the rake in terms of wit, but the audience soon realizes that he lacks the intelligence characteristic of the true wit.

The gender concepts in Restoration comedies appear to be relatively progressive at first sight; male and female characters are shown to be at least intellectually on equal terms. This intellectual equality is demonstrated particularly clearly in the 'wit duels,' which were mentioned above. Nevertheless the society that is portrayed is clearly structured in accordance with patriarchal principles, which means that the agency of female characters, especially their possibility of determining the way they want to live, is severely limited. Ultimately the female characters are largely dependent on decisions on the part of the male characters. Moreover, once they are married, the female characters are often treated as a mere commodity by their husbands. Still, both unmarried and married female characters are regularly shown to rebel more or less openly against the restrictions imposed upon them by patriarchal structures. This defiant stance is arguably most striking in plays by women playwrights, such as Aphra Behn, but it can also be identified in comedies by male playwrights, as, for instance, the famous 'proviso scene' in Congreve's *The Way of the World*, which will be discussed below, illustrates.

As far as their structure is concerned, "multiple interwoven plots" (Bevis 1988: 73) are characteristic of Restoration comedies. Continuing the tradition of Renaissance comedies featuring multiple plots, such as William Shakespeare's *A Midsummer Night's Dream* (1595-96), the juxtaposition of several plots allows for a variety of pleasures and makes it possible to provide variations on particular themes or character constellations. In comedies one may traditionally distinguish between 'high' and 'low' comedy, i.e. between plots that involve upper-class ('high') characters and those that centre on lower-class characters (in particular servants). In comparison to other periods of theatre history, the low plots generally tend to be of minor importance in Restoration comedies, however. In fact, the rude, bawdy type of comedy featuring sexual innuendoes and obscene language, which has traditionally been regarded as characteristic of 'low comedy,' is not restricted to characters from the lower social classes in the Restoration period, but tends to involve the rake and other upper-class characters.

The history of the comedy of manners began in 1668, when George Etherege's second play *She Wou'd If She Cou'd*, which "is widely accepted as the first true comedy of manners" (Bevis 1988: 76), was first performed. As far as the development of the Restoration comedy is concerned, one can distinguish roughly between two different periods. The first period began in 1668 and reached its climax in the mid-1670s, when William Wycherley and George Etherege, two of the most important playwrights of the first period, stopped writing. The first period brought forth plays that are sometimes referred to as 'hard comedy' (cf. Hume 1976), where the rake's egoistic and aggressive stance is almost invariably rewarded and the audience is invited to laugh at those characters who fail to fulfil social norms. Wycherley's *The Country Wife* (1675) and Behn's *The Rover*, which will be discussed below, exemplify many of the characteristics associated with the first period. The plays from the early period also include Etherege's *The Man of Mode* (1676) as well as Wycherley's *The Gentleman Dancing Master* (1672) and *The Plain Dealer* (1676). In the 1690s, a second climax of the Restoration comedy can be observed. The playwrights of the second period of the comedy of manners include John Vanbrugh (*The Relapse*, 1696; *The Provoked Wife*, 1697), William Congreve (*Love for Love*, 1695; *The Way of the World*, 1700), and George Farquhar (*The Recruiting Officer*, 1706; *The Beaux' Stratagem*, 1707). These playwrights introduce a more 'humane comedy' (cf. Hume 1976), where many of the characters show at least some moral scruples. While the early Restoration comedies present an aristocratic lifestyle and a lax system of moral values, the later comedies of manners tend to become more serious in their tone and general orientation. The plays do not advocate promiscuity in the straightforward manner of the early Restoration comedies, and they often criticize the notion of the 'reformed rake,' which one encounters in many of the earlier comedies. In several respects, Congreve's *The Way of the World* is representative of this second period.

1. William Wycherley's *The Country Wife*

The Country Wife (1675) by William Wycherley (1640/41-1715/16) can be regarded as a prototypical example of the Restoration comedy. Like most comedies of manner, *The Country Wife* focuses on upper-class life in Restoration England and is set in London, which is celebrated throughout the play as "the locus of pleasure and sex" (Velissariou 1995: 121). The title of the play already suggests that it draws upon the contrast between the stylish London (high) society and the simple-minded characters from the countryside, which is reiterated throughout the Restoration comedy. In particular, the play makes fun of the title character, Margery Pinchwife, a recently married woman from the countryside who is incredibly naive. Already her very first line in the play is indicative of her ignorance of fashionable life in London; she innocently asks her sister-in-law: "Pray, sister, where are the best fields and woods to walk in in London?" (2.1.1 f.)

Given its obvious endorsement of promiscuity, *The Country Wife* has been one of the most controversial Restoration comedies. Despite the fact that "it succeeded and continues to be revived as one of Restoration drama's major achievements" (Bevis 1988: 83), "for a long time there was only one-sided moral denunciation" (ibid.). *The Country Wife*, which depicts "sexual relationships as a terrain for the exercise of power" (Velissariou 1995: 115), is a paradigmatic example of the loose moral system characteristic of the Restoration comedy. Already in the very first scene of the play, the audience learns that the play's protagonist, the rake Horner, has come up with an unusual strategy which he pursues in order to increase his chances of having affairs with married women. Horner starts the rumour that he is impotent, hoping to convince husbands in this way that there is no harm in him spending time with their wives. The basic idea of *The Country Wife* is reminiscent of Terence's play *Eunuchus* (161 BC). In order to make this rumour more convincing, Horner has made a doctor (the quack) spread reports about Horner's alleged impotence. Horner is sure that married women are hypocritical, avoiding adultery simply because they care about their reputation and not because they are truly virtuous; in other words, he believes that "'tis scandal they would avoid, not men" (1.1.158). This premise of the action in *The Country Wife* shows that the play is "a dramatic satire on hypocrisy and affectation" (Bevis 1988: 85). As far as Horner is concerned, it is clear right from the start that his reputation is less important to him than his pleasure. He happily forfeits his reputation of being a virile man in order to have the opportunity of enjoying sexual intercourse with as many women as possible. His plan turns out to be highly successful. The first woman to grant Horner sexual favours is Lady Fidget, who is keen on having an affair with him without putting her reputation at risk, and most of the other female characters also play along with Horner's plan.

The protagonist Horner is the quintessential rake, and his friends Dorilant and Harcourt can also be categorized as rakes, although they appear to be somewhat less extreme versions of this character type. Harcourt appears to be a 'reformed rake' since he vows constancy after having fallen in love with Alithea. Horner, in contrast, is an extremely inconstant lover, who regards women primarily as "sexual commodities" (Velissariou 1995: 118) and openly declares that "next to the pleasure of making a new mistress is that of being rid of an old one" (1.1.157). He is exclusively interested in his own pleasure and in particular in sexual satisfaction. For Horner, deceiving his lovers' husbands clearly enhances the enjoyment of gratifying his sexual desires. Horner's name thus is clearly a telling name, alluding to his habit of committing adultery, of 'putting horns' on husbands' heads. In *The Country Wife* women's sexuality is shown as "a factor potentially subversive of patriarchal arrangements" (Velissariou 1995: 116), due to "the self-determination of female desire outside such arrangements" (ibid.).

What renders Horner's actions presumably less despicable in the eyes of the audience is the fact that his opponents are presented as equally egocentric and either stupid or even downright cruel characters. His main antagonist, the middle-aged former rake Mr Pinchwife, has married a naïve young woman from the countryside in order to avoid becoming a cuckold and treats her in a very cruel manner, threatening to use physical violence when he fears that she is not the obedient wife he had hoped for.

The play's title character, Mrs Margery Pinchwife, is the prototype of the naive woman from the countryside who is not used to the customs of the city, but who nevertheless displays a lusty interest in the attractive men she encounters in the city and quickly learns what opportunities London offers for satisfying female desire. Thus, she is the perfect (and very willing) victim of Horner's plan. Interestingly, visits to the theatre contribute to Margery's awakening desire: "Not only does the theater turn the actors' bodies into objects of sight, and of desire, but it also exposes the audience to the gaze of others to the same effect. It is in the theater that Margery first learns how to distinguish between her old husband and the young, handsome actors." (Velissariou 1995: 121) The metatheatrical comments referring to the theatre as an eroticized place, where desires can be articulated and fulfilled, provide interesting evidence of self-referentiality in the Restoration comedy. Pinchwife, who used to be a rake himself, originally chose a naive wife because he was convinced that wit in a woman was bound to harm her husband eventually: "What is wit in a wife good for, but to make a man a cuckold?" (1.1.518-20) Although she lacks the wit to forge any plans on her own behalf, Margery Pinchwife resolutely resists her husband's efforts to force her into the role of the obedient and faithful wife. The conflict between Mrs Pinchwife and her husband finally reaches a climax in the "dark violence" (Bevis 1988: 83) of the letter-writing scene, where Pinchwife forces his wife to write a letter in which she rejects the advances of her admirer. In this scene Pinchwife threatens to harm his wife by writing "whore with this penknife in [her] face" (4.2.117 f.) and by stabbing "out those eyes that cause [his] mischief" (4.2.136).

On the whole, *The Country Wife* is exemplary of a relatively rude kind of comedy, drawing its comic effects in particular from allusions to sexual intercourse and impotence. Sexual innuendoes thus play a crucial role throughout *The Country Wife*, reaching a climax in the notorious 'china scene,' where Horner and Lady Fidget talk about 'buying china' in the presence of the latter's husband Sir Jasper Fidget, all the time using the word 'china' as a code for sexual intercourse respectively for male genitalia. Thus, they plan committing adultery in the husband's presence without making the latter suspicious. The china scene contributed very much to the criticism caused by the play; it "provoked a moral reaction leading to revisions and a long eclipse" (Bevis 1988: 84). In *The Country Wife* comic effects are generally often created by discrepant awareness, by situations in which the audience knows more than one of the characters. Due to discrepant awareness, several of the characters become the target of laughter. In act 2, scene 1, for instance, Sir Jasper's frequent asides give away that he believes what he has heard about Horner's alleged impotence and thus he involuntarily exposes himself to laughter. While he is making fun of Horner's situation, the audience realizes that Horner is likely to have the last laugh, given the fact that it is apparently easy to fool Sir Jasper. Besides Sir Jasper the play features further comic characters. One of these is Sparkish, a witwoud, who is totally unaware of the fact that the other characters despise him, or, as Dorilant puts it, "he can no more think the men laugh at him than that women jilt him, his opinion of himself is so good" (1.1.296-98). Disguise is also used to produce comic effects in Wycherley's play. In order to shield his wife from other men's eyes, the jealous Pinchwife at one point forces her to pretend to be a young man. Female characters disguised as men already appear in Renaissance comedies. What makes such scenes arguably more interesting, or perhaps more titillating, in Restoration comedies is the fact that now, in contrast to the Renaissance, women impersonated female characters. As a consequence of the male costumes typical of the period, the actresses inevitably revealed their legs in male attire, instead of covering them with long dresses.

The complex intrigue plot triggered by Horner's stratagem is juxtaposed with a love and courtship plot centring on Alithea and Harcourt. There is a striking contrast between Margery Pinchwife's sister-in-law Alithea and all of the other female characters in *The Country Wife*. Alithea is shown to be an intelligent, honest, and virtuous woman who almost seems to be out of place in the egocentric world depicted in Wycherly's comedy. She for instance shows pity for her inexperienced sister-in-law – an emotion that is quite unusual for a character in a Restoration comedy. Moreover, Alithea's steady character is revealed by her loyalty to her fiancé Sparkish. Yet the witwoud Sparkish is clearly no match for the intelligent Alithea, and finally she is won over by the persistence of the wit Harcourt. Alithea is only persuaded to marry Harcourt, however, after having realized that Sparkish is not in love with her. While Harcourt – similar to many rakes in the comedy of manners – finally marries (and thus becomes a 'reformed rake'), Horner appears to be rewarded for his promiscuity and does not show the slightest inclination to change his behaviour. The grotesque 'dance of the cuckolds,' which constitutes the ending of *The Country Wife*, once more picks up the theme of adultery and emphasizes the satirical character of the play, in which the love between Harcourt and Alithea is the exception rather than the rule.

2. Aphra Behn's *The Rover*

Aphra Behn (1640-1689) is the most prominent of a number of women playwrights from the late 17th / early 18th century. She wrote 17 plays as well as poetry and prose narratives, including *Oroonoko: or, The Royal Slave. A True History* (1688). Her most famous comedy *The Rover* (1677), which was inspired by Thomas Killigrew's play *Thomaso; or, the Wanderer* (1664), is an unusual Restoration comedy as far as the setting is concerned, as was pointed out above. While comedies of manners tend to be set in London during the Restoration period, *The Rover* is set in Naples during carnival time in the period before the Restoration. The play features the adventures of a group of exiled Royalist Cavaliers (Willmore, Belvile, Frederick, and Blunt) and of three noble ladies (Hellena, Florinda, and Valeria), who make use of the liberties offered by the carnival season, wearing masks in order to hide their true identity. The carnival setting of course provides an ideal context for a comedy in which disguise and mistaken identities play a crucial role. In addition, carnival was of central importance to the English aristocracy in the Restoration period, as Beach (2004: 4) points out: "carnival had, quite possibly, never been as closely aligned with an English ruling class as it was in Restoration society," where it "was theorized [...] as a means to maintain social order."

There is a conflict between the English Cavaliers and two noble Spaniards, Don Antonio and Don Pedro, who reside in Naples. This constellation makes it possible to celebrate the superior wit and bravery of the English Cavaliers. Beach (2004: 3) argues that the references to national stereotypes contributed much to the play's success with the 17th-century audience: "a large part of the play's appeal, both before and after the Glorious Revolution, derives from its earnest creation of a nationalist spectacle that fantastically recasts the Stuart exile as another chapter in the venerable English tradition of anti-Spanish privateering." National stereotypes are drawn upon on several levels, including the "presentation of English Cavalier dominance in several fight scenes" (Beach 2004: 3) and the "strategic manipulation of national costume" (ibid.).

While many Restoration comedies predominantly show male characters initiating important plot developments, *The Rover* grants the female characters a strikingly active role. The three 'women of quality' Hellena, Florinda, and Valeria unanimously claim the right to determine their future and in this way they also drive the plot forward. This is highlighted by a comparison with Killigrew's *Tomaso*, as Burke (2004: 122) points out: "In devising their own plan to get out of the patriarchal prison, all three of Behn's virgins also show the initiative and daring reserved for cavaliers and courtesans in Killigrew's play." In particular Hellena shows a type of behaviour that is usually restricted to male characters, since she is "the one who came up with the carnival plan and [...] the one who explicitly expresses the desire to 'Ramble'" (Burke 2004: 122). Hellena resolutely resists her brother's plans for her future, who wants to force her to become a nun. For her as well as for the other female characters, masquerade is a way of defying patriarchal authority. When Hellena disguises herself as a gipsy this is clearly "a form of resistance to the repression of feminine desire" (Hutner 1993: 106). At one point she pretends to be a boy, appearing on stage in men's clothes, which is further evidence of her rebellious spirit and her desire to claim male prerogatives. The way she flirts with Willmore and her attitude towards sexuality even make it possible to categorize Hellena as a 'female rake' (cf. Schabert 1997: 255): When Willmore says to her that "a woman's honour is not worth guarding when she has a mind to part with it" (5.1.533-35), Hellena does not even pretend to be shocked, but readily agrees: "Well said, captain." (5.1.536) Yet ultimately the "freedom to ramble" (Hutner 1993: 107) that is granted to women by their masquerade and by the carnival offers at best a temporary liberty. Finally, Hellena does not have to become a nun, but decides to marry Willmore, thus clearly following patriarchal expectations. Moreover, despite her apparently promiscuous utterances, she remains a virgin right to the end.

The male protagonist and title character Willmore exhibits many of the attributes characteristic of the rake: He is a dashing Cavalier and an inconstant lover and does not even show any traces of guilt because of his inconstancy. Just like other rakes he is only interested in the pursuit of pleasure. The wit duels between Willmore and Hellena provide much of the comic effects of the play. In these wit duels Hellena shows that she is Willmore's intellectual equal and manages to fascinate him by her wit as much as by her appearance. In contrast to many other Restoration rakes, Willmore does not possess a fortune – a fact that may very well serve as an additional inducement to marrying Hellena in the end. As Beach (2004: 2) points out, "many scholars have argued that Behn's play represents an earnest feminist attack on the character of the rake and the sexual audacity of the Stuart court". Yet the rake Willmore in the end is not punished for his 'roving,' but is rewarded by marrying the woman he has chosen.

The Rover juxtaposes several love and courtship plots. In addition to the love plot involving the rake Willmore and the female libertine Hellena there is a more conventional love and courtship plot which focuses on Captain Belvile and Hellena's sister Florinda. Belvile already won Florinda's heart some time ago, during the siege of Pamplona, when Belvile "nobly treated" (1.1.54) both Florinda and her brother, "preserving [them] from all insolences" (1.1.54 f.). Like her sister Hellena, Florinda is the victim of patriarchal power structures. While her brother wants Hellena to become a nun, he intends to force Florinda into a marriage of convenience. In the course of the play Belvile and Florinda, who are both very constant in their affection, overcome all obstacles that prevent them from getting married. Beyond alluding to the threatening marriage of convenience this subplot presents the situation of women in patriarchal society in a yet more bleak way, since "[t]hroughout the play Florinda is subject to a series of attempted rapes, first by Willmore, then by Blunt and Frederick, and finally by a group of men, including her own brother, Pedro" (Hutner 1993: 109). The third (minor) love plot, which takes up very little of the action, involves Belvile's companion Frederick and Hellena's relative Valeria. Frederick's behaviour and his comments show him to be an unabashed womanizer: "I dare swear I have had a hundred as young, kind, and handsome as this Florinda; and dogs eat me if they were not as troublesome to me i'th' morning as they were welcome o'er night." (1.2.39-42) Yet he suddenly decides to marry Valeria, apparently turning into a 'reformed rake.'

In addition to the three 'women of quality,' *The Rover* features the two prostitutes Angellica Bianca and Lucetta, who also turn out to be very interesting characters from the point of view of gender studies. While Lucetta's main function is to deceive the simple-minded Englishman Blunt, the courtesan Angellica Bianca has often been seen as Aphra Behn's alter ego, and in fact "[m]uch of the recent criticism of *The Rover* has focused on the problem of the author's dialectically self-constructed image as the female writer-whore" (Hutner 1993: 103). In contrast to the simple prostitute Lucetta, Angellica Bianca literally advertises herself as a rare commodity by means of her "self-construction as Petrarchan mistress [which] charts the attempt of a woman excluded from the marital marketplace to turn her beauty into an alternative form of power" (Pacheco 1998: 323). Although "her beauty and its proportionately exalted price come close to recreating the physical unattainability of the chaste Petrarchan lady" (ibid.: 336), the image she constructs proves to be no substitute for virginity. Ultimately, in *The Rover* the power of unmarried women depends on withholding sexual favours before marriage. In this respect, the play clearly stays within a patriarchal framework, which regards chastity as the quintessential feminine virtue.

The Rover presents Angellica Bianca's decline from being a strong, apparently independent woman to being a desperate lover, driven to extremes by her jealousy. At first she proudly declares that she is immune to love, in this way emphasizing her independence: "inconstancy's the sin of all mankind, therefore I'm resolved that nothing but gold shall charm my heart." (2.1.145-46) Yet as soon as she meets the rover Willmore, she falls in love with him, which means that she is not in control of her destiny anymore. When he leaves her, her anger and disappointment even make Angellica Bianca threaten to shoot Willmore, the pistol in her hand arguably being "symbolic of her attempt to usurp phallic control" (Hutner 1993: 108) once more. The scene in which the courtesan threatens Willmore does not look very much like a scene from a comedy. Instead, its tone is serious, which makes it more difficult for the audience to take the courtesan's despair lightly. The playwright even uses stylistic means to turn the courtesan into a serious character: "In the first love scene between Angellica and Willmore, the courtesan speaks in blank verse, a form that is generally reserved for serious drama, and after she falls in love in this scene, her allusions to her 'Soul' [...], her 'Virgin heart' [...], and her 'Vows' [...] further link her to the heroines of this kind of drama" (Burke 2004: 126). The way Angellica Bianca is presented is likely to evoke sympathy with the woman who feels betrayed by the rake, despite the fact that she is a courtesan.

In a further plot, focussing on the English country gentleman Blunt being deceived by the prostitute and thief Lucetta, the play provides low comedy, introducing lower-class characters as well as particularly rude language. Blunt, who even refers to himself as an "Essex calf" (3.4.9), is yet another example of the recurring Restoration stock character of the fool from the countryside, who is easily cheated by others. Blunt turns out to be the most openly misogynist character in the play. Having been robbed by Lucetta and dumped in the sewer, he vows vengeance, threatening the virtuous Florinda with rape: "[...] I will kiss and beat thee all over, kiss and see thee all over; thou shalt lie with me too, not that I care for the enjoyment, but to let thee see I have ta'en deliberated malice to thee, and will be revenged on one whore for the sins of another." (4.4.53-57) As this passage illustrates, for Blunt "the boundary separating virgins from whores vanishes for the simple reason that all women are sisters under the skin" (Pacheco 1998: 334). The fact that chaste Florinda is in danger of being raped by Blunt serves to criticize his misogynist views. Thus, all plots of the play support a feminist reading since they draw the attention of the audience to the diverse restrictions a patriarchal society imposes on women, notwithstanding their efforts to resist patriarchal authority.

3. William Congreve's *The Way of the World*

The Way of the World by William Congreve (1670-1729) was first performed in 1700 and thus is a relatively late example of the Restoration comedy. The central plot of Congreve's play, a love and courtship plot, focuses on the male protagonist Mirabell, who is courting the beautiful, wealthy, and witty Millamant. In contrast to rakes like Horner and Willmore, Mirabell is shown to be truly in love with Millamant right from the beginning of the play. Nevertheless Mirabell is not an inexperienced young man, but used to have affairs with other women in the past, which means he represents the character type of the 'reformed rake.' In order to win Millamant's heart and hand, Mirabell has to overcome two major obstacles. His attempts to overcome these obstacles trigger much of the action. Thus, in contrast to the plays discussed above, which feature largely parallel, though intricately interwoven plot lines, the plot of Congreve's comedy is based much more on a single impetus, which gives rise to a relatively complex single plot.

The first obstacle Mirabell has to overcome is the fact that Millamant's aunt, Lady Wishfort, who has the right to deprive her niece of half of her fortune if the latter marries without her consent, despises Mirabell and consequently does not approve of him marrying Millamant. Given the fact that Lady Wishfort heartily dislikes Mirabell, it is anything but easy to overcome this obstacle. The main reason for Lady Wishfort's dislike of Mirabell is the fact that the young man used to pay the 55-year-old lady compliments in order to win her approval and to hide his love for her niece from her. Before she eventually found out the truth Lady Wishfort for a while believed that Mirabell was in love with her. In order to make Lady Wishfort agree to his marriage plans, Mirabell devises a complex intrigue, which involves his servant Waitwell, disguised as the nobleman 'Sir Rowland,' courting Lady Wishfort and Mirabell finally coming to the lady's rescue.

The second obstacle Mirabell has to overcome is Millamant's aversion to giving up her liberty by becoming a married woman. In general, the female characters appear to be much more independent in *The Way of the World* than in many of the earlier Restoration comedies. Especially Millamant is a very strong female character, who repeatedly shows that she is Mirabell's intellectual equal. In the famous 'proviso scene' (act 4, scene 5) Mirabell and Millamant engage in a verbal sparring which appears to be a strategic power struggle between the two characters. Like Hellena and Willmore in *The Rover*, Mirabell and Millamant are a prime example of the 'gay couple,' i.e. "a pair of lively, witty lovers whose love contains an element of antagonism – each desires the other but is wary of commitment" (Howe 1992: 66). Using the diction of legal treaties, the two lovers formulate conditions for becoming married in the proviso scene. In this wit duel Millamant very clearly expresses her misgivings about traditional female role patterns in general and marriage in particular. She thus formulates a number of conditions – including the "liberty to pay and receive visits to and from whom I please; to write and receive letters, without interrogatories or wry faces [...]; to wear what I please; and choose conversation with regard only to my own taste" (4.1.190-93.) – which must be fulfilled before she will even consider 'dwindling into a wife' (ibid.), as she puts it. As her comments on married life and the very notion of 'dwindling into a wife' show clearly, her concept of marriage is anything but romantic. She is aware that a marriage to Mirabell will inevitably lead to a loss of freedom for her. Yet, despite the self-confident behaviour she displays in the proviso scene and elsewhere in the play, Millamant confesses much more conventional feelings in a conversation with Mrs Fainall: "Well, if Mirabell should not make a good husband, I am a lost thing; – for I find I love him violently." (4.1.285 f.) Mirabell likewise lists a number of demands in the proviso scene and in this way provides a satire on current fashions and on women's vanity, but also cleverly pays compliments to Millamant, saying for instance: "I article that you continue to like your own face, as long as I shall: and while it passes current with me, that you endeavour not to new coin it. To which end, together with all vizards for the day, I prohibit all masks for the night, made of oiled-skins and I know not what" (4.1.221-25).

Two other female characters, Mrs Fainall and Mrs Marwood, paint a very bleak picture of married life and of the lack of constancy displayed by men. Mrs Fainall, for instance, says about men: "[...] when they cease to love [...], they loathe; they look upon us with horror and distaste; they meet us like the ghosts of what we were, and as such, fly from us." (2.1.5-8) Being older than Millamant, both women have experience with being left by former lovers. Yet neither of the two female characters is a constant lover herself. Similar to many female characters in Restoration comedy, they regard adultery as a facet of modern life and thus subscribe to the lack of moral principles which is characteristic of the Restoration comedy in general. Moreover, the way the two women interact provides a satire on female friendship, which is shown to be utterly hypocritical. The play even suggests that friendship between men and women is more likely than friendship among women, who are regarded as being natural rivals, competing with each other in terms of looks as well as wit.

The comic effects in *The Way of the World* are largely generated by wit duels, by comic stock characters and by contrasts between the opposition 'city vs. country' and 'old vs. young.' Although many other comedies from the later period use the contrast between city and country in a less stereotypical fashion, *The Way of the World* is relatively 'conservative' in this respect. Sir Wilfull Witwoud, a visitor from the countryside, is not used to city customs, and Millamant does not hesitate to express her disdain of the countryside, saying "I nauseate walking; 'tis a country diversion, I loathe the country and everything that relates to it." (4.1.105 f.) In Congreve's comedy, there are prime examples of the 'witwoud.' Both Witwoud and Petulant exemplify this stock character. Moreover, the play features the stereotype of the 'ageing coquette,' represented by the character of Lady Wishfort, another character with a telling name. Her excessive use of make-up is indicative of her desire to appear youthful and to be courted, preferably by younger men. Her vanity makes her extremely susceptible to flattery and thus an easy target for the attempts to deceive her. Especially the detailed depiction of her efforts to appear in the best possible light for her supposed suitor creates comic effects. The speech in which she ponders how to receive 'Sir Rowland' arguably constitutes one of the great comic moments of the play: "There is a great deal in the first impression. Shall I sit? – No, I won't sit – I'll walk – ay, I'll walk from the door upon his entrance; and then turn full upon him." (4.1.15-18) In addition, applying paint to her face proves to be useless since frowning immediately makes "some cracks discernible in the white varnish" (3.1.130 f.). The comedy thus exploits the contrast between young and old characters to generate comic effects – a strategy that is common in the Restoration period, but that is also one of the features that can be observed in comedies from other periods in literary history. In comedies parents and elderly relatives time and again function as blocking characters, trying to undermine the younger characters' plans and thus are often victims of intrigues on the part of the younger characters.

4. Summary

Bevis (1988: 71) says about the atmosphere of the Restoration comedy that it "resembled that of the pre-Lenten carnival in Europe: a time of masks, sexual pursuits, kidnapping and release." The Restoration comedy, and most of all the plays from the 1660s up to the mid-1670s, celebrated a libertine life style, making regular use of bawdy comedy and sexual innuendoes. The tendency to endorse promiscuity can likewise be observed in poetry from the period, for instance in poems by the Earl of Rochester, who, due to his libertine lifestyle, is also said to have served as an inspiration for the figure of the rake in the comedies of manner. In order to produce comic effects the comedy of manners relied very much on the variation of a limited number of stock characters and on perpetuating clear oppositions such as city vs. country and old vs. young, as was shown above. In some of the later Restoration comedies the opposition city vs. country is seen in a somewhat different light, though. Instead of depicting the countryside simply as the abode of 'country bumpkins,' Vanbrugh's *The Relapse*, for instance, presents the countryside as a place of marital harmony, whereas the city is associated with temptation and brings about the 'relapse' of the reformed rake.

Shifts like the one just mentioned are indicative of a change in terms of values that ultimately prepared the path for the sentimental comedy, which emerged at the beginning of the 18th century, gradually replacing the comedy of manners. The sentimental comedy aimed at a different target audience, the middle class, whose attitudes and interests shaped much of 18th-century literature in general. This new kind of comedy presented morally sound characters and in this way eliminated many of the sources of comic effects that were previously used (e.g. the comic stock characters), which turned the sentimental comedy into a type of play whose primary aim was not making the audience laugh but educating them by showing morally unexceptional behaviour on stage. Towards the end of the 18th century, however, there was a return to the 'laughing comedy,' which revived some of the features of the Restoration comedy. Richard Brinsley Sheridan (1751-1816) and Oliver Goldsmith (1730-1774) wrote plays that departed from the strict morality of the sentimental comedy and drew upon some of the comic elements associated with the Restoration comedy, without returning to the extreme egoism and promiscuity displayed in many Restoration comedies. At the end of the 19th century, Oscar Wilde's (1854-1900) plays once more picked up certain features of the Restoration comedy of manners, celebrating the lifestyle of the upper classes and featuring witty dialogues and aphorisms that are indicative of the rhetorical brilliance of some of the characters. For Wilde's dandies, just as for the rakes in the Restoration comedies, the pursuit of pleasure is the main guiding principle for their actions. As the revival of certain aspects of the comedy of manners in the late 18th and late 19th centuries shows (see chapter 12), the Restoration comedy has proved to provide inspiration for a number of later playwrights, though it has arguably remained unique in terms of its unabashed endorsement of promiscuity as far as the history of the English comedy is concerned, at least if one does not take British film comedies and TV sitcoms into consideration, which often feature exactly the kind of bawdy comedy which led to severe criticism of the Restoration comedy by contemporary as well as by later criticism.

Bibliography

Primary Sources

Behn, Aphra. 1967 [1677]. *The Rover*. Frederick M. Link (ed.). London: Edward Arnold.
Congreve, William. 1970 [1700]. *The Way of the World*. Kathleen M. Lynch (ed.). London: Edward Arnold.
Etherege, George. 2010 [1668]. *She Would, If She Could: A Comedy* [*She Wou'd If She Cou'd*]. Whitefish, MT: Kessinger.
Wycherley, William. 2003 [1675]. *The Country Wife*. James Ogden (ed.). London: A&C Black.

Annotated Bibliography

Bevis, Richard W. 1988. "Mask and Veil: Comedy." In: Richard W. Bevis (ed.). *English Drama: Restoration and Eighteenth Century, 1660-1789*. London/New York: Longman. 71-102.
An older, but still very readable overview of the development of the comedy in the Restoration period.

Canfield, J. Douglas. 2008. "Restoration Comedy." In: Susan J. Owen (ed.). *A Companion to Restoration Drama*. Oxford: Blackwell. 211-27.
A recent, concise overview of the Restoration comedy.
Howe, Elizabeth. 1992. *The First English Actresses: Women and Drama 1660-1700*. Cambridge: Cambridge UP.
The study focuses on the new role of women in the theatre of the Restoration period, including the comedy.
Hughes, Derek & Janet Todd (eds.). 2004. *The Cambridge Companion to Aphra Behn*. Cambridge: Cambridge UP.
One of several recent companions to the works of Aphra Behn, which covers her contribution to literature in general, including her comedies.
Palmes, Maria. 1990. "William Congreve: The Way of the World." In: Herbert Mainusch (ed.). *Europäische Komödie*. Darmstadt: Wissenschaftliche Buchgesellschaft. 73-97.
An interpretation of Congreve's most famous comedy.
Todd, Janet. 1996. *Aphra Behn Studies*. Cambridge: Cambridge UP.
A survey of a range of different approaches to the works of Aphra Behn.
Zimbardo, Rose A. 1989. "William Wycherley." In: Paula R. Backscheider (ed.). *Restoration and Eighteenth-Century Dramatists*. First Series. Detroit, MI: Gale. 263-90.
A concise article on Wycherley's works.

Further Secondary Literature

Beach, Adam R. 2004. "Carnival Politics, Generous Satire, and Nationalist Spectacle in Behn's *The Rover*." In: *Eighteenth-Century Life* 28.3: 1-19.
Burke, Helen M. 2004. "The Cavalier Myth in *The Rover*." In: Hughes & Todd 2004. 118-34.
Hume, Robert D. 1976. *The Development of English Drama in the Late Seventeenth Century*. Oxford: Clarendon P.
Hutner, Heidi. 1993. "Revisioning the Female Body: Aphra Behn's *The Rover*, Parts I and II." In: Heidi Hutner (ed.). *Rereading Aphra Behn: History, Theory, and Criticism*. Charlottesville: Virginia UP. 102-20.
Pacheco, Anita. 1998. "Rape and the Female Subject in Aphra Behn's *The Rover*." In: *ELH* 65.2: 323-45.
Schabert, Ina. 1997. *Englische Literaturgeschichte aus der Sicht der Geschlechterforschung*. Stuttgart: Kröner.
Velissariou, Aspasia. 1995. "Patriarchal Tactics of Control and Female Desire in Wycherley's *The Gentleman Dancing-Master* and *The Country Wife*." In: *Texas Studies in Literature and Language* 37.2: 115-26.

9. RESTORATION TRAGEDY AND HEROIC DRAMA: JOHN DRYDEN'S *ALL FOR LOVE, OR THE WORLD WELL LOST*

INGO BERENSMEYER

1. Restoration Tragedy and Heroic Drama: A Theatre-Historical Introduction

In contrast to Restoration comedy, serious drama of the period 1660-1700 is far less well-known and rarely performed today. The heroic play in particular, a genre which briefly flourished in 17th-century England between 1660 and 1680, is closely tied to the social world and the political thought of its own time. Since both of these are very distant for today's readers, they require a more prolonged historical and contextual introduction. Before turning to a model analysis of John Dryden's *All for Love* (1678) as a key example of later 17th-century serious drama, we are going to look at Restoration tragedy first from the perspective of English theatre history in general and then shed light on the main features of its 'heroic' aesthetics.

Drama was the most public of literary genres in the early modern period. In London, public playhouses flourished between 1580 and 1620, when the most important English plays by William Shakespeare, Christopher Marlowe, Ben Jonson, Francis Beaumont, and John Fletcher were first performed. Large open playhouses like the famous Globe Theatre (1599-1642) could accommodate audiences of between 2,000 and 3,000 people. After c. 1610, smaller so-called private playhouses like the Blackfriars or the Phoenix in Drury Lane (built in 1617) returned a higher profit but, because tickets were more expensive, attracted a more socially homogeneous audience.

Despite, or partly because of, its high popularity, Elizabethan and Jacobean theatre remained a peripheral and not generally accepted cultural institution, relegated to the city margins in the vicinity of brothels and bear-baiting arenas. From the 1620s onwards, theatre moved closer to the city centre, facilitated by its rising social prestige. Elaborate theatrical productions were also staged at court: The fashionable 'court masque' involved courtiers and even the king and queen themselves as actors in allegorical and 'romantic' (romance-based) plays. Both at court and in the city playhouses, there was a growing tendency of more spectacular entertainments that involved visual stage effects which had been largely absent in Tudor drama. Under the Stuarts, during the reign of James I (1603-1625) and Charles I (1625-1649), audiences became more refined and more interested in watching plays that thematized a Neoplatonic concept of "'purity' in love that could not easily be shared by the population at large" (Hunter 1997: 21): plays like John Fletcher's (1579-1625) *The Faithful Shepherdess* (1608-09) or Thomas Heywood's (1574-1641) *Love's Mistress* (1634). Because audiences re-diversified and re-specialized, theatre never reached such a wide consensus again as it had enjoyed under Elizabeth I (for a detailed historical overview of later 17th-century English drama, see Hume 1976).

The public performance of plays can be regarded as a cultural site for addressing relevant social questions and problems (cf. Greenblatt 1988). One could perhaps say that drama, while certainly serving a prime function of popular entertainment, also gives a socially acceptable shape to different, sometimes even dissident, observations and representations of social reality, thus enabling, in the fictional space provided by the stage, a more flexible and less punishable handling of alternative options for living. Theatre probably has the closest and most immediate connection with public social spaces; in the 17th century, it serves as a medium of public representation and discussion of social and political themes, often in the form of allegorical plots that are set in exotic locations (Spain, Portugal, Italy, the Ottoman Empire) and in other periods of history.

In 1642, all theatres were officially closed. The English Civil War (1642-1651) made large assemblies of people appear too dangerous; furthermore, the victorious Parliamentarian party shared the Puritan "antitheatrical prejudice" (Barish 1981: 3). This is why theatres remained closed in the 'Commonwealth' (Republic) of the 1650s and during the Protectorate of Oliver Cromwell (1653-1657). Many royalists – supporters of King Charles I, who was publicly executed in 1649, and of his son Charles II – went into exile to France or the Netherlands. Royalist theatre on the continent during this time is an area that is under-researched; but so is theatre in Cromwellian England. Even though the playhouses remained closed, exceptions were made for semi-private theatricals that included music and were promoted as serving public propaganda for the Republican cause. William Davenant (1606-1668), one of the top theatrical entrepreneurs after the Restoration in 1660, already honed his skills in writing and staging such theatricals in London in the 1650s (e.g. *The Siege of Rhodes* [1656], *The Cruelty of the Spaniards in Peru* [1658]).

In 1660, when monarchy was restored in England, Davenant and Thomas Killigrew secured a duopoly for themselves in running the only two officially licensed playhouses in London. Many older plays, including those by Shakespeare, were revived and rewritten to adapt them to changed audience tastes.

This changed gradually with the establishment of so-called 'private' playhouses and a change of court tastes. When the theatres reopened in 1660, they were popular again, but they were more expensive and socially exclusive than before. This was the short flowering of 'heroic drama,' full of elevated rhetoric and bombastic speeches that reflected an absolutist understanding of monarchical rule, and of the extremely witty and irreverent Restoration comedy which produced cool observations of contemporary city life and satirized its excesses (see chapter 8). John Dryden (1631-1700) excelled in both genres. Other authors connected with serious drama in the later 17th century include, among others, William Killigrew (*Ormasdes* [c. 1664]), Roger Boyle (*The General* [1664]), Elkanah Settle (*Cambyses* [1671]), Thomas Otway (*Alcibiades* [1675]), Nathaniel Lee (*Sophonisba* [1675]), and John Banks (*The Rival Kings* [1677]).

Heroic drama flourished after the Restoration because it united popular taste with strategies of political persuasion. For a while after King Charles II returned to England in 1660, there was a time of conservative, even reactionary cultural stylization of power and absolutist ideology which demanded a highly poetic and heroic style. At the same time, however, the 17th century was a period of latent social unrest and rapid modernization, of which the English Civil War (1642-1651) and the Puritan Interregnum (1649-1660) had been symptoms. In this climate of latent democratization, in which the first recognizable political parties were formed and public opinion first became a significant factor in the realm of politics (pamphlets, the 'mob'), these high-cultural forms had to be tested against social reality (for a more detailed survey of Restoration literary culture, cf. Berensmeyer 2007). For a while, they drew large audiences to the newly reopened theatres to watch and worship spectacles of monarchical power and feats of heroism. After a few years, though, when the first cracks became visible in the ideological veneer of the Restoration settlement, heroic tragedy lost its appeal because it did not stand the test of reality. Unlike Restoration comedy, which continues to find modern audiences, Restoration tragedy has not survived beyond its immediate historical context. However, elements of heroic drama do survive in a different medium: in the highly ornate musical form of baroque 'opera seria' ('serious opera'), e.g. Handel's *Ariodante* (1735) or Mozart's *Idomeneo* (1781). When their emotional core is translated into orchestral music and the singing voice, the dramatic weaknesses of heroic tragedy can more easily be ignored.

2. Major Features of the Heroic Mode: From Epic to Serious Drama

The heroic mode in drama is closely connected to the genre of epic poetry, which was considered as the highest achievement and the most respected form of literature in the early modern period (c. 1500-1700), modelled on classical authors like Homer (c. 8th-7th c. BC) and Virgil (70-19 BC), but also medieval poets like Dante (1265-1321) and Tasso (1544-1595). Homer's *Iliad* (c. 750 BC) recounts many episodes from the Trojan War (c. 1200 BC) that can be considered 'heroic,' especially in its portrayal of individual warriors like Achilles and Hector. For the 17th century, Virgil's *Aeneid* (c. 29-19 BC), the Roman epic about the Greek hero Aeneas, whose adventures lead to the foundation of Rome, was considered most worthy of translation and imitation. John Dryden (1631-1700), the poet and playwright whose name is most frequently connected with heroic drama, also produced a verse translation of *The Aeneid* in 1697.

In Tudor and Stuart England, the production of epic poetry was also considered highly relevant for nation-building, because it could serve as a cultural source of national self-esteem and as a sign of independence from competing continental cultures like Italy, France, and Spain. However, most attempts at composing an English national epic remained incomplete: Edmund Spenser's (c. 1552-1599) *The Faerie Queene* (1590/1596) ends after six (of the projected twelve) books; William Davenant's *Gondibert* (1651) was abandoned by its author after the first three books had received scathing criticism (cf. Berensmeyer 2007: 151-62). There were many attempts at writing an English heroic epic in the 17th century, though most of them are now largely forgotten: e. g. Samuel Daniel's *The Civil Wars* (on the Wars of the Roses) in eight books (1595-1609); Abraham Cowley's *Davideis: A Sacred Poem of the Troubles of David* (1656, in four books) and *The Civil War* (on the Civil War) in three books (the first published in 1679). John Milton's *Paradise Lost* (1667) is the only modern English epic of any lasting significance, and it is often considered as the last great work of the English Renaissance; but its ambitions are no longer national but predominantly religious, and while it does contain a central heroic figure (Christ), its anti-hero Satan has, perhaps ironically, turned out to be a much more memorable and impressive character.

One of the most important aspects of early modern epic poetry is its *allegorical* character. The fictional events recounted in the heroic epic are intended as masked or coded representations – what Edmund Spenser, writing in 1590, calls a "dark conceit" (Vickers 1999: 297) – which the reader has to decode. This is usually intended as didactic "doctrine by example" (ibid.: 299), conveying moral values and sometimes also political messages by telling exemplary stories of 'virtue' or heroic valour. Sometimes, though, the precise didactic content is more difficult to decipher. For instance, Spenser's *Faerie Queene* uses the legends surrounding the figure of King Arthur as an epic framework to signify Glory in the abstract and Queen Elizabeth I in particular; Elizabeth is also present in the poem under the names of Britomart, Belphoebe, Mercilla, and Gloriana. Twelve of her knights, the examples of different individual virtues (e.g. piety, temperance, chastity, friendship, courtesy), each undertake an adventure. Arthur symbolizes the perfection of all the other virtues; he has a vision of the Faerie Queene and, deciding to seek her out, is brought into the adventures of the several knights and carries them to a successful conclusion. This explanation of the plot, given in Spenser's introductory letter to Sir Walter Ralegh, does not emerge from the epic itself; moreover, the poem and the explanatory schema given in the author's introduction do not match (on early modern allegory, see Pfeiffer 2009).

The other major source of 17th-century heroic drama is the 'prose romance,' a popular narrative genre that flourished in the Renaissance. Like the epic, romance writing – an important precursor of the modern novel – focused on aristocratic and courtly values, telling long and episodically structured stories about human identity, agency, and self-fashioning. It was considered appropriate reading matter for young noblemen and -women. Yet despite the lasting success of Sir Philip Sidney's *Arcadia* (c. 1580), which was frequently reprinted and imitated, the romance was usually not considered as a serious literary genre. It appears to have been especially popular with female readers in aristocratic circles. Italian and Spanish romances were translated and printed in England; Sidney's niece, Lady Mary Wroth (c. 1586- c. 1652) is one of the first women to write in this genre (*The Countess of Montgomery's Urania* [1621]). In the mid-17th century, during Civil War and Interregnum, the romance became a hallmark of royalist ideology – a deliberate way of looking backwards to the supposed 'golden age' of Elizabeth and the cliché of 'merry old England.'

In contrast to romance, epic was considered to be a more 'masculine' genre telling about heroic exploits in the world of high politics and warfare. Davenant's *Gondibert* (1651) is of some historical interest because it is an attempt to combine epic with romance: it sets out to tell a tale of chivalry set in medieval Lombardy, but the poem breaks off after some 1,700 quatrains because the first published books were a complete failure with the public – perhaps one of the greatest failures in English literary history – and Davenant was ridiculed for the pompous theorizing with which he introduced his poem and his poetics in the lengthy preface, published separately in 1650. Afterwards, no one attempted such a combination of romance and epic again. Nevertheless, its romantic ideology was to form the core of heroic drama, sponsored by the Court and developed by Davenant and Killigrew after 1660.

The heroic play is geared towards impressing its audience and teaching them about codes of courtly conduct and the virtue of obedience. Dryden cites Davenant's Machiavellian understanding of the author as an absolute sovereign and the audience as his subjects who must be persuaded and conquered (cf. Berensmeyer 2007: 159). These are precisely the terms in which Dryden, in the essay "Of Heroique Playes" (1672), published as a preface to the first part of his play *The Conquest of Granada* (1670), argues for the use of realistic theatrical effects:

> [...] these warlike Instruments, and, even the representations of fighting on the Stage, are no more than necessary to produce the effects of an Heroick Play; that is, to raise the imagination of the Audience, and to perswade them, for the time, that what they behold on the Theater is really perform'd. The Poet is, then, to endeavour an absolute dominion over the minds of the Spectators: for, though our fancy will contribute to its own deceipt, yet a Writer ought to help its operation. (Dryden, *Works* XI: 13 f.)

In the same essay, Dryden gives Davenant credit for having invented the heroic play (cf. Clarke 1932: 438; Kamm 1996: 37). In fact, many of Dryden's aesthetic principles are derived from Davenant – including the principle that, in order to be effective, a play or a poem "ought to be bigger then [sic] the life" (*Works* XVII: 182). The exaggerated passions and, for modern audiences, highly 'unrealistic' plots of heroic drama can be explained as owing to this aesthetics of effect (and affect) intended "to raise the imagination" and "to endeavour an absolute dominion over the minds of the Spectators." The mixture of tragic and comic elements in serious Restoration drama is a shared quality of English and continental, above all Spanish, baroque theatre; it also points forward to modern melodrama, popular on the 19th-century stage and in much of today's world cinema (e.g. Bollywood), which likewise aims at generating powerful emotions.

Yet the didactic and political component is much more pronounced in the heroic aesthetic of the Restoration. In the dedication to his translation of the *Aeneid,* Dryden declares: "The shining Quality of an Epick Heroe, his Magnanimity, his Constancy, his Patience, his Piety, or whatever Characteristical Virtue his Poet gives him, raises first our Admiration: We are naturally prone to imitate what we admire: And frequent Acts produce a habit." (*Works* V: 271)

Earlier, in his dedication of *The Conquest of Granada* to the Duke of York, Dryden had defended the loftiness of heroic drama in similar terms:

> The feign'd Heroe inflames the true: and the dead vertue animates the living. Since, therefore, the World is govern'd by precept and Example; and both these can onely have influence from those persons who are above us, that kind of Poesy which excites to vertue the greatest men, is of greatest use to humane kind. (*Works* XI: 3)

The flowering of English heroic drama was brief; it coincided with the Restoration of a more absolutist kind of monarchy in 1660 and lost its convincing appeal when this type of monarchy lost its powers of persuasion in the political crises of the 1680s and was replaced by a constitutional monarchy after the 'Glorious Revolution' and the Bill of Rights in 1689. A more democratic kind of theatre was called for, one that presented more realistic everyday conflicts and did not call for larger-than-life heroes. Comedy and domestic tragedy were the genres that were best suited to this situation (see chapters 10 and 11).

3. *All for Love, or the World Well Lost*

John Dryden's *All for Love, or the World Well Lost* (1677) is one of the very few tragedies from the Restoration period that continue to be staged in the 21st century. The play was probably first performed by the King's Company at the Theatre Royal, Drury Lane, in December 1677 and first printed in 1678. Its plot focuses on the final hours in the lives of the Roman military leader Mark Antony and the Egyptian queen Cleopatra, observing the neoclassical unities of time, space, and action. The time of the play comprises a single day, and the action takes place in a single setting, the temple of Isis in Alexandria. Unlike most of Dryden's plays, which are written in rhyming couplets, *All for Love* is in blank verse, in deliberate imitation of Shakespeare. But the play is not a direct reworking of Shakespeare's *Antony and Cleopatra* (c. 1606-07). Shakespeare's love tragedy was not considered an artistic success in the 17th century, mainly because of its sprawling plot, which ignored the Aristotelian unities, and its fairly unheroic portrayal of the two lovers. There is no record of a Restoration performance of Shakespeare's *Antony and Cleopatra,* and well into the 19th century stage productions of Shakespeare's play frequently included passages from Dryden's much-loved *All for Love*. Moreover, Antony and Cleopatra were "the subject of innumerable paintings, poems, plays and romances" (Novak 1984: 368), so that Dryden's play is best considered as an original work on a fashionable European theme rather than a reworking of Shakespeare. The rich tradition of Cleopatra plays in early modern Europe include Samuel Daniel's *The Tragedie of Cleopatra* (c. 1594), Thomas May's *The Tragedie of Cleopatra Queen of Aegypt* (1626), as well as French, Italian, and German plays by Robert Garnier, Estienne Jodelle, Cesare de Cesari, Cinthio, and Caspar von Lohenstein. Dryden's play is also often read as a response to Charles Sedley's drama *Antony and Cleopatra,* published in 1677. Furthermore, Dryden's subtitle echoes that of plays like William Rowley's *All's Lost by Lust* (c.

1619, printed 1633); the theme of love-against-the-world was a favourite of 17th-century drama and popular prose.

The play has a classical five-act structure. It begins shortly after the battle of Actium (2 September 31 BC), in which the combined Roman and Egyptian forces of Mark Antony and Cleopatra are defeated by the forces of Octavian (later emperor Augustus). This decisive battle, which ends the Final War of the Roman Republic, would consolidate Octavian's power as sole ruler of Rome. After the death of Julius Caesar in 44 BC, the triumvirate of Octavian, Lepidus, and Mark Antony had ruled the Roman Empire for ten years. Despite marrying Octavian's sister Octavia (for political reasons), Antony continued to spend most of his time in Egypt with Queen Cleopatra, with whom he had formed an alliance and begun a love affair in 41 BC. Like many dramatists who worked with this historical material, Dryden was inspired by the Roman historians, especially Dio Cassius (155-235) and Plutarch (50-120). Dryden's familiarity with these classical sources can be taken for granted; in the 1680s, he coordinated the first complete translation of Plutarch's *Lives of the Noble Greeks and Romans* into English.

All for Love opens with two Egyptian priests, Serapion and Myris, who talk about a series of unusual occurrences (flooding and sudden storms) which they interpret as omens foretelling the downfall of Egypt. They are overheard by Cleopatra's Eunuch, Alexas. He confronts them with his pronounced disbelief in religious superstitions; the real storm about to break, he points out, is the military threat of the Roman forces outside the city. The city is under siege, and Antony appears to have given up the fight: he hides himself in the temple of Isis, "his heart a prey to black despair" (1.1.61). From Alexas, we also learn about Cleopatra's unconditional love for Antony: "O, she dotes, / She dotes, *Serapion*, on this vanquish'd Man" (1.1.76 f.). Their observations about Antony's world-weariness are confirmed by the Roman general Ventidius. Ventidius confirms Antony's heroic and virtuous character (1.1.123-33). The confrontation between the Romans and the Egyptians in this first scene also emphasizes the cultural differences between them: while the Egyptians give orders for a day of "Pomp and Triumphs" (1.1.139) to celebrate Antony and Cleopatra, the Romans see this "Pageantry" (1.1.143) as "degenerate" (1.1.155). Ventidius hopes to goad Antony back into action, placing the blame for his defeat on Cleopatra:

> O, she has deck'd his ruin with her love,
> Led him in golden bands to gaudy slaughter,
> And made perdition pleasing: She has left him
> The blank of what he was:
> I tell thee, Eunuch, she has quite unman'd him:
> [...]
> Unbent, unsinew'd, made a Womans Toy[.] (1.1.170-77)

In a dramatically powerful moment, Antony enters, "*walking with a disturb'd Motion*" (stage direction after 1.1.202). In a soliloquy that is overheard by Ventidius, Antony confirms his despair; throwing himself on the ground, he pathetically declaims: "Lye there, thou shadow of an Emperor; / The place thou pressest on thy Mother Earth / Is all thy Empire now" (1.1.216 ff.). Ventidius upbraids him and tries to rouse him from his inactivity ("Up, up, for Honor's sake; twelve Legions wait you / And long to call you Chief" [1.1.337 f.]), but Antony remains firm: "I will not stir" (1.1.353). He forbids Ventidius to criticize Cleopatra. The topic of love-against-the-world, and the play's subtitle, are invoked in the phrase "No word of *Cleopatra*: She deserves / More World's [sic] than I can lose" (1.1.368 f.). However, his friendship for Ventidius finally makes him agree to leave Cleopatra behind and to join his new troops, ready to fight.

The second act shows us Cleopatra in conversation with Alexas and her maids, Iras and Charmion. Cleopatra has learnt that Ventidius is about to take Antony away; she gives voice to her "transcendent passion" for Antony (2.1.20), a love that knows no bounds, surpassing rational or political considerations. It is above ordinary notions like "that faint word, *Respect*" (2.1.79), a word that, according to Cleopatra, "is for a Wife" (2.1.82) like Octavia but not for a lover like herself. The sober Alexas tells her that erotic love is a bad advisor because passion distorts perception like looking through water (2.1.85 f.). Alexas advises her to desire a personal farewell from Antony. They leave the scene to the Roman commanders; Alexas confronts Antony and Ventidius with Cleopatra's parting gifts (jewels and a ruby bracelet for Antony) and implores Antony to agree to a personal conversation with Cleopatra. Ventidius senses that this will endanger Antony's will to leave, but he cannot prevent the meeting. The ensuing dialogue between Antony and Cleopatra shows Dryden's dramatic and poetic skills to their utmost effect, especially in the quick repartee of its opening lines, which imitates the stichomythies of Ancient Greek drama:

ANTONY. Well, Madam, we are met.
CLEOPATRA.   Is this a Meeting?
Then, we must part?
ANTONY.   We must.
CLEOPATRA.   Who sayes we must?
ANTONY. Our own hard fates.
CLEOPATRA.   We make those Fates our selves.
ANTONY. Yes, we have made 'em; we have lov'd each other
Into our mutual ruin. (2.1.241-45)

Despite Ventidius' warnings, Antony listens to Cleopatra's entreaties; she claims that she was never in love with Julius Caesar, with whom she had an affair before meeting Antony. Her love for him, she claims, is stronger than her attachment to her kingdom or even to her own life. Antony is overwhelmed by renewed passion and renounces the world as a toy that he would willingly pass on to the "Boy" Octavian (2.1.444). Instead of joining his troops, he decides to spend the night with her: "how I long for night! / That both the sweets of mutual love may try, / And once Triumph o're *Cæsar* ere we dye." (2.1.460 ff.)

In act 3, we see Antony and Cleopatra joined in a harmonious embrace. They idealize their love with references to classical mythology, referring to each other as "*Venus*" and "*Mars*" (the Roman goddess of love and the god of war, 3.1.11). Antony wants to avoid Ventidius, who has to physically pull him back in order to talk to him. The general has brought Antony's best friend Dollabella back to Alexandria, in a last attempt to remind him of his military and political duties. But even his wife Octavia and his two little daughters, whom Ventidius brings on next, at first seem unable to make Antony place "duty" above "love" (3.1.316 f.). Both Dollabella and Ventidius urge the wavering and "distracted" (3.1.346) Antony to follow the directions of "Justice and Pity" (3.1.340), which are on the side of his wife and children. Antony, moved by Octavia's pleas, embraces his children: "I am vanquish'd: take me, / *Octavia;* take me, Children; share me all." (3.1.362 f.) Soon after this family tableau, the rival queens meet in a confrontation between law and love. But the audience's sympathy is directed towards Cleopatra, who eloquently overrides Octavia's insistence on her legal status by pointing to the strength and legitimacy of her emotions: "I love him better, and deserve him more." (3.1.450) (Apparently, the original casting of a matronly actress as Octavia opposite a physically attractive Cleopatra contributed to this distribution of sympathies in favour of the mistress rather than the wife.)

But Antony cannot bring himself to part with his mistress. At the beginning of act 4 we see him plead with his friend Dollabella to talk to Cleopatra on his behalf: "tell her […] how much I was constrain'd; / I did not this, but with extreamest force" (4.1.31 f.). Dollabella, left to his own devices, expresses his conflict between his friendship for Antony and his own erotic desire for Cleopatra. At this point, Cleopatra enters, talking with her Eunuch Alexas; they are observed by Ventidius. Alexas develops a plan to make Antony jealous, using Dollabella as a foil. Cleopatra hesitates but finally gives in. Ventidius observes her conversation with Dollabella; she puts on a cheerful face as Antony's "bosom-friend" (4.1.153) delivers Antony's parting message to her. However, Dollabella lies to her, saying that Antony's words of goodbye were harsh and cruel. Hearing this, Cleopatra faints, thus proving her true love for Antony. Dollabella immediately regrets his lie ("O cursed, cursed Wretch! / What have I done!" [4.1.169 f.]) and, as soon as Cleopatra has been revived by her maidservants, confesses and accuses himself of having betrayed Antony for the love of Cleopatra (4.1.189). Cleopatra, in turn, confesses to having feigned her excessive kindness to Dollabella in order to make Antony jealous.

Ventidius, who had left before Cleopatra's swoon, now returns with Octavia to observe Dollabella taking Cleopatra's hand. Octavia and Ventidius are quick to tell Antony about what they take to be Dollabella's and Cleopatra's betrayal. Antony at first does not believe them, but Ventidius' arguments are quite realistic:

ANTONY. My Cleopatra?
VENTIDIUS. Your Cleopatra;
Dollabella's Cleopatra:
Every Man's Cleopatra.
ANTONY. Thou ly'st.
VENTIDIUS. I do not lye, my Lord.
Is this so strange? Should Mistresses be left,

And not provide against a time of change?
You know she's not much us'd to lonely nights. (4.1.295-302)

They call upon Alexas as a witness, who insinuates that, having been rejected by Antony, Cleopatra has indeed turned her affections towards Dollabella. Antony is outraged and pushes Alexas out, telling him to go to hell. Octavia feels confirmed in her opinion of Cleopatra as a "faithless Prostitute" (4.1.389), but Antony will not be rid of his love for Cleopatra, so Octavia decides to leave Antony and Alexandria for good and to transfer her "tenderness and care" (4.1.425) to her children in Rome. Left alone, Antony expresses his thoughts in a soliloquy:

> ANTONY. Why was I fram'd with this plain honest heart,
> Which knows not to disguise its griefs and weakness,
> But bears its workings outward to the World?
> I should have kept the mighty anguish in,
> And forc'd a smile at *Cleopatra*'s falshood:
> *Octavia* had believ'd it, and had staid:
> But I am made a shallow-forded Stream,
> Seen to the bottom: all my clearness scorn'd,
> And all my faults expos'd! (4.1.432-40)

This moment is important for our understanding of Antony's character as pure and honest; using the water imagery that is so frequent in this play (cf. Alexas' line about perception being distorted through water, 2.1.86), he literally makes himself transparent to the audience. We can see him "to the bottom". Thus he gains the audience's sympathy for his inability to put a brave face to the accusations against Cleopatra and to pretend that he is no longer in love with her. At this moment, Dollabella enters to entreat Antony to believe in Cleopatra's true love. They are joined by Cleopatra to bear the brunt of Antony's jealousy and anger at love and friendship betrayed. Cleopatra points out that it was a plot devised by Alexas; Antony, though, will not be moved by their pleas for forgiveness, and sends them away, deploring "That you were false, and I could trust no more" (4.1.597).

Antony banishes Dollabella and retreats to the tower of Pharos, from where he observes the sea battle between the Egyptian and Roman fleets. Cleopatra accuses Alexas of having produced her downfall through his false advice. The priest Serapion enters to report that the Egyptian ships have surrendered to Octavian without a fight. In order to save his own skin, Alexas tells Antony that Cleopatra was innocent and has committed suicide. He assumes that the joy to find her still alive will make Antony forget about his misdeeds; Antony, however, now feels deeply guilty himself and takes responsibility for Cleopatra's presumed suicide. He calls upon Ventidius to kill him with his sword, but Ventidius kills himself instead. Antony falls upon his own sword, mortally wounding himself. Cleopatra and her maidservants rush in, and Antony dies in Cleopatra's arms. His final words are a masterpiece of poetic compression:

> Think we have had a clear and glorious day;
> And Heav'n did kindly to delay the storm
> Just till our close of ev'ning. Ten years love,

> And not a moment lost, but all improv'd
> To th' utmost joys: What Ages have we liv'd!
> And now to die each others; and, so dying,
> While hand in hand we walk in Groves below,
> Whole Troops of Lovers Ghosts shall flock about us,
> And all the Train be ours. (5.1.389-97)

Cleopatra decides to join Antony in death and thus to become his true wife: "my Nobler Fate / Shall knit our Spousals with a tie too strong / For *Roman* Laws to break" (5.1.416 ff.). The maidservants bring her a casket with venomous snakes, with which Cleopatra kills herself. The maidservants also die. The play closes with Serapion, bringing in Alexas as a prisoner to be handed over to Octavian, the new ruler, who is just about to enter the city. His final words are directed to the dead lovers:

> [...] Sleep, blest Pair,
> Secure from humane chance, long Ages out,
> While all the Storms of Fate fly o'er your Tomb;
> And Fame, to late Posterity, shall tell,
> No Lovers liv'd so great, or dy'd so well. (5.1.515-19)

It has to be noted that, in many respects, *All for Love* is a formal departure from the dominant conventions of English Restoration tragedy: there is no double plot, there are no heroic couplets, no "amorous geometries, tragicomic minglings, and quick turns" (Sherman 2004: 29) that characterized Dryden's earlier plays and many other contemporary tragicomedies and heroic plays. As stated above, it observes the neoclassical unities and thus more closely resembles the French tragedies of Dryden's contemporary Racine, whose *Phèdre* also dates from 1677. As in Racine's plays, the action in *All for Love* does not unfold in quick turns and surprises, but in relatively slow movements and static tableaux, culminating in Antony's metadramatic verbal compression of "Ten years love" (5.1.391) into one "clear and glorious day" (5.1.389). Similar to Racine, Dryden's tragedy of affect eroticizes the political and politicizes the erotic (cf. Teuber 2008: 174-77). Its relatively slow pace conceals the fact that, as Stuart Sherman has argued, change and the response to change are key elements of Dryden's theatrical imagination. In *All for Love,* the changes and reversals that Antony undergoes between the roles of lover and husband, soldier and hedonist are ultimately all contained in this final moment of self-recognition: "Antony was always, fundamentally the same, possessed of the passion that suffuses this moment and by expansion the whole decade. The last change now is that he knows it." (Sherman 2004: 30)

The theme of *All for Love* is love against the world, certainly, but the force that drives its plot is the difficulty of being emotionally honest, of knowing the heart of one's lover and of knowing the truth about one's own emotional self. In its rather static presentation, it sometimes gives the impression of a drama of ideas. Characters constantly question their own position in relation to others; they also question the medium of language, holding individual words up for inspection – 'love,' 'respect,' 'friendship.' The falsehood of Alexas – the play's villain – misleads Cleopatra from the straight path of emotional authenticity to the crooked ways of dishonesty and untruthfulness. In contrast, Antony's self-recognition in act 4 allows the audience to see through him as through clear water. The final act, a spiritual recognition scene in the Aristotelian sense of *anagnorisis*, culminates in the lovers seeing themselves for what they really and truly are; its tragedy lies in the fact that by then it is too late for them to turn things around. All the lovers can hope for in the afterlife is fame and renown for their unconditional love.

4. Conclusion

Like many earlier heroic plays, *All for Love* is about the siege of a city, Alexandria. In its style and tone, however, it departs from the bombastic speechifying of Dryden's earlier serious drama, most notably *Tyrannick Love* (1669) and *The Conquest of Granada*. *All for Love* sets out to "Prove […] that Love, being an Heroique Passion, is fit for Tragedy" (Dryden, qtd. from Novak 1984: 371). In its idealization and refinement of sensual love and erotic desire, it follows French tragedies like Racine's *Alexandre le Grand* (1665) and French neoclassical theorists like René and Charles de Saint-Évremond, who argued that love was a suitable topic for tragedy. Critics have pointed out that the portrayal of Antony and Cleopatra, in showing "how sensual passion on the level of a monarch and his mistress might be viewed as an heroic emotion" (Novak 1984: 375) bears out some resemblances to the relationship of Charles II and his mistress, Louise de Kéroualle, Duchess of Portsmouth:

> At a time when the country was enraged by the exalted position of a courtesan in the court, and a French and Catholic courtesan at that, Dryden surrounds such love with some magical virtues. Dryden's Antony and Cleopatra have done great things in their lives, but nothing greater than the degree to which they sacrifice everything for love. (Ibid.: 375 f.)

Their love is certainly sensual and sexual, but it assumes a quality of "innocence and purity" (ibid.: 376) in Dryden's verse. It can even be read as a "moral apology" (Kews 2004: 145) for the lovers, and, by allegorical extension, for King Charles and his mistress. Its success eclipsed Dryden's competitor Charles Sedley's version of *Antony and Cleopatra* (1677), which painted a much more critical picture of the lustful king and his manipulative mistress.

Thus, whereas many other early modern writers tried to draw a moral and political lesson from the erotic and wasteful relationship between Antony and Cleopatra, Dryden's version avoids political allegory. As Richard Kroll observes, "[t]he entire action […] describes a complete political vacuum" (2007: 258), an emptiness in which the characters are "stranded in the midst of the putatively dramatic situation" (ibid.: 259). Nevertheless, the monumentalized ('heroic') lovers manage to gain the audience's sympathies. Dryden's Antony and Cleopatra are ultimately allowed to triumph: even in death, they will receive eternal fame as two of the greatest lovers in history. But the glory they reach is no longer the same as in earlier heroic plays. Antony and Cleopatra escape from the formulaic posturing and rather absurd speeches of heroes and heroines in earlier heroic plays. Their characters are presented in a more domestic, even 'realistic' fashion, occasionally bordering on comedy ("Well, Madam, we are met" [2.1.241]). They are human rather than superhuman, pointing forward to later developments in the history of British drama, such as 18th-century sentimental comedy (see chapter 10) and domestic tragedy (see chapter 11). This is what makes *All for Love* the most accessible of Dryden's serious plays, and Dryden's later statement that "I never writ anything for myself but Antony and Cleopatra [i.e. *All for Love*]" (qtd. from Novak 1984: 389) finds a positive echo in the fact that this is often considered to be his best play.

Bibliography

Primary Sources

Dryden, John. 1956-2002. *The Works of John Dryden*. H. T. Swedenberg, Jr., et al. (eds.). 20 vols. Berkeley/Los Angeles, et al.: U of California P.
—. 1984 [1678]. *All for Love; or, The World Well Lost*. In: Maximillian E. Novak (ed.). *The Works of John Dryden*. Vol. XIII. Berkeley/Los Angeles, et al.: U of California P. 2-111.

Annotated Bibliography

Berensmeyer, Ingo. 2007. *"Angles of Contingency": Literarische Kultur im England des siebzehnten Jahrhunderts*. Tübingen: Niemeyer.
 An investigation into the cultural underpinnings of English neoclassicism, which form the basis of Dryden's work.
Clarke, William S. 1932. "The Definition of the 'Heroic Play' in the Restoration Period." In: *Review of English Studies* 8: 437-44.
 A crucial reference point for modern scholarship dealing with later 17th-century serious drama.
Hume, Robert D. 1976. *The Development of English Drama in the Late Seventeenth Century*. Oxford: Clarendon P.
 The most comprehensive history of English Restoration drama available; useful as a reference tool for the topic.
Kamm, Jürgen. 1996. *Der Diskurs des heroischen Dramas: Eine Untersuchung zur Ästhetik dialogischer Kommunikation in der englischen Restaurationszeit*. Trier: WVT.
 A highly systematic study of communication models in the Restoration period, combined with a detailed analysis of 17th-century heroic drama.
King, Bruce (Ed.). 1968. *"All for Love": A Collection of Critical Essays*. Englewood Cliffs, NJ: Prentice-Hall.
 Contains useful, though in some cases somewhat dated perspectives on Dryden's All for Love.

Kroll, Richard. 2007. "The Political Economy of All for Love." In: Richard Kroll. *Restoration Drama and "The Circle of Commerce": Tragicomedy, Politics, and Trade in the Seventeenth Century.* Cambridge: Cambridge UP. 253-62.

A central chapter on Dryden's All for Love *in a magisterial study on the economic and political contexts of later 17th-century drama.*

Novak, Maximillian E. & Alan Roper. 1984. "Commentary on *All for Love*." In: *The Works of John Dryden.* Vol. XIII. Berkeley/Los Angeles, et al.: U of California P. 363-440.

Provides detailed explanatory notes to All for Love.

Winn, James Anderson. 1989. *John Dryden and His World.* New Haven: Yale UP.

The best and most detailed biography of Dryden to date; also useful as a reference source to Restoration culture.

Zwicker, Steven N. (ed.). 2004. *The Cambridge Companion to John Dryden.* Cambridge: Cambridge UP.

The most comprehensive and student-friendly introduction to the life and works of John Dryden.

Further Secondary Literature

Barish, Jonas A. 1981. *The Antitheatrical Prejudice.* Berkeley/Los Angeles et al.: U of California P.

Greenblatt, Stephen. 1988. *Shakespearean Negotiations: The Circulation of Social Energy in Renaissance England.* Berkeley/Los Angeles, et al.: U of California P.

Hunter, G. K. 1997. *English Drama 1586-1642: The Age of Shakespeare.* Oxford: Oxford UP.

Kews, Paulina. 2004. "Dryden's Theatre and the Passions of Politics." In: Zwicker 2004. 131-55.

Pfeiffer, K. Ludwig. 2009 [1977]. "Struktur- und Funktionsprobleme der Allegorie." In: Ingo Berensmeyer & Nicola Glaubitz (eds.). *Von der Materialität der Kommunikation zur Medienanthropologie: Aufsätze zur Methodologie der Literatur- und Kulturwissenschaften 1977-2009.* Heidelberg: Winter. 159-87.

Sherman, Stuart. 2004. "Dryden and the Theatrical Imagination." In: Zwicker 2004. 15-36.

Teuber, Bernhard. 2008. "Die Tragödie als Theater der Macht: Repräsentation und Verhandlung königlicher Souveränität bei Seneca und im frühneuzeitlichen Drama der Romania." In: Roger Lüdeke & Virginia Richter (eds.). *Theater im Aufbruch: Das europäische Drama der Frühen Neuzeit.* Tübingen: Niemeyer. 155-80.

Vickers, Brian. 1999. *English Renaissance Literary Criticism.* Oxford: Oxford UP.

Womersley, David (ed.). 2000. *Restoration Drama: An Anthology.* Oxford: Blackwell.

10. SENTIMENTAL COMEDY:
RICHARD STEELE'S *THE CONSCIOUS LOVERS*

VERA NÜNNING & IRINA BAUDER-BEGEROW

1. Steele's *The Conscious Lovers*: An Unfashionable Classic?

With 26 performances following the first night on 7 November 1722 at Drury Lane Theatre and re-openings in every London season up to 1775, Sir Richard Steele's *The Conscious Lovers* was spectacularly successful and one of the most influential plays of the 18th century. In print, *The Conscious Lovers* proved to be even more profitable. The three editions published in 1722/23 were followed by 45 in the ensuing 77 years, among them translations into German, Italian, and French (cf. Ellis 1991: 54). Moreover, George I allowed the play to be dedicated to him and awarded Steele (1672-1729) a gratuity to the amount of £500.

In spite of its extraordinary reception history, this famous drama, which has come to be regarded as the prototypical 'sentimental comedy,' did not appeal to later audiences in the same way as it did to contemporary audiences; it began to sink into oblivion in the early 19th century. Especially 21st-century readers find it difficult to relate to the play since they are used to different kinds of character and speech. Furthermore, present-day notions of authenticity and expectations regarding the plot conform to patterns of perception and changing viewing habits based on short-term attention induced by television formats and video clips. Whereas 'Restoration comedies' (see chapter 8) have fared well as far as modern repertoires are concerned, the sentimental comedy is supposed to be unpalatable to the taste of modern theatre-goers.

In order to explain why strikingly few 18th-century plays have gained the status of 'literary classics,' one has to take into account a number of different, yet related factors: the cultural context and the preoccupations of 18th-century readers and authors, the emergent culture of sentiment, the generic features of comedy and the poetological debates of the times (see chapter 9).

Whereas nowadays the terms 'sensibility' and 'sentiment' have decidedly pejorative connotations, smacking of melodrama and sentimentality, these terms carried very positive implications in the 18th century, especially from the 1740s onwards. To say, for example, that someone had 'sensibility' suggested a very attractive character. Originally these terms did not only refer to emotions; up to the middle of the 18th century, 'sentiment' also meant 'opinion,' which only slowly became associated with feelings and 'moral' attitudes. Sensibility referred to a (physical) ability similar to our contemporary term 'sensitivity;' its meanings included a capacity for empathy as well as one's emotional affection by the actions and feelings of others. Such sentimental values were closely connected to a new image of man; in concord with (later) European thinkers like Jean-Jacques Rousseau (1712-1778), latitudinarian clergymen and the Earl of Shaftesbury believed as early as the beginning of the 18th century that man was by nature a 'good' and social animal. Later, philosophers like Adam Smith (1723-1790) and David Hume (1711-1776) presumed that women and men were able to adopt the perspective of others, that they had compassion and naturally felt sympathy when they imagined, for instance, a fellow human being tortured. To be good-natured, to feel benevolence for others, and to express these 'delicate,' kind, and 'tender' feelings in polite behaviour was held to be a natural characteristic of man. Sensibility and sentiment thus had a wide range of positive connotations; they were closely connected to refined emotions and supposed to lead to a kind of behaviour that benefited one's companions as well as the society at large. It has to be borne in mind, however, that these features, which were talked about as if they were common to mankind, were usually related to the middle and upper ranks. The lower classes led a completely different life; physical labour transformed their bodies, and it was believed that they were basically concerned with egotistic aims ensuring their survival; the fashionable values of sentiment were therefore reserved to the upper ranks and served as a means to demonstrate their alleged superiority (for an overview of the most important values of the culture of sensibility cf. Nünning 1996; Barker-Benfield 1992; Todd 1986).

To be sentimental was therefore something very different from our contemporary understanding of the term; as a matter of fact, to be sentimental meant to be both fashionable and good. However, the very popularity of the concept proved to be a double-edged sword later on. On the one hand, the values of the culture of sentiment initiated and strengthened many humanitarian concerns; they led to very diverse movements such as the establishment of the Society for the Prevention of Cruelty to Animals, and, of course, provided a boost for abolitionism. On the other hand, the supposed link between ostensively 'sentimental' behaviour and one's own benevolence was conducive to a rather hypocritical staging of sensitivity. The desire to impress others with one's alleged good nature and fashionable behaviour gave rise to a 'cult of sensibility' in which the emotions were divorced from both reason and action. From the middle of the century onwards, 'sentimentality' for many became an end in itself so that the term eventually acquired ambivalent connotations. 'Languishing ladies,' for instance, preferred lying on the sofa and talking about the acuteness of their emotions to visiting the poor or even a friend in distress: They claimed that they would suffer so much in these situations they would faint – and thus preferred to stay at home.

To modern readers, sentimental values and didactic literature seem to be worlds apart. We know that literature was held to teach by example and that plays were meant to 'entertain and instruct' the audience, but didacticism is nowadays often linked to cognitive aspects of morality: The contents of the 'teachings of literature' are moral precepts or Christian values. However, due to the conviction of the importance of emotions and the intimate relation between emotions and reason (nowadays confirmed by insights from neurobiology), feelings came to be thought of as worthy of being both acquired and taught during the 18th century. As a result, it became particularly important for the middling ranks to display the 'correct' virtuous and tender feelings. After all, the growth of the middling ranks was a relatively new phenomenon, closely related to the demographical and cultural changes and the beginnings of the Industrial Revolution. Since this rising social group was interested in establishing its position in society, it claimed virtue and refined feelings as characteristics of its own class. By means of their virtue, they stressed, they were superior not only to the allegedly immoral lower ranks but even to the aristocracy, which they regarded as insincere and of lax (sexual) morals (cf. Nünning 1995: 19-41). The didacticism of Steele's play is best understood in this context: He wanted to demonstrate what 'good' and 'refined' feelings are, and aimed at inciting these sentiments in his audience so that theatre-goers and readers would learn how to feel these emotions and thus become worthy members of society.

Since the traditional characteristics of comedies did not agree with this kind of teaching, the didactic aim "to chasten wit and moralize the stage" (Prologue 28) heavily influenced the kind of comedy that sentimental writers put on stage. The love affairs and intrigues, the folly and deviant behaviour of the often less than perfect characters in comedies could not incite the proper feelings of tenderness, sympathy and pity. In the 17th century, the audience had roared with laughter when a clever young couple outwitted its elders; they had enjoyed the battle of the sexes and were delighted when the dim-witted 'fops' and lusty old men were punished (see chapter 8). This, however, ran counter to sentimental values: To set up bad examples, to reward cruel egotists, and to laugh at pitiful losers did not contribute to the moral education of the audience.

As early as 1698, Jeremy Collier had acidly criticized earlier comedies in his pamphlet *A Short View of the Immorality and Profaneness of the English Stage*; and even though the plays written in the 1690s did not really deserve this diatribe, his text triggered a controversy which lasted well into the 18th century. This prepared the ground for Steele's success: People recognized that they were faced with a new, morally rewarding kind of play. Unlike its predecessors, this innovative kind of drama, which was influenced by the values of sensibility, lacked the obviously comical. Now stripped of 'low laughter,' the sentimental comedy came to share many features of the tragedy.

As journalist, Member of Parliament, and manager of the Drury Lane Theatre, Steele was in a position to realize his reform agenda on stage. Long before the curtain was raised on *The Conscious Lovers*, the author had propagated the new values of sentiment (as far as they were developed at the time) in his early pamphlet *The Christian Hero* (1701). More importantly, he developed his ideas in the influential journals *The Tatler* and *The Spectator*, two standard-setting moral magazines he co-edited with Joseph Addison. Unlike severer critics who wanted to close the theatres, he saw the potential of combining entertainment and moral advice (cf. *Tatler* 16.4.1709). His early plays *The Funeral* (1701), *The Lying Lover* (1703), and *The Tender Husband* (1705) already showed a departure from traditional comic forms. We can therefore witness a gradual emergence of sentimental features on stage, even though *The Conscious Lovers* is widely regarded as his first full-fledged 'sentimental comedy.' Earlier plays such as Colley Cibber's *Love's Last Shift* (1696) and *The Careless Husband* (1704), for instance, employed conventions characteristic of both sentimental and Restoration comedies.

Nonetheless, the opening night of *The Conscious Lovers* was preceded by an extraordinary publicity campaign between partisans and critics of sentimental values. The prologue (written by Leonard Welsted) advertised the play as an audacious attempt to displace the corrupt and immoral "strategems" (Prologue, 3) of earlier comedy. Obviously, the play annoyed traditionalists, who attacked Steele personally, accusing him not only of commercialism but also of dilettantism since he flouted hitherto widely acknowledged functions of comedy (cf. Hynes 2004: 146).

Sentimental comedies do indeed differ from earlier plays, in particular from Restoration comedies. The characteristics of both sub-genres become most obvious in comparison: Both differ markedly as far as speech and dialogue, the allocation of information, perspective structure, *dramatis personae*, and depiction of characters, plot and closure, norms and values as well as intended effects are concerned (for a detailed overview of the characteristics of sentimental plays as opposed to Restoration plays cf. Barkhausen 1983; Nünning/Nünning 1998: 103-08). Though many critics have pronounced it impossible to define or, indeed, identify the features of the sub-genre (cf. Bevis 1988: 146 ff.; Loftis 1959: 127-32), one can roughly characterize sentimental comedies as being informed by the intended effect on the audience, whose moral emotions were to be incited and developed. This overall aim manifests itself in the conception of the characters, which are mainly used to embody the values of sensibility, compensate for the lack of intrigues and deception, emphasize the 'inner conflicts' and feelings of the protagonists as well as foreground the use of language and dialogue. Our interpretation of Steele's play will show to what extent the typical features of sentimental comedies shape this drama, which can be thought of as a paradigmatic embodiment of the genre. Moreover, we will try to provide an insight into the main features of sentimental comedies in general.

2. *The Conscious Lovers*

In his preface to the play, Richard Steele famously said that his aim was to provide a "joy too exquisite for laughter." This remark is both pertinent – it came to be a kind of motto for his successors – and astonishing: What is a comedy without laughter? What might seem rather quaint and old-fashioned today was both radical and innovative at the time. Steele made an attempt to provide an answer to the harsh criticism of the alleged immorality of comedies, which, in an increasingly moral society, threatened to render them both unattractive and unimportant. As a result, he not only used the stage to promote the new ideas about human nature, but at the same time managed to meet the taste of the audience and make the play as profitable as possible. The sentimental features of Steele's play become particularly evident when one looks at its predecessor and intertextual model, the Latin play *Andria* by Terence (166 BC). While the plot is rather similar to Steele's play, it displays many of the characteristics of comedy and clearly abides by traditional rules.

In *The Conscious Lovers* and in most sentimental plays, the family is shown to be a unit based not only on financial but also on emotional and moral relationships. The parents, and with them characters of the older generation, are shown in a positive light (cf. Ellis 1991: 52), whereas servants represent (now negatively connoted) features of the heroes of earlier comedies. As an important part of the new middle class, rich merchants are now placed on a par with people who were formerly thought to be their superiors. Furthermore, the promotion of new values of sentiment throughout the play deeply informs the structure and diction of the play. Passages with quick repartee are next to non-existent, whereas the integration of many moral speeches is striking. As a consequence, we are not confronted with the suspense of a tight plot but instead with the addition of scenes which at first appear strangely unconnected to the action.

2.1 The 'World of the Story': Characters and Plot

As in most sentimental plays, the constellation of characters is firmly rooted in the middle class; but the main characters are part of the more mundane merchant world. The introduction of a merchant as a positive character is in itself an innovation, since tradesmen were held to be part of the 'monied interest,' which, in opposition to the old 'landed interest,' was supposed to be potentially dangerous: After all, they might profit from a war which would be England's ruin, and were not allowed to vote or have a seat in parliament. While merchants slowly came to be respected as necessary and valuable parts of the commonwealth, they were still widely regarded with suspicion. Nonetheless, merchants are depicted positively in this play. As a foreign trader who has become immensely rich through his involvement in the Eastern trade, Mr. Sealand is presented as a respectable character whose daughter Lucinda is set to marry Jack Bevil, the son of the squire Sir John Bevil, who belongs to the landed gentry.

Although he is a very virtuous character who wants to obey his father, Jack Bevil is not happy with the forthcoming wedding; he is in love with Indiana, a beautiful orphan without any social connections. His bride Lucinda also regards the marriage with dread, since she has lost her heart to Bevil's friend Myrtle, who longs to marry her. What stands in the way of the four lovers is not only the fact that their fathers want to match them in a different way, but that the children are set on respecting the wishes of their parents. Moreover, the nobleman Cimberton, another suitor for Lucinda's hand, enters the stage in the second act. However, he is not taken seriously but ridiculed as a fop throughout the play; a fate often met by the aristocratic characters, who are usually shown to be both lusty and immoral. After the usual number of complications, which in this play cannot be regarded as comic, the orphan Indiana is revealed to be Sealand's first daughter whom everyone had long believed to be lost and dead. After this, everything can end well.

This ending has been read as the triumph of bourgeois sensibility. Nevertheless, one has to take into account that among the middling ranks, both money and reputation were widely held to be more important reasons for marriage than love, at least until the beginning of the 19th century. As in many 18th-century plays and novels, love and fortune coincide, and the protagonists are allowed financially profitable marriages which gratify their feelings at the same time. As co-heiress to Sealand's fortune, Indiana becomes an eligible daughter-in-law for the Bevil family, who are representative of the 'landed interest.' Moreover, Sir Bevil comes to accept love as a positive ingredient of married life and accepts the importance of emotions – as he can now afford to do so. Steele therefore skilfully utilizes the prestigious traditional status of the Bevils in order to demonstrate their compatibility with emerging middle-class values and propagate new ideas of morality.

The hierarchy within the *dramatis personae* also supports sentimental values. The characters are grouped according to their virtue; characters embodying middle-class morals become the protagonists of the play. Though young Bevil may appear to be a boring example of traditional virtue to modern readers, he differs markedly from earlier heroes. His prodigious display of morality marks him as a member of a 'new' and rising social class who reads edifying literature at night. As a representative of a new ideal of the gentleman who embodies sentimental and moral values instead of wit, Jack Bevil is "indeed hard to believe in" (Ellis 1991: 47): Not only does he sport tender but always honourable feelings for the languishing Indiana, he also obediently seeks to obtain his father's consent although he – unlike the hero of Terence's play – is financially independent through a maternal legacy. Thus, he does not need the good will of his father, but still he sees himself bound by a "religious vow" (2.1.) not to marry Indiana without his father's consent. This sentimental hero finds his counterpart in the afflicted heroine Indiana, who enters the stage as an early epitome of the 'damsel in distress:' young, beautiful, impoverished, and orphaned. Just like Antonio Scarlatti's uncomplaining opera heroine Griselda, whom Indiana admires, she patiently endures all tribulations (2.2.). Bevil selflessly supports her to the point of being suspected of secret amorous motives which he, ironically, has, but does not confess to, since they would not be deemed 'right' as he is not in a position to marry her. Even Indiana herself, who is also in love with him, comes to believe in his lack of romantic feelings for her. After his lengthy assurances of being merely motivated by compassion, she finally renounces him in agony. With this altruistic act, she reaches the peak of her ordeals; after all, she has lost her parents in infancy, survived a maritime disaster and was barely able to defend her virginity against a French rogue. The Indiana sub-plot echoes elements of the immoral comedy as it creates suspense, and her relationship to Bevil shows some similarities to that of a kept mistress (2.2.).

However, unlike her alter ego in Terence's play, who is suspected of being a courtesan, Indiana is never supposed to be a 'fallen woman' who has lost her chastity.

Her virtue shines through, even during her hardships. Sir Bevil is taken aback when he first encounters her at a masked ball admiring "[h]er uncommon air, her noble modesty, the dignity of her person" (1.1.). Even Sealand has to forget about his prejudices on becoming acquainted with her; "so worthy an object, so accomplish'd a lady, as your sense and mien bespeak" (5.3.). As a woman who patiently endures affliction and firmly resists harassment, Indiana is a representative of the ideal young woman. In concord with the values of sensibility, the main couple's 'conscious love' (i.e. sentimental love), which the title of the play accentuates, is admirable because of their moral superiority rather than the erotic appeal which characterizes the protagonists of the Restoration comedy. Thus, physical tokens of love like kisses are reserved for the lower classes, as Lucinda's maid Phillis realizes, who is the subject of yet another (low) love plot (cf. 3.1.).

Stock characters like the rake or the coquette, who were of major importance in earlier plays, are doubly marginalized by being either out of fashion or relegated to the servant class. By putting the rogue and the coquette on the level of the lower orders, Steele ridicules the former models of behaviour that were of central importance to the heroes and heroines of Restoration comedies. Jack Bevil's manservant Tom – "the prince of poor coxcombs" (1.1.) – likes to pose as a libertine, and Lucinda's maid Phillis acts out the part of the coquette. Phillis, whom her mistress thinks of as a "pert merry hussy" (3.1.), refers to the negative view of their assumed roles: "O Tom! Tom! Is it not a pity that you should be so great a coxcomb and I so great a coquet, and yet be such poor devils as we are?" (1.1.) Moreover, Sir Bevil's 'good,' faithful servant Humphrey exposes the degenerated image of the rogue when he derides Tom's self-fashioning: "I hope the fashion of being lewd and extravagant, despising of decency and order, is almost at an end, since it is arrived at persons of your quality" (1.1.).

As far as the upper middle ranks are concerned, libertinism is a thing of the past. Sir John Bevil is known to have been a rakish figure in his youth, but he has now changed. His son mentions the comic turmoil on his parent's marriage day which resembles typical elements of restoration comedy:

> I have been told, Sir, that, at the time you married, you made a mighty bustle on the occasion. There was a challenging and fighting – scaling walls – locking up the lady – and the gallant under an arrest for fear of killing all his rivals. (1.1.)

When Sir Bevil and his servant Humphrey wear the clothes of Bevil's father at a masquerade, they are followed by a yelling, masked crowd "as if we had been the most monstrous figures in that whole assembly" (1.1.). In the 18th century, the Restoration is as old-fashioned as the late Baron's garments.

The mockery of obsolete Restoration ideals is mainly located at the level of the minor characters. Lucinda's snobbish mother and especially the "formal, philosophical, pedantic" (2.1.) aristocrat Cimberton appear as figures of fun whose intrigues prove to be futile. Their main function is to set up obstacles for the lovers' union and to add a comic tinge to the main plotline. Despite his long pedigree and being "three hundred years an older gentleman than any lover [...] [Lucinda] ever had" (3.1.), the old Cimberton is a weak antagonist for Jack Bevil. The aristocrat reveals his disregard of sentimental values when he examines Lucinda's body as if he were purchasing a horse: "I am considering her, on this occasion, but as one that is to be pregnant" (3.1.). When Indiana is finally revealed to be Lucinda's elder half-sister who is to share her inheritance, Cimberton realizes that he will get considerably less money if he marries her and breaks off his advances as he "was in treaty for the whole" (5.3.). In consequence, he exposes himself as a lustful and avaricious fop. Moreover, Mrs. Sealand's unproductive efforts to bring about a marriage with an aristocrat are looked upon with derision. Her attempt at pairing her daughter with her noble kinsman Cimberton is exposed as the motive of a "poor troublesome woman" by Myrtle (2.1.). Besides, a merchant's wife – however blue-blooded her own ancestors might have been – in pursuit of a pure noble lineage is a satiric device in itself. Aristocratic values are therefore ridiculed not only through the foppish, weak, and lusty Cimberton, but also through Mrs. Sealand's pathetic efforts to re-establish the alleged link between her family and the nobility.

The distance between the ideal characters and the others is confirmed by the fact that there is general agreement about the traits of good and foolish figures. Except for Mrs. Sealand, the vain Cimberton is condemned by all of the characters. Lucinda sees in him only a "phlegmatic fool," and according to Myrtle he exhibits only "very little judgement: [...] No, no; hang him, the rogue has no art, it is poor simple insolence and stupidity." (2.1.) Similarly, Jack Bevil's filial obedience is universally acknowledged and there is no doubt about the merits of the virtuous, beautiful, and long-suffering daughters of Mr. Sealand and of the two fathers.

2.2 Diction and Structure

In addition to the content and the constellation of characters, the morality and the sentiment of the play also inform the tempo of the dialogic exchange between the characters. Moreover, the register differs considerably from colloquial speech: Exalted elocution und an emotionally charged vocabulary form essential parts of the sentimental characters' dialogues. Jack Bevil and Indiana use a style similar to earlier heroic plays and to the use of language of aristocratic characters in 16th- and 17th-century tragedies: They converse with much pathos and in set phrases (and sometimes in rhymes, cf. 2.2.). The lively exchange of verbal blows in quick repartee that was characteristic of Restoration comedy is debased by the fact that it is used by 'low,' uneducated servants. In analogy to Shakespearean plays, however, the lower orders also provide comic relief: Tom's and Phillis' down-to-earth and juicy flirtations (1.1.) provide a contrast to the 'conscious' lovers. As a result, the servants act out the battle of the sexes which the sentimental couples deny themselves.

Sentimental plays tend to give the characters space to express their views without interruption by others: owing to the overall didactic aim, the worthy sentiments of the characters must be treated with respect; they could not be ridiculed. Consequently, the key scene (cf. 2.1.) between Indiana and Jack Bevil features very little interruption; moreover, entire scenes display a virtually monologic structure "punctuated by the occasional enabling 'phatic' interjection from a supposed interlocutor" (Hynes 2004: 151). Abstract concepts such as love, reason, and understanding are meticulously analysed while standard devices in Restoration comedy such as ambiguity or sexual allusions are omitted. Instead, the diction of the sentimental protagonists is marked by clear propositions and sentimental emphasis (cf. 2.2.).

As the few instances of verbal sparring in the main characters' dialogues do not feature diverging opinions, a conciliatory tenor pervades the play. Even the dichotomy between the traditional values of the landed gentry and the newly emerging merchant elite turns out to be only an outward antagonism. Mr. Sealand and Sir John Bevil may fight a comic verbal duel over the importance of "genealogy and descent" (4.2.), yet their concepts of marriage policy complement one another. Moreover, Sealand's verdict about the rise of the merchant class is often cited as an important statement proclaiming the new prominence of commerce in society:

> We Merchants are a Species of Gentry, that have grown into the World this last Century, and are as honourable, and almost as useful, as you landed folks, that have always thought your selves so much above us. (4.2.)

This demonstrates a new self-assurance of a formerly marginalized group that now confidently claims an exalted place in society. Merchants are said to be a species of 'Gentry,' a title reserved for the 'landed gentry.' Consequently, merchants are not only shown to be respectable – as Mr. Sealand and his perfectly virtuous daughters indicate – they are even explicitly said to be just as important and worthy as the landed gentry, whom Sealand refers to as 'folks.'

Since the interests of the landed gentry and the rich merchants are shown to be intertwined, the play lacks a real social conflict – the aristocrat Cimberton is unanimously criticized, and the lower classes are not taken seriously either. Moreover, Jack Bevil's conflict between his love towards Indiana and duty towards his father turns out to be a pseudo clash of interests in the end. Myrtle's jealousy of his alleged rival Jack, whom he believes to be in love with Lucinda, is ungrounded, nor is it developed into a comic, fast-paced plot. Conflicts such as these only serve to induce edifying speeches and scenes of moral demonstration. In addition, there are no real villains: Even Indiana's French would-be-ravisher "on cooler thoughts" (1.2.) desists from pursuing her further. Based on the belief in the positive nature of mankind, Steele's dramatic world is not a natural habitat for thoroughly wicked villains. Novak (1979: 50) is right when he points out that in sentimental plays, characters' flaws just occur to such an extent that they are "led astray by passion or by a lack of proper polish and civilization." The 'duel scene' (4.1.), which according to Steele was his reason for writing the play, serves as a fine example for this statement: this scene is ultimately all about the necessity and ways of circumventing a duel.

Since Jack Bevil thinks solving a conflict with violence foolish, the 'duel scene' becomes a demonstration scene depicting the virtue and repentance of the central characters. In consequence, the strategic moves and combats of wit which were representative of earlier comedies are now replaced by the representation of insight into higher virtues. The quarrel between Myrtle and Jack Bevil, which leads Myrtle to challenge his alleged rival, culminates in Myrtle's realization of his own rashness. When he displays "quick anger," Jack Bevil meets him in a "cool manner" and with "moderation" (4.1.). As the epitome of sentimental virtue, Jack disapproves of the duel, which continued to be an important way of resolving conflicts of 'honour' until the early 19th century. It is not before Myrtle questions Indiana's virtue that Bevil consents to meet his friend's challenge. Of course, this imprudent move has no impact; when the misunderstanding is cleared, Myrtle admits his defeat and apologizes:

> Dear, Bevil, your friendly conduct has convinced me, that there is nothing manly but what is conducted by reason, and agreeable to the practice of virtue and justice. And yet, how many have been sacrificed to that idol, the unreasonable opinion of men! (4.1)

Critics have stressed that the 'duel' scene is dysfunctional for the play as a whole since it is unconnected to the previous scenes and irrelevant for the progression of the plot. However, the fact that the scene seems rather unrelated to the rest of the play is a typical feature of sentimental drama as well as of sentimental novels. Essential scenes gain their importance not from their position in a causally connected plot, but from the moral lessons which are disclosed by the insights and feelings of the characters. This often leads to long tirades or 'tableau scenes' in which the characters adopt evocative positions and gestures in order to invoke an image similar to a didactic painting.

The lack of external conflicts and a fast-paced plot already points to the sentimental concern with the 'inner world' of the characters. In a crucial scene (2.2.) Jack Bevil and Indiana negotiate sentimental values; otherwise nothing else happens. This dialogue illustrates that possessing sensibility not only entails the ability to have benevolent feelings, but also being aware of and reflecting upon one's emotional world.

> BEVIL JUN. If I might be vain of any thing in my power, Madam, 'tis that my understanding from all your sex, has mark'd you out, as the most deserving object of my esteem. [...]
> INDIANA. [E]steem is the result of reason, and to deserve it from good sense, the height of human glory; nay, I had rather a man of honour should pay me that, than all the homage of a sincere and humble lover.
> BEVIL JUN. You certainly distinguish right, Madam, love often kindles from external merit only –
> INDIANA. But esteem arises from a higher source, the merit of the soul –
> BEVIL JUN. True – And great souls only can deserve it. (2.2.)

In many scenes, the features of love, esteem, merit, understanding, reason, mind, good sense, and judgment, as well as the differences between these emotions are elaborated or at least represented. Modern readers have a hard time reconstructing all the subtle differences of meaning of the terms, but it is this kind of awareness of the 'refined emotions' and the search for even more subtle and delicate feelings, as well as the recognition of their close connection to both reason and virtue, which mark the merit of the sentimental hero or heroine. Just as Restoration protagonists displayed their wit with relish, the central couple in the sentimental comedy delights in this almost ostentatious exhibition of feelings that was meant to stir the emotions of the audience.

2.3 Sentiment and Didactic Impact

Nearly all of the features of Steele's play are influenced by his commitment to the idea that literature should 'teach by example.' In order to inspire altruistic and elevated feelings in his viewers, he uses morally superior characters and puts them in positions in which they could illustrate (and impart) their own refined emotions. In concord with the new – and controversial – belief that man is by nature a good and social being, Steele models his figures on Shaftesbury's positive idea of man and thus constructs his main characters as perfect embodiments of virtue and politeness. The Hobbesian notion *homo homini lupus est* has become outmoded in Steele's dramatic world; instead, benevolence and sympathy are introduced as the main characteristics of the protagonists. Empathy, pity, and charity likewise are held in high esteem, and even the parents, the traditional stumbling blocks in love comedies that usually have to be outwitted by the lovers, mean well. Sir Bevil is far from being a tyrannical father who forces his son into marriage. As the servant Humphrey realizes, the uneasiness of father and son merely results from "their fear of giving each other pain" (1.1.). Even the friendship of Jack Bevil and Myrtle is spotless, in spite of the fact that one of them is engaged to the other's beloved and apart from the near-catastrophe of the duel. Moreover, honesty and frankness replace the deception strategies which determined characters' actions in earlier comedies.

In concord with the values of sensibility, the play represents a new, ideal concept of marriage based on mutual affection, which Steele had propagated in his essays in *The Tatler* and *The Spectator*. In accordance with the concerns of a rising middle class, the characters in the play stress the emotional ties of the nuclear family. Even Mr. Sealand, who arranges the marriage settlement with the Bevil family in a completely businesslike manner, postpones his daughter's impending wedding on the grounds that the bridegroom is obviously in love with another woman. Moreover, despite his declarations of filial obedience, Jack Bevil prefers to marry for love and not for money. Steele therefore attributes clashing interests and a cynical view on marital life only to the elder generation, in particular to the snobbish Mrs. Sealand, who tries to marry her daughter off for purely opportunistic reasons.

Most of the scenes, however, are geared towards moving the audience, if possible even to tears. The melodramatic reunion of Indiana with her long-lost father (5.3.) does not come as a surprise to the spectators, who are already aware of the kinship between the two. Still, the characters on stage lack this knowledge; only Sealand's sister recognizes her brother at first glance. This use of dramatic irony is typical of sentimental plays: The imbroglio is not a means of letting the audience enjoy the comic entanglement on stage and laugh about the (virtuous) characters; rather it serves to enhance the compassion of viewers, thus teaching them how to feel refined emotions.

The reunion between the family members also stresses the importance of poetic justice in the play. In correspondence with prevalent ideas in the 18th century, divine providence orders the events in a benevolent and just way, while the afflicted orphan waits passively for her reward. Interestingly enough, not only the virtue of the female protagonist is rewarded, but the behaviour of Jack Bevil is evaluated according to the same criteria. Thus, Mr. Sealand says about his future son-in-law: "[T]ell him [...] that this day he still shall be a bridegroom [...]. Tell him, the reward of all his virtues waits on his acceptance." (5.3.) In contrast to the traditional idea that men have to be active and fight aggressively for honour and love, the play places the male protagonist in a position that is usually reserved for women. Indiana and Jack "have little to do besides express their mutual esteem and talk about philosophy" and "wait to see what will happen" (Hynes 2004: 150 f.). Instead of relying on the actions of the leading couple, the happy ending results from the coincidence that the central characters are revealed to be closely related. The hero Jack Bevil does not contribute to this discovery at all; he is a quite resigned character who is heard to "sigh in the most heavy manner" about his troubles (1.1.).

Indeed, it is Myrtle who devises comic subterfuge to impede Lucinda's marriage to Cimberton. At first, Myrtle and Tom smuggle themselves into the Sealand household disguised as lawyers who insinuate that because of legal restrictions, Cimberton's elderly uncle Sir Geoffrey must affirm the engagement of the foppish suitor to Lucinda. In their second coup, Myrtle impersonates this noble relative as a preposterous and farcical *senex amans*, thus conveniently ridiculing the aristocracy once again. These stratagems provide a lively counterpoint to the main plot, but they are unnecessary since it is Indiana's status as Sealand's daughter that counts. The ineffectiveness of both ventures thus shows that trust in divine guidance is superior to the deception of others in order to gain one's ends.

A number of heterogeneous dramatic devices thus serve a didactic effect, helping establish the theatre as a "school of morality." In this regard, the comment about *The Conscious Lovers* in Henry Fielding's novel *Joseph Andrews* (1742), uttered by the very likeable, boisterous yet virtuous character Parson Adams, speaks volumes: in his opinion, the drama is the only play that is "fit for a Christian to read" because of the passages that are "almost solemn enough for a sermon" (Fielding 1999: 266). In a comic novel like Fielding's, this is an acid criticism of the morality of the play. But even though both sentimental values and Steele's drama were not to everyone's taste, it is important to remember that the play managed to imbibe, illustrate and popularize new values, making the reading and watching of plays a respectable endeavour.

3. Conclusion

Taking up, negotiating, and shaping current ideas, sentimental dramas helped propagate new values. Arguably, it was the genre of the sentimental comedy that paved the way for the entry of the values of sensibility into the literature of the 18th century. Since in the early decades there was still a very close connection between the finer, social emotions and reason as well as moral principles, it was possible to express such feelings in short monologues and discuss them in the dialogues between the virtuous characters. Moreover, tableaux scenes helped to visualize refined sentiments. The play thus managed to deal with important topical issues of the times as well as propagating the new position of the middling ranks. In addition, the drama expressed the optimistic Enlightenment belief in the understanding and malleability of men: Human beings could be educated and the formerly denigrated stage was held up as the proper place for important parts of this education.

With the development of the culture of sensibility, the greater stress on emotions, and the differentiation between their finer nuances, it became more difficult for plays to express and negotiate current values. While the drama had proved to be the genre most sensitive to the changes in the mental climate, the novel turned out to be better equipped to 'teach' the values of sensibility. As Virginia Woolf argued a century ago, the dramatic mode lends itself to abstraction and the presentation of intense passions, while the epic, narrative mode is geared towards dealing with details, with the development of nuances, and more subtle emotions. Therefore, it does not come as a surprise that from the 1740s onwards, the values of sensibility became more popular in novels than in plays. With the psychological realism that emerged in the novels of Samuel Richardson, Henry Mackenzie, or Frances Burney, prose fiction was technically better equipped to portray the inner worlds of characters. Simultaneously, the epistolary novel, which lends itself to the spontaneous expression of feelings, began its career as the most popular mode of writing of the time. The 'easy and familiar' style of letters appealed to the polite middling ranks, who read, for instance, history books written in letters, political pamphlets, conduct books, and, of course, sentimental novels in epistolary form. The presentation of refined feelings, the delicate forms of perception, and the portrayal of consciousness became a common feature of many novels, even of the late novels of Henry Fielding, the harsh critic of sentimentality.

In this respect it is not surprising that the heyday of sentimental drama was relatively short. Despite the enormous impact of the Theatre Licensing Act (1737), which effectively silenced more humorous and satirical dramatists like Henry Fielding, and irrespective of the tremendous success of plays like *The Conscious Lovers* and *The Provoked Husband* (1728) by John Vanbrugh and Colley Cibber, the genre soon lost its former popularity. In contrast to a commonly held opinion – fostered by Oliver Goldsmith, who claimed to reintroduce laughter into the comedy in the 1770s – the sentimental drama never succeeded in ousting laughing comedies from the stage. Even during Steele's creative period between 1710 and 1728, more 'true comedies' than sentimental plays were presented. As a consequence, the development of English comedy throughout the 18th century is characterized by an alternation of 'truly' comic and sentimental features.

Steele's ambition to moralize the English stage was taken up, however, in the works of his followers Edward Moore (*Gil Blas*, 1751) and Richard Cumberland, whose most successful plays, *The Brothers* (1769) und *The West Indian* (1771), can be regarded as paradigmatic examples of the sentimental genre with long moralizing conversations between altruistic and self-sacrificing characters.

In addition to these plays, comedies conforming to older genre traditions continued to be written and performed. The oeuvres of George Colman, Samuel Foote, and Arthur Murphy show that this tradition was still strong – though it marked a continuation of conventions which cannot be regarded as 'typical' of or specific to the 18th century. Though some of these plays mock sentimental values, not all of them do so; Murphy's plays, for instance, do not completely reject moral sentiments, and especially Oliver Goldsmith's and Richard Sheridan's works feature benevolent, good, and tenderhearted heroes; refined feelings and kindness were still attractive character attributes in their plays (see chapter 12). The culture of sensibility thus continued to influence literature throughout the 18th and 19th century – it was only the choice of genre, modes of writing, and emphasis that changed.

Bibliography

Primary Sources

Steele, Richard. 1723 [1722]. *The Conscious Lovers*. London: J. Tonson.

Annotated Bibliography

Barkhausen, Jochen. 1983. *Die Vernunft des Sentimentalismus: Untersuchung zur Entstehung der Empfindsamkeit und empfindsamen Komödie in England*. Tübingen: Narr.
A survey of the history of the idea of sentimentalism from its beginnings in the works of Locke and Shaftesbury up to Richard Steele; also analyses opposed philosophies such as Calvinism or the thought of Thomas Hobbes.

Bevis, Richard W. 1988. *English Drama: Restoration and Eighteenth Century, 1660-1789*. London: Longman.
This survey links dramatical configurations of the 18th century to contemporary political and social upheaval. With regard to beginning of the 18th century, Bevis highlights the variety of different types of comedy.

Brown, Laura. 1981. *English Dramatic Form, 1660-1760: An Essay in Generic History*. New Haven/London: Yale UP.

The book offers an excellent account of the genre-history of sentimental comedy.

Damrosch, David, Kevin J. H. Dettmar & Stuart Sherman. 2009. *The Longman Anthology of British Literature, Volume 1c: The Restoration and the Eighteenth Century*. New York: Longman.

This anthology contains works of different literary genres and supplements this wide array with non-fictional texts and an excellent introduction. In general, this compilation of canonical and hitherto neglected texts accommodates new research perspectives on the 18th century.

Ellis, Frank Hale. 1991. *Sentimental Comedy: Theory and Practice*. Cambridge: Cambridge UP.

Arguably the best analysis of the genre contrasts the terms 'sentimental,' 'comedy,' and 'sentimental comedy' and discusses a theory of sentimental comedy; it pays regard to both a catalogue of typical structural features and to processes of social change, and applies this theory to ten central plays.

Hynes, Peter. 2004. "Richard Steele and the Genealogy of Sentimental Drama: A Reading of *The Conscious Lovers*." In: *Papers on Language and Literature* 40.2: 142-66.

Discusses The Conscious Lovers *with the twofold aim of showing, firstly, how the play addresses the issue of legitimacy as a social and familial concept and, secondly, Steele's positioning in relation to his literary predecessors.*

Loftis, John. 1959. *Comedy and Society from Congreve to Fielding*. Stanford: Stanford UP.

Outlines the development of English comedy from 1693 to 1737 with regard to the flourishing and decline of Restoration drama.

Novak, Maximillian E. 1979. "The Sentimentality of *The Conscious Lovers* Revisited and Reasserted." In: *Modern Language Studies* 9.3: 48-59.

Takes a stand in the discussion on the genre of sentimental comedy and argues for the term 'sentimentality' as a fitting description for the emotional dimension of the plays.

Schulz, Dieter. 1976. "Richard Steele: *The Conscious Lovers*." In: Heinz Kosok (ed.). *Das englische Drama im 18. und 19. Jahrhundert: Interpretationen*. Berlin: Schmidt. 74-86.

Though some of the terms that are used have been defined in stricter ways later on, this article provides a good general introduction to the play.

Sherbo, Arthur. 1957. *English Sentimental Drama*. Michigan: Michigan State UP.

Important older account that, in contrast to depreciative studies, regards 'sensibility' positively and proposes important criteria for a definition of sentimental drama reaching beyond the emotional dimension.

Todd, Janet. 1986. *Sensibility: An Introduction*. London: Methuen.
A very good introduction into the importance of the concept of sensibility in 18th-century literature, this brief study provides a chapter each on sentimental poetry, plays and novels.

Further Secondary Literature

Barker-Benfield, G. J. 1992. *The Culture of Sensibility: Sex and Society in Eighteenth-Century Britain*. Chicago: U of Chicago P.
Fielding, Henry. 1999 [1742]. *Joseph Andrews and Shamela*. London: Penguin.
Nünning, Vera. 1995. "From 'Honour' to 'Honest': The Invention of the (Superiority of the) Middling Ranks in Eighteenth Century England." In: *Journal for the Study of British Cultures* 2.1: 19-41.
—. 1996. "Die Kultur der Empfindsamkeit: Eine mentalitätsgeschichtliche Skizze." In: Ansgar Nünning (ed.). *Eine andere Geschichte der englischen Literatur: Epochen, Gattungen und Teilgebiete im Überblick*. Trier: WVT. 107-26.
— & Ansgar Nünning. 1998. *Englische Literatur des 18. Jahrhunderts*. Uni-Wissen Anglistik, Amerikanistik. Stuttgart/Düsseldorf, et al.: Klett.

11. Domestic Tragedy:
George Lillo's *The London Merchant, or The History of George Barnwell*

Birgit Neumann

1. Morality Matters: From Heroic Drama to Domestic Tragedy

Beginning in the late 1670s, after heroic drama (see chapter 9) has already replaced the traditionally 'superhuman' characters of classical tragedy with more human ones, the major serious drama of the English theatre becomes increasingly moral, didactic, and, eventually, openly bourgeois: It aims at evoking pity rather than admiration and stresses passive virtue rather than heroic self-assertion; it defines merit in terms of inner moral worth and frequently focuses on domestic material, private citizens, and innocent female protagonists (cf. Brown 1981: 145 f.). The early works in this affective dramatic mode are still indebted to the poetics and politics of the heroic and thus exemplify codes of courtly conduct. Nathaniel Lee's *The Rival Queens* (1677), for instance, features the typical aristocratic and exotic characters of heroic drama. Yet its protagonists are presented in a more domestic, accessible, and sometimes even 'realistic' fashion. What is more, the play portrays its male protagonists "not as active heroes but as passive victims whose dramatic significance is defined by their pathetic situation rather than their aristocratic status" (Brown 1993: 66 f.).

'Domestic tragedy,' a genre which gains in popularity at the beginning of the 18th century, takes this concern with morality and pathos one step further: it essentially eliminates the representation of social status and explores the different facets of inner worth, putting emphasis on sentiment and domesticity. Broadly speaking, domestic tragedy presents us with an action that suggests, "by means of explicit aphorism, exemplary incident, and especially paragon protagonist, a coherent internal moral code that determines our expectations for its characters and our understanding of their world" (Brown 1981: 145). The moral action of domestic tragedy thus involves a pervasive modification of previous dramatic practice and signals a breakdown of classical, mainly aristocratic notions of worth, honour, and decorum that shape the value-system of earlier tragedy. Its concern with the moral significance of private (and not state) affairs deliberately cuts across established generic distinctions between comedy and tragedy. Domestic tragedy substitutes elevation for domesticity, social status for ethical worth, verse for prose and usually features middle-class, and not aristocratic characters. By this token, tragic and comic forms, which are both shaped by a valorization of sensibility, ultimately converge in the moral action and its aesthetics of affect. As a matter of fact, the 'low,' frequently middle-class, protagonist of domestic tragedy and the exemplary hero of sentimental comedy invoke "the same direct internal moral standard as the arbiter of their merits" (ibid.: 147), though the protagonist of domestic tragedy dies a paradigmatic death whilst the hero of sentimental comedy eventually wins the virtuous woman of his choice (cf. ibid.). Intricately bound up with the rising middle class, 18th-century domestic tragedy presents a particularly interesting arena for the discussion of cultural values, frequently indulging in the increasingly pervasive discourse of English national 'character' (cf. Neumann 2009).

The turn of tragedy to domestic affairs and its concern with the moral worth of individual characters is intimately related to larger cultural developments in 18th-century England. Most notably, the emergence of domestic tragedy reflects – and adds to – the growing cultural importance of morality and sensibility, a development which is related to the attempts of the newly emerging middle class to affirm its social status (cf. Feldmann 1983: 24). Sensibility and the sentimental – the affective display of benign generosity – were a matter of vital debate from the 1740s onward. Most contemporary critics maintained that sensibility was a positive influence and a desirable virtue, a virtue that improves the mind of the individual and society in general. Broadly speaking, sensibility valorizes (masculine) sensitivity as a virtue, regarding it as an expression of a natural benevolence, sympathy, and innate goodness (cf. Ellis 1996).

The changes in the understanding of human nature were prepared for by the writings of the latitudinarian clergymen and the Third Earl of Shaftesbury. In his *Inquiry Concerning Virtue and Merit* (1711) he challenged the established view of man as a predominantly evil, corrupt, and egocentric being, striving after ever more power (cf. Feldmann 1983: 27). Instead, Shaftesbury stressed the innate goodness of man. According to Shaftesbury, men and women are endowed with a sense of altruism, social emotions, and even a 'moral sense.' Stressing the benevolent impulses imparted by sentiments, Shaftesbury argued that feelings are an instructive guide to moral conduct, conducive to the improvement of humanity and society. Virtue, Shaftesbury (1790: 81) argues, lies in the natural affections, "such as are founded in Love, Complacency, Goodwill and in a Sympathy with the Kind or Species."

Sensibility and concomitant notions of morality and individual worth had a special appeal to middle-class England at a time of steady economic growth. According to Paul Langford (1989: 461), sensibility allowed the middle class to define and express "a code of manners which challenged aristocratic ideals and fashions" and which provided them with the opportunity to imagine and create responses of individual and institutional reform. As such, the emphasis on feeling, benevolence, and morality is best understood as a part of the reformation of the code of genteel conduct necessary for the middle class to contest the social exclusiveness of the aristocracy and of reconciling the new mercantile system with ethical standards (cf. ibid.).

Given the interest of the middle ranks in morals and reform, it is not surprising that domestic tragedy, a largely 'bourgeois genre' (cf. Brown 1981), is, to a large extent, defined by its didactic intention, i.e. by its perpetuation of moral standards (cf. Adamian 1968). Characteristically, as Laura Brown (1981) has shown, these moral standards are displayed as an inclusive norm. Whereas the central protagonist of classical tragedy embodies an ideal that is defined by its singularity and hence its distance from the behaviour of the common man and from the conventions of the everyday world, the morality of the hero of domestic tragedy is posited as an absolute standard, seemingly immediately accessible and imitable. This is why the moral action of domestic tragedy, quite unlike earlier forms of tragedy, "can make a direct association between the standards of judgment it applies to its characters and the sympathetic emotional responses of its audience" (ibid.: 145), which ideally embraces and imitates those standards in the real world. Because domestic tragedy presents its ethical standards as an inclusive norm it is sometimes considered as a democratic kind of theatre. Domestic tragedy thus illustrates Markman Ellis's (1996: 23) contention that "the choice of genre effects [sic] not only how something is said, but also what is said, and to whom."

2. Some Characteristics of Domestic Tragedy

Viewed formally, domestic tragedy is characterized by a number of features and strategies which serve its didactic aims. Characterization relies heavily on clear contrasts between good and evil characters and is thus marked by simplification and generalization (cf. Nünning 1998). Domestic tragedy centres on a paragon protagonist, an exemplary or reformable character, whose morality, merit, and virtue are illustrated and confirmed in numerous incidents in the plot (cf. Brown 1981: 157). The tragic hero is frequently drawn from the middle class and, accordingly, embodies its moral standards. To throw into relief the virtues of the hero, he is usually contrasted with an evil villain, who serves as a negative advocate for the values put forward by the play. The result of these contrasting character doublings "is a process of continual moral comparison, carefully weighing the relative guilt or innocence of each character" (Mazella 2001: 800).

The tragic action of domestic tragedy is usually set off by the villain's attempt to take advantage of the hero's innocence and exploit his or her benevolence. 'Virtue' or 'innocence in distress' is therefore a common motif of domestic tragedy (cf. Feldmann 1983: 45). Typically, the wickedness of the villain is at least partly responsible for the fall of the hero. Functionally, then, the villain's evilness contributes to the displacement of the hero's guilt and makes his or her fall appear to result from social corruption and injustice.

The plot of domestic tragedy is usually set in contemporary English society. As a matter of fact, the narrative characteristics typically considered as 'realistic' in the 18th century – namely the depiction of everyday life, the portrayal of the workings of society, the enumeration of domestic detail, the concentration upon private experience and the elevation of individual concerns – are also central to the poetics of domestic tragedy (cf. Brown 1981: 146). Characteristically, the plot of domestic tragedy unfolds relatively slowly and is arranged in a rather loose, often inconsistent manner. It is often chance that propels the action. Indeed, it seems that the exemplary virtue of the tragic moral hero can hardly provide adequate motivation for a consistent plot (cf. ibid.: 152). The catastrophe, which aims at the evocation of pity and sympathy, is frequently only vaguely motivated and mainly serves the explicit didacticism of domestic tragedy. To a certain extent, then, the didacticism of domestic tragedy runs counter to the genre's general realism.

Due to the didactic intentions of domestic tragedy, speech is often more important than action. Domestic tragedy is interspersed with manifold sententious dialogues and monologues in which the characters reflect on ethic, usually middle-class standards, thus arresting the progress of the play (cf. Mazella 2001: 800). In its rather static presentation, domestic tragedy sometimes gives the impression of a drama of ideas. Aphorisms as well as pathos, intense emotionality and unusually explicit ideological detail are characteristic of the speech in domestic tragedy. Dialogues often display strong monological tendencies because by and large there is neither conflict nor disagreement between the central (middle-class) characters. Because the speakers' opinions more often than not coincide, so-called 'consensus-dialogues' prevail. Rather than drawing on verse, prose is the characteristic mode of domestic tragedy.

Domestic drama is not an innovation of the 18th century, but dates back to Elizabethan times. Early domestic dramas include *A Yorkshire Tragedy* (1606) and *Arden of Feversham* (c. 1592), which depict the downfall of ordinary men and dramatize recent and local crimes rather than historical events (cf. Adams 1965; Clark 1975). Yet despite the popularity of individual instances of the genre, domestic drama hardly played a major role on the English stage and even appears to have been buried in oblivion (cf. Feldmann 1983). The genre gains in popularity from the beginning of the 18th century onward, at a time which is commonly associated with 'the rise of the middle class.' Generically, the emergence of domestic tragedy has to be seen in the context of the increasing interest in natural pity, benevolence, and sympathy that becomes manifest in the late heroic drama of John Dryden and Nathaniel Lee (see chapter 9). The later plays by Dryden and Lee, especially *The Rival Queens* and *All for Love* (both 1677), respectively, still feature the exotic aristocratic protagonists essential to the heroic form, though their heroes frequently advocate "an effectually antiaristocratic ideology" (Brown 1981: 70). Moreover, these heroes are usually shown at the "tragic and passive close of their careers" (ibid.) and are thus far from embodying the extraordinary qualities of tragedy's classical heroes. The glory and fame they reach is no longer the same as in earlier heroic plays. This, however, also makes these heroes more accessible and allows them to gain the audience's sympathies.

The plays of Thomas Otway (1652-1685), John Banks (c. 1650-1700), and Thomas Southerne (1660-1746) carry affective assumptions one step further (cf. Brown 1981: 86 ff.): They depict a domestic situation and present a passive, even weak hero, either in the form of an innocent female protagonist or a simple, private citizen who cannot control his destiny. In particular, the serious drama by Otway, such as *The Orphan* (1680), makes much of the affective potential of domestic and statusless characters, who are primarily characterized by their benevolence and innocence. Otway's protagonists are neither princes nor larger-than-life heroes, but private men or women, hence domestic beings who are hardly concerned with issues of honour. Southerne's tragedies, in turn, are indicative of the increasing moralization of serious drama at the end of the 17th century (cf. ibid.: 98). *The Fatal Marriage: or, the Innocent Adultery* (1694), for instance, depicts the horrible consequences of inadvertent bigamy, focusing on the sufferings and self-accusations of the ill-fated, but innocent heroine Isabella. The domesticity crucial to the action of these plays is, according to Laura Brown (1981: 86), "the necessary prelude to the 'classless'" domestic tragedy of the 18th century.

Nicholas Rowe's (c. 1674-1718) tragedies take up the affective mode of Otway, Southerne, and Banks, but furnish it with a moral dimension, thus paving the path for the openly moral forms of George Lillo (c. 1691-1739), Aaron Hill (1685-1750), Charles Johnson (1679-1748), and Edward Moore (1712-1757). Rather than focussing primarily on the characters' innocence, Rowe's plays add moral meaning to innocence and thus provide ample space for the didacticism which comes to be typical of domestic tragedy (cf. Brown 1981: 150). Rowe's tragedies, most notably *The Fair Penitent* (1703) and his popular 'she-tragedy' *Jane Shore* (1714), are interested in "private woes, statusless women, exemplary virtue, didactic morality, domestic morality, domestic history, natural effect, and shared emotional experience" (ibid.: 151), all promoting values which are openly affective, and, to varying degrees, bourgeois. Both *Jane Shore* and *The Fair Penitent* use the emotionality of domestic scenes and private distress to morally instruct their audiences and to contest the social exclusiveness of the aristocratic world-view. To this end they feature female protagonists who grapple with everyday conflicts, usually crises in the family, and who are hardly responsible for their tragic fate. The recalibration of the object of tragedy from the domain of the state to the domestic sphere is explicitly stressed in the prologue to *The Fair Penitent*, which maintains that the play has been designed to eschew the typical tragic subject of "the fate of kings and empires" (Prologue, 1) in order to direct the attention to "a melancholy tale of private woes" (ibid.). "Private woes" and everyday conflicts are considered as a more accessible source of pity: "You shall meet with sorrows like your own" (ibid.). All in all, the plays' aesthetic of affect is geared towards generating pity in the audiences and teaching them about the virtue of sentiment. The emphasis on sentiment is not an end in itself and the poetics of sensibilty is far from being apolitical. Rather, they are firmly bound up with the negotation of concepts of class, nation, and gender, thus giving the middle class an arena for the reflection – and celebration – of its values. Often focussing on the sufferings of female protagonists, moral tragedies tend to naturalize newly emerging power relations by making them appear to be the product of natural gender differences.

The affective values and didactic intentions of Rowe's early moral tragedy pave the way for "full bourgeois tragedy" (Brown 1981: 157). Hill, Lillo, Johnson, and Moore, in their respective discussions of domestic tragedy, all stress the significance of private woes, plain emotion, and moral virtue and flaunt their instructive value. In the course of its further development, the moral action of domestic tragedy becomes increasingly didactic, explicitly addressing cultural norms of the reform-minded middle class. Lillo's *The London Merchant, or The History of George Barnwell* (1731), the most famous example of 18th-century domestic tragedy, fully exploits the didactic potential of the dramatic action, using it, as will be shown, for the negotiation of pressing cultural concerns: Politicizing the sentimental, Lillo's domestic tragedy impinges on social and political controversies, whether these involve class-based hostilities or debates on personal integrity, public status, and national character.

3. The Poetics and Politics of Sensibility in Lillo's *The London Merchant, or The History* of *George Barnwell*

Lillo's domestic tragedy, *The London Merchant*, follows the downfall of a young apprentice due to his association with a prostitute, joining sentiment with morality and constructing a comprehensive ethics for the middle-class protagonists. Lillo's aim was to produce a moral tragedy which centres around a private citizen and thus to create a tragedy for a middle-class audience whose identification with the story could ideally effect a moral reformation in the public. This ambition is explicitly formulated in his dedication to *The London Merchant*: "Tragedy is [...] far from losing its dignity by being accommodated to the circumstances of the generality of mankind that it is more truly august in proportion to the extent of its influence and the numbers that are properly affected by it." (Dedication, 19-23) Unlike classical tragedy, then, domestic tragedy claims to speak directly for its audience, with its usefulness becoming the chief aim: "If tragic poetry be, as Mr. Dryden has somewhere said, the most excellent and most useful kind of writing, the more extensively useful the moral of any tragedy is, the more excellent that piece must be of its kind." (Dedication, 5-8) The category of 'utility,' which was well established in scientific and economic contexts of the time, is here applied to literary productions, thus replacing the classical concept of *prodesse et delectare* by notions of moral usefulness. Indeed, the notion of 'utility' is geared towards legitimizing the featuring of middle-class protagonists and thus testifies to the capacity of drama to respond to the needs of contemporary audiences, in this case the need of the middle class for a new set of cultural norms and behavioural codes (cf. Trainor 1978).

The plot of *The London Merchant* is replete with disaster, passionate recrimination, confession, and forgiveness. Building toward emotional climaxes of mistake, misfortune, deceit, and death, the plot is clearly directed at the evocation of a sympathetic emotional response in the audience. The play draws on a local origin, namely the popular 17th-century ballad of George Barnwell who is enticed by an attractive seductress, Millwood, to betray his master and to murder his wealthy uncle. It is significant that Lillo projects the ballad of misguided virtue onto the 16th century, a time of seemingly great national glory, and thus dissimulates the extent to which his play is implicated in contemporary politics. In this way, the Elizabethan age is re-imagined as the origin of mercantile capitalism and the merchant, who, at the beginning of the 18th century, is just about to enter the political scene, appears as a stable pillar of national progress (cf. Scholz 2004: 73).

The ideology of the emerging merchant class shapes the moral assumptions of the play, and all the material of the drama's local contexts help exemplify these standards (cf. Brown 1981: 159). George Barnwell is a young apprentice to the London merchant Thorowgood. Thorowgood is an exemplary representative of middle-class morality, epitomizing the merits of the merchant class. Barnwell, a promising young man, is meant to learn from him so that he too can ultimately become a merchant-gentleman and enhance England's glory. Yet Barnwell is led astray by the wiles of the prostitute Millwood and his passion for her. In fact, the double title of the play – *The London Merchant, or The History of George Barnwell* – can be interpreted as an indication of the ideal and the fatal deviation from it. It is significant that the play's main title does not refer to the tragic hero but to the exemplary merchant.

The play's character constellation is based on clear oppositions. While Thorowgood embodies the ideals of peacefulness, order, civilization, and patriotism, Millwood embodies their opposites, namely war, civil disorder, sexual libertinism, and barbarous exploitation. Millwood is repeatedly called artful and deceitful; she figures as an extremely attractive "sorceress" (4.16.22) and even as a "devil" (4.18.4), who uses her irresistible power to seduce and ruin honest men. She is introduced in the first act, when she schemes to find some innocent young man "who, having never injured women, [would] apprehend no injury from them" (1.3.40 f.) to seduce and exploit for money. Barnwell arrives, almost immediately melts before Millwood's charms, and agrees to stay for the night.

After his night with Millwood, Barnwell agonizes over his disobeying the rules of his master. His guilt is compounded by the loyalty of his fellow apprentice and friend Trueman. Barnwell does attempt to confess his sin to Thorowgood, yet this confession is stymied by the merchant's well-developed qualities of benevolence, pity, and generosity. Thorowgood insists on forgiving Barnwell without hearing what he has done, thus, ironically, preventing a full discovery of the truth and deferring the inevitable punishment of the apprentice (cf. Mazella 2001: 803). With Thorowgood's forgiveness, Barnwell seems to be back on the track ("Why, I renounce her. I give her up! The struggle's over and virtue has prevailed," 2.5.3 f.), until Millwood and her servant Lucy appear with a concocted story about Millwood being evicted and ruined without his help. Assuming responsibility for Millwood's fate, Barnwell finds himself in what he considers a moral dilemma (cf. 2.13.1 ff.). He decides to steal money from his master because he wants to save a helpless, poor woman from "want and misery" (2.14.16). By this view, Barnwell's theft is presented as the consequence of his characteristic benevolence, an almost exemplary capacity for pity, which is betrayed by Millwood's wickedness. Though Barnwell takes responsibility for his deeds, confessing the power of passions, here he is indeed depicted as the "innocent victim of circumstance and sorcery" (Brown 1981: 160).

After stealing the money, Barnwell feels unworthy of his kind master and decides to flee Thorowgood's house forever. He leaves a note for Trueman confessing his crime, and Maria, Thorowgood's daughter, who is secretly in love with Barnwell, volunteers to cover the theft with her own money. Having no other place to go to, Barnwell takes refuge with Millwood, who readily takes advantage of his situation and urges him to steal more money from his wealthy uncle and to kill him. Although Barnwell agrees to Millwood's remorseless demand, the extremity of her villainy, which even shocks her own servants Lucy and Blunt, as well as the circumstances of the murder again tend to exonerate the tragic hero. While his unsuspicious uncle is deep in thought, incidentally pondering the meaning of death, Barnwell, concealed, "*sometimes presents the pistol, and draws it back again*" (stage direction, 3.7.8) finds himself in a state of irresolution, in which reason battles against passion. Ultimately, conscience prevails. He drops the gun crying out, "Oh, 'tis impossible!" (3.7.9) As a reaction to this "*his uncle starts and draws his sword*" (stage direction, 3.7.8), trying to defend himself against what he believes to be an intruder. Consequently, the play suggests, it is primarily self-defence that brings Barnwell to stab his uncle to death. The larger part of the scene explores the moral consequences of this accident. Barnwell's passionate display of guilt and the persistence of his self-accusation anticipate much of the blame that inevitably follows his crime, while also reflecting the sincerity of his remorse (cf. Brown 1981: 160). Promoting the internalization of disciplinary power, the play suggests that Barnwell's conscience has begun punishing him before legal institutions could do so (cf. Mazella 2001: 802).

After the murder, Millwood fears that Barnwell may give the crime and her involvement in it away and so she decides to turn him in to the authorities herself, hoping that this gesture will cover her complicity. Just after Barnwell is arrested, Thorowgood and Trueman arrive at Millwood's home, accusing her of being responsible for Barnwell's fall. In her passionate speech of defiance, Millwood extends the source of evil to which Barnwell succumbs "from the wiles of a single angry woman to the inequalities of a whole society" (Brown 1981: 159). She claims that she is victim of pervasive institutional injustices in the courts, governments, and the church and even maintains that the effects of such practices are more devastating than those of war (cf. 4.18.). Again, her speech of vindication displaces Barnwell's guilt, making his tragic fall appear to be the result of social injustice and political corruption. Even Thorowgood acknowledges her charge: "Truth is truth, though from an enemy and spoke in malice. You bloody, blind, and superstitious bigots, how will you answer this?" (4.18.57-59) By the same token, Millwood's final diatribe, in which she ascribes her ruin to sexual libertinism – a vice that was alleged to be aristocratic and, accordingly, strongly opposed by the middle class – stresses the need for social reform (cf. Brown 1981: 160; Walach 1980: 50). It is significant that Millwood's speeches of accusation, which have been partly cut by translators (cf. Price 1950: 155), insistently highlight the destructive powers of British religious and legal institutions. One could therefore argue that Millwood's accusations question the demonization of this female figure that the play so eagerly promotes.

Like other domestic tragedies, *The London Merchant* is characterized by a fairly closed structure, resolving all value conflicts and enforcing poetic justice. *The London Merchant* ends "with the supreme pathos" (Brown 1981: 162). Barnwell, uplifted now by his newly gained confidence in God's mercy, is visited in his prison cell by Thorowgood, Trueman, and Maria. Trueman and Thorowgood console him and ultimately forgive him, while Maria belatedly confesses her love for him. Despite the extenuating circumstances of Millwood's influence, Barnwell resumes full responsibility for his acts. He accepts his rigorous punishment, i.e. his sentence to death, and thereby gives proof of his repentance. After several scenes of tears, sighs, and pious exclamations, the play concludes with Barnwell, clam and composed, and Millwood, unrepentant to the end, being led to execution. Millwood, it seems, must be sacrificed so that Barnwell can be returned to the bosom of the (male and middle-class) community, epitomized by Thorowgood. Millwood's refusal of divine mercy hints at her malevolent image of humanity and God: Linking all questions solely to power and lacking all compassion, she cannot imagine a merciful God. The tragic hero, by contrast, finds comfort in his self-denial and humility. He can thus die a Christian death, which celebrates his virtue and which can generate pity in the audiences (cf. Mazella 2001: 818).

In *The London Merchant*, Lillo develops a persuasive system of sentimental benevolence that plays an important part in the characterization of the protagonists. More specifically, the play constructs "a strong internal ethical hierarchy by which every character's worth is carefully classified and against which every act is explicitly judged" (Brown 1993: 86). Here as elsewhere sensibility serves to fix social boundaries, thus regulating who belongs to the (moral) community and who does not belong. Thorowgood is a paragon of middle-class morality and his generosity, benevolence, and belief in the virtues of the merchant class establish the ethical standards of the play. It is significant that the play does not open with the tragic hero or with an exposition for the plot. It opens with Thorowgood, who asserts the immense political power of the group he represents; next, he demonstrates his role as an exemplary, generous, and loving father presiding over a well-ordered household (cf. Feldmann 1996: 294). By contrast, Millwood, the sole non-bourgeois character, stoutly resists any sentimental benevolence and thus consistently locates herself outside the bounds of the play's imagined community (cf. Mazella 2001: 798). By constantly pitting itself against Millwood's presumed otherness, this community comes to define itself in terms of class, morality, rationality, and usefulness.

Of course, the greatest challenge of the play is the creation of a tragic middle-class hero who commits a fatal error *and* represents virtue. Barnwell is a criminal, who is guilty of robbery and murder. At the same time, however, the play does a lot to free him from responsibility (cf. Bernbaum 1915: 153; Brown 1981: 162). Most notably, the play's insistence on Millwood's wickedness contributes to Barnwell's extenuation. Even Millwood's best friend does not approve of her behaviour, interpreting it as a removal of Barnwell's virtue. Moreover, somewhat paradoxically, his extreme benevolence both propels his tragic fall and erases the blame for his fate. Time and again, we find assertions of his innate goodness and his natural feelings. His character, for instance, is defined by his possession of a large portion of "the general love we owe to mankind" (1.5.33 f.). It is this intense form of love, the audience is made to believe, that makes him so vulnerable to Millwood's wiles. Even Thorowgood excuses his apprentice by stressing his benign generosity: "Poor satisfaction, for he, innocent as he is compared to you, must suffer too." (4.16.33 f.) Barnwell himself attributes his sins to the victory of passion over reason, acknowledging that "[t]he law of Heaven [...] requires us to govern our passions" (1.8.9 f.). Affectively, then, Barnwell is represented as innocent; morally and technically, however, he is guilty (cf. Brown 1993: 87). He is guilty precisely because he fails to curb his passions.

In *The London Merchant* the ideological persuasiveness of the sensibility becomes a powerful (political) tool for the negotiation of middle-class values, most notably for the promotion of mercantile capitalism. *The London Merchant* is notable for its reconciliation between the trading class and sentiment. Yet it is important to note that while all the male characters who embrace sentimental values are representatives of the trading class, the market itself is depicted as strictly rational and predominantly linked to law and reason (cf. 1.1.). Commerce, in *The London Merchant*, is regarded as the precondition for promoting civilization and for overcoming the chaotic and instinct-driven state of nature. According to Thomas Hobbes' *Leviathan* (1985 [1651]: 161), the state of nature is marked by the "generall inclination of all mankind, a perpetuall and restlesse desire of Power after power, that ceaseth only in Death." Under these conditions, the civilizing process can hardly prosper: "[N]o Arts, no Letters, no Society," as Hobbes (ibid.: 186) has it. Generally, 18th-century apologists of mercantile capitalism argue that trade and commerce are vital to disciplining man's drive for power and to unite individuals into a peaceful community. Thorowgood marshals the same arguments when he explains to Trueman, the exemplary apprentice, the ethics of trade:

> Methinks I would not have you only learn the method of merchandise and practice it hereafter merely as a means of getting wealth. 'Twill be well worth your pains to study it as a science, see how it is founded in reason and the nature of things, how it has promoted humanity as it has opened and yet keeps up an intercourse between nations far remote from one another in situation, customs, and religion; promoting arts, industry, peace, and plenty; by mutual benefits diffusing mutual love from pole to pole. (3.1.1-9)

According to this extremely positive representation, commerce is not a means of accumulating wealth; rather – and here Thorowgood evokes the ideals of the Enlightenment – it is to be understood as a science, which is based on rational insights and which pulls down prejudices. Commerce aims at joining even the most divergent peoples together into one international business community and is thus capable of transforming materialist antagonism into universal harmony and understanding. This euphemistic vision of trade hints at an equally idealized definition of the merchant. The merchant is less interested in his personal wealth than in the progress of the nation. His aim is to promote knowledge, to foster communication between different, trading peoples and to serve the civilization of nature. Against this normative background, the merchant can indeed self-consciously claim to improve humanity and to function as the catalyst of civilization (cf. Scholz 2004: 77 f.).

In *The London Merchant* the euphoric claims about the civilizing and benevolent effects of British trade generate a powerfully evocative expansionist fantasy, which summons Britons to expand their (mercantile) power over the entire globe. According to the play's euphemistic interpretation, the improvement of human existence, enabled by trade, benefits not only Britain but also its colonies and other overseas territories yet to be colonized. Trueman spells out to which end Britons have to teach the native population the workings of mercantile capitalism:

> I have observed those countries where trade is promoted and encouraged do not make discoveries to destroy but to improve mankind – by love and friendship to tame the fierce and polish the most savage; to teach them the advantages of honest traffic by taking from them, with their own consent, their useless superfluities, and giving them in return what, from their ignorance in manual arts, their situation, or some other accident, they stand in need of. (3.1.11-19)

Purveying a benevolent world system, trade has the power to civilize even "the most savage" (Olaniyan 1992: 45). Once being part of the global business community established by Britain, the colonies can easily overcome the state of nature and their allegedly 'superfluous' riches can be transformed into cultured goods in Britain's newly emerging consumer society. By insinuating that the foreign countries have no use for their natural wealth, Trueman justifies the imperial exploitation as a perfectly reasonable redistribution of goods. Indeed, the ideology of imperial capitalism endorsed by *The London Merchant* is suffused with the sense of an almost providential distribution of goods, testifying to the intrinsically rational order of the world and to the divinely ordained obligation of the merchant:

> On every climate and on every country Heaven has bestowed some good peculiar to itself. It is the industrious merchant's business to collect the various blessings of each soil and climate and, with the product of the whole, to enrich his native country. (3.1.23-28)

'Good' commerce relies on the merchant's moral duty to the community. The ideal merchant curbs the effects of individual wealth by continually disciplining his acquisitive instincts.

Against the backdrop of this ideology we can assess Barnwell's fall from a different angle. A young apprentice like Barnwell can fall prey to the exploitive 'nature' of Millwood, the temptress and evil mistress, because in the commercial society the incapacity to control one's passion ultimately yields a relapse into the state of nature (cf. Scholz 2004: 80 f.). The moral legitimacy of the merchant is based on his capacity to discipline his passion and impose constraint by reason. To be aware of the constant threat of one's passions is, according to *The London Merchant*, vital to any form of self-knowledge, and it is exactly this knowledge which Barnwell, the apprentice, lacks (cf. Cole 1995). Hence, for Thorowgood, the apprenticeship ultimately amounts to the internalization of the disciplinary power of reason:

> When we consider the frail condition of humanity it may raise our pity, not our wonder, that youth should go astray when reason, weak at the best when opposed to inclination, scarce formed and wholly unassisted by experience, faintly contends or willingly becomes the slave of sense. The state of youth is much to be deplored, and the more so because they see it not, they being then to danger most exposed when they are least prepared for their defense. [...] Yet, be upon your guard in this gay thoughtless season of your life. Now, when the sense of pleasure's quick and passion high, the voluptuous appetites, raging and fierce, demand the strongest curb. Take heed of a relapse. (2.4.17-31)

The ideal mercantile self – and we find similar conceptions in Daniel Defoe's compendium *The Complete English Tradesman* (1726) as well as in his novels *Moll Flanders* (1722) and *Roxana* (1724) – emerges through a process of constant introspection and self-constraint, in the course of which disciplinary power is internalized and passions are eventually split off as the other of reason (cf. Scholz 2004: 81). Barnwell's struggle for his self, which is represented in great detail (cf. 2.1.2 ff.), should ideally result in the detachment from his passions. In this vein, *The London Merchant, or The History of George Barnwell* suggests that peace and civilization only come as the rewards of the education of the self towards a disciplined behaviour (cf. Feldmann 1996: 299).

Domestic tragedy's concern with middle-class values is intimately related to the negotiation of gender concepts. The ideal bourgeois woman is represented by Maria, an exemplary daughter, who – as suggested by her name – is characterized by her virtue, obedience, passivity, and sentimentality (cf. Walach 1980: 75). Maria observes and investigates her behaviour in terms of sexual morals and has completely internalized the disciplinary power of the patriarchal society (cf. Feldmann 1983: 117). As a matter of fact, the conflict between love and duty, a frequent cause of struggle between parent and child, can be avoided since Maria, the good daughter, fully endorses her father's system of values: "[M]y inclinations [...] shall ever be submitted to your [...] authority." (1.2.67 f.)

The character of Millwood, by contrast, demonstrates how unstable gender relations are as long as they are not domesticated by the disciplinary power of the bourgeois family. In the world of trade unfolded in the play, Millwood's commodity is her body (cf. Scholz 2004: 82). In the midst of a seemingly well-ordered consumer society, pacified by social convention, family life and sentiment, Millwood draws attention to the fact that the market itself establishes a situation which is not unlike the state of nature, i.e. haunted by constant rivalry. In a conversation with her servant and confidante Lucy, Millwood describes the dynamics of the battle of the sexes:

> MILLWOOD. We are but slaves to men.
> LUCY. Nay, 'tis they that are slaves most certainly, for we lay them under contribution.
> MILLWOOD. Slaves have no property – no, not even in themselves. All is the victor's.
> LUCY. You are strangely arbitrary in your principles, madam.
> MILLWOOD. I would have my conquests complete, like those of the Spaniards in the New

World, who first plundered the natives of all the wealth they had and then condemned the wretches to the mines for life to work for more. (1.3.18-27)

Millwood rebels against gender hierarchies, challenging the allocation of women to the private sphere, which is at the heart of the consumer society. It is by no means coincidental that Millwood, the negative advocate for the values put forward by the play, compares her own practices to those of the 'Spaniards' in the New World. To fully appreciate this reference, we have to recall that in the 18th-century struggle for economic hegemony, Catholic Spain was Britain's main rival (cf. Neumann 2009). Millwood's absolutist political ideology, her Hobbesean vision and her exploitation of (social) contracts defy all aspects of civilization, peace, and sustainability through exchange. In this respect, the characterization of Millwood is a powerful means of metonymically denouncing Spaniards and their practices of colonization as barbarous, of discrediting absolutist politics (and, implicitly, the authority of the aristocracy), and of censuring women who mess with the (patriarchal) economic system. Just like Spain, the play suggests, Millwood is set on conquest and upon feeding "her avarice, insatiate as the grave" (3.4.62). Moreover, by linking Millwood to the presumably aggressive, tyrannical, and exploitative policy of Spain, the play "displaces critical recognition of Britain's own colonial exploitation onto its external counterpart" (Feldmann 1996: 297 f.).

At the same time, however, Millwood serves as the hostile other *within* Britain, the alien culture against which British cultural identity and a Protestant, middle-class order can be consolidated (cf. Flores 1987; Scholz 2004: 82). Millwood's crimes belie the claim that trade and the pursuit of profit make people reasonable, and peaceful. Accordingly, Barnwell's tragic fall displaces the external threat of a Spanish invasion onto an internal, distinctly feminine, threat to Britain's civil order. In Millwood's own interpretation of her fate, her crimes cannot be attributed to her character but to the injustices to be found within society: "If such [perfections of mind and body] I had, well may I curse your barbarous sex who robbed me of 'em, ere I knew their worth, then left me, too late, to count their value by their loss." (4.18.10-13) It seems that the same economic principles that have made Thorowgood rich have made a commodity of her virtue. While Thorowgood is the good capitalist, who understands trade as a means of promoting peace and civilization, Millwood identifies herself as the merciless imperialist. She lacks the necessary self-discipline which could curb economic individualism and the drive for power (cf. Feldmann 1996: 299 f.; Kowaleski-Wallace 1997: 125). All in all, the figure of Millwood demonstrates the extent to which notions of gender and nation, domesticity and imperialism, commerce and morality were intertwined in 18th-century Britain.

In the broader context of economic and sexual politics, Millwood serves as a projection of the ethically questionable practices of merchants – self-interest and profit maximization – onto a female figure (cf. Hammer 1990; Scholz 2004: 83). Becoming the play's "incorrigible, irreducible remainder" (Mazella 2001: 798), Millwood stands in for the moral threat and instability of a consumer society in which social recognition relies on possession. Exchange and trade – as long as they are softened by reason, morals, sentiment, and benevolence – hold society together and ensure peace. Yet exchange and trade also spark the exploitative impulses of men, their avarice and self-interest, and thus potentially undermine social harmony. In acknowledging this danger, the play also acknowledges the need for the greatest possible discipline and punishment. Despite his innate goodness, Barnwell must be severely punished because his social disciplining has failed. The rise of 18th-century sensibility, one can conclude, was a powerful tool for fixing social boundaries, helping to create new, more 'enlightened' practices of punishment that are suited to a polite and commercial society (cf. Mazella 2001: 796). By and large, *The London Merchant*, like other domestic tragedies of the age, propounds a "'civilizing' model of political and social assimilation" (Feldmann 1996: 301), which builds on education, reform, self-control, and the internalization of disciplinary power. Basically, this is why *The London Merchant* is a "moral tale" (Prologue, 24).

4. Conclusion

The London Merchant enjoyed enormous popularity in London theatres in the 18th century. Between 1731 and 1747 the play was staged 96 times and, although its vogue began to dwindle, it remained a stock play at theatres until 1776. By the middle of the century it had become the traditional offering for Christmas and Easter holidays. According to Theophilus Cibber, then acting as manager of the Drury Lane Theatre, the play was "judged as a proper entertainment for the apprentices, & c. as being a more instructive, moral, and cautionary drama, than many pieces that had usually been exhibited on those days" (qtd. from McBurney 1965: xiiii). Yet it is significant that *The London Merchant* was rarely presented by itself; during the 1730s it was commonly followed by such favourite afterpieces as Charles Coffey's *The Devil to Pay* (1732) and Colley Cibber's *Damon and Phillida* (1729). Hence, an evening at the theatre with *The London Merchant* as the main fare was a varied pleasure which mixed the useful with the entertaining (cf. McBurney 1965: xx).

As plays such as Lillo's *Fatal Curiosity* (1736), Johnson's *Caelia; or, The Perjur'd Lover* (1732), and Moore's *The Gamester* (1753) show, domestic tragedy continued to enjoy popularity throughout the first half of the 18th century. Given the explicit didactic intentions of the genre, it is hardly surprising that it persistently addressed those groups of British society that had supposedly not yet sufficiently endorsed middle-class values. Because marriage and the family were regarded as the safeguards of middle-class life, numerous domestic tragedies centre around the problems inherent in these social institutions (cf. Feldmann 1983: 156). Johnson's *Caelia; or, The Perjur'd Lover*, for example, explores gender norms and society's double standards concerning male and female morality, once again revealing the power of natural drives over social codes. The play powerfully redefines notions of the gentleman and corresponding concepts of honour, arguing that conscience and virtue are more important than social origin. Generally, later domestic tragedies tend to disentangle personal relations from political matters. Political tensions were privatized to such an extent that it was possible to dissimulate the political dimension of the represented struggles: "[D]omestic tragedies became domestic dramas [...], which exalted the domestic woman." (Feldmann 1996: 301)

In the course of the second half of the 18th century, the genre gradually declines in importance and is replaced by sentimental comedy (see chapter 10) or other, hybrid dramatic forms with happy, more conciliatory endings. Spectacular and melodramatic forms of mass entertainment characteristic of 19th-century theatre increasingly gain in popularity. Richard Cumberland's domestic drama *The Mysterious Husband* from 1783 is typical of this tendency. Although the play still features moral paragons, it also introduces comical characters, who add melodramatic elements and comic relief to the moral action (cf. Feldmann 1983: 208). Moreover, sensational elements, also characteristic of 19th-century melodrama (see chapter 14), gradually replace the representation of contemporary economic and social problems typical of domestic tragedy. *The Mysterious Husband*, for instance, indulges in irrational phenomena and makes a lot out of the revelation of scandals, in particular bigamy and incest.

18th-century domestic tragedy has given the middle class an arena for the reflection of its values, norms, and social status. Criticism and idealization are the paradoxical results of this reflection, results which manifest themselves most forcefully in the figure of the tragic bourgeois hero. It seems that by the end of the 18th century, domestic tragedy can no longer respond to the challenges of contemporary society. Apparently, audiences prefer to be entertained by more spectacular topics beyond the strictures of everyday life. It is only with the emergence of the so-called problem play (see chapter 15) at the end of the 19th century that the depiction of the socio-economic reality and its influence on people's behaviour once again moves centre-stage.

Bibliography

Primary Sources

Lillo, George. 1965 [1731]. *The London Merchant, or The History of George Barnwell*. William H. McBurney (ed.). London: Edward Arnold.

Annotated Bibliography

Brown, Laura. 1981. *English Dramatic Form, 1660-1760: An Essay in Generic History*. New Haven/London: Yale UP.
  Sketching the history of English drama from 1660-1760, this ground-breaking study provides a concise overview of the development of domestic tragedy and of-

fers an in-depth interpretation of Lillo's The London Merchant, focusing on the moral implications of the play.

Feldmann, Doris. 1983. *Gattungsprobleme des Domestic Drama im Literaturhistorischen Kontext des Achtzehnten Jahrhunderts*. Amsterdam: Grüner.

The book offers a very helpful overview of the central characteristics of domestic drama, relating them to cultural issues of 18th-century England.

—. 1996. "Peace as the Result of 'The Method of Merchandise': Ideological Warfare in George Lillo's *The London Merchant* (1731)." In: Paul-Gabriel Boucé (ed.). *Guerres et paix: la Grande-Bretagne au XVIIIe Siècle*. Paris: Presses de la Sorbonne.

This brilliant interpretation is especially useful for its conceptualization of the domestic subject in terms of a political discourse and for its concise analysis of the mercantile ideology.

Hammer, Stephanie Barbe. 1990. "Economy and Extravagance: Criminal Origin and the War of Words in *The London Merchant*." In: *Essays in Theatre* 8: 81-94.

The article offers a good interpretation of the gender concepts that underlie the characterization of the play's central protagonists.

Mazella, David. 2001. "'Justly to Fall Unpitied and Abhorr'd': Sensibility, Punishment and Morality in Lillo's *The London Merchant*." In: *English Literary History* 68.4: 795-830.

The illuminating interpretation focuses on the political implications of sensibility, showing how this concept uses the prospect of punishment to fix social boundaries.

Nünning, Ansgar. 1998. "Das englische Drama des 18. Jahrhunderts aus kulturwissenschaftlicher Sicht: Themenselektion, dramatische Bauformen, Funktionen und Mentalitäten." In: Monika Fludernik & Ruth Nestvold (eds.). *Das 18. Jahrhundert*. Trier: WVT. 109-45.

The article provides a good overview of the genre-specific characteristics of domestic tragedy, relating the genre to major cultural developments of the age, in particular to British nationalism and xenophobia.

Scholz, Susanne. 2004. *Objekte und Erzählungen: Subjektivität und kultureller Dinggebrauch im England des frühen 18. Jahrhunderts*. Königstein: Ulrike Helmer.

The interpretation is especially useful for its sharp contextualization of the play, relating it to contemporary concepts of capitalism, imperialism, and gender.

Walach, Dagmar. 1980. *Der aufrechte Bürger, seine Welt und sein Theater*. München: Fink.

The study offers an overview of the philosophical and economic contexts that are relevant to the characterization of the play's bourgeois protagonists.

Further Secondary Literature

Adamian, Paul Serop. 1968. *Eighteenth-Century English Domestic Tragedy: A World of Woe*. Michigan: Ann Arbor.

Adams, Henry H. 1965. *English Domestic Tragedy or, Homiletic Tragedy, 1575-1642*. New York: Columbia UP.

Bernbaum, Ernest. 1915. *The Drama of Sensibility: A Sketch of the History of English Sentimental Comedy and Domestic Tragedy 1696-1780*. Boston: Ginn.

Brown, Laura. 1993. *Ends of Empire: Women and Ideology in Early Eighteenth-Century English Literature*. Cornell: Cornell UP.

Clark, A. 1975. *Domestic Drama: A Survey of the Origins, Antecedents and Nature of the Domestic Play in England, 1500-1640*. 2 vols. Salzburg: U of Salzburg.

Cole, Lucinda. 1995. "'The London Merchant' and the Institution of Apprenticeship." In: *Criticism: A Quarterly for Literature and the Arts* 37.1: 57-84.

DeRitter, Jones. 1987. "A Cult of Dependence: The Social Context of *The London Merchant*." In: *Comparative Drama* 21.4: 374-86.

Ellis, Markman. 1996. *The Politics of Sensibility: Race, Gender and Commerce in the Sentimental Novel*. Cambridge: Cambridge UP.

Flores, Stephan P. 1987. "Mastering the Self: The Ideological Incorporation of Desire in Lillo's *The London Merchant*." In: *Essays in Theatre* 5: 91-102.

Hobbes, Thomas. 1985 [1651]. *Leviathan*. Harmondsworth: Penguin.

Hynes, Peter. 2003. "Exchange and Excess in Lillo's *The London Merchant*." In: *University of Toronto Quarterly* 72.3: 679-97.

Kowaleski-Wallace, Elizabeth. 1997. *Consuming Subjects: Women, Shopping, and Business in the Eighteenth Century*. New York: Columbia UP.

Langford, Paul. 1989. *A Polite and Commercial People: England 1727-1783*. Oxford: Oxford UP.

McBurney, William H. 1965. "Introduction." In: *The London Merchant*. William H. McBurney (ed.). London: Edward Arnold. ix-xxv.

Neumann, Birgit. 2009. *Die Rhetorik der Nation in britischer Literatur und anderen Medien des 18. Jahrhunderts*. Trier: WVT.

Olaniyan, Tejumola. 1992. "The Ethics and Poetics of a 'Civilizing Mission': Some Notes on Lillo's *The London Merchant*." In: *English Language Notes* 29: 33-47.

Price, Lawrence M. 1950. "George Barnwell Abroad." In: *Comparative Literature* 2: 126-56.

Shaftesbury, Anthony Ashley Cooper, Earl of. 1790. *Characteristics of men, manners, opinions, times, with a collection of letters*. Vol. 2. London: Tourneisen.

Trainor, Stephen L. 1978. "Tears Abounding: *The London Merchant* as Puritan Tragedy." In: *Studies in English Literature* 18: 509-21.

12. EIGHTEENTH-CENTURY COMEDY OF MANNERS: RICHARD BRINSLEY SHERIDAN'S *THE SCHOOL FOR SCANDAL*

JÜRGEN KAMM

1. Comedy Between Manners and Sentiments

'Comedy' as a generic term covers a wide range of literary texts, lyric, dramatic as well as epic, whose common denominator is essentially the invariously happy ending. The earliest extant definition of comedy in Western poetology was proposed by Aristotle in his *Poetics* where he writes:

> Comedy is (as we have said) an imitation of inferior people – not, however, with respect to every kind of defect: the laughable is a species of what is disgraceful. The laughable is an error or disgrace that does not involve pain or destruction; for example, a comic mask is ugly and distorted, but does not involve pain. (Aristotle 1996: 9)

Aristotle's canonical text was not translated until 1789 by Thomas Twining, but the original Greek version was readily available to classically trained intellectuals during the Elizabethan period and after. Whether they really cared about the Aristotelian proposition is a matter of dispute. Around 1600 drama had branched out into numerous subgenres so that in *Hamlet* (1600-01), Shakespeare could poke fun at contemporary attempts at classification by having Polonius proclaim about the company of itinerant actors in the play: "The best actors in the world, either for tragedy, comedy, history, pastoral, pastorical-comical, historical-pastoral, tragical-historical, tragical-comical-historical-pastoral, scene individable or poem unlimited" (2.2.379-382).

If clear dividing lines were difficult to draw 400 years ago, the further development of comedy has rendered any watertight classification of subgenres even more complex. As a result, handbooks on theatre and drama are frequently reserved when it comes to defining the various branches of comic drama:

> English comedies have been classified under various headings – Comedy of Humours, as written by Ben Jonson (q.v.) under classical influence; of Manners as written by Restoration dramatists like Congreve (q.v.) under the influence of Molière; of Intrigue (from Spain via France) as written by Mrs. Aphra Behn (q.v.); and Sentimental Comedy, as written by Steele (q.v.) in reaction from Restoration Comedy. But all these types merge and overlap, and in the theatre of today it is impossible to assign any given play to a specific genre. (Hartnoll 1988: 107)

Despite such obvious difficulties, comedy of manners, as the term aptly suggests, may be defined as being primarily concerned with the manners, behaviour and conventions dominant within a highly sophisticated and not infrequently artificial society. The members of such an elitist, polite, and leisured social class are characterized by youthful wit, a pronounced interest in fashion and the arts, including theatre and drama, as well as in the instigation of amorous intrigues. Any flowering of comedy of manners thus relies on the presence of such a peer group within the contemporary social setup so that the theatre by holding up the mirror may satirically expose the deficiencies and follies of the leisured class through characters, manners, and plots modelled on the behaviour of this clearly defined section of fashionable society.

When looking for the earliest specimen of a comedy of manners in English literature which would fulfil these criteria one is tempted to point at Shakespeare's *Much Ado About Nothing* (1600). Although Elizabethan drama traditionally catered for all strata of society, this particular comedy focuses sharply on the fashionable clique at the court of Messina, its manners and intrigues, contrasting Don John's evil but eventually thwarted design of destroying Hero's unblemished reputation with the joyful bantering of Beatrice and Benedick, arguably the first 'gay couple' on the English stage. However, Shakespeare's comedies of delight were not at all popular with Restoration audiences after 1660. Rather, a group of dramatists who christened themselves "the Sons of Ben" including Thomas Killigrew, Sir William Davenant, William Cartwright, and William Cavendish emulated Ben Jonson's model of comedy of humours. Following the years of austerity during the Cromwellian Interregnum a fashionable society resurfaced and, headed by the Merry Monarch Charles II, was bent on enjoying life to its fullest, often to extremity. This courtly, upper-class in-group provided a fertile breeding ground for comedies of manners such as William Wycherley's *The Country Wife* (1675), George Etherege's *The Man of Mode* (1676), William Congreve's *The Way of the World* (1700), and George Farquhar's *The Beaux Stratagem* (1707). These racy, sexy, and often downright libertine comedies witnessed a flowering during the 1670s and 1680s but came under increasing criticism towards the end of the century. The numerous attacks on Restoration comedies of manners, perhaps most pointedly phrased in Jeremy Collier's pamphlet *A Short View of the Immorality and Profaneness of the English Stage* (1698) eventually spelt out the end of performing manners.

In the course of the next decades, comedy of manners was replaced by sentimental comedy which was decidedly more to the taste of bourgeois audiences. Richard Steele paved the way with *The Conscious Lovers* (1722) in which emotions like love and rage are shown to be controllable by reason (see chapter 10). The play culminates in a moving scene in which the old and rich merchant Sealand identifies the mysterious young and beautiful Indiana as the long-lost daughter of his first marriage. Since such tear-jerking did not go without criticism, Steele hastened to defend the emotional impact of the scene in his Preface to the printed edition:

> But this incident, and the Case of the Father and Daughter are esteem'd by some People no Subjects of Comedy; but I cannot be of their Mind: for any thing that has its Foundation in Happiness and Success, must be allow'd to be the Object of Comedy; and sure it must be an Improvement of it, to introduce a Joy too exquisite for Laughter, that can have no Spring but in delight, which is the Case of this young Lady. I must therefore contend, that the Tears which were shed on that Occasion flow'd from Reason and good sense, and that Men ought not to be laugh'd at for weeping […]. (Steele 1993: 68)

Joys too exquisite for laughter as well as the government of reason and good sense were central to Steele's enlightened aesthetics of comedy which also contain a strong didactic note which is sounded in the appeal to the audience as voiced in the Prologue:

> Your aid, most humbly sought, then Britons lend,
> And Lib'ral Mirth, like Lib'ral Men defend:
> No more let Ribaldry, with Licence writ,
> Usurp the Name of Eloquence or Wit;
> Nor more let lawless Farce uncensur'd go,
> The lewd dull Gleanings of a Smithfield Show,
> 'Tis yours, with Breeding to refine the Age,
> To Chasten Wit, and Moralize the Stage. (Prologue, 71)

Such moralizing of the stage went hand in hand with the notion of the theatre as a school for the refinement of manners, and the rising middle class, still uncertain of its social role, obviously welcomed dramatic performances in which bourgeois values such as family, patriarchy, industry, temperance, and financial success were praised and rewarded. Inspired by Molière's *L'Ecole des maris* (1661) and *L'Ecole des femmes* (1662) the London stage of the 18th century witnessed the production of more than 20 comedies which used the term 'school' in their titles and thus showed a strong didactic interest, e.g. *The School for Husbands* (1761) by Charles Macklin, *The School for Lovers* (1762) by William Whitehead, *The School for Fathers* (1773) by Isaac Bickerstaffe, and *The School for Arrogance* (1791) by Thomas Holcroft, to name but a few.

The triumph of sentimental comedy during the first half of the 18th century was, however, dearly bought by a high degree of repetitiveness as far as character constellations, motifs, and plot lines were concerned. In 1765, Oliver Goldsmith published his essay "Sentimental Comedy" in which he reminded his readers of the Aristotelian distinction between comedy and tragedy and thereby attacked sentimentalism in comedies as being completely out of place:

> Comedy is defined by Aristotle to be a picture of the frailties of the lower part of mankind, to distinguish it from tragedy, which is an exhibition of the misfortunes of the great. When comedy, therefore, ascends to produce the characters of princes or generals upon the stage, it is out of its walk, since low life and middle life are entirely its object. The principal question therefore is, whether, in describing low or middle life, an exhibition of its follies be not preferable to a detail of its calamities? Or, in other words, which deserves the preference – the weeping sentimental comedy so much in fashion at present, or the laughing and even low comedy which seems to have been last exhibited by [John] Vanbrugh and [Colley] Cibber. (Goldsmith 1972: 164)

Goldsmith argues that sentimental comedy has, generically speaking, taken a turn in the wrong direction since it is the task of comedy to expose and to ridicule the follies of mankind rather than to present them for applause. This criticism is combined with the final warning that sentimental comedy may eventually destroy the 'art of laughing':

> Humour at present seems to be departing from the stage, and it will soon happen that our comic players will have nothing left for it but a fine coat and a song. It depends upon the audience whether they will actually drive those poor merry creatures from the stage, or sit at a play as gloomy as at the tabernacle. It is not easy to recover an art when once lost; and it will be but a just punishment that, when, by our being too fastidious, we have banished humour from the stage, we should ourselves be deprived of the art of laughing. (Ibid.: 168)

Goldsmith himself indicated the new direction of comedy in *She Stoops to Conquer; or, The Mistakes of a Night* (1773) and the immense success of the play lent theatrical support to his poetological criticism of sentimental comedy. At the same time Goldsmith's friend and fellow Irishman Richard Brinsley Sheridan (cf. Danziger 1978) was also experimenting with ways of reviving comedy of manners. In 1775, his first comedy *The Rivals* was favourably received and was quickly followed by the two-act farce *St. Patrick's Day* and the comic opera *The Duenna*. In the following year he bought David Garrick's half share of the patent of Drury Lane Theatre and he launched successful revivals of William Congreve's Restoration comedies of manners. It seemed that the time was ripe for the production of a play which would combine in a new and original way the respective merits of comedy of manners and of sentimental comedy. On 8 May 1777, this play had its premiere under the title *The School for Scandal*.

In order to contribute to the success of the play, David Garrick wrote the Prologue to *The School for Scandal*. Although the use of the term 'school' in the title might suggest that Sheridan wanted to place the play in the tradition of school comedies, Garrick points out that there is no need for schooling audiences in the art of scandal-mongering: "*A School for Scandal*! Tell me I beseech you / Needs there a School this modish art to teach you? / No need of lessons *now* the knowing think: / We might as well be taught to Eat, and Drink" (Prologue, 223). Indeed, Sheridan's didactic approach is rather inspired by the satiric thrust of manners comedy in the sense that the play sets out to ridicule and to expose the follies of a leisured society whose members spend their time in ruining the reputation of others. But would a comedy really be capable of educating audiences in such a way that calumny may be completely expunged? While being doubtful, Garrick nevertheless believes in Sheridan's artistic power to convince his audiences of the socially destructive consequences of backbiting and defamation:

> Is our Young Bard so young to think that He
> Can Stop *the full Spring-tide* of Calumny –
> Knows he the World so little and Its trade?
> Alas, the Devil is sooner *rais'd*, than *laid* –
> So strong, so swift, the Monster there's no gagging;
> Cut Scandal's head off – still the tongue is wagging.
> Proud of your Smiles once lavishly bestow'd
> Again our young Don Quixote takes the road:
> To shew his Gratitude – he draws his pen,
> And seeks the Hydra – Scandal in Its den
> From his fell gripe the frighted fair to save

Tho he should fall – th'attempt must please the brave.
For your applause, all perils he would through,
He'll *fight*, that's *write*, a Cavalliero true,
Till Ev'ry drop of Blood, that's Ink, is spilt for *You*. (Prologue, 225 f.)

The Quixotian image is nicely chosen as it presents the playwright in his apparently pointless fight, not attacking windmills with a lance, but the hydra of gossip with his pen.

2. *Dramatis Personae* and Configuration

In order to emerge victoriously from this hopeless battle, Sheridan employs three distinctive but interrelated groups of characters. At the play's centre are Joseph Surface and his younger brother Charles. Their telling names indicate that the comedy employs the motif of reality and appearance: Joseph is a man of sentiment, in appearance the model hero of sentimental comedy who is always quick in producing the proper sentiment on the proper occasion, e.g. "the Heart that is conscious of its own integrity is ever slow to credit another's Treachery" (4.3.275) or "He that is in Distress tho' a stranger has a right to claim kindred with the Wealthy" (5.1.283). Underneath this superficial mask of smug respectability, however, hides a true aristocratic rake driven by egotistic motives, financially as well as sexually. Conversely, his younger brother Charles acts the part of rake and spendthrift merely on the surface while in reality he is, much like the hero in Henry Fielding's *Tom Jones* (1749), a likeable character who has his heart in the right place. Having been orphaned in their infancy, their uncle Sir Oliver has assumed the role of their guardian, but having made his fortune in the East Indies he has not seen his nephews for a considerable time. In the course of the play, he returns to London in order to test the character of the two brothers and will probe beneath their respective surfaces. In order to achieve this aim, he ensures the services of Rowley, an old servant of the Surface family and simultaneously a chorus-like character, and of Moses, a Jewish moneylender.

The character of Sir Oliver also functions to link this first and the second group of characters. On his return to London Sir Oliver learns that his old friend Sir Peter Teazle, a confirmed bachelor, has recently married a young country girl. Sheridan employs the traditional motif of the *senex amans* who had appeared in Greek and Roman comedies of classical antiquity and who had resurfaced in William Wycherley's Restoration comedy of manners *The Country Wife* (1675) as Mr Pinchwife, newly married to Margery, a country girl, and in the course of the play Pinchwife is duly cuckolded by Mr Horner (see chapter 8). While the comedy had been successful among Restoration audiences, the punishment of Pinchwife by his adulterous young wife could hardly be performed on the 18th-century stage. As a result, David Garrick reworked the play, called it *The Country Girl* (1766) and avoided the unpalatable motif of adultery by exchanging the character of the married wife by a single country girl who eventually and happily finds herself in wedlock. Sheridan uses the Teazles in a similar fashion.

Sir Peter is, however, not merely plagued by his disobedient young wife; he is also the guardian of his ward Maria whom he would like to see matched with the apparently exemplary Joseph but who is secretly in love with the more flamboyant Charles. Again the two groups of characters are thus interlinked since Joseph would be quite happy to marry Maria, not least because of her considerable fortune, while he also, in true rakish style, tries every trick in the book to seduce Lady Teazle and to cuckold her husband.

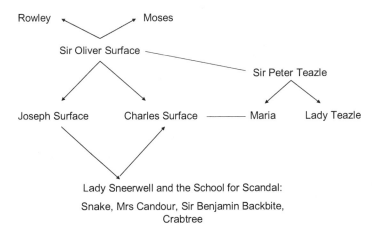

Figure 1: Configuration of Characters

In addition to these two groups of characters, the configuration of the *dramatis personae* is completed by 'the School for Scandal,' presided over by Lady Sneerwell and her back-up team consisting of the fraudulent Snake, the gossiping Mrs Candour, and the scandalmongers Sir Benjamin Backbite and Crabtree. To enhance the complexity of the configurational pattern, the gang around Lady Sneerwell is cleverly integrated into the overall design of the play. In particular, Joseph and Lady Sneerwell have arrived at a clandestine arrangement: since the Lady is, like Maria, secretly in love with Charles, she has agreed to make use of the entire repertoire of the School in order to support Joseph's plans to marry Maria. As a result, the characters within the three groups have numerous connections to each other, but they also pursue different and conflicting aims which are acted out as the plot unfolds.

3. Schemes, Stratagems, and Plotting

The play opens with an exposition set in Lady Sneerwell's house where the School is busy with manipulating the daily newspapers by disseminating misleading information, much in the way which today might be called 'spinning.' Similar to the evil Millwood in George Lillo's *The London Merchant* (1731; see chapter 11), Lady Sneerwell admits that she herself had been the victim of slander in her youth and has ever since vowed to take her revenge by ruining the reputation of other people. As the room gradually fills with the disciples of the School, the scandalmongering soars to incredible heights victimizing various representatives of fashionable London society including Sir Peter and eventually the collective malice is poured on Charles and his financial ruin. Significantly, this is the moment when Maria decides to leave the party, thus not merely indicating her tender feelings for Charles but also the absolute honesty which her name signifies.

In the following scene, one of the School's victims is presented as a completely miserable Sir Peter contemplates on his married state. His relationship to his rebellious wife is the talk of the town and his ward Maria obstinately refuses to marry Joseph but seems to prefer the prodigal Charles. Old Rowley, who embodies the satiric norm of the play, disbelieves in the rumours spread about Charles and reminds his master of the fact that the son may take after his father who was a bit of a spark in his youth but who eventually reformed. However, Sir Peter is not easily pacified, especially because he suspects that his wife conducts a secret love affair with Charles.

Sir Peter's conjugal misery is displayed at the beginning of the second act. As his wife insists on her independence like all fashionable ladies in London he counters by trying to assert his authority as a husband: "Very well! – Ma'am very well! so a husband is to have no influence, no authority?" (2.1.239) The rhetorical nature of the question is instantly revealed in his wife's swift repartee: "Authority! no to be sure – if you wanted authority over me you should have adopted me and not married me. I am sure you were old enough" (ibid.). Even the biting reminder of her humble origins cuts no ice with Lady Teazle who delights in 'teasing' her husband:

> SIR PETER. Yes – yes madam you were then in somewhat an humble Style – the Daughter of a plain country Squire – recollect Lady Teazle when I saw you first – sitting at your tambour in a pretty figured Linnen gown – with a Bunch of Keys by your side, your hair comb'd smooth over a Roll, and your apartment hung round with Fruits in worsted of your own working –
> LADY TEAZLE. O Yes, I remember it very well, and a Curious life I led! My daily occupation to inspect the Dairy, superintend the Poultry, make extracts from the Family Receipt book and Comb my aunt Deborah's Lap-Dog.
> SIR PETER. Yes, yes, Ma'am, 'twas so indeed.
> LADY TEAZLE. And then you know my evening amusements – to draw patterns of Ruffles which I had not the Materials to make – to play Pope Joan with the Curate – to read a Novel to my Aunt – or to be stuck down to an old Spinnet – to strum my Father to sleep after a Fox chase.
> SIR PETER. I am glad you have so good a Memory, – Yes – Madam – These were the Recreations I took you from. – But now you must have your Coach, Vis-à-Vis, and three powder'd footmen before your Chair – and in summer a pair of white Cats to draw you to Kensington gardens – no Recollection I suppose when you were content to ride double behind the Butler on a dock'd Coach Horse.
> LADY TEAZLE. No – I swear I never did that – I deny the Butler, and the Coach Horse.
> SIR PETER. This madam was your Situation – and what have I not done for you? – I have made you a woman of Fashion, of Fortune, of Rank – in short I have made you my Wife –

LADY TEAZLE. Well then and there is but one thing more you can make me to add to the obligation – and that is –
SIR PETER. My widow I suppose?
LADY TEAZLE. Hem! hem! (2.1.240)

Lady Teazle's training in the manners of fashionable London society is completed by the assistance of Lady Sneerwell. In her School, Lady Teazle is instructed about the various ways of destroying the reputation of absent ladies, especially by denigrating their looks and their ungraceful ageing. Joseph uses this moment of merriment to declare his love to Maria, but she does not return his pretended feelings for her. To make matters worse, Lady Teazle has been watching the two and has now every reason to be jealous. Although Joseph manages to appease her eventually, he is afraid that he may finally be found out: "Sincerely I begin to wish I had never made such a Point of gaining so very good a character – for it has led me into so many curs'd Rogueries that I doubt I shall be exposed at last" (2.1.248). His fear is not ungrounded. The second act closes with the happy reunion of Sir Peter and Sir Oliver and with their respective assessments of Joseph and Charles. While Sir Peter admires Joseph's sense of morality and condemns Charles' dissipated lifestyle, Sir Oliver refuses to be biased and decides to put his nephews to the test.

The strategy of scrutinizing the characters of the two brothers is devised in the third act. Rowley informs Sir Oliver that a certain Mr Stanley, a distant relative of the Surface brothers, has become bankrupt and asked Joseph and Charles for financial help. Whereas the older brother politely refused, his younger sibling is anxiously trying to raise money for Stanley although he himself is vastly in debt. Sir Oliver secures the advice of Moses, a Jewish moneylender, who has helped Charles out of his financial trouble before and who knows of a colleague, a Mr Premium, who has agreed to advance a further sum to Sir Oliver's prodigal nephew. As Charles has never seen Mr Premium, Sir Oliver decides to play the role of Premium to Charles while he will present himself as Mr Stanley to Joseph. In order to be really convincing as a moneylender, Moses teaches Sir Oliver a crash course in usury insisting that he must charge at least 40 percent of interest so as to be taken seriously. Interestingly enough, neither usury nor Jewishness is made the butt of satire, but the characters rather quietly acquiesce to the rules of the game.

During the first two acts the audience has heard various reports about Charles and his allegedly dissipated lifestyle, but it is not until scene 3 of act 3 that he has his first appearance. All the rumours about him spread by the School seem to be true as Charles and his friend Careless discuss wit, wine, and women, particularly Maria to whom Charles avows his love. The hilarious juggling with mistaken identities reaches its climax as Sir Oliver as Mr Premium presents himself. Being questioned about his securities Charles admits that he has none left accept his rich uncle Sir Oliver who will bestow his entire fortune on him on the occasion of his death. Not surprisingly, Sir Oliver is taken aback by the thought of his own demise and as Mr Premium assures Charles that Sir Oliver is "as hale and healthy as any Man of his years in Christendom"

(263). His nephew, however, insists on the uncle's extremely bad health: "There again you are misinformed – No, no, the Climate has hurt him considerably – Poor uncle Oliver – yes he breaks apace I'm told – and so much alter'd lately that his nearest Relations don't know him –" (ibid.). Being challenged again whether there is "nothing you would dispose of?" (ibid.) Charles must confess that almost everything of value has been sold to cover his debts, including the family silver and the substantial library. Sir Oliver is deeply shocked by the debauched lifestyle of his nephew and is on the brink of giving him up for good when Charles tells him that the family portraits are still left and that they are now up for sale.

The fourth act opens with the famous "Auction Scene" in which Charles displays the portraits of "the family of the Surfaces up to the Conquest" (4.1.265). One by one his ancestors are knocked down at retail prices, leaving an exasperated and mortified Sir Oliver behind. There is, however, one portrait which Charles is not prepared to part with:

> CHARLES. What that? Oh that's my uncle Oliver, 'twas done before he went to India–
> CARELESS. Your Uncle Oliver! Gad! then you'll never be friends with Charles, That now to me is as Stern a looking Rogue as Ever I saw – an Unforgiving Eye, and a damn'd disinheriting Countenance! an Inveterate Knave depend on't, don't you think so little Premium?
> SIR OLIVER. Upon my Soul Sir, I do not; I think it is as honest a looking Face as any in the Room – dead or alive; but I suppose your Uncle Oliver goes with the rest of the Lumber.
> CHARLES. No hang it, I'll not part with poor Noll – The Old Fellow has been very good to me, and Egad I'll keep his Picture, while I have a Room to put it in.
> SIR OLIVER. [*Aside*] The rogue's my nephew after all! – but, Sir, I have somehow taken a fancy to that Picture.
> CHARLES. I'm sorry for't, for you certainly will not have it – Oons! Haven't you got enough of 'em?
> SIR OLIVER. I forgive him everything! [*Aside*] – but Sir when I take a Whim in my Head I don't Value Money – I'll give as much for that as for all the rest–
> CHARLES. Don't tease me, Master Broker, I tell you I'll not part with it – And there's an End on't–
> SIR OLIVER. How like his Father the Dog is! [*Aside*] well, well, I have done; I did not perceive it before but I think I never Saw such a Resemblance [*Aside*] – well Sir – Here is a Draught for your Sum. (4.1.268)

Charles thus passes his test with flying colours, and his uncle is doubly moved; for one, because Charles was not willing to sell Sir Oliver's portrait and second, because the alleged profligate immediately sent £100 of the auction's proceeds to poor Stanley.

Conversely, the examination of Joseph's character ends in disaster. The third scene of the fourth act has come down in the history of English drama as the "Screen Scene." Set in Joseph's library, the scene opens with Joseph's renewed attempt at seducing Lady Teazle. When she is almost at the point of giving in to his flirtatious offer, her husband is announced and Joseph quickly hides the wife behind a screen from where she will overhear every word of the following conversation. Unaware of his wife's presence behind the screen, Sir Peter confides to Joseph that he is extremely unhappy about his spouse's recent conduct and that, furthermore, he suspects her of infidelity with Charles. Nevertheless, Sir Peter informs Joseph that he has drafted two deeds to settle the financial interests of his wife who will receive an annuity of £800 while he is alive and she will inherit his entire fortune on his death. This conjugal crisis solved, Sir Peter is keen to address his second problem, i.e. Joseph's plan of marrying Maria. Obviously, no topic could be more unwelcome to Joseph at this very moment as Lady Teazle eavesdrops on their conversation. A last-minute reprieve is granted as his brother Charles is announced. Sir Peter tries to hide behind the screen, but since this space is already occupied by his wife, Joseph suggests that he conceals himself in a closet – however, not before Sir Peter has spied a petticoat behind the screen which belongs, as Joseph assures him, to "a little French Millener – a silly Rogue that Plagues me" (4.3.277). Joseph's predicament now becomes even more uncomfortable as husband and wife overhear the ensuing exchange with his brother who refuses to have ever had any design on Lady Teazle since he is in love with Maria while he remembers very vividly the many occasions when "I swear I have seen you exchange such significant Glances –" (4.3.279). Understandably, Joseph is on tenterhooks and must stop his brother from spilling any further secrets. To cut the matter short, he informs Charles that Sir Peter is hiding in the closet to ascertain whether he had any cause for being jealous. The relieved husband is dragged forth from his hiding place and admits that he has suspected Charles wrongfully.

While it seems that Joseph might get out of this scramble unharmed, he finds himself in the next tight spot as Lady Sneerwell is announced. By no means can he allow her to come up even if it entails the risk of leaving Sir Peter and Charles in company together. Still believing in Joseph's virtue and complete honesty, Sir Peter praises Charles' brother as "a man of Sentiment – well! there is nothing in the world so noble as a man of Sentiment!" (4.3.280) while he gleefully admits that Joseph may have his weak spots as he is hiding a girl behind the screen. Charles cannot believe that his sentimental brother may possibly have a girl in his private lodgings and the following stage direction reads: "[*Surface enters just as* CHARLES *throws down the Screen*]" (ibid.). The secret which Joseph had tried to screen off from prying eyes is thus made public as Lady Teazle stands exposed in front of her husband, her would-be seducer and honest Charles who uses this moment of silent recognition to comment on the slim dividing line between morality and hypocrisy:

> CHARLES. Sir Peter – This is one of the smartest French Milliners I ever saw! – egad you seem all to have been diverting yourselves here at Hyde and Seek – and I don't See who is out of the Secret! – Shall I beg your Ladyship – to inform me! – not a word! Brother! – will you please to explain this matter? – what – Morality Dumb too? – Sir Peter – and tho' I found – you in the Dark – perhaps you are not so now – all mute – ! – well tho' I can make nothing of the Affair I Suppose you perfectly understand one another – so I'll leave you to yourselves – [*going*] Brother I'm sorry to find you have given that worthy man so much uneasiness! – Sir Peter – there's nothing in the world so noble as a man of Sentiment! – [*Exit* CHARLES.] (4.3.280 f.)

Joseph's strenuous attempt to exonerate himself remains futile as Lady Teazle, clearly tired of the entire affair and disgusted by her own behaviour, tells her husband the plain truth of the matter:

> LADY TEAZLE. Hear me Sir Peter – I came hither – on no matter – relating to your Ward and even ignorant of this Gentleman's Pretensions to her – but I came seduced by his insidious arguments, at least to listen to his pretended Passion, if not to sacrifice your Honour to his Baseness–
> SIR PETER. Now I believe the Truth is coming indeed–
> SURFACE. The Woman's mad–
> LADY TEAZLE. No Sir – she has recover'd her senses, and your own Arts have furnish'd her with the means. Sir Peter – I do not Expect you to credit me – but the Tenderness you express'd for me when I am sure you could not think I was a witness to it, has penetrated to my Heart and had I left the place without the Shame of this discovery – my future Life should have Spoke the sincerity of my Gratitude – as for that smooth tongue Hypocrite – who would have seduced the wife of his too credulous friend while he affected honourable addresses to his ward – I behold him now in a light so truly despicable – that I shall never again respect myself for having listen'd to him– [*Exit*.] (4.3.282)

Lady Teazle has evidently learned her lesson: not only is she ashamed of having tried to emulate the manners of fashionable London ladies; she also understands that Joseph's passion for her was simply pretended, that she was a mere toy in his game of seducing her while she is deeply moved by the generosity and true affection of her elderly husband. For these reasons her desire to reform seems utterly convincing.

Joseph, on the other hand, has not yet learned his lesson and his punishment is as yet incomplete. His library becomes the scene of his second downfall at the beginning of the fifth act as Sir Oliver, disguised as Mr Stanley, requests financial help. Joseph protests that he cannot be of any service since he himself is rather poor, having given large sums of money to his prodigal brother. Being asked whether he never received any money from his uncle, Joseph avers that he merely obtained worthless trinkets although Sir Oliver knows very well that he sent him the staggering sum of £12,000 – a vast fortune by 18th-century standards. If Charles passed his uncle's examination during the auction scene, Joseph fails miserably in this trial of his character.

Meanwhile the screen incident is the talk of the town and the School is occupied with enlarging on it by inventing further details, including the rumour of a duel in which Sir Peter was seriously, perhaps even mortally wounded, although it is not quite clear whether Joseph or Charles were the attackers. That such ruthless scandalmongering has nothing to do with reality becomes blatantly clear in the second scene of the last act as a completely uninjured Sir Peter enters the stage and peremptorily orders the members of the School out of his house.

At this point towards the end of the play there is only one plot line left unresolved, i.e. Lady Sneerwell's love for Charles. Again Joseph's library is the setting for the defeat of the scheming couple. Sensing that events have taken a turn for the worst since Charles is now reconciled with Sir Peter who will no longer oppose a marriage to Maria, Lady Sneerwell blames Joseph for having wrecked their joint plan of his union with Maria and her marriage to Joseph:

> LADY SNEERWELL. Are not you the cause of it? – what had you to do – to bate in your Pursuit of Maria to pervert Lady Teazle by the way? – had you not a sufficient Field for your Roguery in blinding Sir Peter and supplanting your Brother? – I hate such avarice of crimes – 'tis an unfair monopoly and never prospers. (5.3.292)

This prophecy becomes immediately true. As Sir Oliver enters in the final scene of the play, Joseph mistakes him for poor Mr Stanley whereas Charles gives Mr Premium a hearty welcome. After having revealed his true identity, their uncle assumes the role of a judge who pronounces the punishment of Joseph and offers forgiveness to Charles. Moreover, Charles is rewarded with the hand of the virtuous Maria, thus thwarting Lady Sneerwell's scheme of securing the affection of the younger brother. Even the last trump card up her sleeve, Snake's faked love letters of Charles addressed to her, makes no trick since Snake has been bribed to tell the truth for once. The comedy thus closes on the dismissal of the hypocritical Joseph and the scheming Lady Sneerwell while simultaneously celebrating benevolence, charity, and virtue as embodied in the reformed Charles and in honest Maria.

4. Sheridan, Comedy of Manners, and its Aftermath

The School for Scandal is beyond doubt Sheridan's comic masterpiece and the play "establishes Sheridan as the greatest comic writer of his day" (Booth, et al. 1975: 174). Its major literary merit consists in the fusion of various earlier comic formats, especially of comedy of manners and of sentimental comedy, offering "a major revaluation of seventeenth- and eighteenth-century themes and characters" (Bevis 1988: 229). Well-tried comic conventions are employed in invariably inverted dramatic style: Joseph poses as a man of sentiment and is fashioned as the hero of sentimental comedy although he is at heart a ruthless egotist. As noted at the beginning, the play relies heavily on the comic potential of appearance and reality, signalled by such terms as 'surface' and 'screen:' Joseph screens his stratagems behind a façade of well-rehearsed sentiments, Charles' benevolence is fairly well obscured until the fourth act, and Sir Oliver is a master of assuming disguises in order to probe the moral quality of his nephews underneath their surfaces.

Moreover, the frequent discussions among the characters about wit, its social functions, and individual responsibility clearly underline the two different comic traditions. The gossipers of the School firmly follow the conventions of Restoration comedy of manners, and Lady Sneerwell adamantly insists that there is no true wit without a dose of malice: "Phsaw! – there's no possibility of being witty – without a little ill nature – the malice of a good thing is the Barb that makes it stick" (1.1.231). In the intellectual climate of the 1770s, characterized by reason, understanding, and benevolence, such an attitude, however, did not pass without criticism as voiced by Maria: "For my part – I own madam – Wit loses its respect with me when I see it in company with malice" (ibid.). Comedy of manners meets sentimental comedy on the battleground of wit. Sir Peter for his part sides with Maria when he lectures Lady Sneerwell about the true nature of wit: "Ah! Madam true wit is more nearly allied to good nature than your Ladyship is aware of." (2.2.245) And when the Lady tries to defend the School's privileges of calumny he retorts: "Aye Madam – and then no Person should be permitted to kill characters, or run down Reputations but qualified old Maids and disappointed Widows–" (2.2.246). Sir Peter is well able to lash back himself in the style of manners comedy because his repartee includes "the Barb that makes it stick" being aimed at Lady Sneerwell's unmarried status. While she may be an expert gossiper, she has failed to obtain a male partner in marriage and thus has also been unsuccessful in practising bourgeois values related to family life. As was shown above her design on Charles will eventually come to nothing and Sir Peter's warning that scandalmongering should be the province of "qualified old Maids" may well be a rough sketch of her future life.

In addition, gossiping is not merely concerned with reputation, good or rather bad looks, and failures of refinement. As the case of Charles and his ill fortune indicates, there is a noticeable parallel between slander and money (cf. Leggatt 1998: 48). Both circulate, especially in the hands of Lady Sneerwell's deft media management of the newspapers, both have corruptive powers, and money as well as reputation may be easily lost. Such losses may provoke laughter based on malicious joy which works well on stage but which is hardly socially desirable (cf. Browne 2007). Hence, Sheridan's play invites audiences to partake of the malicious joy of being witty with a little ill nature for the duration of four acts until the School and its spiteful schemes are finally disempowered. Much in the style of sentimental comedy the play ends with the reform of the humbled, but sexually unblemished Lady Teazle who turns her back on the School and is reunited with her husband. Charles also promises to reform and is rewarded financially because he has secured his uncle's affection and fortune (significantly made in the Empire) as well as emotionally through his union with the virtuous, if somewhat nondescript Maria.

The School for Scandal marks the climax of 18th-century comedy (cf. Shepherd & Womack 1997: 169) and of Sheridan's work as a playwright. His last important comedy, *The Critic* (1779), compares unfavourably with the earlier play. Sheridan became increasingly immersed in his duties of managing Drury Lane Theatre and, in 1780, he was appointed Member of Parliament for Stafford, but as a supporter of Charles Fox and the Whig Party he spent most of his time in the opposition. Being continuously harassed by debts, his financial situation deteriorated when Drury Lane burned down in 1809 and when he lost his seat in parliament three years later. Impoverished and ill he died in 1816 and was buried in Westminster Abbey. Although his comic masterpiece was variously criticized in the decades after its first performance on the grounds of alleged immorality, it was also repeatedly revived during the 19th century (cf. Goetsch 1975: 160 f.). It is interesting to note that comedy of manners often flourished towards the end of centuries: Shakespeare's *Much Ado About Nothing*, as suggested earlier in this paper, was premiered in 1600, the major Restoration comedies of manners date from the end of the 17th century, and *The School for Scandal* was first performed in 1777. Sheridan's comedy is thus an important link between Caroline comedies and the revival of manners comedy at the end of the 19th century when Oscar Wilde, yet another Irishman, revived the format in plays like *Lady Windermere's Fan* (1892), *A Woman of No Importance* (1893), *An Ideal Husband* (1895), and in his masterpiece *The Importance of Being Earnest* (1895). If Wilde had any follower, it was Noël Coward who practised the form in the 1920s in plays like *Hay Fever* (1925). While otherwise the theatre has shown little interest in comedy of manners in the 20th century, it might be argued that a number of conventions of this comic format have more recently found their way into situation comedies on television. Fruitful cases for further research might be productions such as *Absolutely Fabulous* (BBC, 1992-2001) and, to give an American example, *Sex and the City* (HBO, 1998-2004).

Bibliography

Primary Sources

Sheridan, Richard Brinsley. 1975 [1777]. *The School for Scandal*. In: Cecil Price (ed.). *Sheridan's Plays*. Oxford: Oxford UP.

Annotated Bibliography

Aristotle. 1996. *Poetics*. Malcolm Heath (ed. & transl.). Harmondsworth: Penguin.
  Poetics *remains the* locus classicus *as regards generic distinctions as well as the specific place of literature as opposed to philosophy.*
Bevis, Richard W. 1988. *English Drama: Restoration and Eighteenth Century, 1660-1789*. London: Longman.
  A well-informed study on the development of English drama from the Restoration period to the beginning of the Romantic age. The book also includes useful references to theatre architecture and audiences.
Booth, Michael R., et al. 1975. *The Revels History of Drama in English*. Vol. VI: *1750-1880*. London: Methuen.
  This eight-volume publication covers the development of drama in English from the Middle Ages right up to more recent trends in American playwriting. Written by various experts in their respective fields, The Revels History is an indispensable companion to drama in English. The sixth volume is of particular interest for dramatic practice in the second half of the 18th century.

Browne, Kevin Thomas. 2007. *Richard Brinsley Sheridan and Britain's School for Scandal: Interpreting His Theater Through Its Eighteenth-Century Social Context.* Lampeter: Edwin Mellen P.

The study traces Sheridan's career as a dramatist and theatre manager as well as a leading Whig politician. Browne argues that Sheridan's artistic and political activities converged in his dramatic practice which shed light on the social struggles over British identity.

Danziger, Marlies K. 1978. *Oliver Goldsmith and Richard Brinsley Sheridan.* New York: Ungar.

More than eighty Irish writers tried their luck in England during the 18th century. This study focuses on Goldsmith and Sheridan as the best-known dramatists of Irish descent during the period. Danziger reconstructs the friendly relations between both writers, their shared ideas on literature and their shaping of an image of Ireland and the Irish for London audiences.

Goetsch, Paul. 1975. "Richard Brinsley Sheridan: *The School for Scandal.*" In: Heinz Kosok (ed.). *Das englische Drama im 18. und 19. Jahrhundert: Interpretationen.* Berlin: Erich Schmidt. 159-69.

Very well-informed essay on The School for Scandal, *providing very detailed information about the composition of the play and its reception.*

Hartnoll, Phyllis (ed.). 1988. *The Concise Companion to the Theatre.* London: Omega Books.

This is an A-Z of the theatre. With entries listed in alphabetical order and numerous cross references the book is easily navigable and provides swift information about almost every relevant topic.

Leggatt, Alexander. 1998. *English Stage Comedy 1490-1990: Five Centuries of a Genre.* London: Routledge.

Leggatt focuses exclusively on the development of comedy as a tool for social criticism. The study discusses all major comic writers in English literature and places them within their respective social contexts.

Shepherd, Simon & Peter Womack. 1997. *English Drama: A Cultural History.* London: Blackwell.

A useful companion piece to Leggatt's study, English Drama *provides a comprehensive account of the cultural history of English drama, especially challenging the often all too tidy way in which previous scholarship has tried to construct distinctive periods within the development of English drama.*

Further Secondary Literature

Goldsmith, Oliver. 1972 [1765]. "Sentimental Comedy." In: John Hampden (ed.). *She Stoops to Conquer*. London: Dent. 163-68.
Shakespeare, William. 1997. *The Norton Shakespeare*. Stephen Greenblatt, et al. (eds.). New York: Norton.
Steele, Richard. 1993. *The Conscious Lovers, The Beggar's Opera and Other Eighteenth-Century Plays*. David Lindsay (ed.). London: Everyman. 65-143.

13. ROMANTIC VERSE DRAMA:
JOANNA BAILLIE'S *DE MONFORT* AND PERCY SHELLEY'S *THE CENCI*

UTE BERNS

1. Romantic Verse Drama

As far as drama is concerned, our genre descriptions for texts written between 1780 and 1830 appear singularly unstable. On the one hand, this instability is due to a shift in modern scholarly perception of the period's drama – a shift first felt some 30 years ago. On the other hand, this instability is due to changes in the period's theatrical and literary culture, which gave rise to an exciting mixture of old and new forms. Both of these factors bear on the current meaning of the term 'Romantic verse drama,' and on recent discussions of Joanna Baillie's and of Percy Shelley's dramatic writing.

In the broadest possible sense, verse drama denotes dramatic writing in verse that is intended for a public performance through actors. Thus described, the roots of this genre go back to the classical Greek and Roman drama of Sophocles (496-405 BC), Euripides (483-406 BC), or Seneca (c. 1-65 AD). In Britain, verse drama of this broad description first flourished in the later Middle Ages and, especially, the Early Modern Period. The tragedies, comedies, and history plays of Christopher Marlowe, William Shakespeare, and Ben Jonson represent prime examples of verse drama, even though they may frequently contain short sections in prose. The enduring verse form these authors perfected in their plays is the iambic pentameter without rhymes, also called blank verse. Later, the Restoration dramatist John Dryden coined the concept of the 'heroic play' cast in rhymed couplets, for instance, *The Conquest of Granada* (1672); a form that soon became the object of satire. By contrast, Thomas Otway's verse tragedy *Venice Preserved* (1682) remained popular right through the Romantic period. After the turn of the century Joseph Addison's verse tragedy *Cato* (1713) stages a classical subject matter in a neoclassical, elevated format. Yet in the course of the 18th century, verse tragedies apparently depending on an aristocratic cast of characters, conflict of national or grave religious import, and on an elevated form of speech continued to lose ground to a proliferation of dramatic prose forms.

Set against this background, the concept of verse drama acquired a more specific meaning when applied to the late 18th and early 19th century – the period referred to as 'Romanticism.' 20th-century literary histories up to about 1990 – if they considered the drama of this period at all – used the generic description 'verse drama,' (sometimes also 'poetic' or 'lyrical drama'), almost synonymously with the description 'Romantic drama' (Fletcher 1966: 19 f.). This term denoted, above all, the dramatic writing of the canonized male Romantic poets William Wordsworth, Samuel Taylor Coleridge, Lord Byron, Percy Bysshe Shelley, and John Keats. Their dramatic texts include Wordsworth's

The Borderers (1799, rev. 1842) and Coleridge's *The Fall of Robbespierre* (1794, written with Robert Southey), *Osorio* (1797) later revised as *Remorse* (1812), and *Zapolya* (1815). Among the second generation of these poets, Romantic verse drama encompasses, for instance, Byron's *Marino Faliero* (1821), *The Two Foscari* (1821), *Sardanapalus* (1821), and *Werner* (1822) as well as *Manfred* (1817), *Cain* (1821), *Heaven and Earth* (1823) and *The Deformed Transformed* (1824), Shelley's *The Cenci* (1819) and *Prometheus Unbound* (1820), and Keats' *Otho the Great* (1819, written with Charles Brown). The dramas thus collected under the generic description of verse drama comprise extremely heterogeneous texts. At the one end of the spectrum there is Byron's *Marino Faliero: An Historical Tragedy* that closely adheres to an Aristotelian structure as it develops a plot modelled on a historical source. At the other end there is Shelley's *Prometheus Unbound: A Lyrical Drama in Four Acts*, inspired by Aeschylus, in which speakers like Prometheus and Jupiter, Spirits of the Hours and Chorus, as well as Earth, Sun, and Moon switch from dialogic utterance to chorus speech or burst into lyrical songs.

Early Modern drama and Shakespeare's plays in particular were extolled as models for Romantic verse drama (cf. Kucich 1998), yet most of the Romantic plays never made it to the stage – Coleridge's *Remorse* and Byron's *Marino Faliero* are notable exceptions. The majority of the Romantic verse plays discussed so far remained unstaged at the time either because the contemporary theatre managers rejected them (as, for instance, in the case of Wordsworth's *The Borderers*), or because they were printed and read, instead of being offered to the theatre.

Earlier critics assembled a number of reasons for what they perceived as the deplorable and bizarre shape of Romantic verse drama. In some accounts, the Romantic poet, primarily concerned with exploring the inner conflicts of the Self, the passions or the imagination, either did not care for external action and plot construction, or did not know how to handle them. Other scholars attributed the specific shape of the Romantic verse play to the authors' disdain for the contemporary theatre that catered to the uneducated masses. Coleridge's applause for efforts to save the British stage "not only from horses, dogs, elephants, and the like zoological rarities, but also from the more pernicious barbarisms and Kotzebuisms in morals and taste [popular plays in the style of the German dramatist August von Kotzebue] [and] the speaking monsters of the Danube [German Gothic drama]" (Coleridge 1983, II: 208) might be quoted as a case in point. Whether for reasons of form and subject matter or because of an unsuitable contemporary theatrical culture – Romantic verse drama, or so the critics argued, was not meant to be staged and watched. It was to be appreciated by a discerning reader in his or her closet. There, the individual reader could enjoy the performance in his or her mind – as 'mental theatre' (cf. Richardson 1988). Romantic verse drama thus became associated with the exploration of the Self – its consciousness and passions – and with a withdrawal from the public stage to the closet.

More recently, however, this characterization of Romantic verse drama has undergone a number of significant qualifications. To begin with, the redeployment of the term 'Romantic' to describe a period rather than a set of aesthetic preferences has opened up a massively extended field of formerly neglected playwrights and dramatic texts. Many of these playwrights are women, some of them famous at the time. Joanna Baillie is a good example, yet Hannah Cowley, Elisabeth Inchbald, and Mary Mitford, among others, also had several of their plays performed, or printed, or both. More importantly, Joanna Baillie (in her cycle *Plays of the Passions* [1798]) and Mary Russell Mitford (e.g. with *Rienzi* [1828] and *Charles the First* [1834]) also wrote verse tragedies. Their plays, both performed and unperformed, together with those of Richard Lalor Sheil, Felicia Dorothea Hemans, James Sheridan Knowles, John Howard Payne Henry Hart Milman, and others have re-established in the minds of modern critics the verse drama of the period as a genre flourishing both on and off the stage.

Moreover, verse drama has become the focus of historicist approaches. Some critics have analysed the extreme mental or emotional states presented in these plays as negotiating the contemporary medical knowledge of psychological or physiological disorders. Other critics have related the plot structures to the historical narrative of the French Revolution and they have foregrounded the hopes and anxieties bound up with this momentous European event as a further, crucial subject matter that complements the explorations of the Self in contemporary verse drama (cf. Hoagwood & Watkins 1998; cf. Simpson 1998). Romantic verse drama has been discussed as a principle medium for conceiving of the relation between introspection and agency, for the performative re-signification of gender roles, and as a platform for forging British national identities.

In addition to these developments in Romantic studies, scholarly interest in late 18th- and early 19th-century theatre has resulted in new insights into the relation between verse drama and theatrical culture. Contemporary theatrical culture was divided between 'licensed theatres' presenting 'legitimate drama,' and a host of unlicensed venues presenting 'illegitimate' theatrical performances in a variety of well-established popular genres, such as farces, burlesques, burlettas, harlequinades, or masques. During the period in question, only two theatres in London, Drury Lane and Covent Garden, were licensed to play serious drama, i.e. tragedies and comedies. These theatres, repeatedly burnt down and rebuilt in enlarged size, could seat between 1500 and 3600 people each and were wholly dependent on commercial success. All the plays presented there had to be submitted in advance to the Examiner of plays, a state official, who could withhold his permission for the performance, or inflict cuts as he thought fit. By contrast, dramatic texts that went to the press did not undergo such advance censorship. On the one hand, this state of affairs offers a plausible rationale for the fact that much politically or religiously sensitive dramatic writing was not submitted to the stage. On the other hand, the censorship pertaining to the stage has rendered critics aware of politically sensitive issues that are frequently displaced onto foreign or orientalized settings in plays written with a view to the stage.

Furthermore, the dichotomy between 'public stage' and 'private closet' has been questioned. On the one hand, this simple opposition neglects the private theatricals in aristocratic households – a practice notoriously described in Jane Austen's novel *Mansfield Park* (1814). On the other hand, the closet was used also for the collective readings of dramatic texts in a circle of friends. Hence, as Kucich (1998), Simpson (1998), and Burroughs (1997) have shown, the possible cultural locations of the period's verse drama, and the ways in which these plays address their spectators or readers are worth attending to and all but straightforward.

Finally, the complex cultural location of Romantic verse drama, its wide range of authors, and its heterogeneous forms have invited a new look at the way in which this drama engages with other dramatic genres of the period. Tragedy and comedy in the licensed theatres competed, in unlicensed theatres, with forms that featured highly corporeal acting styles, music, spectacular stage events, and stunning visual effects. Against the background of the hierarchical genre system produced through the distinction between licensed and unlicensed theatres, the period witnesses the birth of the gothic drama – Gregory Lewis' *The Castle Spectre* (1797) became a hit on stage – and it witnesses the emergence of the melodrama – even before Thomas Holcroft introduced the term 'melodrama' for his adaptation of Pixérécourt's *A Tale of Mystery* in 1802. The verse drama purposefully engages with these contemporary popular forms. For instance Joanna Baillie's *De Monfort* (1798) and Robert Maturin's *Bertram; or, the Castle of St. Aldobrand* (1816) have also been classified as Gothic dramas (cf. Cox 1992) and even Shelley's *The Cenci* could be said to draw on Gothic conventions. Similarly, the texts written in the Hunt-Shelley Circle experiment with generic forms as they combine verse drama and popular forms such as the masque and the harlequinade (cf. Cox 1998: 123-46) – a tendency brought to a climax in Thomas Lovell Beddoes' *Death's Jest-Book* (1827/1850). Rather than meeting its oft proclaimed sad death, the period's invigorated verse drama thus paves the way into the new century – mediating between high and popular culture in intercultural exchanges, forging psychologically intricate as well as proto-modernist forms, and envisioning future types of the stage.

2. Joanna Baillie, *De Monfort*

Today the poet and playwright Joanna Baillie (1762-1851), author of 26 full-length plays, has been firmly established as "the central figure in [the] flowering of new tragedy" (Cox 2003: xviii) at the turn of the 19th century. Byron counted her dramatic power among the greatest the contemporary stage has to offer, and Sir Walter Scott, like many reviewers at the time, proclaimed her the best dramatic writer since Shakespeare. The first volume of Baillie's *Plays on the Passions* appeared anonymously in 1798, containing three plays including *De Monfort*. Moreover, an "Introductory Discourse" prefixed to the plays presents Baillie's theoretical reflections on drama. There she claims that "sympathetick curiosity towards others" (Baillie 2001: 69) forms the basis of our knowledge of others, of ourselves, and of the world. Drawing on this premise she then argues that drama offers a uniquely privileged mode and medium for satisfying this curiosity in a controlled and educational manner. Tragedy in particular can "unveil to us the human mind under the dominion of [...] strong and fixed passions" (ibid.: 86). (In a remarkable footnote she points out that men and women, when placed in similar circumstances, show a kindred spirit and are capable of the same behaviour; cf. ibid.: 89.) Baillie claims that the better tragedy succeeds in showing to us the human mind and passions in their "faithfully delineated nature" (ibid.: 86 f.) rather than through "embellishments of poetry" or "pompous and solemn gravity" (ibid.: 87), the more easily can we appreciate the instructions of drama as pertaining to our own mind and feelings. She thus develops an aesthetics of "simpler constructions, less embellished with poetical decorations" (ibid.: 93) and "true, unsophisticated language" (ibid.: 94), which actually describe very well the structures and supple and versatile blank verse of her own plays. Yet these principles also exerted an enormous influence on Coleridge, Byron, and other dramatists of the period, and they anticipated central claims later made by leading male Romantic poets.

The "Introductory Discourse" sketches an original and ambitious project. Baillie explains that she will tackle the human passions one by one, that each play will focus on a single passion, and that each passion will feature in a pair of plays, i.e. in a tragedy and in a comedy. Within this cycle, the verse tragedy *De Monfort* is dedicated to the passion of hate. As in most of Baillie's other plays, the number of principal characters in *De Monfort* remains small. It encompasses De Monfort and his sister Jane de Monfort, as well as Count Freberg and his wife who befriend both De Monfort and a man called Rezenvelt; added to them are Jerome, with whom De Monfort stays, servants, a page, a monk, an abbess, nuns, etc. The play dramatizes De Monfort's hatred for Rezenvelt; in a moment of frenzy De Monfort attacks him with a sword and is disarmed, yet he eventually murders him in the woods. The corpse is discovered and brought to a small convent, where De Monfort himself seeks refuge in the storm and confesses his crime. His sister and Count Freberg meet him there; he dies before he is officially punished. The scene is a town in Germany and the action is mostly set indoors. In act 1 to 3 the characters move between Jerome's house and the luxurious festivities at Freberg's house; act 4 and 5 are set in the woods and at the convent.

The single plot-line allows for a concentrated depiction of De Monfort's state of mind. As the play opens, and before the protagonist arrives on the scene, the servants and Jerome exchange their observations of De Monfort, formerly "a liberal and quiet man," but "not now the man he was" (1.1.18). From the beginning, this alerts the audience to De Monfort's fits of absentmindedness, erratic changes of topic, and moments of agitation, which are accompanied by a most expressive body language (detailed in numerous stage-directions). As the play develops, De Monfort's inadequate responses to the social life around him signal his gradual loss of control over his passion until Rezenvelt exclaims "De Monfort, thou art mad" (3.3.195). The protagonist's increasing mental derangement is conveyed in a series of well-crafted soliloquies. This somewhat artificial device designed to offer insights into a character's mind experiences a powerful, and final, revival in the Romantic verse tragedy. In Baillie's play, De Monfort's soliloquies swiftly move from snatches of memory to current desperation to dread of future action, as they display the performative, self-intoxicating effects of graphic expressions of hatred. In fact, Baillie's verse drama has been read as a study in mental pathology – a field of knowledge she shared with her brother Matthew, a physician and member of the Royal Society.

Baillie's primary focus is not on a principal event that causes strong passions, but on passions which, in *De Monfort*, appear as grossly exaggerated responses to inconspicuous social events. Yet it is the very lack of a manifest cause for De Monfort's hatred that invites the audience to look at this passion. After all, his hatred is not only founded on personal antipathy. The aristocrat De Monfort characterizes Rezenvelt as his social inferior lately catapulted to the very centre of society through economic success and favourable manners. As if to confirm this account, Count Freberg describes Rezenvelt as "a most accomplished stranger" (1.1.190) and his company "the best banquet-feast I can bestow" (1.2.108); in the social events he takes part in, Rezenvelt commands centre stage. By contrast De Monfort, marginalized by his inadequate behaviour, finds himself threatened in his social position and identity. The pathological hatred staged in this play thus becomes symptomatic of a fundamental social conflict in the wake of the French Revolution that will continue to erupt in Romantic verse drama. What Baillie here thematizes directly through social rivalry along class lines, is just as often cast, in other plays of the time, as a fraternal conflict between brothers, one of them privileged, the other dispossessed – a plot constellation inspired, not least, by Friedrich Schiller's hugely influential play *Die Räuber* (1781).

In addition to the social aspects of De Monfort's hatred, his passion shows remarkable physical, if not erotic qualities – "Oh, the side glance of that detested eye!/ That conscious smile! that full insulting lip!/ It touches every nerve: it makes me mad./ [...] Dost thou woo my hate?" (1.2.197-200) Two instances where it is assumed that his behaviour stems from love (2.1.58 & 2.2.88) add to the impression that De Monfort's feelings are deeply inflected by a homophobic attraction; he repeatedly describes himself unable to fight and repress his passion – "Nature herself does lift her voice aloud,/ It is impossible" (3.1.27). Furthermore, the intimacy between De Monfort and his sister, grown up together as orphans, acquires incestuous overtones – most obviously when Lady Jane, incognito under a mask, searches for her brother at a ball and – initially – talks about herself as if she had been abandoned by a lover (2.1.199-210). De Monfort's passion, thus socially and sexually charged, is shown to gradually emerge from the very centre of the society depicted. Rather than being defused amidst the social entertainments of a class determined on perfecting their luxurious amusements, it is precisely in this complex and open arena of social performances that his passions fester. Yet what initially appears as a mere social friction, in the last two acts is modulated into uncontrollable and monstrous action. This change is emphasized by the Gothic conventions here seeping into the play – the stormy woods at night, the shrieking owl, the bell tolling, a murderer besmeared with blood, maniacal speech, a convent, and a scene of incarceration. Significantly, though, De Monfort's deed does not result in total ostracism and expulsion, even though he finally describes himself as having "no name" (4.3.20; cf. 4.3.35). Instead, his sister is brought to the fore as a commanding and mediating character. In a striking reversal of contemporary gender roles the play portrays the masculine character as a victim of irrational passions while the female character becomes, ultimately, the centre of stability and integration. Lady Jane acknowledges her brother's show of remorse as proof of his humanity and noble nature. And by reminding him of their shared experiences and hardships, she offers him an individualized sense of identity not grounded in class. The play thus not only displays the psycho-sexual forces of the individual as being closely intertwined with fundamental social tensions, but it also contains their eruption through remorse and a female act of re-integration. A final tableau even lends religious pathos to Lady Jane: "([...] *Here they all hang about her:* Freberg *supporting her tenderly*; Manuel *embracing her knees, and old* Jerome *catching hold of her robe affectionately.* Bernard, Abbess, Monks, *and* Nuns, *likewise, gather round her, with looks of sympathy*)" (5.4.104 f.). As Lady Jane, at the centre of the other characters, mourns for her brother, the visual invocation is that of a *pietà*.

Baillie expressly wrote for the stage, but published her work first for a reading audience; only a smaller part of her plays were actually performed. Featuring intense private struggles with closeted and repressed emotions that feed on and spill into public spaces structured by dispersed disciplinary gazes, her plays did not lend themselves easily to performances on the contemporary stage. Facing a huge auditorium, this stage featured demonstrative and emphatically gestural acting styles, as they were famously embodied by the actors Philip Kemble and the famous Sarah Siddons. In her "Introductory Discourse" and especially in her "Preface" to the third volume of *Plays on the Passions*, Baillie therefore thinks up alternatives: smaller architectural spaces, and a different lighting design that would permit for subtler and more nuanced performances of psychological states and development – a vision that would take a long time to materialize (cf. Burroughs 1997: 74-109). Yet whether on stage or in print, Baillie's plays clearly exerted a formative influence on Romantic verse drama.

3. Percy Bysshe Shelley, *The Cenci*

Percy Shelley, canonized first and foremost as a poet, belongs to the second generation of the British Romantic period; he wrote his verse play *The Cenci: A Tragedy in Five Acts* in 1819. In the preface Shelley explains that the events in the play are grounded in historical facts of late 16th-century Italy. During the Pontificate of Clement VIII, the debauched and cruel Count Cenci turns on his children in lethal hatred and submits his daughter Beatrice to incestuous rape. Together with her brother and mother-in-law Beatrice, formerly gentle and amicable, plots her father's death. The deed is soon discovered. And despite interventions in favour of the perpetrators, the Pope, a former beneficiary of Count Cenci's bribes, has them executed.

Whereas Baillie, in her "Introductory Discourse," takes interest in how the principal passions are propelled and shaped by common circumstances, Shelley's preface to

The Cenci sketches a different approach. Shelley insists that "the person who would treat such a subject must increase the ideal and diminish the actual horror of the events [...]" (Shelley 2000: 730). This emphasis on idealizing the dramatic events and characters rather than allowing for their actual and contingent nature has been linked to the neoclassical aesthetics of drama (cf. Curran 1970). And even though Shelley, too, denounces "mere poetry," e.g. the "detached simile" and the "isolated description" (Shelley 2000: 733), he stresses that in drama, the imagery is vital for "the full development and illustration" of the passions (ibid.: 733).

The revenge plot at the core of the historical narrative shapes Shelley's *The Cenci*, and this plot structure reverberates beyond the play. In fact, the Romantic period witnesses a conspicuous revival of the revenge tragedy in verse – whether in Coleridge's *Osorio* and Byron's *Marino Faliero* or in Maturin's *Bertram* and Mitford's *Rienzi*. For playwrights at the time, the pattern of a series of events moving from oppression to violent retaliation seemed to capture, in a prototypical manner, the revolutionary events that had shaped the period – hence the political significance and fundamental ambivalence of this plot (cf. Simpson 1998). In addition, the revenge plot harboured a potential doubling structure that could be invested with psychological interest, since the avenger, ultimately, tends to resemble the perpetrator, whose violence he or she repeats.

Written for the stage, Shelley's *Cenci* is tightly structured, with a sharp focus on the protagonist's development. The events take place in various palaces and houses in Rome and in the Vatican. In act 4 they briefly move to the castle of Petrella, where the murder of Count Cenci takes place, they move back to the hall of justice in Rome and finally to a prison cell. The *dramatis personae* include Count Cenci, his two sons Giacomo and Bernardo, his daughter Beatrice, and his wife, Lucretia, step-mother of all of his children; also Cardinal Camillo Orsino, a prelate who is in love with Beatrice yet deceives her, and the two assassins Olimpio and Marzio, as well as judges, nobles, guards, etc.

Shelley takes great pains, in the first act, to establish the absoluteness of the Count's patriarchal power as well as Beatrice's utter lack of means to escape from her situation. The early scenes show the Count obscenely celebrating the death of two of his sons in Salamanca. His speeches reveal his sadistic desires, which have long moved beyond the mere infliction of death – "I rarely kill the body, which preserves,/ Like a strong prison, the soul within my power,/ Wherein I feed it with the breath of fear/ For hourly pain" (1.1.114-17). With literary ancestors in Elizabethan and Jacobean verse drama and literary relatives in the contemporary Gothic plays, Count Cenci, arguably, stands unsurpassed as the period's embodiment of subtle sadism and ruthless terror combined with considerable self-knowledge.

We also learn that Orsino, for selfish reasons, will not deliver the petition Beatrice has sent to the Pope (1.2.68-71). Furthermore, Beatrice nobly determines that she will not escape from Cenci if that means leaving her brother and step-mother in his power (1.1.16-19). Yet she also fails in her courageous attempt to persuade the visiting nobles that they must save her relatives and herself from her father (1.3.99-164). Beatrice is presented as bold and fearless, as well as possessed with an apparently incorruptible sense of justice and firmness of mind.

As the play progresses, this firmness of mind gives way to distraction in the face of the experience of incest – "I am chocked! There creeps / A clinging, black, contaminating mist about me – 'tis substantial, heavy, thick,/ [...] it [...] eats into my sinews, and dissolves/ My flesh to a pollution, poisoning/ The subtle, pure, and inmost spirit of life!" (3.1.16-23) This sense of corruption and loss of identity is developed further in an intensely poetic language. Beatrice appears to have lost all access to herself when she refers to herself as "I, who can feign no image in my mind/ Of that which has transformed me" (3.1.108 f.). It is in this traumatic situation that the idea of vengeance takes shape: "If I try to speak/ I shall go mad. Aye, something must be done;/ What, yet I know not – something which shall make/ The thing that I have suffered but a shadow/ In the dread lightning which avenges it." (3.1.85-89) Thus framed, vengeance turns into a desperate attempt to upstage a primary, traumatic, and annihilating act of violation. Crucially, the crime itself, the incest, is never named and remains inexpressible throughout the play. Emerging from the father's orgy of destruction, the daughter's thought and act of vengeance thus acquire a twofold quality. On the one hand, vengeance cannot but replicate the father's transgressive violence, thus producing an uncanny and novel kinship between Beatrice and the old Cenci. On the other hand, the act of vengeance acquires a therapeutic quality. The more Beatrice sets her mind on this act, the more she regains a sense of self-possession and agency. Ultimately, she boldly resolves to become her own legislator and judge – "I [...] at length determined what is right" (3.1.221 f.).

This regained self-command characterizes her behaviour to the last, yet it is presented in a highly ambivalent manner. While the other characters either attempt to flee (Orsino), revert to remorse (Giacomo), or lose their grip on themselves (her mother), Beatrice remains admirably firm. This means, however, that she denies the deed and turns against the assassin she engaged, who has accused her. By using her full rhetorical power, she makes him recant and take the blame on himself alone, before he dies on the rack. Beatrice's attitude and lack of remorse thus stand in marked contrast to the ending of Baillie's *De Monfort*, and, as Julie Carlson has shown (1994: 176-83), this contrast can be generalized. Baillie, Coleridge, and Wordsworth, in the wake of the French Revolution, dramatize, first, acts of violence, and then a remorse that refers back to the original political order. The later generation of dramatists tend to have their characters move on into a space where the initial moral categories appear no longer applicable, and new laws have not yet been forged – a space the ethical-political co-ordinates of which still need to be designed.

Shelley dramatizes a conflict in the family in which the father's and daughter's positions signify absolute power and subjection respectively. At the same time, the text also renders explicit the relation between the head of the family and the head of the state. The Pope, described as "a rite, a law, a custom, not a man" (5.4.5) will not be merciful. Urged by Camillo to consider the monstrous crimes which led the Cenci relatives to act, the Pope replies, "Parricide grows so rife/ That soon, for some just cause, no doubt, the young/ Will strangle us all [...] / Authority, and power, and hoary hair/ Are grown crimes capital" (5.4.20-24). By having the Pope realize that the assassination affects his own security, the Cenci narrative is made to resonate on a political plane.

No matter whether Beatrice's action is considered in a domestic context or as a political allegory, Shelley appears to comment on the ambivalence in her portrayal when he emphasizes, in his preface, that the play must not be subservient to a 'moral purpose' in the ordinary sense. Drama "in its highest form" rather aims to "teach [...] the human heart, through its sympathies and antipathies, the knowledge of itself" (2000: 730). The play, he argues, fulfils this purpose because it will push the spectator into "the restless and anatomizing casuistry with which men seek the justification of Beatrice, yet feel that what she has done needs justification" (ibid.: 731). Thus challenging the reader or spectator to fully confront the protagonist's action does not, however, prevent Shelley from offering his own controversial verdict: Beatrice should not have killed her father. Shelley argues that no person can be truly dishonoured by the act of another; and that "revenge, retaliation, atonement are pernicious mistakes" (ibid.: 730).

It is important to note at this stage that Shelley wrote *The Cenci* in 1819, while working on his other drama, *Prometheus Unbound* (1820), and that, in both of his dramas, he sketches a cycle of revenge. In *Prometheus Unbound*, Prometheus, chained to a rock by Jupiter, initially gives vent to his desire for vengeance by cursing his enemy. As the play progresses, the momentous dramatic development consists in the fact that Prometheus changes his attitude, renounces his vengeful curses, and finally adopts a sympathetic and loving attitude. This change of mind and heart effectively sets Prometheus free and disempowers his enemy – it signifies the overcoming of the age-old cycle of oppression and retaliation and announces a revolutionary utopian future lavishly depicted in a variety of visionary lyrical forms.

The different treatment of the topic of revenge in the two verse dramas corresponds to the different *dramatis personae*, settings, and uses of genre. While the utopian transformation of Prometheus' vengeance into love is set in the realm of the Gods in the 'lyrical drama,' the vengeance enacted by Beatrice is set in human history in the 'tragedy.' Moreover, this human history and its specific social and gendered realities are endowed with an overriding force as they shatter and shape the central character. Those realities actually run counter to the idealizing presentation of human nature and character Shelley envisions for his drama in the preface. On this account, as Mark Bruhn has recently argued, "Shelley stands as a pivot in the history of Western dramatic style, poised between the movements we know broadly as neoclassicism and realism" (2001: 714). Unsurprisingly, the reviews did not take kindly to the *The Cenci*'s subject matter of patriarchal tyranny and incest, and the play did not make it onto any contemporary stage. Yet Shelley's verse drama met with great admiration and fascination in later decades. George Bernard Shaw promoted the first private staging of the play in 1886, and Antonin Artaud's adaption *Les Cenci* (1935) inscribed Shelley's text with a disruptive and sensual language as well as a corporeal and gestural acting style.

4. Later Developments

Later in the 19th century, Browning's dramatic monologues will owe much to the Romantic tradition of the verse drama, yet these monologues are read as dramatic poetry. On the stage, the dominantly realist forms of drama (including the melodrama) have little use for the verse form which conveys a sense of decorum and artificiality that is hard to square with the desire for verisimilitude. The revival of the verse drama only comes with the British modernists, and in this context the very artificiality of the verse form becomes attractive as an antidote to the British realist tradition shaped by Shaw and influenced by Henrik Ibsen.

In his attempt to renew Irish drama and revive Celtic legends for the stage, William Butler Yeats, an avid reader of Shelley and, later, Blake, experimented with verse drama as well as the ritualized forms of the Japanese Noh theatre. His early play *Countess Cathleen* (1892), the one act play *The Shadowy Waters* (1900), and the tragedy *Deidre* (1906), all written in verse, present fables from Irish myth. Staged at the Abbey Theatre at the turn of the century, *The Countess Cathleen* helped to launch a new beginning of dramatic writing in Ireland, even though the verse form found few followers. Pruned into a national drama through several revisions, the verse form and the symbolist language of the play combine into a powerful evocation of Irish history and the struggle for liberty (see chapter 17).

In Britain, verse drama in the 20th century is firmly linked to the modernist poet and critic T.S. Eliot. Leaving behind the blank verse, Eliot eventually developed a verse scheme modelled on the late 15th-century morality play *Everyman* (anonymous). His play *Murder in the Cathedral* (1935) successfully rendered Archbishop Thomas Becket's historical martyrdom in the 12th century in the form of a verse drama complete with a chorus. Eliot soon moved beyond the topics then admitted suitable for verse drama – such as remote history or myth. Inspired by Yeats last play *Purgatory* (1938) that treats a family saga, Eliot began to deploy received plots and stock situations from contemporary drama, for instance in his verse plays *The Family Reunion* (1939), *The Cocktail Party* (1949), and *The Confidential Clerk* (1953). In these instances the verse helps both to foreground the formulaic hollowness of social life and to intimate the existence of a spiritual realm. Eliot's influence on British playwriting continued into the post-war period, and can be felt especially in Christopher Fry's verse comedies – best known among them *The Lady's Not For Burning* (1948).

The experimental Group Theatre in London, which staged some of Eliot's plays in the 1930s, also presented W.H. Auden's verse plays and collaborative work by Auden and Christopher Isherwood. These plays cast revolutionary politics into forms that drew on German expressionism and epic theatre alike. *The Dance of Death* (Auden 1934) and *The Ascent of F6* (Auden & Isherwood 1936) merge Freudian and Marxist perspectives as they treat the class war and the ascent of fascism in Europe. More recent examples of verse plays, combining the epic and the parodic, include John Arden's *The Hero Rises Up* (1968) and Caryl Churchill's *Serious Money* (1987, see chapter 22).

Bibliography

Primary Sources

Baillie, Joanna. 2001 (1798). *Plays on the Passions*. Paul Duthie (ed.). Peterborough, ON: Broadview.

Beddoes, Thomas Lovell. 1935. *The Works of Thomas Lovell Beddoes*. H.W. Donner (ed.). London: Oxford UP.

Byron, George Gordon. 1993. *The Complete Poetical Works*. Jerome J. McGann (ed.). Oxford: Clarendon P.

Coleridge, Samuel Taylor. 1983. *Biographia Literaria*. James Engell & W. Jackson Bate (eds.). 2 vols. Princeton, NJ: Princeton UP. 208.

—. 2001. "Poetical Works." In: Kathleen Coburn & J.C.C. Mays (eds.). *Plays: The Collected Works of Samuel Taylor Coleridge*. Vol 3. Princeton, NJ : Princeton UP.

Cox, Jeffrey N. (ed. & intro.). 1992. *Seven Gothic Dramas: 1789-1825*. Chicago: Ohio UP.

Keats, John. 1970. "Otho the Great." In: H. Buxton Forman (ed.). *The Poetical Works and Other Writings of John Keats*. Vol. 5. New York: Phaeton P.

Mitford, Mary Russell. 1854. *The Dramatic Works of Mary Russell Mitford*. 2 vols. London: Hurst and Blackett.

Shelley, Percy Bysshe. 2000 [1817-1819]. *The Poems of Shelley*. Kelvin Everest & Geoffrey Matthews (eds.) Vol. 2. London: Longman.

Wordsworth, William. 1982 [1842]. *The Borderers*. Robert Osborn (ed.). Ithaca/London: Cornell UP.

Annotated Bibliography

Bruhn, Mark J. 2001. "'Prodigious mixtures and confusions strange': The Self-Subverting Mixed Style of *The Cenci*." In: *Poetics Today* 22.4: 713-63.
Considers the relation between Shelley's theoretical writing on the aims of drama and his style in The Cenci.

Burroughs, Catherine. 1997. *Closet Stages: Joanna Baillie and the Theatre Theory of British Romantic Women Writers*. Philadelphia: U of Pennsylvania P.
Focus on drama theory by female playwrights and actresses; re-appreciation of the closet space.

— (ed.). 2000. *Women in British Romantic Theatre: Drama, Performance, and Society, 1790 – 1840*. Cambridge: Cambridge UP.

Covers Baillie, Inchbald, Mitford and less familiar dramatists; rewarding combination of literary and theatre studies.

Carlson, Julie A. 1994. *In the Theatre of Romanticism: Coleridge, Nationalism, Women*. Cambridge: Cambridge UP.

Focus on Coleridge; gender relations, introspection and agency in drama and on the contemporary stage.

Cox, Jeffrey. 1998. *Poetry and Politics in the Cockney School: Keats, Shelley, Hunt and Their Circle*. Cambridge: Cambridge UP.

Chapter four: on generic hybridity in Romantic drama.

— & Michael Gamer (eds.). 2003. *The Broadview Anthology of Romantic Drama*. Peterborough, ON: Broadview P.

Excellent 'Introduction'.

Crochunis, Thomas C. (ed.). 2004. *Joanna Baillie, Romantic Dramatist: Critical Essays*. London/New York: Routledge.

Broad spectrum of up-to-date scholarship on Baillie.

Curran, Stuart. 1970. *Shelley's* The Cenci: *Scorpions Ringed with Fire*. Princeton: Princeton UP.

Full-length study of the play, discussing both poetry and drama.

Fletcher, Richard M. 1966. *English Romantic Drama 1795-1843: A Critical History*. New York: Exposition.

Old style discussion of the canonized male Romantic dramatists; useful for understanding the debates that followed.

Hoagwood, Terence A. & Daniel P. Watkins. 1998. "Romantic Drama and Historical Hermeneutics." In: Terence A. Hoagwood & Daniel P. Watkins (eds.). *British Romantic Drama: Historical and Critical Essays*. London: Associated UP. 22-56.

Situates Romantic verse drama in history; useful collection of articles in this whole volume.

Kucich, Greg. 1998. "A Haunted Ruin: Romantic Drama, Renaissance Tradition, and the Critical Establishment." In: Terence A. Hoagwood & Daniel P. Watkins (eds.) *British Romantic Drama: Historical and Critical Essays*. London: Associated UP. 56-84.

On crucial role of Early Modern drama for Romantic verse drama; revises discussion about 'stage versus closet.'

Richardson, Alan. 1988. *A Mental Theatre: Poetic Drama and Consciousness in the Romantic Age*. University Park: Pennsylvania State UP.

Discusses plays by Wordsworth, Byron, Shelley and Beddoes as dramas of psychology and the mind.

Simpson, Michael. 1998. *Closet Performances: Political Exhibition and Prohibition in the Dramas of Byron and Shelley*. Stanford: Stanford UP.

In-depth analyses of individual plays, their politics, and the way they address their readers.

Wiggins, Kayla McKinney. 1993. *Modern Verse Drama in English: An Annotated Bibliography*. Westport: CT. Greenwood P.

Covers several hundred dramas written in verse or verse and prose between 1935 and 1992 (Eliot, Fry, and Arden as well as lesser-known playwrights); useful 'Introduction'.

14. VICTORIAN MELODRAMA:
THOMAS HOLCROFT'S *A TALE OF MYSTERY* AND
DOUGLAS WILLIAM JERROLD'S *THE RENT DAY*

GABRIELE RIPPL

1. Introduction: The Melodrama Formula

Etymologically, the term melodrama is a composite of two Greek terms: *melos* for 'song' and *drama* for 'action.' It was originally applied to all musical plays, including opera; at the beginning of the 18th century, melodrama was a mode/genre which combined spoken recitation with short pieces of accompanying music so that music and spoken dialogue alternated and in which music sometimes accompanied pantomime; later, in Victorian England it came to be the name for sensational and romantic stage plays produced to emphatic musical accompaniment. As in modern motion pictures, theme music was used in Victorian melodrama to denote stock characters and to manipulate the spectator's emotions; the musical accompaniment underlined pivotal scenes charged with extravagant emotions and heightened meaning, but it also helped to circumvent the Licensing Act of 1737 (repealed in 1843), which confined the performance of 'legitimate' drama, i.e. regular comedy and tragedy, in London to three theatres holding royal patents: Drury Lane, Covent Garden, and, later, the Little Theatre in the Haymarket. Non-patent theatres, so-called minor theatres, were also flourishing, but they had to offer alternative dramatic entertainment such as dumb show, music, melodrama, and spectacle, and were quick to customize melodrama.

Since the 19th century was a century of industrialization in England, melodrama was an immensely popular entertainment for the industrial working class. The rapid growth of metropolitan populations led to an enormous spread of minor theatres performing melodrama (cf. Booth 1965: 52), which eventually became the mass medium of the time. So in England, unlike in France, melodrama was distinctly lower middle-class and working-class entertainment, and has hence been considered a democratic and egalitarian art form:

> Villains are remarkably often tyrants and oppressors, those that have power and use it to hurt. Whereas the victims, the innocent and virtuous, most often belong to a democratic universe: whatever their specific class origin, they believe in merit rather than privilege, and in the fraternity of the good. (Brooks 1976: 44)

Full of spectacular elements, Victorian melodrama relied heavily on a sensational plot and rapid action. It favoured character stereotypes, rewarded virtue and punished vice and, in the majority of cases, had a happy ending. The terms 'melodrama' and 'melodramatic' are still used today to characterize literary works (whole or part), but also movies and TV film productions, which like their stage counterpart rely on sensational action and violently appeal to the viewers' emotions. The constituents required of a good melodrama with its world of rigid moral distinctions and certainty, in which situation and characters are simple and unambiguous, are described as follows:

> Take an innocent man and a defenceless woman, both of them wholly admirable and free from fault. Present them sympathetically, so that an audience will identify with them and share their hopes. And then set against them every obstacle you can devise. Persecute them with villains, dog them with ill-luck, thrust them into a hostile world which threatens at every moment their instant annihilation. Dramatize these excitements as effectively as the resources of the stage will allow, heighten suspense with music, relieve it with laughter and tears. And then, when all seems lost, allow your hero and heroine to win. Let villainy be outwitted, ill-luck reversed, physical danger overcome and virtue finally rewarded with infinite joy. (Smith 1973: 15)

Melodrama scholarship can be divided into historical and trans-historical approaches. The majority of critics have discussed melodrama as a distinct 19th-century genre whose main functions were wish fulfilment and sensory excitement. Due to its formulaic character they use the term derogatively for a minor drama form and infantilizing product of popular culture (cf. Schmidt 1986: 13-15). In the last few decades, however, this mainly negative evaluation has been dramatically reversed as critical interest in popular and mass culture has turned to melodrama as

> a central element of modern narrative culture, finding in it an essential mode of consciousness in the post-sacred world; a core rhetoric of emergent mass discourses of community and identity; a foundational aesthetic in the development of the novel, film, and television; a dominant language in the modern conduct of public life and politics; and a shaping force in the creation of modern conceptions of family, gender, race, and nation. (Buckley 2009: 176)

Subsequently, critics started to de-historicize the genre. By disregarding the specific historical situation and its cultural dynamics, they have discussed melodramas as performed in 19th-century working-class theatres together with early film melodrama, recent bestsellers, or TV soap operas as "the transhistorical marker[s] of a disruptive, modern mode of consciousness and representation" (Hays & Nikolopoulos 1996: vii). Michael Booth's study *English Melodrama* (1965), a work published half a century ago, is still considered "the best formal history of theatrical melodrama" (Buckley 2009: 178). Booth defines melodrama as

> a dream world inhabited by dream people and dream justice, offering audiences the fulfilment and satisfaction found only in dreams. An idealization and simplification of the world of reality, it is in fact the world its audiences want but cannot get. Melodrama is therefore a dramatization of this second world, an allegory of human experience dramatically ordered, as it should be rather than as it is. (1965: 14)

In spite of "an incredible amount of violence, physical disaster, and emotional agony," Booth explains melodrama's unique and enduring popularity by the genre's "romantic and escapist appeal" (ibid.). In a different vein, James L. Smith in the 1970s evaluated Victorian melodrama as a truly popular theatre, which produced many excellent plays and which shows us what life was really like in the navy, on the farm, out of work or down the mine. It charts working-class attitudes to pressgangs, prostitution, alcoholism, rack-rent landlords and colonial expansion. It examines the impact on society of steam looms, iron ships, railways, telegraph systems, wireless, airships, balloons, submarines, imperialist wars and the gold fever. (Smith 1973: 50)

One of the most influential studies on melodrama is Peter Brooks' *The Melodramatic Imagination* (1976), which discusses French theatre from 1790 to 1830 and links melodrama explicitly to Freud's psychoanalysis. He claims that melodrama has become "the principal mode for uncovering, demonstrating and making operative the essential moral universe in a post-sacred era" (Brooks 1976: 15). Arguing that the hystericized body is a key emblem in the performative rhetoric of melodrama, Brooks sees the main function of the genre in the full acting out of moral statements, thus acknowledging their truth. It uses spectacles, hyperbolic situations, grandiose phraseology, and clear body and sign language to bring across its message of simple moral and psychological absolutes. By relying on the body as a site of meaning, it "provides of saying what is in 'real life' unsayable" (ibid.: 41). Its existence, appeal, and persistence are hence founded in an aesthetics of embodiment: the possibility of saying everything through body language, of "rhetorical breaking-through of repression" (ibid.: 42).

In the 1990s, critics such as Jacky Bratton, Jim Cook, and Christine Gledhill saw melodrama's cultural role "in mediating socio-political change" and "as an agent of modernity" and maintained that "melodrama produces the body and the interpersonal domain as the sites in which the socio-political stakes its struggles" (1994: 1). Michael Hays and Anastasia Nikolopoulos suggest that melodrama to some degree

served as a crucial space in which the cultural, political, and economic exigencies of the century were played out and transformed into public discourses about issues ranging from the gender-specific dimensions of individual station and behavior to the role and status of the 'nation' in local as well as imperial politics. (1996: viii)

Due to the fact that melodrama's heroes and heroines, but also its villains and villainesses, are all exiles, Matthew S. Buckley has more recently suggested melodrama as a genre bound intimately to exile and experiences of "dislocation and displacement, loss and fracture" (2009: 175). He analyses what this 'refugee' theatre has to tell us about the formation of modern drama and the production of modern culture and consciousness as such. According to him, the experience people shared during the decade of the French Revolution (1789-1799) was one of fractured domestic community, violent disenchantment with the world, and a post-sacred sense of order and structure of reality. The Revolution brought with it a series of uncontrollable events which ended in terror and extended trauma: "[E]arly melodrama enacted a pattern of events that corresponds recognizably with the crises of revolutionary experience" (ibid.: 180). The genre refigured the traumatic history it rehearsed by offering a conservative moral vision and by framing "its narratives of trauma from the start within closing fantasies of redemptive justice and restored community" and by "reinscribing social and political conflict into the more intensely theatrical dynamics of personal and domestic relations.

The aim of these tactics was not moral didacticism, but emotional force and intensity of effect" (ibid.: 180 f.), for the very reason that the spectators of early melodrama had themselves been all eye-witnesses at the greatest drama of history and were used to a heightened, concentrated reality. Melodrama's formal qualities, such as a fast pace as well as the extreme violence, derive from a "serial aesthetic guided by a successive logic of intensification and acceleration of traumatic shock" (ibid.: 182). Buckley's reading reverses many conventional assumptions about melodrama as an emotionally superficial and thoroughly unrealistic genre and presents it as a form close to

> sensational expressionism, an emotionally harrowing, psychologically incisive drama, populated by characters whose flatness marks them out as figures of emotional projection, structured by conventions that correspond to, and help to create and reinforce, deep-seated patterns of affective response, and credible most to those whose experiences of violence and dislocation were most intensive and sustained. (Buckley 2009: 188)

2. The Development of Melodrama: Gothic to Military and Nautic

While some critics maintain that many Greek tragedies share with Victorian drama a fundamentally melodramatic view of life (Smith 1973: 7), in his classical study of melodrama, Michael R. Booth maintains the line of descent of melodrama in England to start much later: "one could go back as far as the fifteenth-century morality play" (Booth 1965: 40); he also considers Elizabethan and Jacobean tragedy (*Hamlet*, *Macbeth* and *Richard III* are discussed as proto-melodramas) as well as 18th-century sentimental drama as forerunners, for instance domestic tragedies, such as George Lillo's *The London Merchant* (1731) and Edward Moore's *The Gamester* (1753) (cf. ibid.: 40 f.). Other sources, which influenced the development of the genre, are the Italian *commedia dell'arte*, the Gothic and sentimental elements of German *Sturm und Drang* drama (Goethe, Schiller, von Kotzebue) as well as Parisian melodrama of the post-Revolutionary period, notably the sixty-odd plays of the French melodramatist René Charles Guilbert de Pixérécourt. Most critics consider Jean-Jacques Rousseau's monodrama (written for one actor) *Pygmalion* (1775) the first full melodrama, and it was Rousseau who first used the term 'melodrama' in 1772 to describe his technique in *Pygmalion* for expressing by musical means the emotions of a silent character. However, not only did French influences help to shape English melodrama, English sentimental works as well as Gothic plays and novels were also "partly responsible for the creation of a distinctive French melodrama in the 1790's" (Booth 1965: 44). Fully-fledged English stage melodrama developed as a distinctly separate form in the 1790s.

The 19th century produced an extraordinary number of melodramas on the English stage, a large proportion of which were adaptations of French melodramas as well as English and American novels. Gothic melodrama with its suspense, ghosts, mysteries, and tyrannical villains was the earliest type of melodrama and "flowered on the English stage in the 1790's, bloomed luxuriantly for fifty years or so and then slowly withered away" (ibid.: 67). The settings are often gloomy castles, in whose dungeons rightful heirs are incarcerated, or dark forests "illuminated only by lightening, through which the desperate and exhausted heroine, with or without babe in arms, flees the tyrant or robber band, hair streaming out behind her and clothes in disarray" (ibid.: 68). Virtuous woodmen and peasants, distressed fathers, savage bandits, indefatigable heroes, abducted heroines, and apparitions of ghosts (which was facilitated by the immense improvements in stage mechanics) and victims of all kinds are eyewitnesses of hideous crimes and gory combats and fights. The tyrant's victims and wronged heroines have to face unimaginable cruelty, but justice is always brought to their oppressor in the end. For subject matter and emotional extremism dramatists could rely on contemporary Gothic novels such as Horace Walpole's *The Castle of Otranto* (1764), Ann Radcliffe's *The Mysteries of Udolpho* (1794), Matthew Gregory Lewis' *The Monk* (1796), and Mary Shelley's *Frankenstein; or, The Modern Prometheus* (1818). However, they simplified the plots of the Gothic novels, intensified their sensational and supernatural elements and often introduced humorous characters in order to add comic relief to violent scenes of fear and pathos.

By the time René Charles Guilbert de Pixérécourt's first melodramas appeared on the stages of Paris, Gothic melodrama was well-established in the patent theatres of London. Its central aim was to arouse horror and fear and it was one of the most successful sub-genres, sharing many features with later types of melodrama, in particular domestic melodrama (see below). Supernaturalism (e.g. the frequent appearance of ghosts) and the more gloomy meditation and nervous manner of the staple Gothic villain (testifying to his troubled conscience) as well as hired assassins and the restoration of the rightful heir are specific characteristics of Gothic melodrama which can be subcategorized further. Matthew Gregory Lewis' immediately successful *The Castle Spectre* (1797, based on his Gothic novel *The Monk*) belongs to a first type of Gothic melodrama, namely the "castle-dungeon-spectre melodrama" (Booth 1965: 76); the most famous Gothic melodrama, Isaac Pocock's *The Miller and His Men* (1813), is an excellent example of the later "bandit-cottage-forest type" (ibid.) in which the banditti flourish in their secret hideouts and forests, and the virtuous suffer in their humble cottages. Another prolific and successful author of Gothic melodramas was William Dimond who produced a classic with *The Foundling of the Forest* (1809).

A third sub-type of Gothic melodrama is the "monster melodrama" (ibid.: 84) which has been called an early equivalent of the modern horror film: "Here the main attraction is commonly a non-human fiend of terrible powers who makes the lives of hero and heroine even more trying than usual" (ibid.). An example is Henry M. Milner's *The Man and the Monster* (1823), an adaptation of Mary Shelley's *Frankenstein*. Vampires were a popular subject, for instance in James Robinson Planché's *The Vampyre; or, The Bride of the Isles* (1820) and George Blink's *The Vampire Bride* (1834). Also closely related to Gothic melodrama is the so-called 'dog drama,' which put dogs and other animals on stage. English audiences had always been infatuated by performing animals and "enthusiastically applauded Frederic Reynolds' *The Caravan; or, The Driver and His Dog* (1803), in which the dog Carlo leaps into the sea to save a child" (ibid.: 86). Eastern melodrama with its highly imaginative Eastern setting is another sub-species of Gothic melodrama, but is even more romantic and relying more heavily on spectacle than the former. The first Eastern melodrama was George Coleman the Younger's *Blue Beard* (1798), which combines familiar Gothic elements with a Turkish setting; one of the most famous and most spectacular of Eastern melodramas is William Thomas Moncrieff's *The Cataract of the Ganges; or, The Rajah's Daughter* (1823) which contains many grand processions and lavish scenes in a Rajah's palace and a Brahmin temple.

Another popular sub-genre was military melodrama, which was a product of the war with France and the French Revolution and which is replete with patriotic sentiments: It celebrates Britain's military glories on land, including the country's victories against Napoleon. Nautical melodrama, too, celebrated heroes of insular nationalism such as Wellington and Nelson (ibid.: 93-117). Pioneering plays were Edward Fitzball's *The Flying Dutchman; or, The Phantom Ship* (1827, which like many Gothic melodramas includes monsters and supernatural beings) and Douglas William Jerrold's *Black-Eyed Susan; or, "All in the Downs"* (1829). Other examples are Jerrold's *The Mutiny at the Nore; or, British Sailors in 1797* (1830) and Fitzball's *The Red Rover* (1829). Sadler's Wells Theatre, also briefly known as the Aquatic Theatre, specialized in nautical melodrama and marine spectacles.

3. Domestic Melodrama: Thomas Holcroft's *A Tale of Mystery* and Douglas William Jerrold's *The Rent Day*

The sub-categories of melodrama we have discussed so far are heuristically important, but they are also artificial for the very reason that melodrama in general tends to combine elements of several types. The two melodramas at the centre of our interest, Thomas Holcroft's *A Tale of Mystery* (1802) and Douglas William Jerrold's *The Rent Day* (1832), are primarily domestic melodramas, nevertheless Holcroft's play shares features with Gothic melodrama, and it can be argued that Jerrold's melodrama has – at least to a certain extent – a political agenda, even though we might hesitate to call the play a political melodrama.

Nautical melodrama continued to be successful, while domestic melodrama with its several distinct sub-species also started to attract many spectators. According to Booth, domestic melodrama "offered audiences the same escapism as other kinds, that is, an ideal world of dreams fulfilled" (1965: 120). However, the setting is not wildly romantic, fantastical, military, or nautical, but much closer to the audience's own environment of the factory workplace, slums, crowded streets, hunger, and cold. "Dramatists were quick to offer them familiar situations, settings and characters met with every day, all served up, however, with thrills and happy endings *not* encountered in ordinary life: in other words, realistic raw material processed into an end product of fantasy" (ibid.). Booth considers it a curious paradox that a mostly unreal content is combined with "increasingly realistic settings, a dream world disguised as a true one" (ibid.). Very popular were domestic melodramas with metropolitan settings dealing with alcoholism and the dangers of gambling. Examples are Andrew V. Campbell's *The Gambler's Life in London; or, Views in the Country, and Views in London* (1829), Douglas W. Jerrold's *Fifteen Years of a Drunkard's Life* (1828), and W.H. Smith's, *The Drunkard; or, The Fallen Saved* (1844). The sensationalism of these melodramas vividly exhibited the horrible consequences of drink and gambling, thus supporting the moral admonition aimed at by the dramatists. According to Booth, melodrama is in so many ways "a true social reflector of its times that it is not surprising to find it portraying industrial unrest as well as urban squalor and the problems of drink" (1965: 136). Examples of melodramas strongly sympathetic towards the discontent of the factory worker are John Thomas Haines' *The Factory Boy; or, The Love Sacrifice* (1840), set on Merseyside, and John Walker's *The Factory Lad* (1834). The latter is a serious melodrama about a group of honest weavers made redundant by the introduction of steam-looms and offers no comic relief nor does it present solutions to prevent industrial unrest and class hatred. As Simon Trussler maintains in the context of England's emerging industrialized society, it is "possible to propose that the theatre and politics were now becoming inextricably intertwined, and in consequence [...] the drama was perhaps more responsive to the social conditions of the mass of the people than ever before" (Booth 1965: 196). Edward Stirling's *The White Slave, The Flag of Freedom* (1849) is also a domestic melodrama which deals with another pressing social issue of the time, namely slavery.

Thomas Holcroft (1745-1809) was a largely self-educated stable boy who became a shoemaker and successively an actor and author. Sympathetic to the early ideals of the French Revolution, Holcroft assisted in the publication of the first part of Thomas Paine's *The Rights of Man* in 1791. Together with other social reformers like William Godwin, he was politically active and as a result was indicted for high treason in the fall of 1794 and held in Newgate Prison for eight weeks before being discharged. His post-arrest publications achieved little success, although Holcroft was instrumental in bringing melodrama to Britain at the end of the decade with his *Deaf and Dumb* (1801) and *A Tale of Mystery*.

Holcroft's *A Tale of Mystery* was the first play in English to lay claim to the designation of 'A Melo-Drame,' as it is described on the title page. Like so many other English melodramas, *A Tale of Mystery*, too, is an unacknowledged translation or adaptation of a French source, namely René Charles Guilbert de Pixérécourt's Gothic melodrama *Coelina, ou l'enfant du mystère* (1800), but it further heightens the sensational emotional qualities and the affective force of the French original. In Holcroft's *A Tale of Mystery*, as in *Coelina*, dumbness is central to the plot. In fact, the popularity of the dumb character really started with Holcroft's two-act play and lasted for at least half a century. The setting of *A Tale of Mystery* (*TM*) is Renaissance Savoy and act 1, scene 1 shows the Gothic Hall of the House of Bonamo. The story centres around the mysteries of the honest Francisco, a man of "sorrowful looks" (*TM* 9), who due to his dumbness has to mime his emotions by using body language and signs, accompanied by intense music. His muteness is a result of a murderous attack he suffered in the past, and though he knows the name of his attacker, he refuses to reveal it to his benefactor Bonamo. When the haughty Count Romaldi comes on behalf of his son to seek the hand of Selina, Bonamo's rich foster child and orphaned niece (who is actually in love with her cousin Stephano, Bonamo's son), Francisco starts in horror, recognizing Romaldi as his former attacker. Bonamo's candid and faithful servant Fiametta introduces the audience from the very beginning to the real character of Romaldi by saying he is a person looking for "mischief" (*TM* 7). Selina, too, calls Romaldi selfish and points out the "violence of his character" (*TM* 8), while Stephano mentions "the wickedness of his heart" (ibid.). By the time Romaldi enters the stage, the spectators are fully aware of who the goodies and the baddies are in this melodrama.

Holcroft's play is a prime example of how music is used to introduce characters and create or enhance emotional tension. When Count Romaldi's wickedness is discussed, the stage direction is "[*Music to express contention.*]" (*TM* 8). When Francisco informs his hosts about his disgraced family and his attackers by using signs and gestures, the stage directions say "[*Music.*]" (*TM* 11) every time Francisco violently gesticulates, underlining the mood of the scene and heightening tension. Again, when Francisco refuses to inform Bonamo about the identity of his attackers, whom he characterizes as rich and powerful, and his host becomes suspicious because he cannot believe that rich and powerful people can possibly be villains, the conflict is highlighted by music: "[*Music to express disorder.*]" (*TM* 11) Also, when Montano, Bonamo's honest and noble friend, enters the stage and sees Romaldi, the stage directions are "[*Music plays alarmingly*]" and "[*Music loud and discordant* [...] *Montana starts with terror and indignation*]" (*TM* 14). Act 2, scene 1 starts off with "*Joyful Music,*" introducing the spectators to the forthcoming "*marriage festival.*" The setting is "*A beautiful garden and pleasure grounds, with garlands, festoons, love devices*" (*TM* 19), in which the family has gathered for breakfast before they leave for the notary. The scene is accompanied by "[*Sweet music.*]," to which the rejoicing peasants rise from the shrubs and "*suspend their garlands in a picturesque group*" (*TM* 21). Such arrangement of figures in a picture is known as *tableau*: "The Victorian prosceniumarch was a gigantic picture frame which melodrama filled with gigantic pictures. Managers spent huge sums on gorgeous costumes and grandiose scenery. [...] Every act leads up to its 'tableau', where characters 'groupe' or 'form picture' as the curtain descends." (Smith 1976: 26 f.) Gestures and mute action are of crucial importance throughout melodrama, and in particular at the end of scenes and acts there are visual representations of meaning, "where the characters' attitudes and gestures, compositionally arranged and frozen for a moment, give, like an illustrative painting, a visual summary of the emotional situation" (Brooks 1976: 48). In the scene discussed above, the tableau helps to underline the happiness of the morning before Romaldi deceitfully schemes a second attack on Francisco. When Romaldi's accomplice Malvoglio enters the stage, "*the company start up* [...] *all express terror. The peasants, alarmed and watching: the whole during a short pause, forming a picture*" (*TM* 21). Again, the audience is alerted to Romaldi's villainy through a visual element, a picture or *tableau*, whilst the music starts expressing "*confusion*" (ibid.), when he causes credulous Bonamo to believe that Selina is a child of crime and adultery. Throughout the play intensive feelings are visualized by meaningful gestures, for instance when Bonamo turns Francisco and Selina out of his house after Selina is revealed to be the daughter of Francisco. This scene is presented "[*With Affection*]" (*TM* 22) and with "[*Violent distracted music*]" (*TM* 23). Act 2, scene 1 again ends with a *tableau*, which expresses the meaning of the events through agitated body language and whose message is crystal clear:

> [Stephano endeavours to force his way to Selina: Fiametta passionately embraces her; and by gesture reproaches Bonamo, who persists, yet is tormented by doubt. Stephano escapes, and suddenly hurries Selina forward, to detain her; after violent efforts, they are again forced asunder; and as they are retiring on opposite sides, with struggles and passion, the scene closes.] (Ibid.)

This scene is a good example of how the thrilling plot, rapid succession of scenes, and fast moving action of melodrama allow characters only time to express breathless exclamations and how melodrama in decisive scenes reduces verbal language to a minimum and expresses the message through different semiotic systems such as body language.

When Montano in act 2, scene 2 reveals the villainous character of Romaldi and Francisco's innocence, it turns out that Romaldi is actually Francisco's wicked brother, who loved Francisco's wife, "decoyed Francisco into the power of the Algerines, seized his estates, and finding he had escaped, attempted to assassinate him" (*TM* 26). At the end of this scene "*a distant thunder is heard, and a rising storm perceived*" (ibid.), reflecting the strong emotions of the family members and preparing the audience for the last scene of the play full of suspense, peripety, and high emotions. The setting of act 2, scene 3 resembles that of Ann Radcliffe's Gothic novel *The Mysteries of Udolpho*:

> The wild mountainous country called the Nant of Arpennaz; with pines and massy rocks. A rude wooden bridge on a small height thrown from rock to rock; a rugged mill-stream a little in the back ground; the miller's house on the right; a steep ascent by a narrow path to the bridge; a stone or bank to sit on, on the right-hand side. – The increasing storm of lightening, thunder, hail, and rain, becomes terrible. Suitable music. (*TM* 27)

In this storm an exhausted Romaldi disguised as a humble peasant flees from the authorities into the wild mountain region. The terror he feels is aggravated by the storm and loud thunder and also expressed by mournful music. In the final scene of dramatic confrontation and peripety, when Romaldi is disarmed and arrested and Francisco saves Romaldi's life, suspense, exalted emotions, big gestures, and "greatest agitation" (*TM* 32) are prevalent. This scene verifies Brooks' thesis that melodrama chooses extreme physical conditions to represent moral states:

the halt, the blind, and the mute people the world of melodrama, striking examples of past misfortunes and mysteries. [...] The moral drama has physical repercussions which stand before us as its living symbols. (Brooks 1976: 46)

While blindness is central for tragedy because it is about insight and illumination, muteness has a special role in melodramas like Holcroft's *A Tale of Mystery* for the very reason that this genre is concerned with expression (cf. ibid.: 57).

Douglas William Jerrold (1803-57), the son of strolling players, served in the navy as a boy-sailor and was apprenticed to a painter before he finally became a successful dramatic author who called Charles Dickens his friend. He wrote three dozen plays, amongst them classics like *Black-Ey'd Susan* (1829), *Fifteen Years of a Drunkard's Life* (1828), *Martha Willis, the Servant Maid* (1831), and *The Prisoner of War* (1842), but his melodrama *The Rent Day* (*RD*, 1832) about a criminal steward who squeezes ruinous rents out of the peasantry is one of the most popular ones. Jerrold also wrote several novels and his studies of *Men of Character* (1838) were illustrated by Thackeray. Later in his career he turned to political journalism, became the driving force behind the newly established *Punch* (which testifies to his subversive political tendencies in favour of the poor and society's outcasts) and later successfully ran the *Douglas Jerrold's Shilling Magazine*, the *Douglas Jerrold's Weekly Newspaper* and *Lloyd's Weekly News* (cf. Slater 2002).

Jerrold's *The Rent Day* is an example of a domestic melodrama with a rural setting. Though rural poverty and the contrasting extravagance of ennobled and propertied classes shown on stage were harsh social facts, the good village people triggered nostalgia and sentiment in the urban audiences, who had rural roots themselves (Schmidt 1986: 222-76). *The Rent Day* was a popular domestic melodrama concerned with household and family relationships, but published in the politically fraught year of the Reform Bill (1832) and the reaction to the agricultural misery that prompted the Swing Riots. "The years from 1828 to 1832 'were characterized by poor crops, high prices and enormous importations', putting a considerable strain on the capital of farmers. The number of bankruptcies among tenant farmers, burdened by high rents and tithes, was a frequent political theme" (Meisel 1983: 152). While Jerrold's play does not promote radical measures on rural exploitation,

> the relation of the situation to the times, in conjunction with the class bias in domestic drama as a genre, gives the play political bearings. The landowning aristocrat is not the villain in this melodrama, but his agent is. [...] Virtue, however, in the shape of charity, integrity, and industry, is shared by those whom agent and officials oppress. The oppressed are not rioting have-nots, or large, prosperous farmers fallen on hard times, but the modest representatives of an ideal and imperilled domesticity [...]. (Ibid.: 152 f.)

Other critics have pointed out that a melodrama like *The Rent Day* actually supports conservative values by offering in its domestic form "packaged accounts of working-class life within a sentimental frame of family values and a conventional social order" (Cox 1996: 168). Rather than using the oppressed farmers as mouthpiece for sending out a radical political message about unscrupulous landlords, *The Rent Day* "promotes submission and conformity with the system rather than social change" (Ilsemann 1996: 204).

Jerrold's three-act play is famous for its heightened visuality and intermedial quality, which sculptured the action into a series of *tableaux*, i.e. into lit, frozen, and sometimes framed arrangement of figures on stage. When *The Rent Day* was first produced in January 1832 at the Theatre Royal, Drury Lane, it incorporated tableaux "emulating didactic paintings on the rackrenting theme by David Wilkie" (Trussler 1994: 201), an influential 19th-century Scottish genre painter and member of the Royal Academy. Alert to popular taste and feeling, Jerrold turned to two of Wilkie's best-known paintings, for the title and leading feature of his new village melodrama, which was hailed by the reviewers. The *Spectator* observed on 28 January, 1831:

> *Tableaux vivants*, or animated pictures, are the order of the day [...]. Wilkie's famous picture of *The Rent Day* (1807) has given rise to a drama at Drury Lane, which is likely to vie with it in popularity, and which embodies the spirit of that admirable performance in a story of very great interest. Mr. Jerrold, the author, reads 'a great moral lesson' to the absentee landlords, which we wish they could all peruse and profit by. (qtd. from Meisel 1983: 142)

In the original production of Jerrold's *The Rent Day*, the title picture appeared at the rise of the curtain as an opening tableau and is described in the stage direction: *"The Characters and Stage so arranged as to form, on the rising of the Curtain, a representation of Wilkie's Picture of 'Rent-Day'"* (*RD* 5). At the beginning of the second act the second painting by Wilkie, his *Distraining for Rent* (1815), was again presented as tableau. This scene takes place in what is described as *"The Interior of Heywood's Farm. The Scene, Furniture, etc., as in Wilkie's Picture of 'Distraining for Rent.' Martin and Rachel seated at Table, with Tony, Beanstalk, his Dame, and the Children. Ale, Jugs, etc., on the Table"* (*RD* 22 f.). The drama of an unjust and greedy steward Crumbs who makes the tenants pay for misdeeds of the old squire and who is finally found out by the previously absent young master Grantley (who arrives incognito to check on his property and tenants) is intensified in the second act by

> a plot of domestic anguish and traduced and vindicated innocence, where Martin Heywood, the distrained-against young Job of Jerrold's play, finds his wife Rachel locked up with the young squire, as her only means of saving that gentleman's life from some enterprising villains. (Meisel 1983: 152)

While Martin Heywood believes that the squire managed to seduce his wife, the squire is convinced that Martin Heywood conspired against him and is therefore to be shot when Rachel Heywood intervenes. The family is rescued from ruin by a legacy of golden guineas, which Martin's grandfather has hidden in a chair, and which is discovered at the very last minute when the broker's men have arrived to sequester the chair.

To satisfy the eagerness of the 19th-century audiences for pictures, Jerrold's play offers more tableaux than just the two imitating Wilkie's famous paintings. For instance, toward the end of act 2, when Martin is surrounded by his children, there is a tableau which summarizes and punctuates the situation. This is also the case at the beginning of act 3, scene 4, when he is *"seated in his Arm-Chair. His children grouped about him"* (*RD* 41). Later in the same scene Rachel is begging her husband to believe her to be a faithful wife. When Martin separates the children from their mother, she is overwhelmed by the situation and her husband's injustice and faints across her husband's knee. The stage directions read: "[*Faints, and falls over Martin's knee – the Children surround her*]" (*RD* 43). The tableau picturing this heartbreaking scene has – just as genre painting at the time – an iconic quality which demonstrates in a nutshell how melodrama worked on the emotions of the audience. It also shows that early Victorian melodrama in particular is very much based on idealized 19th-century notions of femininity, represented by female heroines who as unprotected and submissive women reinforce rather than subvert Victorian gender politics. To summarize, the "indulgence of strong emotionalism; moral polarization and schematization; extreme states of being, situations, actions; overt villainy, persecution of the good, and final reward of virtue; inflated and extravagant expression; dark plottings, suspense, breathtaking peripety" (Brooks 1976: 11 f.) are typical features of Jerrold's *The Rent Day*. In the tableaux at the beginning and end of scenes and acts, the characters' attitudes and gestures, compositionally arranged and frozen for a moment, give a visual summary of the emotional situation. Emphasis and memorability are two important effects of melodrama's heightened visuality. As "texts of muteness" (ibid.: passim) melodramas such as *The Rent Day* indulge in overstatement and overemphasis, thus in rhetorical excess:

> Melodramatic rhetoric [...] tends toward the inflated and the sententious. Its typical figures are hyperbole, antithesis, and oxymoron: those figures, precisely, that evidence a refusal of nuance and their insistence on dealing in pure, integral concepts. [...] Emotions are given a full acting-out, a full representation before our eyes. (Ibid.: 40 f.)

This explains melodrama's interest in visual elements, its use of striking dramatic postures, its exaggeration of facial grimace (including eye rolling and teeth gnashing), and finally its use of an artificial diction to support a bombastic rhetoric.

4. Further Developments of Melodrama and the Melodramatic Mode

Victorian melodrama is a multimedial art form, which relies as much on silent bodily gestures, music, and tableaux as on verbal language. Tableaux and music highlight significant and decisive scenes of a play; they underpin their meaning and thus help the audience to memorize them easily. The aesthetics of melodrama is thus an aesthetics of excess which tautologically combines several sign systems to produce "moments of greatest intensity" (Brooks 1976: 74) – a feature it shares with silent cinema.

Due to its Protean nature melodrama "continued in several varieties through the nineteenth century, and died lingeringly after the First World War" (Booth 1965: 13, 145-76), when the more serious modern drama with its anti-heroes and reduction of outward action had already become the new legitimate art form. In the mid-19th century, melodramas with urban settings became popular. These include Dion Boucicault's *The Streets of London* (1864) and Watts Phillips' *Lost in London* (1867). In the second half of the 19th century, there was a demand for more spectacle as well as more naturalism, which engendered the so-called 'sensation drama' with its elaborate sets. The term appears to have been invented by Boucicault, whose introduction of one thrilling sensation scene to domestic melodrama had many imitators. The sensation novels of the 1860s and 1870s offered excellent material for melodramatic adaptations. One of the most famous examples of this genre is Elizabeth Braddon's *Lady Audley's Secret* (1862), which was adapted by George Roberts as well as C.H. Hazlewood; and *East Lynne* (1874) based on Mrs Henry Wood's novel *The Bells* (1871).

With the railway boom of the 1850s and the invention of the electric telegraph "most parts of the country [...] within easy and relatively inexpensive reach" (Trussler 1994: 232), melodrama, too, developed and changes took place: the Gothic mode eventually disappeared, the nautical melodrama with its more elaborate sets was still in demand, the domestic continued to be enormously successful although there were changes such as the increasing tendency of the heroines (Lady Isabel in *East Lynne*) to die for their sins; also the villainess or adventuress became an important melodramatic character (Lady Audley in *Lady Audley's Secret*). Likewise, military plays, which covered events and battles such as the Crimean War (c. 1853-1854), the Indian Mutiny (1857-1858), and the Boer War (1880-1881), were performed with great success. Generally, the settings became increasingly realistic (especially those of metropolitan life) due to the improvement of stage mechanics, as did the dialogues; plots were more carefully constructed and religious themes were introduced (cf. Wilkie Collins' *The New Magdalen*, 1873), characters became more natural and credibly depicted and the detective entered the stage. Later domestic melodrama with its sensation scene(s) paved the way for the sensation dramas with their many thrills, which prevailed from 1880 to the First World War and beyond, especially in the provinces where touring melodrama survived much longer, in fact until the 1930s. Essential to later melodrama's appeal were

> speed, a rapid series of short scenes and quick scene changes; sensation, embodying visions and physical thrills of accident and nautical catastrophe; spectacle, with the use of large crowds, elaborate scenery and ponderous sets of great lavishness; and, finally, realistic effects and the mechanical reproduction of scenes and sensations from actual life. (Booth 1965: 181 f.; cf. also 177-89)

Eventually, however, all this could be achieved more easily by motion pictures than on a theatre stage. Early film drew heavily upon theatrical melodrama, and, by 1915, many famous melodramas had been turned into silent films – Booth (1965: 182) lists amongst others the abolitionist *Uncle Tom's Cabin* (1903), *The Colleen Bawn* (1911), *The Count of Monte Christo* (1912), and *East Lynne* (1914). Amongst silent film melodrama, D.W. Griffith's *Broken Blossoms* (1919) was one of the most successful ones. Stereotyped characters and highly emotional scenes remained the most important ingredients of a genre interested in appealing to the emotions of the audience, when 'talkies' superseded silent film melodrama. Scandalous romances, traitorous friendships, strained familial situations, illness, and other tragedies are the plots of many 'mellers,' for instance in the family melodrama of the 1950s, including *Rebel without a Cause* by Nicholas Ray (1950), as well as in Douglas Sirk's popular melodrama films *Written on the Wind* (1956) and *All that Heaven Allows* (1956). Anjelica Huston's 1999 film *Agnes Browne* is a perfect example of a TV melodrama focusing on the effects of alcoholism, domestic violence, rape, etc. Stage melodrama has only survived in the 20th century as "a conscious archaism or as a form of burlesque" (Booth 1965: 177); examples are George Bernard Shaw's 'intellectual' melodrama *The Devil's Disciple* (1897) and his short curtain raiser *Passion, Poison, and Petrification; or, The Fatal Gazogene* (1905). The melodramatic mode in its macabre and burlesque form was still alive in the 1960s in plays such as Joe Orton's *The Erpingham Camp* (1966) and *Loot* (1965), as well as in Tom Stoppard's parodic *The Real Inspector Hound* (1968), but cinema and TV melodrama have now definitively replaced stage melodrama.

Bibliography

Primary Sources

Holcroft, Thomas. 1975. "A Tale of Mystery." In: Wischhusen 1975. 4-32.
Jerrold, Douglas William. 1848. "The Rent-Day." In: *The Modern Standard Drama: A Collection of the Most Popular Acting Plays*. Vol. IV. New York: William Taylor and Co. 1-48.

Annotated Bibliography

Booth, Michael R. 1965. *English Melodrama*. London: Jenkins.
   Although published more than 40 years ago, Booth's book is still an indispensible classic and the best formal history of theatrical British melodrama.
Brooks, Peter. 1976. *The Melodramatic Imagination*. New Haven/London: Yale UP.
   One of the most influential book-length studies of melodrama of the last 40 years which combines an interest in Freud's psychoanalysis with rhetoric.
Kelly, Richard M. 1972. *Douglas Jerrold*. New York: Twayne.
   Kelly's book is a very good introduction to Douglas Jerrold.
Mercer, John & Martin Shingler (eds.). 2004. *Melodrama: Genre, Style, Sensibility*, London/New York: Wallflower P.
   Mercer and Shingler's collection is an accessible overview of melodrama. The book not only discusses melodrama as a genre, originating in European theatre of

the 18th and 19th century, but also as a specific cinematic style, epitomized by the work of Douglas Sirk.

Rosenblum, Joseph. 1995. *Thomas Holcroft: Literature and Politics in England in the Age of the French Revolution*. Lewiston, et al.: The Edwin Mellen P.

This biography of Thomas Holcroft examines his theories and practice as critic, dramatist and novelist, and places his writing and his political views within the context of the revolutionary period in which he lived.

Schmidt, Johann N. 1986. *Ästhetik des Melodramas*. Heidelberg: Winter.

Schmidt's careful study of melodrama as a transhistorical genre and as a successful Victorian drama explains the aesthetics and the socio-political context of Victorian melodrama.

Singer, Ben. 2001. *Melodrama and Modernity: Early Sensational Cinema and Its Contexts*. New York: Columbia UP.

Singer's well written study of early sensational cinema helps us to understand the interaction between stage and screen melodramas. It describes the origins and history of the silent cliffhanger serials and includes an excellent selection of illustrated materials.

Slater, Michael. 2002. *Douglas Jerrold: A Life (1803-1857)*. London: Duckworth.

Michael Slater's richly detailed biography does justice to the greatly underestimated literary figure, Douglas Jerrold, whose works he helps to contextualize.

Smith, James L. 1973. *Melodrama*. London: Methuen.

Smith's concise history of Victorian melodrama helps to familiarize students with the topic of Victorian melodrama, but does not give as much detailed information as Booth's book.

Trussler, Simon. 1994. *The Cambridge Illustrated History of British Theatre*. Cambridge: Cambridge UP.

Trussler's illustrated history is a particularly rich source for all students of British theatre history. Due to the numerous visual sources the book is a treasure box helping us to understand the British stage at different times in history.

Further Secondary Literature

Booth, Michael R. (ed.). 1969. *English Plays of the Nineteenth Century*. Vol. I: *Dramas 1800-1850*. Oxford: Clarendon P.
Bratton, Jacky, Jim Cook & Christine Gledhill (eds.). 1994. *Melodrama: Stage, Picture, Screen*. London: British Film Institute.
Buckeley, Matthew S. 2009. "Refugee Theatre Melodrama and Modernity's Loss." In: *Theatre Journal* 61.2: 175-190.
Cox, Jeffrey N. 1996. "The Ideological Tack of Nautical Melodrama." In: Hays & Nikolopoulou 1996. 167-189.

Franceschina, John (ed.). 1997. *Sisters of Gore: Seven Gothic Melodramas by British Women, 1790-1843*. New York/London: Garland Publishing.

Hays, Michael & Anastasia Nikolopoulou (eds.). 1996. *Melodrama: The Cultural Emergence of a Genre*. New York: St. Martin's P.

Holcroft, Thomas. 2007. *The Novels and Selected Plays of Thomas Holcroft*. Vol 5. Philip Cox (ed.). *Selected Plays*. London: Pickering and Chatto.

Ilsemann, Hartmut. 1996. "Radicalism in the Melodrama of the Early Nineteenth Century." In: Hays & Nikolopoulou 1996. 191-207.

Kilgarriff, Michael (ed.). 1974. *The Golden Age of Melodrama: Twelve 19th Century Melodramas* (abridged). London: Wolfe Publishing.

Krause, David. (ed.). 1964. *The Dolmen Boucicault*. Dublin: Dolmen P.

Meisel, Martin. 1983. *Realizations: Narrative, Pictorial, and Theatrical Arts in Nineteenth-Century England*. Princeton, NJ: Princeton UP.

Wilkie, David. 2010 [1817]. *The Rent Day*. (As engraved by Abraham Raimbach). 8. Nov. <http://www.gis.net/~shepdog/BC_Museum/Permanent/SirDavidWilkie/SirDavidWilkie.html> (last accessed: 8 Nov. 2010).

—. 2010 [1815]. *Distraining for Rent*. 8 Nov. <http://www.archive.com/web_gallery/S/Sir-David-Wilkie/Distraining-for-Rent,-1815.html> (last accessed: 8 Nov. 2010).

Wischhusen, Stephen. (ed.). 1975. *The Hour of One: Six Gothic Melodramas*. London: Gordon Fraser.

15. AESTHETICIST COMEDY OF MANNERS: OSCAR WILDE'S *THE IMPORTANCE OF BEING EARNEST*

PETRA DIERKES-THRUN

1. The Aestheticist Comedy of Manners: Features and Influences

The 'aestheticist comedy of manners' is a late-19th-century development of the comedy of manners in the context of the aestheticist literary style and philosophy which insists on the non-utilitarian purpose of art ('art for art's sake') and the value of aesthetic surface and style over moral contents and social didacticism. Besides harking back to Restoration comedy of manners (the original heyday of the genre in England), the aestheticist comedy of manners was also influenced by important 19th-century dramatic forms and trends such as the 'well-made play' (Eugène Scribe, 1791-1861; Victorien Sardou, 1831-1908; Sir Arthur Wing Pinero, 1855-1934; Henry Arthur Jones, 1851-1929), 'Victorian farce' (W.S. Gilbert, 1836-1911, Arthur Sullivan, 1842-1900), and the 'social problem play' (Henrik Ibsen, 1828-1906; George Bernard Shaw, 1856-1950). The most important example of this mixed dramatic genre is Oscar Wilde's *The Importance of Being Earnest* (1895), which quotes as well as mocks all of these trends, adapting the comedy of manners to a uniquely 19th-century context in which manners are revealed as superficial, arbitrary, and unmoored from moral and social purpose.

The aestheticist comedy of manners has in common with the original comedy of manners its focus on the protagonists' preoccupation with their social standing, questions of decorum and propriety, and epigrammatic, witty dialogue and repartee. While the original roots of the genre go back to Greek and Roman comedies by Menander (342-291 BC), Plautus (254-184 BC), and Terence (195/185-159 BC), and perhaps the best-known comedies of manners are those of Molière (1622-1673) (*L'école des femmes*, 1662; *Le misanthrope*, 1666; *Tartuffe*, 1664), in England the comedy of manners flourished during the Restoration period in the plays of William Wycherley (*The Country Wife*, 1675), Sir George Etherege (*The Man of Mode*, 1676), and William Congreve (*The Way of the World*, 1700), and was revived by 18th-century writers Oliver Goldsmith (*She Stoops to Conquer*, 1773) and Richard Sheridan (*The School for Scandal*, 1777).

The 19th-century aestheticist comedy of manners is inextricably connected with the name of Oscar Wilde (1854-1900). His four society comedies – *Lady Windermere's Fan* (1892), *A Woman of No Importance* (1893), *An Ideal Husband* (1895), and especially *The Importance of Being Earnest* (1895) – make up practically the entire genre. Its popularity died down with Wilde's infamous homosexual scandal and conviction for so-called acts of gross indecency in May 1895, only to be revived in the second half of the 20th century. Wilde's aestheticist comedy of manners has only a few isolated dramatic cousins in W.S. Gilbert's *The Palace of Truth* (1870), *Pygmalion and Galatea* (1871), *The Wicked World* (1873), and especially *Engaged* (1877), mannered farcical comedies that featured satirical attacks on the mores and hypocrisies of Victorian society.

Like the earlier comedy of manners, Wilde's plays are dominantly concerned with the manners, opinions, and the class hierarchy of society, and feature self-interested schemes and cleverly plotted intrigue. Different from the genre's earlier forms, however, is Wilde's comical questioning of society's moral foundations, which are now depicted as arbitrary, self-interested, and merely conventional, rather than naturally or divinely justified. The aestheticist comedy of manners mercilessly reveals the artificiality of decorum and convention, and the characters appear scandalously amoral, egotistical, and vain while retaining a strong charm for the audience because of their verbal acumen and wit. By citing as well as satirizing widely recognized social and moral conventions and stereotypes relating to Victorian opinions about class and social status, marriage, gender, sexuality, and money, and by extending and twisting them to the point of hilarious absurdity, Wilde ironically deconstructs the very bases and sources of Victorian social and cultural authority. As Peter Raby writes, Wilde's play

> functions through the meticulous imitation, and then subversion, of the tribal social customs of upper-class late Victorian society [...,] a society in which each gesture was significant and was duly noted; where questions of rank, parentage, and wealth were paramount; where custom was enshrined by tradition and by upbringing, slightly modified and refined by fashion; where what you wore, what you ate, where you went, and whom you were seen with defined your status. [...] [H]imself a parvenu among the English aristocracy, [Wilde] understood only too well the key relationship between class and money, and his exposure and exploitation of it is one of the sources of comedy within this play. (1995: 41, 49)

While the deconstructive, radically ironic element of Wilde's aestheticist comedy of manners anticipates some central developments of literary modernism, Wilde also worked in close proximity to Victorian theatrical conventions and well-known dramatic techniques of his time. Contemporaries often compared Wilde's society comedies to popular French dramas by Victorien Sardou, who (along with Eugène Scribe) originated the popular *pièce bien faite*, or well-made play. Even though Wilde repeatedly protested against the comparison with Sardou, it is clear that *Earnest* shares a number of features with the well-made play, which, in Victorian London, was especially identified with Arthur Wing Pinero (1855-1934) and Henry Arthur Jones (1851-1929). The well-made play featured intricate, clever plots with unexpected twists and turns that were mainly set in upper-class society (as opposed to Victorian farce and the earlier comedy of manners, which focused on the lower and middle ranks of society). Sudden plot shifts, mistaken identities, misplaced objects, errors, and surprise revelations kept the audience guessing and heightened their anticipation for secrets to be revealed, raising questions about the reality of truth versus mask (which was one of Wilde's favourite themes, too). The dialogue was typically epigrammatic and sparkled with highly entertaining double entendre and brilliant witticisms. A satisfying denouement finally offered a logical and clever explanation of the twists and turns of the plot.

The well-made play also influenced Victorian farce, another popular dramatic genre with which the aestheticist comedy of manners is closely associated. As Sos Eltis points out, *Earnest* "was identified as Gilbertian farce by a number of Victorian reviewers, and a reading of the play is informed by comparison with Gilbert's *Engaged* (1877) and *The Palace of Truth* (1870) and with Pinero's popular farces *The Magistrate* (1885) and *Dandy Dick* (1887)" (2008: 105), also with Pinero's *The Schoolmistress* (1886) and Brandon Thomas' very popular *Charley's Aunt* (1892). Implausible coincidences, double lives, mistaken identities, foundlings, unions of star-crossed lovers, absurd situational clashes and happily reunited families – which are all present in *Earnest* – are typical staples of farce.

Another, more minor influence on the aestheticist comedy of manners was the so-called new drama or social problem play, associated with Henrik Ibsen and George Bernard Shaw's works. Even though Wilde's ironic title *The Importance of Being Earnest* (for a hilarious comedy that embodies the very opposite of earnestness) would seem to suggest non-serious intention, and although in a *St. James Gazette* interview with Robert Ross on 18 January 1895, Wilde characterized the play's philosophy as "exquisitely trivial, a delicate bubble of fancy" demanding "[t]hat we should treat all the trivial things of life very seriously, and all the serious things of life with sincere and studied triviality" (qtd. from Mikhail 1979: 250), the play raises a number of quite serious, controversial social issues indirectly. "[It] is full of comments on marriage, gender, religion, class, wealth, education, and literature" (Eltis 2008: 106 f.), wittily touching on such hot-button issues as class mobility, social status, or hubris, moral bigotry, gender warfare, middle-class women's education and rise in confidence, and moneyed interests masquerading as love. In this regard, too, the aestheticist comedy of manners is a unique form of cultural criticism of the ossified social, cultural, and political configurations of late 19th-century English society, which under the direction of Oscar Wilde enjoyed laughing at its own folly.

2. *The Importance of Being Earnest* in the Context of the Genre and its Development by Oscar Wilde

After three early experimental dramas (*Vera, or the Nihilists* [1880]; *The Duchess of Padua* [1883], and the banned *Salomé* [1891]), Wilde turned a corner with his four popular aestheticist comedies of manners, of which *Earnest* (*E*) was the final and most developed. Despite offering a satirical collage of popular theatrical trends in these works, Wilde actually embraced the commercialized world of fashionable London West End theatre. Wilde's interest in establishing a name for himself as a serious yet popular dramatist was signified by his connection with George Alexander and the St. James Theatre, a beloved institution recognized for its high-quality plays and well-heeled audience. Here *Earnest* premiered on 14 February 1895 to generally positive reviews and enthusiastic audience response. (His *An Ideal Husband* was still running at the Theatre Royal, Haymarket as well.)

Like many original comedies of manners, *Earnest* features a complex marriage plot and satirizes the contradictions between social manners and morality, and sex, money, and class issues. The plot focuses on two men-about-town, Algernon (Algy) Moncrieff and John (Jack) Worthing, who are friends and, as is revealed later, also long-lost brothers. Living double lives in town and in the country, both men have invented fictitious personae that allow them to get away and escape their duties whenever they wish: Jack pretends to have a wicked brother Ernest in town whom he needs to keep in check, and Algy supposedly visits a sick friend named Bunbury. In a double marriage plot, Jack is in love with Gwendolen Fairfax (Algy's cousin and the formidable Lady Bracknell's daughter), while Algy romantically pursues Cecily Cardew, Jack's pretty young ward, against Jack's express wish. Gwendolen and Cecily are in love with the name Ernest as the incorporation of their manly ideal (effectively turning the relation of a man's name to his substance inside out), so both Jack and Algy pretend to be called Ernest Worthing to please their ladies. Hilarious complications ensue (including a famous scene in which Gwendolen and Cecily, who believe they are engaged to the same man, perform a high-society cat fight over cups of tea), which are further heightened when it is revealed that Jack was a foundling child and does not know his family or social background, a fact that renders him unacceptable as a groom. But through an ingenious and unbelievable firework of revelations and plot twists, it turns out that Jack is actually Lady Bracknell's own nephew, inadvertently left behind as a baby in a handbag at Victoria Station by Miss Prism, now coincidentally Cecily's governess; Algy is his own brother; Gwendolen is his cousin; and Jack's actual name, given to him by his late parents, was indeed Ernest. Hence in the end, all nominal social and monetary obstacles to the characters' happiness are removed and a double marriage will soon take place, confirming once and for all "the vital Importance of Being Earnest," the play's famous last line (*E* 144).

In its focus on manners versus morality, Wilde's play highlights the lack of true meaning or moral depth to social principles, decorum, and propriety portraying a decadent middle- and upper-class society in which good manners mainly mean keeping up good appearances without any moral conviction. In this society young men are bored with their traditional moral and social roles as patriarchal gatekeepers and escape by leading double lives; young women like Cecily and Gwendolen have entirely unrealistic romantic ideals and are highly manipulative and self-interested while feigning feminine innocence and altruism; and hypocritical Victorian society matrons such as Lady Bracknell (herself a social upstart by marriage yet one of high-society decorum's staunchest defenders) rule with an iron fist, defending their social status by keeping watch over shallow appearances and moneyed interests and connections. There are also a few direct echoes of earlier comedies of manners in Wilde's play, such as Cecily's ingenious idea to write letters to herself in her future lover Ernest's name, which has a precedent in Lydia Languish in Sheridan's *The Rivals* (1775) (cf. Raby 1995: 30).

Despite such similarities between the aestheticist and the earlier comedy of manners, the key difference between Wilde's play and the earlier expressions of the genre is that the social and moral framework presented in original comedies of manners and in 19th-century well-made plays clearly affirmed society's existing value systems and social structures after the comical turmoil, whereas Wilde's play emphasizes their utter absurdity and artificiality. Previously, the heroes of the comedy of manners successfully pursued their natural instincts, learned to cleverly bend the rules to their advantage, and benefited from some lucky twists of fate. At the same time, however, they duly learned and ingested their lessons, compromised, and ultimately found a secure place within the newly strengthened society as a whole. In Wilde, individuals' superficial loyalties to trivial codes and manners have thus replaced the genuine social or moral intention of many earlier comedies of manners:

> Wilde's comedies emphasize the aesthetically ritualized arbitrariness of decorum, thereby disclosing the superficiality and contingency of conventional social arrangements. Codes of etiquette function subversively for Wilde as mechanisms for forestalling facile puritanical moralizing by forcing a recognition of the *systemic* component of the value system we call morality. (Mackie 2009: 149 f.)

Rather than deploring the decay of the relationship between surface appearance or manners on the one hand, and truthfulness, moral righteousness, and sincere altruism on the other, *Earnest* boldly inverts their unquestioned validity and status. Wilde ironically suspends and hence questions the true validity of moral language, openly favouring a commitment to individualism and aesthetic surface instead. Wilde's play paradoxically, hilariously, and enthusiastically endorses his characters' preference of surface over depth, appearance over meaning, and style or aesthetic taste over substance. He cheerily elevates superficial codes and manners over morals, thereby denying their original social, cultural, and moral function of supporting a universal, ideal *contrat social*: "Surface, style and fashion reign in this play, in physical appearance, in posture, in gesture, in speech" (Raby 1995: 43). Lady Bracknell expresses this world view as a fact when she opines, "We live, I regret to say, in an age of surfaces" (*E* 133), and other characters live and breathe the same conviction. The modern woman Gwendolen – so alike her mother in many respects – affirms that "[i]n matters of grave importance, style, not sincerity is the vital thing" (*E* 128). Similarly, Cecily excuses Algernon/Ernest's "leading such a bad life" with his "wonderfully good taste" (*E* 113).

The elevation of ingenious style and appearance over substance is of course what *Earnest* is all about, and it is reflected in Wilde's verbal style, which recalls the witty dialogue of the original comedy of manners and the well-made play, while taking it to a much more sophisticated level: "His paradoxes and epigrams are far more extreme, more outrageous than the witty expressions of Congreve and his contemporaries," highlighting "the self-dramatizing cleverness of Wilde's arrogant poseurs" with their "sophisticated social repartee" (Hirst 1979: 51). Well-known social sayings and wisdoms are inverted to reveal the characters' shallowness and cynicism, especially about matters of the heart ("Divorces are made in Heaven" [*E* 72], "washing one's clean linen in public" is unacceptable [*E* 78], "in married life three is company and two is none" [*E* 79]). Audiences' expectations and knowledge of traditional values is invoked but then hilariously reversed, as in Lady Bracknell's retort to Jack's admittance that he is a smoker, "I am glad to hear it. A man should always have an occupation of some kind" (*E* 86), or her comment in praise of English ignorance over education: "Ignorance is like a delicate exotic fruit; touch it and the bloom is gone. The whole theory of modern education is radically unsound. Fortunately in England, at any rate, it produces no effect whatsoever" (ibid.). Wilde comically inverts the value system and surprises readers by switching the place of the good and the bad. For instance, upon Algernon's insistence to Cecily that she must not think he is "wicked," Cecily protests by insisting he better be: "If you are not, then you have certainly been deceiving us all in a very inexcusable manner. I hope you have not been leading a double life, pretending to be wicked and being really good all the time. That would be hypocrisy" (*E* 101).

Wilde's language in *Earnest* sparkles with so many brilliant paradoxes, aperçus, and witticisms that it can be argued that they (rather than plot, characters, or any social themes or principles raised) become the true stars, even the play's central *raison d'être*. W.H. Auden characterized *Earnest* as "a verbal opera, […] a universe in which the characters are determined by the kinds of things they say, and the plot is nothing but a succession of opportunities to say them" (qtd. from Gladden 2010: 38). In his review of the premiere in *The Theatrical World of 1895* on 20 February 1895, progressive theatre critic William Archer, also Ibsen's champion in England, commented:

> What can a poor critic do with a play which raises no principle, whether of art of morals, creates its own canons and conventions, and is nothing but an absolutely wilful expression of an irrepressibly witty personality? […] [*Earnest*] represents nothing, means nothing, is nothing except a sort of *rondo capriccioso*, in which the artist's fingers run with crisp irresponsibility up and down the keyboard of life. Why attempt to analyse and class such a play? […] 'farce' is far too gross and commonplace a word to apply to such an iridescent filament of fantasy. (Qtd. from Beckson 1970: 190)

As Auden and Archer recognized, in accordance with aestheticism's doctrine of 'art for art's sake' the playfulness of Wilde's language actively disrupts and disparages any utilitarian social purpose in the aestheticist comedy of manners. Instead, Wilde creates a self-contained dramatic universe in which stylistic artifice and superficiality, surface and physical sensation rather than rational depth or metaphysical thinking become the new values around which the play revolves. "Conventional morality is shown to be only skin-deep, so another skin-deep virtue is put in its place – beauty. Beauty of language is more important than character" (Byrne 2003: 171).

As mentioned above, "sparklingly witty repartee" (Gladden 2010: 13) was also a popular feature of the Victorian well-made play, in addition to structural and plot complexities that "under Wilde's pen, celebrated mistaken identities, not-so-well-kept secrets, [and] amusing double-talk" (ibid.). There are also similar momentous coincidences, such as Algernon's accidental find of Cecily's cigarette case in act 1 (which leads to his discovery of Cecily's hidden existence and courtship), or Lady Bracknell's overhearing of Miss Prism's name in act 3 (which ushers in a dramatic wave of revelations that eventually lead to the satisfying happy ending for all). Wilde's preoccupation with the themes of aesthetic masks, surface and depth, lies and truth throughout much of his work also has a special affinity to the well-made play's focus on double-talk and double lives, both of which feature prominently in *Earnest*. First of all, there are the double lives Jack and Algernon lead with the help of the imaginary Ernest and Bunbury, but there is also the double life of the seemingly respectable Miss Prism with a quasi-criminal past, and Lady Bracknell's own murky social background behind her façade of social superiority. Lady Bracknell is not above spontaneously reversing her rigid moral or social principles when doing so gains her social or monetary advantages. For example, she quickly retracts her rejection of Cecily as Algernon's prospective wife after hearing that Cecily will inherit a large sum of money, exclaiming: "There are distinct social possibilities in your profile. The two weak points in our age are its want of principles and its want of profile. The chin a little higher, dear" (*E* 134). Similarly, her conservative social attitudes ("To be born, or at any rate bred, in a hand-bag, whether it had handles or not, seems to me to display a contempt for the ordinary decencies of family life that remind me of the worst excesses of the French Revolution. And I presume you know what that unfortunate movement led to," *E* 89) can change in the blink of an eye when an opportunity presents itself and appearances can be kept up.

Reality, or what initially seems real and reliable in Wilde's play, is deconstructed and revealed as deceptive and false; truth and pretence even exchange places: "it is Wilde's genius to show us that, unbeknownst to him, Jack *really* is the person he has been pretending to be all along" (Gladden 2010: 22); he is named Ernest, and he actually does have a brother (Algernon). "Thus, Wilde's play closes by asking who has the right to claim truth, the right to occupy the position of transparency: the progressive liar (Jack) or the traditional moralist (Lady Bracknell)" (ibid.). A new reality is assembled, but instead of a systematic rebuilding of truth we are presented with coincidental arrangements that, deus-ex-machina-like, determine the new order. The clever bringing together of diverse strands of plot and such satisfying conclusion of all the mysteries and conflicts raised are original features of the well-made play, but Wilde heaps one upon another in such a firework of wit and surprises at the end that they also appear farcical and absurdly funny at the same time. "Throughout *Earnest*'s seemingly limitless instances of inversion, one thing does indeed become another, polite pleasures do stand in for more visceral ones, and a lie finally and ultimately reveals itself as the truth" (ibid.: 51). Despite the topsy-turvy plot twists in Wilde's play, the protagonists are always fully in control of their emotions and their will; nothing can truly disturb or shake them out of their irrepressibly good humour, self-confidence, and funny self-righteousness. And yet, "[i]t is not a civilized society temporarily disrupted, but a perfect anarchic state in which the characters live, luxuriating in its benevolent lack of rules, morals, and principles" (Eltis 1996: 172). While the well-made play dealt with happy endings and relied on clever twists of plot to achieve its resolution, too, the end was still convincing. In Wilde, we cannot even be sure any more that the play has not poked fun at itself and consequently at us as well. "In Wilde's farce, [...] there is no division between chaos and order, fact and fiction" (ibid.). What are we to think about the author's seriousness, really, when even the last line, which ties it all together, is an ironic pun on e(a)rnestness, following a statement on triviality?

Along with employing some of the popular conventions of the well-made play, *Earnest* also satirizes some of the well-made play's typical features, such as its building of intense dramatic suspense. "The suspense is terrible," Gwendolen says towards the end of act 3 (when Jack's true identity slowly being unveiled), and voices what the captivated audience may feel at this point: "I hope it will last" (*E* 141). Lady Bracknell inadvertently parodies the familiar melodramatic plot element of a daughter's scandalous elopement: "Apprised, sir, of my daughters' sudden flight by her trusty maid, whose confidence I purchased by means of a small coin, I followed her at once by a luggage train" (*E* 130). Wilde subverts other melodramatic conventions which the well-made play had inherited as well, such as the mourning brother, the philandering gentleman, the deceived fiancée, and the devious governess.

The influence of the Victorian farce, which inherited and parodied some of the features of the well-made play and Victorian melodrama, is even more palpable. Originally, Wilde's play was entitled *Lady Lancing: A Serious Comedy for Trivial People* in earlier drafts (the subtitle changed to *A Trivial Comedy for Serious People* in the final version), and was to be a four-act play, but the theatre manager and actor George Alexander asked Wilde to cut down to three acts, perhaps wishing to bring it in line with the typical structure of Victorian farce, which was usually three acts. Thienpont has analysed the major changes from the four- to the three-act version of the play. She argues that Wilde's cutting and revisions (which left out a key subplot involving a debt collector named Gribsby, and further characterizations of the hypocritical Lady Bracknell, or "Lady Brancaster," as well as Miss Prism) "effected a more poignant social subversion caused by a move towards absurdity, a fortification of the position of the play's women, and a heightened identification with Victorian stereotypes" (Thienpont 2004: 246). Such stereotypes were already familiar from Victorian melodrama. They included the Good Woman, on which Cecily is based, and the Gentleman-Dandy to which Jack alludes (ibid.: 250, 253 f.). Wilde's revision process also seems to have eliminated much of the conventional stage business of farce, in particular its physical humour, and transformed it into no less side-splitting verbal sparring. There a few remnants of physical farcical humour, especially in act 2, with Jack's hilarious entrance in full mourning for the death of his imaginary brother Earnest, or Cecily's and Gwendolen's famous tea scene in which the jealous, insulted hostess Cecily excessively heaps sugar into Gwendolen's cup and offers cake instead of the requested bread and butter, turning the mundane social ritual of taking tea into a brilliantly subdued, high-society cat fight. Other critics have pointed out another echo of the physical humour of farce in Algernon's comical obsession with food and Jack's hilarious entrance in full mourning, reminiscent of Gilbert's *Engaged* (1877) and Pinero's *The Magistrate* (1885) (cf. Gladden 2010: 45 f.; Raby 1995: 28 f.). Further influences from popular farces that have been cited by critics are the name Bunbury and an imaginary brother called Ernest, which appear in F.C. Philips and Charles Brookfield's *Godpapa* (1891), as well as the popular farcical device of the foundling child, for which Powell (1990: 108-23) names W. Lestocq and E.M. Robson's *The Foundling* (1894) as *Earnest*'s direct predecessor.

Wilde's play clearly connotes Victorian farce, yet it also transcends it. Wilde "was not imitating standard British farce, in which sheer pace and physicality were major ingredients and in which the performers tended to signal the verbal jokes" (Raby 1995: 68). "Wilde used the form to make a play that is sparkling, but profound as well" (Parker 1974: 47), raising serious questions about human identity, relationships, and the reliability of the social and moral order itself. Even "beneath the most trivial matters, in the heart of a self-avowed trivial play, there is something serious lurking" (Lalonde 2005: 665).

Wilde's representation of the two young modern women Gwendolen and Cecily, as well as "[t]he linguistic gymnastics of *The Importance of Being Earnest* and its punning sexual subtext" (Eltis 2008: 107), shows a perceptible, if subtle influence of the popularity of the gender conflict in the social problem play of the 1880s and 1890s. They "mirror the play's shifting gender roles, and they combine to subvert any stable notion of normality" (ibid.). In their determination, intelligence, and self-confidence, Cecily and Gwendolen allude to high-minded and principled New Woman type developed by Shaw, Ibsen, and other writers of the 1880s and 1890s, but ironically their enthusiastic idealism is avowedly aesthetic and superficial rather than morally oriented. They are "unafraid to admit that their love depends entirely on a superficial quality" (Gladden 2010: 12). Gwendolen says, for example, "We live … in an age of ideals. The fact is constantly mentioned in the more expensive monthly magazine, and has reached the provincial pulpits I am told: and my ideal has always been to love some one of the name of Ernest" (*E* 83). Cecily repeats the same notion with a sensual angle, as if it was the only thing a young woman could truly believe in: The name Ernest "is a divine name. It has a music of its own. It produces vibrations" (*E* 84). Comically inverting traditional Victorian gender roles, masculinity is reinterpreted as a matter of aesthetic taste and attractiveness, as in Gwendolen's description of her father:

> Outside the family circle, papa, I am glad to say, is entirely unknown. I think that is quite as it should be. The home seems to me to be the proper sphere for the man. And certainly once a man begins to neglect his domestic duties he becomes painfully effeminate, does he not? And I don't like that. It makes men so very attractive. (*E* 116)

The indirect sexual and gender innuendo present throughout Wilde's play, together with a prominent emphasis on double lives, frequent references to the German language and culture (associated with advanced sexology and liberal attitudes towards homoeroticism), a joking reference (in Wilde's four-act version) to Robert Hichens' novel *The Green Carnation* (1894) which parodied the extensive homosexual social circle around Wilde and his lover Lord Alfred Douglas (1870-1945), and especially a possible allusion to the homoerotic love poetry collection *Love in Earnest* (1892) by J.G.F. Nicholson in the play's title, have prompted some critics to understand the play as an intimate closet drama (cf. Craft 1994: 106-139; Behrendt: 168). Sinfield (1994), Sedgwick (1997), and Bristow (1997) offer a more balanced view, arguing against the play's reduction to the (homo-)sexual aspect, which tends to occlude the more wide-ranging provocative aspects of the play, particularly Wilde's complex intertwinement of sexual with social questions, the performance of class, and the transgressive and deconstructive features of Wilde's style and language.

Ironically, however, the shadow of Wilde's impending legal conflict and conviction for same-sex practises already hung over *Earnest*'s premiere, which took place under police protection because of threats of disruption by the Marquess of Queensberry, the irate father of Lord Alfred Douglas, Wilde's lover. When news of Wilde's trial and sentence broke in May, Alexander quickly shut the play down. "That the production succeeding *Earnest* [at the St. James Theatre] was entitled *The Triumph of the Philistines* proved an off coincidence" (Gladden 2010: 17). At least in part due to the serious damage to Wilde's personal reputation in Britain, which lasted for decades, the aestheticist comedy of manners so closely associated with Wilde's name seems to have fallen out of favour. In the long term, however, *Earnest* triumphantly survived. Russell Jackson points out that it "is one of the few plays from its period to remain in theatrical repertoires, outlasting most of the trivial and almost all the serious works of Wilde's contemporaries" (1997: 165).

The play was published in book form by Leonard Smithers and Company of London in 1899, and revived on the British stage by George Alexander himself in 1902, only two years after Wilde's death in his French exile, making a windfall profit of £20,000. It has been standard repertory on the British and world stages ever since.

3. Summary and Outlook on the Genre in the 20th Century

Overall, the aestheticist comedy of manners as embodied by Oscar Wilde's *The Importance of Being Earnest* is characterized by more than one genre or style, combining elements of the original comedy of manners with those of Victorian farce, the well-made play, and the social problem play. Wilde offers up a creative *bricolage* of well-known conventions with his own ironic, even sarcastic treatment which have surprised and delighted audiences for over a century. Many scholars have shown that Wilde's general working method was often to masterfully adapt elements from various different genres while making them seem new and original. As Raby writes, "Wilde seems to have absorbed, and to reflect, a number of theatrical traditions and yet to have formulated his own distinctive style and method" (1995: 5). In doing so, "Wilde manages to produce plays which are both funnier than much contemporary comedy and more effective as social critique than contemporary problem plays" (Byrne 2003: 169).

While Wilde's plays were enormously popular before his downfall, they were also unique; in a sense, the genre of the 19th-century aestheticist comedy of manners began and ended with Oscar Wilde.

Scholars have stressed some connections between *Earnest* and later theatrical developments belonging to modernism and postmodernism. Bristow writes, "in *Earnest* – where everything is exceptionally artificial – there are the beginnings of a theatre of 'alienation' or 'estrangement', which would become a cornerstone of European modernism, especially in the dramas of Bertolt Brecht" (1992: 23 f.). The aestheticist comedy of manners also anticipates Alfred Jarry's (1873-1907) surrealist farce and Samuel Beckett's (1906-1989) and Eugène Ionesco's (1909-1994) theatre of the absurd (cf. Worth 1996: 131, 134). Its influence is further apparent in the work of such post-Wildean writers as Noel Coward (1899-1973), John Osborne (1929-1994), Harold Pinter (1930-2008), Joe Orton (1933-1967), Tom Stoppard (*1937), and David Mamet (*1947). For instance, "Joe Orton's sexually anarchic farces of the 1960s, *Entertaining Mr. Sloane* (1964), *Loot* (1965), and *What the Butler Saw* (1969), can be viewed as modern developments of Wilde's techniques and contain numerous linguistic echoes of the sexually punning subtext of *Earnest*" (Eltis 2008: 105). In his farcical *Travesties* (1974), Tom Stoppard also includes some characters and famous lines of *Earnest*. Besides Joe Orton's *What the Butler Saw*, there are also a few more recent dramatic camp adaptations of Earnest, such as Jill Fleming's *The Rug of Identity* (1986) and Mark Ravenhill's *Handbag; or, The Importance of Being Someone* (1998).

Working in the space between Victorianism and modernism, Oscar Wilde's play marked the end of one age, Victorianism, and the dawn of another. It made fun of and subverted traditional Victorian morality and social customs via "a younger, progressive, seemingly superficial perspective" (Gladden 2010: 11). As Richard Le Galienne wrote in *The Romantic '90s*, Oscar Wilde "made dying Victorianism laugh at itself, and it may be said to have died of laughter" (qtd. from Gladden 2010: 11).

Bibliography

Primary Sources

Donohue, Joseph & Ruth Berggren 1995 (eds.). *Oscar Wilde's The Importance of Being Earnest: A Reconstructive Critical Edition of the Text of the First Production, St. James's Theatre, London, 1895*. Gerrards Cross, Buckinghamshire: Colin Smythe Ltd.
Gladden, Samuel Lyndon 2001 [1895] (ed.). *The Importance of Being Earnest: A Trivial Comedy for Serious People*. Peterborough, ON: Broadview P.
Holland, Merlin 1999 (ed.). *Collins Complete Works of Oscar Wilde: Centenary Edition*. Glasgow: Harper Collins.

Annotated Bibliography

Byrne, Sandie. 2003. "Oscar Wilde's *The Importance of Being Earnest*." In: Jay Parini (ed.). *British Writers: Classics*. Vol. 1. New York, NY: Scribner's. 161-78.

Byrne's article is particularly useful as a general orientation about Wilde and the most salient textual and contextual issues regarding Earnest. *After a brief overview of Wilde's life and works, Byrne describes the play's textual history; first performances and early reception; structural and genre aspects as well as the plot; finally, she offers a brief summary of the play's later reception and 20th-century afterlife.*

Eltis, Sos. 1996. *Revising Wilde: Society and Subversion in the Plays of Oscar Wilde*. Oxford: Clarendon P.

In this well-known book on Wilde's dramatic oeuvre (excluding The Duchess of Padua *and* Salomé*), Eltis presents Wilde as a radical innovator with anarchistic, socialist, and feminist leanings. Accordingly, her chapter on* Earnest *seeks to uncover the revolutionary social criticism, biting class satire, and comical anarchy inherent in the play's plot and characters, revealing that it is more than the mere "bubble of fancy" Wilde claimed it to be (cf. Mikhail 1979: 250).*

Gladden, Samuel Lyndon. 2010. "Introduction." In: Samuel Lyndon Gladden (ed.). *Oscar Wilde: The Importance of Being Earnest*. Peterborough, ON: Broadview P. 11-52.

Gladden provides an excellent, comprehensive introduction to Wilde's play that reflects the most recent scholarship; it prefaces this new edition of Wilde's text by Broadview Press that also includes a useful appendix of historical materials and some excised scenes from the original four-act version.

Jackson, Russell. 1997. "*The Importance of Being Earnest*." In: Peter Raby (ed.). *The Cambridge Companion to Oscar Wilde*. Cambridge: Cambridge UP. 161-77.

Russell's article offers another excellent, short general orientation and introduction to Wilde's play. Russell touches on Wilde's careful revision process while moving from four to three acts and the developments surrounding the first performance; influences from popular dramatic genres; the question of the play's coding of homosexual desire; the dandy figure and class issues; the importance of Lady Bracknell; the play's rapidly moving, witty dialogue; and a comparison to Shaw (who was critical of Earnest*), Jones, and Pinero.*

Lalonde, Jeremy. 2005. "A 'Revolutionary Outrage': *The Importance of Being Earnest* as Social Criticism." In: *Modern Drama* 48: 659-76.

Lalonde offers a corrective to exclusively sexualized, queer readings of the dandy figures in Earnest *(Jack, Algernon) by stressing that the dandy's effeminacy is not only a matter of sexuality, but even more importantly of class. Along these lines, Lalonde analyses the play's emphasis on class struggle and social criticism, focusing on Lady Bracknell.*

Mackie, Gregory. 2009. "The Function of Decorum at the Present Time: Manners, Moral Language, and Modernity in 'an Oscar Wilde Play'." In: *Modern Drama* 52: 145-67.

Mackie's article emphasizes Wilde's sophisticated staging and critique of the limits of moral language and decorum: in Wilde, manners take precedence over morals and are hence revealed (as well as celebrated) in all their pretentious superficiality, making Wilde a direct ally of the New Drama's (Ibsen's, Shaw's) social critique in the comic realm. Mackie also draws attention to the influence of Victorian etiquette manuals on Wilde's comedies in this context.

Parker, David. 1974. "Oscar Wilde's Great Farce *The Importance of Being Earnest*." In: *Modern Language Quarterly* 35: 173-86.

Parker's essay compares typical aspects of Restoration comedy, 19th-century farce, and 20th-century drama of the absurd with Wilde's Earnest, focusing on such aspects as stock characters, typical plot elements, structure and style, and moral or social outlook. The article is especially useful for students trying to understand more deeply the old and new farcical elements of Wilde's play in the context of dramatic history.

Powell, Kerry. 1990. *Oscar Wilde and the Theatre of the 1890s*. Cambridge: Cambridge UP.

Powell's book is one of the most important contributions to Wilde studies and remains an excellent resource for studying Wilde's 1890s theatrical and cultural context, including popular drama. Powell's discussion of Earnest *focuses on probable influences of various contemporary melodramas and farces on Wilde's play, especially W. Lestocq and E.M. Robson's popular farce* The Foundling *(1894).*

Raby, Peter. 1995. *The Importance of Being Earnest: A Reader's Companion*. New York: Twayne Publishers.

Raby's book is divided into two parts, "Literary and Historical Context" and "A Reading" of Wilde's play. While the first part places Earnest *in the larger context of Wilde's general literary and aesthetic philosophy and his cultural and theatrical environment, the second part pays close attention to the play's textual genesis (from four to three acts) and early reception (including photographs and cartoons of the original 1895 production); social criticism and class satire; names and places as cultural signifiers; stylized characters and their rapid transformations; dramatic structure and style; and afterlife in the 20th century.*

Sedgwick, Eve Kosofsky. 1997. "Tales of the Avunculate: *The Importance of Being Earnest*." In: Eve Kosofsky Sedgwick. *Tendencies*. Durham: Duke UP. 52-72.

Sedgwick's essay on The Importance of Being Earnest *remains a locus classicus for queer literary theory approaches to the play, and is also one of the most balanced discussions of the play's controversial relation to Wilde's homosexuality. Sedgwick is careful to point out that Wilde's approach in* Earnest *is not reducible to physical (homo-)sexuality or psychological Oedipal parental issues (the name of the Father). The title of her essay ("Tales of the Avunculate") suggests that investigating the roles of uncles and aunts in the play, especially that of Lady Bracknell, offers a fruitful alternative angle to understanding central questions of sexual and gender identity as well as kinship in the play, with important implications for its sibling plot, marriage plot, and anagnoritic ending. Sedgwick's reading of Wilde's play shows the ways in which it actively destabilizes the very foundations of subjectivity, especially the contradiction between names and truth, appearances and reality, and familial origin and social affiliation.*

Thienpont, Eva. 2004. "From Faltering Arrow to Pistol Shot: *The Importance of Being Earnest.*" In: *The Cambridge Quarterly* 33.3: 245-55.

Thienpont argues against the established scholarly view that the original four-act version of Wilde's play (before Wilde agreed to revise and shorten it at the instigation of theater director George Alexander in preparation for the first performance in 1895) is more authoritative than the three-act version. Comparing the four-act to the three-act version, Thienpont shows that the three-act version is both "more subtle and more radical" in its ironic refinement of farcical and melodramatic conventions, as well as more theatrically effective.

Worth, Katharine. 1996. "*The Importance of Being Earnest.*" In: Jonathan Freedman (ed.). *Oscar Wilde: A Collection of Critical Essays*. Upper Saddle River, NJ: Prentice Hall. 122-38.

Worth's article presents Earnest *as a philosophical farce with existentialist leanings, absurdist elements, and a revolutionary moral and social attitude that connect it to the work of Alfred Jarry, Samuel Beckett, Tom Stoppard, Harold Pinter, and Joe Orton.*

Further Secondary Literature

Beckson, Karl. 1997 [1970]. *Oscar Wilde: The Critical Heritage*. London/New York: Routledge.
Behrendt, Patricia. 1991. *Oscar Wilde: Eros and Aesthetics*. New York: St. Martin's P.
Bristow, Joseph. 1992. "Introduction." In: *The Importance of Being Earnest and Related Writings*. London: Routledge. 23-24.
—. 1997. "'A Complex Multiform Creature': Wilde's Sexual Identities." In: Peter Raby (ed.). *The Cambridge Companion to Oscar Wilde*. New York: Cambridge UP. 195-218.
Craft, Christopher. 1994. *Another Kind of Love: Male Homosexual Desire in English Discourse, 1850-1920*. Berkeley: U of California P.
Eltis, Sos. 2008. "An Introductory Approach to Teaching Wilde's Comedies." In: Philip E. Smith II (ed.). *Approaches to Teaching the Works of Oscar Wilde*. New York: MLA. 100-107.
Hirst, David L. 1979. *Comedy of Manners*. London: Methuen.
Mikhail, E.H. (ed.). 1979. *Oscar Wilde: Interviews and Recollections*. 2 vols. London/Basingstoke: Macmillan.
Sinfield, Alan. 1994. *The Wilde Century: Effeminacy, Oscar Wilde, and the Queer Movement*. New York: Columbia UP.

16. NATURALIST DRAMA – 'PROBLEM PLAYS' OR 'PLAYS OF IDEAS'?
BERNARD SHAW'S *MRS WARREN'S PROFESSION*
AND JOHN GALSWORTHY'S *JUSTICE*

GERHARD STILZ

1. Naturalism in Britain: A European Revision

'Naturalism' is not a term originally invented to describe literary or textual phenomena. Taking its origin from the Renaissance assumption that nature (including the physical dispositions of mankind) could be conclusively described without resorting to 'supernatural' or spiritual revelations, the term 'naturalist' came to refer, above all, to natural scientists and their physical worldview. Methodically controlled discoveries of natural laws, after having been promoted in England by Francis Bacon and Henry Newton, were widely augmented and systematized during the Age of Enlightenment by philosophers and scientists from all parts of Europe. This 'progress of knowledge' had produced a discourse on nature which, during the Romantic period and most notably through Wordsworth's efforts at 'naturalising the supernatural,' affected even the theory and practice of poetic creation (cf. Abrams 1971: 65-70). Romantic and early Victorian 'naturalism' (whether in science, morals, and religion, painting, stagecraft, or acting) had therefore become a term universally familiar to British scientists, philosophers, and artists. Reservations and defences were made, to be sure, against the danger of a 'worldly deluge' by eminent men of both religion and classical education, notably in the controversy over Darwin's theory of evolution. But the (modernizing) scientific and intellectual community in Britain, led by T.H. Huxley, John Tyndall, Herbert Spencer, and Matthew Arnold, debated the respective truths and values of idealism and naturalism as a conflict between "two cultures" a hundred years before C.P. Snow offered his famous lecture on this issue (cf. Turner 1974). By 1859, a literary critic like David Masson, founder of *Macmillan's Magazine*, could dispassionately associate the 'real' with the 'natural' by equating 'naturalism' with a consistent mode of 'realism' and by proposing that "the British Novel, in its totality, should be a Natural History of British life" (rpt. in Greiner & Stilz 1983: 114-19).

Such terminological matters suddenly became more complicated over the irritating political and legal case of the French author Emile Zola and the English translations of his novels distributed by the publisher Henry Vizetelli. The latent official British distrust in revolutionary France, which was revived under the Paris commune in 1871 and aggravated by the ongoing libertarian vitality of the French Republic, shaped the atmosphere of hostility against the vices and decadent morals festering on the continent (which included prostitution and early commercial practices of contraception and birth control). In the guise of Zola's novels, such putrefying evils seemed to threaten Victorian morals and respectability. A National Vigilance Association sprang up in 1889, spreading a mentality of 'Britain under siege' and condemning Zola's "pernicious literature" (ibid.: 79-91) along with his theory of 'Naturalism' which he had formulated in 1879 in two strident essays, one concerning the stage and the other concerning the novel (ibid.: 35-69). 'Naturalism,' on grounds of the spectacular sentence passed by the Central Criminal Court against Vizetelli's "vicious" and "obscene" translations in 1888 (ibid.: 85), remained a dirty word in Britain. For more than 20 years, British authors and critics took pains to avoid this risky term and found alternative ways of expressing their ideas and concepts, leading to a 'new realism.' Through much of the 20th century, literary critics and historians tended to be rather reticent about British contributions (and indeed foundations) lent to the Pan-European and American movement of naturalism. Meanwhile, however, intellectual and artistic movements like naturalism or expressionism are accepted as not having passed by John Bull's islands in the shape of unnoticed and unfruitful foreign mysteries. Such a 'European' cultural reconstruction, with particular reference to British drama and theatre, will inform the following.

In any case, the late 19th-century British official repression of 'Naturalism' as a legitimate and respectable literary term has not led to a temporary blindness (healed only by late revisions), but rather to immediate alternative labelling practices, both expedient and inventive. On the one hand, we have Bernard Shaw's integral concept of "Plays Unpleasant," first used in the title of his collection comprising *Widowers' Houses*, *The Philanderer*, and *Mrs Warren's Profession* (1898), his contribution to the Symposium titled "The Problem Play" (1895), or even the somewhat awkward "Objective Anti-Idealist Plays" coined in his *Quintessence of Ibsenism* (1891) in order to characterize the eight plays of Ibsen's middle period. All these can be said to be generic stop-gap terms for what was and would have been identified as obvious instances of naturalistic drama elsewhere in Europe and in America. On the other hand, inventive labels like "The Drama of Discussion" highlighted in *The Times* on 15 November, 1911, seem to have been coined for elevating the plays of naturalism originally intended to shock people out of their self-complacency onto a level of thoughtful and dispassionate recognition. Similarly, "The Drama of Ideas" was first proposed by Arthur H. Nethercot (1941) as a generic term for correlating plays by Henrik Ibsen, Émile Augier, August Strindberg, Gerhart Hauptmann, George Bernard Shaw, Harley Granville-Barker, John Galsworthy, and, eventually, Eugene O'Neill. It was later fully instrumentalized for Bernard Shaw by Martin Meisel (cf. 1963) and recently amplified by Martin Puchner (cf. 2010) in order to cover philosophical drama in the widest possible sense, starting from Plato's dialogues. The common denominator of 'social problem plays' has been seen in the fact that social problems can be studied, discussed, and, perhaps, even solved by 'objectively' presenting and analysing them on the stage – a decidedly naturalistic strategy. Bernard Shaw discussed this in his contribution to the Symposium on "The Problem Play" in *The Humanitarian* (1895, rpt. in Greiner & Stilz 1983: 215-33). At the same time, Shaw notes that those plays that have contributed to the solution of social or political problems may appear to be dated after their mission has been completed. The main question arising from my provocative title and accompanying our analysis of texts is whether and under which conditions 'problem plays' (in the dual sense of 'plays presenting social problems' and 'plays illustrating communicative problems of the theatre') can and should be historically redeemed and canonized as 'plays of ideas' well worth reading and performing even after their original problems may have disappeared.

For a sober conceptual grounding it may be helpful to recall the theoretical statements on a naturalist literary 'mode' or 'method' published by major authors and critics during the late 19th and early 20th centuries (cf. Greiner & Stilz 1983: 35-256).

Based on the success of the natural sciences which, during the 19th century, had facilitated the technological miracles of the industrial revolution, natural philosophers and scientists gained public recognition and educational ground for their discoveries of 'reliable truths' and 'objective natural laws.' Correspondingly, the advocates of naturalism in the social sciences and the arts were fascinated with the mechanisms of progress and the diagnostic instruments available for observing and describing both physical and mental development and change. The great watchword of scientific discourse being 'objectivity,' naturalists in all fields of human activity felt that their mission was to show how the subjectivity of the observer could be made an integral part of the process of 'objective' observation and, possibly, of the object itself. For literature, and particularly for narrative and drama, this meant that the subjectivity of the author as observer, commentator, and evaluator had to be hidden away in a seemingly 'objective' arrangement of characters and circumstances and presented in a language that was designed not to reveal the author's emotions. This was reminiscent of the method of scientific observation and was indeed occasionally called a 'human experiment.' Obviously, however, the sublimation of the author's subjectivity into his (or her) superficial absence could never mean that the author had in fact resigned his interest, commitment, and responsibility. If he had refined himself *out* of his visible personal existence as an explicit speaker, he had at the same time refined himself *into* his work of art as the tacit mastermind of the factual and emotional arrangement and also as the supreme calculator of the audience's responses. Horace's old dictum *ars est celare artem* ("It is an art to dissimulate artistry") gains new relevance in this context.

In the analysis of a literary text we should thus distinguish three major fields where 'naturalistic features' can be discerned:

1. In terms of *subject matter*, the ideal of 'objectivity' privileges, above all, the material world which, for scientists of the late 19th century, increasingly included social and psychological matters and mechanisms. Basically, this could involve realities and characters from all social classes and ways of life. In practice, however, we find that authors, towards the end of the century, tended to shift their focus of interest away from the middle classes (preferred under mid-19th-century realism), in favour of the lower classes. This goes hand in hand with the burning problems of growing unemployment and depression both in London and the industrial cities of the Midlands. Naturalists thus concentrated their analysis on the hitherto neglected reality of 'low life' while at the same time focussing their interest in the middle and upper strata of society on the extent to

which they caused and profited from the exploitation of the poor. They strove to expose the taboos and self-deceptive lies through which respectable Victorians disguised and defended their comfort. In this, British naturalist dramatists felt inspired by Zola and the brothers Goncourt in France as well as by the Norwegian Henrik Ibsen and also by Gerhart Hauptmann and Hermann Sudermann in Germany. In Britain, they were seconded by novelists and story-tellers like George Moore, Arthur Morrison, Somerset Maugham, Rudyard Kipling, George Gissing, and even young James Joyce.

The ideal of 'objectivity' suggested that 'the present' offered a much more suitable range of subjects for 'scientific' analysis than a remote historical past whose presentation would have been difficult without the author's explicit role as a coordinator and interpreter. Likewise, spatial distances would have been hard to bridge by the dry literary concept of presenting to the audience's critical observation a 'slice of life' (cf. Greiner & Stilz 1983: 228) as an immediately convincing 'experiment.' Accordingly, naturalist plays (like naturalist narratives) are usually characterized by presenting unpleasant, previously repressed realities, preferably with a focus on the life of the lower social strata (which might be taken as a distinctive marker vis-à-vis early and mid-19th century realism).

2. The central idea that a semblance of scientific objectivity should replace overt signals of authorial guidance also came to dominate major naturalistic *modes of presentation*. Concerning the *mode of presenting physical reality*, the newly developed technology of photography became a favourite reference point for authors and critics alike. To some, photography seemed to offer, in an exemplary fashion, the truth in every detail: it was praised for its incorruptibility and precision and it could be used as an easily portable document, incontrovertibly proving 'things as they are.' To others, photography remained a questionable and profoundly false comparison for literary description and, particularly, for the selective discretion and perspectival sovereignty of an author (including a photographer). Contemporaries tended to praise or find fault with the naturalists' depiction of seemingly insignificant details, and many critics and interpreters were in fact irritated with giving subtle meanings to the innumerable objects both large and small that crowded the scene, all without a trace of authorial comment. Yet undoubtedly there was a sense of purpose in the implicit task to discover relevance in seemingly irrelevant details. Registering the insignificant and determining its hidden role in the grand plan attributed new values and new dignity to small things and lowly persons.

A second point of comparison was the invisibility of the camera on the photograph itself, which suggested that, like the photographer, the naturalist artist could or should hide away his subjectivity. Similarly, naturalistic theorists like Zola demanded that the comments, hints, metaphors, and pointed comparisons that were still available to an author under realism, should, under the new naturalist programme, give way to the *impassibilité* of a work of art, to the cold, detached, and dispassionate eye of the scientist observer, who withholds his moral conclusions and leaves them to his sensitive audience. Surely, this impassive attitude can only make sense for the *mode* of presentation, not for the calculated *purpose* of a work of art, least of all for a purpose of social commitment.

Concerning the *temporal arrangement* within a work of art, the scientific plausibility of a sequence of events was made the rule of all plot constructions. This meant that, different from the customary order of events (usually prescribed and protected by the genre conventions in both tragedy and comedy, and ardently opposed to the trivial conventions of the 19th century well-made play and melodrama, see chapter 14), naturalist plays were not supposed to present developments without clearly showing their causes and effects. The world was meant to be seen as profoundly determined, yet not only (in a dark, pessimist sense) by inhuman blows and buffets of fate, but also and rather (in an enlightening, possibly meliorist sense) by individual and volitional acts of resistance and reform. The naturalist experiment was meant to be a demonstrative experiment, arranged by the author, plausible to the educated audience and true to life under the auspices of modern science. The truth content of the 'slices of life' presented was intended to be critically discussed by the audience. Theatre should thus again become a 'moral institution.'

'Objectivity' replaces the author's voice – this is also the motto that governs the *mode and presentation of language*, in naturalistic novels as well as in plays. It is just that the withdrawal of epic and authorial voices into the space behind the curtain was felt to be more natural on 19th-century stages in London (most of which had been converted into the semblance of a stage box following the Bancrofts' path-breaking success with their 'stage realism' in the Prince of Wales' Theatre in 1865). Yet it was not enough that the authorial voices disappeared from the stages (and their remaining aprons) along with the prologues and epilogues of earlier times. According to the new ideal of objectivity, the language of the characters, too, was supposed to appear to be increasingly conditioned by origin, class, individual person, and the particular situation in which they spoke. Dialect, sociolect, idiolect, and psycholect were now to be heard on respectable stages without inviting the audience to superior ridicule and condescending laughter. The language of the characters was to become transparent for the 'objective' physical and psychic realities they were meant to embody and that shaped them while they spoke. The development of 'natural acting' during the 19th century had paved the way for these new modes of speaking, but the theoretical rationale for this 'progress' was ultimately supplied by naturalism.

3. The *purpose* of naturalist plays invariably involves the authors' intentions on the one hand and the recipients' cooperative abilities and impediments on the other. Both are vital and indeed constitutive factors in the potential success of naturalist plays. Misunderstanding the authors' calculated intentions, or the audiences' sensitivities and responsiveness, necessarily leads to misunderstandings regarding texts, genres, or the implications of a literary term. Bertolt Brecht, the clear-sighted re-inventor of the Epic Theatre, fell victim to such a misunderstanding when he denounced "the very word of Naturalism [...] as a crime," and continued explaining that "presenting the prevailing conditions between men as natural ones, with man being considered as a piece of nature and therefore unable to change these conditions is just criminal" (Brecht 1963: I, 157, my own translation). Brecht's dismissal of naturalism would be more seriously

debatable if he had taken into account the naturalists' calculated intentions and explicit statements (as well as the audiences' dispositions and reactions) at their historical face value. As it is, he ignored what might be called a fairly reliable contract of mutual expectations between the authors and audiences of naturalist plays. Most naturalists had a deeply reformist agenda in mind when "sharpshooting at the audience" (Shaw 1986: 171). In effect, naturalistic authors and their followers have helped to trigger needful dialogues, develop strong opinions, and eventually resolve conflicts over ignored, repressed, or tabooed problems. Whether such 'problem plays' can or should also be considered as 'plays of ideas' will have to be discussed in more detail on the basis of individual texts.

2. Independent Theatre: Shaw's *Plays Unpleasant*

The London commercial theatre during the 19th century had developed into a big entertainment industry drawing huge profits from staging a single successful play night after night in a 'long run' for months (and in some cases for years) on end. The theatre market produced mainly 'well-made' contemporary English and French melodrama, comedies, and farces, but also Shakespeare's tragedies in spectacular revivals. The laws of the market were profit-oriented, with hardly any concern for education or reform. This accounts for the widely spread historical verdict that British 19th-century theatre was largely slight and trivial. When, in the late 1870s and early 80s, Ibsen's plays and Zola's vociferous revolt against the theatre as "the last fortress of conventionality" (rpt. in Greiner & Stilz 1983: 41) reached British shores, the profitable dynamics of the commercial system were not disposed to accommodate such critical demands. Therefore, like in other European capitals, a new theatre system sprang up in London. The 'Independent Theatre' movement (adopted in London in 1891 by Jack Thomas Grein, a Dutch dramatist, critic, and stage manager) could rely on small but discerning and politically influential audiences as well as deeply committed dramatists. George Bernard Shaw, art critic and failed novelist, was one of them. He decided to meet the demands of the Independent Theatre for "plays which have a literary and artistic rather than a commercial value" (qtd. in Rowell 1978: 129). To this end, he first submitted and staged *Widowers' Houses* (1892), a bitter critique of London slum landlordism which exposed the insidious but intimate correlations of snug middle-class romantic living and loving with the exploitation and oppression of the London poor. *The Athenaeum*, in its comment on the play on the first night (17 December, 1892), did not hesitate to spot Shaw's naturalist cousin in France: "He aims to show with Zolaesque exactitude that middle-class life is foul and leprous" (Black 1995: 157). Numerous other journals seconded this observation with a furious and controversial debate over Shaw's art of destroying ideals.

Considerably louder and longer-lasting was the public uproar around Bernard Shaw's *Mrs Warren's Profession* (1894). This thoroughly uncourteous courtesan play was meant to respond to *The Second Mrs Tanqueray*, Arthur Wing Pinero's Ibsenesque tragedy of a 'woman with a past,' which, from May 1893 to April 1894, had been performed with considerable commercial success in the respectable St James's Theatre of London's West End. Although Pinero had clearly improved on the melodramatic plot of Alexandre Dumas' *La Dame aux Camélias* (1848; dramatized in 1852 and adapted in England as *The Lady of the Camellias* in 1863), Shaw was not satisfied. He radically wished, in his own play, to "make an end [...] of the furtively lascivious Pharisaism of stage immorality, by a salutary demonstration of the reality" ("Advice to a Young Critic," 4 November 1895, qtd. in Meisel 1963: 142). In effect, this intention and its textual product met with the disapproval of the Lord Chamberlain who, in 1894, banned the staging of the play finding that it was "immoral and otherwise improper for the stage" (qtd. in Shaw 1965: 219). Accordingly, *Mrs Warren's Profession* was first offered to the public in print as the last text in Shaw's collection *Plays Unpleasant* (1898) before it could raise its first stage scandal in a private performance of the Stage Society arranged in the New Lyric Theatre in London (1902). Looking back from the year 1930, when wrapping up his "Apology" of 1902 with further observations gathered during and after the first public performance in Britain in 1925 (and after battling against the censorship that had banned part of the first film version), Shaw explained:

> Mrs. Warren's Profession was written in 1894 to draw attention to the truth that prostitution is caused, not by female depravity and male licentiousness, but simply by underpaying, undervaluing, and overworking women so shamefully that the poorest of them are forced to resort to prostitution to keep body and soul together. Indeed all attractive unpropertied women lose money by being infallibly virtuous or contracting marriages that are not more or less venal. If on the large social scale we get what we call vice instead of what we call virtue it is simply because we are paying more for it. No normal woman would be a professional prostitute if she could better herself by being respectable, nor marry for money if she could afford to marry for love. (1965: 219)

This certainly outlines a social problem whose undeniable existence is asserted by flagging the naturalist keyword "the truth." Shaw confirms that he wrote this play with the firm purpose to expose the roots of a repressed social evil and thereby to eventually improve on it. He discloses a chain of causes and effects, indeed a whole network of conditions, which create and maintain prostitution. It is not individual weakness or failure that are made responsible for the commercial success and the huge economic profits drawn from this problem, but the ruthless mechanism of greedy high capitalism at the turn of 20th century. Art, according to Shaw, has a remedial function to offer in this nasty game, for being "the subtlest, the most seductive, the most effective instrument of moral propaganda in the world, excepting only the example of moral conduct" (ibid.: 221). Art therefore is obliged to serve truth, with the help of scientific research and the materials piled up in official reports and documentations – for example the Parliamentary Blue Books, which Shaw claimed he had studied. For Shaw, the artist's duty included not only the charming presentation of sunny surfaces but also that of the repulsive, horrifying, and loathsome dark depths of reality. In his contribution to "The Problem Play – A Symposium: Should Social Problems be Freely Dealt with in the Drama?" in *The Humanitarian* 6 (May 1895; rpt. in Greiner & Stilz 1983: 215-23),

Shaw reveals his proximity to Zola's doctrines of naturalism as far as the political role of the theatre is concerned. But he also clearly points out that he sees the true quintessence of the naturalist doctrine in the trust placed in the hope that the outcome of the conflict between human volitions and conditions is not predetermined by external circumstances. He boils down this demanding concept of the 'problem play' in the 1902 "Preface" to *Mrs Warren's Profession* (*MWP*) to the much-quoted statement:

> [I]t will be seen that only in the problem play is there any real drama, because drama is no mere setting up of the camera to nature: it is the presentation in parable of the conflict between Man's will and his environment: in a word, of problem. (Shaw 1965: 228)

The dramatic demonstration of this dual conflict antagonizes the two main characters in the play: on the one hand, there is Mrs Warren, the externally hardened but inwardly sentimental businesswoman, who made her way from rags to riches through prostitution and the efficient management of continental brothels. She holds the miserable circumstances around her responsible for her morally doubtful career, which in fact turns out to be not only commercially attractive but also honoured and well-protected by influential men from all public spheres. On the other hand, her daughter Vivie comes to learn that only due to her mother's vituperable income and connections has she been able to enjoy higher education in Cambridge as a student of mathematics. Realizing the abyss of corruption and false pretensions that made her who she is, she refuses to enter her mother's business and decides for an emancipated life ("permanently single [...] and permanently unromantic," *MWP* 274) as an actuary in a London insurance office. She believes in the principles of free will and moral choice: "People are always blaming their circumstances for what they are. I don't believe in circumstances. The people who get on in this world are the people who get up and look for the circumstances they want, and, if they can't find them, make them" (*MWP* 246). Yet, what separates mother and daughter in the final scene, coldly and forever, is not Mrs Warren's profession, which is amply defended and condoned within the circumstances that produced and protected it. The point is rather to be taken from Vivie's final charge that her mother is a "conventional woman at heart" who has "lived one life and believed in another" (*MWP* 286). Vivie chooses a life led by her own uncompromising will – even if that may never be as free from its formative and intervening circumstances as she had proclaimed in her discussions with her mother.

Altogether there are three aspects that help us to distinguish Shaw's *Mrs Warren's Profession* as a naturalist problem play from more conventional courtesan plays:

1. In terms of 'character,' the melodramatic prostitute or 'woman with a past' had traditionally been attractive and seductive in her outward appearance including her way of speaking and acting. She was hard to distinguish from the 'stock character' of a 'femme fatale.' Pinero started to change this image by adding the problem of Paula's despair owed to the inexorable process of ageing. Mrs Warren, by comparison, is "a decidedly vulgar, but, on the whole, a genial and fairly presentable old blackguard of a woman" (*MWP* 220). Her vitality is not based on her tempting youth but, much more creditably, on her courage, efficiency, and self-reliance. A conventional stage courte-

san, moreover, used to be careless, wasting away her enviable abundance of money, beauty, and charm, eventually suffering for this through disease, loneliness, and early death. Not so Mrs Warren. Her career does not allow such simple morals. She is clever, far-sighted, thrifty, businesslike, sociable, and quite healthy: in short, she possesses all bourgeois virtues that may be needed to make the best of any profession.

2. In terms of the logic of the plot, conventional courtesan plays insist that the prostitute or woman with a past dies spectacularly on the stage, or in the adjoining room. She expiates her extraordinary and miserable life, largely relieving the society that supported and ruined her from its moral burden. Mrs Warren, however, survives and thrives. She makes money and increases her wealth like any other successful businesswoman. The idea of contrition and return deemed necessary in romantic and melodramatic courtesan plays is explicitly refused by Shaw's Mrs Warren as implausible and false. This problem does not bear heavily on Mrs Warren. Three tolerable ways of survival appear to be feasible: her sister Liz (burdened with a similar past) has found her position as a respectable lady in Winchester; Vivie, who is invited to become involved along her mother's lines, is reassured by her suitor Crofts that there is no safer space for "queer ways" of business than "decent society" (*MWP* 264 f.); and Mrs Warren herself, who does not consider a change of life, is forgiven her uncomfortable past (though not her continuing double morals) by her perceptive daughter.

3. The issue of guilt and responsibility is indeed central, an issue Shaw felt had to be tackled and set right in this play. The melodramatic prostitute used to be ashamed of her position and felt guilty for having 'fallen.' Mrs Warren, however, as amply paraded in the discussion scenes (and confirmed with many flourishes in Shaw's prefatory and apologetic contexts) has no reason to be ashamed of her profession: she followed the logic of her miserable conditions. But the main shift in Shaw's naturalist treatment of the subject is that now the pillars of society are portrayed as the main culprits in the misery of prostitution, not vaguely or anonymously, nor for want of insight, but ruthlessly, systematically, and based on the 'noble' principles of high capitalism. Even the censorship vested with the Lord Chamberlain in order to ban unwelcome plays is seen as part of this guilty system. Shaw's revolt is voiced in the terms of naturalism.

But there is something in the play that escapes and transcends the solid protest uttered with a gesture of socio-political enlightenment. It is an element introduced by the difficult character of Vivie. Her profoundly philosophical and eminently moral boast that she does not believe in circumstances throws up the question of whether men or women really can or even should ignore their deeply conditioned past lives in order to try and shape their circumstances themselves. This is a disturbing thought which, on close consideration, can turn the arguably transient 'problem play' of *Mrs Warren's Profession* into a lasting naturalistic 'play of ideas.'

3. From Province to West End: Galsworthy's *Justice*

Evidently naturalist drama had a hard time in the commercial theatres of London during the 1890s. If performances were at all permitted, the 'new drama' was mostly restricted to the stages of the Independent Theatre and to private theatre clubs. In Dublin and in other provincial cities (like Glasgow, Manchester, Liverpool, or Birmingham), London touring companies had all but gained a monopoly with their lavish stage performances. However, at the turn of the century, Irish national and British regional movements sprang up and demanded the revival of an 'independent' provincial theatre. On the model of the Independent Theatres in European capitals, their repertories explicitly were to include local, 'realistic' plays. Thus an Irish Literary Theatre (1897-1901) was promoted in Dublin by Lady Augusta Gregory, William Butler Yeats, and Edward Martyn. After being transformed by Yeats into the Irish National Theatre Society in 1902, this initiative was rewarded by Miss Annie Elizabeth Fredericka Horniman, the rich and rebellious daughter of a tea-planter's family, with a stage in the Abbey Theatre (1904). Though Yeats emphatically disavowed realism, his companions, strengthened by such Abbey dramatists as John Millington Synge and, later, Sean O'Casey, wrote and produced plays starting from recipes found in Ibsen and Shaw (cf. Stilz 1993). In Manchester, considered at the turn of the century as one of Britain's most lively and progressive cities, Ben Iden Payne formed his repertory company and, with the help of Miss Horniman's favour (which had meanwhile turned away from nationalist Ireland), started his first season with the Gaiety Theatre (1907) staging Charles McEvoy's arguably naturalistic presentation of lower-middle-class life in *David Ballard*. Other notable plays followed in this vein by Allan Monkhouse, Harold Brighouse, and Stanley Houghton (cf. Stilz 1999). Similar movements can be traced in other major cities in the British province. The Scottish Repertory Theatre followed in Glasgow (1909-14), the Liverpool Repertory Theatre opened in 1911 and survived until the 1920s, and the Birmingham Repertory Theatre opened in 1913 and is working still.

In London, naturalist playwrights had to wait for a change of climate. A major breakthrough was achieved by John Galsworthy, whose *Justice*, subtitled "a tragedy in four acts" was first performed in both London and Glasgow on 21 February 1910. Although this play did not become a blockbuster and was only revived once on the stage in 1916, its political success as a professedly naturalistic play must be seen as remarkable and outstanding (cf. Stilz 1980). The way for *Justice* had been paved in the London Court Theatre by *The Silver Box* (1906), where, in a naturalist fashion, Galsworthy confronted his audience with the irritating fact that there was one law for the rich and a different one for the poor. In *Strife* (first performed in 1909 and strongly reminiscent of Gerhart Hauptmann's *The Weavers*, 1893), theatre goers witnessed an embittered industrial strike threatening both workers and employers with ruin, and finally averted only by a compromise at a high cost. Elements of compromise can also help to explain the secret of Galsworthy's political success achieved by *Justice*. This play actually influenced the legislative reform towards reducing solitary confinement, which was filed by young Winston Churchill, then Home Minister. The audience of the play is presented with the misery of William Falder, a junior clerk in a solicitors office, who has forged a cheque. Not knowing the reasons for this crime, James Howe, senior solicitor, overrules the intercession of his son Walter Howe and hands the delinquent over to the police. Act 2 takes us to the Assizes, three months later. Falder's deed is made comprehensible: he had wanted to save Ruth Honeywill, an innocent married woman, from her brutal husband and wished to start a new life with her in South America. Though not without the veiled compassion of some the office-holders, Falder is sentenced to three years of solitary confinement, under the existing Law. In act 3, we accompany Cokeson, Falder's elderly colleague, on a visit to the prison. Cokeson vainly pleads for the culprit who, in a silent naturalist pantomime, is reduced by solitude and despair to a helplessly suffering animal. Act 4 demonstrates that Falder's return to normal life is barred wherever he goes. He cannot resume his job unless he severs his extra-marital relationship with Ruth. Ruth meanwhile falls victim to her lecherous employer. The situation becomes utterly hopeless when Falder is wanted by the police again, this time because he has forged a letter of recommendation in order to find a new job. Falder escapes the Law by committing suicide.

In spite of Falder's deplorable death, his character does not appear to be 'tragic' enough for the genre announced in the play's subtitle. Moreover, the emotional guidance supplied through much of the drama by the elderly, well-meaning fellow Cokeson smacks of a melodramatic compromise. The titular 'tragedy' seems to reside somewhere else: in the failure of the Law (as it is) to produce Justice (as it should be). The covert rhetoric of the play seems intentionally split: Galsworthy's double strategy appears to be directed at the divided powers in the British political system. On the one hand, the play appeals to the persons responsible for reforms in parliament or in the administration of prisons. This can be supported by studying the social contacts Galsworthy sought and mobilized while he wrote this play, which included direct personal correspondence with Churchill and Sir Ruggles Brise, chairman of the parliamentary prison commission (both of whom were present on the first night).

On the other hand, Galsworthy obviously directed his appeal to the electorate whom he believed he could partly reach through the theatre and partly through critical journals. The power of Galsworthy's appeal "to the general public" (Marrot 1935: 266) was explicitly acknowledged by Churchill in his proposal for the reduction of solitary confinement (and a general reform of the criminal law) before the House of Commons on 20 July 1910.

As a 'social problem play,' *Justice* can be convincingly correlated with the movement of naturalism. Here, Galsworthy presented lower-class life and the dark but well-documented reality of a prison house in a naturalist manner. Naturalism also dictates the principle of causality, which holds the plot together in all its fissures and details. The ending seems to be determined once the cheque has been forged and the law takes its inexorable course. Galsworthy, by firmly embedding his characters in their social milieu and by characterizing the Law as a necessarily incorruptible machine, has created a network of inevitabilities in which the human catastrophe is produced without guilty individual agents. Sudden surprises, lucky turns, and happy incidents are not required. Falder's misery is presented as a 'slice of life' in a Zolaesque sense.

We know from Galsworthy's theoretical essays and statements that he was very much aware of writing in a naturalist manner. In summer 1909, about the time when he was researching documents and visiting institutions in preparation for writing *Justice*, he composed an essay with the slightly coquettish title "Some Platitudes Concerning Drama" (rpt. in Greiner & Stilz 1983: 232-40). There he speaks of an "inherent moral" to be brought to light by the dramatist, and he offers three ways of doing so: The first, "most common, successful and popular" way is to "set before the public that which it wishes to have set before it, the views and codes of life by which the public lives and in which it believes" (ibid.: 233). Galsworthy, like Shaw, thus alluded to the popular 'well-made plays' and melodramas of the 19th century. The second way, he continues, is to

> set before the public those views and codes of life by which the dramatist himself lives [and] if they are opposite of what the public wishes to have placed before it, presenting them so that the audience may swallow them like powder in a spoonful of jam (ibid.: 233 f.).

Here Galsworthy seems to have had in mind, above all, Shaw's collection of insidious comedies in *Plays Pleasant*. There is, however, a third way, Galsworthy points out, namely:

> To set before the public no cut-and-dried codes, but the phenomena of life and character, selected and combined, but not distorted, by the dramatist's outlook, set down without fear, favour, or prejudice, leaving the public to draw such poor moral as nature may afford (ibid.: 234).

This course is meant to be Galsworthy's own. It corresponds, in much of its scientific diction and message, with the programmes of European naturalism, wishing to disguise the author's subjectivity behind the 'objective' reality in the work of art created. Explicitly, towards the end of this essay, Galsworthy subscribes to

> the broad and clear-cut channel of naturalism, down which will course a drama poignantly shaped, and inspired with high intention, but faithful to the seething and multiple life around us, drama as some are inclined to term photographic, deceived by a seeming simplicity into forgetfulness of the old proverb 'Ars est celare artem,' and oblivious of the fact that, to be vital, to grip, such a drama is in every respect as dependent on imagination, construction, selection, and elimination [...] as ever was the romantic or rhapsodic play. (Ibid.: 238 f.)

Like Zola, Galsworthy thus defends himself against the charge that the naturalist playwright decided for the easy way in his 'reproduction' of reality. Even more emphatically than Zola he insisted on the imaginative task and achievement of the artist in creating the illusion of reality by the means of naturalism. And he confesses to a hidden rhetoric guiding his calculated effects: "To put it in another way, naturalistic art, when alive, indeed to be alive at all, is simply the art of manipulating a procession of most delicate symbols" (ibid.: 239).

Galsworthy's *Justice* can thus be read as an exemplar of a politically unusually successful stage play balancing a compromise between naturalist revolt and bourgeois reconciliation. The elements of revolt are to be found in the merciless social misery presented before the audience with a barely veiled accusation directed towards conservative defenders of the existing Law. Theatre-goers are made to see, without embellishment, helpless fraud, ruined matrimonial relations, an adulterous and immoral project of escape, forced prostitution, prison life, hopelessness, despair, and suicide. And all this misery is seen to be determined to end in catastrophe by the mechanisms of justice. Yet a direct confrontation with the responsible persons in office is avoided by the anonymity of the accused 'system.' The 'pillars of society' within the play are largely credited with trying to do their best. The author's attack is thus directed against the evacuated apparatus of the Law.

It can be argued that Galsworthy's compromise between the unpleasant presentation of social sores and the forbearing depiction of the people administering the inexorable system has been bought at a price which has marred the play's longevity. After the problem of this play had been removed by appropriate legal and political measures and reforms, this play did not seem worth staging for much longer. Such considerations should not minimize the momentous merit of such a play. But our comparison of Galsworthy's *Justice* and Shaw's *Mrs Warren's Profession* may account for the difference felt in the still vague distinction between a 'problem play' and a 'drama of ideas.'

4. The Fore and Aft

Naturalism, as explained above, was not invented by Zola. Neither did it fall dead after Galsworthy's *Justice* nor after 1920 (which, for reasons of a coherent historical presentation, can be taken as a cut-off point). In a rather uninterrupted sequence, certainly D.H. Lawrence's three (long unpublished and even longer unstaged) Lancashire playscripts, *A Collier's Friday Night* (c. 1909), *The Daughter-in-Law* (1912) and *The Widowing of Mrs Holroyd* (1911-14), some of Shaw's other plays, such as *Major Barbara* (1905) or *Heartbreak House* (1919), or Sean O'Casey's *The Shadow of a Gunman* (1925) and *The Plough and the Stars* (1926), have been and should be considered as dramatic efforts with a solid naturalist agenda. Furthermore, it will be shown in this Handbook that the 'realist plays by the Angry Young Men' of the 1950s and 60s (from Osborne to Wesker, see chapter 18), some of the texts constituting the 'political theatre' of the 60s and 70s (including plays by Bond, Brenton and Hare, see chapter 20), the provocative gesture in Sarah Kane's and Mark Ravenhill's 'in-yer-face theatre' (see chapter 25) and, above all, the 'documentary turn in contemporary drama and the return of the political' (see chapter 27) have used and continue to reactivate quite a number of the features, both structural and strategic, that had shaped and qualified naturalistic drama since the 19th century. Altogether, the documentary character of photography, film, and television has helped to widen the *practice* of naturalism in the new visual mass media. At the same time, the *theory* of naturalism as a reformist political strategy in art and literature has lost its novelty and revolutionary impetus: it is taken for granted.

Bibliography

Primary Sources

Galsworthy, John. 1999. *Five Plays*. London: Methuen.
Shaw, Bernard. 1965. *The Complete Prefaces of Bernard Shaw*. London: Hamlyn.
—. 1986. *Major Critical Essays*. London: Penguin.
—. 2001. *Plays Unpleasant* (contains *Widowers' Houses*, *The Philanderer* and *Mrs Warren's Profession*). London: Penguin.

Annotated Bibliography

Greiner, Walter & Gerhard Stilz. 1983. *Naturalismus in England 1880-1920*. Darmstadt: Wissenschaftliche Buchgesellschaft.
A reader with a German introduction and critical comments on the British debate over naturalism.
Stilz, Gerhard. 1980. "Naturalistisches Drama und bürgerlich-reformerischer Kompromiss: John Galsworthys *Justice*." In: *DVJs* 54: 564-80.
An analysis of the rhetoric of Galsworthy's Justice.

Further Secondary Literature

Abrams, M.H. 1971. *Natural Supernaturalism: Tradition and Revolution in Romantic Literature*. New York: Norton.
Black, Martha F. 1995. *Shaw and Joyce: "The Last Word in Stolentelling."* Gainsville: Florida UP.
Brecht, Bertolt. 1963. *Schriften zum Theater*, I: 1918-1933. Frankfurt a.M.: Suhrkamp.
Marrot, H.V. 1935. *The Life and Letters of John Galsworthy*. London: Heinemann.
Meisel, Martin. 1963. *Shaw and the Nineteenth-Century Theater*. Princeton, NJ: Princeton UP.
Nethercot, Arthur H. 1941. "The Drama of Ideas." In: *The Sewanee Review* 49.3: 370-84.
Puchner, Martin. 2010. *The Drama of Ideas: Platonic Provocation in Theater and Philosophy*. New York: Oxford UP.
Rowell, George. 1978. *The Victorian Theatre 1792-1914*. Cambridge: Cambridge UP.
Stilz, Gerhard. 1993. "Naturalism and the Irish Theatre at the Turn of the Century: The Difficult Case of Yeats, Synge and Lady Gregory." In: Eberhard Bort (ed.). *Irish Drama from Farquhar to Friel*. Bremen: European Society for Irish Studies. 71-87.
—. 1999. "English Naturalism in the Province. The 'Politics' of the 'Manchester School' and Stanley Houghton's Hindle Wakes." In: Jürgen Kamm (ed.). *Twentieth-Century Drama in English*. Trier: WVT. 135-49.
Turner, Frank Miller. 1974. *Between Science and Religion: The Reaction to Scientific Naturalism in Late Victorian England*. New Haven: Yale UP.

17. THE EMERGENCE OF IRISH DRAMA IN THE EARLY TWENTIETH CENTURY: JOHN MILLINGTON SYNGE'S *THE PLAYBOY OF THE WESTERN WORLD* AND SEAN O'CASEY'S *THE PLOUGH AND THE STARS*

Heinz Kosok

1. The Historical Background

Ever since Ireland was invaded from across the Irish Sea by a Norman army under Henry II in the 12th century, the course of Irish history has been dominated by the conflict with England. During the following centuries, Ireland was gradually conquered, the native population was pushed back into the barren, mountainous regions of the West and North West, and English as well as Scottish settlers took over large areas of the country. Although British politicians were always careful to avoid the term 'colony' with reference to Ireland, the country was clearly kept in a semi-colonial state by her larger neighbour. When, in 1800, the Irish Parliament in Dublin was dissolved in favour of direct representation in Westminster, Ireland lost one of the last vestiges of an independent nation. Throughout the 19th century, Ireland saw a number of rebellions against British dominance, but they were hopelessly disorganized and failed miserably.

However, the conflict between Ireland and Britain was not only a matter of military and political supremacy. Irish society itself was sharply divided; it consisted of two unequal groups who largely ignored one another and often, or so it seems, were not even aware of each other's existence. The vast majority of the rural population were Catholics; they spoke a Celtic language called 'Gaelic' (today, for political reasons, the term 'Irish' is preferred), most of them lived in poverty, relying on potatoes as their staple diet and starving when their potato crops failed, they had no access to political or administrative power, and while they had little or no chance of formal education, they retained a wealth of cultural treasures in myth, saga, and legend as well as in formal poetry, often transmitted orally throughout the centuries. By contrast, the members of the 'Protestant ascendancy' were descended from English or Scottish settlers; they occupied dominant positions in society as landowners as well as members of the judiciary and the administration, they spoke English (often, it must be said, with an Irish accent that was ridiculed in England), and they saw themselves as citizens of a larger Empire whose centre was London. The literature produced by the ascendancy class was primarily destined for a reading public in England, and many Irish writers were happy to move across the Irish Sea when the opportunity offered. The gulf between the impoverished country population and the ascendancy became even wider when in mid-19th century the potato crop failed for several years, causing what is known as the Great Famine, the greatest trauma in Irish history. It is estimated that, in the course of the famine, Ireland lost one quarter of her population through starvation or forced emigration to America. The Gaelic language became one of the victims of this catastrophe, because the first prerequisite of emigration was to learn to speak English, and 'Irish' was pushed back to small regions in the far West.

In spite of such traumatic setbacks, Ireland saw, during the last decade of the 19th century, a native movement that has come to be known as the 'Irish Renaissance,' although many aspects of it must be seen as a *naissance* rather than a re-birth. The Irish Renaissance was a cultural campaign that can be explained as a compensatory phenomenon, after various attempts at a military separation from Britain had failed and even the more moderate movement for 'Home Rule,' a kind of regional autonomy, remained without success. Paradoxically (like so many developments in Irish history) it was largely created and sustained by members of the Protestant ascendancy.

Initially the Irish Renaissance pursued three separate but closely related objects. First of all, it was a *language* movement. Under the inspired leadership of Douglas Hyde (who in 1938, when Ireland severed the last ties with Britain, was to become the first President of the newly-created Irish Republic) it attempted to reinstate Gaelic as the country's national language, thereby investing the despised language of the rural population with the dignity it had been deprived of during the centuries of British dominance, and revitalizing the literary heritage of Ireland that was about to be lost to the cultural hegemony of Britain. Secondly it set out to create for Ireland a new and native literature *in English* which would be radically opposed to the citified literature of England that was seen as sick, degenerated, intellectual, and drained of all true emotion. The outstanding figure in this movement was William Butler Yeats (1865-1939) who in 1923 became the first Irishman to be awarded the Nobel Prize for literature in recognition of his efforts on behalf of the literature of Ireland. The third major strand to be distinguished in the complex web of the Irish Renaissance was the Irish Dramatic Movement.

2. The Irish Dramatic Movement

Until the 1890s, Ireland had possessed no tradition in drama to speak of. Since the 17th century, Irish writers had been fascinated by the splendours of the theatrical scene in London. The 18th century alone saw some 70 playwrights who had been born in Ireland but had gone to London to seek success on the English stage, among them some famous names of English literary history like Richard Brinsley Sheridan (see chapter 12), William Congreve (see chapter 8), George Farquhar, Oliver Goldsmith, and Richard Steele (see chapter 10). The theatres in Ireland, which catered almost exclusively for the Protestant ascendancy, imitated the model of London, and until the end of the 19th century there existed no coherent native tradition (isolated plays, like Charles Coffey's *The Beggar's Wedding* of 1729, Charles Macklin's *The True-born Irishman* of 1762, or Dion Boucicault's three great Irish melodramas of the 1860s and 70s serving as the exceptions that prove the rule). It is therefore one of the most amazing developments in literary history to find a dramatic movement emerging from Ireland in the last decade of the 19th century. As in the field of printed literature, its leading spirit was W.B. Yeats, who was not only a highly original poet, perhaps the greatest poet of the 20th century, as T.S. Eliot suggested; he was also an able organizer who regularly succeeded in involving others in his visionary projects.

The outstanding figure in the literary circle surrounding Yeats was Lady Isabella Augusta Gregory (1851-1932). In 1894, when she met Yeats for the first time, she was the widow of the Governor of Ceylon and lived at her small country estate Coole Park in County Galway which in the following years became a kind of unofficial headquarters of the emerging literary movement and a refuge for many of its writers. She had already had some minor literary experience, but nobody would have expected her to develop into a successful playwright at the age of 50; yet in the following years she not only became Yeats's staunchest supporter in his many activities, but she wrote some 40 plays which, together with the works of Yeats, laid the foundation for a specifically Irish repertoire of drama. Another author whom Yeats encouraged to work for the stage was Lennox Robinson (1886-1958), an intelligent, well-educated man of letters who contributed successful plays to an Irish repertoire well beyond the period of the Irish Renaissance. However, the greatest dramatist to emerge from the Irish Dramatic Movement was undoubtedly John Millington Synge (1871-1909), and this although his dramatic oeuvre comprised only six plays.

Yeats's greatest *coup* was when, in 1904, he cajoled Miss Annie Horniman, the heiress of the famous British tea firm, into sponsoring a small theatre in Dublin, and when he found an obscure Irish amateur troupe under the leadership of W.G. Fay and his brother Frank whom he installed as the company of the new theatre. The Abbey Theatre (named after a street near the city centre) opened on 27 December 1904 with a triple bill of Lady Gregory's *Spreading the News* (1904) with *On Baile's Strand* (1904) and *Cathleen Ni Houlihan* (1902), both by Yeats. On the following night Synge's *The Shadow of the Glen* (1902) was included in the programme, thus introducing, at the very start, the three leading figures of the Abbey (who were also its first directors) to the audience. Before this event, Yeats (beginning in 1899) had already organized short seasons of Irish plays (among which his own figured prominently) in hired halls by troupes of actors invited over from England, but the result must have been more than disappointing. The opening of the Abbey Theatre as a permanent home for Irish drama changed all this. Not that it immediately attracted large audiences, or succeeded in rivalling the larger Dublin theatres that followed the fashions set by the London West End. In fact, in the early years it was often ridiculed as 'WBY's toy thing,' and its imminent demise was predicted more than once. But the Abbey acted as a nucleus for an emerging dramatic tradition, attracting writers who under other circumstances would never have dreamed of writing for the stage, and allowing them to try out various theatrical styles and subjects. In the course of the 20th and, indeed, well into the 21st century, the Abbey survived all crises, failures, disasters (including the fire which destroyed its original building in 1951), and it lived down the constant criticism from the Dublin intelligentsia (culminating in the frequently repeated taunt that 'the Abbey is not what it used to be, *and it never was*'). When, in 1924, it was elevated to the status of the National Theatre of Ireland, it became the first subsidized theatre in the English-speaking world, and it has continued to provide theatrical fare of a high standard to the present day.

The greatest achievement of the early Abbey was that it relied primarily on *new* plays and rarely offered 'revivals' of works originally produced elsewhere. During the first ten years of its existence, Yeats's theatre produced no fewer than 110 plays, the vast majority of which had been specifically written for the Abbey. In the beginning this was not surprising, because Yeats and his collaborators had no repertoire of Irish plays to fall back on, but it has continued to be a special feature of the Irish theatrical scene until today. In the course of its history over the past century, the Abbey has probably shown more premieres than any other theatre in the world. In the early years, a large percentage of the Abbey repertoire consisted of 'short plays' (sometimes, rather nonsensically, called 'one-act plays'), a specific genre neglected in the commercial theatres of London, which in Ireland, like the short story, was developed to a high standard. Short plays were usually produced in 'triple bills' which made a high demand on the flexibility of actors and audiences alike.

If some simplification may be allowed, one can distinguish three types of plays in the early Abbey repertoire. The first group includes the plays of Yeats and very little else. They are short plays, primarily in verse, highly stylized both in their language and also (through masks and dance) in their stage presentation, and often turning to Irish mythology for their subject matter – the extreme opposite to the type of realistic problem play that developed on the *English* stage in the early 20th century (see chapter 16). Yeats found few imitators or successors (the plays of Lord Dunsany [1878-1957], perhaps come closest to his style), and he won only a small elitist audience on which the Abbey alone could not have subsisted. The second group of playwrights, represented primarily by Synge, Lady Gregory, and George Fitzmaurice (1877-1963), were much more successful with the Dublin public. Their 'poetic realism,' based on the country dialect that was actually spoken in the Western regions and on actual occurrences among the rural population, achieved a high degree of universality through the combination of closely observed individuality with trenchant symbolism. The third group consisted of comic or tragic works in the realistic style of the contemporary English problem play which became 'Irish' primarily through their setting and their attention to the specific problems of Irish society. Successful playwrights of this group from the early years of the Abbey were William Boyle (1853-1923), Pádraic Colum (1881-1972), T.C. Murray (1873-1959), and St John Ervine (1883-1971) as well as Lennox Robinson (1886-1958). Needless to say, such a classification obscures certain differences between the individual writers; Lady Gregory in particular could be named in each of the three groups.

3. John Millington Synge

Synge came from an ascendancy background and attended Trinity College, the traditional Protestant university in Dublin (where he learnt German, Hebrew, and Irish) as well as the Royal Irish Academy of Music (where he learnt various instruments and played in the student orchestra). However, he rebelled against the religious and moral values of his family which were also the values of his class and for a number of years led a restless life on the Continent, first in Germany and Italy, then in Paris, where he studied French as well as Breton and other Celtic languages (including Old Irish). His existence during these years must have been scarcely different from that of the tramps and tinkers in his plays. It was in France in 1896 that Yeats met him and realized that his abilities lay in a field quite distant from his vague ambitions to become a literary critic. Yeats advised him to go to the Aran Islands off the West coast of Ireland to experience a life that had never found expression in literature. Between 1898 and 1902, Synge spent a number of weeks each year on Aran where he encountered an existence as remote from Parisian society as it was possible to experience anywhere in Europe. However he did not give up his room in Paris until 1903, and the contrast between the harshness, even brutality, but also spontaneous enjoyment of life that he found on the islands – and the refinements of modern civilization in the French capital led to a mental tension that must have been hard to bear. It can be sensed on every page of *The Aran Islands* (1907), a highly personal travelogue that must be considered his most important contribution to Irish literature apart from his plays. From the turn of the century, Synge had become involved with Yeats's seasons of Irish plays in Dublin, in fact his *In the Shadow of the Glen* (1903) and *Riders to the Sea* (1904) were premiered by W.G. Fay's Irish National Theatre Society which became the Abbey company when Yeats's theatre had opened, and in 1905 Synge, together with Yeats and Lady Gregory, was appointed one of its directors. The concluding years of his short life (he died of Hodgkin's disease on 24 March 1909) were mainly dedicated to the Abbey. His *The Well of the Saints* was premiered in 1905 (as early as 1906 it was produced in Berlin in a translation by Max Meyerfeld and in Prague in a version by Karel Musek). 1907 saw the publication and production of *The Playboy of the Western World* (*PWW*), while his *Deirdre of the Sorrows*, a tragedy based on his love for the actress Molly Allgood, remained uncompleted at his death and was finalized by Yeats and Lady Gregory for a posthumous production in 1910. Until his death, Synge also directed a number of other plays, assisted Lady Gregory with her *Kincora* (1904) and accompanied the Abbey company on various tours. *The Tinker's Wedding* (1909), alone among his plays, was considered 'too dangerous' for an Abbey production and was only issued in print, although his other plays also encountered sharp criticism for being too realistic in the portraiture of rural Irish society.

Synge's name became known to the general public in Ireland when in 1907 the first performance of *The Playboy* provoked violent protests from a nationalist section of the audience. Whereas on the first night the protests had remained verbal, on the second night they resulted in violence, and the police had to be called in to protect the actors (who, very bravely, continued to perform in dumb show for the rest of the week). It is to the lasting credit of the Abbey directors, and in particular to Yeats, that the play was neither taken off nor modified to remove controversial passages in the text, insisting that the freedom of expression on the stage was to be placed above political considerations, however important these might be.

4. *The Playboy of the Western World*

Like any major work of literary distinction, Synge's play merits – and, indeed, demands – to be approached from a variety of angles. The most obvious interpretation (and the one the protesters at the first performances acted upon) is to see it as a near-realistic depiction of a West-of-Ireland setting and its population. Just as the play is historically defined by several references to the aftermath of the second Boer War (1902), it is located geographically on the coast of Northwest Mayo, with Castlebar, some 50 miles distant, the nearest town of any importance, and the small fishing port of Belmullet just down the road – at the time one of the remotest locations in the whole of Ireland. The image that Synge creates of this world is not, indeed, a particularly favourable one. His first stage direction begins with the words "*Country public house or shebeen, very rough and untidy*" (Synge 1995: 99), and these adjectives characterize both the physical setting and the mentality of the characters – a harsh counter-image to the romantic vision of the West of Ireland as a world of innocence, purity, and harmony that was created in nationalist circles, and it was easy to blame Synge for continuing to malign Ireland in the tradition of English prejudices. Synge stresses the remoteness of the scene ("lonesome," his favourite adjective, occurs no less than 20 times) by insisting that the only building anywhere near the shebeen is the house of the Widow Quin who is reported to have killed her husband and suspected of having reared a black ram at her breast. Other characters are hardly more likable. The publican is a drunkard who thoughtlessly leaves his daughter over night while he, with his cronies, goes off in search of booze. Pegeen's fiancé is not only stupid but a coward, a farcical character if ever there was one, and (what must have enraged the protesters more than anything else), he is ridiculous because he is totally dependent on the clergy. The village girls are incredibly naive in their inquisitiveness, and the whole population are hopelessly simple in their hunger for sensations and, when Christy tells his story, in their credulity. Undoubtedly this is a near-realistic view of West-of-Ireland society at the turn of the century, but it is a far cry from the romantic image the Gaelic League was trying to fabricate.

The Playboy, however, would hardly deserve widespread attention today if it were merely a portrait of Irish society at the turn of the century. It is, at the same time, a 'comedy' (Synge's term in the title) in the age-old tradition of comedies on the stages of all ages, where an attractive young hero overcomes all the obstacles in his path to gain the hand of the young heroine, while a chorus of farcical characters provide welcome amusement for the audience. In a typical comedy, there is never any doubt whether the hero will achieve his object, however unlikely it might seem at the beginning, and in Synge's play audience expectation is clearly directed towards such a happy ending – if, that is, one ignores the final scene. The conclusion turns the traditional comedy upside down, because it provides a trenchant analysis of crowd behaviour when confronted with reality. Pegeen's phrase "[…] there's a great gap between a gallous story and a dirty deed" (*PWW* 144) encapsulates the lesson in social reactions that Synge, in contravention to all comedy conventions, introduces at the end.

Again seen from a different angle, *The Playboy* has also a substructure of tragic elements which might, at a first glance, be obscured by the farcical scenes around Michael James and Shawn Keogh but which dominate the story of Pegeen. Apart from Christy, she is the only person in this society capable of change. She is known by others as "the fright of seven townlands for [her] biting tongue" (*PWW* 137), and she even sees herself in such a light. Her future life is mapped out quite clearly in the lonely figure of the Widow Quin: it is easy to imagine that, married to a fool like Shawn Keogh (apparently the only road in life open to her), Pegeen may well end up as another harridan capable of all sorts of cruelty and inhuman behaviour. Her encounter with Christy changes all this; to her immense surprise she finds herself in love, and she suddenly gains the ability to express such love in poetic terms. Her life seems to take an unexpected turn for a fulfilled future, imagining a companionship that, until then, had seemed totally out of reach for her (*PWW* 137) – until, in the end, she finds that she is not strong enough to stand up against the conventional judgement of her surroundings. It is from such a height that her downfall must be seen, and her last words (which gain additional weight as the curtain-line of the play) are an expression of unspeakable bitterness, quite comparable to the distress expressed at the end of earlier tragedies: "Oh my grief, I've lost him surely. I've lost the only playboy of the western world" (*PWW* 146).

Christy is, of course, the central character, and the presentation of the play on stage largely depends on *his* portrayal by an actor. It should be added in passing that the term 'playboy' has here to be seen in a much more positive light than its present-day connotations, denoting 'admired hero' or 'golden boy' rather than the conventional meaning current today. If the interpretation of the play focuses on Christy, it may well be understood, in analogy to the 'novel of initiation,' as a 'play of initiation.' In the novel of initiation a young and inexperienced person, often foolish in his actions and inhibited by the pains of adolescence, is led to a mature position in life, but, unlike the traditional *Bildungsroman*, this does not happen through being exposed to the treasures of culture and philosophy but through the encounter with the unmitigated hardships of life: pain, death, brutality, loneliness, despair, and hopelessness. Christy by all accounts must in his youth have led a miserable life, obsessed by all the inhibitions of adolescence and uncertain of a way out – until he knocks down his father and, terrified by his own brutality, descends into the depths of despair. It is the experience of admiration by others, especially by Pegeen, that first raises him from his despondency, and the process of self-recognition, acted out on stage in the looking-glass scene

(*PWW* 115-17), allows him to triumph in the local sports. Nevertheless, he remains highly unsure of himself, and his confidence is shattered when his father reappears. It is his second act of violence that teaches him all he needs to know about himself as well as about society, and in the confrontation with the cruelty of the local population he gains the independence that allows him to leave the scene as "a likely gaffer" who will "go romancing through a romping lifetime from this hour to the dawning of the judgment day" (*PWW* 146). Needless to say his conversion through the series of sudden turns occasioned by the repeated reappearance of old Mahon, is far from a realistic course of events, and so is Christy's sudden ability to express his emotions in poetical terms, when, for instance, he imagines himself "squeezing kisses on your puckered lips till I'd feel a kind of pity for the Lord God is all ages sitting lonesome in his golden chair" (*PWW* 136). It is the plot as well as the language that justifies the term 'poetic realism,' a Chekhovian rather than a Yeatsian concept, to describe Synge's play.

5. The Irish Independence Movement

The watershed in Irish history in the early 20th century came with what is known as the 'Easter Rising.' On Easter Monday 1916, in the middle of the First World War, some 2,000 Irishmen from two semi-secret organizations, the Irish Volunteers and the Irish Citizen Army, occupied a number of strategic positions in the City of Dublin and proclaimed an Irish Republic, acting upon the old adage that 'England's difficulty is Ireland's opportunity.' Their leaders cannot have expected to achieve instant political independence, but they hoped to be represented at a future peace conference. The British side acted swiftly, sending battle troops and a gunboat across the Irish Sea, and after six days, when the inner city lay in ruins, the rebels were forced to capitulate. The Irish population at first reacted with considerable anger at the insurgence, seeing it as a 'stab in the back' of the Irish troops who were fighting in Flanders and elsewhere as part of the British army. When, however, the British command in Ireland treated the insurgents not as prisoners of war but as common criminals, executing 16 of the leaders and placing the rest in internment camps, the public mood began to change. The resentment that built up during the following months was fuelled by the British refusal to honour the promise of Home Rule for Ireland made before the war, and eventually led to the country-wide War of Independence of 1919-20 with its numerous atrocities on both sides. After difficult negotiations, a treaty was reached which gave the greater part of Ireland far-reaching rights as a Free State, but also finalized the partition of the country, with Northern Ireland (practically the old province of Ulster) remaining part of the United Kingdom. As was to be expected, the conflict between the supporters of the compromise treaty and their die-hard opponents resulted in a Civil War, and it was only when this had finally been overcome, that the new free state could settle down to rebuilding the country and to establishing its political identity. Ireland became a state under the strict control of the Catholic Church, with moral supervision of public and private life and an institutionalized censorship to which many of Ireland's prominent writers fell victim. It has been said that condoms and copies of *Ulysses* (1922) became the favourite contraband goods which Irish people hoped to be smuggled into the country by their visitors from abroad.

In the field of drama, one of the early results of the process of nation-building was to establish the Abbey Theatre as the National Theatre of Ireland (1924), albeit under strict state control. It was here that the early plays of Sean O'Casey (1880-1964) were created, among them *The Plough and the Stars*, O'Casey's tragicomedy about the Easter Rising, produced in 1926, only ten years after the actual events.

6. Sean O'Casey

In contrast to Yeats, Lady Gregory, and Synge, O'Casey came from a lower-middle-class family that had sunk into the proletariat. Born in 1880, he was christened John Casey, but Gaelicized his name to Ó Cathasaigh, later shortening it into the name by which he is generally known. Due to poverty and an eye disease, he had little schooling and from the age of 14 worked as an unskilled labourer. However, he involved himself in a variety of charitable, political, and cultural activities and became secretary of the Irish Citizen Army, the political wing of a powerful trade union. From 1916 onwards, he sent play scripts to the Abbey. When the first of his works, *The Shadow of a Gunman*, was staged in 1923 (he was then well into his 40s), overnight his name became well-known in Dublin, and with his second full-length play, *Juno and the Paycock* (1924), he was a minor celebrity. His fame increased with *The Plough and the Stars* (1926), but to many he also became infamous, because they resented his treatment of the participants in the Easter Rising. His early plays, with the exception of the short *Kathleen Listens In* (1923), are set in the world of the Dublin tenements, originally the town houses of the landed aristocracy which had sunk into the squalor of poverty, each room housing a whole family.

With his fourth full-length play, *The Silver Tassie* (1928), O'Casey widened his horizon both historically and technically, depicting the tragedy of a working-class lad from Dublin who is sent to the front in World War I, is maimed in action and returns to his native town as a cripple, encountering total lack of sympathy and understanding, an experience which must have been widespread in all the countries on both sides of the front. Technically, *The Silver Tassie* was a daring experiment, because O'Casey contrasted the three acts set in Dublin, which are in keeping with the symbolic realism of his earlier works, with an expressionist scene on the battlefield in Flanders where all individuality is lost to the horrors of the war. When he offered the play to the Abbey Theatre, it was rejected under the dominant influence of Yeats, a shock that prompted O'Casey to choose, like so many other writers from Ireland, voluntary exile in England. However, he remained a keen (and some say, an unfair) critic of his native country, and most of his following plays deal with conditions in Ireland. Perhaps the best among these is *Red Roses for Me* (1942) where O'Casey goes back to his memories of the 1913 general strike and lockout in Dublin, fusing them with a moving paean on his native city. *Purple Dust* (1945) is one of the few wholly enjoyable comedies to be written in the 20th century, not only in Ireland, but even here O'Casey deals with one of his persistent themes, the relationship between England and Ireland, introducing two ridiculous Englishmen who suffer personal disasters when they try to set themselves up as landlords in rural Ireland. In his later years, O'Casey used Ireland more and more as the scene for modern morality plays in which he castigates those who offend against his personal scale of values, while Ireland became an almost accidental setting for universal concerns. Nevertheless O'Casey's name was always good for controversy in Ireland. His *The Bishop's Bonfire* was heavily criticized for its alleged anti-clericalism when it was produced in Dublin in 1955, while *The Drums of Father Ned* in 1959 was prevented from being staged for the Dublin International Theatre Festival after the Archbishop of Dublin had personally intervened.

When O'Casey died in 1964, he left a large body of work, comprising 14 full-length plays as well as nine short plays, six volumes of autobiography (in which, as some have said, he 'invented his life'), several volumes of miscellaneous prose and four massive tomes of letters.

7. *The Plough and the Stars*

O'Casey's play, directed by Lennox Robinson, was the first of a number of dramatizations of the Easter Rising that were put on stage in Ireland at various times of the 20th century. It was looked forward to with tense expectation, and the opening night at the Abbey Theatre on February 8, 1926, was attended by a distinguished audience, including the Lord Chief Justice, several cabinet ministers, and a large group of well-known writers. The play was well received, and the reviews in the press were favourable. However, during the following days tension seemed to be building up, until on February 12 a riot broke out in the theatre, obviously well planned; it disrupted the performance when members of the audience climbed on to the stage and attacked the actors, until the police were called in to restore order. Yeats, who was in the theatre, made a courageous speech for the freedom of artistic expression which became generally known, although during the turbulence no-one could hear him, because he delivered his notes to the *Irish Times*:

> "Is this," he shouted, "going to be a recurring celebration of Irish genius? Synge first, and then O'Casey! The news of the happenings of the last few minutes here will flash from country to country. Dublin has once more rocked the cradle of a reputation. From such a scene in this theatre went forth the fame of Synge. Equally the fame of O'Casey is born here tonight. This is his apotheosis." (qtd. from Murray 2004: 175)

Yeats's words link *The Plough and the Stars* (*PS*) with the *Playboy* riots of almost 20 years before, although in other ways the two plays are utterly different. Where Synge's location is a remote corner of rural Ireland, O'Casey's is in the centre of the capital; where Synge's play is a domestic scene between a few individuals, O'Casey's is eminently public and political; and where Synge's dialogue is often lyrical, O'Casey's excels in its enormous range of insults and vituperation.

The reasons for the protest lay precisely in one of O'Casey's great achievements: his *objectivity* in presenting the insurrection. While the protesters were demanding an uncritical glorification of the participants and their cause, O'Casey refused to take sides and instead showed the fighting as well as the reactions of the populace from a variety of angles, personified in the *dramatis personae*. Each of them represents a specific attitude to the Rising: Peter is the braggart patriot, Jack the hot-tempered revolutionary, the Covey the confessed Socialist who rejects any national conflict, Fluther the individual who is interested in politics and religion only as the occasion for personal quarrels, Bessie the Protestant Unionist who sides with the Irish soldiers at the front, Nora the selfish housewife who strives for private social advancement, Mrs. Gogan the naive onlooker who is untroubled by all problems, and Mollser the passive victim of social injustice. The tenement building where they all congregate serves as a microcosm of Irish society before and during the Rising, reflecting the confused and confusing background to the events as it must have appeared at the time. In contrast to other dramatists who also employ the symbolism of theatrical space, O'Casey never explicitly states the representative nature of the building, which renders it all the more convincing but has also opened it to a variety of interpretations.

Technically, O'Casey's approach resulted in the unusual device of having *eight* central characters instead of one or two. Occasional attempts at producing the play with Fluther cast as the 'hero' and/or Nora as the 'heroine' turned out to be failures because they missed O'Casey's central point: that the different reactions to the Rising were equally valid. The play therefore resembles what has been called the 'Chekhovian structure' in drama. Instead of one hero it has a whole group of characters who initiate a number of equally important parallel actions. They present divergent aspects of the same theme and finally converge in a synthesis from which the play's central theme emerges. By the end of act 4, Jack, Bessie, and Mollser are dead, Nora has fallen victim to insanity, Brennan, Fluther, Peter, and the Covey are led into captivity, and Mrs. Gogan is overcome by the death of her daughter. The various lines of action are skilfully interwoven, intensifying one another and serving as ironic commentaries on each other. In addition, they are projected on to a sequence of background events running parallel to the stage actions, thus producing an extremely complex structure.

The play is an outstanding example of the mutual interdependence of 'theme' and 'form' in literature. This can be demonstrated by looking at the relationship between 'stage actions' and 'background events.' The background events comprise the history of the Rising: in act 1 preparations for the rebellion are hinted at, the mass meeting of act 2 openly propagates an insurrection, act 3 takes place at the height of the fighting, with defeat already imminent, and act 4 shows the suppression of the rebellion. The stage actions as a whole reflect the background events: by analogy to the British control of the city, in act 1 the characters are confined to the narrow world of their tenement; in the pub scene and mass meeting of act 2 they push beyond this sphere; in act 3 they find themselves driven back to the street in the slums which they can only leave in danger of their lives, while the turbulence of the military events is mirrored in the turbulent stage actions; and in act 4, having been expelled from their flats, they huddle together in the narrowest room of the house and are eventually turned out even from there, while British soldiers re-enact the occupation of the city in the requisitioning of the room.

While O'Casey's play on the one hand provides a convincing image of a large population under the extreme conditions of an insurrection in a modern city, on the other it offers a closely woven network of realistic detail and highly individualized character portrayal. If it has been claimed above that each of the central characters holds equal importance in the structure of the play, this is not to say that *morally* they are to be seen on an equal footing. O'Casey offers, in the characterization of his figures, straightforward indications of their individual worth, which leads to a scale of values where human solidarity in adversity assumes the highest position. When Fluther risks his life searching for Nora at the time of intense fighting, when Bessie furtively looks after Mollser or nurses and shelters Nora, these acts of solidarity are ranked higher than Nora's striving for bourgeois respectability or the Covey's theoretical study of Marxist literature, because the latter are not balanced by practical acts of kindness. The central characteristic by which the characters are judged is their willingness to assist others *despite* their differences of opinion, temperament or belief. This is true of the insurgents, too: admittedly Jack is a loud-mouthed braggart who goes out to fight more for his own ego than for the sake of Irish independence, but at least he lives up to his words "Death for th' Independence of Ireland!" (*PS* 214) when he is killed in battle, while Peter, for all his protestations of patriotism, remains a coward to the end. It is important to realize that O'Casey neither praises nor condemns the rebels but judges them on the evidence of their personal behaviour.

It is the play's title that requires one final remark. It refers to the flag of the Irish Citizen Army (now in the National Museum of Ireland) which shows a stylized plough, seen against the seven stars which form the constellation of the 'Plough.' The implications for O'Casey's work are obvious: the play deals with the clash between reality and ideal, which all too often becomes the conflict between reality and *illusion*. This is true of the Rising in general as well as of O'Casey's individual characters, each of whom lives with certain self-deceptions that are revealed to be mere wishful thinking in the course of the plot (Fluther believes he can give up the drink, Nora dreams of an idyllic family life untouched by her social circumstances, Jack sees himself as a heroic warrior, etc.). These illusions dissolve in the course of the play, just as the illusion of a successful rebellion against British dominance quickly fades away. It is this aspect more than anything else that makes *The Plough* not only a remarkable play about Irish history but also a moving document of the human condition.

8. O'Casey's Successors

Since the beginning of the 20th century, Ireland has made an enormous contribution to the repertoire of drama in the English language – quite out of proportion to the size of the country's population. This is due in part to the founding, in 1928, of another experimental theatre in Dublin, the Gate, where playwrights with an international outlook which did not fit into the Abbey programme, found a better chance of a production. It is also due, from 1957, to the annual Dublin International Theatre Festival which nearly every year saw the world premiere of an important Irish play, while at the same time it gave small enterprising companies the opportunity to present their work to an international audience. Quite regularly it caused stimulating controversies, which sometimes (as in the case of O'Casey's *The Drums of Father Ned*) led to clashes with the political and/or religious establishment.

It is impossible in a brief survey to do more than list a few names or titles, but it should be stressed that they all deserve to be studied in detail. Denis Johnston (1901-84) was for a time closely allied with the Gate Theatre; his *The Scythe and the Sunset* (1958) is (as the title indicates!) a critical response to *The Plough and the Stars*. While John B. Keane (*1928), for a long time based in provincial Kerry, is perhaps the most backward-looking among Irish dramatists, Hugh Leonard (*1926) must be seen as the prototypical 'professional' writer who produced, among his enormous literary output, a number of satirical comedies which criticize the *nouveaux-riches* of the 1960s and beyond. Brendan Behan (1923-1964) became notorious for his political and theatrical antics, but was clearly overrated at the time despite the qualities of his best work, *The Hostage* (1958). Conversely, the plays of Thomas Kilroy (*1934), complex analyses of outsider cases in Irish society as, for instance, in *Talbot's Box* (1979), have taken a long time to find their way into the Irish literary repertoire. Graham Reid (*1945) and Stewart Parker (1941-1988) are two Belfast dramatists who underline the fact that drama in Ulster, confronting the specific problems of the North, has been put on the map of Irish drama, especially since the founding of the Lyric Players Theatre in Belfast in 1951. Further names that cannot go unmentioned in this context are those of Louis D'Alton (1900-51), Tom Murphy (*1935), and Frank McGuinness (*1953). However, the two outstanding dramatists to have emerged after O'Casey are Samuel Beckett (1906-1989) and Brian Friel (*1929). While Beckett's international reputation as a dramatist rests primarily on one work, *Waiting for Godot* (1949), Friel's national importance is based on more than 20 plays among which *Translations* (1980), if not his best, is his most effective in that it successfully tackles the question that has worried Irish dramatists more than any other, the question of Irish national identity.

Bibliography

Primary Sources

O'Casey, Sean. 1963. *Collected Plays*. Vol. 1. London: Macmillan.
Synge, John Millington. 1995. *The Playboy of the Western World and Other Plays*. Ann Saddlemyer (ed.). Oxford/New York: Oxford UP.

Annotated Bibliography

Greene, David H. & Edward M. Stephens. 1961 [1959]. *J.M. Synge: 1871-1909*. New York: Collier.
 The standard biography, based partly on the memories of Synge's nephew who had known Synge personally.
Gregory, Lady Isabella Augusta. 1972 [1913]. *Our Irish Theatre*. Gerrards Cross: Colin Smythe.
 Highly subjective memories of the origins and the early years of the Abbey Theatre by one of its founders, especially informative on Synge and Yeats.
Grene, Nicholas. 1975. *Synge: A Critical Study of the Plays*. London: Macmillan.
 Valuable analyses of Synge's plays in the context of his other writings.
—. 1999. *The Politics of Irish Drama: Plays in Context from Boucicault to Friel*. Cambridge: Cambridge UP.
 Standard history of Irish drama from mid-19th century to the end of the 20th century.
Hunt, Hugh. 1979. *The Abbey: Ireland's National Theatre 1904-1978*. Dublin: Gill & Macmillan.
 Highly informative history of the Abbey Theatre, with a complete list of Abbey and Peacock productions from 1899 to 1978.
Kiely, David M. 1994. *John Millington Synge: A Biography*. Dublin: Gill & Macmillan.
 A fairly recent life history, updating the one by Greene & Stephens 1961.
Kosok, Heinz. 1985. *O'Casey the Dramatist*. Gerrards Cross: Colin Smythe, and Totowa, NJ: Barnes & Noble.
 Detailed analyses of all of O'Casey's plays, plus summary chapters on his themes, his techniques, his models and anti-models, and his influence on others.
—. 1995. *Plays and Playwrights from Ireland in International Perspective*. Trier: WVT.
 Collection of articles on various aspects of Irish drama history as seen from a point of view outside Ireland.

Krause, David. 1975 [1960]. *Sean O'Casey: The Man and His Work*. London: MacGibbon & Key.

The first book to recognize O'Casey's importance as a major writer and the foundation for all subsequent studies; by the editor of O'Casey's voluminous correspondence.

Morash, Christopher. 2002. *A History of Irish Theatre: 1601-2000*. Cambridge: Cambridge UP.

A detailed, carefully researched (and nevertheless highly readable) history of theatre in Ireland (as opposed to Irish drama).

Murray, Christopher. 1997. *Twentieth-Century Irish Drama: Mirror up to Nation*. Manchester: Manchester UP.

Together with the book by Grene, one of the two standard histories of Irish drama.

—. 2004. *Sean O'Casey: Writer at Work: A Biography*. Dublin: Gill & Macmillan.

Highly detailed and reliable biography that renders all preceding biographical studies obsolete.

Welch, Robert (ed.). 1996. *The Oxford Companion to Irish Literature*. Oxford: Oxford UP.

Indispensable reference work on all aspects of Irish literature over the centuries, with a wide range of entries.

—. 1999. *The Abbey Theatre 1899-1999: Form and Pressure*. Oxford: Oxford UP.

The most recent history of the Abbey, based in part on collections of unpublished plays in the National Library of Ireland and the Abbey archive.

18. REALIST PLAYS BY THE ANGRY YOUNG MEN AND KITCHEN-SINK DRAMA: JOHN OSBORNE'S *LOOK BACK IN ANGER* AND ARNOLD WESKER'S *CHIPS WITH EVERYTHING*

KLAUS PETER MÜLLER

1. Kitchen-Sink Drama

'Kitchen-sink drama' is at first a rather useful expression for the subgenre to be discussed here and easier to define than 'realist plays,' as it instantly describes the location as well as indirectly also the class of people who are the protagonists: these plays have moved out of the drawing room settings of the (upper) middle class represented in many plays of the 1930s, 40s and early 50s, e.g. by Noël Coward, *Private Lives* (1930), *Blithe Spirit* (1941), *Relative Values* (1951). Terence Rattigan was another of those playwrights the new realists of the 1950s objected to, criticising their 'well-made plays,' which consisted of three acts, memorable curtain lines, clearly defined characters, and a traditional development of the action towards a climax and solution. Rattigan was "widely admired and set the tone for serious English theatre in the decade after the Second World War" (Innes 1992: 89). He called the general public 'Aunt Edna,' whom he described as "'respectable, middle-class, middle-aged'" (ibid.) and provided with plots revolving around widely relevant moral issues, as in *The Winslow Boy* (1946) or *Separate Tables* (1954), which was still running when *Look Back in Anger* (1957, *LBA*) opened and had a dramatic structure in the first of its two parts that was very similar to Osborne's play: a violent relationship of a married couple leads to separation, but the wife returns to her husband. The women are beautiful, "accused of sexual frigidity and characterized as 'predictable' (Rattigan) or 'pusillanimous' (Osborne)" (ibid.: 91), with weakness beneath their apparent dominance. Both male characters "share much the same passionate verbal monologues and political commitment. What is different is primarily Rattigan's objectivity" (ibid.), which is strongly contrasted by the very subjective worldview of Jimmy Porter that dominates Osborne's play. Rattigan's plays had strong links to reality, too, and "reflected the psychological repressions and hypocrisy of post-war Britain" (ibid.: 96), but they presented a world less and less people in England wanted to be influenced by. People's worldview and value systems were changing, and Rattigan as well as his colleagues came to be regarded as representing establishment values that one wanted to transform fundamentally. The older playwrights thus did no longer "reflect the new concerns of the post-war age." (Sandbrook 2005: 176)

The kitchen-sink plays present the world of the working and lower middle classes, where very ordinary everyday things are done rather than just talked about, and this world is represented in a different language, too. Wesker's *Roots* (1958) begins in a family kitchen, whereas his *The Kitchen* (1959) is set in a restaurant kitchen, neatly described by Wesker (1990: 9) himself: "The world might have been a stage for Shakespeare but to me it is a kitchen." The setting thus is both realistic and allegorical, i.e. it is also an image of the world or life in general. Kitchen-sink drama is a variety of realist plays, for which Bernard Kops, *The Hamlet of Stepney Green* (1956), Shelagh Delaney, *A Taste of Honey* (1958), or Ann Jellicoe, *The Knack* (1961) provide further examples, revealing the diversity in this subgenre, where all sorts of locations are possible, not just the kitchen, so that John Arden's plays, such as *Live Like Pigs* (1958) or *Sergeant Musgrave's Dance* (1959), are also categorized as kitchen-sink drama, mainly because they have "plots revolving around social problems" and deal with "typically naturalistic theme[s]" (Innes 1992: 137). Mel Gussow's description of a revival of *The Knack* in 1983 as the opposite of a kitchen-sink play, namely a "bachelor-pad comedy," provides another indication of the fact that the setting of a play is not such a useful category after all. But in spite of this, 'kitchen-sink realism' was for a long time in the 1950s and 60s a common expression for realist plays, films, or paintings which showed ordinary working class life. Realism was simply in the air at that time (cf. Berger 1960; Grohman 1966; Homberger 1977; Morrison 1980).

2. Reality, Realism / Realist Plays, and Links to the British Reality after World War II

As 'kitchen-sink drama' is a too narrow expression, the term 'realist play' is more appropriate, and it is the category most often used for the work of John Osborne and Arnold Wesker. It is a concept also implied when one speaks about comedies of manners, political plays, history plays, or feminist theatre, in fact all plays meant to show the audience important elements of the reality they live in or the world they have come to be confronted with, e.g. in a history play. This connection to reality is the basic characteristic of realist plays, and it involves a number of highly intriguing questions that have been at the centre of important investigations in the past 50 years and have culminated in the development of the cognitive sciences, which research the ways in which human beings come to an understanding of themselves and of reality (cf. Clark 2001; Eysenck 2006; Kolak, et al. 2006; Lycan & Prinz 2008; Rupert 2009; Wilson & Keil 2001).

We now know, or assume we know, i.e. it is now generally believed that reality is not simply out there for human beings to investigate it properly, in order to understand it correctly. That is an old-fashioned view of reality (convincingly described and rejected, e.g. by Rorty 1979), which has been replaced by the idea that reality is a complex construct involving human participation: reality is now understood as being constructed by a) the material and b) the social worlds people live in as well as c) every individual's holistic participation in these worlds, both physically and mentally. The constant interplay between body and mind is of utmost importance in this holistic concept of reality (cf. Maturana & Varela 1998). Another key factor involved in people's constructions of reality is the language they learn by growing up in a specific culture (cf. Pinker 2008). And eventually reality depends on a majority of people agreeing in calling one thing real and another not.

A wonderful way of expressing this fundamental basis of reality, social consensus and belief, is provided in Tom Stoppard's *Rosencrantz and Guildenstern Are Dead* (1966), which is not a realist play, but nevertheless expresses significant truths about reality and people's understanding of it. One character tells the story of a man who saw a unicorn, a most "alarming" experience that was then also made by more and more people, "and the more witnesses there are the thinner it gets and the more reasonable it becomes until it is as thin as reality, the name we give to the common experience" (Stoppard 1966: 15). A play to be called 'realist' thus needs to show what many people accept as reality and as its representation at a particular time. That is why there have been realist plays or at least realistic passages in all sorts of plays in all epochs (cf. Aristotle 1996 [c. 350 BC]; Auerbach 1988 [1946]). Hamlet's description of the function of plays is in fact still valid today: "the purpose of playing, whose end, both at the first and now, was and is to hold as 'twere the mirror up to nature" (*Hamlet* 3.2.20 ff.). The question, of course, is, what is meant by nature, i.e. how do people define reality? Each epoch has its specific answers, and there are times when realist plays are not seen as important, when they are not fashionable, but there are also periods when they predominate, as, e.g., in the era of bourgeois realism in Germany between 1848 and 1880, or in England in the late 1950s and 60s.

An easily accessible and generally valid definition of realism is provided by Raymond Williams (1977: 61), who distinguishes between realism as "a particular artistic method" and realism as an "attitude towards what is called 'reality,'" but eventually the two are inseparably related to each other. The realist method became clearly evident in "the bourgeois drama of the 18th century" (ibid.: 63). In the 19th century, it was critically defined in contrast to naturalism, which was "originally the conscious opposition to supernaturalism and to metaphysical accounts of human actions" and had become important at that time because people wanted to explain human activity without any religious or other 'super-human' references by focussing on and describing human reality carefully, preferably in an almost scientific manner. 'Naturalism' has since been used in this sense of an empirical representation of life, or generally as "the reproduction of the appearance of everyday reality" (ibid.: 65). 'Realism' has an equally strong link to the visible reality people live in, but it at the same time intends to reveal "the essential historical movements" (ibid.) below this surface, "the movements of history which underlie the apparent reality that is occurring" (ibid.: 72). Naturalism has, therefore, been compared with an ordinary photography, delivering a description of the surface of reality, whereas realism usually also looks beneath the surface and tries to reveal "the laws that decide how the processes of life develop. These laws cannot be spotted by the camera" (Brecht 1965: 27). They evidently depend on the interpretation of the observer, where political convictions and beliefs come into play.

There are thus four basic characteristics of realism: 1) "social extension" (i.e. all classes of society can be represented in all genres and functions, whereas before the bourgeois tragedies of the 18th century, tragedy was the preserve of aristocratic characters); 2) "the siting of actions in the present, making action contemporary" (Williams 1977: 63; with recognizable characters speaking everyday language in historically specific situations); 3) "an emphasis on secular action" (not on metaphysics or religion), where "human action is played through in specifically human terms – exclusively human terms" (ibid.: 64); 4) realism is "consciously interpretative in relation to a particular political viewpoint" (ibid.: 68). This viewpoint is connected with "the movements of history" (ibid.: 72), the 'laws' one finds at work in a particular situation, which also depend on one's belief. Every representation of reality is, therefore, influenced by the point of view of the presenter, and a particular meaning is always connected with "what is apparently the reproduction of what is happening" (70). All techniques employed in any work representing reality "are in the end inseparable from fundamental conscious or unconscious positions, viewpoints and intentions" (71). That is why both "the methods and intentions are highly variable and have always to be taken to specific and social analyses" (73). The effect intended with realism is "the attainment of a new consciousness" (70) of the spectators as well as the producers of the realistic work of art.

People's understanding of reality had significantly been changed by (and before) World War II. It took, however, a rather long time until this change was also noticeably expressed in the theatre. A first general expression was given by the people in the 1945 general election, which was not won by the leader of the coalition government during the war, the Conservative Winston Churchill, but by Labour. People wanted more equality in the class system, better education, housing, and work opportunities than before, and they hoped to get this from the new government under Clement Attlee, who introduced the National Health Service and continued the 1944 Education Act, providing secondary education for all, raised school-leaving age to 15 in 1947 and thus opened universities to a wider range of people. Churchill was re-elected in 1951, though, and the Conservatives remained in power until 1964. Thus the feeling became stronger and stronger in the 1950s that nothing much had changed. There was a growing discontent in society which explains why the term 'anger' in Osborne's play and its protagonist's evident frustration were regarded as an appropriate expression of strong, instinctive feelings of many people at that time: "'The realism of *Look Back in Anger* does not lie in its conventional three-act, one-set, small-cast treatment, but in the fact that people were prepared to accept Osborne's fiction as real.'" (Kenneth Tynan's review in *The Observer* 13 May 1956, qtd. from Hewison 1988: 157)

3. Angry Young Men

Playwrights, novelists, and others giving voice to this discontent came to be labelled 'Angry Young Men,' who indeed expressed the frustrations and malcontent of *young* people. The 1950s was the decade when teenagers first became really noticeable as a social entity, not least because they now also counted economically (cf. MacInnes 1961). The Angry Young Men gave a strong voice to this group, and they were usually men (Iris Murdoch and Doris Lessing were the exceptions; women were despised because the men identified "supposedly feminine values with modernity and mass culture" [Sandbrook 2005: 201], also rejected then), but they were far from being a unified group. There was little contact between them, they hardly knew or liked each other, and they dealt with many different topics in various ways: "The Angry Young Man was a myth, but marketable, and [...] it created a platform for a number of differing protests against the prevailing orthodoxies." (Hewison 1988: XV) Kingsley Amis's novel *Lucky Jim* (1954), e.g., is a funny, satirical protest against traditional universities, and like John Wain's *Hurry on Down* (1954) it shows a rather common human being, not at all a classical hero, as entirely dependent on his own moral resources to make his way. These new heroes needed to reject the conventional paths and the pressures of traditional institutions as well as of the new commercial world, or they strove to be economically successful and improve their social status, like the protagonists in John Braine's *Room at the Top* (1957) or Alan Sillitoe's *Saturday Night and Sunday Morning* (1958) (cf. Hewison: 1988; Maschler 1957).

David Story's *This Sporting Life* (1960) shows a factory worker in the north of England trying to improve his life by becoming a rugby player. Turned into a film by Lindsay Anderson in 1962, it is now a "kitchen-sink classic" (Norman 2010). "'Kitchen-sink' realism" was in fact significantly present not only in plays and novels but also in the "'new wave' of British cinema" (Clarke 1996: 275), inseparably connected with Woodfall Films, the company founded by John Osborne and Tony Richardson. Together with film director and producer Karel Reisz they had created the Free Cinema movement in 1956, demanding socially conscious films and elevating "working-class life from the sideshow of character parts to the centre of the action" (Heilpern 2007: 180 f.). They made films of *Look Back in Anger* (in 1958, starring Richard Burton and Mary Ure), Osborne's play *The Entertainer* (1957, filmed in 1960 with Laurence Olivier) as well as class-conscious accounts of life in England's industrial North, as in *Room at the Top* (1959) or *Saturday Night and Sunday Morning* (1960). Realism thus was significant in this medium, too.

The Angry Young Men agreed on one important point, namely that civilization was in decline, and the reason for this cultural collapse was "the New Barbarism," the "banalities of [...] newspaper and television," the cheap mass culture of the entertainment industries, but also "the British H bomb," and British politics in the post-colonial world, especially the Suez crisis of 1956 (Hewison 1988: 159 f.). There were various causes they could have adopted, such as protesting against the atom bomb (and Osborne as well as Wesker took part in the Campaign for Nuclear Disarmament), or by developing new ideas after the failures of communism and socialism in the brutal subjections of popular movements in East Berlin in 1953 and Hungary in 1956, by imagining a new role for Britain after its loss of the Empire, or creating a new concept of a fair and equal society and turning it into reality. But Osborne (1929-1994) was always rather vague in his politics, whereas Wesker (*1932) did have socialist ideas, but his endeavour to turn them into reality by establishing Centre 42 in 1961, an arts centre offering traditional working class culture, ended in 1970 because of the lack of funding from the unions and because the ideas did not really work in practice (cf. Heilpern 2007; Milne 2000; Wesker 1970; Wesker 1995; Whitebrook 2002; Wilson 2007).

4. *Look Back in Anger* by John Osborne

4.1 The Setting, Cast, Stage Directions, Motifs, and Key Questions

This is the first play connected with the Angry Young Men and has been very influential as such. Its premiere was on 8th May 1956, directed by Tony Richardson at the Royal Court Theatre in London, and it was not an immediate success. It has a conventional three-act structure, easily recognizable characters, and a fairly common action. Its first really extraordinary element at that time was its setting: Jimmy and Alison Porter's "one-room flat in a large Midland town" (*LBA* 9), not London, another big city or a manor house, nor the polite society in conversation, but a provincial place in the North, where a woman irons clothes and men read newspapers in the opening scene. The audience is literally and figuratively confronted with the whole world of this couple. They are allowed to look into every corner of their lives, and they meet young people from different classes. The setting thus is typically realistic, whereas the cast is not so easily definable: Jimmy is "about twenty-five" and possesses "a disconcerting mixture of sincerity and cheerful malice, of tenderness and freebooting cruelty; [...] a combination which alienates the sensitive and insensitive alike" (*LBA* 9 f.). These stage directions correctly define Jimmy as an alienating as well as an alienated character with intriguingly ambiguous qualities. He even "alienates love, [whereas] CLIFF seems to exact it." Cliff, also 25, "is a soothing, natural counterpoint to JIMMY." (*LBA* 10)

Alison, "roughly the same age as the men, [...] is the most elusive personality to catch in the uneasy polyphony of these three people. She is turned in a different key, a key of well-bred malaise that is often drowned in the robust orchestration of the other two." (*LBA* 10) Two important things are done here: Alison is presented as an enigmatic character, which is a fairly common motif, often used for women, and always connected with the intention of creating suspense. The fact that there might be more behind her beautiful appearance is also suggested by one of the next sentences: "There is a surprising reservation about her eyes, which are so large and deep they should make equivocation impossible." (*LBA* 10) Is Alison a deceitful person, does she hide anything the spectators should know? Such questions also arise in the performance, and the spectators will see that Alison has a secret indeed, namely that she is pregnant, something she for good reasons does not discuss with her husband. But the fact that spectators know more than the characters is a traditional device in well-made and in realist plays, and ambiguity or equivocation is already present in the "disconcerting mixture" of Jimmy's character. It is used in the entire play to reveal the complexity of reality.

The second remarkable thing in the stage direction is that the text speaks of the three characters as though they were different instruments in a piece of music. In the entire play, one is indeed presented with an "uneasy polyphony" (*LBA* 10) that allows neither the characters nor the audience any ease or comfort. Alison clearly provides a different key to the robustness of the men, but not, as one might well expect, mainly because of her different sex and gender, she rather offers a melody connected with disease and class, "a key of well-bred malaise" (ibid.). So she is ill at ease, too, and she comes from a class well above Jimmy's, as is revealed later. The musical imagery used here is a strong indication that the play's realism requires different levels of meaning and has a significant emotional quality.

The stage direction thus gives readers helpful information that the spectators of the play have to deduce from the setting, the characters, their actions, and indeed their voices (cf. Gilleman 2002). The first sentence or the beginning of a play is also always important, as it suggests the main topics that will be dealt with. *Look Back in Anger* begins with Jimmy's question, "Why do I do this every Sunday?" (*LBA* 10) The audience can deduce that his behaviour on this day is not unusual, it is fairly common for him, and the play shows that he has behaved as he does here for a long time. He himself in the next sentence regrets the fact that nothing of importance changes. Two further key motifs of the play are directly introduced in this way, change or the lack of it, and this basic question, why? Why does Jimmy do what he does, and why do these people – as is made clear in the first act – waste their lives and throw their youth away? 'Why?' is actually the key question of the entire play, and answers need to be provided by the spectators.

4.2 How the Play Works, or How Key Questions Can Be Answered

How helpful is the play for finding answers to such questions? A stage direction is a very traditional, direct, and reliable form of passing on information, the form with the closest link to the author (Pfister 1988: 13 ff.). The play itself is not so straightforward and offers more of the disconcerting mixture and equivocation already ascribed to the protagonists. There is also not a simple one-to-one relationship between the play and the reality referred to. Jimmy's sentences after the initial question are a good example of how the play works, which forms it employs for its representation of reality and what that reality in fact is. He says: "Even the book reviews seem to be the same as last week's. Different books – same reviews." (*LBA* 10) On the surface, this is utter nonsense and logically impossible. But on another level, this makes perfect sense, because what Jimmy means is that the papers use the same language and express the same mentality in all their reviews. So he is dissatisfied with the way in which people express themselves and how they think, as he has read the "columns on the English Novel. Half of it's in French" (*LBA* 10 f.). This is how the play also often functions: with contradictions, illogical opposites, disconcerting mixtures etc., which, however, make sense on another level, especially when they are related to people's minds, their mentality, or ideology. That this is a play about people's minds in this sense and about how a person's mind gives shape to the form of the reality perceived is already expressed in the title: this is not a neutral way of looking at reality, but one dominated by anger and other passions. The protagonist's looking back in anger affects only in a very small way his view of the past, which he sees rather favourably, almost as nostalgically as his stepfather (*LBA* 17). But it strongly influences his understanding of himself, others, and the world he lives in now. It evidently has a strong effect on the people around him and on the audience, too.

With this beginning, the play instantly highlights what it is all about and how it works. The audience needs to see below the surface, and it must understand not only what is said but above all what is meant and what makes people behave as they do. Jimmy's first question addresses this directly, and his first sentences give a good example of how this works. A high degree of the audience's active participation is thus required. Another consequence is that information about the characters' positions in their reality is passed on fragmentarily, and the audience is required to put the individual pieces together, if they want a more complete picture. They are thus forced to re-construct the reality of the world they are watching, and they learn in this way that Jimmy comes from a working class background (*LBA* 30), has a university education, but now works with Cliff behind a "blinking sweet-stall" (*LBA* 18), i.e. he has no economic, social, or political power and no prospects at all. Alison is from a higher social class, her father was a Colonel in the British army in India (*LBA* 68), and she and Jimmy married four years ago against her parents' will (*LBA* 42 f.). This high degree of audience participation had been prepared by earlier realist plays of Ibsen, Chekhov, and Shaw, but it reaches a new level here through the influences of modernism and Brecht, creating a new kind of realism.

4.3 The Play's Structure, Action, and Minor Characters

Key motifs, hints at how the play works, and its most important topics can thus already be deduced from the initial stage direction and the beginning of the play. The play's structure, the development of the action, and the other characters can also be quickly described as they follow the patterns of traditional realism: Act 1 shows Jimmy and his workmate Cliff reading the Sunday papers while Alison irons clothes. Jimmy turns out endless tirades against everybody and everything, especially his wife. In the men's rather playful struggle, Alison gets hurt (*LBA* 26). Her small physical damage is only an image of the much greater mental pain she has suffered in her marriage. She tells Cliff that she is pregnant and does not know what to do, but then alone with her husband, "[e]verything just seems all right suddenly" (*LBA* 34). Before she can mention her pregnancy, Cliff comes back and tells her that Helena is on the phone. Jimmy is extremely irritated about this, and act 1 ends with his shocking wish, made more poignant by his ignorance, that Alison had a child "and it would die" (*LBA* 37).

Act 2, scene 1 highlights the change that has been brought to the flat by Helena who points out that Alison must make up her mind about what she wants to do now (*LBA* 46). Alison responds by mentioning the game she and Jimmy "play: bears and squirrels". "Playful, careless creatures in their own cosy zoo for two. [...] They were all love, and no brains." (*LBA* 47) The central topic this play addresses is thus pointed out again: people's minds and how human beings use their brains. Alison admits that there have been strong passions in their marriage, but nothing else. Helena warns her: "Fight, or get out. Otherwise, he *will* kill you." (*LBA* 47) The play's tension and suspense is again dramatically increased in this traditional way.

Helena is the catalyst bringing about greater understanding for both the characters and the audience. She also compels Jimmy to ask another important question: "One of us is mean and stupid and crazy. Which is it? Is it me? Is it me, standing here like an hysterical girl, hardly able to get my words out? Or is it her?" (*LBA* 59), referring to Alison. Jimmy's simile is quite telling and reveals an implied criticism of him and his immature gender concepts: if even boys do not behave in this way, why does Jimmy, who is much older? Spectators will distance themselves further from him, when he says to Alison what else he has got in his mind: "I want to be there when you grovel. [...] I want to see your face rubbed in the mud – that's all I can hope for." (*LBA* 59 f.) The scene ends with Alison's refusal to accompany Jimmy to a dying friend. So even this separation that the spectators have been waiting for is ambiguous.

In act 2, scene 2 Alison's father has much understanding for Jimmy, and his function to reveal a bit of the pressure Jimmy was under makes him a rather sympathetic, considerate person. After they have left, Helena demands of Jimmy, raging again, to "stop thinking about yourself for one moment," and she tells him of Alison's pregnancy. Jimmy's response is so significant that it is repeated three times: "I don't care." (*LBA* 73) Helena "*slaps his face savagely* [...] *and a muffled cry of despair escapes him*" (*LBA* 73 f.). Act 2 ends with Helena kissing Jimmy passionately.

In act 3, scene 1 there at first do not seem to be any changes, apart from Helena having taken over Alison's place. Cliff, however, then speaks of leaving and trying something else, Jimmy and Helena want to "make a good double" in the music halls and in this way also start a new life (*LBA* 86), but then Alison returns. In scene 2, the two women agree that Jimmy is someone "born out of his time," but Helena now understands that she must leave. Her reason is not based on an objective logic, but connected with her belief "in good and evil" (*LBA* 90). She simply knows "it's right" (*LBA* 91). She thus follows her mind and her own conscious choice. Alone with Alison, Jimmy first complains about the injustice of the world, then he turns to her, wondering whether there is not really "a kind of – burning virility of mind and spirit that looks for something as powerful as itself?" When he met her for the first time, Alison "seemed to have a wonderful relaxation of spirit" (*LBA* 94). That was what he wanted, "that kind of strength – the strength to relax" (*LBA* 95). She, however, did not have such a state of mind, as she had not yet endured anything difficult. Now she has suffered a terrible loss, her baby, she feels in the mud, "grovelling!" (*LBA* 95) Confronted with her pain, Jimmy begins "*with a kind of mocking, tender irony*" their squirrel and bear game again, and the play ends on a note of tenderness (*LBA* 96).

4.4 The Play's Ending, Inter-Textuality, and Final Evaluations

What looks like a completely unrealistic, fairy tale ending has the same quality as the rest of the play: it, too, is ambiguous. It can be seen as a fantasy world, an escape from reality, but also as the very opposite. Gilleman, e.g., who detects a "postwar language-oriented realism" (1997: 72) in the play, understands the ending "as an intermediary step toward establishing a new code of living together" with the protagonists heading towards a new stage based "on mutual confirmation and care" (ibid.: 84 f.). He thus sees it as an indication of genuine lasting tenderness and an improvement in the couple's relationship, based on a greater awareness gained through the process experienced in the play. It was also interpreted as a misogynist's victory over his wife through her loss of the most vital female potential, motherhood (cf. Wandor 1987: 8 ff.). The play's "ability to change its meaning according to the temper of the times" makes it "a durable work of art, as well as a social phenomenon" (Billington 2007: 98). Both Billington and Sierz (2008: 46-58) give good examples of the variety of interpretations the play has met with, all of which depend on the 'laws' the spectators have detected and their understanding of the reality depicted. It was "first seen as a cry of political protest" (Billington 2007: 98), expressing the opinion of post-war youth in general and the author in particular, then it was regarded as "a genuine state-of-the-nation play," presenting "an astonishingly wide-ranging picture of the divisions within Fifties England." In 1999, it was performed at the National Theatre "as a Strindbergian domestic battle" (ibid.).

All interpretations thus depend on what is regarded as important in the reality of the time in which the play is watched, but they equally require confirmation from the play itself. This text's claim that the play focuses on people's minds and on how the mind influences human understanding of the past, present, and reality in general is itself determined by the current significance of the cognitive sciences, but it gets substantial support from the play, too, its repeated references to 'spirit' and to other literary texts, which are always products of the mind and reflect certain mentalities. One could even claim that this play is particularly realist by pointing out at an early stage what many people have only now become aware of, namely how much human understanding and behaviour depend on the mind. As far as the evaluation of the ending is concerned, the question is, of course, is a change in Jimmy's mind visible or at least imaginable? Alison has clearly changed and made the conscious decision to come back. She had earlier on called Jimmy "this spiritual barbarian" (*LBA* 67), and one could only agree with her. The numerous inter-textual references to literature in the play are not only a significant realist device but also help to characterize Jimmy and his state of mind. When he speaks out against women, he says that he hates "this 'expense of spirit' lark, as far as women are concerned" (*LBA* 35). The quotation is from Shakespeare, Sonnet 129, which is about 'lust in action' that engenders further lust, madness, and woe. It provides spectators with a foil against which Jimmy's behaviour makes immediate sense and gives it a meaning confirmed by other passages in the play: Jimmy is driven by lust, a lust to hate almost everybody and everything, and he in this way wastes his spirit, he has indeed, as Alison already said, no brain in his relationship to her and is in this sense truly a barbarian.

In his diatribes against women, Jimmy also points out that "people of our generation aren't able to die for good causes any longer. [...] There aren't any good, brave causes left. [...] No, there's nothing left for it, me boy, but to let yourself be butchered by the women." (*LBA* 84 f.) The words about his generation repeat very similar sentences in F. Scott Fitzgerald's novel *This Side of Paradise* (1920), where the new generation means young Americans after WWI: "Here was a new generation [...] grown up to find all Gods dead, all wars fought, all faiths in man shaken ...." (Fitzgerald 1971: 270) The novel describes the spiritual development of such a young man who at first is a 'Romantic Egotist' but in the end becomes a 'Personage,' who is disillusioned and regrets his lost youth, "yet the waters of disillusion had left a deposit on his soul, responsibility and a love of life" (ibid.). Fitzgerald's protagonist gains self awareness and clearly begins a new life. Jimmy Porter does not reach this stage, but many critics have found him to be "a whining, egotistical monster" (Billington 2007: 99). There is the potential that he might change, but that is not important. At the end of the play, the only thing that counts is what the audience make of the play and with their own reality, which is what this play forces them to think about very thoroughly and controversially. They have seen that an egotistic and nostalgically romantic look at England does not produce a sound understanding of reality. A change of mind is required.

5. *Chips with Everything* by Arnold Wesker

Chips with Everything (1962) was first performed at the Royal Court Theatre on 27th April 1962, directed by John Dexter, who had also been the director of Wesker's four earlier plays in the same theatre, *The Kitchen* (1959) and the trilogy *Chicken Soup with Barley* (1958), *Roots* (1959), *I'm Talking about Jerusalem* (1960). These plays had made critics describe Wesker as a 'social realist,' concerned with specific historic or contemporary social problems, and *Chips* fit into this category, too, as it dealt with a widely and intensively discussed topic at that time, namely the advantages and disadvantages of conscription or the national armed service (Clarke 1996: 231 f.). The play was Wesker's greatest commercial success and highly praised by critics (cf. Taylor 1969: 147). It came out at a time when the author was consciously thinking of the realist form he had used so far, and he wanted to move away from what he thought was too much of a superficial naturalism. "Art," he said, "is the creation of experience, not the copying of it." But "I will still be trying to re-create the reality of my experience" (Wesker 1960: 16). *Chips With Everything* (*CWE*) thus is an interesting variation of the realist play, putting more emphasis on direct experiences. The setting is an unspecific, but instantly recognizable air force training camp for new recruits, and the audience directly see what happens to them during the eight weeks of service training. The time is the present, and the audience watches something fairly familiar to everybody, either through personal experience or the reports of family members and friends. These traditionally realistic elements are combined with additional characteristics, however, e.g. the use of Brechtian episodes, which in Brecht's own plays are connected with strange making effects meant to destroy the illusion of realism, but which here mainly have the function of presenting typical situations and characters the audience can recognize directly. One could say the episodes are meant to highlight the laws at work in human history, the main stations in human and a soldier's life. Scene 1 in this two-act play thus shows the N.C.O. Corporal Hill with new conscripts, whom he directly distinguishes by means of very simple categories, namely age and size: the oldest conscript becomes senior man, the second oldest the assistant, etc. Then he tells them who he is and what they are to expect:

> My name is Corporal Hill. I'm not a very happy man, I don't know why. I never smile and I never joke – you'll soon see that. Perhaps it's my nature, perhaps it's the way I've been brought up – I don't know. The R.A.F. brought me up. You're going to go through hell while you're here, through scorching hell. Some of you will take it and some of you will break down. (*CWE* 14)

Breaking people's will, making them do what is expected of them, is a motif of key importance in the play. This is what the persons in power try to do, and one essential dramatic question the play raises is whether they will succeed, and if so, why. Hill himself expresses the two reasons commonly put forward by sociologists, psychologists, and everybody who tries to explain why people do what they do: either because it is in their nature or because of the world, the society, or the system they live in. The play does not provide any direct answers itself, but the setting and the characters as well as their actions are clearly meant to be understood on a realistic as well as on an allegorical level: they represent real life people both individually and generically. Hill thus is an N.C.O. whose individuality is sketched with a few general strokes as a "stocky, Northern, collarless man" (*CWE* 13) with an interest in music, and he is at the same time a typical, 'universal' N.C.O. with rather simple expectations of people and easy ways of categorizing them. What he says to the new conscripts corresponds directly with the audience's knowledge of such persons either through its own experience or the representation of such N.C.O.s in the media.

All scenes work in this way and emphasize the class differences amongst the conscripts, with Pip as the only member of the upper class (scene 2), the officers talking to them in speeches that are clearly formulaic, condescending, and inviting questions which are then not answered (scene 4). This basic lack of communication is increased in the following scenes with a first dramatic climax in scene 7, the Christmas Eve Party: the Wing Commander wants the conscripts to present a "dirty recitation, or a pop song," but Pip has warned them and tells Wilfe to recite Robert Burns instead (*CWE* 35). This is both an example of the traditional culture Wesker wanted presented at Centre 42 and an act defying the officer's order, repeated when he wants an Elvis Presley song, because he thinks they are not up to more and just repeat popular trash, whereas they sing "'The Cutty Wren', *an old peasant revolt song*" instead (*CWE* 37). Pip continues his opposition to his own class and superiors, thus increasing the dramatic tension by organizing "a little raiding expedition" (*CWE* 44) and stealing coke, which leads to the big question at the end of act 1: would they "have pinched the coke without Pip's mind?" Hill knows the answer: "You always need leaders" (*CWE* 46), but it is not the solution Wesker's plays support (cf. Müller 1998: 184), all of which ask, who or what determines a person's life?, to which *Chips* adds the question, is there a chance for outsiders like Pip and Smiler in this society?

Act 2 begins with conscripts who need to be broken, especially Smiler and Pip (*CWE* 52 f.), put up for officer training against his will (56). But Pip continues his opposition, which reaches its climax when he in scene 5 refuses to attack the dummy in bayonet practice. Pip turns down the support offered by another conscript (scene 6), but after an officer's accusation that he only seeks power among the other conscripts, "the good-natured yobs," because among his "own people [...] the competition was too great" (*CWE* 60, scene 7), Pip in scene eight obeys the order. When Chas then asks him to teach him something, Pip again refuses to do so, and Chas tells him bluntly "you're a coward. You lead and then you run away. I could grow with you, don't you understand that?" (*CWE* 62, scene 9)

But this is precisely the point the play intends the audience to grasp, they should not expect leaders but grow up without them. Only in this way can the human degradation exemplified in scene 10 by Smiler's suffering be avoided. This scene has a strong expressionist quality, turning Smiler into a mythic type, which is continued in scene 11 in a more realistic context, when he is back in the conscript's hut, but treated like a Christ figure with Chas washing his bleeding feet. Smiler is "lying there like a bloody corpse" (*CWE* 66), and boys singing "'*Auld Lang Syne*'" are heard, thus another Burns poem, introducing the new year (*CWE* 65). This important scene continues mixing realist and expressionist elements intriguingly when an officer appears and wants all of them arrested. Pip interferes and contradicts him again, making audiences instantly wonder, is this real? But then Pip and the officer smile at each other, and Pip "*begins to change his uniform, from an airman's to an officer's*" (*CWE* 67). Now his transformation is complete, but one still wonders what he is doing, because he then praises the conscripts, calls them "the salt of the earth," and promises that nobody will be harmed. He evidently intends to unite conscripts and officers: "We are good, honest, hard-working like yourselves and understanding; above all we are understanding, aren't we, sir?" (*CWE* 67) What the officers understand, however, is made clear in the list of the posts the conscripts are given, they are made administration orderlies, characterized earlier by the Wing Commander as "waste, absolute waste" (*CWE* 54). The audience thus knows what to think of Pip's transformation and praise, which they will identify as lies. The last scene presents the unity that has been achieved quite literally in the parade taking place. It again offers a direct experience and an impressive image of what is expressed here, where the audience is meant to be both positively influenced by the soldiers' skill and deeply shocked by their loss of self-determination. They thus cannot really agree with Hill's comment: "Lovely, that's lovely, that's poetry" (*CWE* 68), but will again look beyond surface appearances to the harsh reality they have been made aware of, where they need to dertermine their own lives.

6. Osborne's and Wesker's Realist Plays and Developments Up to the Present

The plays reveal the influence of a (social) realism that highlights everyday situations which are regarded as typical, therefore important, and above all as changeable through human action and interference. Human beings do not completely depend on nature or the society they live in. As the situation is very relevant, it needs to be represented as concretely and historically accurate as possible, but both plays reveal the importance of feelings: Osborne works with the feeling of anger, and Wesker wants the audience to experience the situation as directly and holistically as possible, not just rationally. The various links to reality are key factors of the plays' realism, which eventually, however, is only a means to an end, the main objectives are a better understanding of reality, social criticism, and hints at the possibilities of human beings to change reality.

The plays discussed here are part of a long tradition of texts giving insight into important aspects of the reality described. They already make evident how diverse the forms employed in realist plays are in their endeavour to create a new awareness about reality in the audience. Wesker's use of both Brechtian and expressionist elements is a symptom of the inclusiveness of realism, which here employs two forms that were originally explicitly meant to oppose realism and provide alternatives, not, however, in order to get away from reality and enter a world of dreams or fantasy, but to achieve a better understanding of reality (cf. Szondi 1973: 115-121; Kuhns 1997). Efforts to go beyond surface appearances became even stronger with the end of British censorship in 1968, which until that time had made overt realistic statements relating to contemporary governments or the monarchy simply impossible, as were free discussions of sexuality or presentations of violence (cf. Nicholson 2003). The political playwrights of the 1960s to the present have, therefore, had a far greater choice in both content and form than was available to Osborne and Wesker (cf. Bull 1984). Realist plays lost some of their significance because of this and because of the general questioning of representing reality in the context of postmodernity (cf. Berg & Fuchs 1995; Henke & Middeke 2007). Self-reflexivity became important, plays dealing with the limits and possibilities of the theatre, the influences of other media, etc. (Huber 2002). But realist plays have – as always – survived or integrated these new perspectives and have been present on the stage, even when they are occasionally not widely deemed important (cf. Luckhurst 2002). People's understanding of reality has also become more complex so that with regard to the incredible increase in violence on stage since the 1990s, the question could now be asked whether 'in-yer-face' theatre, e.g., is perhaps realistic. It was not meant to be realistic, and Sierz (2001), therefore, unfortunately does not even raise this question, but when people's understanding of reality changes, the definition of realist plays must, of course, also be adapted. Whatever the theoretical answers, it is clear that realist plays will survive and that Osborne and Wesker provided strong and typical examples of this subgenre, increasing the demands on audience participation, offering a 'disconcerting mixture' of forms, emphasising the importance of feeling, and advocating the idea that the mind and human action indeed have a strong influence on reality.

Bibliography

Primary Sources

Osborne, John. 1957. *Look Back in Anger*. London: Faber and Faber.
Wesker, Arnold. 1980. *Chips With Everything / The Friends / The Old Ones / Love Letters On Blue Paper*. Vol. 3. London: Penguin.

Annotated Bibliography

Denison, Patricia D. (ed.). 1997. *John Osborne: A Casebook*. New York: Garland.
> Useful collection of articles on Osborne's plays, most of them on Look Back in Anger, a bibliography, and memories by Wesker, David Hare, and John Mortimer.

Dornan, Reade W. (ed.). 1998. *Arnold Wesker: A Casebook*. New York: Garland.
> Perceptive collection of articles on Wesker's plays, their politics, links to his personal and social lives, historical perspectives, and critical approaches.

Goldstone, Herbert. 1982. *Coping with Vulnerability: The Achievement of John Osborne*. Washington: UP of America.
> Compares Osborne's characters to those in Ibsen's, Chekhov's, and Pinter's plays, as they all exhibit conflicting feelings of self-worth, which makes them vulnerable, but they all try not to give in to such negative feelings and attitudes.

Innes, Christopher. 1992. *Modern British Drama 1890-1990*. Cambridge: Cambridge UP.
> A very good survey of the development and main characteristics of British plays in these 100 years. Osborne and Wesker are dealt with in a long chapter on social themes and realistic formulae that begins with Granville-Barker and ends with Howard Brenton and David Hare.

Lacey, Stephen. 1995. *British Realist Theatre: The New Wave in Its Context 1956-1965*. London: Routledge.
> This book is useful in its discussions of contexts, where it gives readers a number of good examples and insights. On realism and naturalism it is unfortunately somewhat disappointing, often too superficial. A bit of a mixed bag also as far as its discussions of plays is concerned, but it clearly shows how important thorough discussions of realist theatre really are.

Leeming, Glenda. 1983. *Wesker the Playwright*. London: Methuen.
> This book offers the perspectives and insights into Wesker that have been put forward repeatedly. It may be useful as a counterfoil for one's own more intricate interpretations.

Müller, Klaus Peter (ed.). 1993. *Englisches Theater der Gegenwart: Geschichte(n) und Strukturen*. Tübingen: Narr.

The focus of this collection of articles is on how plays have told stories and histories and tried to give meaning to human life, histories of and by women, the theatre, genres, political plays, intertextuality, and media.

Rebellato, Dan. 1999. *1956 and All That: The Making of Modern British Drama*. London: Routledge.

A good example of important perspectives on plays at the end of the 20th century, Rebellato uses Foucault and Derrida, offers a revisionist view on the relevance of the 'new' writers and playwrights in the 1950s, provides a good understanding of how people thought and felt at that time, and ends with a strong emphasis on homosexuality, esp. in Look Back on Anger.

Reitz, Bernhard. 1993. *The Stamp of Humanity: Individuum, Identität, Gesellschaft und die Entwicklung des englischen Dramas nach 1956*. Trier: WVT.

Provides a good survey of British plays from 1956 to the 1980s, gives reasons for changes in realist plays, and focuses on how plays have dealt with human identity. A long chapter on Osborne and one on John Arden and Wesker discuss conventions, experiments, and social criticism in the plays.

Shellard, Dominic. 1999. *British Theatre Since the War*. New Haven: Yale UP.

Discusses plays in their cultural contexts from 1945 to 1997 and is useful for the background information and insights into people's mentalities offered.

— (ed.). 2008. *The Golden Generation: New Light on Post-war British Theatre*. London: British Library.

Presents witness accounts, personal impressions, and evaluations of plays, playwrights, actors (Gielgud, Olivier, Ralph Richardson), theatres, the acting profession, and the influence of television from 1945 to 1968, tries to contradict the idea that the first ten years after the war were a theatrical desert.

Wilcher, Robert. 1991. *Understanding Arnold Wesker*. Columbia: U of South Carolina P.

Deals with Wesker's plays and the playwright's endeavours to turn life into art in chronological order, but puts the plays into topical groups. The chapter on Chips *is called "Rebels and Revolutionaries," and the book ends with a chapter on the short dramatic pieces for one actress, in which Wilcher detects not only solo voices but also the voice of the people.*

Further Secondary Literature

Aristotle. 1996 [c. 350 BC]. *Poetics*. London: Penguin.

Auerbach, Erich. 1988 [1946]. *Mimesis: Dargestellte Wirklichkeit in der abendländischen Literatur*. Tübingen: Francke.

Berg, Eberhard & Martin Fuchs (eds.). 1995 [1993]. *Kultur, soziale Praxis, Text: Die Krise der ethnographischen Repräsentation*. Frankfurt a.M.: Suhrkamp.

Berger, John. 1960. *Permanent Red*. London: Methuen.
Billington, Michael. 2007. *State of the Nation: British Theatre Since 1945*. London: Faber and Faber.
Brecht, Bertolt. 1965. *The Messingkauf Dialogues*. London: Methuen.
Bull, John. 1984. *New British Political Dramatists: Howard Brenton, David Hare, Trevor Griffiths and David Edgar*. London: Macmillan.
Clark, Andy. 2001. *Mindware: An Introduction to the Philosophy of Cognitive Science*. Oxford: Oxford UP.
Clarke, Peter. 1996. *Hope and Glory. Britain 1900 - 1990*. London: Allen Lane.
Eysenck, Michael W. 2006. *Fundamentals of Cognition*. Hove: Psychology P.
Fitzgerald, F. Scott. 1971 [1960]. *This Side of Paradise*. London: Bodley Head.
Gilleman, Luc. 2002. *John Osborne – Vituperative Artist: A Reading of His Life and Work*. New York: Garland.
Grohman, Will (ed.). 1966. *Art of Our Time*. London: Thames & Hudson.
Gussow, Mel. 1983. "Stage: 'Knack' Returns." In: *The New York Times* 22 Aug. <http://www.nytimes.com/1983/08/22/arts/stage-knack-returns.html> (last accessed: 22 June 2011).
Heilpern, John. 2007. *John Osborne: A Patriot for Us*. London: Chatto & Windus.
Henke, Christoph & Martin Middeke (eds.). 2007. *Drama and/after Postmodernism*. Trier: WVT.
Hewison, Robert. 1988 [1981]. *In Anger: Culture in the Cold War 1945-60*. London: Methuen.
Homberger, Eric. 1977. *The Art of the Real: Poetry in England and America since 1939*. Toronto/London: Dent.
Huber, Werner. 2002. "Contemporary Drama as Meta-Cinema: Martin McDonagh and Marie Jones." In: Margarete Rubik & Elke Mettinger-Schartmann (eds.). *(Dis)Continuities: Trends and Traditions in Contemporary Theatre and Drama in English*. Trier: WVT. 13-24.
Kolak, Daniel, William Hirstein, Peter Mandik & Jonathan Waskan. 2006. *Cognitive Science: An Introduction to Mind and Brain*. New York: Routledge.
Kuhns, David F. 1997. *German Expressionist Theatre: The Actor and the Stage*. Cambridge: Cambridge UP.
Luckhurst, Mary. 2002. "Contemporary English Theatre: Why Realism?" In: Margarete Rubik & Elke Mettinger-Schartmann (eds.). *(Dis)Continuities: Trends and Traditions in Contemporary Theatre and Drama in English*. Trier: WVT. 73-84.
Lycan, William G. & Jesse J. Prinz (eds.). 2008 [1990]. *Mind and Cognition: An Anthology*. Oxford: Blackwell.
MacInnes, Colin. 1961 [1957]. "Young England, Half English. The Pied Piper from Bermondsey." In: Colin MacInnes. *England, Half English: A Polyphoto of the Fifties*. Harmondsworth: Penguin. 15-19.
Maschler, Tom (ed.). 1957. *Declaration*. London: MacGibbon & Kee.
Maturana, Humberto R. & Francisco J. Varela. 1998. *The Tree of Knowledge: Biological Roots of Human Understanding*. Boston: Shambhala.

Milne, Drew. 2000. "Drama in the Culture Industry: British Theatre After 1945." In: Alistair Davies & Alan Sinfield (eds.). *British Culture of the Postwar: An Introduction to Literature and Society 1945-1999*. London: Routledge. 169-91.
Morrison, Blake. 1980. *The Movement: English Poetry and Fiction of the 1950s*. Oxford: Oxford UP.
Müller, Klaus Peter. 1998. "Dialogic and Monologic Contexts in Arnold Wesker's Monologues and Monodramas." In: Dornan 1998. 179-93.
Nicholson, Steve. 2003. *The Censorship of British Drama 1900 – 1968*. 2 vols. Exeter: Exeter UP.
Norman, Barry. 2010. "My Movies: This Sporting Life." In: *Radio Times* 4-10 Sept.: 39.
Pfister, Manfred. 1988. *The Theory and Analysis of Drama*. Cambridge: Cambridge UP.
Pinker, Steven. 2008. *The Stuff of Thought: Language as a Window into Human Nature*. London: Penguin.
Rorty, Richard. 1979. *Philosophy and the Mirror of Nature*. Princeton: Princeton UP.
Rupert, Robert D. 2009. *Cognitive Systems and the Extended Mind*. Oxford: Oxford UP.
Sandbrook, Dominic. 2005. *Never Had It So Good: A History of Britain from Suez to the Beatles*. London: Little, Brown.
Shellard, Dominic, Steve Nicholson & Miriam Handley. 2004. *The Lord Chamberlain Regrets...: A History of British Theatre Censorship*. London: British Library.
Sierz, Aleks. 2001. *In-Yer-Face Theatre: British Drama Today*. London: Faber and Faber.
— (ed.). 2008. *John Osborne's* Look Back in Anger. London: Continuum.
Stoppard, Tom. 1966. *Rosencrantz and Guildenstern Are Dead*. London: Faber and Faber.
Szondi, Peter. 1973 [1956]. *Theorie des modernen Dramas 1880 – 1950*. Frankfurt a.M.: Suhrkamp.
Taylor, John Russell. 1969 [1962]. *Anger and After: A Guide to the New British Drama*. London: Methuen.
Wandor, Michelene. 1987. *Look Back in Gender: Sexuality and the Family in Post-War British Drama*. London: Methuen.
Wesker, Arnold. 1960. "Discovery." *The Transatlantic Review* V, December: 16-18.
—. 1970. *Fears of Fragmentation*. London: Cape.
—. 1990. *The Kitchen / The Four Seasons / Their Very Own and Golden City*. Vol. 2. London: Penguin.
—. 1995. *As Much As I Dare: An Autobiography (1932-1959)*. London: Arrow Books.
Whitebrook, Peter. 2002. *Angry Young Men*. London: Scribner.
Williams, Raymond. 1977. "A Lecture on Realism." In: *Screen* 18.1: 61-74. <http://www.afterall.org/journal/issue.5/lecture.realism> (last accessed 7 June 2011).
Wilson, Colin. 2007. *The Angry Years: A Literary Chronicle: The Rise and Fall of the Angry Young Men*. London: Robson.
Wilson, Robert A. & Frank Keil (eds.). 2001. *The MIT Encyclopedia of the Cognitive Sciences*. Cambridge, MA: MIT P.

19. THE THEATRE OF THE ABSURD: SAMUEL BECKETT'S *WAITING FOR GODOT* AND HAROLD PINTER'S *THE HOMECOMING*

ECKART VOIGTS-VIRCHOW

1. Beckett, Pinter, and the 'Theatre of the Absurd' – An Overview

The 'theatre of the absurd' emerged in the 1950s in Paris. It was first named in the eponymous 1961 study by Martin Esslin (1918-2002). The 'absurd' can be etymologically derived via Middle French (*absurde*) from the Latin *absurd-us* (inharmonious, tasteless, foolish, *surdus*: deaf, inaudible, insufferable to the ear). The dominant meaning in contemporary usage (also present in Latin) is a figurative one, "out of harmony with reason or propriety" (s.v. "absurd," *Online Etymology Dictionary*; "absurdity," *Oxford English Dictionary*). Esslin's study discussed four key playwrights of the absurd: Samuel Beckett (1906-1989), Arthur Adamov (1908-1970), Eugène Ionesco (1909-1994), and Jean Genet (1910-1986). Ionesco is cited as responding to the *horror vacui* of a universe without purpose: "Cut off from his religious, metaphysical, and transcendental roots, man is lost; all his actions become senseless, absurd, useless" (Esslin 1961: 19). His one-act sketches such as *The Bald Prima Donna* (*La Cantatrice chauve*, 1950), *The Lesson* (*La Leçon*, 1951), or *The Chairs* (*Les Chaises*, 1952), in response to the horrors of World War II, clearly exhibit features of 'absurdism,' such as deranged plots, instable character identities, ambiguous temporal, and spatial structures, failure of communication, undermined metaphors, and, in general, the dissolution of dramatic tradition.

The philosophical foundations of 'absurdism' can be found in the existentialist thinking of Albert Camus, Jean-Paul Sartre, André Malraux, and Martin Heidegger. Although Camus and Sartre both wrote significant plays, however, their work was not seen as a proper formal expression of the ideas articulated. Philosophically, 'the absurd' indicates the impossibility of finding meaning in human life. It is not to be mistaken with the commonplace meaning of 'absurd' as 'silly' or 'ridiculous,' but must be traced to the usage in Albert Camus' *Le Mythe de Sisyphe* (1942), where he coined the phrase. Camus used and popularized the term 'absurd' that had been introduced by Schopenhauer and Sartre and argued that human rationality is ill equipped to find meaning. The failure to grasp the world rationally effects in 'l'homme absurde' an attitude of revolt against the 'absurd' world. Only if they accept the absurd nature of the universe can human beings live passionately and even attain freedom, "la liberté absurd" (Camus 1942: 73). In terms of art, this would require the writer to find adequate expression of the 'absurd,' rather than follow a rational path towards describing it or writing 'about' it. In the genealogy of 'absurdist' thought, theatrical forms came rather late. Precursors include the 'absurd' pseudophilosophy of pataphysics by Alfred Jarry (1873-1907) and the 'theatre of cruelty' of Antonin Artaud (1896-1848). Irreverent, scatological, and blasphemous, Jarry's *Ubu Roi* scandalized the French bourgeoisie in 1896, and its infantile anti-hero may be seen as a possible expression of the 'absurd.' Dadaist and surrealist genealogies in the first decades of the 20th century have also fed into the 'absurdist' break with tradition, exemplified in Antonin Artaud's aversion to literary drama. Kafka's description of unidentified bureaucratic machineries pursuing individuals as well as his affinity for ambiguous terms in his novels such as *The Trial* (*Der Prozeß*, 1925), *The Castle* (*Das Schloß*, 1926), and *Amerika* (*Amerika* or *Der Verschollene*, 1927) may also be seen as an antecedent of 'absurdism.'

Subsequently, a second generation of younger playwrights has been added to Esslin's list: in Britain Harold Pinter (1930-2008), who was championed by Esslin in further editions of *The Theatre of the Absurd*, and Tom Stoppard (*1937); in the USA Edward Albee (*1928), Sam Shepard (*1943), and David Mamet (*1947); in Switzerland Friedrich Dürrenmatt (1921-1990) and Max Frisch (1911-1991); and in Austria Thomas Bernhard (1931-1989), to name but a few.

Martin Esslin's generic pigeonholing of the theatre of the absurd, which has been challenged from its very beginning – not least by Esslin himself –, remains particularly resonant in Germany (cf. Krause 2010). As I have argued elsewhere, Beckett's reception coincided with a belated awakening in Germany to the international trends towards neo-avantgardism such as *Neue Musik* (new music), surrealism, and radical modernism, and Beckett became a figurehead in a counter-reaction against the blind spots of mainstream culture in post-WWII-Germany (cf. Voigts-Virchow 2009).

Prominent Beckett critics such as Porter Abbott, Richard Begam, Steven Connor or Anthony Uhlmann have been involved in a fierce debate with an earlier generation of Beckett critics on whether Beckett might be seen as neomodernist or rather postmodernist and poststructuralist, a debate prompted by French poststructuralist thinking. Just as Theodor Adorno in the late 1950s and early 1960s, Gilles Deleuze, Michel Foucault, and Jacques Derrida have seen Beckett's work as the literary equivalent of their own philosophy (cf. Uhlmann 1999: 7 f.). More recently, Alain Badiou has highlighted categories of beauty and emotion in Beckett's work, and, together with Slavoj Žižek, continues readings of Beckett inspired by Jacques Lacan, which focus on Beckett's work as an expression of 'the Real,' i.e., a precarious presence beyond language (cf. Badiou 2002). Other major trends of Beckett criticism around the centenary celebrations of 2006 have by-passed the epithet 'theatre of the absurd' – such as the focus on the dramaticules and short fiction in his later work, his work for TV, film, and cross-media experimentation (cf. Bignell 2009; Herren 2007) and his interests and influence in the arts and music, his representation in popular culture and visual culture (cf. Giesing, et al. 2007; Hartel & Veit 2006), or work that relates Beckett to bio-aesthetics or eco-criticism. The spatial turn (cf. Sick 2011) and body discourses (cf. Maude 2009) have also left their mark on Beckett studies. Another research focus makes use of the Beckett Collection of the Beckett International Foundation at the

University of Reading, returning to manuscripts, archival and biographical concerns in the wake of the authoritative texts by Jim Knowlson and Anthony Cronin. These approaches, notably by Mark Nixon, focus on Beckett's formative years as evinced by Beckett's 'German diaries' from 1936/37 (which are set to be published by Suhrkamp in 2015) and the specific cultural contexts from which his work emerges.

All in all, Beckett, who left Dublin to travel across Europe in 1931 and who, finally settled in his French retreat Ussy-sur-Marne, wrote 31 plays, 50 poems, 30 short stories, 15 pieces of journalism and 10 novels. His key works and, more specifically, *Waiting for Godot* (1955), emerge from Beckett's epiphanic dissociation from James Joyce around 1945. Having produced unpublished fiction and obscure journalism for a number of decades – often merely copying Joyce – Beckett realised that ignorance and impotence could be pitted against Joyce's exuberant erudition. Thus, Beckett's work is often divided into three phases, his early work (including the novels *Dream of Fair to Middling Women* [1932], *Murphy* [1938], and *Watt* [1953]) the brilliant key texts from the mid-1940s to the early 1960s (including the trilogy of novels *Molloy*, *Malone Dies* and *The Unnamable* [in French, 1950-52] as well as the plays *En attendant Godot* [1952], *Fin de Partie* [1957], *Happy Days* [1961]), and a third phase of increasingly difficult and laboured work. Here, Beckett takes his by then familiar worlds of failed communication, faded pasts and uncertain futures, cruel nature, absent gods and dogged inertia to aesthetic extremes (including *Not I* [1973]), his works for television (SWR), radio, and a film (*Film*, 1965). Beckett's world, marked by futility, exhaustion, repetition, tedium, boredom, reduction, concentration, stasis, dissociation, and fragmentation, is often put in the nutshell of key quotes, such as "[t]he sun shone, having no alternative, on the nothing new" (the first line in *Murphy*, 1957: 1) or "I can't go on. I'll go on" (the final line in *The Unnamable*, 1959: 418).

Harold Pinter is biographically linked to Beckett, having praised his work with a characteristic set of drastic terms and language clichés, highlighting Beckett's resistance to easy and conventional meaning-making:

> The farther he goes the more good it does me. I don't want philosophies, tracts, dogmas, creeds, way outs, truths, answers, *nothing from the bargain basement*. He is the most courageous, remorseless writer going and the more he grinds my nose in the shit the more I am grateful to him. He's not fucking me about, he's not leading me up any garden, he's not slipping me any wink, he's not flogging me a remedy or a path or a revelation or a basinful of breadcrumbs, he's not selling me anything I don't want to buy – he doesn't give a bollock whether I buy or not – *he hasn't got his hand over his heart*. Well, I'll buy his goods, hook, line and sinker, because he leaves no stone unturned and no maggot lonely. He brings forth a body of beauty. His work is beautiful. (Pinter 1998: 45)

Pinter became Beckett's drinking companion and both playwrights sent each other manuscripts for comment (cf. Billington 2007). The private lives of both playwrights have become issues of controversy: Beckett was married to Suzanne Decheveaux-Dumesnil, whom he had met after he had been stabbed by a pimp in Paris in 1938. He also had an extended affair with BBC script editor Barbara Bray from 1957 and shorter relationships with, among others, his cousin Peggy Sinclair in Kassel in the 1930s and the wealthy American art collector Peggy Guggenheim. Pinter was married to actress Vivien Merchant, who starred in many of his early plays, but also had an affair with TV presenter Joan Bakewell in the 1960s, which informed his play *Betrayal* (1978), with the American Barbara Stanton, and a much-publicized relationship with historian Lady Antonia Fraser, since 1975, who became his second wife after a bitter separation from Merchant.

Pinter, the son of a Jewish tailor from the northeast London Borough of Hackney, spent the 1950s as an actor (under the stage-name David Baron) and continued to act on the stage, radio, television, and film during his career as a playwright, notably in his own works and in Beckett's *Krapp's Last Tape* (1958), his final stage performance at the Royal Court in October 2006. His credits testify to his versatility, as a director of many stage, television, and film productions, writer of 27 screenplays, among them screen adaptations of, for instance, L.P. Hartley's *The Go-Between* (1970, dir. Joseph Losey), Attwood's *The French Lieutenant's Woman* (1981, dir. Volker Schlöndorff), Kafka's *The Trial* (1993, dir. David Jones), and the remake of Anthony Shaffer's *Sleuth* (2007, dir. Kenneth Branagh). In 2005, he was awarded the Nobel Prize for Literature, especially on the basis of his 29 original stage plays. In his first years, Pinter wrote enigmatic plays suggesting a Kafkaesque menace and mixing 'the absurd' with British theatrical tradition, such as the drawing-room comedy or social realism (*The Birthday Party* [1957], *The Dumb Waiter* [1959], *The Caretaker* [1959], *The Homecoming* [1964]). In the 1970s, Pinter toned down the violence of his plays and intensified his discussion of the problematic identity construction in memory, in plays such as *Old Times* (1971), *No Man's Land* (1975), *Betrayal* (1978), and, subsequently, *Moonlight* (1993). In the 1980s, Pinter experienced his so-called political turn, addressing issues such as torture (*One for the Road* [1984]), the Holocaust (*Ashes to Ashes* [1996]), and cultural suppression (*Mountain Language* [1988]) and bluntly criticizing American global policies. Whereas discussions of ambiguities and linguistic indeterminacy in his work, therefore, reprise some of the disputes about Beckett, focusing on modernism or postmodernism in his work, the key debates – which intensified after his controversial Nobel speech – address Pinter's aesthetics in the light of his increasingly outspoken politics (cf. essays by Quigley & Aragay in Raby 2001; Merritt 1990: 50-86).

2. Samuel Beckett's *Waiting for Godot*

En attendant Godot was written in French between October 1948 and January 1949 as a recreational exercise after the painful composition of the trilogy. A preliminary abridged studio production for the French Club d'Essai de la Radio took place on 17 February 1952. The play, directed by Roger Blin who also played the part of Pozzo, subsequently premiered on 5 January 1953 in the Théâtre de Babylone. The response to the tumultuous run was general lack of understanding, but the reviews were mixed rather than hostile. The first English-language production (3 August 1955, Arts Theatre, London) was met by incomprehension on the parts of both director (Peter Hall) and cast – there are many stories of actors dropping out of productions as they claimed not to understand the play.

When the run was threatened by a furiously negative critical response, the play was saved by positive reviews from distinguished theatre pundits Kenneth Tynan and Harold Hobson, and *Godot* (*G*) was later presented with the unique award of "most controversial play of the year" (Hall 2003). A brief description of the play will show the strategies used by Beckett to undermine the 'well-made play' and – more specifically – the Aristotelian model of action with a beginning, middle, and ending.

The setting is based on the principle of reduction and indeterminacy. The stage directions merely read: "*A country road. A tree. Evening.*" (*G* 11) The tree is leafless and dead in the first act, but, miraculously, has grown "*four or five leaves*" in the second act, although this takes place "*Next Day. Same Time. Same Place*" (*G* 53). So, is there some validity to Estragon's contradictory response that they must have been in 'another void' the day before? Estragon ironically calls this paradoxical void a "[c]harming spot" and, facing the audience, notes "inspiring prospects" (*G* 15) – clearly inviting a laugh of recognition from the audience and a metatheatrical interpretation. In significant inarticulation, the characters are unable to specify the location – the tree might be a "willow," a "bush" or merely "shrubs" (*G* 15 f.). The tree, however, has invited commentators to speculate on its meanings in the Bible (as a symbol of life and knowledge) or on its function in suicide (of, for instance, Judas) or at the gates of Hell in Dante's *Inferno* (c. 1314). The characters imitate it, they "do the tree" (*G* 71). In performance, it is often modeled on Alberto Giacometti's slender design in the famous 1961 production of the play. It was clearly important to Beckett, however, to leave the setting unspecific and, therefore, universal and ambiguous.

The same holds true of the characters, which are structured into pairs. Vladimir and Estragon, who call each other Didi and Gogo, are paralleled by the appearance of Pozzo and Lucky. These names have an identical number of letters, yet are different and, to all appearances, meaningless. Their ethnicity and background is unclear – a boy who appears calls Vladimir Mister Albert while Estragon answers to the name Adam (Magregor) – and their decontextualized appearance, fluid names, and fragmentary stories about their past never add up to a comprehensive character outline. They are usually dressed and played as unkempt, stinking vagrants, with Vladimir lanky and Estragon stocky in stature, both wearing bowler hats (suggesting Dublin dress codes or Laurel and Hardy props). They are usually played in contrastive ways, too, with Vladimir more active and Estragon passive, likely to doze off and with even faultier memories than Vladimir. Pairings had been used by Beckett in his novels *Murphy* and *Mercier et Camier* (1946) and they may also recall music-hall turns. In this way and in their typical verbal repartee and banter, they are reminiscent of classic pairs of vaudeville acts and slapstick comedy such as Laurel and Hardy or Liesl Karstadt and Karl Valentin, both of whom were well known to Beckett. It is significant that the Beckett pair is suffering from bodily dysfunction (Vladimir's bladder, Estragon's feet) and that both of them are unable to piece together the whys and wherefores of either their stage presence or their past:

> ESTRAGON. We came here yesterday.
> VLADIMIR. Ah no, there you're mistaken.
> ESTRAGON. What did we do yesterday?
> VLADIMIR. What did we do yesterday?
> ESTRAGON. Yes.
> VLADIMIR. Why... (*Angrily.*) Nothing is certain when you're about. (*G* 16)

Vladimir and Estragon are unable to piece together any consistent memories – in the second act they are not even certain that they have met Pozzo and Lucky the day before, and they are stuck in the presumably perennial situation of waiting, spending their time by verbal and physical 'action' merely in order to overcome tedium and boredom.

In both acts, Vladimir and Estragon's exchanges are punctuated by the appearance of Pozzo and Lucky and, finally, a boy. Pozzo and Lucky may be interpreted as radicalized versions of Vladimir and Estragon, as if they have been refracted in a distorting mirror. Pozzo leads Lucky on a rope and commands him to move, and for Lucky's famous logorrheatic monologue, to "think" (*G* 41). Thus, Lucky might be a lackey, or, as Beckett himself has suggested, lucky as he is lacking expectations (Duckworth 1967: 95). The pompous Pozzo, who is irritated at Vladimir's and Estragon's disappointment when they realize he is not Godot, after all, may be modeled on an Irish ascendancy landlord. Estragon wonders if Pozzo, a figure of self-ascribed authority, may in fact be Godot. Interestingly, in an early draft of the play (in private hands) Beckett toys with the idea of actually making Pozzo Godot and the assonance of the names is a clear link. When they reappear in the second act, Pozzo is inexplicably blind and Lucky is dumb. The fact that Lucky stays with Pozzo indicates that their master-slave relationship is not based on Pozzo's dominance, but on a mutual need to continue their role-play in order to occupy their time.

Probably the most important subversion of the well-made play occurs with the plot. The most famous, shortest and, if not entirely accurate then at least most poignant, plot summary was provided by the Irish critic Vivian Mercier (1956: 6): "Nothing happens, twice." In fact, plenty of things happen in *Waiting for Godot* as the four characters pass their time eating – with Vladimir feeding Estragon – arguing, singing and dancing (Lucky), playing games, exchanging hats, and considering suicide. However, all of this action is lacking a *telos* – it is inconsequential, circular, and ends in stasis. The very first line in the play, Estragon's "Nothing to be done" (*G* 11) in reaction to the failure in taking off his boots, is a disavowal of action. Ultimately, Vladimir and Estragon paradoxically reject the very principle of action that they articulate verbally:

> ESTRAGON. [...] Let's go.
> VLADIMIR. We can't.
> ESTRAGON. Why not?

VLADIMIR. We're waiting for Godot.
ESTRAGON. (*Despairingly.*) Ah! (*Pause.*) (*G* 15)
[...]
ESTRAGON. Well, shall we go?
VLADIMIR. Yes, let's go.
(*They do not move.*) (*G* 52)
[...]
VLADIMIR. Well? Shall we go?
ESTRAGON. Yes, let's go.
(*They do not move.*) (*G* 88)

Both acts end in a tableau of inertia, interchangeably articulated by Vladimir and Estragon in Beckett's typical mode of variation with a difference. Dramatic action has led nowhere and might be expressed by the circular logic of Vladimir's song "A dog game in the kitchen" (*G* 53), rendered with characteristic hesitancy and brooding. The language in *Waiting for Godot* is dominated by the stichomythic repartee of Vladimir and Estragon, with Beckett characteristically advising actors to speak with a tone of utmost exhaustion. The language merely serves to cancel out and qualify whatever validity has seemed to be established in earlier exchanges. A good example of the comic and paradoxical quality of these cancellations occurs when Estragon suggests, "let's contradict each other" and Vladimir replies "[i]mpossible," in fact, of course, contradicting Estragon (*G* 59). The stichomythia climaxes in a series of abusive repartee – which, however, is devoid of any expressive function and, just as other occupations, merely serves as pastime:

VLADIMIR. Ceremonious ape!
ESTRAGON. Punctilious pig!
VLADIMIR. Finish your phrase, I tell you!
ESTRAGON. Finish your own!
(*Silence. They draw closer, halt.*)
VLADIMIR. Moron!
ESTRAGON. That's the idea, let's abuse each other.
(*They turn, move apart, turn again and face each other.*)
VLADIMIR. Moron!
ESTRAGON. Vermin!
VLADIMIR. Abortion!
ESTRAGON. Morpion!
VLADIMIR. Sewer-rat!
ESTRAGON. Curate!
VLADIMIR. Cretin!
ESTRAGON. (*with finality*). Crritic!
VLADIMIR. Oh!
(*He wilts, vanquished, and turns away.*)
ESTRAGON. Now let's make it up.
VLADIMIR. Gogo!
ESTRAGON. Didi! (*G* 70)

Estragon is clearly only able to mimic and vary Vladimir's invective, and Beckett again manages to infiltrate the exchange with a passing metatheatrical shot at the "crritics." The majority of verbal exchanges in the play thus consist of a quick succession of questions, with the replies retarded or blank. Misunderstandings, cross-talk, and pauses abound, indicating the dissolution of language and a scepticism that recalls the linguistic turn of the first decades of the 20th century. Often characters repeat or vary other characters' speeches or reverse roles. Speech disorder clearly signals the anomie (alienated dislocation in social interaction) of Beckett's characters. The climax of the Beckettian dissolution of language in functional chaos comes with Lucky's "think" speech, which parades the speech disorders he himself lists in part – apathia or aphasia (schizophrenic loss of language ability), athambia (imperturbability), paraphrasia (compulsory repetition):

> Given the existence as uttered forth in the public works of Puncher and Wattmann of a personal God quaquaquaqua with white beard quaquaquaqua outside time without extension who from the heights of divine apathia divine athambia divine aphasia loves us dearly with some exceptions for reasons unknown but time will tell and suffers like the divine Miranda with those who for reasons unknown but time will tell are plunged in torment plunged in fire whose fire flames […] crowned by the Acacacademy of Anthropopopometry of Essy-in-Possy of Testew and Cunard it is established beyond all doubt all other doubt than that which clings to the labors of men that as a result of the labors unfinished of Testew and Cunard it is established as hereinafter but not so fast for reasons unknown that as a result of the public works of Puncher and Wattmann it is established beyond all doubt that in view of the labors of Fartov and Belcher […] the practice of sports such as tennis football running cycling swimming flying floating riding gliding conating camogie skating tennis of all kinds dying flying sports of all sorts […] I resume flying gliding golf over nine and eighteen holes tennis of all sorts in a word for reasons unknown in Feckham Peckham Fulham Clapham […] I resume the skull fading fading fading and concurrently simultaneously what is more for reasons unknown in spite of the tennis on on the beard the flames the tears the stones so blue so calm alas alas on on the skull the skull the skull the skull in Connemara in spite of the tennis. (*G* 42 f.)

This tirade is full of parodic anti-religious, anti-authoritative, anti-institutional underpinnings. It is set off by putting Lucky's hat on his head – parodying causal connectivity – and it ends in a blasphemous quasi-crucifixion when Lucky is hoisted up. The fragments parody the discourse of academic, religious, or philosophical argumentation ("Given the existence as uttered forth") – mixed with scatological ("Acacacademy," "Anthropopopometry," "Fartov") and sexually connoted ("Testew," "Cunard," "Feckham," "Clapham") and otherwise bodily ("Belcher") low humour. As Lucky makes clear the divine foolishness of his scholarly cum bodily logorrhea is in fact a complete deprivation of human individuality and a reduction to an automaton of speech whose barrage of coincidental and disjointed repetitions destroys any residual meaning. Its main function is to indicate the dissolution of meanings and symbols, as Lucky's gibberish merely provides disordered fragments of the Western intellectual and literary tradition (Shakespeare's Miranda, Johnson, Verlaine, and Hölderlin). Lawrence Graver has decoded Puncher as ticket puncher and Wattman as a tram-driver. "Essy-in-Possy" clearly and crudely invokes 'esse' and 'posse.' In his view, Lucky's "quaquaua" can be seen as "ultimate meaning or ultimate nonsense" (Graver 2004: 47) – with an onomatopoetic infiltration of, maybe, the Latin indication of "'essential being, in the character or capacity of …'" (ibid.; 'qua') or "'wheresoever turned, turned everywhere, sloping downward from the centre in all directions'" (ibid.; 'quaqua-versal'). The critical attitude towards language can be linked to Fritz Mauthner. Having encountered Mauthner's *Beiträge zu einer Kritik der Sprache* (1901/02) via James Joyce, Beckett adopted his view that language is thought, and that both are inane as means of expression – Lucky's hypertrophied inarticulation, his flood of words, is an excellent example of this. Having incorporated the 'linguistic turn' of the first decades of the 20th century in his work, Beckett was inspired by a vast and various reading in philosophy, from rationalists such as Descartes and Kant to the existentialists. Having addressed the German tradition of idealism à la Kant via Arthur Schopenhauer, Beckett adopted the insistence on the state of powerlessness and ignorance from Arnold Geulincx, the philosophical unhappiness, a resigned melancholy, from Schopenhauer, and an existential homelessness or *Geworfenheit* from Heidegger. Via Schopenhauer, one may link Beckett's work to Eastern philosophy and his work has resonated well in Japan, probably as it seems reminiscent of the traditions of static 'No-theatre.'

Waiting for Godot has proven to be a vast receptacle of interpretative machineries, an echo chamber of allusions. The ultimate deferral of clear meaning, however, have referred audiences back to the foundational situation of waiting, shared by Beckett's characters. In the following paragraphs I will briefly discuss attempts to account for the sources of the play and for the identity of Godot as well as his relation to the two character pairs. One should, however, heed Estragon, who responds to Vladimir's claim that "[t]his is becoming really insignificant" (*G* 60) with a laconic "[n]ot enough." Beckett clearly attempted to purge his play of an all-too-obvious referential dimension and, as Ruby Cohn reports, he rejected claims to infuse his play with meaning in an introduction to the first radio performance:

> I don't know who Godot is. I don't even know (above all don't know) if he exists. And I don't know if they believe in him or not – those two who are waiting for him. The other two who pass by towards the end of each of the two acts, that must be to break up the monotony. All I knew I showed. It's not much, but it's enough for me, by a wide margin. I'll even say that I would have been satisfied with less. […] Estragon, Vladimir, Pozzo, Lucky, their time and their space, I was able to know them a little, but far from the need to understand. Maybe they owe you explanations. Let them supply it. Without me. They and I are through with each other. (qtd. in Knowlson & Knowlson 2006: 122)

In spite of these disclaimers, critics have found numerous meanings embedded in the play. The famous atheist had intimate knowledge of the Bible, which inspired investigations into the Christian dimension of his work. Thus Vladimir and Estragon may be cast as the two thieves from Luke (23: 39–43) of which they speak at the beginning of the play. As Beckett has stated, Vladimir hesitantly invokes St. Augustine of Hippo ("Do not despair; one of the thieves was saved. Do not presume; one of the thieves was damned." [Gordon 2002: 112]) and an ensuing debate emerges on the validity and dubious morality of the story. Vladimir and Estragon as the two thieves are a clear indictment of a God whose world is contingent and whose decision cannot be but haphazard, amoral, and possibly unjust. After all, neither of both is damned or saved at the ending of the play and the *absence présente* of Godot as a God who is present only as a projection of the characters is at the very heart of the play. Godot, after all, has been 'translated' as a little or minor God ('-ot' French diminutive) or as the Godo of Irish slang. Existentialist spite heaped on the absent Christian God abounds in the play, as Mary Bryden (1998) and others have explored. Clearly, the appearance of a boy alludes to God's son Jesus in Christian scripture as well as to the conventions of messenger and *deus ex machina* of Greek drama.

It would be misleading, however, to see Godot as a cipher for a transcendental being. The key question of "Who is Godot?" has rendered further suggestions, some of them wildly implausible, such as: 'a hobnailed boot' (French, *godillot*), a pub-crawl (French, *godailler*), an Englishman (*goddam* in French slang), a Cognac, a mug, a bowl of a pipe, glass of wine, a receptacle (French, *godet*), fornication or a skull (French, *godiller*), a joker or misshapen man (French, *godenot*), a business partner who never comes (Godeau in Balzac's *Mercadet* [1851]), a French actor-manager (in Lenz's *Die Soldaten* [1774/75]), a well-known French cyclist called Godeau, for whose arrival a crowd waits (Hugh Kenner) or a street famous for brothels in Beckett's Paris (rue Godot de Mauroy; cf. Graver 2004: 38-42). According to Calderwood (1992 [1986]: 37), Godot is a death dog or a god-death ('god-tod' or, backwards, 'tod-dog'), reminding him of "Pozzo's arresting metaphor, 'they give birth astride of a grave.'"

More generally, Irish literature and drama abounds with portrayals of thieves and beggars as in the plays of John Millington Synge. William Butler Yeat's *The Cat and the Moon* (1926) portrays two beggars, crippled and sightless, on the way to a miracle. Beckett himself has indicated that three paintings may have provided him with a cue for his pairs. A Caspar David Friedrich painting he possibly saw on his German travels – either *Zwei Männer betrachten den Mond* (1819) or *Mann und Frau den Mond betrachtend* (1830-35) inspired Beckett to create Vladimir and Estragon. Jack Butler Yeats's *The Two Travellers* (1942), another of Beckett's favourite painters, is another source of inspiration (cf. Knowlson 1996: 378 ff.). All of these paintings cue solitary humanity in a desolate, moonlit twilight (with trees). The repartee, some commentators and notably Knowlson (1996: 379) have argued, might be based on his quarrels with his wife Suzanne – Beckett half admitted this – or on his chess conversations with Henri Hayden. The well-established fact that one of the tramps was named Lévy in an earlier version cues a specific historical contextualization of the play as it points to the relevance of Beckett's Jewish friend and fellow Résistance collaborator Lévy, who was killed in the concentration camp Mauthausen. In conversation with his grandson Pierre, Valentin Temkine has taken up this interpretation, taking Vladimir's remark that he and Estragon would not be allowed on the Tour Eiffel to suggest that the four characters are Jews in hiding. He somewhat bluntly stated that Godot was a people smuggler and Beckett simply dramatized the situation of waiting on a chalk plateau near the Alps for the smuggler in transit (Temkine 2008: 14-23). This is another attempt to provide a distinct historical context for the metaphysical tramps – and just as the Marxist reading in the wake of Bertolt Brecht it has its limitations. Brecht had asked Giorgio Strehler in 1956 what Vladimir and Estragon had done during World War II, and subsequently Marxists either sought to provide a clear political context for the master-slave relationship of Pozzo and Lucky or simply dismissed the play as decadent and merely laying bare structural problems of monopoly capitalism.

More daring interpretations have been supplied – with psychological readings casting the four characters as four Jungian archetypes (Pozzo = ego, Lucky = shadow, Estragon = female anima, Vladimir = persona), or with Gogo and Didi representing the ego and id (cf. Dukore 1962), or the mental and the physical man, Body and Mind (cf. Cohn 1962). Beckett's play in various ways points out its own metatheatricality in its rejection of any 'about-ness.' Starting with the assumption that "all theatre is waiting" (Foster 2004: 172) you may find numerous examples of metatheatricality indicated in this essay. Ultimately Beckett's theatre eludes attempts to pinpoint specific interpretative dimensions.

3. Harold Pinter's *The Homecoming*

Harold Pinter's *The Homecoming* premiered on June 3, 1965 at the Aldwych Theatre, in Peter Hall's production for the Royal Shakespeare Company. It was indeed this cooperation with Hall as the 'contemporary' aspect of the RSC that gave Pinter's somewhat fledgling early career a boost. The play can be seen as a culmination of Pinter's first phase as a playwright. This phase, in which Pinter was under the marked influence of Beckett, generated the persistent lexicalized eponymous descriptors 'Pinteresque' and 'Pinterese' (Harrison 1998: 196), the generic marker 'comedy of menace' or Pinter's trademark character constellations, the "battle for position" (Quigley 1975: 49), and the 'catalytic stranger' who destroys a precarious balance in an enclosed space. Finally, the play also abounds in Pinter's signature stage directions 'silence' and 'pause' – indicating either that the dialogue has entered a stage of vacuity or a moment fraught with a depth of implicit, subtextual meaning that transcends articulation.

'Pinteresque' has entered the *Oxford English Dictionary*. In analogy with the somewhat synonymous 'Kafkaesque,' it is used to describe a mysterious existential menace, in the case of Pinter often mixed with aggressive obsessions, erotic fantasies thinly veiled by language, hatred, jealousy, and mental disorder ("Pinteresque," *OED*). 'Pinterese' denotes a use of language marked by the use of pauses and silences, by an understated small talk that is suggestive of a veiled subtext of aggression and erotic fantasy, used to dominate other characters or construe an often vague and ambiguous character identity. 'Comedy of menace' (a term coined by Irving Wardle as early as 1958, cf. Merritt 1990: 225) is a pun on the quintessentially English and highly conventional 'comedy of manners,' indicating that the characteristically mysterious threat by unnamed agents and organisations often appears in a slippery language that tends to imply a humorously revealing linguistic subtext – particularly in Pinter's early plays. *The Homecoming* (*H*) is also an excellent example of the foundational character concept employed by Pinter, which is that of a continuous 'battle for positions.' Pinter picked up Beckett's critical attitude towards language and exposing speech as "a constant stratagem to cover nakedness" (Pinter 1998: 20) and showing in his silences the failure of this communicative strategy of masking. His characters attempt to exert dominance by controlling situations through language and spatial positioning.

The Homecoming has a very simple plot, reminiscent of a family melodrama, and, just as *Waiting for Godot*, a two-act structure. In fact, exposing the Freudian subtext, Begley (2005: 64) called it 'Anti-Freudian' as it lays bare not only the family as a Freudian 'patriarchal horde,' but also the conventions of traditional family drama. It portrays an all-male, possibly Jewish, and to all appearances criminal household in North London, composed of foul-mouthed patriarch Max, his two sons Lenny, apparently a pimp, and Joey, a boxer, as well as Max' brother Sam. Together, they exhibit the pathologies of everyday male life – from a general lack of social skill to an array of verbal abuse. This begins with the very first lines, in which Lenny challenges Max' patriarchal power, ignoring his demands for scissors – the first of many phallic objects in the play – and complaining about his cooking. Clearly, Max is ill-equipped to perform 'motherly' roles in this male microcosm governed by masculine and even macho values. Max is continuously challenged on his masculine authority, not least with reference to his deceased wife Jessie's faithfulness. He hits Sam and strikes Joey and uses verbal aggression in order to stabilize his position. When Ruth lies motionless under Joey, Max sardonically comments that she is "a woman of quality" and "a woman of feeling" (*H* 76). The sources of the absurd in *The Homecoming* are frequently the skewered, warped perceptions of the male 'family.' The catalytic stranger is Ruth, formerly of North London, who pays a visit from America, accompanying her husband Teddy, Max' third son. Enigmatically, she inserts herself into this precarious equilibrium of 'phallic' men struggling for dominance.

As a rule, Pinter's characters refuse to corroborate stories about their pasts – an aspect that is given wider scope in his 1970s plays *Old Times* (1970) or *No Man's Land* (1974) – and accordingly Ruth and Teddy's 'back stories' remain mysterious. The fact that the butcher's son Teddy has become a philosophy professor at an American college seems implausible, all the more so as he refuses to adopt an academic register or speak about his profession when challenged. His wife Ruth, apparently a former London fashion model, eventually agrees to a business proposal that casts her as a prostitute, set up by the family and working in a flat in Greek Street. The resolution of Pinter's play baffled audiences: Ruth accepts the plan on her terms and agrees to make Teddy's homecoming her own. Even more disorientating to audiences, Teddy accepts the proposal and leaves for a single return home. The play ends on a tableau which seems to indicate that Ruth has supplanted the old patriarch Max – who had earlier warned against Ruth's increasing influence. The youngest son Joey has his head in her lap, Lenny stands, watching, and Max has collapsed at her feet, weighed down with the recognition that he might have lost the virility to be eligible as Ruth's partner and to command the scenery. The qualities of Ruth as both whore – she spends two hours with Joey in an upstairs room, during which Joey, however, does not 'go the whole hog' – and as comforting, nursing, caring mother are at stake for the men, and she seems to acquiesce in, even thrive on, this dubiously stereotyped image-making of the men.

In his Nobel Prize speech in 2006, which concentrates on Pinter's political positions, he has addressed his aesthetic of ambiguity, his epistemology of unknowability, the instable character identities and his sceptical attitude to language – all of which can be linked to Beckett and 'absurdism':

> In 1958 I wrote the following: 'There are no hard distinctions between what is real and what is unreal, nor between what is true and what is false. A thing is not necessarily either true or false; it can be both true and false.'
> I believe that these assertions still make sense and do still apply to the exploration of reality through art. [...] Truth in drama is forever elusive. You never quite find it but the search for it is compulsive. [...] I have often been asked how my plays come about. I cannot say. Nor can I ever sum up my plays, except to say that this is what happened. That is what they said. That is what they did. Most of the plays are engendered by a line, a word or an image. The given word is often shortly followed by the image. [...] The first line of *The Homecoming* is 'What have you done with the scissors?' [...] I had no further information. [...] [S]omeone was obviously looking for a pair of scissors and was demanding their whereabouts of someone else he suspected had probably stolen them. But I somehow knew that the person addressed didn't give a damn about the scissors or about the questioner either, for that matter. [...] I always start a play by calling the characters A, B and C. In the play that became *The Homecoming* I saw a man enter a stark room and ask his question of a younger man sitting on an ugly sofa reading a racing paper. I somehow suspected that A was a father and that B was his son, but I had no proof. This was however confirmed a short time later when B (later to become Lenny) says to A (later to become Max), 'Dad, do you mind if I change the subject? I want to ask you something. The dinner we had before, what was the name of it? What do you call it? Why don't you buy a dog? You're a dog cook. Honest. You think you're cooking for a lot of dogs.' So since B calls A 'Dad' it seemed to me reasonable to assume that they were father and son. A was also clearly the cook and his cooking did not seem to be held in high regard. Did this mean that there was no mother? I didn't know. But, as I told myself at the time, our beginnings never know our ends. (Pinter 2005: n. pag.)

The play exhibits Pinter's clear focus on dramatic language. Martin Esslin noted the similarity of Pinter's language to poetry:

> Pinter's dialogue is as tightly – perhaps *more* tightly – controlled than verse. Every syllable, every inflection, the succession of long and short sounds, words and sentences are calculated to nicety. And it is precisely the repetitiousness, the discontinuity, the circularity of ordinary vernacular speech which are here used as formal elements with which the poet can compose his linguistic ballet. (Esslin 1976: 48)

This can be exemplified by Lenny's lengthy speeches that, following his advance towards Ruth, seek to intimidate and impress her, focusing on aggression towards a diseased prostitute and another who sought his help with an iron mangle. Lenny both introduces himself as a pimp and his no-nonsense attitude and clichéd view of women (whores, housewives). Unimpressed, Ruth offers Lenny a glass of water, which becomes peculiarly threatening to Lenny and exemplifies her refusal to being intimidated by Lenny's character construction. In vain, Lenny taunts Ruth with insults, implying that she is his brother's whore, in this key struggle for dominance. In a crucial exchange at the beginning of act 2, Lenny seeks to confront Teddy's American identity as a 'doctor of philosophy' and Teddy and Ruth provide conflicting and sketchy narratives about their life in the USA:

> LENNY. Well, I want to ask you something. Do you detect a certain logical incoherence in the central affirmations of Christian theism.
> TEDDY. That question doesn't fall within my province. [...]
> LENNY. Well, for instance, take a table. Philosophically speaking. What is it?
> TEDDY. A table. (67 f.)

Hard words ("theism") are used to signal mastery and competence. The language clearly becomes a weapon in a challenge – to establish the exact scope of Teddy's province and to demarcate his territory. He may or may not be a successful college professor, but this is relevant only in so far as it will help him to claim his stakes in the confrontation with his father's family composed of – as far as we can tell – a butcher, a chauffeur, a boxer, and a pimp. Is he a fraud whose stories about teaching philosophy in a successful department in a clean country and a happy family life with three boys are impromptu inventions intended to trump the old family set-up with a superior American version? Or is he simply deflating the pompous vacuity of Lenny's challenge? Teddy retaliates, describing his family as "objects" who would not understand his "critical works" (*H* 78).

Phallic rule is the key criterion for the men in *The Homecoming*, as Joey has to compensate for not going "the whole hog" (*H* 84) and the talk about getting "the gravy" (*H* 85) or Lenny's protesting about rocks "frozen stiff in the fridge" (*H* 77) makes abundantly clear. Max has to defend his rule against Lenny's suggestion that he is "sexless" (*H* 88) and his struggle with his brother Max focuses on the mastery of the deceased wife Jessie. Control over the memories of Jessie is characteristically strategic – the characters construe their past in order to gain ground in the territorial struggle suggested by the title *The Homecoming*. The title may refer to Teddy's visit to his family or to Ruth's return to an old location and an old profession – although Teddy tries to suggest that it would be best for Ruth to come home with him – a third possible homecoming. Alternatively, it may also allude to the characters being restored to their selfish truths or truthful selves and vocations. The end of phallic rule is signaled when both Lenny's and Teddy's cigars go out (*H* 67). Max ultimately tries in vain to persuade Ruth to kiss him, and he has to acknowledge that his fears about her not being "adaptable" (*H* 97) come true.

Ruth challenges the men's materialist worldview of the table (and, by implication, people) as commodity, initiating her halting speech with a photographic model's characteristic demand to 'look at her':

> RUTH. Look at me. I ... move my leg. That's all it is. But I wear ... underwear ... which moves with me ... it captures your attention. Perhaps you misinterpret. The action is sim-

ple. It's a leg ... moving. My lips move. Why don't you restrict ... your observations to that? Perhaps the fact that they move is more significant ... than the words which come through them. You must bear that ... possibility ... in mind. *Silence* (*H* 69)

This might be read as teasing, with thinly veiled innuendo of 'lips,' but it clearly also refers to the critical attitude towards language inherited from the earlier 'absurdists': actions are simple, but words as clothes invite misinterpretation. As he made clear in his key essay "Writing for the Theatre," language, for Pinter, is "a highly ambiguous business," where "below the word spoken, is the thing known and unspoken" in a "language [...] where under which what is said, another thing is being said" (Pinter 1998: 19). For Beckett, language becomes futile; for Pinter it is a weapon, a stratagem, a creative and slippery tool in creating and erasing identity.

The ending of *The Homecoming* is equally ambiguous. Ruth, calling Teddy for the first time 'Eddie,' asks him not to become a stranger – a proverbial farewell inviting further communication. Divesting the proverb of its colloquial meaning, however, we may, again, find other meanings lurking: A stranger, one may ask, to whom? Himself? His wife? His macho family? His college life? Maybe Teddy, letting his wife go into a future as prostitute/head of the household with his family, is a helpless victim or, indeed in control and "the biggest bastard in a house full of bastards," as director Peter Hall argues (Batty 2005: 160).

4. Conclusion

The influence of the 'absurdist' playwrights continues via contemporary voices such as Jon Fosse (*1959), Sarah Kane (1971-1999), Martin Crimp (*1956), Martin McDonagh (*1970), and others. Remarkably, Beckett and Pinter – both of them recipients of the Nobel Prize for Literature (1969, 2005) – to this day remain the two most discussed 'modern' playwrights and both the contemporary trends of 'in-yer-face theatre' and 'postdramatic theatre' since the 1990s have built upon the radical foundations of the theatre of the absurd. Both trends have emerged from the catatonic dissolution of identity in a theatre for a world without *telos* – in-yer-face theatre intensifying the verbal and physical cruelty present in Beckett and Pinter and the postdramatic theatre abandoning even the fragmentary shreds of character identity and plot that were left by the theatre of the absurd.

Beckett's later plays since the remarkable one-act *Play* (1962), such as *Not I* (1972) or his work for television, have proved more influential on post-dramatic theatre and the expansion of the formal repertoire of theatre than *Waiting for Godot* or his early plays. Pinter's prevalence in West End theatres, on the other hand, shows that there is at least a marginal possibility for subtextually rich, 'absurdist' forms to survive within the conventions and limited scope of commercial theatre.

Bibliography

Bibliographical Note

Beckett's work is intricately and interestingly connected to his French, English, American, and German publishing houses (Editions de Minuit, Faber & Faber, Grove Press, Suhrkamp). His texts are available in an American omnibus edition from Grove Press 2006, edited by novelist Paul Auster, who counts Beckett's among his greatest influences. The complete edition of his work is being republished in new editions by his English publisher Faber & Faber in 2011.

Primary Sources

Beckett, Samuel. 1998. *Waiting for Godot* [1952: *En attendant Godot*]. In: *The Complete Dramatic Works of Samuel Beckett*. London: Faber and Faber.

Pinter, Harold. 1978 [1965]. *The Homecoming*. In: *Plays: Three*. London: Methuen.

Annotated Bibliography

Batty, Mark. 2005. *About Pinter – the Playwright and the Work*. London: Faber and Faber.
> This critical study follows Pinter in roughly biographical structure; includes interviews with Pinter and many of his collaborators.

Billington, Michael. 2007. *Harold Pinter*. London: Faber and Faber.
> Revised edition of the official biography, first published in 1996, by a leading London theatre critic and friend of Pinter's; offers extensive readings of individual plays, too.

Connor, Steven (ed.). 1992. *New Casebooks:* Waiting for Godot *and* Endgame. *Contemporary Critical Essays*. Basingstoke: Macmillan.
> Marks the heyday of poststructuralist interpretations of Beckett.

Gale, Steven H. (ed.). 2000. *Critical Essays on Harold Pinter*. Boston: Hall.
> A useful collection of criticism and academic analysis, with three interviews, a section on Pinter's films and a bibliographical survey.

Gordon, Lois. 2002. *Reading Godot*. New Haven: Yale UP.
> A useful and recent analysis of Godot *that highlights the religious dimensions and also makes use of Beckett's German* Regiebuch *for his production at the Schiller-Theatre.*

Graver, Lawrence. 2004. *Beckett,* Waiting for Godot: *A Student Guide*. 2nd ed. Cambridge: Cambridge UP.
> There is no end of casebooks and guides to Waiting for Godot – relevant authors include Mark Taylor-Batty, Gerhard Knapp, Peter Boxall, Ursula Dreysse, and others; Graver's recently updated introduction represents numerous others.

Hartel, Gaby & Carola Veit. 2006. *Samuel Beckett*. Frankfurt/Main: Suhrkamp.

An accessible up-to-date introduction in German that highlights Beckett as a transmedia author.

Knowlson, James. 1996. *Damned to Fame: The Life of Samuel Beckett*. London: Bloomsbury.

The definitive, authorized biography, written by an intimate friend and knowledgeable critic of Beckett's.

Merritt, Susan Hollis. 1990. *Pinter in Play*. Durham/London: Duke.

A survey on existing Pinter criticism.

Pilling, James (ed.). 1994. *The Cambridge Companion to Beckett*. Cambridge: Cambridge UP.

A useful collection or introductory aspects of Beckett's entire work in 13 chapters.

Quigley, Austin. 1975. *The Pinter Problem*. Princeton: Princeton UP.

A significant turning point in Pinter criticism, focusing on his linguistic strategies.

Raby, Peter (ed.). 2001. The *Cambridge Companion to Harold Pinter*. Cambridge: Cambridge UP.

A representative collection; a number of essays discuss the 'political' turn of Pinter and apply postmodernist theories to his work, or address his status as theatre celebrity and his precarious generic pigeonholing as either 'absurdist' or 'kitchen-sink.'

Scott, Michael (ed.). 1986. *Harold Pinter*: The Birthday Party, The Caretaker, The Homecoming. Basingstoke: Macmillan.

A good overview over the 'classic' responses to Pinter, with the debate between Trussler and Esslin on The Homecoming.

Further Secondary Literature

"absurdity." *Online Etymology Dictionary*. Douglas Harper. <http://dictionary.reference.com/browse/absurdity> (last accessed: 6 Feb. 2011).

"absurd, adj. and n." *Oxford English Dictionary Online*. <http://www.oed.com/view/Entry/792> (last accessed: 8 June 2011).

Alighieri, Dante. 1833. *The Inferno of Dante*. London: C. Roworth and Sons, Bell Yard, Temple Bar.

Badiou, Alain. 2003. *On Beckett*. Alberto Toscano & Nina Power (transl. & eds.). London: Clinamen P.

Baker, William. 2008. *Harold Pinter*. London: Continuum.

Begley, Varun. 2005. *Harold Pinter and the Twilight of Modernism*. Toronto: U of Toronto P.

Bignell, Jonathan. 2009. *Beckett on Screen*. Manchester UP.

Bryden, Mary. 1998. *Samuel Beckett and the Idea of God.* Basingstoke/Hampshire: Palgrave Macmillan.
Burkman, Katherine H. & John L. Kundert. 1993. *Pinter at Sixty.* Bloomington: Indiana UP.
Calderwood., James L. 1992 [1986]. "Ways of Waiting in *Waiting for Godot.*" In: Steven Connor (ed.). *New Casebook on* Waiting for Godot *and* Endgame. Basingstoke: Macmillan. 29-43.
Camus, Albert. 1942. *Le Mythe de Sisyphe: Essai sur l'Absurde.* Paris: Les Éditions Gallimard.
Carter, Steven. 1997. "Estragon's Ancient Wound: A Note on *Waiting for Godot.*" In: *Journal of Beckett Studies* 6.1: 125-33.
Cohn, Ruby. 1962. *Samuel Beckett: The Comic Gamut.* New Brunswick: Rutgers UP.
Cronin, Anthony. 1997. *Samuel Beckett: The Last Modernist.* New York: Da Capo P.
Duckworth, Colin. 1967. "The Making of *Godot.*" In: Ruby Cohn (ed.). *Casebook on* Waiting for Godot. New York: Grove. 89-101.
Dukore, Bernard. 1962. "Didi, Gogo, and the Absent Godot." In: *Drama Survey* 1: 303-05.
Esslin, Martin. 1961. *The Theatre of the Absurd.* Garden City, NY: Doubleday.
—. 1976. *Pinter: A Study of His Plays.* Expanded Edition. New York: Norton Library.
Fletcher, John. 2006. *About Beckett.* London: Faber and Faber.
Foster, Verna A. 2004. *The Name and Nature of Tragicomedy.* Hants: Ashgate Publishing Limited.
Giesing, Michaela, Carola Veit & Gaby Hartel (eds.). 2007. *Das Raubauge in der Stadt: Beckett liest Hamburg.* Hamburg: Wallstein Verlag.
Gontarski, Stanley E. (ed.). 2010. *A Companion to Samuel Beckett.* Oxford: Blackwell.
Hall, Peter. 4 Jan 2003. "Godotmania". In: *The Guardian* <http://www.guardian.co.uk/stage/2003/jan/04/theatre.beckettat100> (last accessed: 6 Feb. 2011).
Harrison, Martin. 1998. *The Language of Theatre.* New York: Routledge.
Herren, Graley. 2007. *Samuel Beckett's Plays on Film and Television.* London: Palgrave Macmillan.
Krause, Mine. 2010. *Drama des Skandals und der Angst im 20. Jahrhundert: Edward Albee, Harold Pinter, Eugène Ionesco, Jean Genet.* Frankfurt/Main: Lang.
Lahr, John & Anthea Lahr (eds.). 1974. *Casebook on Harold Pinter's* The Homecoming. London: Davis-Poynter.
Maude, Ulrika. 2010. *Beckett, Technology and the Body.* Cambridge: Cambridge UP.
Mercier, Vivian. 1956. "Review of *Waiting for Godot.*" In: *Irish Times* 18 Feb.: 6.
Merritt, Penelope. "Wham bam! Thank you, Sam!" In: *Notes on* Waiting for Godot. <http://www.samuel-beckett.net/Penelope/Godot_intro.html> (last accessed: 22 June 2011)
Münder, Peter. 2006. *Harold Pinter.* Reinbek: Rowohlt.
Naismith, Bill. 2000. *Harold Pinter*: The Birthday Party, The Caretaker, The Homecoming. London: Faber and Faber.

Pinter, Harold. 1998. "Writing for the Theatre." In: *Various Voices: Prose, Poetry, Politics: 1948–2005*. 16-20.
—. 2005. "Art, Truth and Politics." <http://nobelprize.org/nobel_prizes/literature/laureates/2005/pinter-lecture.html> (last accessed: 22 June 2011).
"Pinteresque, adj." *Oxford English Dictionary Online*. <http://www.oed.com/view/Entry/144333> (last accessed: 8 June 2011).
Sick, Franziska (ed.). 2011. *Raum und Objekt im Werk von Samuel Beckett*. Bielefeld: transcript.
Temkine, Pierre. 2008. Warten auf Godot: *Das Absurde und die Geschichte*. Berlin: Matthes & Seitz.
Uhlmann, Anthony. 1999. *Beckett and Poststructuralism*. Cambridge: Cambridge UP.
Voigts-Virchow, Eckart. 2002. "Face Values – Beckett Inc., The Camera Plays and Cultural Liminality." In: Steven Connor, Daniela Caselli & Laura Salisbury (eds.). *Other Becketts*. Tallahassee/FL: Journal of Beckett Studies Books. 119-35.
—. 2009. "Shades of Negativity and Self-Reflexivity: The Reception of Beckett in German Literary Studies." In: Mark Nixon & Matthew Feldman (eds.). *The International Reception of Samuel Beckett*. New York/London: Continuum. 97-107.

20. POLITICAL DRAMA:
EDWARD BOND'S *SAVED* AND DAVID EDGAR'S *MAYDAYS*

ANETTE PANKRATZ

1. Political Drama after 1945: Anger and Agitprop

"All theatre is political" (Itzin 1980: x; Patterson 2003: 1; Kritzer 2008: 1). In the context of British theatre, however, the term 'political drama' denotes plays which explicitly aim at changing the world or at least at challenging the status quo. More often than not, the means advocated for doing so stem from a Marxist analysis of society which focuses on economics and hegemonic class structures (cf. McGrath 1981: 22; Beyer 1993: 307-9; Patterson 2003: 1-3).

The grand narrative about British political drama relies on three core dates: 1956, 1968, and 1979, the premiere of John Osborne's *Look Back in Anger*; the students' revolution and, last and worst, the beginnings of Thatcherism. Recent studies add two more dates: 1990, the end of Communist regimes in Eastern Europe ushering in a climate of uncertainty (cf. Pattie 2006: 392-95), and 2001, the terrorist attacks on the World Trade Center and the subsequent war on terror (cf. Sierz 2007: 203). Although these dates provide pithy and memorable labels (and will also be used as basis for the following brief survey), they cover up the complexities, contradictions, and fuzzy edges. They imply abrupt changes, mythical origins, and equally clear-cut endings. But history is not a well-made play and British political drama did not emerge out of thin air in 1956. There already was a tradition of political drama associated with Bernard Shaw's plays, and, more importantly, with German theatre of the 1920s and 1930s (cf. Patterson 2003: 1; Sierz 2007: 206).

In his seminal book *Das politische Theater* (1929), German director Erwin Piscator stipulates a propagandistic theatre which revolutionizes the masses: "Die Aufgabe des revolutionären Theaters besteht darin, die Wirklichkeit zum Ausgangspunkt zu nehmen, die gesellschaftliche Diskrepanz zu einem Element der Anklage, des Umsturzes und der Neuordnung zu steigern" (1929: 132). This entails a deconstruction of the traditional fourth-wall realism, the integration of film, projection, puppets, and the use of scaffolding or a conveyor belt instead of the classical stage. At about the same time, Piscator's "alter Freund" (ibid.: 211) Bertolt Brecht worked on a politicized theory of epic theatre with similar approaches. In contrast to the traditional theatre, which, according to Brecht, keeps its audience in docile passivity, epic theatre makes people think by means of alienation effects: "Die neuen Verfremdungen sollten nur den gesellschaftlich beeinflußbaren Vorgängen den Stempel des Vertrauten wegnehmen, der sie heute vor dem Eingriff bewahrt. [...] Das lange nicht Geänderte nämlich scheint unänderbar" (Brecht 1993: 81; cf. Kritzer 2008: 17).

In Britain before the Second World War, a socialist, avant-garde author like Wystan Hugh Auden and members of the British Workers' Theatre Movement knew and employed Piscator and Brecht's new approaches (cf. Craig 1980b: 31 f.; Cave 1999: 34), but they only became popular to a broader public after the visit of the Berliner Ensemble in London in 1956. The same year also saw the "revelation of John Osborne" (Kenneth Tynan qtd. from Craig 1980a: 11), the critically acclaimed premiere of *Look Back in Anger* (cf. Patterson 2003: 27; see chapter 18).

The play's success and the subsequent emergence of the new wave of politically committed playwrights resonate with the changes in British culture at large. The postwar consensus between Conservatives and Labour with its agreement on a Keynesian mixed economy and the welfare state had brought material security to the members of the working class. Like most European states, Britain, too, experienced a phase of affluence in the 1950s, which made capitalism no longer look like a threat, but a promise. Hence, Conservative Prime Minister Harold Macmillan proclaimed: "The classwar [sic!] is over and we have won" (qtd. from Lacey 1995: 11). Macmillan's triumphalism was aided by the Cold War. Soviet politics had discredited Communist positions. After the Soviet invasion of Hungary in 1956, 7,000 members left the British Communist Party (ibid.: 35). In this situation, the New Left advocated an undogmatic form of socialism positioned beyond Labourite consensus and Stalinist discipline. This was a stance many of the New Wave dramatists sympathized with or even openly supported (ibid.).

The extent to which this manifested itself in their plays, however, varied. *Look Back in Anger* transposes the well-made play to a then unconventional setting, a bedsit in the Midlands; its protagonist Jimmy Porter with his angry rants against the establishment and a yearning for "good, brave causes" (Osborne 1983 [1956]: 84) represents a merely "proto-political social rebellion" (Lacey 1995: 30). Arnold Wesker's so-called "chicken-soup trilogy," *Chicken Soup with Barley* (1958), *Roots* (1959), and *I'm Talking about Jerusalem* (1960), negotiates more explicitly socialist options. The trilogy draws a panoramic portrait of the Kahns, a Jewish and staunchly socialist working-class family, from the time of the Spanish Civil War (1936-39) to the end of the 1950s. The initial opposition between an impoverished working class and the wealthy upper classes that makes socialism seem as the only viable solution gradually gives way to disillusionment with the policies of both the Labour Party and the Soviet Union as well as the lure of consumerism: "There's nothing more to life than a house, some friends, and a family" (Wesker 1973: 62; cf. Mengel 2002: 81; Beyer 1993: 310).

Despite its novelty value and cultural impact, the New Wave was criticized for "turning authentic working-class experience into satisfying thrills for the bourgeoisie" (McGrath 1981: 11), or rather, for the upwardly mobile younger generation who – like its angry hero Jimmy Porter – tried to leave their origins and rise into the establishment (cf. Craig 1980a: 13). Alternatives could be found in John Arden's disturbing and decisively counter-realistic *Serjeant Musgrave's Dance* (1959) or at the Theatre Royal, Stratford East. The collective of the Theatre Workshop around Littlewood,

MacColl, and Goorney offered Brechtian epic and popular working-class entertainment, merging alienation and the music hall, and they explicitly targeted a working-class audience (cf. McGrath 1981: 44-46; Lacey 1995: 135-36). The Theatre Workshop left its mark with productions of the classics, premieres of Brendan Behan's *Quare Fellow* (1956) and *The Hostage* (1958) and collaborative new plays like *Oh What a Lovely War* (1963). But due to its innovative productions, the troupe soon became patronized by (and dependent on) the middle classes and the West End. Other playwrights and companies began to look for more radical options. Fuelled by non-parliamentarian protest movements such as the Campaign for Nuclear Disarmament (CND) and the protests against the Vietnam War formed around the middle of the 1960s, the new political theatre gained momentum around 1968 and flourished in the 1970s (cf. Itzin 1980: xiv). Constantly merging and changing groups like CAST (Cartoon Archetypical Slogan Theatre), 7:84, Red Ladder, Joint Stock, or Portable Theatre used agitprop and French situationism in order to mobilize people who normally did not frequent the theatre (ibid. 14; Craig 1980a: 15; Bull 1984: 18). If people did not bother to go to the theatre, the theatre came to them. Fringe groups toured the country and played in pubs, clubs, or community centres. This necessitated minimal sets and intentionally non-elaborate forms of presentation (cf. Bull 1984: 16). As Roland Muldoon, one of the founding members of CAST, explains: "We soon learned that we had to work fast, cut fast, to get at least a laugh a minute, if we were to stop the bastards going for a beer in the middle of it. This became the pattern of our work" (qtd. from Itzin 1980: 14).

Despite these common theatrical and political grounds, fringe authors did not form a homogeneous front. First, because in the 1970s politics also covered questions of sexuality, gender, ethnicity, and regional identity, and different fringe groups focused on different special issues – as names like Monstrous Regiment, Siren Theatre Company, Gay Sweatshop, or Black Theatre Co-operative indicate (cf. Pattie 2006: 388). Secondly, authors differed in their artistic approaches. While McGrath and 7:84 intentionally steered clear of all institutionalized forms of theatre and oriented themselves towards a working-class audience with clearly socialist messages (Bull 1984: 19), Trevor Griffiths, Howard Brenton, Howard Barker, David Hare, and David Edgar began to see the shortcomings of agitprop, collaboration, and working for companies which were running on a shoestring. As David Edgar remembers: "I was fed up with seeing agitprop plays that were messy, and I was also increasingly thinking that the politics you could get across were very crude, whereas the world about us was getting more complicated" (qtd. from Bull 2006: 442). The big national companies seemed more appropriate venues for staging complex, sophisticated plays with a large cast. Moreover, the Royal Court, the Royal Shakespeare Company, and others had appropriated the attitudes and techniques of the fringe to a certain extent, creating spaces for experimental drama and commissioning fringe authors and directors such as Max Stafford-Clark (cf. Kritzer 2008: 5). Thus, parts of the fringe moved closer to the mainstream.

With the victory of the Conservatives in the general elections of 1979, the belief in the efficacy of theatre as political weapon declined (ibid.: 6). Many fringe companies had to close due to cuts in funding, justified by Thatcher's neo-liberal ideology and motivated by her neo-Victorian values. Nevertheless, as Howard Brenton asserted, politically committed left-wing playwrights, "are fertile and optimistic in [their] macro overview" (qtd. from Müller 2001: 83) and took a pronounced oppositional stance against Thatcher and all she stood for. State-of-the-nation plays such as Churchill's *Serious Money* (1987) or Brenton and Hare's *Pravda* (1985) provided critical 'macro overviews,' offering portraits of society on a large canvas and often in a 'culinary' style (cf. Reitz 1993: 48).

2. Edward Bond, *Saved*

Edward Bond (*1934) started as a member of the Royal Court writer's group, a latecomer to the New Wave associated with Osborne, Wesker, Arden, and Delaney, and a dramatist who was to create a critical stir which went beyond the famed reception of *Look Back in Anger*. With their surface realism, Bond's early plays – *The Pope's Wedding* (1962) and *Saved* (1965) – suggest a classification as 'kitchen-sink' plays, realistically depicting working-class life, if it were not for their deliberate minimalism and the intensity of violent images. The third play, *Early Morning* (1968), features Queen Victoria as lesbian cannibal as well as her ahistorical Siamese twin sons Arthur and George. Bond remained stylistically versatile in the Shakespeare adaptation *Lear* (1971), for example, the parodist *Restoration* (1981) or the agitprop satire *Passion* (1971). The forms may vary, but the political message always stays the same, namely that socialism is the only 'rational' alternative to the present capitalist system (cf. Innes 1992: 157).

In his political commitment to socialism, Bond clearly stands in the tradition of Brecht, although their theatrical methods differ (cf. Spencer 1992: 6). As Brechtian alienation "can deteriorate into an aesthetic style" (Bond qtd. from Köppen 2004: 76), prone to not fulfilling its aim of making people think, Bond wants to "emotionally commit the audience" (ibid.). In order to do so, he employs so-called aggro-effects, usually representations of violence (cf. Spencer 1992: 8), which serve as symptoms of societal repression. According to Bond, human beings are not born violent, they are socialized in a competitive capitalist culture and thereby become violent. Violence "is caused not only by physical threats, but even more significantly by threats to human dignity. That is why, in spite of all the physical benefits of affluence, violence flourishes under capitalism" (Bond 1997: 13). The stoning to death of a baby in *Saved* (*S*) serves as a case in point.

Saved presents characters from the affluent working class who seem to profit from the political status quo. All are employed and live in restricted, but more or less comfortable conditions. "There's plenty of left-overs" (*S* 46) and there's "[p]lenty [of tea] in the pot" (*S* 52) in the family of Harry, Mary, and Pam. Radio, TV, cinema, and the jukebox provide plenty of entertainment. The younger generation earns enough to buy cigarettes and fashionable clothes. Going out after work and having sexual relationships signal the spirit of a care-free permissiveness. "This is the life." (*S* 23) Len tells Pam when they engage in heavy petting on the sofa. In the course of the play, however, it becomes clear that under this veneer, the characters' lives are shaped by bleakness and barrenness created by the very same structures which guarantee a certain amount of material well-being (cf. Hay & Roberts 1980: 39).

This is indicated by the tensions between Len, Pam, and Fred. Pam leaves Len for Fred and has his baby. While Len stays on as a lodger in Pam's family, who takes care of both her and the baby, Fred cultivates his reputation as a hunter who has as many women as possible (cf. *S* 65), degrading Pam to a mere "lay" (*S* 61). She in turn takes out her frustrations on the baby. Its murder is foreshadowed in scene 4. Pam prepares to go out with Fred while the rest of the family watch TV and have dinner. "*Slowly a baby starts to cry. It goes on crying without a break until the end of the scene*" (*S* 46). Everyone notices the noise: Mary complains; Len worries about the child's future, but none of the characters tries to calm the baby down. This scene indicates that "the child in the pram is dead long before scene six" (Hay & Roberts 1980: 51). Later in the park, Pam has sedated the baby, in order to win Fred back: "Won't wake up till t'morra. It won't disturb yer" (*S* 68). But he is indifferent to her pleas and to the baby, which she leaves behind. Lack of concern also motivates the young men's torturing of the child, "their cruelty is cold, unfeeling" (Hirst 1985: 52). They push the pram around and start torturing the baby, pulling its hair, smearing its face with faeces. The baby turns into an animal, a despicable other, an object:

MIKE. [...] no feelin's.
PETE. Like animals. [...]
MIKE. What a giggle!
PETE. Cloutin's good for 'em. I read it. [...]
COLIN. Looks like a yeller-nigger.
BARRY. 'Onk like a yid. [...]
MIKE. Reckon it'll grow up an idiot.
PETE. Or deformed. (*S* 77 f.)

So far, Fred has ignored the torture of his child. But taunted by Pete, he eventually joins in the stoning. After the brutal communal murder the young men leave the park producing a "*curious buzzing*" (*S* 82), which symbolizes their metamorphosis into "some animal state" (Bond qtd. from Hay & Roberts 1980: 50).

Saved refrains from putting the blame on the young men alone, but confronts the audience with a series of ambivalences. Everyone appears equally as victim and perpetrator; as responsible individual and member of a dehumanizing society. This is to make the audience wonder "'How did this come about?'" (Hay & Roberts 1980: 39). Tentatively, the play itself offers some answers. When we first see the young men in the park in scene 3, their banter already contains the aggression and tendency to objectify anyone deemed inferior or weaker. Pete boasts that he ran a child over with his lorry:

> 'E come runnin' round be'ind the bus. Only a nipper. Like a flash I thought right yer nasty bastard. Only ten or twelve. I jumps right down on me revver an' bang I got 'im on me off-side an' 'e shoots right out under this lorry comin' straight on. (*S* 38)

Pete gets away with it, because "[a]ccidents is legal" (ibid.); a smoothly running economy and making profit are more important than the life of a child. Barry tries to move up in the hierarchy of the group by bragging about his time in the army: "I done blokes in. [...] More'n you 'ad 'ot dinners. In the jungle. Shootin' up the yeller-niggers. An' cut 'em up after with the ol' pig-sticker" (*S* 39). Rather unsurprisingly, Fred moves to the top of the hierarchy after his release from prison. His friends cheer him on and he dominates the conversation in the café (cf. *S* 108-15; Jenkins 1993: 105).

This negligent attitude towards human lives is not restricted to the younger generation. The 68-year-old Harry likewise cherishes reminiscences of the army where institutionalized violence and strict hierarchies provided "peace an' quiet" (*S* 128) and a perspective: "Yer never killed yer man. Yer missed that. Gives yer a sense a perspective. I was one a the lucky ones" (ibid.; cf. Hay & Roberts 1980: 55). But the war also destroyed the lives of Harry and Mary. Their son was killed in the park by a bomb, an event which brought aggressive quiet to the couple (cf. *S* 34); a quiet that also erupts in physical violence (cf. *S* 117-20).

The web of references to the world of work, education, war, and the army connects the young men's murder to generally accepted structural and physical violence. *Saved* depicts a society based on competition and difference, on always finding someone weaker to dominate and to exploit. As Mary explains to Len: "things don't turn out too bad. There's always someone worse off in the world" (*S* 98). If one's superiority is not obvious, it has to be created by verbal and physical means, as in the aggressive jokes of Len directed against Harry or in the comic routine offered by Colin, Barry, and Mike:

> COLIN. It was in the park, yer 'onour!
> MIKE. This girl come up t'me.
> COLIN. An' drags me in the bushes.
> BARRY. Yer 'onour.
> *He laughs.*
> COLIN. I knew she was thirteen.
> MIKE. But she twisted me arm.
> COLIN. An' 'er ol' dad 'd bin bashin' it off for years.
> BARRY. Yer 'onour.
> *He laughs.* (*S* 41)

This parody of a court scene can be associated with Fred's reactions before he has to face trial for the murder of the baby. Again, Fred rejects all responsibility and accuses Pam, "[y]er ruined my life, thass all!" (*S* 83). He even invents a 'bloody gang roamin'' and claims that "[t]he bloody police don't do their job" (*S* 85). Pam in turn attacks Len: "PAM (*pointing to* LEN). 'E started this!" (*S* 115). Just as everyone hears the crying baby, but does nothing about it, most of the characters externalize their guilt by putting the blame on someone else.

Len is the only one who feels responsible. He watched the stoning of the baby and did nothing about it, "[w]ell, I should a stopped yer" (sc. 7.86). He is also the only one who wants to find out why Fred committed the murder and what it felt like. Moreover, he still cares about Pam, even when she violently rejects him, and supports her when she is rejected by Fred. Len's ambivalent position as catalyst of violence and passive (often voyeuristic) observer disqualifies him as representative of a moral norm. Instead he serves as stand-in of the (conventional) audience member who also merely watches and refrains from action (cf. Spencer 1992: 35; Lacey 1995: 149; Mangan 1998: 15). Nevertheless, his behaviour in the very last scene of the play indicates a "social stalemate" which, according to Bond, makes *Saved* an "irresponsibly optimistic" play (Bond 1977: 309). Despite a violent row, Harry can persuade Len to stay in the house. The next day, we see him mending a chair while the rest of the family are involved in their quotidian tasks.

Saved premiered as a private club performance, because Bond had refused to change the play according to the demands of the Lord Chamberlain's office. It had stipulated several cuts, the entire scenes 6 and 9 (a sexually charged scene between Len and Mary) among them. Despite the performance for members of the English Stage Society only, the play created an immediate public debate about the representation of violence. When the Lord Chamberlain's office sued the Royal Court for producing *Saved* without a licence, this elicited a public debate on stage censorship (Hay & Roberts 1980: 41 f.; Mangan 1998: 11). It was to take three more years and two more – supposedly incriminating – plays, Osborne's *A Patriot for Me* (1965) and Bond's *Early Morning*, until theatre censorship was officially abolished. This ties in with the emergence of the fringe.

3. David Edgar, *Maydays*

Although Bond occasionally wrote for fringe companies, he remained attached to the big national companies. It was younger playwrights like David Edgar, who profited from the abolishment of stage censorship in 1968 and the mushrooming of the fringe. Edgar started out at the beginning of the 1970s with agitprop plays in collaboration with Portable Theatre, General Will, and 7:84, fusing journalistic inquiry with popular genres and epic techniques (cf. Bull 1984: 155 f.; Swain 1986: 16). *Tedderella* (1972), for example, is a satirical mock-pantomime on Conservative Prime Minister Edward ("Ted") Heath. *Dick Deterred* (1972) stars US president Richard "Tricky Dick" Nixon in a parodic rewriting of Shakespeare's *Richard III*. But gradually Edgar grew sceptical about the efficiency of agitprop in a world which "was getting more complicated" (qtd. from Bull 2006: 442). *Destiny* (1976), *Mary Barnes* (1978), and *The Jail Diary of Alby Sachs* (1978) were staged by the Royal Shakespeare Company and the Royal Court, and mark his move towards social realism, psychological drama, and a broad scope both in terms of time covered and characters employed (cf. Swain 1986: 193).

Maydays (1983, *M*) fits into this phase of Edgar's development as playwright. Its political thrust is influenced by the changes in Britain after 1979. While Bond's *Saved* enquires into the reasons for violence and makes the audience ask why a baby could have been stoned to death, *Maydays* tries to find out how Margaret Thatcher could have come to power and why people turn from socialism to autocratic conservatism. It is "a big public play on a big public theme. Its territory is nothing less than the map of post-war politics" (Billington, qtd. from Swain 1986: 283), covering the time between 1945 and the early 1980s, set in the Soviet Union, Hungary, Great Britain, and the United States. In order to cover this vast terrain, Edgar adapts Brechtian and filmic techniques, frequent changes of locale and intercutting of scenes (cf. ibid.: 297; Bull 2006: 445). Instead of alienation and de-personalization, the play uses a psychologically grounded realist framework, a "'dialectical' tension between subjective and objective factors" (Innes 1992: 182), focusing on the lives of three characters, Jeremy Crowther, Martin Glass, and Pavel Lermontov. The fervent enthusiasm of the young socialist Jeremy at the end of the Second World War gives way to disillusionment, compliance with the norms of the establishment, and the adoption of conservative values. Martin's political positions develop similarly over the course of the 1960s and 1970s. This cyclical movement from revolutionary youth to the belief in authority in middle age (cf. Schäffner 1988: 294) is somewhat countered by the subplot focusing on Lermontov. He, too, loses faith in Communism. First doubts arise in 1956, when he is confronted with insurgents in Hungary. After the suppression of the Czechoslovakian protests in 1968, he actively works against the Soviet regime and is put into a labour camp. Released from imprisonment in the late 1970s, he goes to exile to Great Britain where he is courted by the Conservative Committee for Liberty. In contrast to Jeremy and Martin, however, he refuses to cooperate, because he realizes the structural parallels between Soviet oppression and the Committee's promotion of "Authority" (*M* 120; 134), which boils down to the persecution of critics as "traitors," "subverters," and "parasites" (*M* 3.6.134). Concomitant to Lermontov's resistance is the countercultural opposition of Martin's former lover Amanda.

The title *Maydays* ambiguously and ironically refers to both the socialist May Day celebrations and the international distress signal (cf. Bull 1984: 223). Moments of elation, marked by versions of Lenin's dictum that "revolutions are festivals" (*M* 1.1.13; 1.8.54), are dialectically juxtaposed with moments of crisis. The bureaucratic and autocratic socialism of the Soviet Union is directly discredited by the suppression of the Hungarian uprising and the Prague Spring. Indirectly, references to "Kronstadt," the violent putting down of a sailor's revolt by the Bolshevics in 1921, and "Red Barcelona," the overthrow of anarchists by communists in the Spanish Civil War, serve as *leitmotifs* to indicate the suppression of socialist initiatives by socialists (cf. Swain 1986: 297; Schäffner 1988: 288).

Just as in Bond's *Saved*, post-war affluence and consumerism have a negative impact. Where *Saved* operates with implications and allusions, *Maydays* explicitly foregrounds their detrimental consequences, most directly so in Phil's manifesto:

One.
Karl Marx was wrong. The working class has not become more immiserated and thus more conscious of itself. It has become richer and less conscious of itself.
Two.
What happened is that capitalism has mutated. Mass production has led to an increasing, stultifying, numbing universe of things. A stereo in every fridge. A family saloon in every tumble-dryer. (*M* 2.1.63)

The play focuses on the attempts to find socialist solutions for this cultural change. Like Osborne's Jimmy Porter, Jeremy Crowther feels that "we were fifteen years too young" for fighting in the Spanish Civil War and the Second World War (cf. 1.3.30) and like Wesker's Kahn family, his belief in socialism is severely shattered by the events in Hungary (cf. 1.3.29). Martin embodies the post-war generation. When still at school he joins the liberal and mainly middle-class CND, and gets more radical at the end of the 1960s in the protests against the Vietnam War. In the 1970s, Martin is looking for directions. One option is the anarchism promoted by Phil:

Five.
The old left is trapped in old ideas. The real revolutionaries in our society are blacks, gays and women, disaffected youth who demand the right not to be forced to work, the so-called mad refusing to accept the "logic" of an insane world. Six. [...]
To unite these groups we must provide examples of the possibility of change. The bullet and the bomb are not the real revolution but they are real metaphors of revolution. Seven.
An action of guerilla warfare serves to show that the power of the state can never be invincible. (*M* 2.1.63f.)

Martin veers between Phil's anarchism, Amanda's counter-cultural opposition and the strict party discipline of the Socialist Vanguard led by James Grain. For Grain, the "festival of the oppressed and the exploited" has to be based on authoritarian hierarchies, following and quoting Lenin, "we shall be traitors and betrayers of the revolution, if we do not use the festive energy of the masses to wage a ruthless and self-sacrificing struggle for the direct and decisive path" (*M* 1.5.36).

When Martin is expelled from the Socialist Vanguard, he gradually starts turning his back on the entire socialist movement. Unlike Jeremy Crowther, he does not succumb to the fascist catchphrases of the Committee for Liberty, which tries "to reassert the basic, fundamental instincts of the nation [...] the reassertion of authority" (*M* 3.6.133). Nevertheless, he joins a Thatcherite think tank and moves into his parents' house, working for the local church community which only supports the "conspicuously needy" (*M* 3.7.143). *Maydays* ends in subdued optimism. Amanda and Martin meet again. The feminist, socialist, and pacifist works in a protest camp which clearly reflects Greenham Common (cf. Swain 1986: 293). And Soviet dissidents continue working against an oppressive system.

4. Conclusion

British theatre survived Thatcherism and the Premiership of Tony Blair; but it could not change the world. After the Fall of the Wall and the end of the Cold War, it no longer attempted to do so, either. As literary agent Mel Kenyon puts it: "To write these big political plays full of certainties and resolution is completely nonsensical in a time of fragmentation. When you want to create a political piece of drama, there's no point in mimicking the form of resolution and certainty in a time of complete uncertainty" (qtd. from Saunders 2008: 20). Hence, established writers forego clear-cut political messages. Churchill's *Mad Forrest* (1990), Brenton's *Berlin Bertie* (1992), and Edgar's *Pentecost* (1994) emphasize the instability and insecurity of the situation after the regime changes in Europe. For a while, Hare turned towards realist psychological drama (e.g., *Skylight* [1995] or *Amy's View* [1997]) in which the political becomes the private; Churchill engaged with postdramatic forms which represented the *status quo* as an eerie and surreal nightmare (e.g., dystopian *Far Away* [2000]) (cf. Sierz 2007: 208).

The new generation of post-Thatcher dramatists foregrounded uncertainties and violence. Although critical of the *status quo*, Mark Ravenhill's *Shopping and Fucking* (1996) or Sarah Kane's *Blasted* (1995) no longer assumed to know the solutions (see chapter 25) – as Bond had done in his foreword to *Saved* –, nor did they offer grand narratives about the metamorphoses of socialist ideas in the vein of Edgar's *Maydays*. Instead they offered "little stories" (Ravenhill 1996: 12.64) based on "personal pain rather than public politics" (Sierz qtd. from Saunders 2008: 5), full of deconstructions of meanings and 'in-yer-face' violence (cf. Saunders 2008: 3). Critical assessment of these new plays varies. While Aleks Sierz and Kenneth Urban concede a political component, "demolishing the simple binary oppositions that hold society together" (Sierz 2001: 9) and challenging ethical norms (cf. Urban 2008: 39), Klaus-Peter Müller amongst others emphasizes their solipsism, pessimism, and de-politicized glamorization of violence (cf. Müller 2002: 15; Saunders 2008: 5-8).

Dramatists became more overtly political again at the end of the 20th century. Howard Brenton and Tariq Ali's *Ugly Rumours* (1998) and Alistair Beaton's *Feelgood* (2001) satirized New Labour as Thatcherism with spin (cf. Tönnies 2003). Verbatim plays based on interviews, newspaper reports, and political documents critically dealt with the politics of Blair's governments in both domestic (cf. Hare's *The Permanent Way* [2003]) and international affairs. After 9/11 and Britain's support for the wars in Afghanistan and Iraq, playwrights took an explicitly oppositional stance emphasizing that "politics matters because politics kills" (Edgar 2010: n. pag.). This was discernible in Harold Pinter's 2005 Nobel Prize speech as well as in Hare's *Stuff Happens* (2004), Robin Soans' *Talking to Terrorists* (2005), or Victoria Brittain and Gillian Slovo's *Guantanamo* (2004).

While verbatim theatre lost steam, the critical political attitude continues at the end of the decade, invigorated by the global economic crisis and Britain's ongoing search for a national identity. Brenton's *Never Had It So Good* (2008) once again returns to history to examine the gestation of 1950s affluence. Hare's *The Power of Yes* (2009) and Lucy Prebble's *Enron* (2009) analyse the pitfalls of a globalized economy. Jez Butterworth's *Jerusalem* (2009) confronts the audience with an energetic drug dealer and 'gyppo' at the centre of a multi-layered portrait of England between Morris dancing and asbos. In an article for the *Guardian* published in February 2010, David Edgar announces yet another new wave of political playwrights which are about to change the world. Again.

Bibliography

Primary Sources

Bond, Edward. 1997. *Plays: 1: Saved; Early Morning; The Pope's Wedding*. London: Methuen.
Edgar, David. 1983. *Maydays*. London: Methuen.

Annotated Bibliography

Bull, John. 1984. *New British Political Dramatists*. Basingstoke: Macmillan.
By now classical study on politically committed playwrights of the 1970s and 1980s with a focus on Brenton, Hare, and Edgar.
Craig, Sandy. 1980a. "Reflexes of the Future: The Beginnings of the Fringe." In: Sandy Craig (ed.). *Dreams and Deconstructions: Alternative Theatre in Britain*. Ambergate: Amber Lane P. 9-29.
—. 1980b. "Unmasking the Lie: Political Theatre." In: Sandy Craig (ed.). *Dreams and Deconstructions: Alternative Theatre in Britain*. Ambergate: Amber Lane P. 30-48.
Sometimes polemical surveys of the fringe and alternative theatre from the perspective of a practitioner trying to come to grips with the changing situation in Britain after Thatcher's new regime.
Hay, Malcolm & Philip Roberts. 1980. *Bond: A Study of His Plays*. London: Eyre Methuen.
Monograph on the plays combining interviews with Bond, accounts of the production history, and interpretations.
Hirst, David L. 1985. *Edward Bond*. Houndmills: Macmillan.
A survey of the plays.
Itzin, Katherine. 1980. *Stages in the Revolution*. London: Methuen.
Broad overview of the sprawling fringe companies, their theatrical strategies and political positions.

Kritzer, Amelia Howe. 2008. *Political Theatre in Post-Thatcher Britain*. London: Palgrave Macmillan.

Focusing on In-Yer-Face drama and putting it in the framework of political theatre.

Mangan, Michael. 1998. *Edward Bond*. Plymouth: Northcote House/British Council.

Concise survey of Bond's career as a playwright.

Painter, Susan. 1996. *Edgar: The Playwright*. London: Methuen.

The monograph analyses Edgar's developments as playwright and the related revisions of his political attitudes.

Patterson, Michael. 2003. *Strategies of Political Theatre: Post-War British Playwrights*. Cambridge: Cambridge UP.

Survey of politically committed socialist theatre from Arnold Wesker to the early work of Caryl Churchill.

Roberts, Philip. 1985. *Bond on File*. London/New York: Methuen.

Production history of the plays with the most important critical reactions.

Saunders, Graham. 2008. "Introduction." In: Rebecca D'Monté & Graham Saunders (eds.). *Cool Britannia? British Political Drama in the 1990s*. Houndmills: Palgrave Macmillan. 1-22.

Like Kritzer's monograph an attempt to integrate the new In-Yer-Face playwrights into a broader framework.

Schäffner, Raimund. 1988. *Politik und Drama bei David Edgar: Eine Studie zum politischen Gegenwartstheater in England*. Essen: Blaue Eule.

The theory-based monograph analyses Edgar's developments as playwright and the related revisions of his political attitudes.

Sierz, Aleks. 2007. "'Political What-Do-Ya-Call-It': British Drama and Its Politics." In: Sabine Volk-Birke & Julia Lippert (eds.). *Anglistentag 2006 Halle: Proceedings*. Trier: WVT. 203-13.

Concise, sometimes polemical look at recent British drama.

Spencer, Jenny S. 1992. *Dramatic Strategies in the Plays of Edward Bond*. Cambridge: Cambridge UP.

Seminal work on Bond's œuvre, combining formal analysis with sociopolitical contextualizations.

Swain, Elizabeth. 1986. *David Edgar: Playwright and Politician*. Frankfurt/Main: Peter Lang.

The monograph analyses Edgar's developments as playwright and the related revisions of his political attitudes.

Further Secondary Literature

Beyer, Manfred. 1993. "Politisches Theater und Medien: Ansätze zu einer Gattungspoetik." In: Klaus-Peter Müller (ed.). *Englisches Theater der Gegenwart: Geschichte(n) und Strukturen*. Tübingen: Narr. 307-37.
Brecht, Bertolt. 1993. "Kleines Organon für das Theater." In: Bertolt Brecht. *Schriften 3: 1942-1956*. Werner Hecht et al. (eds.). Frankfurt a.M.: Suhrkamp. 65-97.
Bull, John. 2006. "Left in Front: David Edgar's Political Theatre." In: Mary Luckhurst (ed.). *A Companion to Modern British and Irish Drama: 1880-2005*. Oxford: Blackwell. 441-53.
Cave, Richard Allen. 1999. "Twentieth-Century English Theatre and Drama." In: Jürgen Kamm (ed.). *Twentieth-Century Theatre and Drama in English: Festschrift for Heinz Kosok on the Occasion of his 65th Birthday*: Trier: WVT. 17-54.
Edgar, David. 2010. "Enter the New Wave of Political Playwrights." *The Guardian* 28 Feb. <http://www.guardian.co.uk/stage/2010/feb/28/david-edgar-new-political-theatre> (last accessed: 22 June 2011).
Elsom, John. 1976. *Post-war British Theatre*. London: Routledge & Kegan Paul.
Innes, Christopher. 1992. *Modern British Drama: 1890-1990*. Cambridge: Cambridge UP.
Jenkins, Anthony. 1993. "Edward Bond: A Political Education." In: James Acheson (ed.). *British and Irish Drama since 1960*. Houndmills: St Martin's P. 103-16.
Köppen, Ulrich Rainer. 2004. *Edward Bond und die Postmoderne*. Mainz: Phil. Diss.
Lacey, Stephen. 1995. *British Realist Theatre: The New Wave in its Context 1956-1965*. London: Routledge.
McGrath, John. 1981. *A Good Night Out: Popular Theatre: Audience, Class and Form*. London: Methuen.
Mengel, Ewald. 2002. *Das englische Drama des 20. Jahrhunderts: Eine Einführung in seine Klassiker*. Tübingen: Stauffenburg.
Müller, Klaus Peter. 2001. "British Theatre in the 1980s and 1990s: Forms of Hope and Despair, Violence and Love." In: Bernhard Reitz & Heiko Stahl (eds.). *What Revels are in Hand? Assessments of Contemporary Drama in English in Honour of Wolfgang Lippke*. Trier: WVT. 81-107.
—. 2002. "Political Plays in England in the 1990s." In: Bernhard Reitz & Mark Berninger (eds.). *British Drama of the 1990s*. Heidelberg: Winter. 15-36.
Patterson, Michael. 2006. "Edward Bond: Maker of Myths." In: Mary Luckhurst (ed.). *A Companion to Modern British and Irish Drama: 1880-2005*. Oxford: Blackwell. 409-18.
Pattie, David. 2006. "Theatre since 1968." In: Mary Luckhurst (ed.). *A Companion to Modern British and Irish Drama: 1880-2005*. Oxford: Blackwell. 385-97.
Piscator, Erwin. 1929. *Das politische Theater*. Berlin: Adalbert Schultz Verlag.
Rabey, Ian David. 1986. *British and Irish Political Drama in the Twentieth Century*. Houndmills: Macmillan.

Reitz, Bernhard. 1993. *The Stamp of Humanity: Individuum, Gesellschaft und die Entwicklung des englischen Dramas nach 1956*. Trier: WVT.
Sierz, Aleks. 2001. *In-Yer-Face Theatre: British Drama Today*. London: Faber and Faber.
Tönnies, Merle. 2003. "'New Lingo – New Theatre'? New Labour's Rhetoric and Political Drama in Contemporary Britain." In: Merle Tönnies (ed.). *Britain under Blair*. Heidelberg: Winter. 169-91.
Urban, Kenneth. 2008. "Cruel Britannia." In: Rebecca D'Monté & Graham Saunders (eds.). *Cool Britannia? British Political Drama in the 1990s*. Houndmills: Palgrave Macmillan. 38-55.

21. BIOGRAPHY, HISTORY, AND MEMORY PLAYS:
BRIAN FRIEL'S *MAKING HISTORY* AND PETER SHAFFER'S *AMADEUS*

ANSGAR NÜNNING & SIBYLLE BAUMBACH

1. On the Rise of Biography, History, and Memory in Contemporary Drama

Interest in biography, history, and memory has become one of the hallmarks of contemporary British, and even more so Irish, drama. Especially since the end of the 1970s, there has been a remarkable rise of new kinds of revisionist, metafictional, and self-reflexive history and memory plays that testifies to a reawakened interest in both history and memory as themes and modes of dramatic representation, indicating "a broader cultural longing for – and inability to – return to and have done with, the past" (Malkin 1999: 10). The present chapter will examine postmodernist modes of representing the past in contemporary British plays as well as the changed attitudes to, and notions of, history and memory that such plays express.

The 'history play,' the 'memory play,' and plays that revolve around the biography of real persons are paradigmatic examples of what has come to be known as hybrid genres because they use fictional techniques to present historical facts and figures. Despite the fact that this hybrid quality has been one of the key features of the history play ever since its beginnings in Greek theatre with Aeschylus' *The Persians* (cf. Favorini 2008), and its proliferation in the Early Modern era (see chapter 5), the postmodernist history play, just like the memory play, distinguishes itself in many ways from the traditional model of the genre represented in the works of earlier playwrights, such as George Bernard Shaw, Stephen Phillips, and T.S. Eliot, who have displayed interest in the past.

In addition to the crossing of boundaries between fact and fiction, history and myth, historiography and historical drama, it is especially the self-conscious exploration of the different modes available for the recuperation of the past that has not only been a major concern in the theory of historiography but has also become one of the hallmarks of postmodernist history and memory plays. More often than not the emphasis in these plays is not on the past as such, but on the presence of the past in the present, or the reconstruction of the past from the point of view of the present. Rather than displaying any nostalgic interest in the past, contemporary British dramatists have deployed methods of fragmentation, demythologization, and deconstruction of 'history,' and thereby also raised questions of narrativizing history. The themes and forms of postmodern history and memory plays express revisionist notions of history, focusing on the perception of history in the minds of average people rather than on key historical events, and undermining the basic assumptions of positivist historiography.

Moreover, many postmodernist history and memory plays display that "crisis in representation" which Hans Bertens in his survey *The Idea of the Postmodern* has identified as the "common denominator to all these postmodernisms [...]: a deeply felt loss of faith in our ability to represent the real" (1995: 11). The high estimation in which playwrights who have specialized in history and memory plays, e.g. Brian Friel, Howard Barker, Edward Bond, Howard Brenton, David Edgar, Michael Frayn, and Peter Shaffer (see Krieger 1998: 145 ff. for an introductory overview), are currently held may in part be attributed to the fact that the blurring of genre distinctions has opened up new possibilities for representing history, biography, and memory on stage. Many history and memory plays exhibit textual features that are, by common consent, characteristic of postmodernist literature, while displaying an interest in dramatic storytelling that is not usually associated with either drama or postmodernism. On the one hand, they are often characterized by temporal discontinuity, fragmentation, indeterminacy, a juxtaposition of numerous competing accounts of the past, decentring of 'great' historical events, intertextuality, metafictionality, and reflexivity. On the other hand, they often use dramatic, narrative, and performative features as means of representing or staging biography, history, and memory.

The main goals of this chapter are to give a brief outline of a typology and poetics of postmodern history plays and memory plays, providing an overview of both their main generic features and the different kinds of generic variants that have emerged over the last three decades. While refraining from making any sweeping generalizations about postmodernism, this chapter will survey the range of British history plays and memory plays, from the thematic innovations of revisionist history plays and memory plays that present history in the decentred and subjective manner associated with the *histoire des mentalités* (cf. Scanlan 1990: 10) to metahistorical plays, or historiographic metadrama, and metamnemonic plays that serve to foreground the dynamics of remembering rather than events lying in the past. These developments will be further illustrated by an exemplary interpretation of two plays that represent many of the new trends, Brian Friel's *Making History* (1989) and Peter Shaffer's *Amadeus* (1979).

2. History Plays and Memory Plays: Definitions, Generic Features, and Different Kinds

Located on the border between historiography and literature, fact and fiction, contemporary history plays and memory plays (as well as plays that are concerned with biographical subjects) have shown a pronounced tendency to cross boundaries of genre distinctions. The resulting proliferation of hybrid genres and new generic variants bears witness to the fact that a dichotomy between fact and fiction has of late been called into question. Yet the ways in which genre conventions are blurred in contemporary drama are so multifarious that it does not make much sense to subsume all the plays in question under one label, be it history plays or memory plays.

Definitions of the genre known as history plays usually focus on the representation and dramatization of past historical events or, in a somewhat looser sense, the impact of these events on the lives of the *dramatis personae*. By contrast, memory plays are not so much concerned with delineating the past as they are with the dynamics of remembering. The term 'memory play' was coined by the American playwright Tennessee Williams in connection with his non-realistic drama *The Glass Menagerie* (1945), in which the audience experiences the past as it is remembered by the main character. Especially since the 1970s, there has been a great increase in plays preoccupied with questions of memory "both in terms of their *thematic* attention to remembered (or repressed pasts), and in terms of the plays' 'memoried' *structures*" (Malkin 1999: 1). In contrast to history plays, memory plays often include one (or several) narrator(s), who recollect(s) events in the past, which are represented in contradictory images, destabilized perspectives, overlapping or echoing voices, and other deconstructive techniques, such as repetition, conflation, and regression.

Given the great number of differences in themes and techniques in contemporary history plays and memory plays, a typology is needed that takes into account both the thematic innovations and the dramatic devices that distinguish different kinds of these subgenres from one another. For convenience sake, the various traditional and postmodern manifestations of the genre may be organized under typological rubrics, such as 'documentary history plays,' 'realist history plays,' 'revisionist history plays,' 'metahistory (or metahistorical) plays,' and implicit and explicit forms of 'historiographic metadrama.' Although the documentary history play and the realist or traditional history play belong to the group of generic hybrids which integrate factual material, it is the remaining three types that are of particular interest for anyone trying to come to terms with generic innovations in contemporary British drama. Revisionist history plays rewrite history, but, in contrast to what has come to be known as 'historiographic metafiction' (cf. Hutcheon 1988), they lack any elements that break the aesthetic illusion and foreground the fictionality of a text or a play. In this respect, many recent history plays resemble the postmodernist historical novel, which, according to McHale, is revisionist in two senses: "First, it revises the *content* of the historical record, reinterpreting the historical record, often demystifying or debunking the orthodox version of the past. Secondly, it revises, indeed transforms, the conventions and norms of historical fiction itself" (1987: 90). It often does so by violating one or even all of the constraints on the insertion of reality references that realist fiction adheres to. McHale has shown that in the traditional history play, the insertion of historical facts is governed by a number of constraints: "the 'dark areas' constraint," "a constraint on anachronism," and a third constraint which postulates that the "fictional world obeys real-world physics and logic" (ibid.: 87 f.). In contrast to the traditional history play, postmodernist variants of the genre tend to foreground the seam between the fictional version of the past delineated in a play and historical reality in various ways.

As far as the content is concerned, revisionist history plays have extended the conventional boundaries of the traditional history play in a number of significant ways.

They have increasingly incorporated those thematic domains that such recent historiographic developments as the history of mentalities, women's history, oral history, history from below, and the history of everyday life (*Alltagsgeschichte*) deal with. The formal innovations concern the revision and transformation of the realist conventions which predominated in historical drama up to the 1960s. The adaptation of postmodern dramatic techniques has changed the history play into new kinds of revisionist or 'metahistory plays.' Revisionist history plays are inspired by the wish to rewrite history, particularly from the point of view of those all too long ignored by traditional historiography. One of the most important innovations in contemporary British historical drama is the tendency toward marginalizing the great events of history and highlighting instead the experience of ordinary human beings. Plays like David Hare's *Plenty* (1978) focus on the lives, manners, and morals of those that historiography tended to overlook rather than on the historic victor. By focusing on "the ex-centrics, the marginalized, the peripheral figures of fictional history" (Hutcheon 1988: 114), revisionist history plays present "a decentred view of history" (Scanlan 1990: 10). Frank McGuiness' *Observe the Sons of Ulster Marching Towards Somme* (1985), Tom Murphy's *Famine* (1968), and David Edgar's *Destiny* (1976) provide typical examples of this revaluation and inversion of centre and periphery. The revisionist impact of revisionist plays, such as those by David Hare and Howard Brenton, for instance, also depends on formal properties: in their fictional explorations of Britain's imperial past, such literary devices as time-structure, the semanticization of material possessions, the use of recurring metaphors, and the inversion of roles, attitudes, and beliefs undermine the ideological justification of the British mission. Revisionist history plays tend to make historical events and persons peripheral to a fictional plot and to focus instead on everyday aspects of past reality.

The impulse to rewrite history from the points of view of those whom traditional historiography tended to ignore becomes particularly apparent in some history plays by female playwrights (cf. Kramer 2000). Like other recent women's history plays and memory plays, Caryl Churchill's *Cloud Nine* (1979) and *Top Girls* (1982), and Timberlake Wertenbaker's *Our Country's Good* (1988) and *The Grace of Mary Traverse* (1989) attempt to supplement those incomplete and partial accounts of the past which systematically ignore the viewpoints and roles of women. Instead of contenting themselves with reconstructing particular areas of women's history, however, these plays exemplify a specifically feminist approach to history, politics, gender, and historiography. They focus on such feminist issues as women's rights movements, the sexual double standard, women dying in childbirth, and the inequality of men's and women's education. Approaching the past from a feminist point of view, these revisionist history plays describe and polemicize against not only the discrimination of women in former periods, but also the thoroughness of the erasure of women from the historical record. Like many other revisionist history plays, these postmodernist texts incorporate hitherto neglected themes and explore new modes for the representation of history in fiction.

It is the intricate structure of many contemporary history plays and memory plays rather than their content, however, that offers the best example of the plays' revisionary historical interest. Instead of merely revising the content of the official historical record, another innovative type of historical drama, namely metahistory or metahistorical plays, explores, revises, and transforms the formal conventions of the traditional history play. In contrast to historiographic metafiction which addresses problems related to the writing of history explicitly in metafictional comments, metahistory plays focus on the continuity of the past in the present, the interplay of different time-levels, forms of historical consciousness, and the recuperation of history.

Metahistory plays and memory plays, just like recent metadrama, in general (cf. Hauthal 2009), represent significant innovations in the treatment of history as a literary theme because what they highlight is the process of historical reconstruction and the protagonists' consciousness of the past rather than a represented historical world as such. Instead of portraying a historical world on the diegetic level of the characters, metahistory plays are generally set in the present but are concerned with the appropriation, revision, and transmission of history. Such plays typically explore how characters try to come to terms with the past and how to relate the past to the present, making key historiographical issues a matter for self-conscious literary examination. Metahistory plays and memory plays portray the past as liable to the distortions that subjective reconstructions and recollections entail. What is highlighted in these plays are the historiographical endeavours of the protagonists living in the present, rather than the past itself.

Two further features that characterize many metahistory plays are what can be called 'semanticization of space' and dense 'intertextual networks.' Contemporary history plays and memory plays incorporate a great number of 'echoes' of the national past that will resonate with the educated spectator or, as it were, reader. Through the numerous intertextual allusions that are woven into his plays' settings, characters, and incidents, Friel, for instance, formally foregrounds Ireland's cultural heritage. The persistent use of almost every conceivable mode of intertextuality keeps reminding the reader of how literature and other works of art have contributed in significant ways to defining a sense of cultural nationality.

Any discussion of the broad spectrum of contemporary history plays and memory plays would, of course, be incomplete without a consideration of the existence of historiographic metadrama, which is the dramatic equivalent of historiographic metafiction, and which explicitly undermines the conventional borders between historiography and fiction. According to Hutcheon, the self-conscious reworking of documentary material in contemporary fiction is a key characteristic of the postmodern, which "effects two simultaneous moves. It reinstalls historical contexts as significant and even determining, but in so doing, it problematizes the entire notion of historical knowledge" (1988: 89). Historiographic metafiction inscribes and analyses its mimetic engagement with the past in order to enquire into the epistemological status of history, historical explanations, and historiography. The basic confrontation that characterizes postmodernism, Hutcheon maintains, is that of "documentary historical actuality" with "formalist self-reflexivity and parody" (1989: 7). Using history as both a reference to the real past world and as a discursive construct, historiographic metafiction "differs substantially from the use of history in the traditional history play where history, as a group of facts which exists extra-textually and which can be represented as it 'really was,' is never in question" (Lee 1990: 35).

Among the other contemporary history plays and memory plays that have significantly transformed the conventions of the traditional history play are such metahistoriographic works as Friel's *Making History*. Still other writers, like Howard Brenton and David Hare, have experimented with innovative modes of not only representing the past in drama, but of questioning the very representability of history. In Brenton's *H.I.D. (Hess is Dead)* (1989), which is devoted to exploring the death of Hitler's deputy Rudolf Hess, the process of constructing events through history is at stake. In the quest for what truths are 'hid' in Hess' suicide, the play implicitly puts key concepts of positivist historiography like objectivity, unity, continuity, causality, and linear teleology under scrutiny.

Given the multitude of different forms, it is useful to differentiate between the various forms that historiographic metadrama – just like the different types of metafiction (cf. Wolf 1993: 230-59) – may take. It may either be explicit, that is, it may use the devices of metafictional reflection to self-referentially explore the epistemological, methodological, and linguistic problems connected with any attempt to construct coherent accounts of the past, or implicit. In the latter case, its metahistoriographic concerns are incorporated formally in the structure of the play and its performance. Implicit forms of historiographic metadrama are represented by those postmodernist history plays and memory plays whose structure and dramatic techniques reflect the insights of modern theories of history. The polyphonic and fragmentary structure of Samuel Beckett's *That Time* (1975), *Endgame* (1956), or *Krapp's Last Tape* (1958), for instance, emphasizes the discrepancy between the real past and the remembered version of that past, between events and their representations. The inability to grasp and narrate the complex processes that make up historical reality is implicitly expressed through the juxtaposition of different characters' heterogeneous observations on the key events of the play which remain enigmatic. The multiperspectival structure and the montage of texts from different genres draw attention to the distorting effects of selecting sources, to the historian's problem of having to rely on scanty evidence, to the partiality, contradictoriness, unreliability, and questionable authenticity of historical sources and documents, and to the close affinity between history and story.

The impossibility of synthesizing contradictory accounts of the same course of events serves to undermine the belief that historical processes can ever be objectively known. By presenting randomly incompatible versions of different witnesses, many of the plays mentioned above, just like those discussed in greater detail in section 3, illustrate that (wo)man's models of history do not mirror any particular aspects of a past reality. Instead of one authentic representation of the past, the audience is confronted with a plurality of competing versions.

As opposed to implicit or structural variants, explicit forms of historiographic metadrama overtly discuss epistemological and methodological problems of reconstructing the past: historiographical issues are directly addressed by characters, often first-person narrators. With the benefit of hindsight, a good case might be made for Friel's *Making History* being an early forerunner of this new hybrid genre of 'metahistoriographic drama' since its metafictional questioning of the conventions of historiography anticipates many of the concerns and dramatic strategies that have been identified by Hutcheon and others as characteristics of historiographic metafiction.

By undermining the notion of historical truth, historiographic metadrama calls into question the ontological boundary between fact and fiction, the real and the imaginary, and suggests a profound scepticism of man's ability to acquire objective knowledge of the past with metahistoriographic reflections foregrounding the interpretive role of the historian. The implication is that historiography is inevitably a process of subjective construction. What emerges in contemporary history plays and memory plays, then, is a pattern of retrospective projections. Despite the overt scepticism, however, it is not the factual existence of past events that these plays call into question, but only man's ability to ever know the true course of history. Both Friel's *Making History* and Shaffer's *Amadeus* are by now famous cases in point since they abound with reflections on the selectivity and constructivity of memory, and the unbridgeable gulf that separates the present from the past, historiography from bygone events.

3. 'History and Historiography in the Making': Exemplary Interpretations of Brian Friel's *Making History* and Peter Shaffer's *Amadeus*

The construction of history and the risk of oversimplification and mystification in the process of 'recording' the past take centre stage in Brian Friel's *Making History* (*MH*), which premicred at the Guildhall in Derry on 20 September 1988. The play focuses on a pivotal moment in Irish history, the defeat at the Battle of Kinsale in 1601, and the subsequent fall of the Gaelic aristocracy. It revolves around the Earl of Tyrone, Hugh O'Neill (1550-1616), the chief leader of the Irish clan, who led an Irish and Spanish alliance against the army of Queen Elizabeth I, aiming to drive the English out of Ireland. The four scenes of the two-act play capture different stages of O'Neill's life: first we meet him at his home in Dungannon, Ireland in late August 1591, the night after the 41-year-old Catholic Irishman married his third wife, the Protestant Mabel Bagenal, who is not only 21 years his junior, but an 'upstart,' to boot: the daughter of new Elizabethan settlers and sister of the Queen's Marshall in Ulster. Then there is a time leap of about a year, in which Mabel has converted to Catholicism and the battle looms on the horizon. The second act sets in "[a]*bout eight months later* [...] *somewhere near the Sperrin mountains*" (*MH* 43) after the rebellion is crushed. On top of the political defeat, the fugitive O'Neill experiences a personal tragedy when he learns that his wife and newborn son died in childbirth. The final scene takes us to Rome, "*many years later*" (*MH* 54), where the now exiled hero spends his sunset years, his temper bitter, his body in decay, and confronted with a history that is not his own.

To an even greater extent than Friel's earlier play *Translation* (1980), which also deals with Ireland's ambiguous and troubled past, more precisely with the decline of the Irish language, *Making History* explores the relationship between fact and fiction, language and reality, and dramatizes the transfer, transformation, and 'bringing across' (*trans-latere*) of the past into the present. The play experiments with linguistic, temporal, political, cultural, and religious boundaries and the crossing thereof, while illustrating the loss and gain experienced in the transfer. Shifting between momentary snapshots of O'Neill's life – suggesting that "[m]ost history is private, uncelebrated, unobserved" (Pine 1990: 212) – and reports of the political environment that are carried into the private space, the action moves between the private and the public. The linchpin keeping these different strands together is the protagonist, who serves as mediator and translator, caught "between two opposing worlds, seeking [...] a defeated Gaelic culture and an advancing English civilization" (Connolly 1993: 163). His hybrid identity is introduced linguistically in his shifting from the dominant "*upper-class English accent*" (*MH* 1) to his native Tyrone accent in moments of anger. Questions of identity and hybridization are central issues in this play, as suggested by the key imagery of culture and cultivation, which is introduced in the first scene when we meet O'Neill in his home, arranging flowers, and is further developed in the following scene when Mabel's sister Mary brings seeds from her homeland to Dungannon in the hope of persuading her to come home.

Making History is not only the main theme and concern of the play: it is also an appeal, a challenge, and a command to the audience, who are involved in the reconstruction of the past insofar as they have to fill in the blanks between these snapshots of O'Neill's life to piece together his (hi-)story. The play centres on and is framed by a 'history' of O'Neill, which is announced in the first scene and read out by its author, the Catholic Archbishop, and self-appointed biographer, Peter Lombard, before the curtain falls. By dramatizing the beginning of Lombard's early, hagiographic account of O'Neill's life (which preceded Sean O'Faolain's famous biography of 1942) and including a historiography within a historiographic play, Friel succeeds in taking the process of 'making history' to centre stage.

As its ambiguous title already serves to show, Friel's plays subtly explores the double meaning of the phrase 'making history,' referring to both "history in the making" and to "historiography in the making," to quote Elisabeth Wesseling's formulations (1991: 135, 120). In doing so, this fine exemplar of historiographic metadrama not only reflects upon problems and constraints involved in historical research and narration, *Making History* also foregrounds "the constitutive role of the imagination in producing versions of history" (ibid.: 120). The question of what the historian's functions and responsibilities are is explicitly discussed by the characters; as early as the first scene, the protagonist expresses his discomfort with the proposed 'history:'

> O'NEILL. But you'll tell the truth?
> LOMBARD. I'm no historian, Hugh. I'm not even sure I know what the historian's function is – not to talk of his method. [...] Maybe when the time comes my first responsibility will be to tell the best possible narrative. Isn't that what history is, a kind of story-telling? [...] Imposing a pattern on events that were mostly casual and haphazard and shaping them into a narrative that is logical and interesting. (*MH* 8)

As this example serves to illustrate, the dialogue, in a slightly anachronistic fashion, revolves around some of the key problems discussed by metahistorians like Hayden White (1978). The idea of the narrative quality and inevitable distortion that comes with historical work is presented as part of the deal. Eventually, Lombard discloses his true motives and abandons the idea of an objective 'truth' in favour of a greater purpose:

> Think of this as an act of *pietas*. Ireland is reduced as it has never been reduced before – we are talking about a colonized people on the brink of extinction. [...]. Now is the time for a hero. Now is the time for a heroic literature. So I am offering Gaelic Ireland two things. I'm offering them this narrative that has elements of myth. And I'm offering them Hugh O'Neill as a national hero. (*MH* 67)

Another time might have given rise to another history. In presenting a purpose-built narrative, the historian serves the political needs of his time, culture, and society. After the battle is lost, O'Neill's 'history' becomes the foundation upon which a future Gaelic Ireland can be created: the making of a national hero welds its people together. For O'Neill to be installed as an unblemished Irish patriot, who at the time of the Counter-Reformation leads his people in a war of faith against heretical foreign forces, his actions have to be presented as a heroic crusade before they are positioned in a text, and perpetuated in a constructed narrative – a mythologized past flagged as history. What O'Neill qualifies as "a lie" (*MH* 65) is defended by Lombard as "[m]erely a convention. [...] You lost the battle – that has to be said. But the telling of it can still be a triumph" (*MH* 65). In Lombard's history, quite unlike in Friel's drama, there is no room for the love relationship with the passionate Mabel nor for anti-heroic images of an aging, impoverished, bitter protagonist, such as are presented in the final scene of *Making History*. Friel's O'Neill is tortured by 'his' biography that is incongruous with the past and fails to translate his character and his story. His pleading to assign Mabel a leading role is to no avail. Asserting that one history can only accommodate one hero, Lombard suggests that Mabel will eventually get a story of her own ("[i]t will be a domestic story Hugh; a love story," *MH* 69). "[I]n the overall thing" (*MH* 69), however, in the glorified account of O'Neill's life, there is no room for her. Instead, Lombard proudly engages in "the first public recital of *The History of Hugh O'Neill*" (*MH* 70), which drowns out O'Neill, who is in tears by the time the lights are dimmed: "Mabel, I am sorry ... please forgive me, Mabel ..." (*MH* 71). The hero's final words are "both an apology and an excuse" (Pine 1990: 213). Even though Lombard proposed to "rewrite it in any way you want" (*MH* 66), O'Neill never interfered in the process of 'making history,' but connives in what he knows to be "a lie" (*MH* 65).

By presenting 'his' story of O'Neill, in which the love relationship with Mabel plays a leading part, rather than 'history,' Friel challenges Lombard's account and follows a desideratum expressed by the historian O'Faolain, who suggested how O'Neill's history should be written:

> If anyone wished to make a study of the manner in which historical myths are created he might well take O'Neill as an example ... a talented dramatist might write an informative, entertaining, ironical play on the theme of the living man helplessly watching his translation into a star in the face of all the facts that had reduced him to poverty, exile and defeat. (O'Faolain 1942: 280 f., qtd. from Connolly 1993: 160)

The way in which Friel's play makes history not only adds to the postmodern notion that all narrative records, fictional or historical, are ideological constructs, but makes a strong case "for the primacy of fiction," offering "the prospect of liberation from the demands of history" (Pelletier 2006: 76). As Friel writes in a programme note:

> *Making History* is a dramatic fiction that uses some actual and some imagined events in the life of Hugh O'Neill to make a story. I have tried to be objective, faithful – after my artistic fashion – to the empirical method. But when there was a tension between historical 'fact' and the imperative of the fiction, I'm glad to say I have kept faith with the narrative. For example, even though Mabel, Hugh's wife, died in 1591, it suited my story to keep her alive for another ten years. [...] I remind myself that history and fiction are related and comparable forms of discourse and that an historical text is a kind of literary artefact. (Programme *Making History*, Field Day 1988)

Friel frees himself from historical constraints. Even in his note on his revisionist history play he intensifies the notion that history is continuously in the making and that there is no one history, but, instead, many histories: His remark on having granted Mabel an extra ten years breaks not only with the chronology suggested by history but also with the one observed in his play: the historical Mabel died in 1595, not in 1591, nor in 1601 (when the historical battle of Kinsale took place); in the play, however, the fight is over and Mabel deceased by spring 1593. By this "subtle practical joke at the expense of the hapless academic fact checker" (Connolly 1993: 160), Friel confers the authority over history to drama, which not only selects "the best possible narrative" (*MH* 8), but stages history in performance, and offers a seemingly unmediated *hic and nunc* encounter with O'Neill. Friel draws together the different strands of history and historiography in a play that brings history to life through a performance which is both a reflection and a product of 'making history.'

Like Friel's play, Peter Shaffer's acclaimed two-act memory play *Amadeus* (*A*), which opened in London in 1979, shares both a revisionist interest in challenging and debunking the official historical record, and a concern for metahistorical and metabiographical issues like "the partiality of historical knowledge" (Wesseling 1991: 120), "the unreliability of the sources" (ibid.: 122), and the inevitable selectivity, narrativity, and dubious reliability of any historical or biographical narrative. In Shaffer's play, which is both a fictional dramatic biography and a metabiographic play (cf. the typology outlined by Kramer 2000), the two strands of 'history in the making' and 'biography, or even hagiography, in the making' are knit together at the outset of the action, while the historiographic process and the demystification of a historical figure is taken one step further. The starting point is the rumour surrounding the mysterious and untimely death of Wolfgang Amadeus Mozart (1756-1791), who was said to have been poisoned by his rival Antonio Salieri (1750-1825). The latter fuelled the suspicion surrounding himself by writing a confession of the deed 30 years after Mozart's death, and by attempting to commit suicide. At the outset of the play, set in 1823, Salieri's name resounds throughout the stage, as the Venticelli, the 'little winds,' purvey the rumour, inducting the audience into the Viennese gossip of the time. Then the aged Salieri introduces himself directly to 'his' audience, announcing an exclusive performance of "[his] last composition, entitled *The Death of Mozart; or, Did I Do It?*" (*A* 17). In the mode of epic theatre, the fourth wall is broken and the audience made aware that they are watching a play. Unlike in Brechtian theatre, however, Shaffer does not use epic elements for any didactic or ideological purpose but puts them into service to dramatize Salieri's subjective recollection of the past, introduce him as unreliable narrator, and impede audience identification with the (historical) figures, thus supporting a critical reflection on the story presented. While the latter, which expands and alters historical data, is clearly marked as fictional, it is rooted in the audience's historical awareness, which provides the foundation for Salieri's version and makes it work.

Through the play's complex communication structure (cf. Nünning 1994), Salieri is established as narrator and 'translator' of events. He is situated on the same time-level as the audience and guides them through his dramatized flashbacks, which constitute the main part of the play. Salieri reconstructs the past while, at same time, commenting on it. Even though the play continuously crosses temporal boundaries, integrating the past into the present, the present into the past, the fictional illusion is never broken, as Salieri's comments are part of his process of remembering and the past is constituted only by his recollection of it. It is Salieri, therefore, who holds together the different levels of time and space opened up in the play. He introduces the audience to the action and bids them farewell in the final scene, thus providing a frame of reference, which intensifies the notion that all that happened in-between sprang from his personal memory. This notion is intensified by rapid shifts in time (and place), omissions, foreshadowing, and flashbacks in this metamnemonic play, which further points to the episodic memory on which the action is based.

As suggested by Werner Huber and Hubert Zapf,

> the structure of the play resembles that of an *interpretive act*: Salieri is interpreting his relationship with Mozart during (apparently) the last hour of his life (November 1823), for an audience of the future (his 'Confessors' [...]), in the form of a continuous interplay between narrative-reflective interpretations and scenic reconstructions of the past (from 1781 onward) culminating in the death of Mozart (1791). (1984: 301)

The relationship of story and storyteller differs from *Making History* insofar as Salieri does not have to endure 'history' being imposed upon him, but – at least within the logic of the play – gets to tell 'his' story on the last night of his life (cf. *A* 17). From the very beginning, the audience are prepared for the unfolding of a story that is based on highly subjective, selective, and relative recollections, and is invited to put Salieri's account to the test and compare it with their own historical knowledge. In other words: the audience, which Salieri addresses as "Ghosts of the Future" (*A* 14), are involved in the process of making history.

Amadeus does not provide a chronological account of Mozart's life. Instead, this metabiographic memory play is a (re-)collection of Salieri's most decisive memories of and intrigues against his despised rival, which, at the same time, marks his attempt at coming to terms with the past and justifying his actions. The night he met Mozart, Salieri recalls, "[t]hat night changed my life" (*A* 24). He confesses to the audience the "terrible and thrilling purpose" (*A* 61) his life acquired after perusing the genius' manuscripts, and goes on to tell how he slandered Mozart and how he resolved "to hasten him toward madness, or toward death" (*A* 104). As narrator, Salieri fulfils several functions within this memory play: he establishes a frame of reference for the audience and mediates the action, guiding their reactions to the dramatic flashback; he introduces characters, provides historical background information ("The year – to begin with – 1781. The age still that of Enlightenment," *A* 18); and establishes cross-references within the play ("We were *yet again* in the library of the Baroness Wald-städten," *A* 81). His limited knowledge as a narrator who is part of the story he presents comes to the fore when he starts speculating on other characters' intentions: "Would she come? I had no idea" (*A* 52). Salieri blurs the past, present, and future, blending the fictional time of 'his' story and the real time of the performance by addressing the audience ("You see how it was," *A* 63). At the beginning of act 2, for instance, Salieri, according to the stage directions, "*comes downstage and addresses the audience directly*" to announce, "[t]his is now the very last hour of my life. You must understand me. Not forgive. I do not seek forgiveness" (*A* 61). Occasionally, he lets his *dramatis personae* freeze, such as in his encounter with the enraged Constanze, who holds in her fury while Salieri discloses to the audience, "I would have liked her – oh, yes [...]. But I wanted nothing petty! ... My quarrel wasn't with Mozart – it was *through* him! Through him to *God*, who loved him so" before she "*runs from the room*" (*A* 63).

Throughout the play, Salieri longs to make the audience his confederates in his envious resentment towards Amadeus, the 'beloved of god.' It is to the spectators, his "*Amici cari*" (*A* 117), that the 'everyman' Salieri discloses his true motives ("I wanted Fame," *A* 16). He even involves them in his scheming: "How could I stop it? ... How could I block this opera of *Figaro*?" (*A* 61). When Mozart dies, Salieri seems to have achieved his aim, but the death of his rival backfires on him. Mozart's music is more popular than ever while Salieri lives to experience his downfall: "I must survive to see myself become ... *extinct*" (*A* 115). After his suicide attempt, Salieri, who now refers to himself as "Patron Saint of Mediocrities" (*A* 117), turns to the audience to release them with a benediction: "I absolve you all. Amen!" (*A* 118) Ultimately, however, it is the audience that has the power of absolution: they have to judge Salieri's character and weigh the remarks of this unreliable narrator against the scenic display of the action. For this reason, as Peter Hall remarks, the story is not presented "entirely through Salieri's eyes. There must be a tension between what the audience sees and what Salieri describes" (Hall 1984: 465).

"Did Salieri leave poisoned wine for Mozart, or was he content in tormenting him emotionally? ... What exactly did kill Mozart?" (Klein 1993 [1979]: 164). These questions are left unanswered by both history and the playwright. Instead of providing solutions, Shaffer stages a search for truth, which remains unresolved in Salieri's "changing images of memory" (*A* xii). Although many early reviewers felt appalled by his demythologization of Mozart (cf. Gelatt 1980), Shaffer's depiction of the genius' childish, irresponsible, and irreverent character and his "linguistic eccentricities" "follow[s] factual sources to a remarkable degree" (Gianakaris 1991: 129, 131). Some of these are "quoted verbatim" (*A* xvi) in the play. While in relation to Salieri's character Shaffer took some dramaturgical liberties, regarding Mozart there was little that he felt history had omitted, except "a serious emotional confrontation" (*A* xvi) between Salieri and Mozart. As Shaffer himself remarks, "there *needs* to be such a Scene [...]. The objection that no evidence exists for such an encounter is no excuse for not providing one" (*A* xvi).

Amadeus is a drama of genius and mediocrity, in music as in historiography. Ironically, the text of this metahistoriographic play itself poses similar questions and problems to historiographic accounts, as there is not one but multiple *Amadeus* (cf. *A* xvi-xxxiv). Shaffer, for instance, changed the openings for performances in British and American theatres, respectively. If one further takes into account that each performance is unique, the complexity of making history in drama gains yet another level. As Peter Hall remarked, "[s]cholars will have a merry time with the text of *Amadeus* in the future: there are so many versions – even published ones. They will be able to worry and fret over the differences well into this century" (*A* x f.).

To an even greater extent than *Making History*, Shaffer's play suggests that there is not one truth about the past, no one 'history,' but rather a plurality of conflicting (hi)stories, which are dependent on and constructed by various observers and historians. By exploring both "history in the making" (Wesseling 1991: 135) and "historiography in the making" (ibid.: 120), recent biography, history, and memory plays like Friel's and Shaffer's have not only dramatized and fictionalized their respective historical subjects, but also foregrounded some of the key issues and problems involved in any attempt to reconstruct the past and produce coherent versions of history.

4. Textuality, Constructivity, Narrativity: Postmodernist Attitudes to History

The broad range of new modes that have recently been used for representing the past and the multitude of generic crossovers should not obscure the fact that all of the postmodernist kinds of historical drama that have been identified have fundamental things in common. These similarities concern that complex of new attitudes to the experience and representation of history which is regarded as specifically postmodern. First, foregrounding the textual form through which history is mediated, these postmodernist history plays present a "world viewed in terms of 'textuality'" (Waugh 1984: 15): "What emerges [...] is history as text: history as personal reconstruction" (ibid. 107). These plays therefore illustrate one of the crucial insights of Fredric Jameson and Hayden White, namely that the events, personages, and material structures of the past are indistinguishable from the textual or medial forms of documentary representation:

> That history [...] is *not* a text, for it is fundamentally non-dramatic and non-representational; what can be added, however, is the proviso that history is inaccessible to us except in textual form, or in other words, that it can be approached only by way of prior (re)textualization (Jameson 1981: 82).

In addition, many recent biography, (meta)history and memory plays, and historiographic metadramas can be understood as plays about the reconstruction and recording of history, plays which illustrate Michel de Certeau's thesis that "the past is the fiction of the present" (1988: 10). By exposing the insurmountable gap between historical events and their narrative representations, contemporary biography, history and memory plays testify to what de Certeau regards as the central paradox of historiography, which applies just as well to the problems of biography:

> Historiography (that is, "history" and "writing") bears within its own name the paradox – almost an oxymoron – of a relation established between two antinomic terms, between the real and discourse. Its task is one of connecting them and, at the point where this link cannot be imagined, of working *as if* the two were being joined. (de Certeau 1988: XXVII)

Despite the fact, then, that the terms biography and historiography suggest that biographers and historians create a nexus between life or history and writing, contemporary biography, history and memory plays remind the audience that the gulf between the real past and discourse, between history as it is experienced and history as it appears in the form of the product of researchers' investigations is, in the end, unbridgeable. Moreover, the implications of the structure of contemporary biography, history and memory plays reflect a deep-rooted scepticism about the objective nature of biographical narratives and historiographic constructions and, even more so, about the ability of any biographer or historian to know the past by any other than textualized means. History will thus inevitably be re-written again and again and our (changing) views of the past can, as de Certeau observes, indeed be nothing but constructions projected from the present.

By crossing borders and blurring genres, contemporary biography, history, and memory plays continuously remind us of what Hayden White has demonstrated in his enquiries into the epistemological status of history, namely that historical discourse "*constitutes* the objects which it pretends only to describe realistically and to analyse objectively" (1978: 2). Contemporary history plays and memory plays can thus be read as an expression, in theme and form, of the constructivist view of historiography that the study of history is a method for the construction of coherent stories of the otherwise vacuous and elusive nature of the past, and that historiography is a dramatic process which does not reproduce the past, but is something we construct, just like the fictional worlds projected in the plays.

Bibliography

Primary Sources

Friel, Brian. 1989. *Making History*. London/Boston: Faber and Faber.
Shaffer, Peter. 2001 [1981]. *Amadeus*. New York, et al.: Harper Perennial.

Annotated Bibliography

Acheson, James (ed.). 1993. *British and Irish Drama since 1960*. Basingstoke/London: Macmillan.

A fine collection of 15 essays on British and Irish theatre, including essays on history plays by Brian Friel, Peter Shaffer, Howard Brenton, and Timberlake Wertenbaker.

Bertens, Hans. 1995. *The Idea of the Postmodern: A History*. London/New York: Routledge.

A brilliant, illuminating, and highly recommended guide to the characteristics, key theories, and critical debates of postmodernism.

Favorini, Attilio. 2008. *Memory in Play: From Aeschylus to Sam Shepard*. New York/Basingstoke: Palgrave Macmillan.

A useful survey of the history and development of memory plays.

Harben, Niloufer. 1988. *Twentieth-Century English History Plays: From Shaw to Bond*. Totowa, NJ: Barnes & Noble.

A helpful introduction to the genre including analyses of plays by George Bernard Shaw, Reginald Berkeley, T. S. Eliot, Robert Bolt, Peter Shaffer, John Osborne, and Edward Bond.

Hutcheon, Linda. 1988. *A Poetics of Postmodernism: History, Theory, Fiction*. London: Routledge.

A groundbreaking study on the cultural practice and theories of postmodernism.

Jameson, Fredric. 1981. *The Political Unconscious: Narrative as a Socially Symbolic Act*. Ithaca, NY: Cornell UP.

This highly influential study by the renowned American Marxist literary and cultural critic, which opens with the slogan 'always historicize,' explores the complex function of literature and the interpretative frameworks by which narratives are constructed.

Klein, Dennis A. 1993 [1979]. *Peter Shaffer*. New York: Twayne Publishers.

An excellent introduction to Shaffer's dramatic works; each chapter is devoted to one play and summarizes major criticism, sources, performance history, reviews, and critical analyses.

Malkin, Jeanette R. 1999. *Memory-Theater and Postmodern Drama*. Ann Arbor: U of Michigan P.

An insightful study of the representation of memory vs. history in postmodern theatre with a good introductory section and close readings of Samuel Beckett, Heiner Müller, Sam Shepard, Suzan-Lori Parks, and Thomas Bernard.

Peacock, Alan J. (ed.). 1993. *The Achievement of Brian Friel*. Gerrards Cross: Colin Smythe.

A collection of essays on Friel's dramatic art and his achievement in "Translating History" (S. Connolly, 149-63) and "Marking Time" (F. O'Toole, 202-14), and "The Use of Memory" (S. Heaney, 216-19).

Roche, Anthony (ed.). 2006. *The Cambridge Companion to Brian Friel*. Cambridge: Cambridge UP.

A collection of introductory essays to Friel's drama both as literary texts and in performance.

Further Secondary Literature

de Certeau, Michel. 1988. *The Writing of History*. New York: Columbia UP.

Connolly, Sean. 1993. "Translating History: Brian Friel and the Irish Past." In: Peacock 1993.149-63.

Gelatt, Roland. 1980. "Peter Shaffer's *Amadeus*: A Controversial Hit." In: *Saturday Review* Nov.: 11-14.

Gianakaris, Constantine John. 1991. "Fair Play? Peter Shaffer's Treatment of Mozart in *Amadeus*." In: Constantine John Gianakaris (ed.). *Peter Shaffer: A Casebook*. New York/London: Garland. 127-31.

Hall, Peter. 1984. *Peter Hall's Diaries*. John Godwin (ed.). London: Harper & Row.

Hauthal, Janine. 2009. *Metadrama und Theatralität: Gattungs- und Medienreflexion in zeitgenössischen englischen Theatertexten.* Trier: WVT.

Huber, Werner & Hubert Zapf. 1984. "On the Structure of Peter Shaffer's *Amadeus.*" In: *Modern Drama* 27: 299-313.

Hutcheon, Linda. 1988. *A Poetics of Postmodernism: History, Theory, Fiction.* New York/London: Routledge.

—. 1989. *The Politics of Postmodernism.* New York/London: Routledge.

Kramer, Stephanie. 2000. *Fiktionale Biographien: (Re-)Visionen und (Re-)Konstruktionen weiblicher Lebensentwürfe in Dramen britischer Autorinnen seit 1970. Ein Beitrag zur Typologie und Entwicklung des historischen Dramas.* Trier: WVT.

Krieger, Gottfried. 1998. *Das englische Drama des 20. Jahrhunderts.* Stuttgart: Klett.

Lee, Alison. 1990. *Realism and Power: Postmodern British Fiction.* London/New York: Routledge.

McHale, Brian. 1987. *Postmodernist Fiction.* London/New York: Methuen.

Nünning, Ansgar. 1994. "Be my Confessors! Formen und Funktionen epischer Kommunikationsstrukturen in Peter Shaffers *Amadeus.*" In: *Forum Modernes Theater* 9.2: 130-48.

Pelletier, Martine. 2006. "*Translations*, the Field Day debate and the re-imagining of Irish identity." In: Anthony Roche (ed.). *The Cambridge Companion to Brian Friel.* Cambridge: Cambridge UP. 66-77.

Pine, Richard. 1990. *Brian Friel and Ireland's Drama.* London/New York: Routledge.

Scanlan, Margaret. 1990. *Traces of Another Time: History and Politics in Postwar British Fiction.* Princeton: Princeton UP.

Waugh, Patricia. 1984. *Metafiction: The Theory and Practice of Self-Conscious Fiction.* London: Routledge.

Wesseling, Elisabeth. 1991. *Writing History as a Prophet: Postmodernist Innovations of the Historical Novel.* Amsterdam/Philadelphia: Benjamins.

White, Hayden V. 1978. *Tropics of Discourse: Essays in Cultural Criticism.* Baltimore/London: Johns Hopkins UP.

Wolf, Werner. 1993. *Ästhetische Illusion und Illusionsdurchbrechung in der Erzählkunst: Theorie und Geschichte mit Schwerpunkt auf englischem illusionsstörenden Erzählen.* Tübingen: Niemeyer.

22. FEMINIST THEATRE:
PAM GEMS' *QUEEN CHRISTINA* AND CARYL CHURCHILL'S *TOP GIRLS*

BEATE NEUMEIER

1. Feminist Theatre

The term 'feminist theatre' has always been a contested area, raising questions about politics and aesthetics. The more inclusive and seemingly less politically charged terms 'women's drama' or 'women playwrights,' however, have had an equally debated history. The evaluation of these terms is "determined by the material, political, cultural, geographical, and theatrical circumstances of the historical moment," as Elaine Aston und Janelle Reinelt (2000: 3) have argued persuasively. While "women playwrights have broadened the agenda of British drama" since the 1960s (Stephenson & Langridge 1997: ix), British theatre still is a male-dominated business with a majority of male writers and artistic directors.

Of course women have played an important role in English theatre as actresses since the Restoration period, when the tradition of boy actors playing the female parts came to an end. This is also the time when the plays of the first professional woman writer, Aphra Behn (1640-1689), were being staged, although the history of women playwrights actually begins with Elizabeth Cary (1585-1639), whose plays, such as *The Tragedy of Mariam* (1613), were, however, never performed during the late Renaissance period. Despite Aphra Behn's success as a Restoration playwright it remained difficult for women writers to make it in the theatre business. It was only in the 20th century and in the context of the women's movement and changing gender roles that women dramatists gained a lasting voice and visibility.

The Cambridge Companion to Modern British Women Playwrights starts out with a chapter on early 20th-century suffrage drama, but it was only during the 1950s and early 1960s that a new generation of women playwrights like Shelagh Delaney, Ann Jellicoe, and Margaretta d'Arcy gradually began to change the theatrical landscape. However, "the major changes took place" in the 1970s in the context of Second Wave feminism (cf. Wandor 2000: 63). Women playwrights like Michelene Wandor, Caryl Churchill, and Pam Gems aligned themselves with the Women's Liberation movement, discussing the issues raised in their work. New possibilities for women in the theatre opened up with the foundation of women's theatre groups, such as the Women's Company and the Women's Theatre Group (now renamed the Sphinx) in 1974, followed by Monstrous Regiment in 1975 (operative until 1993), Gay Sweatshop's women's company in 1977, Siren and Clean Break in 1979, and Theatre of Black Women in 1982. Moreover, a number of important, innovative, and "politically conscious" (Reitz 1998: 151) established theatres like the Royal Court started supporting plays by women, many of whom considered themselves socialist-feminist dramatists.

The common association of the terms women playwrights and feminist theatre with the Women's Liberation movement thus is connected to the increasing visibility of women playwrights from the 1960s onwards and to the foundation of feminist theatre collectives in Britain enabling young female dramatists to get their plays produced. Experiments with an all-female cast, with cross-dressing, or multiple casting, as in Churchill's *Top Girls* (1982) and *Cloud Nine* (1979), were encouraged by the collaboration with women's theatre collectives. Moreover, after the abolition of censorship (1968) the use of gender-specific locations, like a public women's lavatory (Maureen Duffy, *Rites* [1969]) or a public women's bath (Nell Dunn, *Steaming* [1981]), allowed for an unprecedented innovative exploration of questions of the interrelation between the public and the private, the personal and the political.

In this context Susan Bassnett has marked out "a series of quite distinct shifts of emphasis" in the development of feminist theatre:

> [...] mid-way through the 1970s, women's theatre began to shift away from its initial socialist agenda to an exploration of broader debates about gender and sexuality. [...] By the early 1980s, gay and lesbian theatre was increasingly important [...]. This emphasis on the body, which was directly connected to feminist politics in general, was also accompanied by a growing interest in exploring theatre form. (Bassnett 2000: 73)

In terms of politics, however, the 1980s was also the decade, when the "promise of a 'democratic opening' end[ed] in reactionary closure, marked by the 1979 election of Margaret Thatcher – Britain's first woman Prime Minister" (Aston & Reinelt 2000: 13). Caryl Churchill's famous analysis of historical and contemporary *Top Girls* expresses the discontent and frustration with this conservative political shift from a socialist-feminist perspective, foregrounding the political success of Thatcher as the problematic result of an ideology of bourgeois feminism, based on the belief in individual success within a patriarchal system discarding any interest in female solidarity. Ironically, despite Thatcher's 'iron' rule and the concomitant financial cuts in the arts, the period of the 1980s was marked by a veritable "explosion of new women's theatre" (Edgar 1999: 8) with the rise of young playwrights like April de Angelis, Sarah Daniels, Deborah Levy, Liz Lochhead, Louise Page, and Timberlake Wertenbaker. This was also the time when plays addressing intersections of gender, race, and ethnicity gradually gained wider public attention, such as Caryl Churchill's successful exploration of these issues from the Victorian Empire to the present in *Cloud Nine*. Theatre companies like the Black Theatre Cooperative (1979), the Theatre of Black Women (1982), Talawa (1985), Tamasha (1989), and Kali (1991) and the emergence of writers like Winsome Pinnock, Tanika Gupta, and Meera Syal have contributed to a radical questioning and a re-definition of notions of Britishness in terms of cultural hybridity (cf. Bassnett 2000: 78). Thus, while the political visibility of Thatcher guaranteed an increased public interest in gender issues, it also provided the basis for a critical alliance between the left-wing part of the still male-dominated theatre business and women playwrights: "For women playwrights it was a terrific time. [...] It was a time when women were prominent at the Royal Court." (Wertenbaker, qtd. from Stephenson & Langridge 1997: 137)

Timberlake Wertenbaker's statement about the 1980s is in striking contrast to her diagnosis of the 1990s, as "slightly more reactionary times [...] not the most welcoming moment for women" (ibid.). According to many critics the most important theatrical innovation of the 1990s was in-yer-face theatre (cf. Sierz 2001), advocated by a young generation of playwrights using aggression and shock tactics to attain immediate audience response. Although a number of women playwrights like Sarah Kane, Rebecca Prichard, and Phyllis Nagy have been associated with this trend, in-yer-face-theatre has been predominantly seen as an expression of a crisis of masculinity by male playwrights in reaction to 1980s feminism, centering on male characters ("the 'new lad' culture that emerged in the 1990s was effective in silencing (degrading, even) women's representation" [Aston 2003: 4]). Few women playwrights like Timberlake Wertenbaker in *The Break of Day* (1995) attempted a theatrical reassessment of the feminist movement since the 1970s at that time (cf. Neumeier 2010). The label woman writer, let alone feminist writer, became increasingly unfashionable or was deemed obsolete, as Sarah Kane's statement proves: "I have no responsibility as a woman writer because I don't believe there's such a thing" (qtd. from Stephenson & Langridge 1997: 134 f.). However, despite this resistance of an association with feminism, Sarah Kane's plays addressing the destructive effects of violence do testify to ongoing gender concerns and implicitly acknowledge the inevitably gendered notions of violence.

The often-stated prognosis of a permanent disappearance of women playwrights as a political force has not come true after the turn of the millennium. Instead, Elaine Aston argues, a form of "bad-girl drama" by writers like Emma Frost, Stella Feehily and Lucy Prebble has emerged in continuation of the "hard-hitting, brutal drama by women" (2006: 74) of the 1990s. Despite or because of the persistent 'laddism' of the theatrical world (cf. Aston 2003) and the survival of only a few women's theatre companies (like Clean Break founded in 1979) there is a continuous interest in exploring issues of gender and politics within British theatre in general and by women playwrights in particular, who, however, seem increasingly skeptical towards party politics. Significantly, this is also true for recent plays by feminist playwrights who became prominent in the 1970s and 1980s "such as Caryl Churchill, Timberlake Wertenbaker, or Bryony Lavery [who] present us with drama that grows increasingly dark" (Aston 2006: 72).

2. 'Top Girls' of Feminist Theatre: Pam Gems and Caryl Churchill

Pam Gems (*1925) and Caryl Churchill (*1938) are clearly "the most canonical" modern British women playwrights, whose plays have been produced "by the most prestigious and well-funded of Britain's theatres, the Royal National theatre, the Royal

Court, and the Royal Shakespeare Company" (Aston & Reinelt 2000: 152). Both of them have been associated with the Women's Liberation movement, have collaborated with women's companies, and have identified themselves as feminist playwrights. Some of their most successful plays, like Pam Gems' *Queen Christina* (1977), *Piaf* (1978), and *Marlene* (1996) as well as Caryl Churchill's *Top Girls* (1982) and *Cloud Nine* (1979), probe into the complex relations between public and private, fact and fiction, past and present, and engage in questions about historiography and biography (see chapter 24). An even closer connection exists between Gems' *Queen Christina* and Churchill's *Top Girls* insofar as both plays do not only contribute to a revision of history from a feminist perspective, but also specifically address the debate about the compatibility of career and motherhood (cf. Neumeier 1990).

Despite these commonalities, the differences between the two playwrights and their plays have often been emphasized. Pam Gems has been acclaimed as a "herstorian dramatist" (Godiwala 2006: 28) whose plays are variations on the recurring formula of the 'one-woman show' focusing on central female icons, while Caryl Churchill has been admired for her variety of topics and innovative styles. Read along those lines, Pam Gems explores in *Queen Christina* the implications of being a 'top girl' of history from a feminist perspective decidedly refraining from party politics, while Caryl Churchill in *Top Girls* criticizes the very notion of the 'top girl' as a bourgeois feminist concept from a firmly socialist-feminist perspective. The reduction to such a contrastive reading, however, tends to overlook the complexity of the theoretical implications of the plays.

3. De- and Reconstructions: Feminist Theatre and Life Writing

Many contemporary women playwrights have investigated the lives of women of the past and their historical representations (cf. Kramer 2000). This can be seen as part of a general interest in biographical drama, shared by male playwrights from Edward Bond and Howard Brenton to Tom Stoppard and Martin Crimp. Women writers like Caryl Churchill, Pam Gems, Liz Lochhead, or Timberlake Wertenbaker have focused on implications of gender in life writing as part of their feminist project of rewriting history and revising the literary canon. This endeavor has taken different directions, ranging from a celebratory acclaim of exemplary women's achievements to a critical questioning of their roles as token women within patriarchal society. Moreover, the focus on the lives of outstanding women of the past inevitably evokes notions of biography and autobiography, thus raising questions about intertextuality, narrativity, and identity. While the enthusiastic re-appraisal of a particular female heritage implies the belief in the existence of a unified subject, the skeptical re-evaluation of the past tends to foreground the cultural constructedness and performativity of gendered identities.

The concept of performativity as "that reiterative and citational practice by which discourse produces the effects that it names" (Butler 1993: 2), developed by feminist philosopher and theorist Judith Butler in *Gender Trouble* (1990) and *Bodies That*

Matter (1993), decisively shaped the performative turn in contemporary culture and in the field of cultural theory both in the humanities and social sciences. Butler's original introduction of the concept of the performativity of identity foregrounded the links between performativity and performance in theatre:

> Hence, gender – and by implication identity in a more general sense – is an act which has been rehearsed, much as a script survives the particular actors who make use of it, but which requires individual actors in order to be actualized and reproduced as reality once again. (Butler, rpt. in Case 1990: 272)

Despite Butler's later emphasis on the differences between performance and performativity, the theatre proves a particularly productive space for the exploration of their complex interrelation through de- and reconstructions of theatrical identities with a "focus on real-life acts and transgressive gender performances" (Claycomb 2004: 527). Drama and theatre thus are at the very centre of the wider contemporary performative turn which is inevitably linked to the turn towards life writing discernible in contemporary culture and cultural theory (cf. Smith & Watson 2001, 2002).

Ryan Claycomb (2004: 526) has argued that

> staged feminist biographies respond to the imperative to place women in the pantheon of history but avoid the patriarchal trappings of the biographical tradition, by contextualizing and calling attention to the construction of their narratives and projecting the significance of their biographical subjects into the present and the as-yet-unformed future.

Thus the tension between life writing as a liberal humanist project of revealing the whole truth and a postmodern insistence on the decentered, fragmented subject can be foregrounded, challenged, or eventually be re-solved in the theatrical production. Performativity can be thematized and/or staged in its coercive and/or subversive implications. Pam Gems recreates the life of Queen Christina of Sweden, disrupting the romantic myth of the Hollywood Garbo movie to reveal the coercive power of – as well as the struggle against – cultural gender-construction. Caryl Churchill radically deconstructs not only the lives but the very notion of 'top girls' of the past – and the present. In each play the concept of the life story is used as exemplary form of textualization, the constitutive elements of which – namely identity and narrativity – are questioned. Both playwrights use the exploration of the past as a "call to action in the present" (Claycomb 2004: 531), though, in significantly different ways, investigating possibilities of agency and strategies of change by creatively prefiguring later developments in feminist theory.

4. 'Bodies that Matter': Pam Gems' *Queen Christina*

Since the 1970s Pam Gems has written and adapted plays about famous historical or literary women, from Queen Christina and Rosa Luxemburg to Edith Piaf and Marlene Dietrich, from Guinevere to Camille, in an attempt to "deconstruct patriarchal cultural ideologies operative in politicized private and public spaces" (Godiwala 2006: 28). Moreover, as Dimple Godiwala has pointed out, Gems' exploration of the implications of female power and fame, particularly with regard to notions of the body and sexuality, seems to coincide with or anticipate theoretical texts about writing the body (Cixous 1976), gender performativity as a normative citational practice (Butler 1990, 1993), and agency as repetition with a critical difference (Hutcheon 1985). ("Gems' plays written since the early 1970s construct the woman not only as *subject* but one possessing *agency*, ..., acknowledge a range of sexualities and gendered positions, ..., all of which no Anglo-American white middle-class feminist theorist was able to conceptualize till the 1980s." [Godiwala 2006: 15])

Queen Christina (*QC*) is a particularly interesting example, insofar as the play draws upon the historical figure and the film version of the life of the 17th-century Queen of Sweden, revealing different strategies of gender-construction. This is achieved in the play by first conflating and then separating historical and cinematic images of Christina. In her afterword to *Queen Christina* Gems explains: "I'd seen the Garbo movie ... I had the idea, like, I suspect, many people, that Christina had been a shining, pale, intellectual beauty" (1986: 47 f.), who as Mary Remnant specifies in her introduction to the play, "abdicates in order to marry her lover, who is immediately killed in a duel, leaving her tragically alone and kingdomless to make her way in the world" (ibid.: 8).

Pam Gems' two-act life chronicle opens with the episode of a miscarriage, one of the numerous failures of Christina's mother to deliver an heir and the subsequent decision to educate the female offspring Christina for the throne, which means educating her as a man. Thus the very first scene establishes a rigidly divided world in which the female is linked to private life and breeding, the male to public power and duty. At the same time, however, the performativity of gender is implicitly acknowledged by the very fact that Christina is supposed to be able to transcend the female gender stereotype through education. Christina's cross-dressing as outward sign of the subsequent nature/nurture debate is reminiscent of English Renaissance plays written during and after the reign of Elizabeth I, from Shakespeare's *Twelfth Night* (c. 1601) to Dekker's and Middleton's *The Roaring Girl* (c. 1607-10) and Fletcher's *Love's Cure, or The Martial Maid* (c. 1612-15), which playfully toy with cultural fears and fantasies about women's ability to defy gender boundaries. While these comedies predictably end (at least on the surface) with an acknowledgment of 'natural' boundaries reaffirming the patriarchal system, Pam Gems' 20th-century presentation of Queen Christina foregrounds the fundamentally subversive implications of the debate.

Based on the cultural memory of the Hollywood movie (1933) featuring Greta Garbo, the audience easily accepts a beautiful cross-dresser as part of an eroticized game of disguise. This expectation is, however, shattered in the second scene which centers on a prearranged betrothal between Christina and a German prince, who is shocked to find out that she is a manly, "slightly crippled," "battered figure in hunting clothes" (*QC* 18) with a lesbian relationship to her beautiful lady-in-waiting Ebba. Pam Gems thus engages the spectator in a critique of the cinematic production of gendered images and their effects. At the same time, however, she makes use of cinematic techniques herself ("the techniques I use are filmic: the short scenes, jump cuts" [Gems, qtd. from Stephenson & Langridge 1997: 95]), thus foregrounding the constructedness of all representation.

Throughout the remainder of the first act, which functions as a kind of parody of the 'female' life-cycle between birth-giving, betrothal, and wedding, Christina is presented as a 'man' trapped in an 'imperfect' woman's body, deploring the "ludicrous patterns in nature" (*QC* 19) such as her monthly cycle, abhorring the sight of pregnancy in Ebba, and deriding the hysterical emotionality displayed by her mother. At the same time, however, there is a growing awareness of unfulfilled desires, like the unrequited love for a man who prefers the beauty of Ebba. In a confrontation with the chancellor of the state, Christina expresses the incompatibility of his demands on her "unique position," combining "both the manly qualities of a king, and the fecundity of a woman" (*QC* 29). She convincingly argues that by having been made into "a man, despising women" (*QC* 29), she has been cut off from the roles of wife and childbearer. Contrary to the Hollywood myth Gems' Christina abdicates to avoid marriage and childbirth and to seek personal freedom instead. The play ironically foregrounds the falsity of the Hollywood solution of the victory of love as a 'natural' cure of gender transgression, focusing on the effects of an education as a 'top girl' within a patriarchal system based on contempt for women.

The second act of the play starts where the Hollywood movie ends, tracing Christina's life after her departure from Sweden and – by implication – from an enforced gender-construction. Yet, the resultant feelings of uncertainty and the fear of an impending loss of identity lead to her retreat into the world of her education with its patriarchal mindset based on violence resulting in her attempts to secure the throne of Naples through warfare and eventually in her murder of a lover turned political traitor as the ultimate act of assertion of masculine power. This deed, however, marks the turning point in Christina's development and initiates her descent into madness and her 'rebirth' as a woman.

Critics have read this second act as "Christina's period of self-discovery and growth" (Godiwala 2006: 34) ending in a "resolution of Queen Christina's identity" (ibid.: 38), in the course of which she blames her education for her childlessness. In contrast to readings of the play as a plea for either a retrieval of a 'female nature' or for a vision of androgynous harmony, I would like to argue that this development, rather than being naturalized is (at least to a certain extent) ironized as yet another example of gender performativity as a citational practice (cf. ibid.: 38 f.). Thus, significantly, Christina's education as a woman after her breakdown starts by her being fed, scolded, and slapped as a sort of substitute doll by the child of Christina's maid. In a further step, Christina is presented in feminine attire trying to please the visiting Cardinal, who, she imagines, has come as her suitor. When she complains that one room "is now my whole world. To go as far as [the] door fills me with terror" (*QC* 43), this can be read not only as a reference to her state of recovery, but also as an ironic comment on the limitations of the 'female sphere' in general. Christina's self-liberation from this extreme confinement is linked to her saving the life of her maid's daughter in an act of instinct leading to an incipient re-evaluation of her life:

> I have been as a man. I have commanded. I have signed death warrants, consigned regiments to the sword. All done in my name. I have even committed murder. What more do you want?
> [...] By God, half the world are women...they've learned subversion, to keep their teeth in their mouths and the rope off their backs, why not try that?
> [...] I was bred as a man, despising the weakness of women. I begin to question the favour.
> [...] They know how to share rather than take...by god, they share their very bodies with their own young, with us!
> [...] I begin to perceive that I am a woman. What that is, heaven knows...the philosophy is yet to be written, there is a world to be explored. (*QC* 44 f.)

Although this could be read as an advocation of an essentialized 'feminine' counter culture, it also can be seen to signal a resistance to such an easy solution and an openness to change. Moreover, the play does not end here and on a note of triumphant resolution, but rather on an ironic insistence on the coercive power of cultural gender-construction, contrasting Christina's sudden hysterical sexual advances towards the Cardinal after the end of her speech with his and her maid's pitiful comments on Christina's lack of beauty, echoing statements from almost all the characters throughout the play.

The persistence of gender stereotypes is further emphasized by the portrayal of the other women characters in the play. Christina's mother is presented as the victim of an oppressive system perceiving women as breeding machines, which has turned her into a hysterical creature knitting and eating chocolates in compensation for a lack of emotional attachment. The suffragettes in the play are depicted as advocates of an equally oppressive counter system. The beautiful Ebba, finally, is representative of all those who smoothly fit into and take advantage of the existing system, and thus lack any personal reason for promoting structural change. The play leaves the main characters with a partial awareness, but presents them as still caught in the web of the old cultural text, the patriarchal system. This is reflected in Pam Gems' particular use of the traditional biographical form of the exceptional life story, whose narrative sequence is still adhered to, but whose identity concept is disrupted. Gems' play not only deconstructs a specific myth of the historical Christina, but foregrounds gender performativity as a citational practice in its implications for contemporary society calling for action and change. Written more than a decade before Butler's groundbreaking *Gender Trouble*, Pam Gems' *Queen Christina* seems to prefigure positions central to Butler's analysis of the interrelation of sex, gender, and sexuality. In contrast to earlier literary and theatrical uses of cross-dressing and in contrast to the Garbo version of Christina, Gems does not use cross-dressing as a device to mark a distinction between a culturally constructed gender and a biological sex implying a naturalized gender hierarchy. Thus the emphasis on Christina's lack of conventional 'feminine' beauty and on her bisexuality is used to disrupt notions of an ahistorical androgynous ideal, turning Christina into a historically situated sign of radical ambiguity, "a 'misfit' body which invites us to question gender roles, identity and behaviour" (Aston 2000: 160).

5. The Politics of 'Gender Trouble': Caryl Churchill's *Top Girls*

Caryl Churchill has been called "the most successful and best-known socialist-feminist playwright to have emerged from Second Wave feminism" (Reinelt 2000: 174) with an immense impact on "the evolution of a contemporary feminist theatre practice and scholarship on the English stage and in the theatre academy" (Aston 2003: 18). Churchill's history plays of the late 1970s and early 1980s in particular, *Cloud Nine*, *Top Girls* and *Fen*, with which she "established herself as a major international playwright" (Reinelt 2000: 179), have been celebrated as part of a feminist historiography written "in light of the feminist activism and feminist theory of the 1970s" (ibid.). However, like Gems, Churchill seems to anticipate feminist theory of the 1990s in plays, which probe into notions of performance and performativity through cross-dressing, but also through multiple casting, and the disruption of chronology. In contradistinction to Gems' plays the deconstruction of conventional notions of individual identity and progressive history in Churchill's plays is bound to a decidedly socialist-feminist perspective. In her reading of *Top Girls* (*TG*) Elaine Aston (2003: 20) puts it in a nutshell: "If earlier drama had signaled the difficulty of socialism without feminism, *Top Girls* shows the dangers of feminism without socialism." The lasting impact of *Top Girls*, evident in revivals, TV broadcasts, and popular as well as scholarly attention, testifies to the continuous relevance of issues such as the compatibility of career and motherhood raised in the play.

The play opens with the main character Marlene's promotion to managing director of the employment agency 'Top Girls,' which the heroine celebrates together with other 'top girls' from the past in a (fantasy) restaurant scene. Scenes 2 and 3 of the first act present Marlene in her new position, and the dreary country life of her sister Joyce and daughter Angie, who rightly suspects her admired aunt Marlene to be her real mother. The final act presents Angie's visit to Marlene's office and ends on a troubled reunion between Marlene and her sister, which actually took place one year earlier in Joyce's kitchen. Thus, as often pointed out by critics, the movement of the play turns backwards, from a refined place of opulent consumption to a simple place of basic production, thereby disrupting the audience's sense of chronological progression. The play's last word, Angie's remark "frightening" (*TG* 87), refers not only to a nightmare Angie has had, but also to women's future beyond the limits of the play. Significantly this bleak picture is reinforced by the chronologically last line of the play, which is a comment by Marlene on the prospects of her daughter Angie: "She's not going to make it" (*TG* 66). The assumption, that she seems to have to make it within a patriarchal structure, is, however, the really frightening thought according to the play's logic.

In marked contrast to Gem's play *Queen Christina*, which centres on one specific historical 'top girl,' Churchill reveals the marginality of the achievement and of the very notion of the 'top girl' by presenting the first scene as a "dramatized Women's Studies class" (Brown 1988: 127), as Marlene's introduction of the women to each other shows:

> This is Joan who was Pope in the ninth century, and Isabella Bird, the Victorian traveler, and Lady Nijo from Japan, Emperor's concubine and Buddhist nun, thirteenth century [...] and Gret who was painted by Brueghel. Griselda's in Boccaccio and Petrarch and Chaucer because of her extraordinary marriage. (*TG* 20)

By first presenting and then discarding this illustrious assembly after the first scene, Churchill can foreground the continuity of female struggles and the historicity of individual achievements at the same time. The overlapping dialogue of the women at the dinner table is not a reproduction of the cliché of feminine chatter, but foregrounds the isolation of the 'top girls' from each other. The separate life stories, which emerge in the course of the scene, prove the women's identities to be just as culturally constructed as their historical costumes. Marlene's hope for a universal sisterhood, shared by Second Wave feminism, applies – if at all – to a unison in distress (MARLENE. "O God, why are we all so miserable?" [*TG* 18]), but not to common views or characteristics, as the conversations about a variety of subjects (love, family, religion, morals) unmistakably demonstrate. Ironically the women spot the injustices within other historical contexts, but are blind to those of their own time. The performativity of gender is further emphasized by Churchill's multiple casting, the 'doubling' or 'tripling' of roles played by the same actress, which is not used as a means to suggest an underlying essentialism but on the contrary to stress gender as citational practice (e.g., patient Griselda, homely Jeanine, and 'emancipated' Nell are played by the same actress). Moreover, the fact of an all-female cast avoids any potentially naturalizing visualization of the gender binary, the cultural constructedness of which the play wants to unravel.

The play's foremost target of criticism is the bourgeois feminist notion of the 'top girl' personified in Marlene and her celebration of egoistic individualism and Thatcherism (MARLENE. "She's a tough lady, Maggie." [*TG* 84]). Her sister Joyce's advocacy of altruism and socialism, however, is rendered impotent by passive suffering and subdued bitterness, and therefore in its present form does hardly represent an alternative vision. It has been argued that

> [i]n the place of an *authentic* female voice there is nothing but a void, which none of the characters manages to fill with alternative contents. The play leaves the spectator deeply unsettled by providing no positive role models, no obvious figures of identification and no suggestion of a better future. (Rubik 1996: 181, emphasis added)

Along those lines Churchill has been criticized for not turning to appreciative readings of her chosen historical top girls (cf. Eichler 1990: 146). Significantly, Churchill's opening restaurant scene draws on Judy Chicago's famous installation artwork, *The Dinner Party* (1974-1979) in honor of famous historical women (among them Pope Joan and Isabella Bird). Churchill, however, ironizes the essentialist implications of Chicago's celebration of the body and of a universalized 'authentic' female experience, foregrounding the coerciveness of gender performativity within a patriarchal system. Thus the play indeed deliberately creates a gap which remains to be filled, an absence which is made present by the evocation of existing gender images without providing the reassurance of an identifiable role model. This deconstructive thrust of notions of individualized identity is linked to Churchill's disruption of history and narrativity as constitutive elements of life writing. The play's aim is thus to reveal the interrelation between victimization and success in the women's life stories, and to emphasize the necessity of a structural change for women *and* men who are equally presented as victims of a coercive gender system (as the conversations about Howard and about Marlene's and Joyce's father reveal). In this sense Churchill's *Top Girls* differs from Gems' *Queen Christina,* with which it shares the central question about the compatibility of rule and reproduction.

In contrast to Gems' depiction of Queen Christina, who is torn by the conflicting dynastic demands made on her, Churchill presents this dilemma from a wide variety of very different perspectives through the stories told by the women in the play: The emperor's concubine Lady Nijo had to abandon her children conceived by her lover, Pope Joan had to die because the onset of labour and delivery revealed her as a woman, obedient Griselda consented to give up her children, the traveller Isabella Bird remained childless, Gret lost two of her children in war atrocities, and Marlene handed her daughter over to her sister Joyce. Despite the differences, however, between those who were forced to give up their children, and those who decided to leave them behind or not to have them in the first place, the incompatibility of career and motherhood is emphasized. In contrast to Gems, however, Churchill links this issue to that of "the social reality for young, disadvantaged girls" (Aston 2003: 25) like Angie, who is judged and discarded without any compassion by her mother Marlene who stands for a merciless meritocracy.

Ironically, despite its direct political engagement with a specific historical moment (Thatcherism) and its criticism of a specific form of feminism (bourgeois feminism), Churchill's play has been misread sometimes in the 1990s as a criticism of feminism as such, "uncomfortably close to the recent calls for women to stay at home with their children" (Reinelt 2000: 181). This misreading of the play is indicative of the "reactionary times" (Wertenbaker, qtd. from Stephenson & Langridge 1997: 137) of the 1990s, characterized by the rise of the concept of postfeminism in Europe and the USA as an ideological weapon in what Susan Faludi described as *Backlash: The Undeclared War Against Women* (1991). The claim that feminist (by implication: bourgeois feminist) aims have been reached in the West rendering feminism obsolete, is precisely what Churchill's play argues against. Instead of satisfying the demand for thematic solutions and formal closure, Churchill's play foregrounds gender performativity in order to encourage the feminist belief in the possibility of personal *and* political change. *Top Girls* is a diagnosis, but also a call for therapy.

Since the 1970s Pam Gems and Caryl Churchill have decisively contributed to the rise and shaping of feminist theatre in Britain. Very often their positions have been presented in terms of a polarization ignoring the significant links between them. Gems' 'one woman shows' about historical and literary 'top girls' as cultural icons in connection to her focus on the body and on sexual desire have often been misread as celebration of essentialist notions of femininity. In contradistinction, Churchill's plays have been misread either as a celebration of socialism as a cure-all, or – as in the case of *Top Girls* – as a bleak picture without any vision for change, or sometimes even (in the postfeminist 1990s) as a renunciation of feminism as such. However, the analysis of the plays has revealed the many features shared by both playwrights who have turned – yet in decisively different ways – to life stories foregrounding the constructedness of gendered oppositions between private and public, fact and fiction, to explore possibilities of agency as a call to action for the audience. These commonalities and this insistence on difference and diversity, combined with a refusal of clear-cut solutions and the comforts of closure links the feminist perspectives of Pam Gems and Caryl Churchill with the new women playwrights emerging in the 21st century who write "out of a contemporary moment in which a generalized myth of postfeminism collides and is in conflict with particular social, sexual and cultural experiences" (Aston 2006: 84).

6. Feminist Futures?

The fact that women playwrights have gained a decisive and enduring status within British theatre has been inevitably and intricately linked to feminist politics and practice. Even if the term feminist theatre remains a contested area, the thematic and formal links between many contemporary plays written by women foreground the lasting urgency of the issues addressed by feminism. Over the past decades exciting innovative plays by women have continuously but differently centered on the gendered implications of issues like violence (Sarah Daniels, *Masterpieces* [1983]; Sarah Kane, *Blasted* [1995]), physical and mental disease (Louise Page, *Tissue* [1978]; Sarah Daniels, *The Madness of Esme and Shaz* [1994]), sexual desire and sexual identity (Bryony Lavery, *Her Aching Heart* [1990]; Sarah Kane, *Cleansed* [1998]), reproduction and motherhood (Timberlake Wertenbaker, *The Break of Day* [1995]; Helen Cooper, *Three Women and a Piano Tuner* [2004]), genetic engineering (Sarah Daniels, *Byrthrite* [1987]; Caryl Churchill, *A Number* [2003]), aging and death (Laura Wade, *Colder than Here* [2005] and *Breathing Corpses* [2005]; Sarah Kane, *4:48 Psychosis* [2000]), as well as on questions about the future in increasingly global terms (Caryl Churchill, *Far Away* [2000]; Timberlake Wertenbaker, *Credible Witness* [2001]). Often this exploration of pressing problems of the present and the future is linked to an intertextual engagement with and a re-evaluation of the past.

In her investigation into *Feminist Futures?* (2006) after the turn of the millennium, Elaine Aston maintains that "in contradistinction to the idea of a postfeminist society, social realities would seem to argue that the idea of a more progressive future, for women especially and for society generally, is further away from our grasp than it was in the 1970s" (Aston 2006: 72). This is reflected in recent plays by feminist playwrights who emerged in the 1970s, like Caryl Churchill and Pam Gems, as well as by a new generation of women playwrights. In view of the global concerns of the 21st century, feminist issues and aims pose themselves in new ways and with new urgency. But the hope for or belief in political solutions has considerably diminished. In this context the call for a 'new' feminism in recent years signals less the necessity for a new theory than the ongoing topicality of feminist concerns in an increasingly globalized world where gender is of decisive importance for inter- and transcultural issues. The necessity of the 21st century to develop strategies of survival needs feminist theatre in all its diverse political and aesthetic implications countering stagnation and imagining answers for the future.

Bibliography

Primary Sources

Churchill, Caryl. 1982. *Top Girls*. London: Methuen.
Gems, Pam. 1985. *Queen Christina*. In: *Plays by Women*. Vol. 5. Mary Remnant (ed.). London: Methuen. 13-46.

Annotated Bibliography

Aston, Elaine. 1995. *An Introduction to Feminism and Theatre*. London: Routledge.
This book provides an indispensable wide-ranging introduction to feminist approaches to theatre studies, theatre history, the impact of feminist theories, and gender theory in the theatre including a variety of specific case studies of individual plays.
—. 1997. *Caryl Churchill*. Plymouth: Northcote.
The volume offers a comprehensive study of Churchill's theatre from her early writing for radio and television through the decisive 1970s and 1980s to her more recent plays. Close readings of her plays focus on Churchill's involvement with feminism, socialism, and theatrical experiment.
—. 2003. *Feminist Views on the English Stage: Women Playwrights, 1990-2000*. Cambridge: Cambridge UP.
Aston offers "a feminist view of the 1990s" countering notions of postfeminism with feminist readings of plays by Caryl Churchill, Sarah Daniels, Bryony Lavery, Phyllis Nagy, Winsome Pinnock, and Timberlake Wertenbaker, as well as Sarah Kane, Rebecca Prichard, and Judy Upton.
— & Janelle Reinelt (eds.). 2000. *The Cambridge Companion To Modern British Women Playwrights*. Cambridge: Cambridge UP.

This volume presents an indispensable survey of women playwrights from the 1920s to the 1990s as well as a number of sections, each introduced by the editors, on national tensions and intersections (focusing on Welsh, Scottish, and Northern Irish playwrights), on questions of the canon (focusing on Pam Gems, Caryl Churchill, and Sarah Daniels), and on non-mainstream writing (focusing on black and lesbian playwrights).

— & Geraldine Harris (eds.). 2006. *Feminist Futures? Theatre, Performance, Theory*. Houndmills: Palgrave.

This book brings together theatre scholars and practitioners, exploring feminist futures of the theatre from a variety of perspectives engaging in debates about women writers and directors, addressing questions about the interrelation of theatrical style, performance, and political agency with a focus on different geographical regions (Europe, Africa, America, Australia).

— & Elin Diamond (eds.). 2009. *The Cambridge Companion to Caryl Churchill*. Cambridge: Cambridge UP.

This companion offers readings of Churchill's plays with regard to topical contemporary issues such as the ecological crisis, sexual politics, revolution, and terror, as well as essays concerned with Churchill's formal innovations, collaborations, and influences on new generations of playwrights.

Case, Sue-Ellen (ed.). 1990. *Performing Feminisms: Feminist Critical Theory and Theatre*. Baltimore: The Johns Hopkins UP.

This canonical book on feminist theory and the theatre opened up the field with sections on questions of representation, intersections of gender, class and ethnicity, as well as on performing gender (including Judith Butler's essay on "performative acts and gender constitution").

Freeman, Sandra. 1997. *Putting Your Daughters on the Stage: British Lesbian Theatre from the 1970s to the 1990s*. London: Cassell.

This comprehensive study explores the emergence of lesbian theatre in Britain from the 1960s to the 1990s, examining the impact of particular theatre companies, as well as on the role of the Arts Council, including readings of plays by Phyllis Nagy, Bryony Lavery and Sarah Daniels.

Godiwala, Dimple. 2006. *Queer Mythologies: The Original Stageplays of Pam Gems*. Bristol: Intellect Books.

This book provides a detailed analysis of Pam Gems' plays as "queer mythologies" unsettling notions of identity with regard to class, ethnicity, gender, and sexuality.

Goodman, Lizbeth & Jane de Gay (eds.). 1998. *The Routledge Reader in Gender and Performance*. London: Routledge.

This book is a comprehensive study on gender and the performing arts by major critics in the field, including sections on the history of women in theatre, on their changing status in contemporary theatre, on feminist approaches to performance, on notions of the body, on sexualities, on different performance cultures, on multimedia technologies, and on questions of reception theory.

Griffin, Gabriele. 2003. *Contemporary Black and Asian Women Playwrights in Britain.* Cambridge: Cambridge UP.

This groundbreaking book on Black and Asian women playwrights in Britain explores questions of diaspora, migration, un/belonging, culture clashes, and the racialization of sexuality in connection to readings of plays by writers such as Tanika Gupta, Winsome Pinnock, and Amrit Wilson.

Wandor, Michelene. 2001. *Post-War British Drama: Looking Back in Gender.* London: Routledge.

This revised edition of Wandor's Look Back in Gender *(1987) traces "the imperative of gender in the playwrights' imagination" in British drama from the 1950s to through the 1990s juxtaposing feminist readings of plays by male playwrights like Osborne, Beckett, Pinter, Wesker, Hare, Friel, and Ravenhill to those of plays by women playwrights like Jellicoe, Churchill, Daniels, Wertenbaker, and Kane.*

Further Secondary Literature

Aston, Elaine. 2000. "Pam Gems: Body Politics and Biography." In: Aston & Reinelt 2000. 157-73.

— . 2006. "'Bad Girls' and 'Sick Boys': New Women Playwrights and the Future of Feminism". In: Aston & Harris 2006. 71-87.

Bassnett, Susan. 2000. "The Politics of Location." In: Aston & Reinelt 2000. 73-81.

Brown, Janet. 1988. "*Top Girls* catches the Next Wave". In: Phyllis R. Randall (ed.). *Caryl Churchill: A Casebook.* New York: Garland. 117-30.

Butler, Judith. 1988. "Performative Acts and Gender Constitution: An Essay in Phenomenology and Feminist Theory." *Theatre Journal* 40.4: 519-31. Rpt. In Case 1990. 270-82.

—. 1990. *Gender Trouble: Feminism and the Subversion of Identity.* New York/London: Routledge.

—. 1993. *Bodies That Matter: On the Discursive Limits of "Sex".* New York/London: Routledge.

Cixous, Hélène. 1976. "The Laugh of the Medusa." Keith Cohen & Paula Cohen (transl.). In: *Signs* 1.4: 875-93.

Claycomb, Ryan. 2004. "Playing at Lives: Biography and Contemporary Feminist Drama." In: *Modern Drama* 47.3: 525-45.

Edgar, David (ed.). 1999. *State of Play: Playwrights on Playwriting.* London: Faber and Faber.

Eichler, Rolf. 1990. "Caryl Churchills Theater: Das Unbehagen der Geschlechterdifferenz." In: Bernhard Reitz & Hubert Zapf (eds.). *British Drama in the 1980s: New Perspectives.* Heidelberg: Winter. 139-52. Rpt. In: Therese Fischer-Seidel (ed.).

1991. *Frauen und Frauendarstellung in der englischen und amerikanischen Literatur*. Tübingen: Narr. 199-216.
Faludi, Susan. 1991. *Backlash: The Undeclared War Against American Women*. New York: Crown Publishers.
Hutcheon, Linda. 1985. *A Theory of Parody: Teachings of Twentieth-Century Art Forms*. New York: Methuen.
Kramer, Stephanie 2000. *Fiktionale Biographien: (Re-)Visionen und (Re-)Konstruktionen weiblicher Lebensentwürfe in Dramen britischer Autorinnen seit 1970*. Trier: WVT.
Neumeier, Beate. 1990. "Past Lives in Present Drama: Feminist Theatre and Intertextuality." In: Bernhard Reitz & Hubert Zapf (eds.). *British Drama in the 1980s: New Perspectives*. Heidelberg: Winter. 63-77. Rpt. in: Therese Fischer-Seidel (ed.). 1991. *Frauen und Frauendarstellung in der englischen und amerikanischen Literatur*. Tübingen: Narr. 181-98.
—. 2010. "Women's Drama: Timberlake Wertenbaker." In: Merle Tönnies (ed.). *Das englische Drama der Gegenwart: Kategorien – Entwicklungen – Modellinterpretationen*. Trier: WVT. 173-92.
Reinelt, Janelle. 2000. "Caryl Churchill and the Politics of Style." In: Aston & Reinelt 2000. 174-93.
Reitz, Bernhard. 1998. "'Shedding the Panty-girdle': The Women Playwrights and the Issue of Feminism." In: Barbara Korte & Klaus Peter Müller (eds.). *Unity in Diversity Revisited? British Literature and Culture in the 1990s*. Tübingen: Narr. 147-58.
Remnant, Mary. 1986. "Introduction." In: *Plays by Women*. Vol. 5. Mary Remnant (ed.). London: Methuen. 7-11.
Rubik, Margarete. 1996. "The Silencing of Women in Feminist British Drama." In: Gudrun M. Grabher & Ulrike Jessner (eds.). *Semantics of Silences in Linguistics and Literature*. Heidelberg: Winter. 177-90.
Sierz, Aleks. 2001. *In-Yer-Face Theatre: British Drama Today*. London: Faber and Faber.
Smith, Sidonie & Julia Watson (eds.). 2001. *Reading Autobiography: A Guide for Interpreting Life Narratives*. Minneapolis: U of Minnesota P.
—. 2002. *Interfaces: Women, Autobiography, Image, Performance*. Ann Arbor: U of Michigan P.
Stephenson, Heidi & Natasha Langridge (eds.). 1997. *Rage and Reason: Women Playwrights on Playwriting*. New York/London: Methuen.
Wandor, Michelene. 2000. "Women Playwrights and the Challenge of Feminism in the 1970s." In: Aston & Reinelt 2000. 53-68.

23. NEW FORMS OF (TRAGI-)COMEDY: ALAN AYCKBOURN'S *ABSURD PERSON SINGULAR* AND *COMIC POTENTIAL*

ALBERT-REINER GLAAP

> I don't think there is any area that can't actually employ comedy, providing it's truthful comedy. There was a movement where comedy belonged here, and tragedy belonged there and, really, to get laughter in a tragic scene was considered to be unfortunate. My contention was that if you don't have comedy in a tragedy people will laugh anyway and probably laugh at the wrong bit. They'll laugh at a big emotional moment because they are just drained of emotion. (Glaap & Quaintmere 2004: 239)

These are words from Alan Ayckbourn, the author of more than 70 English comedies which have been translated into more than 40 languages. Indeed, his comedies do have a tragic potential. It was Friedrich Dürrenmatt who is reported to have said: "Komisch muß es sein, wenn das Tragische sichtbar werden soll." However, Ayckbourn's plays are not tragicomedies in which the action is basically serious and seems to threaten disaster to the protagonist, but ends in a happy ending. They are 'tragicomedies' as plays in which serious and comic elements are combined throughout the action, either as double plot or as alternating episodes of seriousness and humour.

1. Ayckbourn's Plays as a Mixture

Ayckbourn's primary target is to keep his audience in their seats for two or three hours and hold their attention. But under a veneer of entertainment, we always discover characters, situations, and conflicts that make us ask ourselves and each other far-reaching questions. Ayckbourn once said that a comedy is just a tragedy stopped at a certain point, and – in a conversation with me – he referred, with a twinkle in his eyes, to a lady who – having seen one of his plays – came up with the following remark: "I would not have laughed had I known what I was really laughing about" (unpublished interview). The playwright himself has this to say:

> I like to find in my plays a mixture... I mean, there are moments in the play where you can look at the audience, and half of them are laughing and half of them aren't, and some of them say, 'I'm sorry, I find this too upsetting to laugh at' and other people say, 'I found it upsetting, but I still laughed.' And I like both. It's a recognition mixture and sometimes things are so close that you can no longer laugh. There are things in my plays that I don't laugh at, that other people do. (Glaap & Quaintmere 2004: 41)

Some critics refer to Ayckbourn's plays as 'comedies of embarrassment,' others place them between 'comedies of manners' and 'comedies of menace' (this in the Pinteresque sense of the term) or call them farces. Are his plays comedies or farces? Ayckbourn could not care less about terminological hair splitting. Comedy and farce merge in most of his plays: *Taking Steps* (1979) is engineered as a farce, *Bedroom Farce* (1975) – despite the word 'farce' in the title – is basically a comedy. But what makes comedy? How is comedy defined? Generally speaking, it is a broad category of drama ranging from slapstick and farce through burlesque and parody to forms bordering on tragedy – black comedy and tragic-comedy, for instance. To Ayckbourn, comedy is a straight play with a sense of humour. Farce, however, is one which leads the audience beyond the laws of human probability. As the playwright said to me in one of our many conversations:

> The first act is all on the ground. In the second act we begin to lead the audience slightly up the wall and with any luck, they won't notice we are walking. By the third act we should be walking around the ceiling and we may drop them on their heads just before we finish. And they say, "How did we get up here?" (Glaap & Quaintmere 2004: 74)

Farce is by no means 'comedy with the meaning left out.' English farces (apart from 'cardboard' farces) are not just medleys of jokes and japes. Their illogicality is most logical – like many things in our everyday life. Farces often use tragedy's raw materials but produce caricatures of the cruelty of our world.

2. Other Writers of Farces

Comedies with farcical elements have long been very popular in British theatre. A playwright as prolific as Ayckbourn and with whom he is often compared was Noël Coward (1899-1973). Towards the end of World War II, London theatres had staged a remarkable recovery, and Noel Coward's *Blithe Spirit*, written in 1941, "had achieved 1,716 consecutive performances" (Shelland 1999: 2) by 1945. In the late stages of decrepitude light comedies were particularly appealing. They are one facet of the wide variety of comedy as a genre. In the 1980s, when London musicals increasingly attracted crowds of people, from all over the world, it came as no surprise that some playwrights tried to win back theatregoers by writing light comedies. Ray Cooney (*1932) is still considered to be one of the contemporary masters of English farce. In *Run For Your Wife* (1982) a bigamous husband tries to keep his two wives from a catastrophic meeting. This may be an absolute tragedy in real life; in farce it is meant to get laughs. Light comedy is a subgenre of comedy which is loathed by most theatre sophisticates but appealing to audiences who do not want anything but entertainment. And in Ray Cooney's plays there often seems to be a point at which 'comedy' becomes 'farce.' What is more, Cooney has been very instrumental in working on contemporary issues. Internet dating in *Caught in the Net* (2001), a sequel to *Run For Your Wife*, is but one example.

The playwright who, apart from Ayckbourn, uses the conventions of farce innovatively is Michael Frayn. His *Noises Off* (1982), a particularly well-crafted farce, has been a big hit over the past three decades. Cooney's farces provide the bones of *Nothing On*, the play-within-a-play in *Noises Off*, which deals with the aspirations and frustrations of a group of actors as they tour the provinces with *Nothing On*. At the beginning of *Noises Off*, we see this farce in dress-rehearsal. A cleaning woman (as a stock character) fails to remember what she is meant to do with the plate of sardines she is carrying. A real estate agent is bringing his girlfriend to one of the houses he is meant to sell, for a love affair, needless to say. When the married owners suddenly return from Spain, where they had gone to avoid income tax, one can well imagine that everything is bound to go topsy-turvy. The same scene we see in the second act but from the backstage side of the set. Half the cast is drunk, and the sexual rivalries of the actors lead to a total disaster. The third act is a logical consequence of the middle act. Now we see an onstage performance, in which nothing works anymore. No one knows who is on and who is off. The company has disintegrated and the play degenerated into chaos. *Noises Off* is farce proper. We get it in triplicate: a farce inside a farce, a farce behind a farce, and a farce of a farce. The farcical elements cannot be separated from the philosophical basis of Michael Frayn's plays which is the idea of order and disorder on stage and in life. He belongs to the playwrights who believe that farce is often more appropriate than tragedy as a way of looking at the world. But "fortunately," says Frayn, " no one ever notices this philosophical basis is there. If they did, they probably wouldn't come to see the play" (Bach & Glaap 2008: 65). *Noises Off* is a serious comedy.

3. Ayckbourn's Early Plays

One of Britain's most important and commercially successful playwrights is Alan Ayckbourn (*1939). He is the very theatrical craftsman, whose work covers the full range of comedies from light comedies to farces to so-called dark comedies. He has exerted a strong influence on the British theatrical scene for more than 40 years, starting as an actor and stage manager. In the 1960s, he began directing and writing plays. Theatre critics have referred to him as 'great farcist' or 'funny joker,' 'Mr Sit(uational) Com(edy),' as the 'Molière of our time' and 'England's most prolific present-day bard,' or 'playwright of the middle-middle class.' Only a few of these labels do justice to Ayckbourn's work. Some reflect the fact that he was critically underestimated, due to his theatrical ingenuity and his aversion to political avant-garde experimental theatre. The truth, however, is that he regards himself as a 'director who happens to write.' He is indeed a director-playwright; he starts writing with the theatre in mind, in particular 'his' Stephen Joseph Theatre in the Round in Scarborough, North Yorkshire, at the end of the railway line. Many of his entertaining and well-structured plays have transferred to London.

It is not only his remarkable skill in playwriting and an eye for detail, but also his insights into present-day life that make him the successful writer he is. Some of our friends and neighbours and we ourselves shine through some of his characters. Sir Peter Hall, for many years head of the National Theatre in London, recognized this when, as early as in 1986, he wrote: "In 100 years' time, when he's been forgiven for being successful, people will read his plays as an accurate reflection of English life in the 1960s, '70s and '80s. They present a very important social document" (Glaap 1993: 345).

So far, Alan Ayckbourn has written 74 plays, two of which will be discussed in the following part of this essay – one written in 1972, *Absurd Person Singular*, the other in 1999, *Comic Potential*. Prior to this, however, a brief survey of Ayckbourn's work before 1972 may give an insight into the very early stages of this playwright's comedy-writing.

His first success was *Meet My Father* (1965), later retitled *Relatively Speaking*. Stephen Joseph, the most important influence on his work, had advised him to learn playwriting by starting off with an actor-proof play, which, once its mechanism has been set in motion, moves on by itself like a clockwork. But it was absolutely clear, even in those early days, that Ayckbourn would never spoonfeed his audience, but rather provide them with subliminal clues, seamless plotting, and his unique way of handling the English language and its many possibilities of being misunderstood.

Relatively Speaking (1965) is a conventional comedy in two acts and four scenes. Ginny and Greg are a young couple who live together and who are about to get married. She tells him that she is going to her parents' home in the country. But she is really going to her former lover's home to retrieve their letters. Greg, wary as he is, follows her. In turn each of them is welcomed in the country home. The result is a chapter of misunderstandings. Philip is the ex-lover who won't give up, and his wife Sheila is too polite to throw them all out. Ayckbourn "gives us a classic comedy […]. Scene I: We meet couple A. Scene II: We meet couple B. Scene III: Sparks fly when the two couples meet. Scene IV: All is resolved and the participants are sadder but wiser as a result" (Benedictus 1986: 23 f.). *Relatively Speaking* is a farce of mistaken identities.

How the Other Half Loves (1969), Ayckbourn's first play to reach Broadway (1971), is about three couples connected by an extramarital affair and divided by class. They are representative of middle-class gentility, but none of them are happy. The men work for the same company, but are separated by subtle differences in position and background. Fiona Foster and Bob Philipps have an affair, and the Featherstones – a little accountant and his wife – are their mutual alibi. The play is basically about evil and how people cover up their disappointments and cruelties by hurting each other. *How the Other Half Loves* and some other early plays by Alan Ayckbourn were classed as 'lightweight' comedies in the 1960s and 1970s. But later on when this play was revived it was no longer seen in opposition to Ayckbourn's later plays which some critics have labelled his 'darker' plays.

From the beginning, the 'dark,' or rather the 'serious,' element has been part of this playwright's work, more prominent than before in *Time and Time Again* (1971), which is markedly different from the two previous plays. There are Leonard, an ex-teacher, Anna and her husband Graham, one of Graham's employees, and Peter with his girlfriend Joan. Both Graham and Leonard feel attracted to Joan. A few months later, Joan is thinking of marrying Leonard, who, however, has not yet plucked up the courage to tell Peter who – in Leonard's view – has a violent temper. He never tells him, and Joan finally thinks that Leonard does not want her enough. They drift apart. This play is about two people who are not destined to get together.

Contrary to what one expects, the central character in *Time and Time Again* is not the driving force, but a misfit, a loser, whom Ayckbourn makes a fascinating character. "I have upset the balance," he says, "[...] I wanted to write a total vacuum, a central character who took no decisions , did nothing, everything was done for him and by simply taking no decisions he affects the whole course of the play. Doing nothing, he upsets about five lives" (Ayckbourn 1972: 28 f.). In this play, Ayckbourn, to a large extent, dispenses with funny lines and cares as much about the characters' feelings as about structure, as he writes with reference to *Time and Time Again*: "I prefer to regard it as the play when I first began to attend to people as well as plot" (Glaap & Quaintmere 2004: 31).

4. Farcical Humour, Offstage Action, and Social Criticism

Absurd Person Singular (1972) marked the beginning of something completely new in the 1970s, by being more serious in its social criticism of the English middle-middle class of the time. What made this play successful was its combination of symmetrical perfection and exploration of sex, class, and power. What was stressed more when the play was produced again in 1990 was that it foresaw Thatcherism long before it came into existence, as Michael Billington states: "This is one of the great plays of the Seventies, precisely because it foresaw what would happen in the Eighties: the decline of the professional classes at the expense of thrusting opportunities" (Billington 1990). *Absurd Person Singular* (*APS*, 1991) is indeed a comedy, but it is also a sad reflection on how people treat each other, and how the weak are (un)likely to make it in this world. It has certain elements of the 'well-made play': it consists of three acts, the characters are three married couples who get together on three successive Christmases in three different kitchens. And it is about the rise of two and the downfall of four of the characters, and about complex situations and misunderstandings. Farce and comedy emerge as opposite sides of the same coin. Typical features of farcical humour, black comedy, and social satire can be ferreted out in the respective acts of the play. Excerpts from the stage directions at the beginning of the three acts provide a springboard for an analysis of *Absurd Person Singular*:

First Kitchen	*Second Kitchen*	*Third Kitchen*
modest scale; model kitchen; gadgetry	untidiness; a room continually lived in; natural scrubbed wood	modernized to some extent; still retains a lot of the character of the original room
suburban house	fourth-floor flat	big old Victorian house
Jane: unimaginatively made up: her hair tightly permed	Eva: unmade, unkempt and baggy-eyed	Ronald: sitting in an armchair; wears a scarf and a green eye-shade
Sidney: a small dapper man; has a small trimmed moustache, and a cheery, unflappable manner	Geoffrey: his voice is heard off	Eva enters: She wears a winter coat and carries an empty teacup and a plate

(Glaap 1979: 46)

The kitchens are very important in *Absurd Person Singular*, because they reflect the social and spiritual strata of the couples. Sidney Hopcroft is an ambitious shopkeeper, his wife Jane a house-proud woman, one might even call her a cleaning maniac. They want to impress their guests with a successful party. Geoffrey and Eva Jackson live in a very informal way without following accepted rules of behaviour. Ronald and Marion Brewster-Wright are rich, fashionable people, the smart set. The three couples have become acquainted through business. But why did Ayckbourn set the scene in the kitchens?

> I was pleased to have discovered the idea of 'offstage-action,' to be sure. It seemed an interesting solution to set the scene apparently in the wrong room, i.e. their kitchen. [...] Where we should have been, surely, was in the sitting-room. That's where the main action (apparently) was happening. Of course, it rarely was. The really interesting things, the things people want to say to each other in private were said in here by the sink. (Glaap & Quaintmere 2004: 34)

Apart from indicating the different social levels, the offstage action helped to centre the play away from its principal setting which contained Dick and Lottie Potter. "It seemed," says Ayckbourn, "an audience would only thank me for keeping us all out here [i.e. in the kitchen], away from his [i.e. Dick's] jokes" (ibid.). Dick and Lottie are offstage characters. Every now and then, reference is made to them in the kitchens, and we hear their voices, from time to time, drifting in from the sitting room before the kitchen door closes. Their functions are to provide the party, to throw light on onstage characters, who, for their part, have different attitudes to Dick and Lottie. Marion and Ronald find them interesting, Sidney finds them admirable and jolly, and Geoffrey ogles at Lottie in her long knitted dress. For the audience they are just an element of fun. The two are boring, and the audience should be sure that they will never meet them. Offstage characters – always and here in particular – add a perspective beyond the action itself.

What gives the play unity is that it is related over three successive Christmases. Each act is or becomes a Christmas party. In the first act, Sidney's party is ruined by his wife's absence. Jane, who is expected to be the efficient wife, is outside in the pouring rain looking for the tonic water bottles which she has over-zealously tidied away. Meanwhile, Dick and Lottie have arrived. The following scene ensues:

> SIDNEY. It's a good job it's only Dick and Lottie out there. It might have been the Brewster-Wrights. I'd have had a job explaining this to them. Walking in and out like a shoe salesman. All right?
> JANE. Yes.
> SIDNEY. Right. (*He throws open the door jovially.*) Here she is. (*Pushing Jane ahead of him.*) Here she is at last.
> *Hearty cries of 'Ah ha' from Dick and Lottie.*
> JANE (*going in*). Here I am.
> *Jane and Sidney exit.*
> SIDNEY (*closing the door behind him*). At last.
> *A silence. A long one.*

Sidney returns to the kitchen. Conversation is heard as he opens and closes the door. He starts hunting round the kitchen opening drawers and not bothering to shut them. After a second, the door opens again, and Jane comes in.

JANE (*as she enters*). Yes, well you say that to Lottie, not to me. I don't want to know that... (*She closes the door.*) What are you doing? (*She hurries round after him, closing the drawers.*)

SIDNEY. Bottle-opener. I'm trying to find the bottle-opener. I can't get the top off Lottie's bitter lemon.

JANE. It's in there.

SIDNEY. In there?

JANE. Why didn't you ask me?

SIDNEY. Where in there?

JANE. On the mantelpiece?

SIDNEY. The mantelpiece?

JANE. It looks nice on the mantelpiece.

SIDNEY. It's no use having a bottle-opener on a mantelpiece, is it? I mean, how am I...?

The door chimes sound.

JANE. Somebody else.

SIDNEY. All right, I'll go. You open the bitter lemon. With gin.

JANE. Gin and bitter lemon.

SIDNEY. And shake the bottle first. (*APS* 8 f.)

Jane's return to the kitchen is a sad moment, and what Sidney does to her is appalling. This is only a short scene, but it is symptomatic of much more. Sidney is the epitome of men whose only interest is to 'make it' and rise to the top in their jobs. He wants to impress his influential guests whatever the cost, even if it means having to 'sacrifice' his wife. Later, in the third act, he dominates the party games. He can make architects and bank managers dance to his tune. As regards Jane, "the audience is remorselessly buffeted between the comedy and a sense of anger on her behalf," writes Paul Allen (2004: 27).

Act 2 again presents the audience with the alternative either to laugh and enjoy or identify and be angry. Here, Ayckbourn deviates from the conventional lines of comedy to try something new: this act is about a woman committing suicide. The trivial upsets of the Hopcrofts' party are here replaced by disasters on a larger scale. When the curtain rises, Eva is sitting at the table in her dressing-room, unmade and baggy-eyed. She lives on pills and is trying to commit suicide while Geoffrey entertains the other couples. He delivers a long monologue and reminds her that they agreed that he should leave her and live with Sally and that they are having a Christmas party tonight. During his monologue, Eva does not say one word, signalling that their world is one without communication. She tries to hang herself from the kitchen ceiling light fixture which she pulls down, but is believed by the others to be changing a bulb. She climbs out onto the window ledge. She runs toward a bread knife wedged in the half-opened drawer. She empties the oven, puts a tea napkin down inside and tries laying her head on it. Whatever she tries is misunderstood and misinterpreted. It does not dawn on her guests that she is trying to commit suicide. Ayckbourn, with all his knowledge of farce, makes the action work well.

The idea of centring the second act round a woman committing suicide seemed to be a dangerous undertaking to Ayckbourn himself. Would he be accused of bad taste? Was he (ab)using human tragedy to get laughs? "I resolved," he writes, "that whatever happened the humour would never be directed against the luckless Eva herself. The comedy [...] would arise from the other misguided blunderers who had totally misread her intentions" (Glaap & Quaintmere 2004: 34). Ayckbourn admits that "as performances went by, I was to learn a vital comic lesson. Namely that a single, truthful, serious event can become funny when set alongside a parallel series of equally serious, contrasting events" (ibid.).

The tone in act 3 is much more subdued. This party is hosted by the Brewster-Wrights. They live in a Victorian house, and their kitchen, though modernized to a certain extent, still retains a lot of the original room. Ronald is sitting in an armchair, reading a soft porn novel without really enjoying it. He has lost any feelings – if he ever had them. Marion is a drunken monster. Geoffrey and Eva's fight has come to a standstill. Sidney and Jane demand that the others dance to their tune. Four of them have a weakness in their characters: "'Marion through her vanity,' asserts Ayckbourn, 'Ronald his remoteness and indifference, Geoff his sexual and professional arrogance and Eva her self-centred obsession'" (Glaap & Quaintmere 2004: 35). Only Sidney and Jane seem to have what it takes to survive. But their relationship is confined to an unfeeling partnership of social climbers. The characters are recognizable people, whose personal traits have been exaggerated.

As *Absurd Person Singular* moves across its three acts it reveals three different social layers: the Hopcrofts are very much up-and-coming, the Brewster-Wrights (with their double-barrelled name) stand for the upper-middle class, and the Jacksons are 'bohemians.' *Absurd Person Singular* is a pun. It satirizes the characters who are all lonely and absurd, and what happens is not overlaid on the action but developed naturally from the conflict of characters. When the play was remounted in 1990, a theatre critic had this to say:

> Comedies are the white wine of theatre beside the heavy reds of drama. They are best consumed young and few have the quality to become vintage [...]. It says a lot then for Alan Ayckbourn's 1973 play [...] that it still has people clutching their sides even in a midweek matinee performance. (Hassell 1990)

5. The Canvas Widens

Absurd Person Singular marked the beginning of something new by its social criticism of the English middle-middle class. *Way Upstream* (1981) deviated from the mere 'domestic' comedies. With its political overtones, it is often referred to as a state of the nation play. During the 1980s, Ayckbourn began to write what are called his 'darker' plays: *Woman in Mind* (1985), a tragicomedy about a woman who tries to cope with the stresses and strains of her life by inventing in her imagination a loving and caring family; *A Small Family Business* (1987) about a world which no longer has a moral code to measure things by. *Henceforward* (1987) deals with life in a future in which arts and love do not count any more and violence and riots prevail.

Ayckbourn's plays of the 1980s and '90s illustrate his versatility. The canvas has widened: from family-based plays to plays about our modern society. Technological developments, the ever-increasing role of the mass media, in particular TV, and life in our computerized world have become issues in Ayckbourn's plays. He says worrying things while still gripping and entertaining his audience. Theatre critic Charles Spencer writes: "The truth is that, at his best, Ayckbourn is simultaneously the funniest and the darkest playwright. [...] What makes his greatest plays so astonishing is that we laugh uproariously as we pity his characters" (Spencer 2002).

6. *Comic Potential* – A Comedy with Tragic Potential

This applies in particular to the play that premiered in 1998, *Comic Potential* (*CP*), which – in common with many Ayckbourn plays – also has a tragic potential. It is a play whose subject is 'comedy,' a man falling in love with a robot being its central theme. It is also a futurist romantic comedy. The play is set 20 years into an imagined future, in which comedy is dead and has been replaced by daytime TV soaps, in which so-called actoids are programmed to produce emotions and laughter. Actoid is Ayckbourn's term for a robot which can remember the lines and seems to cause less trouble than real actors.

The play starts with a hospital scene in a soap opera which is being recorded in a TV studio. An android doctor is telling a young man, in the presence of his weeping mother, that the X-rays show that there is massive damage to his foot.

> "I'm going to remove the temporary pluster cust and umputate just above the unkle." Chandler Tate, the director, reals: "Hold it! Hold it! What is it saying? Prim, what the hell is it saying now? Umputate his *uncle*. Is that what I heard? [Prim, the programmer]: I'm sorry, Chance... It's not my fault..." (*CP* 2)

Chandler Tate is a burnt-out American film director in his late 50s who has seen better days. The once-good director – faced with shrinking budgets – can only employ actoids to act in his low-level soaps. Adam Trainsmith, his nephew, is to recreate a comedy, a genre which has long since gone out of fashion, and he believes in the androids' abilities. When he comes into the studio, he meets an actoid whose giggle captivates him. Her name is JC 333 (Jacie Triplethree). She has not been programmed and is not meant to laugh but cannot help it, thereby setting herself apart from the others in that she has a sense of humour. Jacie as an actoid can merely draw on the characters she has already played and repeat chunks from horrible melodramas. Nevertheless, Adam gets increasingly infatuated with her and conceives of a comedy to be tailor-made for her. She must learn to read, later in the play, when he teaches her with the aid of the *Book of Genesis* in the *Bible*:

Adam opens the Bible at the beginning.
ADAM. Right. You understand the general principle of reading? All these different little clumps of words, do you see?
JACIE. Yes.
ADAM. And every word is made up of letters. And there are only twenty-six letters to remember but they make up hundreds of different words. Thousands and thousands of words. Look at this. That is an I, you see. Then that is an N, and those two together make the word IN, you see.
JACIE. IN...
Adam. Next word – this is ridiculous –
JACIE. The next word...?
ADAM. Next word, T – H – E – that makes THE, you see? So we get IN THE... (*CP* 89)

Adam continues teaching her letter by letter, how words are constructed and result in the sentence: "In the beginning God created the Heaven and the Earth" (*CP* 90). By putting the letters together the two are creating a world for themselves. Adam teaching Jacie, a machine with possibilities. Even more, he humanizes the actoid, recognizes a spark of 'comic potential' in her and teaches her some of the basics of comedy – the 'double take,' for instance, and a few other Buster Keaton tricks. *Comic Potential* is about a future bordering on our days in which human beings are increasingly being replaced by machines and hardly count at all in a computerized world. But there is more to it than this. *Comic Potential* poses the fundamental question of what makes us human, what it means to be human. Can a machine show us what makes us human? Ayckbourn confronts us with an image of today's multi-channel popular culture, of machinery and cyberspace. But his play is ultimately about growing up, about being aware; it is a warning against letting the development continue.

The relationship between Adam and Jacie – similar to that of Professor Higgins and Eliza Doolittle – has developed into a love story, but there is a scene in *Comic Potential*, where Jacie for the first time finds her voice,

> and she finds it out of an anger, desperation and frustration, a fear about what the future holds for her and a fear of the love she feels inside her, which is an unfamiliar, frightening thing to have in what is ostensibly a logical machine. (Ayckbourn qtd. from Glaap & Quaintmere 2004: 178)

"I am not Jacie, Adam, I am JCF 31 triple 3. There is no Jacie. There is no real me. I'm a machine Adam." And she continues:

> I can *play* your Jacie. I can play her just as you want her to be. I'm good at that. That's what I was made for. But I can never *be* your Jacie. Do you see the difference? I've been miscast, you see. Please. Take me back. Audition failed. [...] I want to melt down. [...] I can't control me. (*CP* 99)

In this scene, Willy Russell's *Educating Rita* (1980) and *Shirley Valentine* (1986) come to mind.

When Carla Pepperbloom, the company's Regional Director, a snake in the grass, interferes and wants the film done on her terms and orders Jacie to be melted down, she and Adam run off together into real life – shopping in a boutique, having a meal in a restaurant. Carla is sacked and Jacie is offered Carla's job and will thus not be able to appear in the film herself. An ambiguous ending. Ayckbourn himself comments: "I like to think, personally, that Jacie will manage to balance a career and a relationship. She is certainly not going to be a pushover in the business world" (Glaap & Quaintmere 2004: 175).

7. The Serious and the Comic Side by Side

In the 1990s, critics put the question if Ayckbourn's plays are comedies or farces. Theatre critic John Peter gave this answer:

> If you have prejudices, prepare to shed them now: if you think that definitions are essential, take early retirement. Is Alan Ayckbourn's new play a farce, a comedy-farce, a black farce or a tragical-comical psycho-medical entertainment? The one categorical imperative in Ayckbourn country is that on your way in you must leave your categories in the cloakroom. (Peter 1990)

Most of Ayckbourn's plays are indeed amalgams of several constituents, some of which emerge in this or that play. In comedies, we are amused by the mental and emotional turmoil brought about by the characters. We laugh *at*, or rather *with* them, as we discover a neighbour, a friend, or even ourselves in the character's behaviour.

The 'comedy of manners' is concerned with behaviour and speech patterns which are socially accepted. It examines the validity of the surfaces behind which characters seek social acceptance. Such plays were very popular, particularly in the early part of the 20th century. The 'comedy of embarrassment' mostly deals with the middle-class governed by a code of ethics and dos and don'ts that one should follow. Breaking these taboos can produce great humour. Some of Ayckbourn's early plays form a bridge between the comedy of manners and serious comedy. Over the years he has moved closer to his ideal of writing 'serious comedies' that will "make audiences laugh, gasp, laugh, gasp," as he put it in conversation with me.

Comedy is an integral part of all his plays, but under a veneer of entertainment, audiences would like to find something serious. Ayckbourn reiterates that when he sits down to write he will never say 'I'm going to write a comedy' but 'I'm going to write a play.' What is to be entertaining and/or serious or tragic in the script is dependent on the theme and the characters. "I was once asked by a journalist if I ever had ambitions to write a serious play. I think my face must have said more than I intended, for she instantly dived back into her notebook and asked me whether I preferred cats to dogs" (Ayckbourn 2002: 4).

Some of Ayckbourn's comedies border on farce, which – in the past – was often misunderstood as a play that evokes laughter but requires only minimal expenditure of mental effort. Farce and farcical elements in Ayckbourn's plays cannot be defined by negatives only, like crude coincidences, pie-throwing, ludicrous situations, and one-dimensional characters. Here, farcical and comical effects serve the purpose of revealing the frustrations, the disappointments, and the cruelties of some of the characters.

Topic-wise, Ayckbourn moved from social criticism of the English middle-middle class in the 1960s and '70s to exploring new areas in the 1980s, more female-oriented comedies, for instance, and plays on the English society of the time. His writing does not any more exist in one pocket only. Death, violence, a threatening future, and technological advances are some of the issues dealt with in the 1990s (cf. Glaap & Quaintmere 2004). But Ayckbourn is still interested in running the serious and the comic side by side. *Comic Potential* is about love as well as laughter.

"One hopes," writes Ayckbourn, "[...] that there will still be room for comedy with increasing technology. I've never ever laughed at a joke on the Internet yet. It's full of very solemn people airing useless, and occasionally some useful, information, but if you want a good night out, the theatre is the answer" (Glaap & Quaintmere 2004: 179).

Bibliography

Primary Sources

Ayckbourn, Alan. 1977. *Absurd Person Singular*. A.-R. Glaap (ed.). Berlin: Cornelsen.
—. 1991. *Absurd Person Singular*. Geoff Barton (ed.). Harlow: Longman.
—. 1999. *Comic Potential*. London: Faber and Faber.

Annotated Bibliography

Allen, Paul. 2001. *Alan Ayckbourn. Grinning at the Edge: A Biography*. London: Methuen.
 In this biography, Allen explores Ayckbourn's background and how he became an outstanding comic playwright and observer of the English middle-class. On the back-flap of this book, Peter Hall is quoted: "If, in a hundred years, anyone wants to know what it was like to live in the second half of the 20th century, I am quite sure they will turn to the plays of Alan Ayckbourn before they look at historians and sociologists."
—. 2004. *A Pocket Guide to Ayckbourn's Plays*. London: Faber and Faber.
 This book lists all of Ayckbourn's plays (up to 2003) in chronological order with a plot breakdown for each play. It also provides useful hints on productions.
Glaap, Albert-Reiner. 1993. "Ayckbourn, Frayn and all: Zur Entwicklung der englischen Komödie in den siebziger und achtziger Jahren." In: Müller 1993: 341-63.
 In this essay, which lends itself to familiarizing students with English comedy and farce as special subgenres of drama, reference is made to the most prominent modern comedy writers in England and their work.

— & Nicholas Quaintmere (eds). 2004. *A Guided Tour Through Ayckbourn Country*. Trier: WVT.

This guide has been put together from many sources: interviews with Alan Ayckbourn, statements made by the playwright on his plays, and articles on the Ayckbourn phenomenon. As the book provides a broader picture of Ayckbourn the writer, the director, and the man, it can act as a springboard for experiencing his work first-hand.

Holt, Michael. 1999. *Alan Ayckbourn*. Plymouth: Northcote.

Michael Holt, who has worked with Alan Ayckbourn for 25 years, in this book, explores the range of Ayckbourn's work and the playwright's dramatic technique and theatrical experiment.

Page, Malcolm. 1989. *File on Ayckbourn*. London: Methuen.

This is one of the "Writer Files" published by Methuen Drama which contain a checklist of the particular playwrights' work, excerpted reviews and comments as well as comments from the writers themselves.

Reitz, Bernhard (ed.). 1994. *Contemporary Drama in English: New Forms of Comedy*. Trier: WVT.

A collection of twelve essays on various facets of contemporary comedy in some English-speaking cultures such as Britain, Canada, or the US.

Scott, Andrew. 2005. *Comedy*. New York/Abingdon, Oxon: Routledge.

This is a guide for those studying comedy in its many forms, theories, and techniques.

Smith, Leslie. 1989. *Modern British Farce: A Selective Study of British Farce from Pinero to the Present Day*. London: Macmillan.

The volume traces the continuity of farce tradition from Pinero to Orton, Cooney, Ayckbourn, Frayn, and Stoppard.

Further Secondary Literature

Ayckbourn, Alan. 1972. "The Joan Buck Interview." In: *Plays and Players* Sept.: 28-29.

—. 2002. *The Crafty Art of Playmaking*. London: Faber and Faber.

Bach, Susanne & Albert-Reiner Glaap (eds). 2008. *Frayn in Germany: Plays and Novels*. Trier: WVT.

Benedictus, David. 1986. "Review of *Relatively Speaking*." In: *Plays International* June: 23-24.

Billington, Michael. 1990. "Review of *Absurd Person Singular*." In: *The Guardian* 17 May: n. pag.

Glaap, Albert-Reiner. 1979. *Das englische Drama seit 1970: Hintergrundinformationen und Unterrichtsvorschläge für die Sekundarstufe II*. Limburg: Frankonius 1979.
Griffiths, Trevor R. 2003. *The Theatre Guide*. London: A&C Black.
Hassell, Graham. 1990. "Review of *Absurd Person Singular*." In: *What's On* 28 May: n. pag.
Müller, Klaus-Peter. 1993. *Englisches Theater der Gegenwart: Geschichte(n) und Strukturen*. Tübingen: Narr.
Peter, John. 1990. "Review of *Body Language*." In: *The Sunday Times* 27 May: n. pag.
Shelland, Dominic. 1999. *British Theatre Since The War*. New Haven/London: Yale UP.
Spencer, Charles. 2002. "Ayckbourn reveals his secrets." In: *The Daily Telegraph* 31. Aug.: n. pag.
White, Sidney Howard. 1984. *Alan Ayckbourn*. Boston: Twayne Publishers.

24. ADAPTATION, INTERTEXTUALITY, AND METADRAMA: TOM STOPPARD'S *ROSENCRANTZ AND GUILDENSTERN ARE DEAD*, PETER NICHOLS' *A PIECE OF MY MIND*, AND MICHAEL FRAYN'S *LOOK LOOK*

JANINE HAUTHAL

1. Adaptation, Intertextuality, Metadrama

The art of theatre relies on an audience's "willing suspension of disbelief" (Coleridge, qtd. from Greenblatt 2006: 478) allowing them to enjoy artifice as 'reality.' Comprising scripts written to be performed, drama is a mixed genre; its intermediality shows in the performative potential of plays and their inherent theatricality. As a consequence, drama developed throughout its history an established set of medium-specific conventions distinguishing it from other literary genres such as poetry or prose. With respect to the textual *mise en page* (cf. Worthen 2005: 11), the canonical form we know today, with its (graphic) differentiation of primary and secondary text, emerged in the 16th century when, with the invention and proliferation of printing, drama emancipated itself from the theatrical spectacle. Regarding the theatrical *mise en scène*, the most significant convention is probably the 'fourth wall.' Established with the advent of theatrical realism in the 19th century, this had a strong influence not only on playwriting but also on theatrical architecture and stage design. The proscenium pictureframe stage (*Guckkastenbühne*), which divides stage and auditorium, became prevalent in the 19th to 20th century.

Plays which refer to and reflect on drama as theatrical fiction or literary form, and thus raise recipients' awareness of medium-specific or genre-specific conventions, are generally known as 'metadrama.' Metadramatic devices are manifold and comprise (a) the classical play within the play, which enjoyed great popularity in Shakespearean and Elizabethan drama, (b) metafictional characters, as in e.g. Samuel Beckett's *Waiting for Godot* (1953) and *Endgame* (1957) (cf. Schlueter 1979), (c) plays set in the theatre or featuring actors, like George Villiers' *The Rehearsal* (1671) and other rehearsal plays of the 17th and 18th centuries, (d) narrator figures and other epic devices such as prologue, epilogue, or chorus, which often feature in plays by Bertolt Brecht and other representatives of the so-called epic theatre, (e) role-doubling and multiple casts (i.e. allotting several roles to one actor or actress), and (f) techniques of directly addressing the audience. All these metadramatic devices remind an audience of the fact that what they see on stage is not a 'slice of life,' but a fictional construct. In accordance with the *theatrum mundi* metaphor of the world as a stage, these devices can also draw an audience's attention to the theatrical aspect of social role-playing in everyday life.

Furthermore, metadramatic devices can refer to and reflect the theatre rather than the drama itself. This occurs, for instance, when characters connected with the theatre apparatus – directors, stage managers, or theatre critics – enter the stage, as in Tom Stoppard's metadramatic 'whodunnit' *The Real Inspector Hound* (1968). Moreover, the creation of secondary roles in which actors step out of character and reveal their 'real' self 'behind' the character they embody unfolds a metatheatrical potential. This often yields a comic effect, as in Thornton Wilder's *The Skin of Our Teeth* (1942), when Miss Somerset performs the maid Lily Sabina. Such fictionalizations of the *mise en scène* draw recipients' attention either to the process of theatrical production in general or to the 'here and now' of the particular performance. As a result, the dramatic illusion is disturbed or broken. A similar effect is achieved when a play as a whole explicitly addresses the audience, as is the case in Peter Handke's *Offending the Audience* (1966).

Finally, the notion of metadrama also applies to plays that fictionalize the writing process by showing characters on stage who are conscious of their own fictional status, or by depicting dramatists. Featuring a playwright called Harry Luckless, Henry Fielding's *The Author's Farce* (1729) demonstrates how this device can also yield a comic effect. Whilst such elements mainly affect the theatre audience, a dramatist can also make use of self-referential stage directions and directly address actors, directors, stage designers, or readers in the secondary text. Such references to the writing process, or to the medium of print, draw attention to the theatricality of the play-text itself.

A play-text's theatricality becomes explicit when its *mise en page* does not comply with dramatic convention. Gertrude Stein's landscape plays, written between 1913 and 1946, for instance, no longer differentiate between primary and secondary text, i.e. between speech and stage directions. Moreover, they leave the spatio-temporal context undefined, or contain speech without specifying how many characters are talking and what gender or age they possess. These at times 'anti-theatrical' tendencies not only disappoint reader expectations, but also present an aesthetic challenge to directors, actors, or stage designers seeking to put on a theatrical performance. The textual ambiguity of such *mises en page* can form a considerable obstacle to the *mise en scène* in contemporary writing for the stage (cf. Puchner 2002; Worthen 2005; Hauthal 2009: 300-29).

Hence, the object of metareference in drama is twofold: On the one hand, metadramatic elements comprise genre-specific references to dramatic conventions and reflect on drama's ontological status as fiction, and, on the other, metatheatrical elements – as well as the theatricality of the play-text itself – reflect the intermedial relationship between text and performance.

As this medium-specific theorization of metareference in drama indicates, there are many different ways of incorporating a meta-level and functionally eliciting recipients' metareferential awareness of both medium and genre. Accordingly, theories of metadrama commonly distinguish between different forms of metadrama (cf. Hornby 1986; Vieweg-Marks 1989; Hauthal 2009), of which adaptive and intertextual variants represent one important type.

Metadrama first received theoretical attention when Lionel Abel coined the term in 1963 (cf. Abel 2003 [1963]). Since then, researchers have focused on the play within the play as an Elizabethan dramatic device in general, and on William Shakespeare's plays in particular, especially on *Hamlet* (c. 1600), probably the most canonical text with respect to metadrama. The continuous broadening of theoretical and historical focus, however, has revealed instances of metadrama not only in plays of antiquity (cf. Bierl 1991), but also in North American and Continental European literatures of the 20th and 21st centuries, where it takes the form of metaplays by such authors as Sam Shepard, Paula Vogel, Thornton Wilder (USA), Rainald Goetz, Martin Heckmanns, Händl Klaus, Heiner Müller, Botho Strauß (Germany), Thomas Bernhard, Peter Handke, Elfriede Jelinek (Austria), Jean Genet (France), Luigi Pirandello (Italy), and José Sanchis Sinisterra (Spain).

Metadrama, however, does not feature with equal prominence in all periods. As far as the history of British metadrama is concerned, the earliest extant secular British play, Henry Medwall's *Fulgens and Lucres* (1497), already comprises a play within the play and thus anticipates later Elizabethan and (post-)modernist developments. British metadrama's initial heyday dates back to Thomas Kyd's *The Spanish Tragedy* (1584-89) and the plays of Shakespeare, as well as of his contemporaries such as Francis Beaumont, John Fletcher, and Thomas Middleton. In the 17th and 18th centuries, the popularity of metadrama diminished, but it remained present, as John Gay's *The What D'Ye Call It* (1715) and Richard Brinsley Sheridan's *The Critic* (1779) show. With the rise of literary realism in the 19th century, metadrama disappeared almost completely from the theatre. Since the beginning of the 20th century, however, metadramatic elements have fanned out again in an ever-growing variety of forms and functions (cf. Boireau 1997; Fischer & Greiner 2007).

In recent decades, numerous British playwrights have written at least one metaplay, contributing to the spread of self-reflexivity in the context of postmodernism. The following analysis will focus on metaplays by Tom Stoppard, Peter Nichols, and Michael Frayn. Further examples of contemporary metadrama can be found in the works of such dramatists as Alan Ayckbourn (see chapter 23), Howard Brenton, Edward Bond, Martin Crimp (see chapter 26), Christopher Hampton, Sarah Kane, and Timberlake Wertenbaker (cf. Krieger 1998: 155-61). The significance of these metaphenomena in contemporary arts and media is, however, still open to debate (cf. Wolf 2011). Are they symptomatic of postmodern nostalgia, marking what Barth calls "aesthetic exhaustion" (cf. Barth 1967); or do they, on the contrary, indicate an increasing (and presumably ironic) medium-awareness, thus signifying "aesthetic replenishment" (cf. Barth 1980); finally, do they point to current concerns with reality and identity and thus reveal a level of epistemological criticism?

2. Adaptive and Intertextual Metadrama

The three plays in the following case study contain explicit metadramatic and metatheatrical reflections and therefore have a strong metareferential potential. Whilst *Rosencrantz and Guildenstern Are Dead* (1966) explores theatrical and social roleplaying by staging metafictional characters, *A Piece of My Mind* (1987) shows a playwright struggling with writer's block, and hence draws attention to the writing process. In *Look Look* (1990), a metaplay that depicts the thoughts of fictional spectators and actors alike, the reception process and the 'here and now' of theatrical performance are reflected upon. Hence, the three plays differ in their use of metareferential devices with respect to object, focus, and function.

2.1 Staging Metafictional Characters: Tom Stoppard's *Rosencrantz and Guildenstern Are Dead*

Metadrama is a central feature of *Rosencrantz and Guildenstern Are Dead* (*R&G*). Stoppard's play is an absurdist adaptation of *Hamlet* in which Rosencrantz and Guildenstern, two minor characters in Shakespeare's play, appear as protagonists. Retaining the Shakespearean plot, Stoppard incorporates verbatim passages and quotations from *Hamlet* into his play (see, for instance, the title) while Ros and Guil are on stage, or which they evidently overhear. In other scenes he reconstructs their off-stage life. In these scenes, the two Elizabethan courtiers often interact with The Player and a group of Tragedians, and these characters are likewise given more weight than in *Hamlet*.

Rosencrantz and Guildenstern Are Dead is based on the (limited) information given in Shakespeare's tragedy. This creates the impression that Stoppard's play is set off-stage with respect to *Hamlet*. The Player seems to allude to this when he invites Ros and Guil to "look on every exit being an entrance somewhere else" (*R&G* 28). As an audience is likely to recognize Stoppard's borrowings from Shakespeare, whether narrative, figural, or textual, the play's intertextuality has a strong metadramatic and comic potential.

Thus, introducing the dress rehearsal of a dumb-show that summarizes the plot of Shakespeare's *Hamlet* and ends with Rosencrantz' and Guildenstern's death (cf. *R&G* 84-95), Stoppard uses the device of the 'play within the play' to establish a meta-level of reflection. For the play's (literate) recipients know (or can presume from the title) that Ros and Guil are doomed to die, but Ros and Guil themselves do not know this, and thus fail to recognize the anticipation of their death in the Tragedians' pantomime. The dramatic irony resulting from this discrepancy in levels of information makes recipients reflect on their own horizons of expectation and thus raises their self-awareness.

Moreover, a strong metadramatic potential stems from the extensive reflections on theatre and drama that characterize Ros' and Guil's dialogues with The Player. Frequently discussed topics are, for instance, theatre and commerce (cf. *R&G* 21-29), audience expectations (cf. *R&G* 89, 94 f., 139), theatre's dependency on an audience (cf. *R&G* 67 ff.), and dramatic genres as well as theatrical styles (cf. *R&G* 33 f., 88). In their conversations with the Tragedians' "*Spokesman*" (*R&G* 20) Ros and Guil advocate high art, Aristotelian poetics, and mimetic realism. Their position, however, is subjected to considerable irony and is challenged by The Player's more pragmatic and popular approach to theatre. A climax in this respect is a scene at the end of the third act in which Guil – enraged by The Player – tries to murder the latter with a dagger. The Player 'dies;' but while the Tragedians "*watch with some interest* [...] [and] *applaud with genuine admiration*" (*R&G* 138 f.), Guil remains unaware of the skilful enactment and only later realizes that the dagger is a theatrical prop and The Player's death a performance.

Furthermore, continuous reference to theatre or drama-related topics distances spectators from what is presented on stage and disturbs the dramatic illusion. This distancing effect is further intensified by Stoppard's use of epic devices, as when Ros and Guil look at, or indirectly address, the audience (cf. *R&G* 32, 45, 61 f., 63 f.). The implicitness (and effectiveness) of metareference in Stoppard's play shows, for instance, when Ros yells "Fire!" (*R&G* 63) in order to "demonstrat[e] the misuse of free speech" and – when only Guil reacts – "*regards the audience, that is the direction, with contempt*" (*R&G* 64). The ambivalence of this and other, similar moments is striking because, inasmuch as Ros and Guil stay in character, the theatrical fiction is left intact. Nevertheless, the self-awareness expressed by the metafictional characters tends to break the fourth wall and thus weakens the dramatic illusion of a realistic (i.e. heteroreferential) fiction.

In contrast to *Hamlet*, the main objects of metadramatic philosophical reflection in Stoppard's play are not issues of guilt and revenge, but postmodern notions of identity and predetermination. This shows in the peculiarities of character conception, namely in the fact that Ros and Guil (as well as other characters) tend to repeatedly mix up their names (cf. *R&G* 21 f., 37, 39, 50 f., 56, 58, 115, 117 f., 136, 142), making instability and confusion of identity and role into a recurrent theme.

The intertextuality of Stoppard's play is, again, evident in Ros and Guil's vain struggle against their predefined destiny. This is hinted at in The Player's answer to Guil's question "Who decides?" (*R&G* 88): "PLAYER (*switching off his smile*). *Decides*? It is *written*" (ibid.). The predetermination Ros and Guil experience throughout the play leads them to compare their situation in its passivity to that of a 'spectator' (cf. *R&G* 45). Such a reversal of roles also occurs when the two Elizabethans first meet The Player and he greets them with the words "An audience!" (*R&G* 20), but later adds: "I recognized you at once [...] as fellow artists" (*R&G* 22).

In its recourse to the metaphor of the world as a stage, Stoppard's play conforms to, and implicitly reflects, what Manfred Pfister calls the "absolute nature of dramatic texts" (1991: 4). The literal conception of the world as a stage through which the play explores drama's 'absolute nature' manifests itself in the conception of characters and the treatment of space. Ros and Guil remain on stage for the duration of the play. Their restriction to the stage as location confirms that their status as characters is essentially textual. Moreover, the entire play is set in a single (undefined) space in which realistic probabilities are no longer effective. Instead, the fictitiousness of this textual world is exposed right at the beginning of the play when a tossed coin lands on 'heads' 90 times in a row (cf. *R&G* 12). Thus the fictional world of *Rosencrantz and Guildenstern Are Dead* does not amount to a hetero-referential representation, a 'slice of life,' modelled on the lived-in world and conforming to dramatic convention. Instead, the play depicts an intertextual world linked thematically and structurally with other dramatic texts.

In accordance with the literal conception of drama's 'absolute nature' in Stoppard's play, the moment when Ros and Guil leave the stage for the first time and disappear into the wings not only marks the play's ending but also their own death. Their theatre-specific way of dying as vanishing matches Guil's description of death from the point of view of a dramatic character: "Death is [...] the absence of presence, nothing more ... the endless time of never coming back" (*R&G* 140). As this description is grounded in the principles of presence and absence, which implicitly allude to definitions of the theatrical sign as a presence referring to an absence (cf. Pavis 1996: 302 f.), the play's ending reflects specificities of theatrical performance. These metatheatrical reflections, however, are implicit and occur only as the play ends. In their isolation, they highlight the metareferential character of the play as a whole.

Referring to and at the same time reflecting on its intertextual relations with *Hamlet*, *Rosencrantz and Guildenstern Are Dead* confirms the canonical status of Shakespeare's tragedy. Stoppard's play thereby contributes to the circulation and preservation of cultural norms, and thus to 'literature's memory' (cf. Lachmann 1997). Moreover, the play's metareferences reflect individual notions of memory and identity: By transposing Shakespeare's classic into a fragmented world in which certainty is unachievable, and where the construction of identity through memory fails, the play demonstrates memory's crucial role with respect to human agency.

2.2 Staging the Process of Writing for the Stage: Peter Nichols' *A Piece of My Mind*

Like Stoppard's *Rosencrantz and Guildenstern Are Dead*, Peter Nichols' *A Piece of My Mind* (*PMM*) possesses a strong metareferential potential. Nichols' play, however, differs significantly in focus, as its metadramatic and metatheatrical potential stems mainly from four elements (cf. Hauthal 2009: 185-214): 1) a dramatist as protagonist, 2) a *mise en abyme*-structure with several diegetic levels, 3) a mix and reflection of literary genres and medial modes, and 4) the staging of a writing process.

A Piece of My Mind centres on the character of Ted Forrest, a dramatist suffering from writer's block who is struggling to write an autobiographical novel. Throughout the play, everything Ted writes, reads, or thinks is immediately shown on stage. This complicates matters for recipients, as the action divides into a number of diegetic levels.

The primary diegetic level (DL1) shows the 'present state' of the writing process. This level complies with Aristotelian conventions, as it encompasses one day and is spatially confined to a single room ("the writer's study," *PMM* 8). In this respect the spatiotemporal deixis of Nichols' play resembles that of *Rosencrantz and Guildenstern Are Dead*. The fact that Ted – like Ros and Guil – remains on stage for the entire play leads to anti-illusionist scene-changes (cf. *PMM* 15, 18, 23) that expose the textual status of characters and events in much the same way as in Stoppard's play. In contrast to *Rosencrantz and Guildenstern Are Dead*, however, Ted's continuous stage presence is realistically motivated by his status as writer-protagonist and suggests that the play takes place in Ted's head (showing a 'piece of his mind'). Compared to Stoppard's play, the metareferential potential of spatio-temporal deixis in *A Piece of My Mind* is, therefore, diminished. Instead, the illusion that the play depicts an act of writing is confirmed.

The secondary diegetic level (DL2) is embedded in the first. It comprises the fictional worlds Ted invents as a writer. These worlds either belong to the novel that Ted is currently trying to write or to a sitcom he once wrote and which he now re-reads and remembers. Both novel and sitcom form an autobiographical flashback covering the last 20 years of Ted's family life and his career as a dramatist. Furthermore, there are tertiary diegetic levels (DL3-n) which possess a different ontological status, as they show (pipe) dreams of Ted's and things he fears (like, for instance, his play being badly reviewed by critics; cf. *PMM* 20). As events on DL2 and DL3-n are told from Ted's subjective point of view, significant parts of *A Piece of My Mind* are structurally comparable to novelistic I-narration. They introduce a level of mediation into the play that deviates from traditionally multi-perspective storytelling in drama.

Ted, however, is not completely in control of the secondary diegetic levels. His attempts to change the past in his own favour by inventing twists in the storyline which will allow him to avoid meeting his rival, a dramatist with the telling name Miles Whittier, fail. Moreover, Ted's wife Dinah can abort or alter scenes against Ted's will (cf. *PMM* 41, 45, 84 f.). As these and other mutual influences between DL2 and DL3-n indicate, the play's diegetic levels cannot be easily organized into a hierarchy, even though visual or acoustic markers such as dry ice or alterations in music and light signify changes of level. In contrast to other metaplays, which make use of the 'play within the play'-device (e.g. Shakespeare's *A Midsummer Night's Dream* (1594-96); see also chapter 4), the common autobiographical denominator of interlocking diegetic levels in *A Piece of My Mind* makes it even more difficult to differentiate between them.

This superimposition of diegetic levels is further enhanced by implicit and explicit metatheatrical references to the 'here and now' of an actual performance and the use of a multiple-character cast. As the list of *dramatis personae* decrees that two actors and two actresses are to perform the cast of 20 characters (with the exception of Ted who is enacted by a fifth actor), numerous relations of correspondence and contrast between characters are formed, and the fictitious nature of theatrical performance is foregrounded. This effect is further enhanced when actors address the audience *ex persona* (cf. *PMM* 14). As in *Rosencrantz and Guildenstern Are Dead*, however, such references to the theatre are scarce. As a consequence, their metatheatrical potential remains isolated.

The illusion that what is depicted on stage amounts to acts of autobiographical writing underlies the mix of literary genres and medial modes in *A Piece of My Mind*. The fictional worlds of DL2 each display different aesthetic techniques according to the target medium of either novel or sitcom. In the sitcom scenes, for instance, not only does the story gain a comic edge, but also discursive strategies slightly change as sitcom music (cf. *PMM* 50, 68) and canned laughter are used (cf. *PMM* 9, 36, 39, 44 f., 50, 54, 57 f., 87). Similarly, scenes belonging to the novel introduce techniques of narrative mediation into the play (cf. *PMM* 10, 13, 14 f., 19, 23 f., 27 f., 38, 42, 56 f., 59 ff., 66, 70 f., 74 f.). The play, however, also contains scenes that are disclosed as acts of novel-writing but still contain generic markers of sitcom. They suggest that Ted, to a certain extent, fails to rewrite his script into a novel, and thus confirm his lack of control over the storytelling process.

At first, this integration of other literary genres and media into the play has a strong metareferential impact that complements Ted's continuous reflections on the function of art in general (cf. *PMM* 23) and of drama in particular (cf. *PMM* 68, 83 f.), as well as his thoughts on the differences between writing a novel and writing for the stage (cf. *PMM* 7, 10, 55 f.). Medium and genre-specific characteristics of these various types of writing are contrasted and reflected. A closer look reveals, however, that the mix of genres and modes in Nichols' play corresponds to Ted's adaptation of scenes from the novel or sitcom for the stage. The metadramatic potential created by the use of narrative or sitcom techniques in drama is thereby reduced. A similar observation can be made with respect to Nichols' use of multiple casts and of actor's falling out of role, which indicate a gap between actor and role. In contrast to Brechtian forms of epic theatre, where this gap functions as a distancing device, the visibility of actor and role in *A Piece of My Mind* tends, however, to authenticate the dramatic illusion of the writing process. It shows how Nichols creates new ways of presenting consciousness on stage through the use of metadrama.

In the highly self-referential final scene of the play, Ted decides to turn the novel into a play, and the recipients (and Ted) become aware that the actual play proves that this transformation has already taken place. At this moment DL1 and DL2 coincide: the diegetic levels are no longer differentiated. As a result, Ted experiences himself as part of his own play (cf. *PMM* 84 f.). Dramatic conventions are thus once more disturbed or broken, but at the same time the illusion of depicting an act of writing on stage is – yet again – confirmed. The realistic motivation of metadramatic techniques can therefore be considered the central feature of metadrama in *A Piece of My Mind*.

Hinting at the clichéd character of the scenes that Ted invents, the use of canned laughter indirectly criticizes the schemata and stereotypes that are used in (contemporary) life-writing or biopics. Moreover, the play's pessimistic outlook on a "new Dark Age" (*PMM* 87) in which theatres are closed and television dominates the cultural sphere indicates that the cultural function of metadrama in Nichols' play lies above all in its criticism of contemporary media culture.

2.3 Staging the Audience: Michael Frayn's *Look Look*

In contrast to the plays by Stoppard and Nichols, Michael Frayn's metadrama *Look Look* (*LL*) lacks realistic motivation. The two-act play, which premiered in the Aldwych Theatre in London on 17 April 1990, focuses neither on actors nor on writers, which would implicate the literary or theatrical production of a play; instead, it takes the idea of the 'play within the play' further by staging an audience. *Look Look* can therefore be considered a complement to Frayn's successful metadramatic comedy *Noises Off* (1982), which is also set in the theatre and shows a group of actors during a dress rehearsal (act 1), a matinee (act 2), and the last British tour performance (act 3) of a comedy called "Nothing On." Besides its slapstick elements, the comic potential of *Noises Off* derives from the fact that in each of the three 'performances within the play' the off-stage action increasingly impacts and undermines the on-stage performance. Moreover, the contrast between characters' on-stage and off-stage personalities forms a pattern of comic dissonances.

Set in a theatre auditorium, *Look Look* fictionalizes the process of watching a play, directly confronting a real audience with its fictional double. The fictional performance remains invisible to the 'real' spectators, as it takes place in the auditorium where the latter are sitting. Finding themselves confronted with a fictional auditorium, spectators become aware of their own act of watching. Moreover, the play's metatheatrical spatial construction reveals its potentially unsettling side, making an audience the object of a second (acted) audience's attention. *Look Look* thus seems to suggest a reversal of roles: It evokes the impression that the actor-spectators, engaged in watching the 'real' audience as if they were an imaginary play, expect them to perform.

The meta-level of reflection that emerges from the play's spatial construction is enhanced by the metadramatic comedy of the first act. Frayn's play holds a mirror up to theatre audiences by revealing the foibles and boredom of eleven fictional spectators. Frayn's stereotypical portrayal of an audience shows how spectators' thoughts wander, how their individual perceptions differ, and what happens as their expectations are confronted with the play unfolding before them. Having these fictional spectators think aloud, the play gives insight into their worlds of thought, and thus reflects on reception processes in the theatre. On the whole, the play seems to imply that, to a certain extent, spectators only perceive what they expect.

Frayn introduces a playwright, Keith, into his play as the author of the invisible 'play within.' The playwright's comments are juxtaposed to the reactions of the other spectators and establish an explicit level of reflection. As his comments disclose, Keith is anxious about the spectators' response to his play and hopes they will connect with the characters he has created. Oblivious to all of this, his fellow members of the audience produce a string of misinterpretations, laugh in the wrong places and, as Keith increasingly bemoans, generally fail to pay attention to his play. Eventually, however, they stagger into comprehension, find common ground with the characters they are watching, and – to the playwright's relief – are at last emotionally moved.

The second act of the play takes the idea of mirroring further by depicting the (previously invisible) on-stage action in the form of the second act of Keith's play. As a variation of the first act, the play's focus shifts from auditorium to stage. This shift in focus is discernible in the change of scenery. The auditorium moves backwards and gives way to a stage area, "the garden" (*LL* 44), where the second act of Keith's play is set. In the background, the fictional audience remains dimly visible: According to the stage directions, it should be impersonated by "understudies, [or] dummies" (*LL* 46).

This prepares for another metatheatrical twist likewise announced in the stage directions: "the cast of KEITH's play [...] look[s] like the cast of our play" (*LL* 46). Presenting the fictional audience as characters in Keith's play results in a doubling of the cast. This twofold *mise en abyme*, however, is not the only meta-reflexive layer Frayn establishes in his play.

The second act makes the thoughts of the (fictive) actors audible while they are enacting their roles (cf. *LL* 62-110). Showing how the actors react to each other's thoughts as in a conversation, the play highlights their mutual professional understanding. The device reaches a climax when the playwright within the play ('Keith') himself delivers a speech on how individual members of the audience have been changed by the play, and how this will affect their future behaviour. At the same time, however, the 'Keith'-actor recalls an encounter with the play's author who asked him to "pla[y] the full stops" (*LL* 101). This memory causes him to forget his lines so that he needs prompting (cf. *LL* 102 ff.) and another actor jumps in, ending the scene by presenting awards to members of the audience – which comprises yet another metadramatic twist, given that audiences usually bestow rather than receive theatrical prizes.

The speech of 'Keith' is metareferential not only in content, but also in delivery. Technically, making two utterances (speech and thoughts) from the same source (the Keith-actor) audible at the same time means that the actor's words 'in role' must have been previously recorded and are now played simultaneously with the thoughts he is articulating on stage. In this play-back, the character's speech and the actor's thoughts are dissociated, giving rise to an interesting insight into the acting profession and actors' professionalism: An actor does not have to be affected by or 'live' the role he or she enacts; on the contrary, during performance, actors' thoughts take on a life of their own.

This insight into actors' thought-worlds distances spectators from the characters being portrayed, inasmuch as it undermines common expectations about psychological acting – the assumption that actors have to feel what they act in order to convincingly embody a character. The process is complex if not, indeed, contradictory: on the one hand, the live presentation of the actor's thoughts provides a moment of 'authenticity' that breaks through the fictional levels of the play; on the other, it heightens still further the metatheatrical potential of the scene, as the dissociation of speech and thought emphasizes and draws recipients' attention to the divide between actor and role.

In sum, both metatheatrical content and form of Frayn's *Look Look* distance an audience from what is depicted on stage. Although spectators might recognize themselves in their alter egos enacted on stage, identification on the whole is prevented by the clichéd caricatures presented in Frayn's satire.

3. Summary

Adaptation and intertextuality play a central role in the metadramatic interplay of dramatic forms, and often initiate a cross-fertilization of historical traditions. Thus, Stoppard's *Rosencrantz and Guildenstern Are Dead* merges metadrama and theatre of the absurd (see chapter 19), integrating them into the tradition of biographical drama by addressing issues such as (postmodern) identity and determination (cf. Südkamp 2008: 86-107). The combination of metadramatic and absurdist elements forms a tendency, initially prevalent in modern British drama, that can be associated with the works of Peter Shaffer, Caryl Churchill, Martin Crimp, the innumerable well-made metaplays of Alan Ayckbourn (see chapter 23), or recent plays by former in-yer-face author Anthony Neilson, such as *The Wonderful World of Dissocia* (2004) and *Realism* (2006).

Like Nichols' *A Piece of My Mind*, many of these plays also feature new, 'undramatic' ways of depicting consciousness on stage. In Nichols' play, these new forms emerge from adapting other, non-dramatic literary genres or medial modes for the stage – namely novel and sitcom. Such intermedial and intermodal forms of metadrama amount to a second trend in contemporary British drama (cf. also Pietrzak-Franger & Voigts-Virchow 2009). Further examples of intermedial metaplays reflecting (trans-)generic conventions are, for instance, David Hare's *A Map of the World* (1983) and Marie Jones' *Stones in His Pockets* (1996).

The strong metareferential potential of Nichols' play stems from its depiction of an author-figure and an act of writing on stage. In this way, *A Piece of My Mind* is also indicative of a third trend in contemporary British playwriting. This trend is responsible for populating the British stage with author-figures. Examples of it are Tom Stoppard's *Travesties* (1974) and *The Real Thing* (1982), and Patrick Marber's *Closer* (1997; see chapter 26). Depicting an (autobiographical) writing process triggered by memories, Nichols' play, moreover, draws attention to the peculiarities of staging memory and biography and thus metadramatically reflects on the subgenre of the memory play.

Whilst the metaplays by Stoppard and Nichols reflect on acting and writing for the stage, and thus challenge conventions of the *mise en scène*, Frayn's *Look Look* thrusts the audience more directly under the spotlight, explicitly reflecting the relationship between recipients and performance. Frayn's play also challenges conventions of the textual *mise en page* by, for instance, dividing the page into two columns in order to signify simultaneous actions on stage (cf. *LL* 48-56, 62-110). This discovery of the page as space in writing for the stage marks a fourth, increasingly medium-specific tendency in British metadrama today. Martin Crimp's *Attempts on Her Life* (1997) and his trilogy *Fewer Emergencies* (2005), as well as Sarah Kane's *Crave* (1998) and *4.48 Psychosis* (2000), for example, cease to define characters in terms of gender, age, or number and also leave the setting undefined. Leaving characters or context undefined in the medium of the written text raises the question of how to project a place without any visible character on stage, and how to enact characters without specifying their gender, age, or number. Using the written medium to reflect and disturb the transformation from page to stage, these postdramatic theatre texts thus exhibit a theatricality of their own which, as an overt hindrance to the *mise en scène*, can be described as anti-theatrical (cf. Puchner 2002).

As the example of *Look Look* demonstrates, not only its adaptive and intertextual variants, but metadrama as such relates to aesthetic conventions developed throughout the history of drama with respect to both theatrical *mise en scène* and textual *mise en page*. One of the dominant aesthetic functions of metadrama therefore consists in the shaping and negotiation of literary drama's generic memory. At the same time, by breaking received conventions and challenging audience expectations, metadrama also allows for and promotes generic developments, for instance the evolution from drama to postdramatic theatre texts (cf. Hauthal 2009: 331-47).

The study of metadrama thus reveals not only that postdramatic forms of theatre revive established aesthetics of performing and playwriting, but that new forms of writing for the stage invigorate theatrical aesthetics. Contemporary metaplays demonstrate that both the opposition of text and performance and the nexus between realist aesthetics and playwriting often proclaimed in postdramatic theatre practices can be overcome, and that the theatricality of these texts is comparable to that of postdramatic performance. Hence, many metaplays conceptualize text as indeterminate material lacking linearity and sequential logic; they are more concerned with circumstance or condition than with action and plot (cf. Barnett 2008). Further research, however, is needed to clarify whether the history of metadrama allows one to assume a linear development from anti-dramatic to anti-theatrical tendencies.

Bibliography

Primary Sources

Frayn, Michael. 1990. *Look Look*. London: Methuen.
Nichols, Peter. 1987. *A Piece of My Mind*. London: Methuen.
Stoppard, Tom. 1985 [1967]. *Rosencrantz and Guildenstern are Dead*. Stuttgart: Reclam.

Annotated Bibliography

Abel, Lionel. 1963. *Metatheatre: A New View of Dramatic Form*. New York: Hill and Wang. Rpt.in: *Tragedy and Metatheatre: Essays on Dramatic Form*. New York/London: Holmes & Meier, 2003.
Abel's pioneering essay coined 'metatheatre' as a generic term with a specific cultural and historical poetic function. Abel claims that metatheatre emerged in the 17th century when antiquity's conception of tragedy was no longer reconcilable with the idea of life as 'already theatricalized.'

Boireau, Nicole (ed.). 1997. *Drama on Drama: Dimensions of Theatricality on the Contemporary British Stage*. Basingstoke: Macmillan.
The 15 articles of Boireau's anthology demonstrate the vitality and variety of reflexivity in British drama of the last three decades. Part I explores the crossfertilization of historical traditions in contemporary re-appropriations of Greek

myths, medieval forms, Jacobean dramatic patterns, and traditional Japanese forms. Part II shows how major contemporary authors undermine realism by foregrounding the theatrical medium as 'the real.' Part III focuses on the interplay of codes in community theatre and other theatrical practices, in translations and adaptations of foreign plays as well as in musicals.

Fischer, Gerhard & Bernhard Greiner (eds.). 2007. *The Play Within the Play: The Performance of Meta-Theatre and Self-Reflection.* Amsterdam/New York: Rodopi.

Fischer and Greiner's volume is devoted to the topic of 'the play within the play.' 30 articles cover a broad spectrum of historical periods, genres, and approaches. Drawing on recent debates in postcolonial studies, game and systems theories, as well as media and performance studies, authors explore a wide range of poetic, (inter-)cultural, and philosophical issues associated with this metadramatic device, including the baroque idea of theatrum mundi, *the 'Hamlet paradigm,' postmodern play and intercultural appropriations as well as intermedial transformations of the 'play within the play' in opera, film, and narrative fiction.*

Hauthal, Janine. 2009. *Metadrama und Theatralität: Gattungs- und Medienreflexion in zeitgenössischen englischen Theatertexten.* Trier: WVT.

At the intersection of literary and theatre studies Hauthal's dissertation modifies existing theories of metadrama in order to account for medium-specific reflections of performance and print in contemporary theatre texts. Drawing on intermedial and narratological approaches to drama, Hauthal uses the concept of (text)theatricality to distinguish metadramatic reflections of dramatic form and function from metatheatrical notions, reflecting the theatrical mise en scène *on the one hand and the textual* mise en page *on the other. Analyses of postdramatic theatre texts show how these metaplays undermine conventions of layout and dramatic form and thus exhibit a theatricality that forms a hindrance to the mise en scène.*

Hornby, Richard. 1986. *Drama, Metadrama, and Perception.* Lewisburg: Bucknell UP.

In the first part of his study, Hornby delineates a theory of metadrama by identifying five 'varieties of the metadramatic.' These include the 'play within the play,' the 'ceremony within the play,' 'role-playing within the role,' 'literary and real-life reference within the play,' and self-reference. Based on Hornby's premise that, to a certain extent, 'all drama is metadramatic,' the second part of the study focuses on a selection of six plays ranging from antiquity to modernity and revolving around issues of 'drama and perception.'

Schlueter, June. 1979. *Metafictional Characters in Modern Drama.* New York: Columbia UP.

Following Abel, Schlueter deals with metafictional characters in modern drama that remind audiences of the duality of theatrical role-playing, i.e. the simultaneous presence of actor and character. Revealing rather than concealing the fictional nature of the dramatis personae, *the plays Schlueter focuses on range from Pirandello's* Henry IV *to Handke's* The Ride Across Lake Constance *as an exam-*

ple of 'metafictional theatre' in which metadramatic self-consciousness is not confined to characters, but applies to the play as a whole.

Vieweg-Marks, Karin. 1989. *Metadrama und englisches Gegenwartsdrama*. Frankfurt a.M.: Lang.

Vieweg-Marks' influential theory of metadrama distinguishes six forms of metadrama, namely thematic, fictional, epic, discursive, figural and adaptive metadrama. Focussing on fictional metadrama, Vieweg-Marks' study explores its formal and functional variations by comparing comedies and farces by Tom Stoppard (Michael Frayn and Alan Ayckbourn) with political plays by Edward Bond (Howard Brenton and Peter Nichols).

Further Secondary Literature

Barnett, David. 2008. "When is a Play Not a Drama? Two Examples of Postdramatic Theatre Texts." In: *New Theatre Quarterly* 24.1: 14-23.
Barth, John. 1967. "The Literature of Exhaustion." In: *The Atlantic Monthly* 220: 9-34.
—. 1980. "The Literature of Replenishment: Postmodernist Fiction." In: *The Atlantic Monthly* 245: 65-71.
Bierl, Anton F. Harald. 1991. *Dionysos und die griechische Tragödie: Politische und 'metatheatralische' Aspekte im Text*. Tübingen: Narr.
Greenblatt, Stephen (ed.). 2006 [1962]. *The Norton Anthology of English Literature*. Vol. 2. New York/London: W.W. Norton & Company.
Krieger, Gottfried. 1998. *Das englische Drama des 20. Jahrhunderts*. Stuttgart: Klett.
Lachmann, Renate. 1997. *Literature and Memory: Intertextuality in Russian Modernism*. Minneapolis: U of Minnesota P.
Pavis, Patrice. 1996. *Dictionnaire du Théâtre*. Paris: Dunod.
Pfister, Manfred. 1991. *The Theory and Analysis of Drama*. Cambridge: Cambridge UP.
Pietrzak-Franger, Monika & Eckart Voigts-Virchow (eds.). 2009. *Adaptations: Performing Across Media and Genres*. Trier: WVT.
Puchner, Martin. 2002. *Stage Fright: Modernism, Anti-Theatricality, and Drama*. Baltimore/London: Johns Hopkins UP.
Südkamp, Holger. 2008. *Tom Stoppard's Biographical Drama*. Trier: WVT.
Wolf, Werner (ed.). 2011. *The Metareferential Turn: Forms, Functions, Attempts at Explanation*. Amsterdam: Rodopi [forthcoming].
Worthen, William B. 2005. *Print and Poetics of Modern Drama*. Cambridge: Cambridge UP.

25. Contemporary British Drama: In-Yer-Face or Post-Political Theatre? Sarah Kane's *Blasted* and Mark Ravenhill's *Shopping and Fucking*

Roger Lüdeke

1. In-Yer-Face Theatre and Its Discontents

Definitions of concepts, or terms, form the foundation of literary theory. They allow us to select and circumscribe the phenomena we want to describe and for which we intend to find persuasive explanations. Aristotle's *Posterior Analytics* (c. 1st c. BC) determines some basic requirements of a successful definition. Accordingly, definitions are based on a process of abstraction and differentiation. Therefore, the term or observable phenomenon in question has to be situated in a class of similar elements that share crucial characteristics (or semantic features) with the one to be defined. The process of abstraction aims at eliminating certain particular characteristics in order to categorize more general features. However, as promising as abstraction is, it must not lead to over-generalization. When you want to find out, for example, what a birch tree is, it is not a good idea to categorize it as forming part of nature; not because this would not hold true, but because this classification would make it very difficult to determine the specificity that allows you to distinguish the birch tree from any other element forming part of the class of nature. Similarly, over-differentiation is to be avoided; when you want to know what a birch tree is, it would make very little sense to start your thought process with setting up the class of the *betula cylindrostachya* because this category will cover only very particular features of the phenomenon in question while eliminating the more general ones that would allow you to situate the phenomenon in a wider context. Moderate abstraction and adequate differentiation guarantee the descriptive power and explanatory strength of conceptualizations in literary studies and makes for their epistemic value. Based on this understanding of the nature and function of generic definition in literary criticism, the problematic nature of the following definition of 'in-yer-face theatre' becomes apparent.

> The widest definition of in-yer-face theatre [embodied in the work of playwrights such as Sarah Kane, Mark Ravenhill, Philip Ridley, and Martin McDonagh] is any drama that takes the audience by the scruff of the neck and shakes it until it gets the message. It is a theatre of sensation: it jolts both actors and spectators out of conventional responses, touching nerves and provoking alarm. Often such drama employs shock tactics, or is shocking because it is new in tone or structure, or because it is bolder or more experimental than what audiences are used to. Questioning moral norms, it affronts the ruling ideas of what can or should be shown onstage; it also taps into more primitive feelings, smashing taboos, mentioning the forbidden, creating discomfort. Crucially, it tells us more about who we really are. Unlike the type of theatre that allows us to sit back and contem-

plate what we see in detachment, the best in-yer-face theatre takes us on an emotional journey, getting under our skin. It is experiential, not speculative. (Sierz 2001: 4)

The problems of theatre critic Alex Sierz' definition of in-yer-face theatre are manifold. This definition amasses too many features that are situated on entirely heterogeneous levels of description: aesthetic rules, moral norms, the empirical recipients' emotions, anthropological constants ('primitive feelings'), and so on. It is circular and opaque to the extent that it uses metaphors to paraphrase the metaphorical *definiendum* (hard to imagine, by the way, how a play is in-yer-face by shaking the recipients' neck). First and foremost, however, the definition of in-yer-face is far too general. Attributes like 'bold,' 'experimental' can probably be assigned to any art form that, since the early modern period, to say the least, has been bound to fulfil the norm of being new, original in terms of what is shown and how. Phrases like "takes the audience by the scruff of the neck and shakes it until it gets the message" and key words like "sensation" or "shock tactics" suggest that the main focus of Sierz' concept seems to lie in the new British playwrights' blatant depiction of corporeal violence or obscenities. The problem, however, with this definitional feature is that it is also too general. There are so many different instances of theatrical violence in various aesthetic or dramatic contexts that we tend to lose sight of the specific function that the representation of violence is to fulfil in each of these cases. The instances of violence shown in *Sir Gawain and the Green Knight* (late 14th c.), in *Titus Andronicus* (1594), in Antonin Artaud's *théâtre de la cruauté*, in Bret Easton Ellis' *American Psycho* (1991), and in Sarah Kane's *Blasted* (1995) are pretty much in-yer-face; however, having categorized these phenomena under this label, we can be absolutely sure that we have lost track of all the features that make the dramatic depiction of violence intellectually and aesthetically interesting.

Furthermore, it seems that Sierz wants to abstract the functional context in which violence is used in in-yer-face theatre to the field of 'morals' in the widest possible sense. What has been said in terms of the far too general concept of the violation of aesthetic norms turns out to be even more problematic in the general field of morals. Stating that plays by author X 'smash taboos,' 'jolts both actors and spectators out of conventional responses,' or 'questions moral norms' implicitly affirms these norms from the very start, and what is more, it reduces the plays in question to a secondary, or entirely parasitic, phenomenon. The role that violence plays in contemporary British drama is however much more complex and needs a concept that is nuanced enough to go beyond the smug notion of an aesthetic provocation that always, and necessarily therefore, affirms the norm. By drawing on the well-established concept of 'political theatre,' I will try to show how violence in contemporary drama is connected to an aesthetic stance that allows for a more extensive critique of social relations of power. Different from the 'agitprop' tradition of political theatre contemporary drama is 'post-political' to the extent that it aims at questioning 'politics' and 'policies' on the level of their conditions of possibility, namely on the level of 'polities.'

2. The Concept of Political Theatre

Especially in the broader Anglo-American context of cultural studies the phrase 'political theatre' has been used in a very far-reaching and correspondingly vague way. By using it as a synonym of whatever is of public and of social interest, the 'political' has thereby been expanded into "individual and collective experiences formerly considered 'private' or 'personal'" (Holderness 1992: 13). Similar to Marxist critique of ideology, this implies that, under the conditions of societal battles for power and domination, whether determined by economic factors or driven by an anonymous urge for control and disciplinarization, the personal or intimate sphere in which societal subjects can fulfil themselves independently is rather limited. Be this as generally debatable as it may – for the problem we are concerned with it should be clear that when "everything is considered politics, that is, strategies in different types of struggles for power, whether they are economic, cultural, ethnic, or based on sexuality or gender" (Nielsen & Jørgensen 2004: 62), the chances for a workable and sufficiently selective notion of political theatre as a specific dramatic subgenre are rather low.

From a historical point of view, the disadvantages of such an infelicitously broad concept of the political become even more apparent. The origins of political theatre in the narrower sense, namely as a specific subgenre in the history of drama, is usually traced back to the Agit-Prop movement of the 1910s and '20s. When setting down the possibly most comprehensive manifesto of political theatre in his 1929 essay collection *Das politische Theater*, Erwin Piscator (1963 [1929]) had, however, a comparatively precise agenda of political issues in mind. He aimed at revising programmatic guidelines and decisions of contemporary policies and at transforming patterns of political practices that concerned, for example, the working conditions of the lower classes, the equal distribution of economic goods, the social welfare or, later, the traumatic experience of the Shoah. For Piscator, Holderness's (1992: 14) remark "that plays about sexism in language, or male prostitution, or the personal experience of racism, have just as much claim to the status of 'political theatre'" would probably have counted as a typical example of middle-class self-mystification.

On the other hand, there is no doubt that an important current within contemporary British drama can be seen as renewing the dramatic techniques of political theatre according to Piscator. The same strive towards socio-political relevance can, however, also be found in much earlier playwrights of the 20th century. Few would question that the flagships of the 1950s and '60s New English Drama such as John Osborne, Anne Jellicoe, Arnold Wesker, John Arden, Edward Bond, or David Storey as well as the major representatives of the second generation including authors like David Edgar, Howard Barker, Howard Brenton, Trevor Griffith, David Hare, or Caryl Churchill were motivated by a critical stance towards the particular socio-political situation they were living and writing in.

What is required then is a more feasible concept of the political that allows us to comprise and compare the varied set of political theatre in a more systematic way and which would make it possible to grasp the specificity of the two playwrights in question here. A closer look at different concepts in the field of political science can help us in this endeavor. Typically, political scientists distinguish between 'polity' as opposed to 'policies' and 'politics.' 'Policies' refers to any political content which defines the political aims and purposes pursued by political players and factions. In order to enforce such (semantic) policies their representatives are required to undergo a process which involves conflict and in which the struggle for power and influence is negotiated. Policies thus presuppose 'politics' (in a narrower sense of the word) insofar as politics can be seen as a set of specific (pragmatic) strategies or tactics that allow the representatives of certain policies to realize their particular claims. Even more fundamental than policies and politics, then, is the term of 'polity.' For polities define the (syntactic) conditions of the political and juridical order under which policies can be thought out and/or under which politics can be put into practice. Hence, polities determine the discursive, epistemological, and linguistic setting that causes political orders to emerge in the first place (cf. *OED*, s.v. 'policy,' 'politics,' and 'polity;' for the German debate about these terms, cf. Rohe 1994).

Several of the playwrights forming part of the New English Drama belonged to a working class environment, some of them were committed to everyday party politics; consequently, their plays can be considered an aesthetic instrument of promulgating certain political concerns (policies) including, for example, the threat of nuclear war, the inhumane bureaucracy of the welfare state, social injustice, the growing cleft between the city, and the industrialized countryside, miners' problems, or the oppression of women. Even authors who did not refer to political issues that were considered of urgent importance at the time struggled at least with an abstract concept of society (cf. Zapf 1988) and were consequently dealing with practices of opinion-forming, distribution of information, and the possibilities of self-articulation that would allow all the people to actively participate in the political and economic developments of contemporary society (politics).

> BEATIE. […] I didn't know how to talk see, it was all foreign to me. Think of it! An English girl born and bred and I couldn't talk the language---except for to buy food and clothes. And so sometimes when he were in a black mood he'd start on me. 'What can you talk of?' he'd ask. 'Go on, pick a subject. Talk. Use the language. Do you know what language is?' Well, I'd never thought before – hev you? – it's automatic to you isn't it, like walking? 'Well, language is words,' he'd say, as though he were telling me a secret. 'It's bridges, so that you can get safely from one place to another. And the more bridges you know about the more places you can see!' [*To* JIMMY] And do *you* know what happens when you can see a place but you don't know where the bridge is? (Wesker 2001 [1959]: 22 f.)

Although authors like Mark Ravenhill (*1966) or Sarah Kane (1971-1999) share with these writers a deep depreciation of what they see as the outdated conventions of the well-made play, the political agenda of plays like *Blasted* (1995), *Phaedra's Love* (1996), *Cleansed* (1998) as well as *Shopping and Fucking* (1996), *Citizenship* (2005), *Pool (No Water)* (2006), *Shoot/Get Treasure/Repeat* (2008) is situated on an entirely different level. Roughly speaking we can say that Ravenhill and Kane produce test cases of political de-legitimation and re-legitimation. Their plays try to come to terms with the ethical and juridical conditions, or frameworks, of socio-political orders under which policies (political contents, or programs) can be conceived of and under which politics (political performances, procedures, or interactions) can be put into practice. Hence, the two exemplary plays we will deal with in this article are primarily situated on the more fundamental level of polity.

3. Sarah Kane's *Blasted* and the Force of Law

When Sarah Kane's play *Blasted* was first performed at the London Royal Court in 1995, the *Daily Mail* (Tinker 1995) hastened to label it a "feast of filth," while the *Guardian* (Billington 1995: 22) deliciously dwelled on the "scenes of masturbation, fellatio, frottage, micturition, defecation – ah, those old familiar faces – homosexual rape, eye gouging and cannibalism."

In terms of violence, *Blasted* (*B*) certainly does not fall short. A racist middle-aged journalist with lung cancer rapes epileptic Cate in a Leeds hotel room. Then war breaks out, a nameless Soldier comes on stage and tells Ian about the agonies of fighting. After raping Ian and sucking out his eyes, he shoots himself. In the last scene, Cate returns with a baby given to her by a victim of the war raging outside. When it dies, starving Ian tries to eat it. Notwithstanding its controversial reputation, *Blasted* was a huge theatrical success. It occasioned a mass media hype which at the time assured a sold-out run and thus made for the rampant, albeit short, career of the author who died in 1999.

Far from exploiting violent scenes as a mere eye-catcher, violence is intrinsically related to Kane's dramatic analysis of political power. This can be shown by a short digression into the history of political philosophy. As long as political sovereignty seems to be guaranteed by a divine agency, the political act of stating sovereign power represents what seems to be pre-existent, God-given, and eternally true. A prime example of this political paradigm is what Ernst Kantorowicz (1981) described as the medieval concept of political sovereignty, namely the notion of the sovereign's body natural being transcended by the body politic. The ideal foundation of this model of political embodiment was the double nature of Christ, his human and his divine nature that lies at the heart of the Christian *ecclesia* such as developed in Saint Paul's *Epistle to the Romans*: "For as we haue many members in one body, and all members haue not one office: So, we beyng many, are one body in Christe, and euery one members one of another" (*Bishops' Bible,* Rom. 12:4-6; see also 1 Cor. 12:12-27). Saint Paul thus intends to repeal any distinction between the political, the social, the individual, and the religious by seeing them unified in the ubiquitous presence of the Saviour, the *corpus mysticum Christi*. As a consequence of this, the symbolic representation of power on earth, too, seems to be secured by a transcendent force that guarantees a substantial relation between the symbolic acts of empowerment and the contents of what is thereby politically symbolized. Once this divine guarantee is problematized, however, the act of 'stating' political power becomes a performative act, that, instead of representing the supposedly divine right post factum, must be seen as creating, or producing, its proper foundation.

> Since the origin of authority, the foundation or ground, the position of the law can't by definition rest on anything but themselves, they are themselves a violence without ground. Which is not to say that they are in themselves unjust, in the sense of "illegal." They are neither legal nor illegal in their founding moment. (Derrida 1992 [1990]: 14)

Kane's *Blasted* is equal to this level of political reflection as the second part of the play presents a state of war highly reminiscent of the violent conflicts that took place between 1991 and 2001 in the territory of the former Socialist Republic of Yugoslavia. In one of her last interviews, Kane mentioned the following media experience at the time when she was writing her play:

> At some point during the first couple of weeks of writing [in March 1993] I switched on the news one night while I was having a break from writing, and there was a very old woman's face in Srebrenica just weeping and looking into the camera and saying – 'please, please, somebody help us, because we need the UN to come here and help us'. [...] I asked myself: 'What could possibly be the connection between a common rape in a Leeds hotel room and what's happening in Bosnia?' (Sierz 2001: 100 f.)

By broadcasting such scenes of violence and horror, the world wide mass media coverage of the conflict deliberately focused on aspects of international polity. As emotionally charged as these documentary impressions were, they also furthered the contemporary discussion about whether NATO's intervention into Yugoslavia would be legitimate, or whether it would contradict the United Nations' political principle of national sovereignty. Moreover, the decisive question of whether the Srebrenica massacre was to be categorized as genocide or not, concerned matters of polities, too. For, this eventually allowed the invocation of the 1948 United Nations "Conventions" according to which genocide is a punishable international crime which legitimized a state of exception that made it legally possible for the prosecutors to suspend the political sovereignty of the accused state in question and perform an act of usurpation in the name of a greater justice.

The legitimacy of such performative institutionalizations of political justice would require that what is being institutionalized is already in effect. It is only this that would provide the act of empowerment with legality and make the political force of justice a lawful one. Claiming sovereignty under the conditions of a lost transcendence, therefore, turns out to be a highly paradoxical act. And as a consequence of this, any form of political sovereignty is structurally bound to the epistemological impossibility of distinguishing between 'law' and 'violence,' i.e. between what is 'just' and 'justice' and what is not.

In the middle of Kane's *Blasted* the nameless soldier talks to Ian about the agonies of civil war, and the Soldier remembers what the enemy troops did to his former girlfriend Col: "[…] they buggered her. Cut her throat. Hacked her ears and nose off, nailed them to the front door." (*B* 47) Earlier in the scene, he describes the revenge he took:

> Went to a house just outside town. All gone. Apart from a small boy hiding in the corner. One of the others took him outside. Lay him on the ground and shot him through the legs. Heard crying in the basement. Went down. Three men and four women. Called the others. They held the men while I fucked the women. Youngest was twelve. Didn't cry, just lay there. (*B* 43)

At first glance, the actions described by the soldier seem to form part of what Francis Bacon described as the practice of *private revenge*: "a kinde of Wilde Iustice [...]. For as for the first Wrong, it doth but offend the Law; but the *Reuenge* of that wrong, putteth the Law out of Office" (Bacon 1966 [1625]: 18). A second glance at Kane's play, however, makes clear that, under the exceptional conditions of civil war, the soldier's actions are rather equivalent to what Bacon calls *public revenge* which for him "are for the most part, Fortunate" (ibid.: 19). Contrary to private revenges, public revenges are typical of *coups d'états*. Killing the sovereign can thus constitute a legitimate 'state of exception' during which the validity of the given law is suspended so as to re-enforce an institutionalizing contract that is bent on re-establishing the political order.

> That he should be conveyed to the Place from whence he came, and from thence to the place of Execution, and there to be hanged until he were half dead, his Members to be cut off, his Bowels to be cast into the Fire, his Head to be cut off, his Quarters to be divided into four several parts, and to be bestowed in four several Places. (Salmon 1719: 144)

The ritualized form of violence perpetrated on a nobleman found guilty of state treason in 1589, is quite similar to the fierce states of exception that Kane depicts in her play. Both constitute a transitory zone where the distinction between just and unjust, between law and violence is held in abeyance. Acts of public revenge such as committed by Kane's unnamed soldier or by the official executioner of Bacon's contemporary thus lay bare the wilderness of public justice on which the supposed validity of the given political law is based and founded.

Of course, Kane can also be seen to follow playwrights like Beckett (1906-1989), Pinter (1930-2008), and Bond (*1934) or avant-garde traditions such as Artaud's 'theatre of cruelty.' More adequately, however, it can be seen to draw on the rather ferocious heritage of early modern 'in-yer-face theatre' such as represented by *Titus Andronicus* as well as by Marlowe's *Tamburlaine* (1590), Webster's *Duchess of Malfi* (1614), or *King Lear* (1605).

> I was doing a workshop with this person who script edited it [*Blasted*] and he said, 'right I'm going to the toilet, and when I come back tell me what the title of the play is you're going to write', and I thought 'oh, for fuck's sake', and I knew it was about someone who got drunk a lot, so he came out and I said 'I'm going to call it *Blasted*. '[sic] It was only when I was into about the fourth draft I suddenly thought, 'of course, it's the blasted heath!' And by that time I was already reading *Lear, and* [sic] it was beginning to influence it, but it was just sheer coincidence, but once that happened I thought maybe this is – I hate to say destiny and things – but I thought maybe there's some subconscious drive to rewrite the play. (Saunders 2002: 58)

Sarah Kane's drawing on early modern forms of dramatic violence is an aesthetic method intended to make us re-experience the transcendent boundaries of political authority. Plays like *Blasted* can hence be seen as a dramatic practice that allows for imagining the lack of transparency of political power by staging discernible symbolic forms of political legitimation or de-legitimation within a context of historical change and political crisis. What Ravenhill once called Kane's 'classical' style rather results from her tendency to adopt political archaisms which make it possible for her to relocate the question of polity in much older mechanisms of political sovereignty based on the ruler's boundless and excessive power over life and death.

Due to Kane's dramatic technique, the political world of her play is thus eventually transformed into a *universal* state of exception which actualizes the intrinsic contradictions of polities in the performative mode. The logical plot of the well-made play, the well-ordered synopsis or syntagma of the myth of tragedy, is thereby transformed into an endlessly repeatable series, or paradigm, of violent 'actings' and gesticulations on stage. It is this particular quality of theatrical *opsis*, or theatrical performance, which makes Kane's play – contrary to Ravenhill's reading again – rather archaic than classic.

As is well known, *opsis*, or performance on stage, according to Aristotle is the least important quality of tragedy: "Spectacle, while highly effective, is yet quite foreign to the art and has nothing to do with poetry. Indeed the effect of tragedy does not depend on its performance by actors." (Aristotle, *Poetics* 1450b) And "to produce the tragic effect by means of an appeal to the eye is inartistic and needs adventitious aid, while those who by such means produce an effect which is not fearful but merely monstrous have nothing in common with tragedy" (ibid.: 1453b). For Aristotle "opsis is to be transformed into syn-opsis," and, as a consequence of this, the scenic medium is reduced to a mere surplus that "allows the plot to emerge" (Weber 2004: 101). In contrast, the intrinsic necessity and verisimilitude of what is dramatically represented has to guarantee the audience's aesthetic illusion while providing them with the occasion to identify with the characters' thoughts and actions represented on stage. The overall mimetic nature of tragedy is thus related to the discursive and logical order of a verisimilar, a uniform, and a complete story. The coherent plot of myth is able to transform the contingencies of the human actions and events (pragmata) into what Michelle Gellrich felicitously termed "calculable, intelligible possibilities, which are conformable to the precept of the usual, or the likely" (1988: 111 f.). This explains why Aristotle's theory of tragedy concentrates on how the tragic plot is to overcome the paradoxical reversal of the tragic shock (peripeteia). It is *anagnorisis*, or recognition, that is bound to put a definitive end to the potentially endless series of tragic reversals: "anagnorisis reassembles what peripeteia has overturned" (Weber 2004: 263). In contrast, the scenes from *Blasted* quoted above rather aim to delay the moment of anagnorisis, they tend to interminable repetition, one shock following another and spectacular "surprise piling up on surprise" (ibid.: 261).

Nevertheless, "*Blasted* is a hopeful play," Sarah Kane claims in one of her last interviews (Sierz 2001: 103). And from what we have said concerning the anti-classical quality of her dramatic art, it should be clear that the dramatic re-constitution which *Blasted* attempts to offer cannot but be closely related to *opsis*, the force of theatrical performance.

> [CATE] pulls a sheet off the bed and wraps it around her. She sits next to IAN's head. She eats her fill of the sausage and bread, then washes it down with gin. IAN listens. She feeds IAN with the remaining food. She pours gin in IAN's mouth. She finishes feeding IAN and sits apart from him, huddled for warmth. She drinks the gin. She sucks her thumb. Silence. It rains. IAN. Thank you. (*B* 60 f.)

By means of very basic, albeit ambiguous, gestures of shelter, comfort, need, and support, Cate overcomes the mass media discourse of revenge and counter-revenge represented in the play by her torturer Ian who dictates journalistic hate speeches over the phone. Cate's decision to forego any possible measures of revenge exceeds any psychological plausibility and goes beyond any conceivable syntagma of the dramatic plot. The form of a forgiving justice is purely situated on the level of the dramatic performance. This means that the "iterative quality of all performances, which imitate or actualize a rehearsed 'model'" (Wald 2007: 12) is deliberately glossed over by the sheer power of an apparently singular theatrical presence. Directly addressed to the audience, this strategy aims at transforming dramatic representation into a unique scene of community in which interpersonal proximity can be experienced in a new way.

This is how Kane's theatrical practice of countering mass media promises to release the characters from the interrelated discourse of violence and power. As a consequence they are enabled to refrain from using this exceptional situation as an instrument for empowerment. Instead, they are allowed to 'perform' the complete consumption or exhaustion of the political law and thereby dismiss their violent claim to sovereignty. Of course, (psycho)logically speaking, Cate seems to have all the right to take revenge on Ian for the suffering he caused her. When refraining to do so, however, she performs an ethical act from which a future post-civil order might emerge.

Like some of her early modern predecessors, Kane succeeds in re-locating the question of justice radically outside any human or secular frame of reference. Thus in Kane as well as in early modern tragedy the void left by the loss of what was *sacred*, provokes new forms of dramatic presentations that provide specific secular ways of experiencing the latencies, the epistemological blindness, of political institutionalization. The political theatre of *Blasted* aims at restoring a transcendent form of justice *post mortem*, a form of justice that is dissociated from the location of any human jurisdiction. "Thought you were dead," says Ian after Cate has had one of her epileptic states, and it is Cate who answers: "I suppose that's what it's like. [...] The world don't exist, not like this. / Looks the same but – / Time slows down. / A dream I get stuck in, can't do nothing about it. [...] Blocks out everything else. / Once –." (*B* 10, 22)

4. Mark Ravenhill's *Shopping and Fucking* – Debunking Polities

Shopping and Fucking (1996) is among Ravenhill's first plays; it premiered at Royal Court Upstairs before it became a worldwide success. Similar to Kane and other contemporary playwrights, it questions political systems on a fundamental level that concerns the conditions of the possibility of polities. Short-lived criticism has classified *Shopping and Fucking* (*SF*) as another prime example of British in-yer-face theatre of the 1990s although, as we will see, it works completely differently than Kane's *Blasted*. Whereas Kane's dramatic art reduces politics to an archaic level of ineluctable violence that is only overcome by a scenic performance of a mutual acceptance of the irreducible needs and fragility of the other, Ravenhill's play sets out to liquefy and debunk the various narratives of political legitimation that claim to narrate the origins of power.

> LULU. Tell us the shopping story.
> MARK. Please I want to …
> ROBBIE. Yeah, come on. You still remember the shopping story
> MARK. Well all right. I'm watching you shopping.
> LULU. No. Start at the beginning.
> MARK. That's where it starts.
> ROBBIE. No it doesn't. It starts with ›summer‹.
> MARK. Yes. OK. It's summer. I'm in a supermarket. It's hot and I'm sweaty. Damp. And I'm watching this couple shopping. I'm watching you. And you're both smiling. You see me and you know sort of straight away that I'm going to have you. You know you don't have a choice. No control. Now this guy comes up to me. He's a fat man. Fat and hair and lycra and he says: see the pair by the yoghurt? Well, says fat guy, they're both mine. I own them. I own them but I don't want them – because you know something? – they're trash. Trash and I hate them. Wanna buy them? How much? Piece of trash like them. Let's say … twenty. Yeah, yours for twenty. So, I do the deal. I hand it over. And I fetch you. I don't have to say anything because you know. You've seen the transaction. And I take you both away and I take you to my house. And you see the house and when you see the house you know it. You understand? You know this place. And I've been keeping a room for you and I take you into this room. And there's food. And it's warm. And we live out our days fat and content and happy. (*SF* 275)

Contrary to the conventions of drama, Ravenhill's play is mostly not action shown but a serialized performance of stories told. These stories exhibit the force that narratives possess in terms of the formation of communities. The fact that the characters' names (Mark, Robbie, Gary, and Lulu) refer to the boy band *Take That* and to the singer Lulu, who joined them on their hit single *Relight My Fire* (1993), shows the degree of irony to which such foundational narratives are to be exposed in the course of Ravenhill's play. Strategies like these can be seen as a dramatic act of political criticism (in the sense of performative analysis) because they show "the potential of theatrical performance to foreground the workings of [social] performativity through marking them as theatrical, that is, as representational rather than authentic" (Wald 2007: 23). More foundation myths, similar to the one the play starts off with, are performed by various characters throughout *Shopping*; they, too, evoke a rather mixed set of intertextual references ranging from the musical *Lion King* (based on the 1994 Disney movie) to Shakespeare's *Hamlet* (1600) (BRIAN. And there's this moment. This really terrific moment. Quite possibly the best moment. Because really, you see, his father is dead. Yes? The Lion King was crushed – you feel the sorrow welling up in you crushed by a wild herd of these big cows. One moment, lord of all surveys. And then ... a breeze, a wind, the stamping of a hundred feet and he's gone. Only it wasn't an accident. Somebody had a plan. You see? ... it was arranged by the uncle. Because. LULU. Because he wanted to be King all along. BRIAN. Thought you said you hadn't seen it. LULU. I haven't. Instinct. I have good instincts. That's one of my qualities. I'm an instinctive person; *SF* 277 f.) This indicates that Ravenhill's dramatic approach, unlike Kane's, is not so much about the violent impact of these archaizing myths but about staging theatricalized failures of such allegedly *grand récits*:

> GARY. I think we all need stories so that we can get by. And I think that a long time ago there were big stories. Stories so big you could live your whole life in them. The Powerful Hands of the Gods and Fate. The Journey to Enlightenment. The March of Socialism. But they all died or the world grew up or grew senile or forgot them, so now we're all making up our own stories. Little stories. It comes out in different ways. But we've each got one. (*SF* 335)

What Ravenhill indeed shows in the course of his play is how, based on their only very restricted validity, these 'big stories' can be made use of, can be repeated and appropriated in very specific contexts, in varied frameworks of interaction and based on highly individualized pragmatic needs.

> MARK. The important thing for me right now, for my needs, is that this doesn't actually mean anything, you know? Which is why I wanted something that was a transaction. Because I thought if I pay then it won't mean anything. Do you think that's right – in your experience?
> GARY. Reckon
> MARK. Because this is a very important day for me. I'm sorry, I'm making you listen.
> GARY. Everyone wants you to listen.
> MARK. Right. Well. Today you see is my first day of a new life. I've been away to get better well to acknowledge my needs anyway, and now I'm starting again and I suppose I wanted to experiment with you in terms of an interaction that was sexual but not personal or at least not needy, OK?
> A distant sound of coins clattering. (*SF* 294)

Ravenhill's play offers a site in which the difference between private and public, between systemic structures and individual practices, centre and periphery, between micropolitics and macropolitics is blurred by means of the characters' actively appropriating and thus liquefying socio-political models of order. This practice provides the subjects of power with at least a certain degree of autonomy. Ravenhill's debunking of the foundational *récits* of polities are realized through the character's interactions with these narratives. Running counter against systemic closure, social interaction is, as it were, 'naturally' inclined to exceed the codified boundaries and super-frames of social systems, because you can never be quite sure in which context you are actually situated. This explains why social interaction, in general, is characterized by a particular openness, and why this openness is theatrically exploited, institutionalized and made a general rule in Ravenhill's playful dramatic discourse. It is the histrionic playfulness ruling the characters' appropriative practices of social interaction that guarantees their liberty even in the worst of power games whereas in comparable struggles the protagonists of Kane's *Blasted* simply succumb to an authoritative and excessive power over life and death.

> GARY. Because – look – this bit. In my story. My story doesn't end like this. He doesn't fuck me. […] No. Because in the story he's always got something. It depends, changes. He gets me in the room, ties me up. But he doesn't just wanna fuck me does he? Cos it's not him, it's not his dick, it's a knife. He fucks me with a knife. So … […].
> LULU. You could die.
> GARY. No. I'll be OK. Promise.
> ROBBIE. It'll kill you.
> GARY. It's what I want.
> LULU. Go home. […]
> GARY. Listen, right. When someone's paying, someone wants something and they're paying, then you do it. Nothing right. Nothing wrong. It's a deal. So you do it. […] I thought you were for real. […] Pretending, isn't it? Just a story [...] I wan you to do it. Come on. You can do it. I've been looking. Looking and I can't find him. You knew that, didn't you? Because he's not out there. No. Because he's been here all the time. I've got this unhappiness. This big sadness swelling like it's gonna burst. And it's hurting me. I'm sick and I'm never going to be well again. I want it over. And there's only one ending.
> MARK. I understand.
> GARY. He's got no face in the story. He's in my head – waiting – but. I want to put a face to him. Your face. Do it. Do it and I'll say 'I love you.' (*SF* 352-54)

Whereas social macro-systems of law, economy, or politics, can only be described as being indifferent to interaction-related contingencies, interactional communication is characterized by what André Kieserling has recently described as "Distanzierung von der Gesellschaft in der Gesellschaft" (1999: 62). Thus, the general codes and programs on which the social macro-systems are based do not fully and securely apply here; instead they can be put to a series of rather ludic tests. Contrary to Kane's political theatre, Ravenhill reveals polities to be based on individualized and thus highly flexible practices of symbolic exchange due to which the legitimising narratives of societal power lose their monolithic force and can enter a playful state of dynamic transaction and revision. Entirely different from Kane's scenic acts of archaic (self-)sacrifice, it is rather the subversive power of symbolic interaction that constitutes the promise of bliss and of freedom which propels Ravenhill's dramatic economy. Especially, the last scene of *Shopping* shows how dramatic interaction can expose the structure of micropolitical performatives as highly individualized repetitions based on which the allegedly general patterns of social power systems and their prescriptions can "be investigated and reimagined" (Wald 2007: 17).

It's three thousand AD. Or something. It's the future. The earth has died. Died or we killed it. The ozone, the bombs, a meteorite. It just doesn't matter. But humanity has survived. A few of us ... jumped ship. And on we go. So it's three thousand and blahdeblah and I'm standing in the market, some sort of bazaar. A little satellite circling Uranus. Market day. And I'm looking at this mutant. Some of them, the radiation it's made them so ugly, twisted. But this one. Wow. It's made him ... he's tanned and blond and there's pecs and his dick ... I mean, his dick is three foot long. This fat sort ape-thing comes up to me and says ... See the mute with the three-foot dick? Yeah. I see him. Well, he's mine and I own him. I own him but I hate him. If I don't sell him today I'm gonna kill him. So a deal is struck, a transaction, I take my mutant home and I get him home and I say: I'm freeing you. I'm setting you free. You can go now. And he starts to cry. I think it's gratitude. I mean, he should be grateful but it's ... He says – well, he telepathizes into my mind – he doesn't speak our language – he tells me: Please. I'll die I don't know how to ... I can't feed myself. I've been a slave all my life. I've never had a thought of my own. And I say: That's a risk I'm prepared to take. (*SF* 358)

5. Further Developments in Contemporary British Drama

An important current within more recent contemporary British drama is characterized by a decisive renewal of documentary techniques of dramatic representation. For several years now, the London Tricycle Theatre, too, has been a major forum for contemporary documentary drama. The way in which the productions combine personal statements, letters, political speeches, legal and medical comments can hardly be distinguished from the kind of docu-montage the genre's precursors had practised long before them. However, similar to what we have observed in Kane and Ravenhill, the political impact of these performances has to be situated on the more fundamental level of polity.

One of the more recent Tricycle productions is Victoria Brittain's and Gillian Slovo's *Guantanamo: 'Honor Bound to Defend Freedom'*. First performed in 2004, it has since achieved worldwide success. *Guantanamo* uses interviews with detainees freshly released from the detention centre, situated at the Bahía de Guantánamo in Southern Cuba. The narrative of *Guantanamo* is characterized by a dialectic structure of personalization and de-personalization that, contrary to the literary tradition of docudrama, refuses to provide the audience with any socio-historical or socio-political explanation. Consequently, the transition from the societal state before and after the event of Guantanamo remains utterly incomprehensible. The individualization of history excludes more general and analytically valid forms of socio-political explanation, whereas the uncanny similarities between the different individual stories indicate an external dynamics of a historical process whose principles and laws nevertheless remain absolutely impenetrable.

It can be argued that these strategies of de-historicizing and depersonalizing have to be seen within the political context of the play. It is a dramatic means that allows the documenting of the political status of a socio-political order at the interstice of law and violence, and is eventually used to document the discursive position of juridical subjects at the intersection between man and animal. To corroborate this point, we only have to consider the beginning of the play. There the audience can witness a programmatic speech given by Lord Justice Johan Steyn on the 23rd of November 2003 at Lincoln's Inn, London. In his speech, Steyn calls the United States' naval base at Guantanamo Bay "a legal black hole" (Brittain & Slovo 2004: 5). According to Steyn the "purpose of holding the prisoners at Guantanamo Bay was and is to put them beyond the rule of law, beyond the protection of any courts, and at the mercy of the victors" (ibid.). As is generally known, after the 2002 US invasion in Afghanistan more than 1000 persons from more than 40 countries were classified as assumed Taliban and Al-Qaida members and brought to Guantanamo Bay. Instead of being categorized as Prisoners of War, they were termed as so-called *unlawful combatants*. As POWs the 1907 Hague Conventions and the 1949 Geneva Conventions would have applied, but the Bush administration decided to claim the supposed Taliban and Al-Qaida members were, what they called, *illegal combatants*. The term and category of illegal combatants were first introduced by the US Supreme Court in 1942. At the time, the Supreme Court upheld the jurisdiction of a military tribunal over the trial of several German saboteurs in the United States. The decision of the Court states:

> [...] the law of war draws a distinction between the armed forces and the peaceful populations of belligerent nations and also between those who are lawful and unlawful combatants. Lawful combatants are subject to capture and detention as prisoners of war by opposing military forces. Unlawful combatants are likewise subject to capture and detention, but in addition they are subject to trial and punishment by military tribunals for acts which render their belligerency unlawful. (Ex parte Quirin, 317 U.S. 1 [1942])

This also affects the testimonial strategy of Brittain and Slovo's *Guantanamo*. Instead of giving voice to its protagonists, the play bears testimony to societal subjects that have lost the possibility of speaking and thus oscillates between an animal-like state of being and the ultimate reduction to identifiable patterns of juridico-political discourse. Between mumbling, whispering and remaining silent on the one hand and repeating the prefabricated samples of a legally testifying subject on the other, the detainees' speeches are presented in their empty relation to a discourse the individuals cannot take responsibility for anymore.

> MR BEGG. One night two Pakistanis ... two American soldiers, assisted by two Pakistani officers, burst into [Moazzam's] house [in Pakistan], took him as prisoner, threw him to the floor, bundled him up and put him into the boot of their car – in front of other neighbours and the little child, she saw that and - they took him away. I received a telephone. ...it was whispering...I think he had his mobile with him or what ...he said – just like that *Mr Begg drops his voice and whispers* 'Dad,' *Raising his voice to normal.* I said: 'Who is that?' He said: *Dropping to a whisper again.* 'Moazzam.' *Normal voice.* I said: 'Why you are talking like that?' 'I have been arrested.' I said: 'By whom?' He said: 'two Pakistanis ... two American soldiers and two Pakistanis soldiers.' I said: 'Where are you?' He said: 'I'm in the car and they are taking me away, I don't know where. My wife and children are in Pakistan, please take care of them and don't worry,' and then either somebody saw him talking or something... (Brittain & Slovo 2004: 23).

By confronting the intrinsic tensions of the documentary tradition of political theatre, *Guantanamo* manages to refrain from naturalizing its demands for historical truth and individual authenticity. By giving up docudrama's epistemological claim to understanding the principles and rules of socio-political and historical processes, Brittain and Slovo succeed in documenting a state of society where the possibility to distinguish between law and violence has been forfeited. On the other hand, by problematizing docudrama's traditional claim to authentic representation of the outlawed subject, *Guantanamo* manages to stage the voicelessness of legal subjects that have been deprived of their right to political discourse in an extra-juridical state of exception. The individuals who are given the power to speak here are at the same time social representatives of those who have officially and, as it were, legitimately been deprived of any right to political discourse or juridical *logos*.

Since the time of Aristotle's *Politics* (c. 329-26 BC), discourse or speech has been considered the condition of possibility for any political or jurdical order, for:

> now, that man is more of a political animal than bees or any other gregarious animals is evident. Nature, as we often say, makes nothing in vain, and man is the only animal whom she has endowed with the gift of speech. And whereas mere voice is but an indication of pleasure or pain, and is therefore found in other animals (for their nature attains to the perception of pleasure and pain and the intimation of them to one another, and no further), the power of speech is intended to set forth the expedient and inexpedient, and therefore likewise the just and the unjust. And it is a characteristic of man that he alone has any sense of good and evil, of just and unjust, and the like, and the association of living beings who have this sense makes a family and a state. (Aristotle, *Politics* 1252b)

Contrary to these premises of polities, the societal subjects documented in *Guantanamo* are situated in the interstice between man and animal, between a surrender to the power of offical discourse and mumbling silence. Brittain and Slovo's indirect approach using discursive and narrative structures thus constitutes a new form of documentary theatre that stages a *drama of polity*.

Similar to the productions of Kane and Ravenhill, *Guantanamo* could, of course, also be described as taking "the audience by the scruff of the neck and shak[ing] it until it gets the message;" "a theatre of sensation [that] jolts both actors and spectators out of conventional responses, touching nerves and provoking alarm" (Sierz 2001: 4). This type of generalization does not, however, account for the specific function of violence which is characteristic of each of these plays. Rather, harnessing models of political philosophy allows us to view the plays in terms of a fundamental critique of polities. In other words, a more specific classification shows that these plays do more than merely tapping "into more primitive feelings, smashing taboos, mentioning the forbidden, creating discomfort" (Sierz 2001: 4). Furthermore, a conceptualization of contemporary drama as a political theatre that is so radically situated on this self-reflexive level of polity has allowed us both to distinguish it from immediate precursors of the 1950s and '60s New English Drama and at the same time become aware of how intimately they are affiliated to the earlier modern tradition of questioning the potentiality of sovereignty on stage. In the case of *Blasted* and *Guantanamo*, polities are shown to be intrinsically related to an exceptional power over life and death. Ravenhill, on the other hand, scenically explores questions of micro-political tactics of resistance against an agency of power that re-affirms itself through foundational narratives. All of these plays, however, go far beyond sheer scandal and sensation so that the gains of viewing them through the lens of in-yer-face seem to be after all rather meagre.

Bibliography

Primary Sources

Kane, Sarah. 2001 [1995]. "Blasted." In: Sarah Kane. *Complete Plays*. David Greig (introd.). London: Methuen. 1-61.

Ravenhill, Mark. 2001 [1996]. "Shopping and Fucking." In: Graham Whybrow (ed.). *The Methuen Book of Modern Drama: The Plays of the '80s and '90s*. London: Methuen. 271-359.

Annotated Bibliography

Holderness, Graham (ed.). 1992. *The Politics of Theatre and Drama*. New York: Macmillan.
A comprehensive overview of contemporary forms of political theatre; most of the articles are situated in the theoretical context of cultural studies.

Howe Kritzer, Amelia. 2008. *Political Theatre in Post-Thatcher Britain: New Writing 1995-2005*. New York: Palgrave.
A useful survey of recent British playwrights and their works which focuses on the socio-political and historical context. Additionally, this work engages with questions raised by Sierz (see below); particularly useful in terms of her analysis of contemporary reactions to performances.

Fischer-Lichte, Erika. 2005. *Theatre, Sacrifice, Ritual: Exploring Forms of Political Theatre*. London/New York: Routledge.
Based on ritual theory and theory of interaction, this book shows the societal force of performance with case studies ranging from Max Reinhardt's Oedipus Rex to the 1919 Soviet production of The Overthrow of Autocracy.

Nielsen, Ken & Lisbet Jørgensen. 2004. *Political Theatre Revisited and Redefined*. Copenhagen: Föreningen Nordiska Teaterforskare.
Theoretically advanced study on contemporary forms of theatre; situated in the context of cultural studies; especially dedicated to the 'politics' of gender, class, and race.

Piscator, Erwin. 1963 [1923]. *Das politische Theater*. Hamburg: Rowohlt.

The most comprehensive manifesto of early 20th century political theatre. This includes original documents and images of Piscator's productions.

Saunders, Graham. 2002. *'Love Me or Kill Me': Sarah Kane and the Theatre of the Extremes*. Manchester: Manchester UP.

Useful introduction into the life and work of the British playwright. This work includes insightful close readings of her work in addition to interviews and useful background information concerning the production and performance of her plays during her lifetime.

Sierz, Aleks. 2001. *In-Yer-Face Theatre: British Drama Today*. London: Faber and Faber.

Apart from the conceptual problems discussed in this article, this is a well-documented survey of theatre in Britain in the 90s; it focuses on the attitude of the major plays and playwrights of this decade based largely on the author's interviews and personal experiences of the performances.

Wald, Christina. 2007. *Hysteria, Trauma and Melancholia: Performative Maladies in Contemporary Anglophone Drama*. New York/Basingstoke: Palgrave Macmillan.

Based on psychoanalytical approaches and performance studies, Wald shows the gendered nature of the extreme states of mind exhibited in plays by Kane and others.

Zapf, Hubert. 1988. *Das Drama in der abstrakten Gesellschaft: Zur Theorie und Struktur des modernen englischen Dramas*. Tübingen: Niemeyer.

This study shows how playwrights of the New English Drama and beyond perform their experience of society as abstract and impersonal. This work focuses on Osborne, Wesker, Arden, Stoppard, and others.

Further Secondary Literature

Aristotle. 1982 [1967, c. 350 BC]. *Poetics*. Gerald F. Else (transl. & intro.). Ann Arbor, MI: U of Michigan P.

—. 1984 [c. 329-26 BC]. *Politics*. Carnes Lord (transl.). Chicago: U of Chicago P.

—. 2009 [1930, originally published as part of *Organon* c. 1st c. BC]. *Posterior Analytics*. E.S. Forster & Hugh Tredennick (transl.). Cambridge, MA: Harvard UP.

Bacon, Francis. 1966 [1937, 1625]. "Of Reuenge". In: Francis Bacon. *The Essays or Counsels, Civil and Moral*. Brian Vickers (ed.). London: Oxford UP.

Billington, Michael. 1995. "Review of *Blasted*." In: *The Guardian* 20 Jan.: 22.

Brittain, Victoria & Gillian Slovo. 2004. *Guantanamo: 'Honor bound to defend freedom.'* London: Oberon.

Derrida, Jacques. 1992 [1990]. "Force of Law: The 'Mystical Foundation of Authority.'" In: Drucilla Cornell, Michael Rosenfeld & David Gray Carlson (eds.). *Deconstruction and the Possibility of Justice*. London/New York: Routledge. 3-67.

Gellrich, Michelle. 1988. *Tragedy and Theory: The Problem of Conflict since Aristotle.* Princeton: Princeton UP.

Kantorowicz, Ernst. 1981. *The King's Two Bodies: A Study in Medieval Political Theology.* Princeton: Princeton UP.

Kieserling, André. 1999. *Kommunikation unter Anwesenden: Studien über Interaktionssysteme.* Frankfurt a.M.: Suhrkamp.

Lüdeke, Roger. 2007. "The Politics of Documentary Drama: 'Honor Bound to Defend Freedom.'" In: Klaus Stierstorfer (ed.). *Anglistentag 2007 in Münster: Proceedings.* Trier: WVT. 115-23.

Rohe, Karl. 1994. *Politik: Begriffe und Wirklichkeiten: Eine Einführung in das politische Denken.* Stuttgart: Kohlhammer.

Salmon, Thomas (ed.). 1719. "The Tryal of Philip Howard, Earl of Arundel, the 18th day of April, 1589. and in the 31st Year of the Reign of Queen Elizabeth." In: *A Compleat Collection of State-Tryals, and Proceedings upon Impeachments for High Treason, and other Crimes and Misdemeanours; from the Reign of King Henry the Fourth, to the End of the Reign of Queen Anne.* Vol. 1. London. 140-44.

Supreme Court of the United States. 1942. "Ex parte Quirin, 317 U.S. 1." 31. July. <http://www.law.cornell.edu/supct/html/historics/USSC_CR_0317_0001_ZS.html> (last accessed: 15 Nov. 2007).

Tinker, Jack. 1995. "This Disgusting Piece of Filth." In: *Daily Mail* 19 Jan.

Weber, Samuel. 2004. *Theatricality as Medium.* New York: Fordham UP.

Wesker, Arnold. 2001 [1959]. "Roots." In: Graham Whybrow (ed.). *The Methuen Book of Sixties Drama.* London: Methuen. 1-92.

26. Drama and Postmodernism: Martin Crimp's *Attempts on Her Life* and Patrick Marber's *Closer*

Sarah Heinz

1. The Postmodern Condition: Delight or Trouble

Like all periodizations, the era of postmodernism is not a historical fact but rather a discursive construction (cf. McHale 1992: 1). Although the prefix 'post' seems to imply a clear-cut historical beginning of a period after modernity, to date there is no consensus on the status or definition of postmodernism and its relation to modernity (for an overview cf. Zima 2001).

In the sense of an artistic movement and a description of developments in industrialized, Western societies, the beginning of postmodernism can be located after the Second World War but it has many connections to society and the arts before the War. It can therefore be defined as both a breach with and as a continuation, acceleration and radicalization of modern developments (cf. Zima 2001: 36; Welsch 2008). In the sense of a cultural and literary theory with different schools of thought like deconstruction, poststructuralism, or discourse analysis, it has been claimed that postmodernism is a phenomenon that started in the 1960s (cf. Butler 2002: 2 f.). Students of postmodernism will soon realize that an additional problem with defining the notion is the heterogeneity of the thinkers, disciplines, and attitudes that are often subsumed under the umbrella term of postmodernism. These include historical studies like Michel Foucault's discourse analyses, Jacques Derrida's studies on language and philosophy or Jean-Francois Lyotard's studies on philosophy and Enlightenment thought, studies on media and society like Jean Baudrillard's, on postcolonial aspects like Homi K. Bhabha's, gender theory like Judith Butler's, or on sociological and economic aspects like Fredric Jameson's.

Generally, postmodernism describes, analyses, and criticizes the condition of Western society and its technological, social, cultural, and economic developments. These developments can be described in terms of globalization and an increasing dependence upon technology, especially media technology, in warfare, communication, transportation or consumption, and in terms of differentiation and specialization. Since the Second World War, it has become increasingly difficult or even impossible to grasp our world or even a single society in its totality. Thus, postmodern societies have not only become specialized and differentiated but also increasingly abstract (cf. Zijderveld 1970). In this context, postmodernism has been assessed as a reaction against modern thought in the sense of Enlightenment thought with its vision of one whole and knowable world and attached values like objectivity, rationality, and science. The basis upon which these values rest is accordingly rejected as well: the stable, coherent, and self-conscious subject which Descartes defined in the famous formula "I think therefore I am" (cf. Zima 2001: 26 f.). As a result, postmodernism is concerned with the crisis of modern societies and modern individuals, and it reflects this crisis by becoming self-reflexive and meta-historical. If there is no objective world outside the self and if this self is also a construction, of language, of discourse, of media, then the only thing which culture and theory can look at are the processes and means of constructing the world and the self.

These insights into the fundamental constructedness of self and world result in an ongoing decentring and pluralization of collective and individual identities and in a questioning and destruction of clear-cut boundaries and their ensuing hierarchies and oppositions. In this vein, Lyotard defined postmodernism as "incredulity towards metanarratives" or so-called "grand narratives" (1986: xxiv). The most prominent oppositions to be questioned in the last few decades have been male/female and mind/body; subjective/objective, fact/fiction, and rational/irrational; or self/other, centre/margin, and colonizer/colonized. 'The world' turns into a plurality of worlds, history turns into a myriad of equally true stories, and the self turns into a multiplicity of incoherent or even mutually exclusive selves.

Due to this dissolving of certainties, one major effect of postmodernism has been a feeling of loss: the loss of the stable subject and the individual's authenticity, the loss of truth, objectivity, and universality or the disappearance of reality. Consequently, an absence and insecurity emerges at the centre of contemporary society (if there still is such a thing as a centre), a development which has been described as an increasing indifference and exchangeability of all values, identities, and also of capital and objects (cf. Zima 2001: 44 f.). But apart from this negative assessment of postmodernism as loss and insecurity a positive assessment is equally possible. The insight into the world's and the self's fundamental constructedness can have a liberating effect because the world as we see it can and must be changed, if only by constantly questioning the status quo of our constructions and by playfully rearranging the fragments of modernity. It is this value of constant questioning and rearrangement that most postmodern art and literature share. It forces us to tolerate any cultural, political, racial, or gendered other and to re-assess our own positions in the light of cultural relativity. This playful questioning constitutes the much-discussed ethical impetus of postmodernism (cf. Bauman 1993). Postmodern paradoxes can delight or trouble as Hutcheon has pointed out (1988: x), but they will always stimulate reactions.

2. Drama and Postmodernism

As a direct consequence of this relativist and pluralist thinking and the resulting questioning attitude, postmodern art and postmodern theatre test our intellectual responses towards a work of art or a theatrical performance and suggest that notions of beauty, coherence, and absolute aesthetic evaluations are suspect. We are not simply able to lean back and enjoy the performance in the safety of the auditorium. Quite the contrary, postmodern drama aims at making us feel disturbed and insecure, an approach it shares with in-yer-face theatre, which aims at "questioning moral norms" and jolting "both actors and spectators out of conventional responses, touching nerves and provoking alarm" (Sierz 2000: 4, see chapter 25). Postmodern drama thus questions our processes of making sense, very often by making it impossible or at least very difficult to create any stable meaning at all. And it is the spectator and not the author or the director who creates that (always temporary) meaning.

Hans-Thies Lehmann (2006: 27 f.) has summed up this tendency of drama after postmodernism in his term 'postdramatic theatre,' which again implies something that has ended, traditional dramatic theatre, and something which comes after it, questioning but also continuing and radicalising its tradition. Lehmann locates postdramatic theatre in scenic practice since the 1970s which rejects the conventions of traditional theatre, namely imitation, character, action/plot, the fourth wall and a play's social function of bringing about "affective recognition and solidarity" (ibid.: 21) by the moment of catharsis. The stage in traditional theatre represents and therefore is the world, "abstracted but intended for the imagination and empathy of the spectator to follow and complete the *illusion*" (ibid.: 22). Traditional theatre therefore aims at not only representing but *being* a world as a totality: "Wholeness, illusion and world representation are inherent in the model 'drama'; conversely, through its very form, dramatic theatre proclaims wholeness as the *model* of the real" (ibid.: 22).

It is obvious that postmodern drama cannot subscribe to these notions of either theatre or reality as whole and representable. Postmodern drama therefore experiments with fragmentation, self-reflexivity, and metadramatic modes by pointing to and performing its own constructedness instead of performing a coherent story with individual characters on a realistic background. This is not entirely new as examples like Luigi Pirandello's *Six Characters in Search of an Author*, first performed in 1921, show. Indeed, postmodern drama has many connections to theatrical movements before the Second World War like epic theatre, surrealist and avant-garde theatre, or Artaud's *theatre of cruelty*. Nevertheless, British drama after the 1970s and increasingly from the late 1980s onwards take these older anti-illusionist approaches one step further by embedding a rejection of concepts like plot, character, representation, and realism into a radically relativist but also playful illustration of the way that language, media, and discourses construct our worlds and selves. One example would be Sarah Kane's *4.48 Psychosis* (2000) in which there are no explicit characters and the text consists mainly of a series of numbers, monologues, or bits of poetry, or Caryl Churchill's *Blue Heart* (1997), two one-act plays that start out as seemingly naturalistic pieces that are then increasingly infused with anti-naturalistic wordplay or repetitive dialogue.

As language is one of the central means of creating self and world, postmodern drama often plays with language via repetition, linguistic ready-mades, and intertextual quotation, often from popular media like advertisement or film, rather than staging a dialogue between two realistic characters (cf. Agusti 2005). Together with plot, character, and imitation, notions of individual and collective history as truth are also dismissed, as can be seen in Michael Frayn's *Copenhagen* (1998) where characters are trying to find out about the true version of their past and the meaning of universal history. Needless to say, they find neither the truth nor universal history. Instead, the play presents circular and repetitive retellings of history without any recognizable direction which result in contradictory, multiple, and subjective versions which are all equally true. Martin McDonagh's *The Pillowman* (2003) takes an even more radical look at history and stories by assessing the futile attempt to make fiction, stories, and reality correspond in the story of a writer who is accused of murder because his grisly stories about child murder seem to be enacted in real life. This play takes postmodern incredulity towards history one step further by showing that not even an individual's life story can ever be recounted 'as it really happened.' Postmodern drama therefore shares many characteristics with biography and the memory play (see chapter 21) and with metadrama (see chapter 24).

Formal experiment is not an end in itself though. By making it impossible to sit back and enjoy the performance, postmodern drama addresses central issues of contemporary society and stages their contradictions. Gender roles are deconstructed by plays like Marina Carr's *Low in the Dark* (1989) where men and women create images of each other by retelling their unsuccessful relationships or fantasizing about the ideal woman in a self-reflexive and decidedly anti-realistic play. And racial boundaries and images of the other are questioned in plays like debbie tucker green's *Stoning Mary* (2005) in which the play's black characters are performed by white actors and one character is sometimes played by two actors who engage in a highly stylized internal dialogue reminiscent of poetry and rap music (see chapter 28).

The following two interpretations will outline to what extent and to what effect drama after postmodernism breaks with but also how it continues and radicalizes tendencies of modernity and traditional theatre.

3. Martin Crimp's *Attempts on Her Life* and Patrick Marber's *Closer*

Martin Crimp's play *Attempts on Her Life* (*AHL*) premiered at the Royal Court Theatre Upstairs in London in March 1997, Patrick Marber's play *Closer* (*C*) was first performed at the Royal National Theatre in London in May of the same year. 1997 was a decisive year in which Britain saw the death of Lady Di, the election of Tony Blair, the publication of the first book of the *Harry Potter* series, and the beginning of devolution. It was the year the British left Hong Kong, the Rodney King trial started the Los Angeles riots and the year of the cloning of the sheep 'Dolly.' 1997 thus marks both endings and beginnings at the dawn of a new millennium and at the close of an old one, and it is very fitting that Crimp and Marber deal with postmodernism in the sense of loss and endings as well as potential new beginnings and rearrangements. Both plays have won numerous awards, transferred successfully to Europe and the USA and were translated into several languages. They are frequently revived and in early 2001

Closer became one of the first plays from the 1990s to be performed in the new millennium. In 2004, Marber's play was adapted into a major Hollywood film with a cast including Julia Roberts, Natalie Portman, Jude Law, and Clive Owen.

The following interpretation of the two plays as representatives of postmodern or postdramatic theatre is based on three categories: formal aspects, the problem of character, selves and identities, and the role of media, images, and the disappearance of reality. However, other categorizations of *Attempts on Her Life* and *Closer* have included in-yer-face theatre, metadrama, or contemporary tragicomedy (cf. Sierz 2000: 187-95; Saunders 2008: 29-32). The following interpretation will therefore focus on the specifically postmodern aspects of the two plays, only touching upon features that Crimp and Marber share with these and other theatrical movements.

3.1 Formal Aspects

Crimp's and Marber's plays can both be described as postdramatic in their formal construction as they reinterpret and question all the basic ingredients of traditional theatre: character, action and plot, and its naturalistic modes of representing these elements on stage as imitation. They also use elements, quotations, and references from a multiplicity of genres and texts to create a heterogeneous, open structure that refers to both popular and high-brow culture. Thus, they draw attention more to *how* theatre presents and creates meaning and less to *what* is being presented. And yet, both plays are also connected to the ideal of traditional theatre of presenting a world on stage, because it is the fragmented, multiple, and mediatized world of contemporary postmodern societies that is being performed in all its ambiguity.

Of the two plays, *Attempts on Her Life* is the more openly anti-illusionistic. It has no directions as to what the stage or the actors should look like, and the only information on the actors is that "[t]his is a piece for a company of actors whose composition should reflect the composition of the world beyond the theatre." (*AHL* v) In the first production the company consisted of eight actors, four male and four female of mixed ethnic background, but it has been performed with different numbers of actors and changing mixtures of ethnic groups. Speeches are not assigned to specific actors; dashes indicate a change of speaker, while a slash marks the point of interruption in overlapping dialogue. The play is set in no specific time or place, features no discernable, named characters who actually appear on stage and has no coherent plot. Instead of acts, it is divided into 17 scenarios which can be played in any order and of which the first, "All Messages Deleted," may be cut in performance. If there is a plot in *Attempts on Her Life*, it can be described as "a rollercoaster of late twentieth-century obsessions" as it is called on the dust jacket. These obsessions include unprotected sex and pornography as well as terrorism and ethnic cleansing, advertising, art as well as consumption and personal relationships. In all scenarios, different generic forms and languages are used, quoted, and ironically rearranged, for example the conventions of Hollywood romance in the second scenario, the language and style of advertisement in the seventh scenario, or the language and conventions of art criticism in scenario eleven. This juxtaposition of completely different discourses with their languages and conventions creates a kaleidoscopic image of postmodern society as an era of indifference and relativity, but also of the possibility of combining, rearranging, and re-evaluating things that traditionally are not assessed together. The audience is asked to scrutinize its values and identities when they witness that the description of an advertisement for a new car is presented next to a conversation about ethnic cleansing and dead babies, or when a discussion about suicide as art or about pornography stands next to a text about communicating with aliens or about particle physics.

Compared to this open rejection of realism and the fragmented, intertextual and multi-generic form of Crimp's play, *Closer* seems to be a much more traditional piece. It at least has a rough outline of a plot, a setting, and characters who are established as protagonists with a name and some background. The play is set in London in the 1990s and follows the lives of its four characters over four and a half years in twelve scenes which are presented chronologically. There is Dan, a newspaper obituarist, who meets Alice, a stripper, and begins a relationship with her. And there is Anna, a photographer, who begins a relationship with Larry, a dermatologist, but who also has an affair with Dan. The couples break up, change partners and reunite, only to finally separate at the end of the play to never meet again after Alice has died in an accident. This seems to be a very traditional story along the lines of romance and tragedy. And yet, *Closer* shares many of Crimp's postdramatic features. Although Marber's play somehow retains features of the well-made play, it is self-consciously modern, aggressive in language, and depicts or at least heavily hints at violence and sexual acts. Except for a few props the stage is empty and although the four characters have names and a bit of their biographical background is sketched in the early scenes they remain flat stereotypes or "vivid cartoon shapes" (Dromgoole 2000: 193). Alice is described as "a girl from the town," Dan is "a man from the suburbs," Larry is "a man from the city," and Anna is "a woman from the country" (*C* n. pag.). Much in the style of Jacobean or Restoration drama characters are "represented through type" and "based on class/social position rather than individual psychology. So while on the surface *Closer* seems realistic, conventional patterns of characterization are largely absent" (Saunders 2008: 21). This also becomes obvious in the generic hybridity of the play which is comedy and tragedy, satire and romance, and which uses conventions, language and images from all these generic traditions. In its reinterpretation of character, plot, and the conventions of imitation it is thus very similar to the playful rearranging and questioning attitude of Crimp.

3.2 The Problem of Character, Selves, and Identity

Postmodernism and its drama revolve around the question of the self and its identity. What is this 'I' that I am, what is the 'I' that is addressing me from the stage and what makes it what it is? Am I an effect of circumstances or am I also a free agent? These questions are at the heart of most plays that have been assessed as postmodern or post-dramatic like Frayn's *Copenhagen* or Churchill's *Blue Heart* and thus also at the heart of Crimp's and Marber's plays. In their form and content, the plays oscillate between selves and characters as fragmented effects of circumstances and discourses on the one hand and moments of self-conscious decisions and a rejection of preformed images on the other.

This becomes obvious in *Attempts on Her Life* which, despite the formal fragmentation outlined above, has a certain unity in the character that all the scenarios are about, the woman implied in the title, whose name is alternately given as Anne, Ann, Anya, Annie, Anny, or Annushka. Scenario 1, "All Messages Deleted," combines these multiple constructions of Anne into one scene in which we hear voices from an answering machine that foreshadow the other scenarios of the play and that address the woman the play is looking for.

And yet, this woman with these multiple but also similar names is never present on stage herself. Just as postmodern societies are formed around an emptied centre, the play is formed around an absence that all 17 scenarios are trying to recreate on stage: "Anne's contradictory character indicates that she's an absurdist notion, an absence filled by other people's opinions and ideas" (Sierz 2006: 52). The attempts on her life of the title are therefore both the suicide attempts talked about in scenario eleven as well as the actors' and the audience's attempts at creating Anne's life out of the material that is presented to us. In that sense, in spite of its rejection of character, plot, and their coherence the play also maintains at least traces of the unified subject and a unified story in our struggle to make sense of Anne. The incidents happening to Anne in the play are therefore "only as significant as the manner in which they are interpreted, understood and represented" (Dromgoole 2000: 62). It is no surprise that the attempts on Anne's life fail in establishing a round character. Instead we are presented with fragmented parts of a whole multiplicity of Annes that fail to combine into one coherent whole. The absent Anne is created as a dead child or an older woman, as a terrorist, wife or daughter, as a porno actress, a rock star, as a performance artist, and in one scenario even as the make of a car.

In this rejection of character and plot Crimp's play is, together with plays like Kane's *4.48 Psychosis*, one of the most radical plays of the 1990s because the absence of Anne is presented by being told rather than shown to the audience. In this sense, the actors are "speakers not characters" (Zimmermann 2003: 74). There is no action on stage and the spoken text of the scenes creates the impression that what is being told to us is not a finished script but is being created on the stage at the moment of utterance. One example of this is the second scenario in which Anne is a young, idealistic woman who has an affair with an older, richer and powerful man in an unnamed European city. Their reconciliation after a dispute is described as follows: "He kisses her and presses her back down onto the bed. Or she him. Better still: *she* presses *him* back down onto the bed such is her emotional confusion, such is her sexual appetite, such is her inability to distinguish between right and wrong in this great consuming passion

[...]" (*AHL* 16). This is a succinct description of the audience's experience. We are confused by what and how things are presented to us and we are not able to distinguish between right or wrong as we have never actually seen the scene or the described characters on stage. We only see actors on stage telling us about them. The use of the generic conventions of romantic Hollywood movies and the obvious construction and rearrangement of what is being told to us in a language heavily influenced by conventional discourses on sexuality, gender, consumption, and luxury reinforce this feeling of unreliability, insecurity, and a loss of a tangible, coherent reality.

Marber's *Closer* makes a very similar statement on postmodern identities and the circumstances which influence their shaping and reshaping but puts its emphasis on personal relationships and love. Saunders has stated that the overall impression that *Closer* creates is that of "a fluidity of identity, where none of the characters are what they seem. [...] Character development in the play is shown more as a form of slippage" (2008: 21). All four characters seem to be superficial, empty, and dependent on the images other people have of them. Nearly the only information we get on Anne is that she takes portrait photographs of strangers, otherwise she remains an enigma as far as her feelings or motivations are concerned. The same holds true for the male characters, Larry and Dan. In scene 3, in which the two men chat over the Internet, Dan takes on the persona of Anna, engages in cybersex with Larry and accidentally arranges a meeting between Larry and the real Anna that ironically ends with the two beginning a relationship. Why these people do things, why they fall in love or separate is one of the central blank spaces in the play (cf. Sierz 2000: 194). To the audience they remain what Dan calls "known strangers" (*C* 107).

This postmodern fluidity and constructedness of identity becomes most obvious in the character of Alice Ayres, the young stripper about whom Larry says at the end of the play "She made herself up" and who herself answers the question of who she is with "I'M NO ONE." (*C* 115, 111). In Alice, gender, body, and sexuality become the focus of attention and the idea of the skin and the body as a last resort of authenticity is rejected in scenes like scene 7, which is set in a strip club where Larry meets Alice after Anna has left him (cf. *C* 62-73). Here, Larry craves for intimacy and closeness and tries to get both by having Alice strip for him, mistaking nakedness for authenticity. However, the more naked Alice gets and the closer Larry looks at her body, the more distant and anonymous she becomes. Larry therefore tells her that she is "wearing armour" and summarizes his sexual experience as "[e]verything is a Version of Something Else" (ibid.: 67, 63). Both male and female gendered identities are here exposed as effects of a discourse on sexuality and the body that is highly influenced by media images and pornography, an analysis which *Closer* shares with *Attempts on Her Life*, especially with scenario 16, "Pornó," in which violence against women is contrasted with the sanitized images of the porno industry (cf. *AHL* 71-79). The two plays are thus set at a specific juncture in the 1990s when the discussion of gender, the New Man, and feminist politics had reached a point where, as Marber said in an interview, "no one knows what's going on anymore" (Sierz, qtd. from Saunders 2008: 9). Gendered identities, the body, and sexuality are therefore as relative, multiple, and constructed as all other identities that the postmodern self might want to go back to. Male and female qualities become equally contingent and arbitrary, as Alice points out by describing the ideal woman of male fantasy in scene 1: "Men want a girl who looks like a boy. They want to protect her but she must be a survivor. And she must come ... like a *train* ... but with ... *elegance*" (*C* 11). The ideal woman is both a boy and a girl, tough but also vulnerable, elegant but also violent in her sexual appetite, or, in a nutshell, she must be a coherent unit of incoherent paradoxes. This is one of the most succinct comments on postmodernism in the play and a statement on an ambivalent and contradictory age that is fascinated with surfaces, mirrors, and endlessly repeatable media images but that simultaneously pines for the real, the authentic and its innermost, true self (cf. Rabey 2003: 200 f.). In this sense, *Closer* is a play about relationships and intimacy in which the word 'love' is the most brutal of the play's many four letter words (cf. Raab 2002: 145). At the same time, it is a declaration of the indifference and exchangeability of roles and values in postmodern society because the female body can be bought by money as easily as male fantasies can be produced by the porno industry or as partners can be exchanged.

Alice, whose real name is Jane Jones, constantly constructs and reinvents herself in the course of the play, taking on a series of names, wigs, clothes, and pasts which accompany the different roles that she inhabits. She adopts the name Alice Ayres from a London memorial that commemorates "ordinary people who died saving the lives of others" as she explains to Dan in scene 1 (*C* 5). But Alice is also constructed by circumstances and the desires and expectations of the people around her: "Victorian waif, loyal lover, temptress and victim: these roles are at times self-consciously adopted – while at other times imposed by others" (Saunders 2008: 22). Alice or Jane thus becomes an allegory of everyone's unstable identity and, like the origin of her question mark-shaped scar, she remains a mystery until the very end of the play (cf. Raab 2002: 140 f.). According to Marber, Alice is the "soul of the play" (qtd. from Saunders 2008: 22). As in *Attempts on Her Life*, the soul and centre of *Closer* therefore is an absence. In Alice, this can be interpreted both as isolation, loneliness, and a need to cover up a lack of identity as well as a presentation of a sense of liberty and freedom from the constricting roles imposed by social discourses, especially of gender and class (cf. Innes 2002: 432). Yet, whether one interprets her as representing the potential or the danger of postmodern identities, Alice is a character who stands for the discursive, multiple, and fragmented nature of self and world. This is underlined by her adopted name which connects her to *Alice in Wonderland*, and her comment in scene 1 is highly reminiscent of Lewis Carroll's heroine and her reaction to the inverted realities of Wonderland: "It's most *curious*" (*C* 5).

3.3 The Role of Media, Images, and the Disappearance of Reality

This inversion and multiplication of the world that the characters inhabit are connected to what has been described as the disappearance of reality and the role of the media and simulations in postmodern societies. Indeed, truth, reality, and the images that the media create are among the central topics of the two plays tying in with the postmodern assumption that "[w]e live, not inside reality, but inside our representations of it" (Butler 2002: 21). Crimp and Marber share this preoccupation with media and simulation with many playwrights of their generation, for example Mark Ravenhill, whose play *Faust (Faust is Dead)* from 1997 is a discussion of the death of reality, or Abi Morgan's *Splendour* from 2000 whose central metaphor is the photograph which is proof and manipulation of an individual's past at the same time (cf. Pankratz 2004).

In *Attempts on Her Life*, the topics of media, images, and the disappearance of reality already become obvious by the epigraph of the play: "No one will have directly experienced the actual cause of such happenings, but everyone will have received an image of them" (*AHL* n. pag.). This is a quotation from Jean Baudrillard and a reference to both our world and contemporary theatre not being modelled on reality but on representations that are created by media like television or the Internet. Baudrillard's pessimistic theory states that our reality has been replaced by a hyper-reality that bears no relation to any reality whatsoever. In this hyper-reality, the borderline between copy and original has been annihilated and we are inescapably distanced from real experiences. This theory is vividly illustrated by Crimp's play. The audience neither sees the real Anne nor directly witnesses any of the action described by the actors. We might live in what is often called an information society, but most of this information is to be distrusted as we cannot assume that reality has ever been part of its construction. "The postmodernist attitude is therefore one of a suspicion which can border on paranoia" (Butler 2002: 3).

This paranoia and suspicion becomes obvious in many of the 17 scenarios of *Attempts on Her Life*. It can take the form of direct quotation from media like the small print of advertisements in scenario 7 or from popular culture as in the case of information signs or instruction plates on products as in scenario 4. It can also take the form of direct references to cameras, photography, or video clips as in most of the scenarios. And it can take the form of imitating the discursive style of media genres like the short, explosive sentences from abusive talk shows or the unconnected fragments of modern video clips. Overall, it is obvious that the play's model is film (cf. Zimmermann 2002: 114-17). Scenario 5, "The Camera Loves You," combines all these references to media and the hyper-reality they construct in the form of lyrics that are frequently performed as a rock or rap song. The lyrics here criticize the superficial hollowness of media images, the consumption they advertise, and the selves they create in repetitive, hammering rhythms:

The camera loves you
The camera loves you
The camera loves you

We need to sympathise
We need to empathise
We need to advertise

We need to realise
We are the good guys
We are the good guys

We need to feel
what we're seeing is real (*AHL* 25).

In *Closer* the setting of the play already points to this intersection of media, images, superficiality, and the disappearance of reality as the metropolitan London of the 1990s is shown as being preoccupied "with the surface appearance of things and an accompanying cynicism and bleakness as audiences witnessed the machinations of its characters" (Saunders 2008: 9). The quick dialogues, the memorable funny lines, and intense but hollow and short-lived emotional moments of the play remind one of television soap operas or situation comedy and simultaneously create pleasure and dismay at the way the four characters deal with each other. A major part of this superficial feeling that the play creates is the presentation of new media like the Internet and new technologies like the mobile phone. Scenario 3, in which Larry and Dan chat with each other, was one of the first onstage representations of people communicating over the Internet and is usually one of the most successful scenes in performances of *Closer*. In this scene it becomes clear that information society with its possibilities of immediately communicating with others all over the world does not shrink the world but rather distances and isolates people who lead a lonely "fishbowl existence" (Innes 2002: 433; cf. Rabey 2003: 199 f.). Much in the sense of Baudrillard, the media are shown as not representing reality or expressing real selves but as creating only self-referential simulations. On the Internet chat, Larry and Dan create fake images of their selves and others while at the same time exposing intimate details about their sexual fantasies and their innermost needs. Even the orgasm of Dan, who is pretending to be Anna, is fake and expressed in a random outburst of letters, turning the human body into a hyper-real simulation. The body is no last resort of authenticity. Both men therefore gain no real closeness or intimacy from their virtual encounter as Dan's comment at the end of the scene shows: "Desire,like the world,is am accident. The bestsex is anon. We liv as we dream, ALONE" ([sic!] *C* 27). The audience does not even get the feeling that Dan and Larry have gained sexual gratification of any kind. The Internet scene thus combines a simulation of intimacy with the isolation of the two characters (cf. Phillips 2001). In this sense, Crimp and Marber are indeed representatives of contemporary theatre's tendency to include the media, their languages, and modes of perception into their form, content, and performance.

4. Conclusion

Linda Hutcheon has stated that postmodernism is about "what happens when culture is challenged from within: challenged or questioned or contested, but not imploded" (1988: xiii). Postmodernism indeed challenges most of the central issues of societies today: the role and use of technology and media, the possibility of interpersonal relationships, love, and individual agency, the position and function of the individual and its body or the role of cultural differences. Consequently, drama after postmodernism encapsulates all these issues and puts its audience to the test by denying simple formulas and ready-made meaning. On the one hand, it therefore transgresses conventions, forms, and much of the content of traditional drama and reflects the openness and processuality of human knowledge and the instability and constructedness of our selves. On the other hand, it also acknowledges the human need for meaning and coherence by hinting at the opportunities of a new, if only temporary arrangement of traditions, conventions, and roles into some kind of unity.

Crimp and Marber create this paradoxical incoherent unit by plays that seem to be pessimistic about the future of contemporary society and our futile attempts at creating a meaningful self and life. By the ending of *Closer* the three remaining characters, Larry, Dan, and Anna all "exit separately" (117), leaving an empty stage and the basic question who these people really were, or rather, whether they ever were someone at all. At the end of *Attempts on Her Life* the audience does not have the feeling that they ever got to know the person that the play is looking for, Anne or Annie or Anya or Annushka. And yet, the plays succeed in making the audience ask questions and remain sceptical when it comes to the 'grand narratives' of modernity and of their individual lives. This is an entirely optimistic stance which states that asking questions about our society is worth it because only thus society has a future. Theatre, no matter how open and postmodern, appeals to us and the society in which it is performed and points out the freedom of our acts of reading. It is this ethical demand of drama after postmodernism that authors have taken up today, even if some of them return to more realistic modes of presentation and more direct political claims (see chapter 27). New writing after 2000 includes an enormous number of stories about groups and people that are different due to religious, racial, gendered, psychological, generational, educational, or other characteristics. Thus, it can be interpreted as a continuation and adaptation of the postmodern project.

Bibliography

Primary Sources

Crimp, Martin. 2007 [1997]. *Attempts on Her Life*. London: Faber and Faber.
Marber, Patrick. 1999 [1997]. *Closer*. New York: Grove Press.

Annotated Bibliography

Agusti, Clara Escoda. 2005. "Short Circuits of Desire: Language and Power in Martin Crimp's *Attempts on Her Life*." In: *Ariel* 36.3-4: 103-26.
An interpretation of the play in the context of postmodern theory with a focus on language and language games which argues in favour of Crimp's ethical, yet postmodern position.

Butler, Christopher. 2002. *Postmodernism: A Very Short Introduction*. Oxford: Oxford UP.

A concise and comprehensible introduction to the development, theories, and concepts of postmodernism.

Henke, Christoph & Martin Middeke (eds.). 2007. *Drama and/after Postmodernism*. Trier: WVT.

A comprehensive collection of essays covering theoretical approaches as well as case studies from British and American drama in the context of postmodernism.

Lehmann, Hans-Thies. 2006. *Postdramatic Theatre*. New York: Routledge.

One of the major studies on the connection between contemporary theatrical practice and postmodernism with a special focus on the German context.

Phillips, Doug. 2001. "Patrick Marber's *Closer* and the Plague of Fantasies." In: *Text & Presentation* 22: 127-34.

A concise analysis of Marber's play with respect to desire, sexuality, and the hyper-real simulations of both in postmodern media society.

Raab, Michael. 2002. "'Post-Feminist masculinity and all that shit': Patrick Marber's *Closer* in London and Munich." In: *Anglistik & Englischunterricht* 64: 137-48.

A comparison of the English and the German version of Marber's play with a variety of critical positions and information on the play's translation and actual performances.

Rabey, David Ian. 2003. "Coming Closer." In: David Ian Rabey. *English Drama since 1940*. London: Longman. 195-201.

A concise analysis of the play in the context of Marber's other work of the 1990s.

Saunders, Graham. 2008. *Patrick Marber's* Closer. London: Continuum.

A compact study guide on Marber's play with information on background, performances, character and genre analyses and interpretations of central scenes.

Sierz, Aleks. 2001. "Patrick Marber's *Closer*." In: *In-Yer-Face Theatre: British Drama Today*. London: Faber and Faber. 187-95.

The first major discussion of Marber's Closer, *here in the context of in-yer-face theatre, but also touching upon many points relevant to a postmodern interpretation of the play; includes interview material with Marber and actors.*

—. 2006. *The Theatre of Martin Crimp*. London: Methuen.

A study of all of Crimp's plays, translations and other works up to Fewer Emergencies *(2005) and the translation of Chekhov's* The Seagull *(2006).*

Zima, Peter V. 2001 [1997]. *Moderne/Postmoderne*. München: Wilhelm Fink.

A classic study giving an overview of the connection between modernity and postmodernism and its most important thinkers and theories (in German).

Zimmermann, Heiner. 2002. "Martin Crimp, *Attempts on her Life*: Postdramatic, Postmodern, Satiric?" In: Margarete Rubik & Elke Mettinger-Schartmann (eds.).

(Dis)Continuities: Trends and Traditions in Contemporary Theatre and Drama in English. Trier: WVT. 105-24.
One of the earliest discussions of Crimp's work in the context of postdramatic theatre with references to other contemporary British playwrights and novelists.

Further Secondary Literature

Bauman, Zygmunt. 1993. *Postmodern Ethics*. Oxford: Blackwell.
Dromgoole, Dominic. 2000. *The Full Room: An A-Z of Contemporary Playwriting*. London: Methuen.
Hutcheon, Linda. 1988. *A Poetics of Postmodernism: History, Theory, Fiction*. London: Routledge.
Innes, Christopher D. 2002. *Modern British Drama: The Twentieth Century*. Cambridge: Cambridge UP.
Lyotard, Jean-Francois. 1986 [1979]. *The Postmodern Condition: A Report on Knowledge*. Manchester: Manchester UP.
McHale, Brian. 1992. *Constructing Postmodernism*. London: Routledge.
Pankratz, Annette. 2004. "Signifying Nothing and Everything: The Extension of the Code and Hyperreal Simulations." In: Hans-Ulrich Mohr & Kerstin Mächler (eds.). *Extending the Code: New Forms of Dramatic and Theatrical Expression*. Trier: WVT. 63-78.
Welsch, Wolfgang. 2008 [1987]. *Unsere postmoderne Moderne*. Berlin: Akademie Verlag.
Zijderveld, Anton C. 1970. *The Abstract Society: A Cultural Analysis of Our Time*. New York: Doubleday.
Zimmermann, Heiner. 2003. "Images of Women in Martin Crimp's *Attempts on Her Life*." In: *EJES* 7.1: 69-85.

27. THE DOCUMENTARY TURN IN CONTEMPORARY BRITISH DRAMA AND THE RETURN OF THE POLITICAL: DAVID HARE'S *STUFF HAPPENS* AND RICHARD NORTON-TAYLOR'S *CALLED TO ACCOUNT*

ANNEKA ESCH-VAN KAN

1. Throwing the Spotlight on Current Events: Documentary Plays in the 21st Century

The first decade of the 21st century has surprised many by an astonishing number of documentary plays. It is notoriously claimed that the terrorist attacks of 11 September 2001 in conjunction with the wars on Afghanistan and Iraq stirred a wave of political theatre in Great Britain and the United States (cf. Carlson 2004; Billington 2003). David Edgar envisages the history of political theatre as a series of cometary impacts and claims: "We were due for a whoosh" (qtd. from Kellaway 2004). The most recent "whoosh" sets in motion a sudden blooming of various forms of documentary theatre in Great Britain – reaching from a series of so-called 'tribunal plays' at the Tricycle Theatre that reenact public inquiries to diverse variants of verbatim plays that are edited from or incorporate real-life material, mostly interviews.

The agglomeration of 'documentary plays' that are centring on themes surrounding terrorism, the Iraq War, and the conflict in the Middle East validate the claim that the aesthetic shift in direction was in parts triggered by current events: Robin Soans' *Talking to Terrorists* (2005) intercuts interviews with people who were involved in terrorist movements with others who were affected by terrorism; Victoria Brittain and Gillian Slovo's *Guantanamo: "Honour Bound To Defend Freedom"* (2004) explores the inhuman conditions under which prisoners are unlawfully held captive in US prison camps; Gregory Burke's *Black Watch* (2007) follows Scottish soldiers on their tour of duty in Iraq; Alan Rickman and Katherine Viner's *My Name is Rachel Corrie* (2005) commemorates a young American activist who got run over by a bulldozer while protecting a Palestinian home from being destroyed; this list could easily be extended and the mere number of major plays suggests the assumption that breaking with the disenchantment of past decades politics has all of a sudden returned onto British stages with a "whoosh" of topical documentaries.

Cutting across the discourse of a sudden emergence of documentary theatre Derek Paget insists that "[t]he documentary theatre form is always already *there*, but [that] its fate – seemingly – is to be perennially out of sight until it is needed" (2009: 234). In his seminal book *True Stories: Documentary Drama on Radio, Screen and Stage* (1990) he traces back the history of documentary theatre from its coinage by Erwin Piscator via the living newspapers of the Federal Theatre Project in the United States as well as the Worker's Theatre and the Unity Theatre in Britain through to the documentary plays of the 1960s and 1970s such as Peter Weiss' *The Investigation* (1966). Paget suggests bewaring the rhetoric of radical breaks to keep the continuities in mind. The practice of Theatre in Education groups and the popularity of the theatre of Peter Cheeseman in Britain or Emily Mann and Anna Deavere Smith in the United States are proof enough that documentary theatre never entirely got out of vogue. While the recent documentary turn in contemporary drama could with quite some justification be identified as a fourth point of culmination, Paget emphasizes that dominating forms such as the Tribunal Theatre and verbatim techniques are not an invention of the new millennium and that neither the co-existence of diverse forms of documentary theatre nor their history should be lost off sight (cf. Paget 2009: 232f.).

2. A Janus-Faced Genre: Between Non-Art and Avant-Garde

A quick survey of the seminal literature on documentary theatre reveals that the field is mined with an irritating plurality of designations. Each time and profession champion a specific terminology indicating a shift in perspective and fundamentally different, yet at times very compatible conceptions of what documentary theatre is: a genre, a mode, or a set of techniques (cf. Hammond & Steward 2008).

Notions such as 'documentary drama,' 'documentary theatre,' and 'documentary play' refer to a literary or theatrical genre. 'Documentary drama' is nowadays almost out of use based on its terminological closeness to 'docudrama' that "is at cross-purposes with a rule of accuracy in the documentary play" (Dawson 1999: xiv). The terms 'documentary theatre' and 'documentary play' are often used interchangeably even though the first one emphasizes a focus on the performance event and staging, whereas the second tends to centre on or solely refer to the drama or literary script. Terms such as 'non-fictional theatre,' 'faction,' and 'theatre of fact' describe a mode of plays that is characterized by a specific relation between reality and fiction. This perspective is often accompanied by the attribution of educational or political purposes or functions. Designations such as 'theatre of testimony,' preferred by leading American documentary playwright Emily Mann, and the currently in vogue notion of 'verbatim theatre,' coined in the late 1980s by Paget (1987), stress the mediality of source material and identify the term with a set of aesthetic strategies or techniques. The compatibility of these approaches shows in various definitions that combine several or all three conceptions (cf. Paget 1990; Favorini 1994; Dawson 1999). Documentary theatre is defined as a literary, or theatrical genre (cf. Dawson 1999; Paget 1987, 1990) that uses pre-existing documentary material (such as newspapers, interviews, official transcripts of trials, or government reports) and claims to offer access to a hidden truth (cf. Dawson 1999; Norton-Taylor 2004; Weiss 1968).

Contrasting documentary theatre with the new journalism that "used to be described as 'art of fact,'" Michal Lachman suggests that "verbatim drama should [...] be seen as 'fact with no art,' meaning no artificiality or artefact" (2007: 317). This definition partakes in the well-established prejudice, reaching as far back as to Plato, that there is "an inverse ratio between documentary purity [that is its inherent truth claim] and [its] aesthetic value" (Bruzzi 2000: 14). In tune with this it is demanded that documentary theatre should shun all artificiality to be turned into a suitable medium for the revelation of a truth that is obscured by mass media.

A consequence of the assumption is that the documentary play is frequently denied the status of an artwork. Referring to the tribunal plays at the Tricycle Theatre, *Guardian* journalist Norton-Taylor states that "some still question whether such pieces of verbatim theatre can be called plays at all" (qtd. from Hammond & Steward 2008: 129). This assertion is widespread and was impressively exemplified by the highly controversial disqualification of Anna Deavere Smith's *Twilight: Los Angeles, 1992* by the Pulitzer Prize jury in 1993, based on the fact that it was non-fictional and could therefore not be regarded as a play. Today, one might assume that British playwright David Hare pushes at an open door when he defends verbatim plays as works of art based on a comparison of the process of editing quotes with the shaping of raw material by a sculptor (cf. Hammond & Steward 2008: 130), yet a number of creators of documentary plays themselves decide to be identified as editors rather than playwrights emphasizing the affair of editing "as a craft rather than an art" (ibid.: 139). Norton-Taylor answers Hare's defense of the genre by admitting that "[t]o be honest, *pace* Hare, I do not regard myself as an artist" (ibid.: 130).

Starting from this situation it appears natural that scholars and critics alike tend to foreground the topicality of documentary plays, concentrating on "the veracity of the document, ethical representation and documentary theatre's place in the greater political discourses of the day" (Ferguson 2009: 9). In consequence of the alignment of documentary theatre with non-art, "what is uniquely theatrical about this kind of theatre [and] what the mechanics are that make documentary theatre more than just a report or another kind of journalism" (ibid.) is considered insignificant and therefore ignored. This vision of documentary theatre, however, only tells half the story.

Piscator's *In Spite of Everything!* (1925), which "in retrospect may be named the Ur-text of the documentary theatre movement" (Favorini 1994: 33), introduced stage technology such as "multi-level sets, projections, loud-speakers, and an ironic juxtaposition of live stage image with cool and objective projected image" (ibid.: 35). Joan Littlewood's legendary *Oh, What a Lovely War* (1963) introduced Brechtian and Piscatorian approaches to the British theatre. It was improvisational in nature and assembled musical numbers, projections of films and photographs, a news panel and Pierrot show acts in a revue-like structure. It is therefore surprising that the idea of a documentary theatre that strives at its own dissolution into life dominates, even though the history of documentary theatre was marked by its experimentation with stage technology and alternative, non-Aristotelian, multi-vocal, and at times even non-narrative dramaturgies (cf. Dawson 1999). Paget characterizes documentary theatre as "a theatre of interruption" and contrasts its "rapid real-time transformations of time, place and purpose" and "2-D acting" (2009: 229) with the preference of rounded characters in naturalism. Documentary theatre in its avant-garde tradition is many-voiced, foregrounds the performance event, and embraces the aesthetic experiment.

While documentary theatre started off as a genre that conflated artistic innovation with journalistic impulses, it seems as if in contemporary theatre the internal divide is turned outwards: one strain of recent documentary plays bonds with naturalism and strives for the uncovering of a hidden truth, the other strain emphasizes the experimental aesthetics of documentary theatre and self-reflexively explores the relationship between representation and reality.

3. The End(s) of Representation: True Stories vs. Deconstructive Meta-Theatrics

In his 2004 *New Statesman* article "Spirit of Inquiry," Norton-Taylor reflects on the Tricycle tribunal plays and announces that "[t]he role of the theatre in exposing the truth and reality, unvarnished, is making a welcome comeback." He floats the question if theatre could "really be a more effective and honest medium than newspapers, television or radio" and answers it with a clear "Yes" (ibid.). Quoting his collaborator and artistic director of the Tricycle Theatre, Nicolas Kent, he avers that "[y]ou can get nearer to the real truth" (Kent, qtd. from Norton-Taylor 2004) since the editing "for a two-hour script" is far less subjective than the editing "for an article of a few hundred words, or a television clip of a few moments" (ibid.). The fact that some of the most prominent documentary plays of recent years have been co-authored by *Guardian* journalists (Brittain & Slovo 2004; Norton-Taylor 1999, 2003, 2005, 2007; Viner & Rickman 2005) lends credence to the conception of documentary theatre as an extension of journalism by other means. Kent repeatedly emphasized that the initial impulse to set up tribunal plays has been triggered by the deficiency that public hearings were not being televised. He even considers the possibility that once they actually will be televised the format of the tribunal play might be rendered superfluous (cf. Hoggard 2005). Theatre appears as a substitute for journalism entrusted with the task of mending journalism's failures.

Contemplating on the recent convergence of documentary theatre and journalism Lachman finds that both "share the view that truth can be fully disclosed and objectively described once appropriate methods of investigating, recording and reporting of material are established" (2007: 314). Common to both documentary theatre and journalism is furthermore that they are generally conceived as "*utile* forms" that to differing degrees aim to "*reassess* international/national/local histories," "*celebrate* repressed or marginalized communities and groups," "*investigate* contentious events and issues in local, national and international context," and "*disseminate* information" (Paget 2009: 227 f.). Despite his general suspicion towards the presuppositions and aesthetics of tribunal theatre Chris Megson argues that "the theatrical re-playing, in edited form, of [...] seminal inquiries has exposed audiences to the internal workings of government, raising crucial questions about parliamentary accountability [and] the ideological manipulation of state institutions" (2008: 110). In stark contrast to the realization of theatre's inefficacy that followed the utopian belief in art's revolutionary potential in the 1960s and 1970s, it is generally acknowledged that the Tricycle tribunal plays have had a substantial impact. *The Colour of Justice*, Kent and Norton-Taylor's 2003 documentary on the murder of Stephen Lawrence, is still used by British police forces for training purposes against institutional racism (cf. Hammond & Steward 2008: 109). In spite of everything that theatre actually makes a measurable difference is rather the exception than the rule and it hardly applies to the documentary turn in British theatre in general.

The contributions to the 2006 *TDR* issue which pioneered a systematized analysis of the recent blooming of documentary theatre all sing from the same hymn sheet: they express a deep mistrust in the development and question its politics. Stephen Bottoms pointedly accuses "the current 'verbatim theatre' trend in London" of "lioniz[ing] plays that are both manipulative and worryingly unreflexive regarding the 'realities' they purport to discuss" (2006: 67). Carol Martin prizes the work of artists such as Lebanese Walid Raad and German director Hans-Werner Kroesinger over the wave of verbatim theatre and tribunal plays in Britain, arguing that the former "invite contemplation of the ways in which stories are told" and "examine the ways in which documentary functions" (2006:12) while the later entirely lack a level of self-reflexivity. Other scholars follow the line of argument initiated in the *TDR* issue (cf. Young 2009; Innes 2007). The many examples of meta-theatrical performances invoked in various essays allow Alison Forsyth and Chris Megson to open their compendium *Get Real* with the proclamation that "instead of reaching for a whilly objective representation of 'truth', much documentary theatre has functioned to complicate notions of authenticity" (2009: 2) and, in the same volume, Paget echoing Martin (cf. 2006: 13) brings in the interrogation of "the very notion *documentary*" (2009: 227 f.) as a fifth function of documentary theatre.

Janelle Reinelt strikes the core of the debate when she lays stress on three pivotal hypotheses in recent theorizations of the genre: She acknowledges that "[t]he value of the document is predicated on a realist epistemology" (2009: 7), yet she emphasizes that "the experience of documentary is dependent on phenomenological engagement." She furthermore locates the documentary "in the relationship between the object, its mediators [...] and its audiences" rather than "in the object" (ibid.) and concludes that "[t]he experience of documentary [...] is in fact constitutive of the reality it seeks" (ibid.). Rather than concluding with the affirmation of a documentary theatre that embraces self-reflexivity over other forms, Reinelt offers a theoretical lens that can be applied to any form of documentary theatre.

Referring to variants of verbatim theatre that would probably be classified with those that conceal employed aesthetic strategies, Edgar interestingly emphasizes that "much verbatim theatre is double-coded, not just sourced from interviews but about the interview process [itself]" (2008). He instances the visibility of the earphones in productions of Blythe's Recorded Delivery Theatre Company and the appearance of the playwright as a character in Burke's *Black Watch*. Affirming the constructed nature of documentary plays, Hare, who in his plays *The Permanent Way* and *Stuff Happens* blends fact and fiction, points out that "[i]t's a total misunderstanding of documentary theatre to think that it's all about just presenting a load of facts on stage" (qtd. from Hammond & Steward 2008: 59). He emphasizes that "you have to organize the material just as you organize the material as a playwright" (ibid.). Experimental productions as well as rather conservative ones increasingly render the "creative work" that happens in "[t]he process of selection, editing, organization, and presentation" (Martin 2006: 9) visible and thereby acknowledge that "documentary theatre creates its own aesthetic imaginaries" (ibid.: 10).

The address of the interview process and the realization of its constructed nature alone, however, does not guarantee that "the highly selective manipulation of opinion and rhetoric" (Bottoms 2006: 57 f.) coming with many documentary plays is elucidated. Celebrating the work of the Tectonic Theatre Project and directly addressing his remark to the recent documentary turn in British theatre Bottoms demands that "other artists working in the liminal space between 'art' and 'life' that is documentary theatre should also think actively about developing their own forms of theatrical and textual reflexivity by way of reminding audiences that history itself is necessarily complex, uncertain, and always already theatricalized" (ibid.: 67).

4. The Performance of Politics: David Hare's *Stuff Happens*

Since the 1990s Erika Fischer-Lichte has unremittingly announced a double 'performative turn' in terms of the staginess and adoption of performance elements in media and politics as characteristics of contemporary society as well as in the form of an overall shift in perspective towards unstable meanings, process, and transformation in the humanities (cf. 2008). Beyond Erving Goffman's analysis of performance in everyday life that employs the notorious metaphor of the *theatrum mundi* and finds that we are all constantly acting parts (cf. 1959), the role of performance in the shaping of public personae and political candidates engaged academic interest at least since Ronald Reagan, an actor by profession, was elected President of the United States in 1981.

The performance of politics is what Hare's *Stuff Happens* (*SH*), which premiered at London's National Theatre in 2004 (followed by a New York run at the Public Theatre in 2006), is all about. The play is based on the reporting of the run-up to the Iraq War as presented by newspapers and television and merges verbatim quotes by politicians with imagined scenes "[w]hen the doors close" (*SH* "Author's Note"). Nicholas Hiley, writing for the *Times Literary Supplement*, finds that *Stuff Happens* "perhaps isn't so much a political play as a play about politicians" (2004). The play starts off with an introduction of its protagonists Dick Cheney, Colin Powell, Condoleezza Rice, Donald Rumsfeld, Paul Wolfowitz, and Tony Blair, as well as two minor characters Hans Blix and Kofi Annan both granted with a neglectable small number of lines (thereby mirroring the rather ornamental function of the United Nations in the lead up to the Iraq war). The introduction of these eight characters is followed by the statement of "An Actor" who reappears throughout the play as a narrating voice which is occupied in turn by the entire cast: "These are the men and women who will play parts in a defining drama of the new century" (*SH* 9). In an ironic twist, George W. Bush, who has often been blamed to be nothing but a lay figure, "steps among them" (ibid.) immediately after this utterance.

The introduction of the main characters reveals that the often-met accusation that *Stuff Happens* espouses a political position is well justified, yet it can be put into doubt if this happens in a manipulative way (cf. Bottoms 2006) or rather with the cards on the table. The "'continuous commentary'" by the narrating voice "leads to a particular type of distancing effect" (Innes 2007: 443) when it is ironically juxtaposed to character speech as in the above-mentioned example. The bias of the play eventually becomes blatantly obvious in the satirical exaggeration of personal characteristics and the use of nicknames such as "Rummy," "Wolfie," and "Condi" (*SH* e.g. 20, 44, 49) that invite a cartoonish realization on stage. Instead of claiming objectivity and truthfulness, the play rather openly airs its partisanship.

Stuff Happens often serves as the butt of carping criticism directed against the recent blooming of documentary theatre. At the centre of this criticism, next to its manipulative partisanship, are the allegation of authenticity and the claim that documentary plays offer the audience access to a hidden truth. The author's note to the published version of *Stuff Happens* is notoriously quoted to prove Hare's alleged naive belief in the veracity of representation: "What happened happened" (*SH* "Author's Note"). Regardless of Hare's own attitude that may be derived from diverse interviews and whatever the overall reception of its performances might suggest, the play including the author's note hardly supports such a disambiguate reading. To the contrary, it can well be argued that *Stuff Happens* accepts the inaccessibility of the 'events' themselves and is enmeshed in the web of stories that make those events intelligible. Following this reading, one could find the play to explore the blurring of reality and fiction and destabilize the supposition of an allocatable historical truth and the attribution of any truth-value to documents.

Hayden White renownedly laid bare the fictional dimension of historiography by introducing a distinction between 'events' and 'facts' (cf. 1973). Acknowledging the actual advent of events, he found that "there is no such thing as raw facts but only events under different descriptions" (White 1999: 9). His argument that "[s]tories are told or written, not found" and that therefore "[a]ll stories are fictions" (White 1999: 9) lead him to a conclusion that challenges the documentary project altogether, namely that "the notion of a true story [...] is virtually a contradiction in terms" (ibid.). Interestingly, Hare's explicit claim that *Stuff Happens* is a history play (*SH* "Author's Note") and not a documentary is often rejected as irrelevant and misleading. The declarations that "[w]hat happened happened" and that "[n]othing in the narrative is knowingly untrue" (ibid.) are taken as evidence that *Stuff Happens* actually is a documentary and does claim to present the 'true story' behind the manipulative concealments of mass media. While these readings are justified in the sense that they mirror a certain reception that seems to be evoked by the play, it is surprising that the rather obvious link between Hare's statements and the core ideas of White is not brought into focus. The occurrence of events is affirmed ("[w]hat happened happened") but the version of it presented in the play is identified as a "narrative" and ultimately as an interpretation of the events it depicts. *Stuff Happens* neither stands in contrast to nor tries to occupy the position of a 'reality behind the stories,' but it presents a story that is meant to destabilize master-narratives created by mainstream media. Interestingly, media images and coverage are the documents that *Stuff Happens* is based on. In effect this topples the widespread assumption that documents are always already linked to a truth for which they provide evidence: The play uses snippets of mass media representations as documents to unsettle the story that is promulgated in these very media. Thereby it builds its own version of the story on documents that are revealed as unreliable.

The unreliability of documents and the need to interpret them explicitly becomes a topic in two scenes of the play. During an early internal meeting of Bush's inner circle a map of Iraq is presented that is meant to provide evidence concerning a possible threat by means of weapons of mass destruction. The understanding of the map as evidence by Rumsfeld and as a document inviting contradicting interpretations by Tenet is contrasted in a collage of ellipses:

> RUMSFELD. It's grainy, but you can see…
> TENET. This looks to us…
> RUMSFELD. You can see clearly…
> TENET. I think the CIA believes…
> RUMSFELD. Even I can see, and I'm nearly seventy […]. (*SH* 13)

The second scene that questions the reliability of documents follows later in the play when "*General Hassan Muhammad Amin sets out a table with twelve thousand pages of documents for the world's press to photograph*" (*SH* 86). Documents are produced to be photographed rather than to be read and analysed. The character Blix makes the impossibility to master all available information even more visible when he states: "To be honest, I was happy for the document to go first to Washington. They have the logistical capacity to make fifteen copies of twelve thousand pages. We don't" (*SH* 87). This could of course be read as a joke about this specific report about chemical facilities by the Iraqi government, but it could as well be understood as a more general questioning of the truth value associated with documents. "One memorable image, repeated several times," that Reinelt treasures in her memory of the London performance "showed the press grouped together in a clump in one corner of the mammoth stage, looking like a many-headed hydra, creating both an amusing effect and a gestus of journalistic cowardice and competition, all in one image" (2005: 305). The excretions of this beast at odds with itself are the fertile soil of *Stuff Happens*.

5. The Theatre as a Courtroom: Richard Norton-Taylor's *Called To Account*

Norton-Taylor's *Called To Account: The Indictment of Charles Anthony Linton Blair for the Crime of Aggression Against Iraq. A Hearing* (*CA*) which premiered at the Tricycle Theatre in 2007 turns the theatre into a courtroom and investigates the basis of an indictment of former Prime Minister Tony Blair for an act of aggression against Iraq. The play engages in the interpretation of documents and the meta-reflection on the process of meaning making throughout the play. Referring to the claim that an "unequivocal decision [...] to go to war" (*CA* 29) in Iraq had been taken by April 2002, defense lawyer Julian Knowles asks newspaper journalist Michael Smith: "That's your evidence is it?" Smith answers: "That's my belief yes," just to be countered by Knowles conclusion: "That's your interpretation of the documents" (*CA* 29). Former commissioner for the Intelligence Service, Sir Murray Stuart Smith, differentiates between different forms of intelligence and evaluates their reliability. He finds that human intelligence "can vary enormously [...] in reliability" and that "although the camera doesn't lie it's not always easy to interpret actually what...what you're seeing" (*CA* 31). Time and again, witnesses are asked to read out and interpret paragraphs of crucial documents that are also made accessible to the audience projected on plasma screens (cf. Stoller 2005). The entire play is preoccupied with the confrontation of different interpretations of a certain set of official documents and it very much stresses the point that there is no one truth but that valuation is only possible within a given discursive frame (for instance legal, political, or moral; cf. *CA* 10, 17, 72, 87).

Called To Account stands in the tradition of the tribunal plays that since the 1994 production of *Half the Picture* have been associated with the Tricycle Theatre, its artistic director Kent and *Guardian* journalist Norton-Taylor. Tribunal theatre is based on a "meticulous re-enactment of edited transcripts of state-sanctioned inquiries that address perceived miscarriages of justice and flaws in the operations and accountability of public institutions" (Megson 2009: 195). *Called To Account*, however, radically differs from other tribunal plays in not being based on an actual inquiry but setting up a hearing of its own. The theatre hired a legal team to investigate the grounds for an indictment of Blair and left no stone unturned to gain public figures and people with insights into or directly involved in the decision-making process as witnesses. The script was then edited from the recordings of those hearings. Far beyond the often acknowledged structural parallels between performances in law and theatre (cf. Hammond & Steward 2008: 139), *Called To Account* – blurring the lines between art and life – actually transforms the stage into a courtroom – with the judge missing, "leaving [...] the audience [...] in the role of the jury, to make up its own mind" (ibid.: 112).

Norton-Taylor accentuates that "[e]xposing the truth has been the goal of each of our tribunal plays" (qtd. from Hammond & Steward 2008: 106). He entrusts an educational role to the theatre that "allows a writer to explain and contextualize a running controversy that otherwise would be lost in (necessarily) erratic journalistic coverage"

(Norton-Taylor 2007). Contrary to Hare, who insists that "[t]heater [...] is not journalism" (2005: 27 f.), Kent (qtd. from Stoller 2005) in line with his collaborator Norton-Taylor condemns the conflation of fact and fiction in Hare's plays and is convinced that documentary plays should strictly adhere to journalistic standards, that is a) they should only include verbatim material or quotes from official documents and b) they should follow the actual sequence of events or the chronological order of witness reports. Asked if theatre just as journalism needed several sources to claim something as a 'fact,' Kent emphasizes that he has "never done plays that do that because [he is] always using what people have said" (Kent, qtd. from Stoller 2005). It is questionable if the interplay of subjective truths ever arrives at a more objective one. Yet this seems to be suggested by the artistic duo that aims to take the lid off institutional failures.

The claimed objectivity, however, can hardly be ascribed to tribunal plays for real. In fact, the illusion of objectivity and authenticity are effects of the performances. "Typically, tribunal productions take the form of a forensic simulation of the inquiry's disputations and setting, with actors playing the roles of the actual witnesses and judicial personnel" (Megson 2009: 195). The striking "anti-theatricality of the Tricycle tribunals" (cf. Edgar 2008) has repeatedly been pointed out. Kent himself suggests that "[t]he hyper-naturalism of everything being very low-key means it's nearer to the truth" (qtd. from Hammond & Steward 2008: 156). This effect is created by several staging devices that turned into conventions for tribunal productions: the stage set replicates the hearing room, there is no stage action, the lighting remains unchanged, and the house lights are up throughout the performance, the audience is surrounded by plasma screens that project the documents in question, the programmes for the productions include copied documents, actors speak in an accelerated naturalistic TV-like fashion – striving for a high degree of verisimilitude and avoiding caricature and impersonation –, voices are amplified with microphones, and the actors do not return onstage to take their applause (cf. Hammond & Steward 2008; Stoller 2005). Kent claims that "[w]ith a tribunal play, whenever you do anything for dramatic effect it's wrong" (qtd. from Hammond & Steward 2008: 156), yet in fact all the above-listed devices are obviously used for effect and attune to create the illusion of authenticity. In addition to the staging devices the play script already includes authentifying devices such as superfluous information: a witness asking for a marker pen (*CA* 32) or the specification that "[t]he page number is in the right hand corner" (*CA* 35). These details are explicitly introduced to "make[s] the whole thing so much more believable and truthful" (Kent qtd. from Hammond & Steward 2008: 156).

Contemplating on the "fetishization of political personality" (Megson 2008: 116) that marks out the reception of *Called To Account*, Megson finds the "hardcore illusionism in much Tribunal theatre" at odds with its "disruptive potential" (ibid.: 114). The pleasure derived from the naturalistic doubles of public personae elides the critical endeavour and turns the play into "a popular political entertainment rather than a fully-rounded investigation or a traditionally well-made piece of theatre" (Fisher 2007). Despite the formal structure of the inquiry that gives voice to "friend and foe alike"

(Norton-Taylor 2007), *Called To Account* is of course not unbiased. The project came into being based on the artists' strong opinion that Blair should be called to account for his actions in the run-up to the Iraq War and obviously this shows in the play script as well as in the performance. Beyond the artistic decisions taken in the selection of volunteering witnesses and the editing of the interview material, there are a couple of rather unambiguous scenes. The second act begins with a short tête-à-tête between a witness and a defence lawyer who pours him a glass of water and provides him with a document to hold onto during the hearing. The witness counters: "I might need something stronger by the time I finish this." (*CA* 48) Later on in the hearing the same witness at several times expresses his insecurity as to which kinds of information he is allowed to share publicly. The play finally culminates in a striking moment that turns the bias blatantly obvious: "As the defense rests, an image of a grinning Blair appears on a screen above the proceedings" (Benedict 2007).

The scepticism towards tribunal theatre is viable. Immediate judgments, however, block the view onto perchance more interesting aspects of each singular performance. *Called To Account* does not attempt to represent a real-life event, but it simulates an inquiry that was realized several years after the performance – calling some of the original characters of the play as witnesses – and thereby causes the relation between representation and reality to sway. It does not represent a given reality but it pretends to represent a trial that will only have taken place in the future.

6. The Politics of Performance and the Return of the Political

Irrespective of the biases that drive the Tricycle tribunal plays, their story of success is remarkable and it cannot be denied that they actually do reverberate. The tribunal plays reached more than 25 million people all over the world, attracted unlikely audiences, were presented to government officials, and triggered public debates. This has been acknowledged when the Tricycle theatre was awarded with the 2006 *Evening Standard*'s Special Award for its 'pioneering work in political theatre' (cf. www.tricycle.co.uk). The political brisance of Hare's *Stuff Happens* is far more controversial. While many acknowledged the critical potential of the play at the time of its London premiere, J. Chris Westgate – referring to the 2007 production in Seattle – concludes that "play and production implicitly reinforce complacency by first turning controversy into entertainment – [...] confirming ideological or political beliefs instead of challenging them – and second by transforming controversy into commodity" (2009: 405).

The commodification of political theatre becomes blatantly obvious when tribunal Theatre is turned into a trademark of the Tricycle Theatre and when audiences and media evoke more excitement about the true-to-life impersonation of public personae than about the core issues of the plays. Beyond this eventual continuation of consumer culture, the political efficacy of *Stuff Happens* as well as *Called To Account* is generally rated by its potential to resonate in the daily news and political discourses.

Recent theatre theory, however, suggests that what attributes a political twist to performances is exactly the impossibility to translate the phenomenological experience of performances back into political discourses. Hans-Thies Lehmann (cf. 2002) poignantly remarked that the political can only surface in the interruption of politics and French philosopher Jacques Rancière champions the view that "[t]he dream of a suitable work of art is in fact the dream of disrupting the relationship between the visible, the sayable, and the thinkable without having to use the terms of a message as a vehicle" (2004: 63). He continues that a political work of art should always oscillate "between the readability of the message that threatens to destroy the sensible form of art and the radical uncanniness that threatens to destroy all political meaning" (ibid.). Theories of the political in art rather than political art, furthermore, elide the sharp distinction between art and politics and shift the focus towards the aesthetics of politics as well as the politics of aesthetics.

In his *Theatre Survey* article "Counterbalancing the Pendulum Effect: Politics and the Discourse of Post-9/11 Theatre," James M. Harding suggests "that 9/11 has pushed the discourse of our discipline back toward a conventional, indeed reactionary, understanding of politics, theatre, and performance" (2007: 20). He criticizes the "decidedly conventional and conservative theatrical terms" (ibid.) framing Hare's *Stuff Happens* and questions the "clean distinction between the artist and the citizen" (ibid.: 23) that is proclaimed in Harold Pinter's notoriously quoted Nobel Lecture (2005), in which he states that as a writer he still believes that "[t]here are no hard distinctions between what is [...] true and what is false," when "as a citizen today he cannot" (Harding 2007: 22). The endeavour of the tribunal plays as well as most forms of verbatim theatre to influence public opinion by using theatre as a vehicle for a political message certainly is part of this 'pendulum effect' and it can justifiably be claimed that the productions lack a disruptive potential beyond signification, yet it is intriguing how both plays at the same time correspond to certain aspects of advanced theorization. *Stuff Happens* destabilizes the relation between fact and fiction and focuses on the performance of politics while *Called To Account* throws the distinction between representation and reality off balance.

Critics and scholars alike tend to dismiss much of the recent "whoosh" (Edgar, qtd. from Kellaway 2004) of documentary plays and turn a blind eye to the fact that they are an outcome of our contemporary culture and that they in many ways interact with advanced theory. Their ignorance, however, in many ways continues the reactionary momentum. Instead of wearily swinging with the pendulum, academic reflections on recent documentary theatre should spice the pendulum up and trace an oscillation between art and life that might very well bear witness of a return of the political.

Bibliography

Primary Sources

Hare, David. 2004. *Stuff Happens*. London/New York: Faber and Faber.
Norton-Taylor. 2007. *Called To Account: The Indictment of Charles Anthony Linton Blair for the Crime of Aggression Against Iraq. A Hearing*. London: Oberon Books.

Annotated Bibliography

Dawson, Gary Fisher. 1999. *Documentary Theatre in the United States: An Historical Survey and Analysis of Its Content, Form, and Stagecraft*. Westport: Greenwood Publishing.
   Dawson's study sketches the development of documentary theatre in the United States not Great Britain, yet it sorts out definitions of the genre and relates those to the overriding genre of the history play.
Forsyth, Alison & Chris Megson (eds.). 2009. *Get Real: Documentary Theatre Past and Present*. Basingstoke: Palgrave Macmillan.
   Get Real *focuses on the recent upsurge of documentary theatre in Great Britain, offers a historical perspective on the development in GB and elsewhere and engages in a theorization that continues the critical project of the* The Drama Review *Special Issue on Documentary Theatre.*
Hammond, Will & Dan Steward (eds.). 2008. *Verbatim: Techniques in Contemporary Documentary Theatre*. London: Oberon Books.
   Verbatim *compiles interviews with the major representatives of verbatim theatre, namely Soans, Hare, Blythe, Norton-Taylor, Kent, and Max Stafford-Clarke.*
Martin, Carol (ed.). 2006. *Documentary Theatre*. Special Issue of *TDR* 50.3.
   The TDR Special Issue pioneered the systematized analysis of the recent blooming of documentary theatre. The contributions tend to offer a critical perspective onto verbatim theatre and tribunal plays and favour performances that become self-reflexive.
Paget, Derek. 1990. *True Stories? Documentary Drama on Radio, Screen, and Stage*. Manchester: Manchester UP.
   Paget considers major examples from past and contemporary documentary practices in theatre, radio, film, and television in the UK and US.
Piscator, Erwin. 1979. *The Political Theatre: A History 1914-1929*. New York: Avon.
   Piscator is often claimed to be the originator of the documentary theatre genre. This volume assembles writings on major productions and on political theatre.

Weiss, Peter. 1968. "Fourteen Propositions for a Documentary Theatre." In: *World Theatre* XVII: 375-89.

This article sums up the positions and techniques of German documentary playwright Peter Weiss. It has turned into a notoriously quoted manifesto for documentary theatre.

Further Secondary Literature

Austin, John Langshaw. 1962. *How To Do Things With Words*. Oxford: Clarendon P.

Benedict, David. 2007. "Review of *Called to Account*." In: *Variety* 26 April. <http://www.variety.com/review/VE1117933454.html?categoryid=33&cs=1> (last accessed 8 June 2010).

Billington, Michael. 2003. "Drama Out of a Crisis." In: *The Guardian* 10 April. <http://www.guardian.co.uk/stage/2003/apr/10/theatre.artsfeatures> (last accessed 26 Oct. 2010).

Bottoms, Stephen. 2006. "Putting the Document into Documentary – An Unwelcome Corrective?" In: Martin 2006. 56-68.

Bruzzi, Stella. 2000. *New Documentary: A Critical Introduction*. London/New York: Routledge.

Carlson, Marvin. 2004. "9/11, Afghanistan, and Iraq: The Response of the New York Theatre." In: *Theatre Survey* 45.1: 3-17.

Deavere Smith, Anna. 1994. *Twilight: Los Angeles 1992*. New York: Anchor Books.

Edgar, David. 2008. "Doc and Dram." In: *The Guardian* 27 Sept. <http://www.guardian.co.uk/stage/2008/sep/27/theatre.davidedgar> (last accessed 26 Oct. 2010).

Favorini, Attilio. 1994. "Representation and Reality: The Case of Documentary Theatre." In: *Theatre Survey* 35.2: 31-43.

Ferguson, Alexander. 2009. *Productive Tensions: A Theory of Documentary Theatre*. M.A. Thesis. U of British Columbia, Vancouver. <https://circle.ubc.ca/handle/2429/12639> (last accessed 8 June 2010).

Fischer-Lichte, Erika. 2008. *The Transformative Power of Performance: A New Aesthetics*. New York: Routledge.

Fisher, Philip. 2007. "Review of *Called to Account*." In: *The British Theatre Guide*. <http://www.britishtheatreguide.info/reviews/calledaccount-rev.htm> (last accessed 8 June 2010).

Goffman, Erving. 1959. *The Presentation of Self in Everyday Life*. New York: Anchor Books.

Harding, James M. 2007. "Counterbalancing the Pendulum Effect: Politics and the Discourse of Post-9/11 Theatre." In: *Theatre Survey* 48.1: 19-25.

Hare, David. 2005. *Obedience, Struggle & Revolt: Lectures on Theatre*. New York: Faber and Faber.

Hiley, Nicholas. 2004. "Review of *Stuff Happens*." In: *The Times Literary Supplement* 17 Sept.: 20.

Hoggard, Liz. 2005. "Out of Crises, a Drama." In: *The Observer* 27 Mar. <http://www.guardian.co.uk/stage/2005/mar/27/theatre> (last accessed 26 Oct. 2010).

Innes, Christopher. 2007. "Towards a Post-Millennial Mainstream? Documents of the Times." In: *Modern Drama* 50.3: 435-52.

Kellaway, Kate. 2004. "Theatre of War." In: *The Observer* 29 Aug. <http://www.guardian.co.uk/stage/2004/aug/29/theatre.politicaltheatre> (last accessed 26 Oct. 2010).

Lachman, Michal. 2007. "The Colours of History or Scenes from the Inquiry into Verbatim Drama." In: Christoph Henke & Martin Middeke (eds.). *Drama and/after Postmodernism*. Trier: WVT. 311-23.

Lehmann, Hans-Thies. 2002. "Wie politisch ist postdramatisches Theater?" In: *Das Politische Schreiben*. Berlin: Theater der Zeit. 11-21.

Littlewood, Joan & Charles Chilton. 1965. *Oh, What a Lovely War*. London: Methuen.

Luckhurst, Mary. 2008. "Verbatim Theatre, Media Relations and Ethics." In: Nadine Holdsworth & Mary Luckhurst (eds.). *A Concise Companion to Contemporary British and Irish Drama*. Oxford: Blackwell. 200-22.

Martin, Carol. 2006. "Bodies of Evidence." In: Martin 2006. 8-15.

—. 2009. "Living Simulations: The Use of Media in Documentary in the UK, Lebanon and Israel." In: Forsyth & Megson 2009. 74-90.

Megson, Chris. 2008. "'The State We're In': Tribunal Theatre and British Politics in the 1990s." In: Daniel Watt & Daniel Meyer-Dinkgräfe (eds.). *Theatres of Thought: Theatre, Performance and Philosophy*. Newcastle: Cambridge Scholars. 110-26.

—. 2009. "'Half the Picture': 'A Certain Frisson' at the Tricycle Theatre." In: Forsyth & Megson 2009. 195-208.

Norton-Taylor, Richard. 2004. "Spirit of Inquiry." In: *New Statesman* 7 June: 39-40.

—. 2007. "Blair in the dock." In: *The Guardian* 16 April. <http://www.guardian.co.uk/politics/2007/apr/16/politicsandthearts.theatre> (last accessed 26 Oct. 2010).

Paget, Derek. 1987. "'Verbatim Theatre': Oral History and Documentary Techniques." In: *New Theatre Quarterly* 3.12: 117-27.

—. 2009. "The 'Broken Tradition' of Documentary Theatre and Its Continued Powers of Endurance." In: Forsyth & Megson 2009. 224-38.

Pinter, Harold. 2005. "Nobel Lecture: Art, Truth & Politics." 7 Dec. <http://nobelprize.org/nobel_prizes/literature/laureates/2005/pinter-lecture.html> (last accessed 8 June 2010).

Rancière, Jacques. 2004. *The Politics of Aesthetics: The Distribution of the Sensible*. London/New York: Continuum.

Reinelt, Janelle. 2005. "Review of *Stuff Happens*." In: *Theatre Journal* 57.2: 303-06.

—. 2009. "The Promise of Documentary." In: Forsyth & Megson 2009. 6-23.

Stoller, Terry. 2005. "Tribunals at the Tricycle: Nicolas Kent in conversation with Terry Stoller." In: *Hunter Online Theatre Review*. <http://www.hotreview.org/articles/tribunalsatthet.htm> (last accessed 8 June 2010).

The Tricycle Theatre. Homepage. <http://www.tricycle.co.uk> (last accessed 8 June 2010).
Weiss, Peter. 1966. *The Investigation: Oratorio in Eleven Cantos.* London: Marion Boyars.
Westgate, J. Chris. 2009. "David Hare's 'Stuff Happens' in Seattle: Taking a Sober Account." In: *New Theatre Quarterly* 25.4: 402-18.
White, Hayden. 1973. *Metahistory: The Historical Imagination in 19th Century Europe.* Baltimore: Johns Hopkins UP.
—. 1999. *Figural Realism: Studies in the Mimesis Effect.* Baltimore: Johns Hopkins UP.
Young, Stuart. 2009. "Playing with Documentary Theatre: Aalst and Taking Care of Baby." In: *New Theatre Quarterly* 25.1: 72-87.

28. BLACK BRITISH DRAMA: DEBBIE TUCKER GREEN AND KWAME KWEI-ARMAH

DEIRDRE OSBORNE

1. Introduction

Ian Rickson, formerly Artistic Director (of ten years) at the Royal Court Theatre, London – a venue known for its nurturing of cutting edge writing since the 1950s – believes that "the best plays come from the edges or corners of society" (Rickson 2004). Black playwrights working in Britain today provide salient examples of this viewpoint in their dramatizations of voices that until now have been only sporadically produced for mainstream British stages. Although black dramatists born outside the UK such as Una Marson in the 1930s, Wole Soyinka and Barry Reckord in the 1950s, and Mustapha Matura in the 1970s did have plays staged to acclaim, the territory has remained ostensibly white and male-dominated. Notwithstanding this fact, black women like Yvonne Brewster, Carmen Munroe, Mona Hammond, Denise Wong, and Jacqueline Rudet spearheaded the establishment of significant black-led theatre companies in the 1980s. As recipients of Arts Council of England subsidy, these companies operated in community to middle-scale touring capacities rather than gaining traction in mainstream cultural venues. From the mid-1980s, a time of Conservative Government arts disinvestment, which saw myriad black arts organizations cease activity, playwrights such as Winsome Pinnock and directors like Paulette Randall pioneered their own mainstream as women *and* as indigenous black British women, achieving longevity in a theatre world where white men unilaterally retain artistic and commercial hegemony. In the new millennium, British-born black playwrights Kwame Kwei-Armah, Roy Williams, debbie tucker green, and Bola Agbaje have achieved a certain permeation of this complex but concomitant to this is a stifling generic association with social realism to which, arguably, tucker green is the only challenger in her experimental and experiential adventurousness. Given its history to date, this raises questions regarding the artistic evolution and sustainability of Black drama for the future, the positioning of black women playwrights and on whose terms this will be negotiated.

2. Historical Overview: A Brief History of Black British Drama

Archaeological evidence proves the existence of black people in the British Isles at the beginning of the first millennium (notably the Roman ruler Septimius Severus [193-211 AD]) and indicates both the degree of heterogeneity of the ancient population, and an African presence despite admixture. In recent research funded by the Wellcome Trust, King and others "found that one third of men with a rare Yorkshire surname carry a rare

Y chromosome type previously found only amongst people of West African origin" (www.medicalnewstoday.com). However, it is from the Middle Ages that accounting for blackness overtly configures physiological difference (foremost in religious and travel writing) to mark out the polarity between Christian and non-Christian, by implication white and non-white people, thereby continuing a classical narratology of negotiating otherness established by Herodotus (485-c. 425 BC) and Pliny (c. 62-114 AD). As Sue Niebrzydowski (2001) demonstrates, medieval England's knowledge of non-European races was derived from direct contact through warfare (such as the Crusades) and vicariously through travel literature (such as the translation of John Mandeville's travel writing [1356-57]), religious exegesis, secular poetry (John Gower [1330-1408], Geoffrey Chaucer [1343-1400]), and encyclopaedia (such as Caxton's Middle English *Mirrour of the World* [1481]). This knowledge was primarily symbolic rather than produced in reference to an abiding, actual presence. The inscribing of blackness prior to the Renaissance represents the articulations of the divergent cultures created by the intersectional epicentre of Europe, the imperial powers, Portugal, Spain, France, and England as they vied for material and territorial superiority. The representtations in writing reveal how tropes of blackness in the medieval world view were already intertwined with ideas about female beauty and male power, which became voiced increasingly through the language of racial difference, overwriting the previous representational motivation of forging religious distinction between Christian and Muslim.

To date, no evidence exists of any plays written or devised by black writers in Britain until the 20th century. Of course black characters were penned by white writers well before this. As women were played by men and boys on the British stage until 1660, so too did white people apply make-up and accessories that supposedly conveyed blackness to audiences. Black-faced devils in medieval morality plays wore black stockings and masks in performance and this racialized, prosthetic technique remained entrenched in British culture most especially through the make-up of minstrelsy until the late 20th century. Michael McMillan (2004: 54) notes: "It wasn't until the mid-1970s that the BBC, bastion of 'balanced' broadcasting decided it was time to take *The Black and White Minstrel Show* off the air." Any survey of the presence of black people in early British theatre history thus resides in the vicarious and inauthentic black characters that white writers created from the 16th to 19th centuries. Playwrights who produced images of black people in their plays include Jonson (1572-1637), Dekker (1572-1632), Heywood (1575-1641), Webster (1758-1847), Middleton (1580-1627), and Chapman (1559-1634). Early imaginative treatments of black people are also captured in the form of some 17th-century dialogue poems: George Herbert's (1593-1633) "A Negro maid woos Cestus, a man of a different colour," Henry Rainolds's "A Black-moor Maid wooing a fair Boy: sent to the Author by Mr. Henry Rainolds," "The Boyes answer to the Blackmoor" by Henry King, and "A Fair Nymph Scorning a Black Boy Courting Her" by John Cleveland. As the titles indicate, the ubiquitous theme of cross-race courtship implies a negotiating of desire, transgression, and miscegenation. Anu Korhonen poses the question: "What did people actually see when they encountered darker-skinned individuals, either real people, or textual and visual representations of black Africans?" (2005: 94) Black skin became pivotal to constructions of white identity. Even at this time, before the honing of racist ideology that accompanied the imperial enterprise and the trans-Atlantic trade in enslaved people from the African continent, conceptions of black skin were entwined with judgements and distinctions between white and black, beauty and defect, the civilized and brutish.

Dark skin was unavoidably observable in a white-majority society. There tended to be a collapsing of distinctiveness into a generalizing physical category that denoted blackness based upon lips, skin colour, and hair. The physical accounting for blackness created expectations in audiences (spectator, listener, or reader), of associated behaviour. Traits of character developed dramatically from this. *Ipso facto*, blackness came to signify evil, hell's agency, and sin as seen in Elizabethan plays: Shakespeare's *Titus Andronicus* (1592) and Dekker's *Lust's Dominion* (1599). Works were weighted with racializing assumptions and cultural judgements as was Jonson's Jacobean *Masque of Blackness* (1605) in which royal maskers darkened their skin. Devised in response to Queen Anne's request to play a "black-more" (Barthelemy 1987: 20), the white women's prosthetic blackness is removed ultimately, by the King's power. The blackened performers are restored to their rightful white beauty in a spectacle of authority which Kim Hall (1994: 183) describes as "a defining moment of the British empire which used blackness to privilege white beauty."

The Moor in 16th- and 17th-century drama typifies the agent of ruin and duplicity in a range of murderous, raping, cruel, vengeful, exotic, and untrustworthy representations. Yet scattered amongst the endless negative versions, ethnologically and dramatically, there are favourable glimpses which reveal the (possibly unconscious) ambivalence harboured by the playwrights towards their black subjects. In this way, the narrowness of dogma and culturally restricted viewing is offset against dramatic characterization and balance. However, as Elliot Tokson (1982: 135) observes, "[w]henever a black character exhibits a sign of decent behaviour, either it is so buried among acts of evil that it fails to leave any lasting impression, or it appears conditioned by a recognition of the higher virtue of the white culture." The humanizing of black people represented in Renaissance drama relied upon their Christianizing and adoption of recognizably white culturally-associative customs, speech, and manners.

The fluctuating numbers of black people in the population was precipitated by various historical events. Black soldiers fleeing to England after the British defeat in the American War of Independence triggered a repatriation of 459 black people to Sierra Leone in 1783. Caribbean plantation owners relocating their households to England (most noticeably after the abolition of the Slave Trade Act in 1807) also increased the black servant class visible on London streets who were often resented by the white working classes (with whom they also intermarried) as pampered accessory to the wealthy classes (see *Below Stairs* exhibition, National Portrait Gallery 2003-2004). Literary and historical scholarship from the late-20th century has unearthed the degree to which black people in Britain participated in cultural and commercial life up to the abolition of slavery throughout the British Empire in 1833 (cf. Carretta 1996; Dabydeen 1985; Fryer 1984; Gerzina 1995; Innes 2002; Waters 2007). However, the visibility of black people and representations of black experience are primarily glimpsed through paintings by white artists or else in the writings of visiting black writers, poets like Phyllis Wheatley (1753-1784), the memoir, letters, diaries, and life-writing of people such as Mary Prince (b. c. 1788), Quobna Ottobah Cugoano (c. 1757-c. 1801), Ukawsaw Gronniosaw Olaudah Equiano (1745-1797), and Ignatius Sancho (c. 1729-1780), thereby in many ways mirroring the popular true-heritage-disclosed novels such as Henry Fielding's *Tom Jones* (1749) where everything is not as it first seems – rather than in any writing for the stage. Slave portrayals in the theatre and engravings of the late-18th century were frequently vulgar satires, farces, or sentimental poems featuring Africans wrongly enslaved who were in fact nobility (in real-life, the prince of Annamaboe, William Ansah Sessarakoo [1736-1749] who attended a performance of Southerne's *Oroonoko* Theatre Royal, Drury Lane, 1759 or John Henry Naimbanna [1767-1793]). Shakespeare's *Othello* (1604) and Thomas Southerne's dramatized adaptation (1696) of Aphra Behn's novella *Oroonoko* (1688) continued to be particularly popular in theatres throughout the 18th century as comic operas in which black characters, played by white actors, dominated the theatre seasons (*Love in the City* [1767], *The Padlock* [1768], and *The Sultan* [1773] by Isaac Bickerstaffe, *The Black-a-moor Wash'd White* [1776] by Henry Bate). Like the two-act farce, James Townley's *High Life Below Stairs* (1759) featuring two black servants, these productions were the vehicles for white performers only. Hence the most literally live arena (aside from daily living) for encountering blackness, the theatre, continued to be off-limits to black people as playwrights and actors despite the numbers of black people in London's population throughout the 18th and 19th centuries.

It was not until the mid-19th century, with the presence of Ira Aldridge (1807-1867), a black American actor (who escaping segregation, came to Britain and adopted British nationality), that there is the first public example of a black performer achieving agency in the kinds of roles he interpreted in mainstream theatre. Having exhausted the number of black characters he could play by the late 1820s, Aldridge took on white roles while writing his own melodramas and doggerel verses with political overtones. Although he played black and white roles in classical plays to international acclaim, toured provincially and throughout Europe, the actor also suffered the racism of West End theatre critics who ensured his London season was truncated. Throughout the mid-19th to early-20th centuries, black performers were to be found ostensibly in circuses, sideshows, and musicals. In 1911, African American intellectual W.E.B. Du Bois (1868-1963) commented upon the racial diversity he witnessed in Edwardian London.

> The empire is a colored empire. Most of its subjects – a vast majority of its subjects – are colored people. And more and more the streets of London are showing this fact. [...] There must be thousands of colored people in the city. [...] There is color prejudice and aloofness undoubtedly here, but it does not parade its shame like New York or its barbarity like New Orleans. (Du Bois 1911: 159)

This observation connects to that made by another intellectual, Henry Louis Gates Jr., at the end of the century, when he noted, "[m]y initial travels through black London, then, were for me a succession of spit-takes: black people who sounded English without even trying." (2000: 169) Twenty-five years later he observes, "a culture that is distinctively black *and* British can be said to be in full flower, both on the streets and in the galleries" (ibid.: 171) one, where he is, "always struck by the social ease between most blacks and whites on the streets." (Ibid.: 176) Black people in Britain have had a perpetual association with cosmopolitanism and internationalism which remains largely under-explored. From the Fisk Jubilee Singers (1874-75) onwards, touring shows from the United States abounded, such as: *In Dahomey* (1903), *Plantation Days* (1923), *Dover Street to Dixie* and *Blackbirds* starring the African-American singer Florence Mills in 1923 and 1926, African American émigré Elisabeth Welch (1904-2003) in *Dark Doings* and *Nymph Errant* (1933). Together with musicals such as *Show Boat* (1928) and *Porgy and Bess* (1952) in West End theatres, throughout the 1920s and 30s, the revue was the primary performing context for black performers who were invariably from abroad.

In terms of drama, the pre-World War II, white-majority, British public like their American counterparts continued to be exposed to white playwrights' representations of black characters, writers who generally knew no black people personally nor had experience of black citizens' lives. Furthermore, there was not yet the concomitant demographic mass in Britain that had produced American black intellectuals and artists behind organizations such as the NAACP, cultural movements like the Harlem New Renaissance, or the Historical Black Colleges and hence representational agency. In the first decades of the 20th century, black intellectuals from abroad often settled in London for periods of time and there was a developing internationalism politicized by the common ground of the racial injustices experienced. Writers and politicians such as Claude McKay (1890-1948), C.L.R. James (1901-1989), Marcus Garvey (1887-1940), George Padmore (1903-1959), Kwame Nkrumah (1909-1972), Paul Robeson (1898-1976), and Una Marson (1905-1965), and medical doctor Harold Moody (1882-1947) were all activists in various organizations which spoke out against imperialism and critiqued colonization. Marson in particular, as a woman in a man's representational world deserves some further commentary. She was a published poet, worked for the BBC radio and was a pioneering figure for black women – although not universally recognized as such. In an unheeded facet of black theatre history, her biographer, Delia Jarrett-Macauley notes that black Jamaican feminist Marson directed her play *At What a Price* (1932) which was performed by members of the League of Coloured Peoples "at the YMCA hostel Central Club...23 November 1933" and that "the play transferred for a three-night run, beginning on January 15, at the Scala Theatre, central London," receiving favourable reviews and making history as "the first black colonial production in the West End" (Jarrett-Macauley 1998: 53 f.).

Prior to Marson's landmark achievement, Robeson had starred in Eugene O'Neill's racially problematic *The Emperor Jones* (1920) at the Ambassadors Theatre in 1925 and in 1930, and was the first professional black actor to play Othello in Britain since the 19th century. Drama productions in mainstream theatres which cast black actors throughout the 1930s ostensibly featured Robeson. Many were staged by Unity Theatre and were penned by white writers: *Basilik* (1935) by Peter Garland, *Stevedore* (1935) by Paul Peters and George Sklar, and *Plant in the Sun* (1938) by Ben Bengal. Black actors featured in productions of O'Neill's *All God's Chillun' Got Wings* (1924), first staged in England at the Royal Court with Jim Harris, Emma Williams, and Henry Brown in 1929 and revived with Robeson in 1933. The one exception to Robeson's singularity was C.L.R. James's *Toussaint L'Ouverture* (1936) for the Stage Society, which also included other black actors: Robert Adams, Orlando Martins, R.E. Fennell, John Ahuma, and Lawrence Brown. The cultural presence of black people in the context of theatre and performance drew upon many strands of the African diaspora and its trans-Atlantic and colonial manifestations but was overwhelmingly within white creative frameworks. Casting opportunities did not improve as Robert Adams and Ida Shipley were the only two black actors in London Unity Theatre's 1946 production of *Toussaint L'Overture* (1936), the rest of the cast consisted of white people having been blacked up. Colin Chambers (1989: 400) notes, "[u]nity had always taken a stand on racism, particularly against anti-semitism" and "during the war had refused membership on the grounds of racial attitude." However, their progressiveness regarding racial inclusiveness was not sustained as Chambers explains, "when Britain had become more multi-ethnic after recruiting Commonwealth labour, Unity, like most of the left, remained overwhelmingly white though it continued to be staunchly anti-imperialist" (ibid.).

World War II had engendered a transitory population of black servicemen and women from the colonies and the United States to create, especially in London, a mobilized and variegated demographic. Intermixing also left a legacy of biologically mixed children, many of whom were placed in orphanages, evidence of taboo-defying, cross-race, and frequently out-of-wedlock or extra-marital sexual relationships. The reconstruction of Britain after 1945 relied upon the labour from invited Commonwealth migrants and generated the largest mass migration to its shores in British history, changing the racial and cultural landscape forever. As Robert Adams had co-founded the wartime London Negro Repertory Theatre (with Peter Noble), other black-led drama organizations in the post-war period include: the West Indian Drama Group, founded in 1956 by Joan Clarke (who specialized in directing plays with all-black casts) and based at the West Indian Students' Union, and the Ira Aldridge Players, established by Herbert Marshall in 1961 as a permanent black theatre company. Inconsistencies abound in accounts of these early Black theatre companies, many of which folded soon after their founding. For example, despite Adams and Clarke's groups, Bruce King states that "Lloyd Reckord tried to establish the first Black theatre company in London. His New Day Theatre Company began in 1960 with two short plays by Derek Walcott" (King 2004: 76 f.). He also notes another group, "Edric and Pearl Connor then formed the Negro Theatre Workshop (1963) which rehearsed plays at the West Indian Students Centre and Africa Centre" (ibid.). Pearl Connor was to go on to form the first agency representing black performing artists in Britain. The prominence of a woman director such as Clarke together with Marson and Connor's achievements form a compelling but unrecorded antecedent for women director-producers, Joan-Ann Maynard, Yvonne Brewster, Paulette Randall, Patricia Cumper, and Josette Bushell-Mingo later in the century.

Throughout the 1950s and 60s, black male writers born outside Britain had some success with productions of their work at the Royal Court Theatre (locus of the Angry Young Men generation) and Theatre Royal, Stratford East (home of Joan Littlewood's Theatre Workshop). Errol John's *Moon on a Rainbow Shawl* (1956) was staged at the Royal Court in 1958 while Barry Reckord had three plays produced there: *Flesh to a Tiger* (1958) starring indigenous black British actor and singer Cleo Laine (with Tamba Allen, Pearl Prescod, James Clarke, Lloyd Reckord, Johnny Sekka, Nadia Cattouse, and Connie Smith), *You in Your Small Corner* (1960), and *Skyvers* (1963), produced with white actors as the Royal Court claimed it could not find any black actors! In 1960 the New Negro Theatre Company at Theatre Royal Stratford East staged white writer Paul Green's *No Count Boy* with a black cast including Allen, Mark Heath, Sekka, Neville Munroe, Clifton Jones, Gloria Higdon, and Carmen Munroe, and Jones's double-bill *La Mere/The S Bend* – clearly not suffering from the Royal Court's inability to find black actors. In the West End however, the staging of black plays remained those by African American writers: Langston Hughes' musical *Simply Heavenly* (directed by white actor Laurence Harvey at the Adelphi in 1958) was followed by Lorraine Hansberry's *A Raisin in the Sun* at the same theatre in 1959 directed by its black Broadway director, Lloyd Richards.

Reflecting upon 1970s theatre, Roland Rees (1992: 24) founder of Foco Novo noted, "[o]nly in recent years …[the late 80s]…would upward mobility and class assimilation of a black character have been possible to contrive in a British play" in reference to the plot of *The Electronic Nigger* (1968) by American Ed Bullins, a Black Panther activist. The play, part of Ed Berman's InterAction lunchtime plays staged at the Ambience café in Queensway, provided a powerful impetus for writers working in Britain. *Black Pieces* (1970) by Mustapha Matura was staged for the (Berman produced) Black and White Power season at the ICA. Two members of the cast, Alfred Fagon and T. Bone Wilson, went on to write their own plays. In particular, Fagon's own reaction to Matura's first play shows the degree to which watershed innovation occurred, not only in the experiences dramatized but also the use of idiom and vernacular which characterized the work of the Caribbean Artists Movement (1966-72). Roland Rees recounts Fagon's reaction: "He looked at the script and said: 'I cannot read this.' I said: 'Why?' He said: 'I dare not read it.' Alfred explained he had never seen anything written down in the way he spoke…To him it was a momentous occasion. And indeed those early plays by Mustapha broke that ground." (Rees 1992: 106) Theatre-making drew together a close network of immigrants. Matura knew Stefan Kalipha (an East 15 Drama School graduate) and film maker and photographer Horace Ove who were all to record the period of the 1970s and 80s in their different artistic media.

The lack of roles for black actors led to the further establishment of black companies in the 1970s and '80s. Examples of this proactive redress are seen in the Temba Theatre Company, founded in 1970 by Alton Kumalo and Oscar James, an ex-Royal Shakespeare Company actor who had no opportunity for major roles. Similarly, the Black Theatre Co-operative was formed by Mustapha Matura and Charlie Hanson (in 1978), Theatre of Black Women by Patricia Hilarie, Paulette Randall, and Bernardine Evaristo (in 1982), Imani-Faith by Jacqueline Rudet (in 1983), Umoja (founded in 1983) by Gloria Hamilton and Alexander Simon to encourage and create opportunities for black people in field of theatre arts, Black Mime Theatre by Denise Wong (in 1984) and Talawa by Yvonne Brewster, Carmen Munroe, Mona Hammond, and Inigo Espejel (in 1985). Ria Lavrijsen notes how insertion into culture impelled these practitioners, "[t]he black population was shut out of British society and that was questioned by 'black theatre'" (1990: 78).

By the end of 1985, the Arts Council changed its policy to target white institutions to support black artists so that integrated casting became standard. However, black theatre groups argued that funding to them should have been direct, rather than via white-dominated elitist institutions. In that connection, Lavrijsen cites the American playwright August Wilson's argument in relation to integrated casting – that it was "no more than an excuse not to perform any plays by black writers" (1990: 81) – to suggest that a whitening process still pervaded British theatre – despite certain superficial changes. On the other hand, while the proliferation of black-led companies facilitated black performance from the 1970s, this did not always equate with generating new writing or promoting black playwrights. Temba's final Artistic Director, Alby James, pointed to the developmental torpor and incessant identity politics trope that led to a narrowing of the scope of black work in the 1990s. This is arguably one of the progenitors of contemporary limitations in black dramatists' experimentation – something which does not characterize other forms of writing such as poetry, lyrics, or novels. Caryl Phillips (*1958) argues retrospectively that there was a relative dearth of new black writing for theatre in the 1980s and 1990s.

> The establishment and funding of black theatre groups such as Talawa Theatre Company meant that there was a black stage presence during this period, but not necessarily new writing. Second, the increased availability of television and film commissions, with the opening up of Channel 4, and the last glorious flourish of BBC television drama, meant that writers began to look to the screen both for a larger audience, and for more immediate financial rewards. Third, it became increasingly commonplace for directors to move between mediums and venues, and in such circumstances it was very difficult for working relationships to be established and nourished. (Phillips 2005: 16)

However, this same period saw the flourishing of many women playwrights who worked far more experimentally with language and physical theatre than their male contemporaries. Corresponding to the male-dominated worlds created by Matura, Tunde Ikoli, and others was the emergence of black women's theatre and performance, and most particularly the work of playwrights such as Rudet, Pinnock, Trish Cooke, Jenny McLeod, Maria Oshodi, and Jackie Kay, who entered the mainstream with varying degrees of longevity, as well as the staging of plays by less established writers: Grace Dayley's *Rose's Story* (1985), Killian M. Gideon's *England is De Place for Me* (1987), Sandra Yew's *Zerri's Choice* (1989), Lisselle Kayla's *Don't Chat Me Business* (1990), and Valerie Mason-John's *Brown Girl in the Ring* (1999). It is also due to the work of women editors that this legacy of black women playwrights at work during that period did not disappear, as sampled in Wandor's *Plays by Women*, Vol. IV (1985), *Plays by Women* (1986, 1990), Brewster's *Black Plays* (1987, 1989, 1995), Griffin and Aston's *Lesbian Plays* (1987), Consodine and Slovo's *Dead Proud* (1987), Gray's *First Run: New Plays by New Writers* (1989), and George's *Six Plays by Black and Asian Women Writers* (1993, reproduced with a new Introduction in 2004).

It should also not be forgotten that the lack of staying power attributed to black theatre finds explanation in the perennial pruning of its funding. Rees's Foco Novo – the company that nurtured black playwrights Matura, Fagon, Ikoli, and others – was a typical casualty of funding cuts made in the 1980s and 1990s. Ikoli's pioneering plays address the experiences of indigenous black Britons and people of dual heritage, marking a new direction in Black drama in the 1980s. Foco Novo produced Ikoli's *On the Out* (1978), *Sink or Swim* (1982), *Sleeping Policeman* (1983) with Howard Brenton, *Week in Week out* (1985), *The Lower Depths* and *Banged Up* (both 1986). In 1992, in a conversation with Rees, Ikoli described the demise of Foco Novo:

> Ikoli: We were told all these appraisals...[by the Arts Council]...were really for our own benefit, and if we did what we were supposed to, we would find ourselves leaner and more efficient in the future.... Then we disappeared overnight.
> Rees: After sixteen years! (Rees 1992: 133 f.)

The cut raised an uproar, but it also created an opportunity to discuss the implications of different sorts of funding appropriations. Talawa Theatre Company, which seemed to have planted itself permanently in the British theatrescape, was set to develop the old Westminster Theatre (in London) into Britain's first black-led, black-managed, dedicated theatre with Paulette Randall as Artistic Director. By May 2005, the company faced decimation in funding as its board members clashed with a chair (a Labour Party peer with a formidable record in campaigning for racial justice), who, without theatre experience, applied business management criteria that threatened to strangle the company artistically leading to Randall's departure. Unfortunate occurrences of that sort have underlined the need for a dedicated black theatre. As *Time Out*'s Theatre Editor Jane Edwardes reports: "Does black theatre really want to be ghettoized in a specific building?" (2005: 157). A similar pattern was repeated in the new millennium when longstanding black arts enterprises such as the Black Arts Alliance and Centreprise were disinvested after drawn out appraisals, demands for restructuring in unrealistically limited time frames and conclusions that there was no need for the kind of black specialist arts hub both organizations offered.

Internal strife unfortunately has played a part in the difficulties faced by Black theatre in Britain, already not made any easier by the white-dominated funding criteria and closed-shop white coterie of drama critics. Racist attitudes have produced paternalism and discrimination against black arts organizations and artists throughout the 20th century as black writers have faced hindrances simply because they did not belong to the ethnic majority. A Eurocentric and Western benchmark has served as the definitive, critical indicator of quality. When practitioners did not attain instant expertise (meaning compliance with conventional norms of British discourse or stagecraft) and success (meaning financial support and critical acclaim in the mainstream media), this benchmark ratified conveniently the charges of poor quality. Notable also is the differential treatment where the white playwrights are categorized collectively as innovative in developing a new and explosive genre of theatrical experience, be it in-yer-face (Sierz 2000; see chapter 25) or verbatim (the darling of the fabulation, tribunal, factual-fictional interface plays), and the black playwrights are found to be merely slipping towards melodrama or writing poetically not dramatically when they adopt similar dramatic strategies to express a contemporary aesthetic.

Moreover, black British dramatists seeking to have their work produced at the end of the 20th century faced a split between (a) identifying with collective interests of the black community (in a society which until the mid-1990s grouped black and Asian experiences under the one multicultural and discriminatory umbrella) or (b) attempting to move ahead and try for something more like artistic individualism. Funding cuts, inconsistent archiving, and minimal critical attention has resulted in the disappearance of much material evidence of Black drama in British theatre and literary historiography. The perceived lack of continuity between the decades is an effect of scholarly neglect and means essentially that, as Kwei-Armah remarked, "every generation then has to build again, start again, and believe they are actually the beginning" (Osborne 2007: 253). The perception also underscores the fact that the critical infrastructure and archiving processes assumed for white dramatists – who automatically take their place in a centuries-old discursive field – have not habitually accompanied the achievements of black theatre practitioners.

3. debbie tucker green's and Kwame Kwei-Armah's Plays

To date, tucker green (*1964) is the most radical black British experimenter along these lines, with her unique re-workings of norms in language, casting demands, and treatments – while Roy Williams (*1968) is the most prolific playwright of the leading contemporary and confrontational black dramatists. Both have been part of the Royal Court's new writing commissioning initiative, but not exclusively affiliated to the venue. Whereas tucker green foregrounds women-centred themes and interrogates the role of women in the crush of capitalism and violence, both global and domestic, Williams together with Royal National Theatre commissionee Kwei-Armah (*1966) tends to write drama of black working-class experiences and explores the ramifications of violence and crime in a society that has disenfranchised a significant section of its own citizens. While Williams continues to produce work associated with this demographic, Kwei-Armah has moved into other representational territory creating overtly political theatre syntax in his more recent plays by which he scrutinizes the mores of Britain's black middle-classes and stages a more variegated migrant experience incorporating recent East European presences. All three writers have captured the public imagination through their mainstream theatrical successes but tucker green with her experimental techniques that create multi-receptive and performative potential on both page *and* stage and Kwei-Armah as the first black British playwright to conquer the West End, best exemplify watershed moments for contemporary Black British drama.

Kwei-Armah has been thrice commissioned by the Royal National Theatre. *Elmina's Kitchen* (2003) explored familial impoverishment in the setting of drug-related black on black violence for which he won the *Evening Standard* and Charles Wintour awards for Most Promising Playwright and a nomination for a Laurence Olivier Award for Best New Play 2003. *Fix Up* (2004) followed the quest of mixed-race teacher Alice to find her biological father and cultural roots in a black bookstore where material acquisition of the current generation was pitted against knowledge retrieval. Both plays were directed by Angus Jackson. As well as a national tour, *Elmina's Kitchen* was aired on BBC Radio 3 (produced by Claire Grove) and BBC4 television, with a season in Baltimore USA (2005). The revival of *Elmina's Kitchen* (in which he starred) was the first Black British play to transfer to London's West End (Garrick Theatre). The third RNT commission *Statement of Regret* (2007) was an overtly state-of-the-nation play, using the setting of a black think tank to probe intra-racial tensions between black people's African or Caribbean heritage identifications, reparations for slavery, and the notion of the blaxpert vs. the black professional. *Seize the Day* was part of the Tricycle Theatre, London's *Not Black and White* season (2009) and in exploring the campaign of a black London mayoral candidate, returns to the subject matter of black people in public and professional life of *Statement of Regret*. Both plays hammer out the participation of black Britons in political and economic citizenship, offering a powerful counterpoint to the press and media stereotypes of under-achievement that still prevail. Kwei-Armah chides an audience's potential incredulity regarding a middle-class, black, politicized mainstream, thus disabling ideological barriers to this being credible. He states unequivocally that he writes from a standpoint of –

> Let's not mince words here, my work is political work. I say my work is coming from a cultural perspective that is supported by my Pan-Africanist politics. Which is why for instance, the American black establishment have looked at *Elmina's Kitchen* [...] performed at the Center Stage, Baltimore, directed by August Wilson's director, Marion McClinton. [...] My politics is a diasporic, black politics influenced by the philosophies of Marcus Garvey and Malcolm X and the writings of James Baldwin and Amiri Baraka. It is non-apologetic politics. I make no bones in talking about the cultural specificity of my work. (Osborne 2007: 253)

Elmina's Kitchen (*EK*, referring to the notorious Ghanaian slave fort) captures a very specific period of working-class black London history. With an all-black cast, Kwei-

Armah creates a compelling portrait of familial disintegration as an older embattled male migrant generation (Clifton and Baygee) are unable either to protect or offer a moral model to second- and third-generations (Deli and Ashley) in the face of their own failed attempts at entrepreneurship and competing lures of quick money through drug-dealing and violence (Digger). Identity as derived from the country of origin, cultural antecedents, and its relationship to Britishness is apparent. The local gangster Digger is described as having come from Grenada and emigrated at 14 with an accent that "*swings from his native Grenadian to hard-core Jamaican to authentic black London.*" (*EK* 4) Nuance countermands the discriminatory generalizing of a historically racist society when Digger refers to British-born Deli as "You British blacks" (*EK* 14) in a putdown, yet Baygee, "*the last of the West Indian door-to-door salesmen*" (*EK* 13) in turn labels Digger "White boy." It is this interrogation of the mosaic of British-ness, the assertion of voices that exist and represent experiences beyond mainstream critical vision that frequently appears in Black British drama. In the cultural output characterized as British there is a changing landscape transformed by political struggle in representing identity-shaping institutions of family, law, and education. Kwei-Armah plants his protagonists' indigenousness as distinct from the migratory or arriviste sensibility, while at the same time embroidering his dramatic tapestry with the threads of its heritages. Only the older generation who emigrated from the Caribbean refer to the effects of colonization: "BAYGEE. *(conversationally)*...when a black man tief one man cry, when the European dem tief, whole continents bawl" (*EK* 19) and Clifton's "The most witchcraft is practise by the white man. How do the arse you think he managed to take Africa from we" for which Deli, his son, exhibits little tolerance, "Don't bring none of your white this and dat in here, Clifton. I don't want to hear that." (*EK* 38) As Gates Jr. (2000: 170) quoted John La Rose's comment of fellow ex-patriots: "'How can they be English?' [...] 'Their entire culture is West Indian,'" Kwei-Armah unequivocally locates his British characters' identities as not being derived in relation to the colonizing enterprise but from their strategic survival in a specific urban context of Hackney. He writes from a British-born standpoint and creates a play which negotiates the complexity of identity affiliations (cultural, geographical, and ethnic) possible for black citizens. Deli's generation are confounded by what Sandhu identifies as the acute differences in cultural expectations and political realities of generations separated rather than joined by the legacy of migration.

> If migrants do contemplate the past, it's the past of their parents and grandparents, of the colonial city or village from which they hail. This ancestral realm is alien to their children who don't share the same geographies, memories or idiolects. What can second-generation migrants do to locate themselves? Where are the contours of their sense of self? [...] Those who grew up in the 1980s hoping to assert their Englishness knew that, as far as Margaret Thatcher was concerned, they were a threat to national cohesion. (Sandhu 2003: 284)

From such a discarded, disregarded, and discredited generation, Kwei-Armah implies plausibility for Ashley's actions, the youngest in three generations of men, in only seeking self-respect through embracing the drugs world the gangsta Digger offers, quick fix symbols of material success and status that Deli, his father cannot.

> ASHLEY *stares at* DELI *with hate in his eyes...*
> ASHLEY. He takes away your pride, then your livelihood, and all you can do is stand dere like a fish? You've lost it blood.
> DELI. (*flash of temper*) I'm not no blood wid you.
> ASHLEY. Regrettably, that's exactly what you are. (*EK* 25)

Male shame which has been propagated by social inconsequentiality and disenfranchisement is barren ground upon which to propagate seeds of self-worth in future generations. In this fallow environment it is notable that mothers are absent – either dead or offstage. Elmina is simply the dead woman, idealized by her son and complained about by his father, her ex-husband who had absconded from the marriage and child-rearing responsibilities. Although she is present in the name of the café and in her portrait on its walls, she exerts no moral influence. There are two passing mentions of Ashley's mother (who has left Deli) while Anastasia the sole on-stage woman has lost her child and thus, tangible motherhood. Moreover, the sexual denigration of women takes on many forms. Kwei-Armah's stage directions at Anastasia's first entrance suppose a universal salaciousness: "*we can see that she has the kind of body that most men of colour fantasise about. Big hips and butt, slim waist and full, full breasts*" (*EK* 15) compared to Deli, "*a happy spirit...a born struggler...slightly overweight*" (*EK* 3), or Digger "*looks every bit the 'bad man' that he is. His hair is plaited in two neat sets of cane rows*" (*EK* 4) while Clifton is "*large-built...a boastful man*" (*EK* 32). When pressed upon this Kwei-Armah responded,

> [w]hen Anastasia walks into the room, they go, 'I will give you attention'. The only way you get attention in that world, is either by being as masculine and vocal as they are or, by being something that they want to fuck – as opposed to being the *only* way that I would describe a female. (Osborne 2007: 259)

In addition, Anastasia's moral compass (which the audience or reader have been able to follow through the brutal male-male contestations) is inexplicably not allowed to hold steady when she sleeps (implausibly) with Clifton while in a relationship with Deli.

The dramatic arc (following Aristotle's template for tragedy) works to bring Deli to his lowest point: unable to trust the woman he loves, betrayed by his concupiscent father, informing on Digger in return for money that he hopes will win Ashley back. Yet, Kwei-Armah compounds this with absolute loss. Ashley, in Digger's crew (in an almost Oedipal moment) goes to shoot his own father in order to not be 'the informer's boy,' privileging his street credibility over blood ties he considers demeaning:

> ASHLEY *slowly takes out his gun.* DELI *just stares at him.*
> ASHLEY. You let me down Dad...
> DIGGER. Alright, now point the gun at your punk-arsed dad. The one that gets beat up and does nothing, has his business near taken away and does nothing, but then informs on a brother man...*(screams at him)* Is this the type of people we need in our midst?
> ASHLEY. No.

DIGGER. OK then, raise the gun, point it.
ASHLEY *does*.
DIGGER. Good. Is your finger on the trigger?
ASHLEY. Yes.
DIGGER. Good. (*EK* 93 f.)

In a grim coup-de-theatre however, "DIGGER *pulls out his gun and shoots* ASHLEY *dead*," proclaiming: "... Yes. Ah so dis war run!" (Ibid.) The expulsion of the younger generation offers a bleak inversion of nature's expected cycle and underscores the contorted legacy of inheritance. Meta-narratively, the play asks audiences to consider the consequences of continuing to alienate and marginalize black citizens born in this country. Given the majority of British theatre-goers are white (and Kwei-Armah acknowledges this as the host community, suggesting black writers are interlopers to a degree), this play taps into the limited representations of blackness that have permeated the British theatre complex in which misogyny, young men dying of wounds centre-stage, and futility have become rewarded. These kinds of plays have prompted the ire of Talawa's current artistic director, Patricia Cumper who responded with,

> [y]oung black people are growing up in a society where they are frequently stereotyped and alienated. They respond in many creative and dynamic ways – but we don't hear much about that. What makes it into the newspapers and on to the stage is dysfunction, criminality and violence. (Cumper 2009)

Kwei-Armah works within the armour of social realism which means he has not been catalogued by Aleks Sierz's notion of in-yer-face theatre and its limited canonization of (white) *fin-de-siècle* writers. Sierz characterized in-yer-face this way:

> How can you tell if a play is in-yer-face? Well, it really isn't difficult: the language is filthy, there's nudity, people have sex in front of you, violence breaks out, one character humiliates another, taboos are broken, unmentionable subjects are broached, conventional dramatic structures are subverted. At its best, this kind of theatre is so powerful, so visceral, that it forces you to react - either you want to get on stage and stop what's happening or you decide it's the best thing you've ever seen and you long to come back the next night. As indeed you should. (http://www.inyerface-theatre.com/what.html)

The disentanglement from social-realism's restrictions lies in linguistic and generic experimentation for dramatists and aesthetic engagement with the work by critical writers. Although Sierz has roped tucker green into his framework of in-yer-face, her plays actually assert a challenging alternative to its white-exclusivity and its dependence upon staged brutalities. tucker green's body of work places her at the centre of contemporary, experimental play writing for theatre. She has followed American cultural critic bell hooks (and Gertrude Stein before her) in her stances against bigotry and capitalization, to wage her own campaign of anti-realism and linguistic inventiveness. Her trans-generic form draws into its compass a number of drama and performance heritages (Ntozake Shange, Suzan-Lori Parks, Caryl Churchill, Jill Scott) as well as addressing experiences and standpoints untypical in Britain's theatre programming. tucker green's corpus of work to date, not only undercuts expectations of the topics she, as a black British dramatist should address, but also defies conventional approaches to form and dramatic language, staging, and casting determiners.

Her work can also be examined via the critical field of performance poetics. Reading her plays (paradoxically), pluralizes appreciation of their linguistic repertoire as their page life offers a range of options (by which to appreciate the text's complexity), which are reduced by the selection process required for acting the play on stage. To read tucker green's play texts is to be aware that normal (or normalizing) reading is being obstructed. Likewise, its auditory and physicalized life when performed in the theatre, also obstructs the automatic attribution of a number of conventional receptive frameworks. Her texts provoke new relationships with competence: performatively through active silences and overlapping dialogue (which must be recognized by the staging apparatus of actor, director, technical team) and competence linguistically, in testing how far audiences are conversant with vernacular and its resonances with Jamaican patois, estuary English, dub poetry, and jazz lyrics.

Although her first play *Two Women* (2000, *TW*) – her only unpublished play – adheres to conventional spelling, punctuation, and standard English, it displays the origins of tucker green's stylistic and aesthetic trajectory and her characteristic *topoi* of women's social oppression as refracted through race. The characters speak in a phonetically-rendered slang set down with customary spellings to denote Jamaican patois-derived street parlance. "Yu looking fine star. Yeah, yu *da lick* as you 'two's' it through the barriers pleading poverty 'bout buying a ticket." (*TW* 3) In this early play, there is little overlapping dialogue. The overlap occurs through the structural interweaving of both characters (in the stated textual division of prologue, scene, and epilogue) – Sweet (UK Black young woman of W. I. parentage. Aged 15) – and Roni, (Mixed race [black / white] woman approx. 30) as they articulate the plot through indirect dialogue. Sweet and Roni act as barometers of each other's experiences to register and acknowledge what each is going through – a poignant recognition given that both have quite bleak prospects in regards to their (yearned for) emotional happiness and financial security. Never present in the same stage-time as characters, tucker green creates opportunities for inter-referential acknowledgement by the actors as bearer of their character's story. The opening presents the two protagonists self-consciously narrating their lives for the audience or reader whilst drawing attention meta-textually to the work that goes into maintaining their stage roles.

> RONI. I'll be going first.
> **(To Sweet)** We'll start with me.
> **Mine.**
> SWEET. **(Introducing)** Roni.
> RONI. Me just sittin.
> SWEET. As in Saffron.
> [...]
> SWEET. Cos she light.
> As in yellow.
> As in Saff*ron*
> As in *Ron*i.
> [...]

> RONI. Them 'I'm serious' lines showin all here [...] Imitate the 'yeah I'm really interested,' and them falling for my fraud 'attentiveness,' if nothing else – (*TW* 6)

tucker green instructs the audience or reader on the derivation of Roni and plays upon the shifting stress of 'ron' when positioned in a word, pointing to the flexibility of language, something which is developed more explicitly in an exchange between characters in *born bad* (2003, *bb*). In this play, the characters' titles: Dad, Mum, Dawta, Sister 1, Sister 2, and Brother, form the "blood related black family" (*bb* 1). The precision of blood related becomes a disturbing requirement in a play that dramatizes the consequences of incest. The uses of Sister numbered 1 and 2 and Brother creates a sibling group in relation to each other and also highlights Dawta's sequestration (as the one *selected* by Mum for Dad to abuse). She is the only child whose identity is derived from and verified by her parents' biological relationship to her. In naming Dad as her incestuous abuser, Dawta propels the play's accountability narrative to ensure all family members acquire the whole story. tucker green's montage approach to creating her text is transposed to this piecing together of each of the other family members' perspectives. She also infuses her characters' inconstant recollections with implied revenge motives. In scene 3, Sister 1's affirmation that Mum chose Dawta for Dad to abuse, "She chose/I remember," becomes, "I recall...sorta...something...'alf arsed remember like that, y'know?" (*bb* 8) The elliptical vagueness is reinforced by the question mark which undercuts assurance. Lines later, an epanalepsistic passage demonstrates tucker green's linguistically transformative, Chomsky-evoking, second degree grammaticalness as Sister 1 restores Dawta by verifying Mum's facilitation:

> SISTER 1. It wasn't by misfortune. It weren't.
> It weren't all your misfortune
> You weren't borned misfortunate.
> More misfortunate.
> Unfortunate.
> Unfortunately.
> Born bad. No.
> Nature nurture. None a that not knowin.
> Wondering long over which one.
> No.
> She knew.
> She chose. (*bb* 8 f.)

The shifting definitions of the base word "fortune," as it gains and sheds prefixes and suffixes, requires a verbalized dexterity, lyricized by the actor's tone and articulating emphasis in performance, and the reader's cerebral cognizance of the ceaseless potential of language associations. The reassuring alliterative sibilance of "Nature nurture" as a rhythm is negated by the impact of "None a that not knowin," the final assonance underscoring the intentionality and the shared knowledge of what the situation should be, compared to what it is. Together with the double negatives, this linguistic strategy pluralizes ambiguity just as it pares down the very vehicle for its conveyance, via syntax and vocabulary. Mum's wondering "long over" could mean a past decision or signal her deliberating over which child she would pick for Dad to abuse. This presents a chilling juxtaposition between: sacrifice of her child or, judicious selection to appease Dad – that an actor must choose between in delivering emphasis and sense – while a reader can understand both possibilities. Similarly, a reader will see the difference between "No" as a negative and its homophone "know" (as present tense of 'knew') on the page, while an audience member might hear "No" as "know," because it is followed directly by "She knew."

tucker green's genre-refusenik style oversteps acceptable boundaries for theatre's critical custodians. If it is not her works' poeticity that is so alarming, it is that she excludes them from full participation, unless it is under her textual terms. She writes beyond the epistemological framework of playwright and critic's white maleness. Influential broadsheet reviewer Michael Billington habitually laments that tucker green's plays are poems not drama, "more like an acted poem than a play" as he writes of *stoning mary* (2005) which displays "a pungent poetic voice and an eye for detail. But fine writing is not the same as drama" (2006: 38). Although disparaging in his observations, Billington is on the right track, tucker green's plays *are* like a poem. Dialogue groupings on the page evoke stanzaic clusters, as words and phrases are repeated in shifting contexts. Communality is fundamental to the art form of performance poetry and spoken-word poetry as it is to staging play texts. Novelist Dreda Say Mitchell affirmed that as a black British woman she immediately recognized the rhythms and interactions, sayings and rules of the family rituals *random* (2008) captures that are specifically related to black family dynamics – its poetic rendering did not present an obstacle to this (cf. BBC Radio 4, 2008). In contrast, Quentin Letts's review lamented, "[t]he 50-minute poem is hard for a middle-class white ear to follow" (2008: 284), *his* white middle-class ear perhaps! Of course drama-poetry inter-referentiality proves unproblematic when applied to (white men) such as Samuel Beckett (1906-1989) and Harold Pinter (1930-2008). As Keith Peacock (1997:161) writes: "Like Beckett, Pinter's whole career in the theatre […] has been characterised by a poet's search for economy and clarity of expression in words, movement and visual imagery." Precisely the same description applies to tucker green.

4. Some Further Developments

As mainstream theatres have responded to funding requirements that promote more egalitarian representation of Black British theatre, to the demographic realities in Britain today, and to charges of outmoded elitism and theatrical gerontocracy over the past decade, the staging of black writers' works has subsequently burgeoned, in part stimulated by New Writing initiatives for the Royal Court, Soho, Hampstead, Tricycle, and Oval House Theatres and supported by public agencies, including the British Council, the Arts Council, and other local entities, as well as by private grants of various sorts. As the nation's leading black playwrights, it is notable that Williams, Kwei-Armah, and tucker green have not had their work developed via Talawa although under Cumper's artistic direction there has been a clear shift towards nurturing a diverse range of representations of blackness in the next generations of black dramatists. Looking back over the first ten years of the 21st century, there has been a clear shift in the direction of a more multicultural representation in the theatrical mainstream and one which has clearly uncoupled British Asian theatre's dramatic writing and practice from that of Black British drama. Williams received establishment recognition in the awarding of an MBE in 2008 but he, Kwei-Armah, tucker green, and Agbaje are by no means the only black Britons writing scripts. Notable among the panoply of names in contemporary Black British drama are Rhashan Stone, Mark Norfolk, Cumper, Valerie Mason-John, Sol B. River, Linda Brogan, Lemn Sissay MBE, SuAndi OBE, Michael Bhim, Mojisola Adebayo, Biyi Bandele, Courttia Newland, Lennie James, and Oladipo Agboluaje to name just a few of the writers who – besides novels, poetry, and live-word performances – have written play scripts that have led to successful theatrical productions for stage, radio, television, or cinema. Undoubtedly the continuation of this neo-millennial legacy is dependent upon plays being revived, published, and taught. It can only be hoped in the economic austerity of the century's second decade, that black people's self-actualization across many representational disciplines does not become co-opted to white-centring agendas nor diluted by the still white-hegemonic cultural institutions, and that the uniqueness of Black British artistic expression remains a vital constituent of national culture.

Bibliography

Primary Sources

Green, Debbie. 2000. *Two Women.* London: British Library. MS. 9391.
Kwei-Armah, Kwame. 2003. *Elmina's Kitchen.* London: Methuen Books.
tucker green, debbie. 2003. *born bad.* London: Nick Hern Books.

Annotated Bibliography

Barthelemy, Anthony Gerard. 1987. *Black Face Maligned Race: The Representation of Blacks in English Drama from Shakespeare to Southerne.* Baton Rouge/London: Louisiana State UP.
This study analyses representations of blackness in English Renaissance Drama.
Fryer, Peter. 1984. *Staying Power: The History of Black People in Britain.* London: Pluto P.
This comprehensive account traces the history of Africans, Asians, and their descendants in Britain, illustrating how profoundly they shaped British history over the course of the last two thousand years.

Gerzina, Gretchen (ed.). 2003. *Black Victorians: Black Victoriana*. New Brunswick: Holbrook.

The essays investigate the ways blacks were represented in popular Victorian culture, revealing Victorian attitudes toward race.

Innes, C.L. 2008 [2002]. *A History of Black and Asian Writing in Britain*. Cambridge: Cambridge UP.

The volume offers detailed readings of several black and Asian writers in Britain over the last 250 years, focusing on prose writing.

King, Bruce. 2004. *The Oxford Literary History, 1948-2000: The Internationalization of English Literature*. Vol.13. Oxford: Oxford UP.

The book provides a survey of the poetry, fiction, and drama produced by Black British and Asian British writers since 1948.

Owusu, Kwesi (ed.). 2000. *Black British Culture and Society: A Text Reader*. London/New York: Routledge.

The reader brings together major writings on the Black community in Britain, from the Windrush immigrations to contemporary multicultural Britain. It also provides insights into contemporary Black theatre and performance.

Walmsley, Anne. 1992. *The Caribbean Artists Movement, 1966-72*. London: New Beacon P.

The study offers a concise literary and cultural history of the Caribbean Artists Movement.

Waters, Hazel. 2007. *Racism on the Victorian Stage: Representation of Slavery and the Black Character*. Cambridge: Cambridge UP.

The book investigates the black presence on the Victorian stage, illustrating the development of racism under the influence of slavery in the West Indies and America.

Further Secondary Literature

BBC Radio 4, *Saturday Review* 15 March, 2008. <http://www.bbc.co.uk/radio4/arts/saturdayreview_20080315.shtml> (last accessed: 22 June 2011).

Below Stairs curated by Anne French and Giles Waterford, National Portrait Gallery, London. 16 Oct. 2003-11 January 2004. <http://www.npg.org.uk/whatson/exhibitions/2003/below-stairs.php> (last accessed: 22 June 2011).

Billington, Michael. 2005. "Review of *stoning mary*." In: *The Guardian* 6 April: 38. <http://www.guardian.co.uk/stage/2005/apr/06/theatre1> (last accessed: 22 June 2011).

Brewster, Yvonne (ed.). 1987. *Black Plays*. London: Methuen.

—. 1989. *Black Plays Two*. London: Methuen.

—. 1995. *Black Plays Three*. London: Methuen.

Carretta, Vincent (ed.). 1996. *Unchained Voices: An Anthology of Black Voices in the English-Speaking World of the 18th Century*. Lexington: UP of Kentucky.

Chambers, Colin. 1989. *The Story of Unity Theatre*. London: Lawrence and Wishart.

Considine, Ann & Robyn Slovo (eds.). 1987. *Dead Proud: From Second Wave Young Women Playwrights*. London: The Women's P Ltd.

Croft, Susan (ed.), with Stephen Bourne & Alda Terracciano. 2002. *Black and Asian Performance at the Theatre Museum: A User's Guide*. London: Theatre Museum.

Cumper, Patricia. 2009. "I Will Not Put Another Dead Young Black Man on Stage: Forget the Vogue for Tales of Knife Crime and Hoodies – I'm Interested in the Full Range of the Black British Experience." In: *The Guardian* Theatre Blog 4 March. <http://www.guardian.co.uk/stage/theatreblog/2009/mar/03/dead-young-black-man-stage> (last accessed: 22 June 2011).

Dabydeen, David. 1985. *Hogarth's Blacks: Images of Blacks in Eighteenth Century English Art*. Kingston-upon-Thames: Dangaroo P.

Donnell, Alison (ed.). 2002. *Companion to Contemporary Black British Culture*. London: Routledge.

Du Bois, W.E.B. 1911. "Editorial." In: *The Crisis: A Record of the Darker Races* 2.4: 157-59.

Edwardes, Jane. 2005. "Race and Favour." In: *Time Out London* 1814: 157.

Gates, Henry Louis Jr. 2000. "A Reporter at Large: Black London." In: Owusu 2000. 169-80.

George, Kadija (ed.). 2005 [1993]. *Six Plays by Black and Asian Women Writers*. London: Aurora Metro P.

Gerzina, Gretchen. 1995. *Black England: Life before Emancipation*. London: John Murray.

Gray, Frances (ed.). 1990. *Second Wave Plays: Women at the Albany Empire*. Sheffield: Sheffield Academic P.

Griffin, Gabriele. 2003. *Contemporary Black and Asian Women Playwrights in Britain*. London: Cambridge UP.

— & Elaine Aston (eds.). 1991. *Herstory*. 2 Vols. Sheffield: Sheffield Academic P.

Hall, Kim. 1994. "'I Would Rather Wish to Be a Black-Moor': Beauty, Race and Rank in Lady Mary Wroth's *Urania*." In: Margo Hendericks & Patricia Parker (eds.). *Women, 'Race' and Writing in the Early Modern Period*. New York: Routledge. 178-94.

Jarrett-Macauley, Delia. 1998. *The Life of Una Marson: 1905-65*. Manchester: Manchester UP.

Korhonen, Anu. 2005. "Washing the Ethiopian White: Conceptualizing Black Skin in Renaissance England." In: T.F. Earle & K.J.P. Lowe (eds.). *Black Africans in Renaissance Europe*. Cambridge: Cambridge UP. 94-112.

Lavrijsen, Ria. 1990. *Black Theatre on the Move*. Amsterdam: Nederlands Theater Instituut.

McMillan, Michael. 2004. "Re-Baptizing the World in our Own Terms: Black Theatre and Live Arts in Britain." In: *Canadian Theatre Review* 118: 54-61.

Niebrzydowski, Sue. 2001. "The Sultana and Her Sisters: Black Women in the British Isles before 1530." In: *Women's History Review* 10.2: 187-210.

Nkrumah, Afia. 2000. "Introduction." In: Cheryl Robson (ed.). *Black and Asian Plays: Anthology*. London: Aurora Metro P. 7-9.

Osborne, Deirdre. 2007. "'Know Whence you Came': Dramatic Art and Black British Identity." In: *New Theatre Quarterly* 23.3: 253-63.

Peacock, D. Keith. 1997. *Harold Pinter and the New British Theatre*. Westport, CT: Greenwood P.

Phillips, Caryl. 2005. "Lost Generation." In: *The Guardian* 23 Apr.: 16.

Pinnock, Winsome. 1999. "Breaking Down the Door." In: Vera Gottlieb & Colin Chambers (eds.). *Theatre in a Cool Climate*. Oxford: Amber Lane P. 27-38.

Ramdin, Ron. 1999. *Reimaging Britain: 500 Years of Black and Asian History*. London: Pluto P.

Randall, Paulette. 2006. *Personal Interview by Deirdre Osborne*. 21 Jan.

Rees, Roland. 1992. *Fringe First: Pioneers of Fringe Theatre on Record*. Oberon Books: London.

Rickson, Ian. 2004. *Personal Interview by Deirdre Osborne*. 22 Mar.

Sandhu, Sukhdev. 2003. *London Calling: How Black and Asian Writers Imagined a City*. London: HarperCollins Publishers.

Shyllon, Folarin. 1977. *Black People in Britain, 1555-1833*. Oxford: Oxford UP.

Sierz, Aleks. 2001. *In-Yer-Face Theatre: British Drama Today*. London: Faber and Faber.

Thomas, Helen. 2000. *Romanticism and Slave Narratives*. Cambridge: Cambridge UP.

Tokson, Elliott H. 1982. *The Popular Image of the Black Man in English Drama, 1550-1688*. Boston, MA: G.K. Hall and Co.

Walvin, James. 1973. *Black and White: The Negro in English Society 1555-1945*. Harmondsworth: Penguin.

Wandor, Michelene (ed.). 1985. *Plays by Women*. Vol. IV. London: Methuen.

WVT-HANDBÜCHER
zum literaturwissenschaftlichen Studium
Herausgegeben von Ansgar Nünning und Vera Nünning

- **Handbuch 1** • Ansgar Nünning (Hg.): **Literaturwissenschaftliche Theorien, Modelle und Methoden. Eine Einführung.** ISBN 3-88476-698-8, 272 S., kt., € 19,50 (4., erw. Aufl., 2004)

- **Handbuch 2** • Ansgar Nünning (Hg.): **Eine andere Geschichte der englischen Literatur. Epochen, Gattungen und Teilgebiete im Überblick**
  ISBN 3-88476-701-1, 328 S., kt., € 20,- (3., erw. Aufl., 2004)

- **Handbuch 3** • Christoph Bode: **Einführung in die Lyrikanalyse**
  ISBN 3-88476-478-0, 204 S., kt., € 17,50 (2001)

- **Handbuch 4** • Ansgar Nünning, Vera Nünning (Hg.): **Neue Ansätze in der Erzähltheorie**
  ISBN 3-88476-546-9, 288 S., kt., € 19,- (2002)

- **Handbuch 5** • Vera Nünning, Ansgar Nünning (Hg.): **Erzähltheorie transgenerisch, intermedial, interdisziplinär.** ISBN 3-88476-547-7, 312 S., kt., € 20,- (2002)

  Pressestimme: "Alles in allem sind die beiden vorliegenden Bände unerläßliche Wegweiser in einem stark expandierenden Gebiet [...], sie sollten in keiner Bibliothek fehlen, die auch nur im entferntesten Sinne etwas mit 'Erzählen' zu tun hat."
  C. Reinfandt, *Literatur in Wissenschaft und Unterr.* (Rezension zu HB 4 und HB 5)

- **Handbuch 6** • Peter Wenzel (Hg.): **Einführung in die Erzähltextanalyse. Kategorien, Modelle, Probleme.** ISBN 3-88476-700-3, 252 S., kt., € 19,50 (2004)

  Pressestimme: "Besonders positiv ist allen Autorinnen und Autoren anzurechnen, dass sie darauf geachtet haben, ihre theoretischen Grundlagen durch Beispielmaterial aus der (englischsprachigen) Primärliteratur zu belegen. [...] In keiner anderen Publikation wird eine so umfassende und didaktisch aufbereitete Einführung in zentrale erzähltheoretische Modelle und Methoden geleistet wie in dieser."
  S. Buchholz, *Anglistik*

- **Handbuch 7** • Peter Childs, Jean Jacques Weber, Patrick Williams:
  Post-Colonial Theory and Literatures. African, Caribbean and South-Asian
  vergriffen (2006)

- **Handbuch 8** • Tobias Döring (Ed.): **A History of Postcolonial Literature in 12½ Books**
  ISBN 978-3-88476-969-0, 228 S., kt., € 23,50 (2007)

- **Handbuch 9** • Vera Nünning (Hg.): **Der zeitgenössische englische Roman. Genres – Entwicklungen – Modellinterpretationen**
  ISBN 978-3-88476-970-6, 268 S., kt., € 24,50 (2007)

  Pressestimme: "Umso besser, wenn Bände wie dieser ausgezeichnete Führer zu aktuellen Romanen, Genres und Analyseverfahren zeitnah veröffentlicht werden, so lesbar sind und so repräsentative Werke und Autoren vorstellen und beispielhaft ausdeuten."   M. Bracht, *Mitteilungsblatt fmf Westfalen-Lippe*

- **Handbuch 10** • Sven Strasen: **Rezeptionstheorien. Literatur-, sprach- und kulturwissenschaftliche Ansätze und kulturelle Modelle.** ISBN 978-3-86821-050-7, 372 S., kt., € 30,00 (2008)

Wissenschaftlicher Verlag Trier · Bergstr. 27 · 54295 Trier
Tel.: 0651/41503 · Fax: 0651/41504 · www.wvttrier.de · wvt@wvttrier.de

WVT-HANDBÜCHER
zum literaturwissenschaftlichen Studium
Herausgegeben von Ansgar Nünning und Vera Nünning

- **Handbuch 11** • Vera Nünning (Hg.): **Der amerikanische und britische Kriminalroman.**
  Genres – Entwicklungen – Modellinterpretationen
  ISBN 978-3-86821-071-2, 250 S., kt., € 24,50 (2008)

  Aus dem Inhalt: Britische und amerikanische Kriminalromane: Genrekonventionen und neuere Entwicklungstendenzen · Klassische Detektivgeschichten im *Golden Age*: Agatha Christie · *Hard-Boiled*-Erzählungen: Raymond Chandler · Thriller: Patricia Highsmith · Doppelt marginalisiert: Barbara Neely · Thriller und Psychopathen: Thomas Harris · 'Sprechende Körper': Kathy Reichs · *Police Procedurals* als hybrides Genre: Ian Rankin · Anti-Kriminalromane: Paul Auster · Erweiterte Erzählform und zeitgeschichtliche Perspektive: Robert Wilson

- **Handbuch 12** • Herbert Grabes, Klaus Schwank (Hg.): **Das neuere amerikanische Drama.**
  Autoren – Entwicklungen – Interpretationen. ISBN 978-3-86821-079-8, 300 S., kt., € 28,50 (2009)

  Aus dem Inhalt: Darbietungsformen des neueren amerikanischen Dramas · Vietnamkriegstragödie als Aufruf zum Pazifismus: David Rabes *Streamers* (1976) · Subversives *Rewriting* orientalistischer Traditionslinien im chinesisch-amerikanischen Drama: David Henry Hwangs *M. Butterfly* (1988) · Die Geschichte des amerikanischen Feminismus als dramatisierte Biographie: Wendy Wassersteins *The Heidi Chronicles* (1988) · Afroamerikanische Dekonstruktion des Lincoln-Mythos: Suzan-Lori Parks' *The America Play* (1993) und *Topdog/Underdog* (2001) · Die Aufarbeitung von Kindesmissbrauch als *Memory Play* und Metadrama: Paula Vogels *How I Learned to Drive* (1997)

- **Handbuch 13** • Merle Tönnies (Hg.): **Das englische Drama der Gegenwart.**
  Kategorien – Entwicklungen – Modellinterpretationen
  ISBN 978-3-86821-080-4, 272 S., kt., € 26,50 (2010)

  Aus dem Inhalt: Das zeitgenössische englische Drama: Kategorien und Schreibweisen · *In-Yer-Face Theatre*: Sarah Kane · *State-of-the-nation*-Satire: Alistair Beaton · Politisches Drama zur Außen- und Weltpolitik · *Documentary Drama*: David Hare · Dystopisches Drama: Caryl Churchill · Geschichtsdrama: Shelagh Stephenson · Postmodernes biographisches Drama: Michael Frayn · Psychologisches Drama: Joe Penhall · Postdramatisches Theater: Martin Crimp · *Queer Drama*: Mark Ravenhill · *Black British Drama*: Kwame Kwei-Armah · *British Asian Drama*: Ayub Khan-Din · Komödie und Farce: Tom Stoppard

- **Handbuch 14** • Michael Basseler, Ansgar Nünning (Hg.): **A History of the American Short Story.**
  Genres – Developments – Model Interpretations
  ISBN 978-3-86821-302-7, 444 S., kt., € 35,00 (2011)

  Aus dem Inhalt: Theories and Typologies of the Short Story · Early American Short Narratives: The Art of Story-Telling Prior to Washington Irving · Stories of the Puritan Legacy: Myth and Allegory in Nathaniel Hawthorne's "Young Goodman Brown" and "Rappaccini's Daughter" · Feminist Voices around 1900: Kate Chopin's "Désirée's Baby" and Charlotte Perkins Gilman's "The Yellow Wall-Paper" · The Beginnings of the Modernist Short Story of Consciousness: Henry James's "The Beast in the Jungle" · Short Stories of the 1920s and 1930s between Tradition and Innovation: F. Scott Fitzgerald's "May Day" and Ernest Hemingway's "The Short Happy Life of Francis Macomber" · Middle-class Life in the (Realist) Short Story: John Cheever's "The Enormous Radio" and John Updike's "The Music School" · Minimalism and the Return to Realism in the 1970s and 1980s: Raymond Carver's "Why Don't You Dance?" and "Cathedral"

Wissenschaftlicher Verlag Trier · Bergstr. 27 · 54295 Trier
Tel.: 0651/41503 · Fax: 0651/41504 · www.wvttrier.de · wvt@wvttrier.de